DATE DUE			

IN TIME OF WAR

By the same author

The Point of No Return: the Strike which Broke the British in Ulster

Robert Fisk

In Time of War

Ireland, Ulster and the price of
neutrality 1939–45

UNIVERSITY OF PENNSYLVANIA PRESS
PHILADELPHIA
1983

First published in the United States by the
University of Pennsylvania Press, 1983

First published in the United Kingdom by
André Deutsch Limited, 1983

Printed and bound in Great Britain by
Robert Hartnoll Limited, Bodmin, Cornwall

Library of Congress Cataloging in Publication Data

Fisk, Robert.
  In time of war.

  Bibliography: p.
  Includes index.
  1. World War, 1939–1945 – Diplomatic history.
2. Ireland – Foreign relations – Great Britain. 3. Great
Britain – Foreign relations – Ireland. 4. Ireland –
Neutrality – History. 5. World War, 1939–1945 – Secret
service – Germany. 6. Espionage, German – Ireland –
History – 20th century. 7. De Valera, Eamonn, 1882–1975.
I. Title.
D754. I6F57   1983   940.53'2   83–3627
ISBN 0–8122–7888–7 (case)

FOR LOUIS HEREN
*who understood why I wanted
to return to Ireland*

Contents

Preface

Neutrality in war has never been regarded as an act of much honour; and self-interest on the part of a nation fighting for its life can take on an ugly shape when it threatens the freedom of a country which has chosen to stand aside from the conflict. If, therefore, the history of both parts of Ireland in the Second World War and the record of Anglo-Irish relations during that period has been largely ignored in Britain – and until recently in Ireland as well – it is not difficult to see why. Churchill, de Valera and the powerful little Unionist government in Belfast were all involved in an intrigue and mutual suspicion more than seven centuries old, adopting familiar attitudes which became grotesquely distorted in the context of the world war. Since then, neither Britain nor Ireland have seen much advantage in analysing the complex and occasionally tragic events that took place as a result.

Even today, forty-three years after Britain – as well as Germany – planned an invasion of the south of Ireland, forty-two years after the Luftwaffe fire-bombed the almost defenceless city of Belfast and thirty-eight years after the Irish Taoiseach expressed his formal condolences on the death of Hitler to the German Minister in Dublin, not all the archives have been opened. Quantities of wartime British intelligence papers on Ireland are still closed – many hundreds of them have been 'destroyed under statute' in London – while in 1945, the Irish authorities shredded about seventy tons of documents which were considered too sensitive for the scrutiny of historians. In the archives of the Northern Ireland Government, too, there is evidence of extensive 'weeding' among the records. The wartime history of Ireland was not, it seems, something which civil servants wished future generations to examine too closely.

Over the past four years, however, I have been very fortunate in my research for this book. I have been able to read through well over 11,000 wartime documents and memoranda in London, Dublin and Belfast, most of which were until recently closed to the public. The Irish Government and the Northern Ireland Office, the constitutional descendant of the old Government in Belfast, also released more than a thousand confidential wartime papers specifically for this book. These were supplemented by interviews with British and Irish ministers, soldiers, civil servants, intelligence officers and former German agents, and by a study of personal papers and diaries. Together, they have provided the material for what has hitherto been a largely unknown and comparatively unwritten chapter in the history of the Second World War.

Throughout these files and memoranda, letters and memoirs, there runs a common theme: the partition of Ireland, which characterised the framework of relations between Dublin, London and Belfast. For during the war, the border between the province of Northern Ireland and Eire was not just a physical symbol of different national aspirations but a bargaining point at one of the most critical moments in modern European history. In the early years of the war, Ireland sometimes dominated Cabinet discussions in Downing Street and in the last half century, the only offer Britain ever made of a 'solemn undertaking' to bring about a United Ireland came when the German armies stood on the beaches of Dunkirk and when England – and Ireland – hourly expected invasion from the Continent.

On another level, therefore, this book sets out to examine the degree to which decision-making by the British, Irish and Northern Ireland Governments immediately before and during the war was influenced by the domestic considerations and distrust springing from Anglo-Irish relations and the extent to which each administration was reacting to the larger European crisis and the threat of attack or invasion.

There is sometimes no clear division between the various motives which prompted governmental initiatives, especially in the spring and summer of 1940 when the German advance across Holland, Belgium and France changed the contours of political expectation in Britain and both parts of Ireland as much as it did the military map of Europe. Ministers occasionally found it prudent to combine domestic aspirations with the necessities of defence. Yet from the events of those years, certain conclusions can be drawn about the priorities and self-interest of nations at a time of war; about the obligations placed upon them to respect the territorial integrity of their neighbours; and about the principles underlying a policy of neutrality. To this day, partition remains the tumour in Anglo-Irish relations and this study is perhaps all the more topical because the conflict which still divides Catholic nationalist and Protestant unionist in Ireland has changed little in the past forty years.

It would turn a preface into a chapter if I was to recall in detail here the individual help afforded me over the last four years, although the names of all those to whom I owe thanks can be found in the Acknowledgements. It would be ungrateful of me, however, if I did not mention now those to whom I am particularly indebted.

The late Mr Malcolm MacDonald, Britain's former Dominions Secretary and Minister of Health, and Mr Frank Aiken, the wartime Irish Minister for the Coordination of Defensive Measures, spent hours talking about the negotiations for the Treaty ports and explaining why Britain's offer of a declaration in favour of Irish unity was rejected by Eamon de

Valera's Cabinet. Lord MacDermott, the former Northern Ireland Minister of Public Security, gave up most of a day to recall the Luftwaffe raids on Belfast and the conscription crisis in the province. Colonel Dan Bryan, who was director of Irish military intelligence (Chief Staff Officer G2), met me five times to discuss his wartime activities, while in London Mr 'Spike' Marlin, formerly of the American Office of Strategic Services, recounted his 1942 assignment to Eire. In Dublin, Herr Helmut Clissmann, one of the German Abwehr officers with special responsibility for Ireland, and Herr Gunther Schütz, who parachuted into Eire as a German agent, talked about Berlin's fascination with the Irish Republican Army and German espionage in the country.

A special debt of gratitude is owed to a host of British and Irish civil servants, particularly to Dr Peter Smyth of the Public Record Office of Northern Ireland, Mr David Gilliland of the Northern Ireland Office and Mr Breandán Mac Giolla Choille, the Keeper of State Papers at the State Paper Office, Dublin; to the staff of the Public Record Office, London, who sought out not only thousands of pages of diplomatic correspondence but British intelligence records on Eire as well; to Mr Philip Reed of the Department of Documents at the Imperial War Museum in London who in less than twenty-four hours unearthed the complete German Army plans for the invasion of Eire, the envelope still bearing the wax eagle and swastika seal of the Wehrmacht; to the staff of the Taoiseach's Department in Dublin who allowed me to read through a series of apparently innocuous, blue-covered files which turned out to contain de Valera's secret contingency plans for Eire in the event of British or German invasion; and to Mr Michael P. Healy, Secretary to the Irish Department of Defence until 1981, for permission to tour the restricted military areas of the three Atlantic Treaty ports which Winston Churchill vainly attempted to secure for the Royal Navy in the Second World War. Lieutenant Colonel James Dawson, Commandant Patrick Rohan and Company Quartermaster Sergeant William Robinson of the Irish Army spent three days conducting me round the installations; if those great forts, with their tunnels, underground railways, dark granite walls and heavy guns, have turned out to be the most powerful though silent figures in this account of the war years in Ireland, then it is at least partly due to the enthusiasm of these soldiers.

My thanks must also go to Professor Basil Chubb and Dr Patrick Keatinge of Trinity College, Dublin, who allowed me to use material from my thesis for the Department of Political Science. I could not have done without the help of Tony Raven, who valiantly undertook the task of indexing. I am especially grateful to Mr Louis Heren who, as Foreign Editor of *The Times* in 1977, unhesitatingly gave me leave to go to Dublin, and to Sir William Rees-Mogg who, as the Editor of *The Times*, generously granted me a sabbatical for my research. Lastly, and above all others, my thanks go to Olivia O'Leary, who will not need me to explain why this book could not have been written without her.

None of those who helped me are responsible for any errors or for the conclusions I have drawn, although readers who may – and probably will – find some of the facts in these pages distasteful may reflect that virtually every statement is based on contemporary archive material or on the recollection of those who took part in the wartime events discussed here. While this book is intended as a contribution to the study of Anglo-Irish relations and partition in the Second World War, however, it does not attempt to be a comprehensive history of that period nor to supplant those books which have been published about specific aspects of the war years in Ireland.*

In the course of writing, I have several times been faced with problems of nomenclature. During the war years, for instance, many British people (and quite a number of Irish as well) continued to refer to Irish towns by the English names which had been in popular use at the beginning of the century; thus Cobh was still known as Queenstown and Dun Laoghaire as Kingstown. Unless they are used in quotation, I have dealt with them under the names by which they were known in Eire, preferring to adopt the titles officially in use within the state. For identical reasons, Northern Ireland's second city is referred to here as Londonderry rather than Derry, which is the older, Irish form of the English name always used south of the border. Similarly with nations: throughout this book, Eire denotes the twenty-six counties that now constitute the Republic of Ireland. The six-county province which the British sometimes call Ulster (historically a nine-county province of Ireland) is identified by its official United Kingdom designation of Northern Ireland. The use of the term 'Ireland' indicates the whole island, irrespective of the border.

There is one final apology to be made for a few abrupt changes in style. Much of this book was written in the Middle East and my work on it was interrupted by journalistic assignments. Even so, there were occasions when this proved advantageous to someone born after the Second World War; experiencing an Israeli airstrike in a Lebanese village in March of 1978 conferred new meaning on those clinical Northern Ireland Govern-

---

* Carolle J. Carter's *The Shamrock and the Swastika: German Espionage in Ireland in World War II* (Pacific Books) California 1977 and Enno Stephan's *Spies in Ireland* (Four Square) London 1965 are unequalled in their accounts of German espionage in Eire. T. Ryle Dwyer's *Irish Neutrality and the USA 1939–47* (Gill and Macmillan) Dublin 1977 is a major study of Irish-American relations during the war. Joseph T. Carroll's *Ireland in the War Years 1939–1945* (David and Charles) Newton Abbot 1975 and Bernard Share's *The Emergency: Neutral Ireland 1939–45* (Gill and Macmillan) Dublin 1978 recapture the mood of wartime Eire and no book is ever likely to describe Northern Ireland's role in the conflict in such detail as John W. Blake's monumental *Northern Ireland in the Second World War* (Her Majesty's Stationery Office) Belfast 1956. Four of these books owe a debt to *Ireland in the War Years and After 1939–51*, edited by Kevin B. Nowlan and T. Desmond Williams (Gill and Macmillan) Dublin 1969.

ment reports of the 1941 Luftwaffe blitz when I read them again on my return to Belfast.

Perhaps it is also ironic that I should have completed my manuscript in the Lebanon, a country that has been savagely divided by two communities whose frustrations and anger are not dissimilar to those which have manifested themselves in Belfast. And like Eire in the war, Lebanon has found herself a more or less helpless spectator in the larger conflict going on around her, and at the mercy of belligerent neighbours.

Beirut, 1982

Acknowledgements

In the research and writing of this book, I received generous help from many people, sometimes in the form of reminiscences, at other times with encouragement and advice. I can only list them briefly here although their contribution to this study of wartime Ireland was often considerable and I am indebted to them all: to Mr Bruno Achilles; Mr Frank Aiken; Professor John W. Blake; Mr Ende Boland; Mr Kevin Boland; Mr Michael Bowles; Mr John Bowman; Mrs Regina Boyd; Mr Conor Brady; Senator Seamus Brennan; Mr Michael Brick; Lord Brookeborough; Mr Paddy Brosnan; Col. Dan Bryan (ret'd.); Miss Margaret Byrne; Mr Helmut Clissmann; Mr Tim Pat Coogan; Lt-Col. Colm Cox; Dr Cornelius Cremin; Ms Catriona Crowe; Lt-Col. James Dawson; Mr Paddy Devlin; Mr James Dillon; Mr Sean Donlon; Lt-Col. John Duggan (ret'd.); Mrs Florence Dunleavy; Mrs Peggy Fanning; Dr Ronan Fanning; Mr Joe Farrell T.D.; my parents Peggy and William Fisk; Mr Victor Fiorentini; Dr Garret FitzGerald T.D.; Mr John Furlong; Mr Douglas Gageby; Mr Tom Garvin; Dr Martin Gilbert; Mr David Gilliland; the late Professor Rodney Green; Col. John Griffin (ret'd.); Lt-Col. John Hamill; Mr Shay Howell; Mr Brian Inglis; Dr Patrick Keatinge; Mr James Kelly; Mr William Kennedy; the Very Reverend the Dean of Kerry; Commandant George Kirwan (ret'd.); Mr Tommy Lyttle; Mr Adian Maher; Dr Maurice Manning; Mr Ervin Marlin; Mr Sam McAughtry; Mr Joseph McCann; Mr Seamus McConville; the late Lord MacDermott; the late Mr Malcolm MacDonald; Mr Stuart McIvor; Mr David McKittrick; Mrs Rita McKittrick; Dr Deirdre McMahon; Mrs Felicity Ó Broin; Ms Fionnuala O'Connor; Mr Mort O'Leary; Ms Olivia O'Leary; Mr Michael O'Sullivan; Sir Richard Pim (RNVR ret'd.); Quartermaster Sgt. William Robinson; Commandant Patrick Rohan; Mr William Rose; Mr Gunther Schütz; Dr Peter Smyth; Mr Francis Stuart; Mr Kenneth Taylor; Mr Frank Ward; Mr William Warnock; Professor T. Desmond Williams; Mr Bruce Williamson; Mr Hugh Wren; Commandant Peter Young.

I would also like to thank those who kindly gave their permission for me to quote from private and government papers in Britain and Ireland. I owe my thanks to the Admiralty Records Office (London); to Barrie & Jenkins, now part of the Hutchinson publishing group, for permission to quote from David Thomson's *Woodbrook*; to Lady Mairi Bury for permission to quote from a letter which her father, Lord Londonderry, wrote to

Beaverbrook; to the Blackstaff Press for permission to quote from Sam McAughtry's *The Sinking of the Kenbane Head*; to Lord Caldecotte and Churchill College, Cambridge, for permission to quote from the Inskip Diaries; to Houghton Mifflin Co., Lady Spencer Churchill, the Hon. Lady Sarah Audley and the Hon. Lady Soames for permission to quote from Winston S. Churchill's *History of the Second World War* Vols I, II, III and IV; to Alfred A. Knopf, Inc. for permission to quote from Nicholas Monsarrat's *The Cruel Sea*; to Mr Winston Churchill M.P. for permission to quote from his grandfather's article on Ireland in the *Daily Mail*; to Mr Seán Cronin for permission to quote from the Ryan–Kerney correspondence in *Frank Ryan: The Search for the Republic*; to André Deutsch, Publishers, for permission to quote from Brian Moore's *The Emperor of Ice-Cream*; to Faber and Faber for permission to reproduce *Neutrality* by Louis MacNeice; to the late Mr Donal Foley for permission to quote from *Three Villages: An Autobiography*; to Gael-Linn and Mr Dónall Ó Moráin for translating state papers in the Irish language; to Gill and Macmillan, Publishers, for permission to quote from Frank Forde's *The Long Watch: The History of the Irish Mercantile Marine in World War Two*; to Lord Halifax and Major T. L. Ingram and to Churchill College, Cambridge, for permission to quote from the Hickleton Papers; to Mr Michael P. Healy, former Secretary of the Department of Defence (Dublin) and to the Department of Defence for permission to tour the restricted military areas of the ports of Cobh, Berehaven and Lough Swilly; to the Controller of Her Majesty's Stationery Office for permission to quote from British Government documents in the Public Record Office (Kew) and from German diplomatic reports contained in *Documents on German Foreign Policy 1918–1945* Vols. VIII, IX, X and XI; to the House of Lords Record Office (London) and to the Beaverbrook Foundation for permission to quote from letters in the Beaverbrook papers; to Mr H Montgomery Hyde for his kind advice and his permission to quote from his book *The Londonderrys: a Family Portrait*; to the Imperial War Museum (London) for permission to quote from the German *Fall Grün* file, from a letter in the C. V. Mann papers and from a document in the C. V. Jack papers and to Dr Peter Thwaites and Mr Philip Reed of the Department of Documents, Imperial War Museum; to the Ministry of Defence (London) Historical Branch; to the Diplomatic Branch of the Civil Archives Division, National Archives (Washington DC) to quote from documents on the visit of an Irish military delegation to the United States in 1939; to Miss Ann Gallagher and to the Trustees of the National Library of Ireland (Dublin) for permission to quote from the papers of the late Frank Gallagher; to Mr Brian Trainor, Director of the Public Record Office of Northern Ireland (Belfast) for permission to quote from the documents of the Northern Ireland Government and associated papers; to Miss Ursula Schickling for her translation of German military documents; to Mrs D. Dingwall for permission to quote from the diaries and private papers of her father, the late Sir Wilfrid Spender; to Mr Brendán Mac Giolla Choille, Keeper of State Papers, for permission to quote from documents in the State Paper Office (Dublin); and to the Archives Department of University College Dublin and to the Mulcahy Trustees for permission to quote from the papers of the late Richard Mulcahy.

In my search for photographic material for this book, I am especially grateful to the *Belfast Telegraph* and its indefatigable librarian Mr Walter McAuley; to the Imperial War Museum; to the *Irish Press* and its picture editor, Mr Liam Flynn; to EMI Films (Pathé News) for stills from their wartime newsreels of Ireland; also to Mr Larry McKinna, the EMI Librarian, who spent hours of his time running through old monochrome films for me; and to Radio Telefis Eireann.

If by chance I have neglected to mention any names or accidently infringed any copyright, the fault is mine and I apologise for the unintended omission.

Chapter 1

The Sentinel Towers

> To violate Irish neutrality should it be declared at the
> moment of a great war may put you out of court in the
> opinion of the world, and may vitiate the cause by which
> you may be involved in war. If ever we have to fight
> again, we shall be fighting in the name of law, of respect
> for the rights of small countries . . .
>
> Winston Churchill 5 May 1938

Shortly after 1800 hours on 11 July 1938 a hundred men and four officers of the 2nd Heavy Regiment, Royal Artillery, abandoned the fortifications of Spike Island to the Irish Army and stepped out across the wooden drawbridge of Fort Westmoreland for the last time, to their regimental march of 'The British Grenadiers'.[1] The Irish Army No.2 Band, which led the British down to the stone embarkation jetty, had only discovered the score in an old pianoforte tutor a few days before but they played it at the correct British parade-ground cadence of 116 beats to the minute.[2] Across the bay that separated the island from the town of Cobh, with its grey-steepled cathedral, dockside railway terminal and Atlantic quays, dozens of small boats crowded with spectators rode the swell in the evening sunshine; each flew a Union Jack pennant from its mast, while a few hundred yards from the harbour the British destroyer *Acasta* stood on station, with steam up for departure.

Given the depressed state of relations between Britain and her southern Irish dominion before 1938, the ceremony of transfer was a dignified affair, although the worsening crisis in Europe had added an undertow of anxiety, even haste, to the arrangements for the British evacuation.* In

---

* The British and Irish Governments had originally proposed to transfer Spike Island and the adjacent forts around Cobh on June 29, but at a meeting at their High Commissioner's Office in London on May 25, the Irish were informed that the deadline could not be met because the British War Office was experiencing 'considerable difficulties' in the disposal of civilian personnel.[3] At a meeting in the same office two days later, the British also said they desired notice of 'at least 3 months' before leaving the other two ports of Berehaven and Lough Swilly.[4] When military representatives of both parties met on Spike the following month (after the July 11 date had been settled), the Irish officer Commanding Southern Command, Colonel Sean McCabe, still felt it necessary in his opening remarks to express Eire's desire for an 'early agreement' on transfer arrangements.[5]

March, while the Irish Taoiseach,* Eamon de Valera, and the British Prime Minister, Neville Chamberlain, had been negotiating an end to the tariff war and the cession of the three Atlantic naval ports of Cobh, Berehaven and Lough Swilly (retained by Britain under the 1921 Articles of Agreement), Germany had incorporated Austria into the Reich. Within a month of the signing of the new agreement, reports of German military manoeuvres on the border of the Czech Sudetenland had panicked European governments into preparing for hostilities. At such a moment, Britain had chosen to abandon three of her most valuable naval bases in order to guarantee Eire's friendship, if not her allied participation, in a future war; and since possession of the ports would also assist her in maintaining a relatively independent policy of neutrality in war, Eire had no wish to allow the British Government time to change its mind.

On July 7, there was a small celebration, pregnant with the new spirit of Anglo-Irish relations which de Valera and Chamberlain had conceived in London, to mark the forthcoming transfer at Cobh. Fifteen British officers under Lieutenant Colonel R.H.A.D. Love, who commanded what the War Office in London called its South Irish Coast Defences, were entertained at Collins Barracks in Cork City as guests of Frank Aiken, de Valera's Minister for Defence. The Crown was now acknowledged in Eire only for the very limited and symbolic purposes of appointing diplomatic representatives and concluding international agreements but on this occasion Aiken, a man of impeccable Republican antecedents,† felt able to propose a toast to His Majesty[6] before the Irish Army's band played sixteen bars of 'God Save the King', having this time turned up the score, with metronome markings, in a redundant British Army manual of regulation music. On the same night, the Irish Advance Party, already installed at Fort Camden on the headland south of Spike Island, was invited by the departing 33rd (Fortress) Company, Royal Engineers, to the Warrant-Officers' and Sergeants' Mess for a 'free night' which, as the British regiment recorded with slightly condescending humour, 'Officers and NCOs carried . . . out to the utmost meaning of the word. Some were even carried out afterwards. Our Irish friends sang many popular melodies . . .'[7]

Evidence of haste, however, persisted into the morning of the 11th. The Irish military authorities gave Second Lieutenant John Griffin and ten corporals only a few hours notice to put on spurs and artillery badges, decamp from the Curragh and travel the 120 miles to Cobh.[8] Griffin, who the previous month had been transferred from the infantry to the newly-created Irish Coast Defence Artillery, was informed that his ten NCOs were to be the new Master Gunners. Of the Irish Army band that day, only the bandmaster, Second Lieutenant Michael Bowles, was wearing

---

* Irish for the title of Prime Minister (literally: 'chief' or 'leader').
† Born in 1898, Aiken joined the Irish Volunteers in 1913, became Commandant of the IRA's 4th Northern Division in 1921 and was appointed IRA Chief of Staff in 1923.

the full dress uniform of 'dark blue tunic with red cuffs, gold-over-red epaulettes, heavy gold-cord lanyard with ornamental knots, black barathea overalls with a red stripe, two inches wide, down each leg'.*

From the packed promenade at Cobh, the Irish troops were ferried across the bay, past the *Acasta*, to Spike Island. The photographs of the event show them to have been mostly very young men with well-polished brass buckles but still wearing the strapped long leggings above their boots that other armies had discarded years before; the British, who offered the Irish officers an informal glass of sherry on their arrival at Fort Westmoreland on the summit of the island, [10] still wore the same style of flat khaki peaked cap that their predecessors had used in the 1914–18 War.

A Union Jack flew from the temporary flag staff which the British had erected on the barrack square and at 1800 hours, British and Irish guards of honour, each a hundred strong, were drawn up on either side of the flag. For seven minutes, surrounded by the austere late Georgian barrack buildings of the old fortress, the soldiers of the most powerful empire on earth and of one of the world's smallest nations stood facing each other. It was an unparalleled moment in Anglo-Irish history, a ceremony of military respect and political friendship between Britain's most fractious dominion and Ireland's oldest enemy, unwitnessed before and never repeated since. The Irish band played the British national anthem as the Union Jack was lowered and both companies presented arms as a British soldier handed over the fort record book. [11] To 'The Soldier's Song', the green, white and orange Tricolour of Eire was run up the temporary mast. Then an Irish private, speaking in the Irish language, took over the guard.

Within an hour, the British troops, who were to travel home to England on the motor vessel *Innisfallen*, had boarded the tender at the embarkation pier. Colonel Love was so impressed by the 'remarkable' send-off accorded his men – he regarded the unofficial presence of John Dulanty, the Irish High Commissioner in London, as 'a particularly graceful act' – that he was moved to dispatch a three-page report to the British General Officer Commanding Western Approaches, describing the event. '. . . as the last hawser was loosed,' he wrote, 'the Eireann† band on the pier

---

* Bowles, who three years later was to establish the Radio Eireann Symphony Orchestra and to become Professor of Music at Indiana University in 1954, recalled much later how a Sandhurst-educated British subaltern on Spike Island, confused by his bandsman's regalia, 'seemed to have developed a notion that I was some exalted member of the Irish Army, maybe a staff man from GHQ. Eventually, politely and with excellent finesse, he got round to prompting me to tell him what I did. "Me," I said, "oh, I'm just the bandmaster." Our conversation fell apart. He drifted smoothly into the background and I never saw him again.' [9]

† When the name of the Irish Free State was changed to Eire under the country's 1937 Constitution, the British Government generally adopted 'Eireann' as an Anglicised adjectival version of the new name. In Northern Ireland, however, it was used to describe a *citizen* of Eire and in this context became a term of contempt. Since the word is now also archaic in the English language, the less specific adjective 'Irish' has been used throughout this book unless 'Eireann' appears in quotation.

played the National Anthem right through. All officers stood at the salute, all NCOs and men at attention, and every civilian within hearing, either on the pier or in boats and vessels nearby, had his hat off. There was no necessity to call for cheers from the British troops in answer to this compliment.'[12]

In so blithe a manner did the British take leave of their imperial holdings. As the twin-funnelled *Acasta* turned south to escort the *Innisfallen* out of Cobh, the Irish soldiers who now manned the four 18-pounders by the Spike Island drill shed fired a farewell 21-gun salute. They understood that the occasion was one of historic importance for the British as well as themselves[13] and were aware that some of the young men whose departure they were honouring might shortly die in a war which Eire would hopefully be spared. Indeed, in just over two years time, the *Acasta* herself would be sunk in action off northern Norway while engaging the German battle cruisers *Scharnhorst* and *Gneisenau*.

Sketch map of Ireland showing the Treaty Ports

4

The British also left behind some ghosts of history. There were three embossed eighteenth-century cannon still in place outside the gates of Fort Westmoreland;* and in Cobh churchyard and by Fort Carlisle there were some neat rows of naval graves which the Irish promised to safeguard.[15] There were, however, other, sadder memorials left behind which could arouse harsher emotions. Beside the British garrison cricket pitch on Spike Island, scarcely five hundred yards from the commanding officer's shore-line residence, the Irish came across an overgrown cemetery. It was untended and, because it had no walls, bracken and long grass had over the past ninety years smothered all the graves. There were several dozen of these, many of them unmarked; others were recorded by broken headstones bearing only initials and serial numbers. They contained the anonymous remains of the convicts who had died of typhus and dysentery within the walls of Fort Westmoreland while awaiting transportation to a penal colony for felony or treason against the Crown during the years of the Famine.[16]

But the greatest memorials which the British bequeathed were the ports themselves. At the north-western corner of Ireland, the eighteen-mile inlet formed by the Knockalla Mountains and the Inishowen Peninsula provided the deep-water anchorage of Lough Swilly, while four hundred miles down the coastline, a mile-long channel behind Bere Island at the mouth of Bantry Bay and beneath the two thousand foot mountain of Hungry Hill created a natural harbour along one of the westernmost landfalls of Europe. One hundred miles to the east, past the Old Head of Kinsale, a narrow, fiord-like gorge half a mile wide and guarded by headlands more than two hundred feet in height opened into a sheltered pool dominated by Spike Island and the little town of Cobh. This was probably the oldest of the three naval anchorages, for a small rectangular bastion was built on Haulbowline Island next to Spike in 1601 after the Battle of Kinsale;[17] by 1783, at the end of the American War of Independence, there were batteries on Spike Island and on the headlands to the south, each containing 24-pounders, mortars and howitzers.[18] The year after Wolfe Tone's attempt to land with a French fleet during the 1798 rebellion, the War Office built a barracks at Fort Dunree on the hills to the east of Lough Swilly, a position which was already defended by a round tower, some irregular earth parapets and nine cannon.[19]

The cost of the ports gives some idea of the military value which the British placed upon them. In 1804, an average of £4000 – an immense figure at that time – was being spent monthly on the Spike Island and Bere

---

* There was an exhaustive correspondence on this subject between the British and Irish Governments after the transfer, in which the Irish evinced a curator's interest in the provenance of this antiquated British ordnance. The War Office in London eventually tracked down a retired Battery Commander who suggested that one of the guns, a 24-pounder, had been part of the first battery installed on the island. The British were still providing the Irish with such information in January, 1939.[14]

Island forts and Spike merited an inspection two years later by Arthur Wellesley, a Dublin-born veteran of the wars in Flanders and India who was to become Chief Secretary of Ireland in 1807 and later the first Duke of Wellington. By 1812, the cost of the Spike Island works alone was put at one million pounds.[20] Successive British administrations continued to pile fortifications around the ports with little opposition,* until a hundred years later they were among the finest defended harbours in the realm.

In the 1914–18 War, Lough Swilly and Berehaven became assembly points for the convoys to the United States, created when Germany began unrestricted submarine warfare. All three ports served as bases for naval flotillas on Atlantic convoy escort duty and for a time the entire British Grand Fleet retreated to the safety of Lough Swilly when fear of submarines and mines forced it to abandon its own base at Scapa Flow in Scotland.[22] Photographs taken in Cobh during the First World War illustrate the reliance which the Royal Navy placed in the harbour. Warships moored in line abreast and line astern before the town, using the cover of Spike Island to provide visual concealment from the Atlantic; in Berehaven, when the American fleet arrived to join the British, the anchorage was so crowded that it was almost possible 'to walk from the island to the shore across the decks of battleships'.[23]

Over a period of a century and a half, therefore, changing political alliances and the advancing science of warfare had caused the three ports to grow rather than diminish in importance. Forming a five-hundred-mile semi-circle of naval defence around the western perimeter of the United Kingdom, they came to be associated not only with protection against foreign invasion but with Britain's economic survival in a European war. It was consequently not surprising that when the Irish achieved their partial independence under the 1921 Anglo-Irish Treaty, Britain ensured that the defended ports stayed in her hands for the foreseeable future. As a result, the Union Jack continued to fly over Cobh, Berehaven and Lough Swilly, even though the twenty-six counties, now officially known as the Irish Free State, were no longer part of the United Kingdom.

The black stone and concrete fortresses remained a massive barrier against attack by Britain's enemies and a formidable achievement of military engineering, which could in theory withstand sieges of up to four months duration and protect more than a hundred warships. In the charge of care and maintenance parties, the forts were also self-contained British military townships with barracks, married quarters, mess, canteen,

---

* In September 1888, General Edward Saxe Meir, the General Officer Commanding Ireland, suggested in a report to the Adjutant General in London that Lough Swilly should be abandoned. If an enemy cruiser was observed sheltering in the Lough, so his theory went, heavy guns could be made ready in Dublin and then sent the 150 miles to Co. Donegal by rail. On arrival, they would then be used to shell the enemy vessel, assuming it had been unwise enough to delay its visit.[21] The General's plan, which was intended to save money, was very sensibly turned down.

shops, sports facilities and garrison chapels. Apart from troops' living quarters and canteens, Fort Westmoreland on Spike Island could boast two officers' messrooms, a sergeants' mess, three oak-panelled billiard rooms, three tennis courts, two cricket pitches and a gymnasium as well as the commanding officer's six-bedroomed house overlooking the bay. The fort's largest artillery, two 6-inch guns on the southern bastions, were furnished by more than a dozen ammunition stores built twenty feet beneath the ramparts and linked by a series of underground passages.[24]

Fort Camden, on the western of the two headlands, contained almost equally fine accommodation (with three more tennis courts, mess and billiard rooms) although its fortifications were much more impressive than Spike. Over a mile and a half of tunnels catacombed the solid rock beneath the fortress and two narrow-gauge underground railways ran through them, transporting shells from bunkers which had concrete walls eight feet thick. Electrically operated ammunition escalators lifted the rounds to two heavy guns, a 9.2-inch and a 6-inch, whose barrels, over twenty-five feet in length, projected over the south-eastern parapets. They were supported by two 18-pounders and Vickers and Lewis machine guns. At the foot of the sheer precipice on which the fort was built, ran another railway system with points and sidings that served a military dock where the tide surged through the narrow passage between the headlands.

On the other side of this neck of water stood Fort Carlisle, complementing its near-twin with equal defence works and two 6-inch guns. Each fort controlled double torpedo tubes on a permanent setting that could send their projectiles at 90 degrees directly across the gorge. Camden was reinforced by another large installation, Fort Templebreedy, on the cliffs immediately to the south-west. Templebreedy was smaller but still contained barracks, canteen, mess, underground stores, steel ammunition lockers and two 9.2-inch guns with a range of five miles. These were the defences only of Cobh.

The British also retained possession of the defences on Bere Island, and at Lough Swilly they maintained Fort Dunree and Fort Lenan. All of these included redoubts, moated ramparts, ammunition stores, underwater torpedo tubes, machine guns, howitzers and heavy artillery.* Three of the Cobh forts held reserves of water sufficient to last 995 men a minimum of three and a half months without resupply and even the fourth, Templebreedy, could hold out for six weeks with a strength of 200 before

---

* In 1937, the Committee of Imperial Defence listed Cobh's armament as two 9.2-inch and four 6-inch guns, six 18-pounders and fourteen machine guns.[25] This did not include a 9.2-inch and a 6-inch gun officially listed in the following year as reserve artillery (in Fort Carlisle and Fort Westmoreland respectively).[26] At Berehaven, there were two 6-inch and two 4.5-inch guns, two 12-pounders and five machine guns. The forts at Lough Swilly were defended by two 9.2-inch, two 6-inch and four 4.5-inch guns and four machine guns. The Irish told the British in 1938 that they did not want the 18-pounders and the machine guns.[27]

running dry.[28] All told, almost four thousand officers and men – 2377 of them at Cobh, 866 on Bere Island and 565 at Lough Swilly[29] – would defend these mighty forts, guarding scores of merchant ships and at least a hundred naval vessels.* Their occupation added between 200 and 400 miles to the Royal Navy's radius of operations in the Atlantic.[31] It was no idle metaphor when Winston Churchill, inveighing against their transfer in the House of Commons in May of 1938, described the ports as 'the sentinel towers of the western approaches'.[32]

Their strategic military importance was scarcely acknowledged in the Irish festivities that followed the British departure from Spike Island on July 11. For the Irish, these were a celebration of political independence, one that should have followed the end of the Anglo-Irish guerrilla war in 1921 but which had been indefinitely postponed in December of that year when the Treaty signatories had returned to Dublin without the inclusion of Northern Ireland in their promised jurisdiction and with a parliamentary oath of faithfulness to the British monarch in the Articles of Agreement. The Union Jack had been struck in Dublin in 1922 but the shadow of its falling had darkened any jubilation as the opponents of the British-imposed Treaty conditions, including de Valera, fought their old comrades of the Anglo-Irish war who had formed the Government of the new Irish Free State. The British agreement to abandon the three naval ports sixteen years later, however, did not necessitate any concessions from the Irish; and since their original retention by Britain had been specifically embodied in the 1921 Articles, de Valera's acquisition of Cobh, Berehaven and Lough Swilly had struck a very considerable blow at the sanctity of the Treaty. It was by no means the first damage to be inflicted upon it – nor was it intended to be the last – but the transfer of the ports to Eire represented a substantial assertion of Irish sovereignty. That this achievement belonged to a man who had so constantly and virulently opposed the terms of the Treaty made the events of July 11 all the more important for those Irishmen who believed that the civil war had not been fought in vain and all the more humiliating for those who had accepted the 1921 Agreement and who had won that civil war against the forces led – in theory, at least – by de Valera.

He had decided to hold no national celebrations on the 11th, apparently reasoning that since the Irish had yet to regain the six counties of Northern Ireland, they 'must not make it too difficult for the British to give them back'.[33] It is also likely that he feared the British might delay their final

* In July 1939, when the ports were already in Irish hands, the Admiralty in London calculated the number of Royal Navy vessels that might use the ports if permitted to do so by the Eire authorities. Cobh was to be an operations base for 20 auxiliaries and five escorts, and Lough Swilly for 44 auxiliaries and five escorts. Berehaven would have 20 auxiliaries and act as a base for a channel force.[30] These figures do not include the large number of merchant ships that would gather in Lough Swilly before crossing the Atlantic in convoy.

departure from Berehaven and Lough Swilly, which were to be evacuated later the same year, if the Cobh transfer prompted any embarrassing displays of Anglophobia. Nevertheless, a large crowd appeared at Kingsbridge Station to see the Taoiseach leave for Cobh and as his special train steamed through the Dublin suburb of Inchicore – the locomotive appropriately decked out with a giant Tricolour – the employees of the famous old engine works lined the tracks to cheer him.

Although he was only fifty-five, de Valera's eyesight was already very weak and he could have seen clearly only those of his friends and political supporters who sat closest to him on the train. 'Old comrades of the Anglo-Irish war,' the *Irish Independent* called them, coyly avoiding any mention of their civil war allegiance.[34] All but one of the TDs* travelling in the crimson-painted carriages of the Great Southern Railways were members of de Valera's Fianna Fail party and many of them had been active in the anti-Treaty forces. Yet the description was not inaccurate and three of the Government ministers on the train shared not only the same railway compartment but the particular distinction of a role, albeit a modest one, in the 1916 Dublin Easter Rising. Oscar Traynor, the Minister for Posts and Telegraphs, had been a member of the Irish Volunteers during the insurrection and Gerald Boland, the Minister for Lands, served with Thomas MacDonagh's 2nd Battalion in the Jacob's factory behind Dublin Castle. James Ryan, the Minister for Agriculture, had been a medical officer in the Dublin GPO under Patrick Pearse, the Commander in Chief of the Army of the Provisional Republic who, with fourteen others, was put before a firing squad by the British. Pearse's sister was on the train to Cobh on July 11. And so was one of the only two battalion commandants in the Rising to have escaped execution: de Valera.

The explosion of fog signals accompanied the arrival of their train at Cork and the sirens of the other Tricolour-draped locomotives in the station hooted when it set out again ten minutes later on the branch line down to Cobh harbour. In the town, buildings were festooned with streamers and bunting. In the bay, the yachtsmen had replaced their Union Jack pennants with Tricolours. The Royal Cork Yacht Club decided that day that it would in future fly the Irish flag, its officials declaring with perhaps unnecessary sensitivity that the Club ensigns previously displayed by their institution had carried 'no national significance'.[35]

HMS *Acasta* and the *Innisfallen* had cleared the harbour half an hour before de Valera's arrival and were out of sight round the headlands when his train pulled into Cobh. Dressed in a long black coat, black jacket, dark tie and hat, he stood on the quayside with his eldest son Vivion and Frank

---

* Members of the Irish parliament, the Dail (Teachta Dala, literally: Representative of the Dail).

Aiken, although it was Second Lieutenant Griffin who held the arm of the partially blind Taoiseach and guided him onto the boat, speaking to him all the while in Irish.[36] The ministers and parliamentarians were ferried across to Spike Island in a fleet of motor launches which the British War Office had at the last moment handed over to the Irish with something approaching bad grace.* On the island's jetty, the military band played the national anthem again as de Valera stepped ashore and, followed by Aiken and the Irish Chief of Staff, Major General Michael Brennan, walked to Fort Westmoreland. There on the ramparts, he handed his hat to Aiken and ran the Tricolour up the main flagmast.[38] Thus to another 21-gun salute, the flag of the Young Irelanders was raised above the forts that had, long before and in a different world, been named in honour of three unloved imperial Viceroys.

By no stretch of the imagination could the British evacuation have been regarded as a large-scale colonial withdrawal but it was the first time that the Irish had been given an opportunity to celebrate their national independence without at the same time emphasising the divisions within their young state. July 11 also marked the 17th anniversary of the Truce in the Anglo-Irish war, the last occasion on which Irish republicans fought together against the British before turning against each other in civil war. It was therefore natural that the Cobh ceremony should have been an essentially domestic political event and that the strictly military implications of the transfer – though they were understood – should have taken second place.

De Valera's tour of military inspection that evening seems to have been a formality and the fact that both of Fort Templebreedy's 9.2-inch guns were out of commission escaped the notice of the press.† In the speeches that were to follow, there was no word of the international dangers which threatened European peace and no public suggestion that the transfer of the ports would enable Eire to disentangle herself from British involvement in a future war. In a general election the previous month, the Fianna Fail party which de Valera founded in 1926 had won more than 50 per cent of the votes, a result that partly reflected the popularity of the Anglo-Irish settlement. De Valera therefore gave to the night's proceedings a party political flavour. From Cobh he travelled to the Cork town of Midleton to open a Volunteer hall for the part-time military reserve force which his

* The Eire authorities believed that at least seven of the nine small War Department boats at Cobh should be considered part of the 'fixed defences' and transferred to them free. The British took the view that only three of the vessels might 'perhaps' be regarded as such. The Irish eventually received six of them and for years afterwards the boats plied around Cobh harbour, betraying their English origins with names like *Raven*, *Jackdaw* and *Rover*.[37]
† One of the guns had steel choke – a decrease in calibre caused by the movement of the lining against the outer sleeve of the barrel during firing exercises – and the other had a cracked 'A' tube. The British promised to make good these deficiencies by the end of the year.[39] The damaged tube was replaced by October when Irish artillerymen test-fired the gun, hitting a 12-foot target at five miles' range.[40]

Fianna Fail Government had created four years before.* Throughout the day, de Valera's son Vivion had been wearing the uniform of a Volunteer officer.[43] At midnight, the Taoiseach returned to Cork city to attend a Fianna Fail 'victory ceilidhe', a social evening which by its very nature emphasised his party's responsibility for this new manifestation of Irish sovereignty.

When de Valera spoke at Midleton, he coupled the transfer of the ports with an invocation to God 'to restore unity to our country and bring the whole of this island again into the possession of the Irish people'.[44] In Cork he told his audience that without the restoration of the Irish language, 'what has happened today at Spike Island and Cobh will be very incomplete indeed, even if it is followed by our getting back in a very short time the whole of this country for the Irish people.'[45] The British evacuation was conceived by de Valera as a phase in the destruction of the Treaty, to be consummated when the British relinquished Northern Ireland, and a stage in the regeneration of the Irish nation. Events on the Continent – Germany's military ambitions, the continued growth of fascism and the strategic importance which the ports might soon acquire for the British – played no part in that night's considerations.

The moment was an emotional one for de Valera. On his way from Cobh to Midleton, he had asked his military escort to wait while he sat beside the country road, 'head in his hands in meditation or prayer'.[46] He did not consider the 1938 Anglo-Irish agreement a personal triumph, only 'a rectification of injustices' about which there was no bargaining to be done.[47] For de Valera, these injustices went back for several hundred years although the victories, humiliations and personalities which immediately shaped that day – and which were to influence political and military decisions on Ireland over the next seven years – all lay within the span of the last half century.

The history of the struggle for Irish freedom since 1900 is a familiar one but in 1938 the emotional if not the physical wounds of those who took part were still deep and painful. There was some inevitability about this since the three principal parties to the Irish crisis in the twentieth century – the Irish nationalists, the Irish unionists and the British – had shared one dominant characteristic: the almost constant preparedness as well as the

* The Volunteer Force was intended to capture the energies of young men who might otherwise have joined the Irish Republican Army. But it served a dual purpose for it also allowed de Valera to inject Fianna Fail blood into the army – the same army which had fought for the first Government and for the Treaty in the civil war. The political leaning of Volunteer recruits was acknowledged in a semi-official handbook in 1968. It said that 'a large proportion of its members, certainly of its officers and NCO members, joined because the force was sponsored by a government other than that which had held office from 1922 to 1932.'[41] Regular soldiers used to complain that Volunteers received speedy and unfair promotion.[42]

capacity to use armed force to support their demands. Britain and Ireland and that semi-distillation of both nations in the north-east of Ireland, exhibited almost identical degrees of self-interest in their dealings with each other.

For more than two hundred years, England's behaviour towards Ireland had been governed by considerations of national defence and by the need to preserve the realm. It was also coloured by hundreds of years of mainly Catholic revolt and consequent suppression, of famine, agrarian unrest and further suppression, the latter all the more cruel because of the Irish practice of appealing for foreign assistance against their rulers. For more than a century, Catholics were excluded from all political power and the Famine in 1847, with its resulting emigration, almost halved the population in twenty years. By the late nineteenth century, the worst excesses of English and Ascendancy coercion were less frequent and the corruption and inefficiency at Dublin Castle, the seat of the British administration in the country, had for the most part been expunged. Yet in London, magazines still caricatured the Catholic population of Ireland as an ignorant and dissolute peasantry, clothed in dirty rags and usually holding a cudgel. That a race which the British considered benighted should have produced organisations of intellectual standing as well as subversive power – the Young Irelanders or the Fenians – served to enrage them rather than create a new understanding of the nation which they had governed for so long. Liberalising legislation did not produce the desired stability in Ireland and the British came to regard the Irish as a people who clung to abstract, unrealistic ideals of freedom. The British habit of crushing any serious demonstration of these ideals had not faded with the years.

Irish attitudes towards the British were more single-minded even if they were often politically divided. While national liberation came throughout the nineteenth century to be sought chiefly through political means, armed rebellion remained a permanent and practised option. In the Westminster parliament, Irish MPs pursued an agitation so destructive that it made and broke British governments, a parallel to the physical violence that always lay beneath the surface. Gladstone's conversion to home rule in the 1880s temporarily muted the protests of nationalists but gave rise to a new movement among Irish loyalists – or Unionists as they now called themselves – who were fearful of native government. For the most part descendants of Protestant planters who had colonised Ireland in the seventeenth century, they were alarmed for their economic well-being, political security and religious freedom,[48] as well as their political supremacy.

Such independence as the British seemed anxious to grant the Irish, however, was of a strictly limited nature. An Ireland under home rule was to be an integral part of the Commonwealth. On this basis, Winston Churchill, the converted British Liberal and First Lord of the Admiralty, felt able to brave the 'fearful imprecations' of a Belfast Unionist mob in 1912[49] to support the doubtful concept of a united, free but British Ireland. With the Irish parliamentary leader John Redmond beside him, he told a Catholic rally that 'the flame of Irish nationality is inextinguishable'.[50] But 'nationality' did not mean separatism, even less republicanism.

A Government of Ireland bill had meanwhile been making its passage through the Commons in London under Asquith's Liberal Government. It proposed to give Ireland a separate parliament with jurisdiction over her internal affairs but without control of revenue, defence or relations with the Crown. Redmond accepted this rather deluded bill although the Unionists, led by Sir Edward Carson and James Craig – whose respective professions of barrister and stockbroker typified Unionist admiration for law and big business – refused to countenance its enactment. Carson organised the formation of the Ulster Volunteers, an army of Protestants pledged to resist Irish home rule, and in 1914 he authorised the importation of 19,100 rifles and two million rounds of ammunition from Germany,[51] a classic exercise in gun-running organised by Major Frederick Crawford, a Belfast businessman and experienced arms smuggler.

The formation of the Ulster Volunteers in the north-east of Ireland, where the majority of Protestants lived, had already provided the inspiration for the Irish Volunteers, a militant nationalist force whose founders were mostly members of the secret Irish Republican Brotherhood. There was an initial link with Redmond's parliamentary party but it did not last long. The young de Valera joined the Irish Volunteers, convinced that home rule would be won 'not by ballots but by bullets'[52] now that the British Conservative party was giving its support to the Ulster Volunteers. Nationalist suspicion of British intentions was further increased by what became known as the Curragh mutiny. When it seemed that British troops would be sent from the Curragh to keep order in Belfast on the introduction of home rule, Brigadier General Sir Hubert de la Poer Gough made it known that he and his fellow officers in the Third Cavalry Brigade would accept dismissal rather than move against Ulster. Churchill, on the other hand, was prepared to coerce the Northern Irish Protestants and secretly ordered a Royal Navy battle squadron to the Scottish port of Lamlash in readiness for an approach on Belfast. But the confrontation did not materialise. The home rule bill was placed upon the statute book in September 1914 but with two limiting clauses: it was not to come into operation until the end of the war that had just begun and until parliament had had an opportunity of creating special amending legislation for Ulster.[53]

Carson and Craig gave Lord Kitchener 35,000 Ulster Volunteers to send to the Western Front and many thousands of Redmond's followers joined the British ranks as well, at the enthusiastic bidding of their party leader. A minority of the Irish Volunteers would not serve the King, and in 1916 the two streams of Irish nationalism – for the Ulster Protestants had clearly developed their own strain of independent patriotism – achieved their appropriate apotheoses. In April, the Irish Volunteers, with James Connolly's Citizen Army, staged the rising in Dublin which was to prove the genesis of the final war against the British. Three months later, Carson's Ulster Volunteers attacked the German lines at Thiepval on the Somme, demonstrating their loyalty to the Crown with 5500 officers and men killed, wounded and missing. In Belfast afterwards, 'in house after house, blinds were drawn down, until it seemed that every family in the city had been bereaved.'[54]

Throughout the First World War, Germany itself showed little interest in Ireland although the Irish nationalists had expected more of her. Sir Roger Casement had prayed for Germany's salvation in 1914 because 'God Save Ireland is another form of God Save Germany',[55] and in December of that year he signed a 'Treaty' with Germany which tentatively proposed a landing in Ireland by a German-equipped Irish Brigade.[56] German guns had found their way to the Ulster Volunteers in 1914 and, in fewer numbers, to the Irish Volunteers in the same year. Just prior to the 1916 Rising, the Germans shipped arms for the Irish Volunteers but the vessel carrying them was forced to blow itself up, together with its cargo, after it was captured by the Royal Navy and put under escort to Queenstown. Germany, one of the 'gallant allies' boasted by Patrick Pearse when he read the Proclamation of the Republic from the steps of the Dublin GPO in 1916, was of little use to the Irish, as Casement realised.[57] Save for the shelter which U-boats occasionally sought in the remote bays along the west coast of Ireland, German military involvement in the island was virtually non-existent. The British, however, convinced themselves that the Irish, who had rebelled during England's moment of peril in 1916, were capable of more sinister dealings and in 1918 an 'Irish–German conspiracy' was discovered.[58] De Valera was imprisoned in the wave of detentions that followed although no proof of the conspiracy was ever made public.

When the world war had ended, nationalists and Unionists returned to their struggle to find that the field of battle had changed in the intervening years. The 1916 Rising, condemned at the time by the Redmondites, had given birth to a new and less moderate nationalism which was no longer satisfied with the kind of independence offered in the pre-war home rule bill. The Sinn Fein movement founded by Arthur Griffith ran in the general election of 1918, treating it as a poll for an Irish assembly, Dail Eireann, a separatist legislature which denied the legitimacy of British rule and was refused recognition by the British. In January 1919 the Dail formally established the Irish Republic; de Valera, who escaped from Lincoln jail in February, was in April elected President of the Dail – in effect, the Prime Minister – with Griffith as his Vice President. The last Irish war against the British, a conflict of assassination and reprisal by both sides, began that same year. The nationalist guerrillas claimed to be the army of the Republic – they were to become known within months as the Irish Republican Army – although the agreement which their leaders were finally to reach with the British Government provided for nothing like a Republic.

In 1920, a Government of Ireland Act at last came into being. It now proposed the setting up of two parliaments in Ireland, one for the six counties in the north-east and one for the rest. It thus protected the Protestant heartland in Ulster though the Unionists were forced to sacrifice three of the nine counties of the province in order to maintain a sizeable Protestant majority over the Catholic nationalist inhabitants. There was to be a Council of Ireland containing representatives of both parliaments, a piece of standing machinery for Irish unity should the two legislatures choose to end partition. The Act was ignored by Sinn Fein but shrewdly observed by the Unionists who in 1921, after bloody anti-Catholic riots in Belfast, formed the first Government of Northern Ireland.

When the British and the IRA agreed to a truce in July of 1921, therefore, partition was a fact and the Irish delegates to the subsequent Treaty negotiations were in no position to prevent the division of their country – only to campaign against it. De Valera, as President of the Dail, sent his delegates to talk to Lloyd George, the British Prime Minister, without preconditions and the Irish representatives – Arthur Griffith, Michael Collins, Robert Barton, E.J. Duggan and George Gavan Duffy – were divided among themselves. De Valera himself stayed in Dublin.

The negotiations involved three fundamental issues: the form of Irish civil government to be set up and its relationship to the Crown, partition, and British security arrangements. Under Lloyd George's final threat of 'war within three days', the Irish came away on 6 December 1921 not with a republic but with a dominion whose parliamentarians swore faithfulness to the British monarch. The ultimate unity of Ireland was only guaranteed by the promise of a Boundary Commission which would – so the Irish hoped – further curtail the size of Northern Ireland and thus make it impossible for the truncated province to exist as a separate entity. In contrast, the Irish spent surprisingly little time debating Britain's demands for the use of naval bases. Given the great constitutional issues at stake this was perhaps understandable but, as one historian has remarked, the Irish agreement to allow Britain the use of these bases even in peacetime 'would seem to have made nonsense of any claim to real independence, for such an arrangement would in any major war have made it wellnigh impossible for Ireland to preserve that neutrality which is the ultimate hallmark of sovereignty.'[59]

Yet that is just the arrangement which Griffith, Collins and the other plenipotentiaries accepted. Article 6 of the Treaty[60] stated that the British forces would undertake Ireland's naval defence 'until an arrangement has been made between the British and Irish Governments whereby the Irish Free State undertakes her own coastal defence' although it was Article 7 which contained the trap-door through which Irish sovereignty would disappear if Britain went to war. The Irish Free State, it said in paragraph b, 'shall afford to His Majesty's Imperial Forces . . . in time of war or of strained relations with a Foreign Power such harbour and other facilities as the British Government may require for the purposes of such defence as aforesaid.' An Annex[61] listed the specific facilities as Berehaven Dockyard, Queenstown and Lough Swilly. Belfast Lough in Northern Ireland was also included since the Treaty envisaged an end to partition, and the Annex contained a requirement for fuel stocks on Haulbowline Island and aviation facilities 'in the neighbourhood' of the ports.

In the context of the world war that was to break out less than eighteen years later, the discussions which took place on this issue were prescient, sometimes to the point of prophecy, although when Griffith raised the question of Irish neutrality with the British representatives on the first day of the conference, October 11, he did so in a general discussion of foreign policy rather than of British defence requirements. He indicated that Ireland would 'want to be free to be neutral' in the event of a war declared by Britain; Lloyd George countered by recalling that Cape Colony had not been compelled to introduce conscription during the 1914–18 war and that South Africa had sent troops to the war as a voluntary act. But, he said, South Africa 'could not be neutral. She would still be at war with Germany. So it would be with Ireland.'[62] Britain could not 'compel Canada to put her resources in but to allow her to be neutral would be to repudiate the King's sovereignty'.[63] To this, Griffith replied that the Irish could not enter a war freely 'if it is not a free choice', adding that he personally thought that Britain's position 'would be stronger in time of war if Ireland were neutral . . .'[64] This argument, in slightly different form, was to be heard again within twenty years.

Lloyd George had spoken of the Irish ports earlier that day, referring to the original British proposals sent to de Valera in July in which it was stated that Britain 'should maintain control of the sea, should have recruiting and air base facilities'.[65] The coast of Ireland, he told the Irish delegation, 'is essential to us, largely for the defence against submarines. You ought not to put us in the position of having to break a treaty in order to defend ourselves.'[66]

Winston Churchill, now Secretary of State for War and Air, had been instructed to prepare that part of the Agreement which dealt with strategic reservations[67] and for him, England's security and status were ruling considerations – a viewpoint that was entirely in accordance with previous British priorities in Ireland and which was to be demonstrated again in this same sphere in later years. Yet his attitude towards the ports, as it emerges in the account of Lloyd George's secretary Thomas Jones, seems to have been quixotic, flexible almost to the point of complaisance in discussion with his government colleagues but adamant when confronted by the Irish. On October 13, after consulting Earl Beatty, the First Sea Lord, Churchill told a preliminary meeting of the British representatives that 'what struck him was the little importance attached by the Admiralty to the Irish stations. There were a few guns at Bear [sic] Island. The Admiralty did not want Haulbowline. Beatty wanted one or two wireless stations.'* Lloyd George hoped that Beatty was 'not thinking too much of the Grand Fleet and forgetting all about submarines' but Churchill suggested that Queenstown† could be given to the Irish on the same terms as the Simonstown naval base which was maintained by South Africa but partly financed by Britain. Lloyd George demurred, suggesting that 'later we will hand over Bear Island, Queenstown, etc.'[69] Austen Chamberlain, the Lord Privy Seal, said that he too was 'doubtful about handing over Queenstown now', to which Churchill replied with panache: 'You can keep a man and boy there.'[70]

Churchill was not suggesting that the ports were unimportant, merely that they were unimportant at that moment, a realistic view but a dangerous principle upon which to work during a conference on Irish independence, as he himself realised. 'Our position,' he concluded, 'is "We must have free use of the Irish coasts in peace or war for Imperial defence." ' An Irish memorandum rejected the initial British demands for naval facilities, claiming neutrality for Ireland and this was discussed at the sixth session of the conference on October 21. 'We cannot be sure,' Churchill then argued, 'that the Irish would have power to keep an effective neutrality. We could not guarantee the confluence of trade in an area where submarines were lurking unless we had Queenstown and other ports . . . Our destroyers would have to go out to meet the enemy with a radius of operation reduced by 100 miles. We have the support of all our naval experts in the view we take . . . a completely honest neutrality by Ireland in the last war would have been worse for us.'[71] If Ireland bore Britain ill will in the future, Churchill also suggested, the ports might become 'nesting places for our enemies'.

The Irish began to bend on the ports three days later. Curiously, it was Birkenhead, the British Lord Chancellor, who pointed out to them the full implications of British naval occupation. It would, he told them, 'entitle other nations with whom we were at war to make you an enemy'. Collins replied that there would be a compensating point. 'A country refusing to

---

* Churchill's briefing by Beatty left something to be desired. Stressing Lough Swilly's importance for the protection of Liverpool commerce, Churchill said that arrangements over the port could be made with the 'Dominion of Northern Ireland'. He had to be told later that Lough Swilly was not in Northern Ireland at all but in County Donegal, which would fall under a new Dublin administration.[68]

† Queenstown gained its regal title when it afforded Queen Victoria her first landfall in Ireland. For the same reason, the name was not destined to endear itself to the Irish after independence, when it was officially referred to by the Free State authorities as Cobh.

recognise Ireland's neutrality,' he said, 'would make Ireland an enemy.'[72] This extraordinary *non sequitur* seems to have passed without comment save for a remark by Birkenhead that 'it might not pay to take advantage of the fact that you had departed from neutrality.'[73]

By the last day of negotiations, the Irish had gained one military concession, the right to a share in their own coastal defence after five years. But there the matter stood. It was understandable that British retention of harbour facilities would seem of less immediate consequence to the Irish than the declaration of faithfulness to the King and Britain's retention of Ireland's six north-eastern counties. Even de Valera, who was to become one of the Treaty's most implacable opponents, was prepared to accept a limited British presence in the ports.* His Document No.2 – the first being the actual Articles of Agreement – was twice put before the Dail and it would have accepted a five years' occupation of the ports.[75] Nonetheless, Irish preparedness to accept a British military presence in *both* parts of Ireland is a striking feature of the Treaty. It is clear that not only partition but the symbols of sovereignty – exemplified in the negotiations over the parliamentary oath and Ireland's dominion status – assumed far more importance in 1921 than the unneutral position into which the future Irish Free State would be thrust by Britain's physical hold on the ports, albeit on a 'care and maintenance' basis.

What the Irish got from all this was, in Churchill's phrase, 'dominion home rule'[76] and he at least was satisfied with the offer's acceptance. Erskine Childers, the Irish delegation's Secretary, was appalled at the outcome; his 'abiding image' of the last few hours of negotiation was Churchill, 'striding up and down the lobby lowering and triumphant, all heavy jowl and huge cigar projecting like the bowsprit of a ship'.[77] De Valera, 'an almost broken man',[78] had been given no warning that the delegation would sign such an agreement, the terms of which were in his view 'in violent conflict with the wishes of the majority of this nation'.[79] He vainly attempted a compromise that would have taken Ireland out of the Empire, recognising the King only as head of an External Association which would loosely bind the Irish nation to the Empire though not as a member. In May 1922 he walked out of the Dail.

Griffith was elected President in his place and the division in Irish nationalism was consecrated in Dublin in June when, with British encouragement, the new national army opened fire on members of the republican wing of the IRA who had taken over the Four Courts in protest at the Treaty. Churchill, as Colonial Secretary, had warned that the occupation

---

* De Valera had, however, appreciated their political importance. In 1919, he had been asked by the *Christian Science Monitor* whether he would hand the Irish ports to Germany if Ireland was free, and had replied that 'to be free means to be free, not to have a master. If England took away her troops and our independence were acknowledged, we would fight to the last man to maintain that independence. It is not a change of masters we want, though I do not know that the change would be for the worse.'[74]

must end if the Treaty was to be implemented but it was the kidnap of the national army's Deputy Chief of Staff, General J. J. O'Connell, that provoked the attack. According to Rory O'Connor, the leader of the republicans in the Four Courts, 'Mr Churchill cracked the whip . . .'[80] De Valera fled Dublin at the start of the civil war to join the republicans, by whom he was re-elected president of a rival 'government', a nominal leadership with little real power since the IRA Chief of Staff controlled military activities.

The republicans acknowledged defeat in May 1923. The probable casualty figure of just under four thousand dead[81] did not include Griffith, who died suddenly in June 1922. But among that number was Childers, shot by a pro-Treaty Government firing squad the following November. Michael Collins, the Commander in Chief of the national army, was killed in a republican ambush near Bandon in County Cork less than two weeks after Griffith's death. His body was taken by sea from Cobh for a state funeral in Dublin, a mournful night-time voyage which gave the British the opportunity to pay their martial respects. As the boat journeyed up the coast, its crew heard the Last Post sounding across the sea from a British naval squadron;[82] in the darkness, hundreds of Royal Navy ratings stood at attention along the decks of the warships as the funeral boat passed, in honour of the Irishman who had kept his word by the Treaty even at the cost of allowing Ireland's illusory revolution to devour its step-sons.

For it transpired that there had in fact been no revolution and that, despite the rhetoric of the first nationalist leaders, the institutions of the new state were fundamentally the same as the old British ones.[83] Legislature, executive and judiciary all functioned in a recognisably British pattern. W. T. Cosgrave, who became acting chairman of the pro-Treaty Government after Griffith's death and was to become President of the Executive Council of the Irish Free State, was a conservative who – when the civil war had ended – took his country along a constitutional path with little or no change in the culture of Irish political life. A British Governor General sat in Dublin and those TDs who supported the Government swore their faithfulness to 'King George V, his heirs and successors by law'. The remainder, the forty-four Sinn Fein members, refused to take their seats.

The Government's adherence to the Treaty, however, caused other problems. The civil war had left a spirit of lawlessness behind it. In the seven months from August 1923 there were 738 cases of arson and armed robbery[84] and in March 1924 armed men fired on British troops in the Treaty port of Cobh, killing one and leaving twenty wounded. That same year, General Richard Mulcahy, who had taken over as head of the army after Collins' murder and who was now Minister of Defence, faced a mutiny of old IRA men among the ranks of the Government forces. They reminded Cosgrave's administration that the IRA had only accepted the Treaty as a means of bringing the Republic into existence. In the Cabinet,

Kevin O'Higgins, the Vice President and Minister for Home Affairs, insisted that the army should be brought under Government control. Mulcahy resigned and O'Higgins, who was to be assassinated three years later by unknown gunmen, also demanded that the Adjutant General and two other senior officers relinquish their posts. It was as well for Cosgrave that the mutiny was suppressed for the following year the Boundary Commission, which the Treaty and its Irish adherents had enshrined as the ultimate security of national unity, fell apart when it became clear that Northern Ireland stood to gain rather than diminish in size as a result of its findings. At a hurried meeting in London, Cosgrave, Craig and the British Prime Minister, Stanley Baldwin, agreed that the existing boundary between Northern Ireland and the Irish Free State should remain unaltered.

In 1926, de Valera broke with Sinn Fein, founded his own party and entered the Dail, informing the officer who was supposed to administer the oath that his signature was given only to gain entrance to the parliament and that 'no other significance' should be attached to it.[85] It was an unsubtle form of conceit but one which would be exercised again when constitutional niceties had to be observed in order to be broken.

The Cosgrave Government was now faced with a growing world economic crisis and the unpopularity which the depression inevitably visited upon the administration was heightened in 1931 by a Draconian piece of legislation which set up a military tribunal with powers of capital punishment to deal with political crime. This placed the IRA further behind de Valera and in the 1932 election, Fianna Fail emerged as the largest party in the Dail. Although he did not possess an overall majority, de Valera was appointed President of the Executive Council, taking on in addition the portfolio of External Affairs. Before the election, the British Dominion Secretary, J.H. Thomas, had warned the Cabinet that 'if the General Elections in the Free State should result in the return of Mr de Valera, a difficult situation would be produced . . .'[86] It needed no great powers of foresight to grasp this point and in his first six years of office, de Valera's exertions were principally devoted to the dismemberment of the Treaty against which he had campaigned for so long. The first symbol of monarchical authority to be made redundant was the post of Governor General. In November 1932, de Valera requested the King to remove his representative and substituted in his place a Fianna Fail shopkeeper from Maynooth.

Land annuities were no longer to be paid to the British Treasury. The withholding of these funds – interest payments on loans which the British government had advanced to Irish tenant farmers at the end of the nineteenth century so that they could purchase their lands – coincided with de Valera's declared intention of abolishing the oath of allegiance. To the British, this sounded akin to conspiracy; J.H. Thomas 'sniffed the approach of treason in every tainted breeze'.[87] De Valera's biographers went to some lengths to prove that the Irish leader wanted these two issues to be considered separately[88] although it is doubtful if he cared very much. The abolition of the oath and the ending of annuity payments – financial transfers which had been guaranteed by the Cosgrave Government – were contained in the Fianna Fail election manifesto, and when the British Attorney General, Sir Thomas Inskip, spoke on the annuities question in August 1932, he understood what was happening in the Free State even if he underestimated de Valera's political abilities. 'It is not money that stands in the way of peace,' he said. 'There is something bigger and deeper. Does Mr de Valera want to be a partner in the Empire, or is he pursuing the will-o'-the-wisp of a republic?'[89] There was no doubt that de Valera was looking to a republic and there was nothing elusive about his purpose when he spoke at Arbour Hill in 1933:

> Let it be made clear that we yield no willing assent to any form or symbol that is out of keeping with Ireland's right as a sovereign nation. Let us remove these forms one by one, so that this State that we control may be a Republic in fact; and that, when the time comes, the proclaiming of the Republic may involve no more than a ceremony, the formal confirmation of a status already attained.[90]

These aims were easier to state in 1933 after he had secured a working majority with the support of eight Labour members at a further general election. The oath of allegiance, which for de Valera was 'an intolerable burden to the people of this State',[91] was removed by the Dail in May 1933 despite the opposition of Cosgrave's Cumann na nGaedheal party.

Britain reacted to the default on the land annuities – which with other payments totalled about £5 million – by placing a 20 per cent duty on all Irish goods entering Britain. The Irish Free State in its turn imposed protective tariffs and so began the economic war that was to bring much hardship and considerable social unrest to Ireland before it was brought to an end in 1938. But de Valera's accession and the consequent souring of relations had inspired other concerns within the British Government. By April of 1932, the British General Staff had been asked to produce a memorandum for the Cabinet's newly-formed Irish Situation Committee on the extent to which the application of economic sanctions against the Free State would affect the garrisons of the three British-occupied Treaty ports.

Since 1922, Cobh, Berehaven and Lough Swilly had settled into that trough of military inactivity which usually accompanies a period of international peace. Expenditure had been 'pared to the limit'[92] and the ports were in the hands of care and maintenance parties comprising a total strength of only 728 officers and men.[93] When the Committee of Imperial Defence discussed the 'unsatisfactory state of the coast defences of the Empire' in 1931, it was conceded – notwithstanding the growing importance of air power – that the British Air Staff could not offer RAF protection in place of the artillery defences at Cobh and Lough Swilly.[94] During Cosgrave's term of office, just two British destroyers based on Plymouth were maintained in Free State waters; according to a later Dominions Office report – and contrary to the impression which was to be given by Churchill – the Cosgrave Government was less than enthusiastic about its obligations under Articles 6 and 7 of the Treaty and reluctant to allow the British naval presence to be increased. The Free State, it said,[95] had been 'averse to visits by other vessels of the Royal Navy on account of the risk of incidents' and in 1930, when HMS *Tiger* visited Buncrana in Lough Swilly, Cosgrave's administration had given its approval 'rather reluctantly'.*

This restricted use of the ports was unlikely to change in the immediate aftermath of de Valera's election victory but the support given to Fianna Fail by the outlawed IRA, the liberty which the IRA expected under de Valera's Government and the military threat which this could present to the ports – with or without official sanction from the Irish authorities – brought forth some unhappy conclusions from the British General Staff. Their secret memorandum stated that if the British garrisons there were cut off from the mainland by an economic boycott, then the troops could be supplied and maintained 'only at considerable cost and inconvenience'. If relations became strained:

> there might be a possibility of raids, though such might be carried out by irresponsible people rather than as recognized agents of the Irish Free State; that is, they might be either merely countenanced by the authorities or they might, in certain eventualities, be directed by the authorities.
>
> In either event, the situation would be not only unpleasant but dangerous.[96]

The garrisons were 'weak and scattered' and 'not in a position to resist organized attack, without reinforcements'. The War Office had a reinforcement contingency plan but were worried that if the additional troops reached the ports before an attack – which they would have to do in order to be effective – then this would be regarded as a provocation. The General Staff's final conclusion was unambiguous:

> Owing to uncertainty as to the future of these ports, our present policy is to do the bare minimum for the comfort of the isolated garrisons . . . If it were not essential, for reasons of security, to hold the ports, the War Office would be glad for the occupation to come to an end and to be rid of an awkward commitment. It is for the Admiralty to advise as to the possibility of evacuation.[97]

* Proposals that a British destroyer or cruiser should visit Dublin for the Horse Show Week in 1931 collapsed because the Irish Government would only allow a daytime call by the vessel. It is unclear, however, why the British felt that a naval presence in the Irish capital would be welcomed at such a difficult period in the life of the Cosgrave administration even though the annual equitation festivities were supposed to be an international affair. Dublin was in any case not a reserved port.

The Admiralty subsequently told the Irish Situation Committee that it was 'necessary for the Navy to be able to rely on these ports being available at any time . . .' adding that

> Unless we maintain the British garrisons as at present, in the event of political conditions in the Irish Free State being hostile to this country, it might be found that the British Navy would be denied the use of these harbours. The situation might even become so serious that these harbours might be open to use by fleets hostile to this country. In each case the strategic position would be such that it would be impossible to ensure the safe arrival in war of the seaborne supplies essential to this country . . . the Admiralty consider that it is essential that the British garrisons should be maintained in the ports of Berehaven, Queenstown and Lough Swilly.[98]

The Admiralty, therefore, temporarily scotched any plans to pull out of the Treaty ports. The two memoranda largely conformed to the traditional structure upon which political and military decisions over Ireland had been taken in the past. The reliance on Irish defences as a protection for Britain, the possibility of foreign interference, distrust of the Irish authorities and fear of internal Irish subversion were historical preoccupations. Nonetheless, the General Staff's document was a significant one, for this was the first time that British military authorities had cast such serious doubt on the strategic importance of the facilities along the Irish coast. The idea that the ports were a liability – an 'awkward commitment' – rather than a necessity for survival was a comparatively new one and in the years to follow, this argument would influence not just the Admiralty but the British Cabinet as well.

The discussions on the ports were all the more problematical because of the unknown relationship between the IRA and the new Fianna Fail Government. The Irish Situation Committee in London agreed in August 1932 that 'as a matter of principle any attack must be resisted', concluding that if the port garrisons were threatened and British reinforcements sent in, the British should 'inform the Irish Free State, contemporaneously with the action, but without giving details'. As the conclusions decorously put it, the Committee was worried that information about plans for British resistance to an IRA attack 'might possibly come to the knowledge of the revolutionary bodies concerned'.[99]

De Valera's election victory had indeed been welcomed by the IRA. The organisation had withdrawn its allegiance from the 'president' of the non-existent republic and its 'Dail' in 1925 because of the apparent political impotence of his Sinn Fein movement. But his stated belief that the IRA could claim some continuity as a republican army – even if its members were 'misguided'[100] – gave it some credibility and de Valera was rewarded with its support in the 1932 poll. On March 9, Aiken, his new Minister for Defence, paid a friendly visit to an IRA leader in the jail at Arbour Hill Barracks and on the following day every prisoner there was

23

released. De Valera then revoked the orders proscribing the IRA. But his decision to fracture the Treaty and the imperial connection by constitutional rather than revolutionary methods ensured that this cordial honeymoon was short-lived.

In June, Sean Russell, an IRA leader since the civil war, addressed more than 15,000 members at Wolfe Tone's grave at Bodenstown.[101] The IRA began training and drilling with arms, generating as they did so a rival paramilitary organisation among the old Treaty supporters and former Free State soldiers who had fought in the civil war against republicans. Mulcahy, Cosgrave's former Minister for Defence, and Dr Tom O'Higgins, a brother of the murdered Kevin O'Higgins, were among the first committee members of this Army Comrades Association which, like veterans' movements elsewhere in Europe, rapidly developed along quasi-fascist lines with military parades, blue-shirted uniforms, Nazi-style salutes and anti-Communist speeches. By the autumn of 1932, the IRA was openly threatening Cosgrave's Cumann na nGaedheal and pro-Treaty supporters. Frank Ryan, one of the IRA's most prominent members, told a public meeting in Dublin that 'while we have fists, hands and boots to use, and guns if necessary, we will not allow free speech to traitors.'[102] This sort of thing went much further than the abuse and official coldness displayed in the Dail between Fianna Fail and Cumann na nGaedheal and in February 1933 the IRA's Army Council issued a directive to its units, denouncing Fianna Fail's 'capitalism' and stating that 'the policy of the Fianna Fail "Government" is bound to lead to widespread disillusionment amongst a great proportion of its Republican supporters . . .'[103] In the years that followed, the IRA and the Blueshirts fought each other in riots on the streets of towns in almost every part of the Free State and the military tribunal which had originally been introduced by Cosgrave's Government, was used to sentence arrested members of both organisations. By 1937, the court had convicted 868 supporters of the two groups, exactly half of whom were IRA members and half Blueshirts,[104] a figure which suggested a numerical if not a personal impartiality on de Valera's part.

Throughout this internal unrest, de Valera had gone on with his dismemberment of the Treaty. The Irish Nationality and Citizenship Act and the Aliens Act of 1935 – which theoretically made British citizens aliens if they were not citizens of the Free State – was followed in 1936 by the External Relations Act, legislation which removed the King from the Constitution in all but external diplomatic affairs and which was facilitated by Edward VIII's abdication. The economic war had also continued, affording some relief to small Irish farmers who received rebates on annuities and benefited from import protection, but causing great financial hardship to owners of larger farms who found their British markets closed to them.

In 1935, however, the British and Irish Governments took tentative steps to end their mutual political and economic isolation. In Geneva, where the Free State had been a member of the League of Nations for the past twelve years, Joseph P. Walshe, Secretary to the Irish Department of External Affairs, told the British Foreign Secretary, Anthony Eden, that de Valera would look favourably upon a British initiative to break the impasse.[105] At the same meeting, which took place in October shortly before the British elections, Walshe said that if the conditions of the 1921 Treaty could be revised, the Irish Free State was 'perfectly prepared to set aside the necessary money to carry out the defence of the ports' in consultation with British experts.[106] This, he said, 'would certainly involve the Irish Free State in a considerable expenditure, as it would involve the construction of destroyers' but the Irish were prepared to carry this out because they realised Britain's interest and the need for the 'close coordination' of the two countries' defences.[107]

Here was a critical extension of de Valera's domestic interests into questions of military strategy, a new approach that not only went to the heart of the sovereignty issue but also stretched far outside the constitutional and economic problems with which he had until now contented himself. Lobbying was at the same time going on in Dublin, where the press was informed that de Valera too had 'discussed matters' with Eden in Geneva. *The Times*, which tended to adopt a liberal attitude towards Anglo-Irish affairs at this period and whose staff were sometimes manipulated by governments to advance political proposals, carried a long article from its Dublin correspondent at the end of October. He suggested that Fianna Fail's anxiety not to lose an early opportunity of regaining the six counties in Ulster made the party 'more ready now to come to terms than it might be a few years hence.' Then he went on to consider the Treaty ports:

> The Governor-General will disappear in a few months' time. Then all that will remain of Dominion status will be the occupation by the British Navy of Lough Swilly and Bantry Bay. The Government is most anxious to get the warships out on purely sentimental grounds, and I believe that it would be ready to give Britain a very firm undertaking as to its attitude in time of war in return for a voluntary withdrawal. It is argued here that the strategic value of the Irish ports has diminished since the development of the air arm, that the success of aircraft against warships was demonstrated in striking fashion by the Greeks some time ago, and that Britain's security hardly would be affected by a withdrawal from Lough Swilly and Bantry Bay, particularly if the Free State Government should promise to allow free access to the British Fleet in time of war. In fact, the Free State Government probably would be willing to negotiate a treaty of mutual defence . . .[108]

The enticement of 'free access' to the Royal Navy in time of war and the assurance that the Irish only sought a British evacuation 'on purely sentimental grounds' seemed designed for those British ministers who — if they could disregard the rather startling omission of Cobh from the list of ports – would be interested in the possible benefits of a *détente* with de Valera.

It was fortunate for the Irish Government that Malcolm MacDonald, the 34-year-old son of the former British Prime Minister, took over as Dominions Secretary from J.H. Thomas in the autumn of 1935. MacDonald had been Parliamentary Under Secretary at the Dominions Office since 1931 and had been upset by Thomas's antagonism towards de Valera. Thomas, he felt, regarded de Valera's refusal to abide by the Treaty as 'a revival of old Irish hostility towards Britain'.[109] Thomas did not like the Irishman's 'terrifically sincere rigidity' and, according to MacDonald, 'used to refer to de Valera as "the Spanish onion in the Irish stew" '. MacDonald's own motives, however, were not chiefly altruistic. He was concerned lest the Irish Free State leave the Commonwealth and was conscious that Canada and South Africa – the latter with an interest in secession – might take de Valera's side if she did. More important was the international crisis. Hitler had been Reich Chancellor for almost three years and Germany had begun a programme of rearmament in 1934. In October 1935 Italy started to fulfil her fascist ambitions by invading Abyssinia. MacDonald thought that a major war was probably inevitable and remembers having 'a vague impression that Ireland might become an enemy' in such a war even though Britain had the right to use the Treaty ports.

MacDonald told his Prime Minister, Stanley Baldwin, that he believed a meeting should be arranged with de Valera. Lord Hailsham, the Lord Chancellor, was a right-wing Tory with a strong bias towards Northern Ireland and since he might have persuaded the British Cabinet to veto a meeting of this nature, MacDonald secured Baldwin's 'acquiescence' in keeping the plan from his fellow ministers.

The Committee of Imperial Defence was consequently asked to re-examine British defence requirements in Ireland and in February 1936 the Deputy Chiefs of Staff produced a curiously ambivalent and at times contradictory report which seems to have owed as much to a desire to facilitate MacDonald's policies as it does to naval strategy. The document[110] commenced by recalling a statement which de Valera had made nine months previously to the effect that the Irish Government 'would not allow their country to be made the base of attack on Great Britain'. This, said the Deputy Chiefs of Staff, was satisfactory 'but it does not go far enough'. The 1921 Treaty articles on the ports were not dictated primarily by any fear that the bases would be used for a hostile attack on Britain. 'The all-important consideration was that we wished to be certain that our Fleet and Air Force would have all the facilities which they would need in time of war for use against the forces of an enemy, more especially in the protection of the vital trade routes concentrated off the Irish coasts, in the security of which the Irish Free State is almost as much concerned as the United Kingdom.'

But after this very straightforward historical summary, the report went on to say that 'the present time seems a propitious one for the transfer since the immediate importance of the reserved ports has somewhat decreased in view of the recent re-orientation of the defence policy of this country.' This 'reorientation' involved a conviction that air power would in the future make ideas of naval supremacy redundant, and a desperate faith in Britain's ability to curb Germany's growing military strength. Exactly a year earlier, Britain and France had proposed an arms equality agreement with Germany which would, they hoped, put an end to fears of German aggression by 'legalising' the rearmament programme that Hitler had undertaken in violation of the 1919 Versailles Treaty. This idea collapsed when Hitler established conscription almost immediately after the proposals were put before him, but an Anglo-German naval agreement later in the year theoretically restricted Germany's warship production by allowing her to build a navy only one third the size of Britain's. The British took confidence from this, although they permitted Germany to build a submarine tonnage 60 per cent of Britain's; the agreement only encouraged Hitler to expand his rearmament still further.[111]

It was therefore perhaps not surprising that the contradictions inherent in Britain's international defence strategy should, in somewhat different form, have found their way into the memorandum on Ireland prepared for MacDonald:

> It is not suggested for a moment . . . that the free and unimpeded use of these ports is in any way less vital to our Fleet than it has been in the past, but rather that they have assumed a somewhat lower place in the order of priority for the modernisation of defences than they had previously held, consequent upon the changed international situation.[112]

The Deputy Chiefs of Staff then proposed that the Irish Free State should be asked to place airfields at the disposal of the RAF in the event of war – this was a tightening up of the Annex to the 1921 Treaty rather than a relaxation – and that the Irish should not be discouraged from supplying 'a small force of destroyers of their own' if they wished to do so. The second of six conclusions at the end of this perambulation stated baldly: 'Provided improved relations are assured, despite the risks involved, it would be desirable to offer to hand over the complete responsibility for the defences of the reserved ports to the Irish Free State.'

In this proposal, and in however confused a fashion, lay the fundamental element of trust which the British – or at least MacDonald and his colleagues in the Dominions Office – were trying to inject into Anglo-Irish affairs, a demonstration of confidence that would hopefully be rewarded not by further demands but by a new relationship between the two countries. This same statecraft, applied to other nations, would carry the badge of appeasement two years later and in Britain, long after the end of the Second World War, the transfer of the Irish ports would be seen as one with the nationally humiliating policies pursued by Chamberlain's Government in the face of war.

De Valera cautiously agreed to meet MacDonald in London on his way to Switzerland for eye treatment and in March 1936 Dulanty, the Irish High Commissioner, conducted MacDonald unobtrusively to de Valera's rooms in the Grosvenor Hotel above Victoria Station.[113] MacDonald recalled later[114] that he had arrived at the tradesman's entrance of the hotel in order to avoid publicity and had been taken through the kitchen and up the servants' back stairs before 'slipping into de Valera's room'. He found de Valera 'by far the most rigid, obstinate man I have ever negotiated with as well as being the most charming and genial'. At the start of the discussions, MacDonald made it 'absolutely clear that there was no chance of the British Government revising its views on partition' and de Valera replied that he could not alter his own views on the matter. The financial dispute, constitutional questions and the ports occupied their time. At the end of their talk, His Majesty's Secretary of State for Dominion Affairs left the hotel by the same route as he had entered, through the tradesman's door.

MacDonald wrote a paper based on this and further discussions with de Valera and submitted it to the British Cabinet in May.[115] It said that the absence of agreement between the United Kingdom and the Irish Free State was 'the most serious aspect of inter-Imperial relations' and that it tended 'to weaken the moral authority of the British Commonwealth of Nations in world affairs'. Parliament and public opinion were increasingly impatient with this situation, MacDonald said, and an early agreement was 'all the more desirable in the light of the dangers of the present international situation'. The paper – which was basically a proposal to open formal negotiations with de Valera – covered the economic war, trade relations, constitutional issues and defence; on the ports, MacDonald submitted the report prepared by the Deputy Chiefs of Staff, which had not yet been studied by the Committee of Imperial Defence.

Baldwin had agreed that MacDonald's memorandum should be placed on the Cabinet agenda with the proviso that it should not be discussed until a meeting of the Irish Situation Committee, which included those ministers most concerned with Anglo-Irish affairs. The committee subsequently met in the Prime Minister's room at the House of Commons on May 12. MacDonald, who felt that the meeting was 'very tense', sat opposite Baldwin, who at this point chose to take no side in the debate. Hailsham condemned the memorandum and made, in MacDonald's words, 'a brilliant attack on everything in the paper'. He believed that the problem was a hopeless one and predicted that a failure in negotiations would lead only to a further deterioration in relations with the Irish Free State. MacDonald was dismayed when the division bell rang and Baldwin hurriedly adjourned the meeting. As the ministers were leaving, however, Neville Chamberlain, the Chancellor of the Exchequer, asked Mac-

Donald to visit him in his room after the vote. MacDonald did so, to find Chamberlain writing at his table. Chamberlain then asked him to give the replies which he would have made to Hailsham if the meeting had not been interrupted by the division bell. When MacDonald had finished, Chamberlain said that he supported the idea of formal negotiations, adding: 'You can count on my help.'[116]

When the committee met again on May 25, Chamberlain had been lobbying on MacDonald's behalf. Sir John Simon, the Home Secretary, was now favourable, though 'naturally and typically critical of some things'. MacDonald thought that the British might be able to coax de Valera into settlement talks if the Government made a declaration 'to the effect that the Irish Free State is mistress of her own destiny'.[117] This, it was hoped, would prevent de Valera from taking the Free State out of the Commonwealth. Baldwin regarded the threat to the Empire represented by a possible Irish secession as the principal reason for starting negotiations with de Valera. MacDonald held to his views about a declaration although his explanations suggested an attitude towards the Irish which bordered on condescension. 'It is well known,' he said, 'that Mr de Valera himself attaches very great importance to such a declaration being made and public opinion in the Irish Free State, which is greatly interested in questions of abstract freedom, would also warmly welcome such a declaration . . . Irish mentality being what it is, abstract considerations of this kind have a very great importance.' De Valera and many of his supporters were 'obsessed with the feeling that so long as they might be subject to any restriction they were not in enjoyment of full political freedom.' The declaration – which would rule out any British military coercion if the Irish Free State decided to leave the Commonwealth – would have a beneficial effect on de Valera and also 'on the more extreme Republicans, who would no longer be able to make use of this imaginary grievance'.[118]

This was misleading. The physical partition of Ireland – about which there was nothing abstract – was just as important a grievance within the IRA as any subservience to Britain, and de Valera, while he does not seem to have entertained any serious idea of taking over Northern Ireland by violent means, shared the same scale of political values. MacDonald judged that de Valera's chances of obtaining a united Ireland were higher if the Free State remained within the Commonwealth, yet he quite misunderstood how this idea would be received in the Free State. 'Responsible politicians,' MacDonald said, '. . . would be forced by circumstances to realise that . . . in order to secure a united Ireland they would have to give up their Republican ideal.' Such phantom expectations – for this was a ghost of the old dominion home rule idea – should have been forsaken long before.

It was Chamberlain who pointed out that if MacDonald's declaration was made, 'it would be exceedingly difficult to bring effective pressure to bear on the Irish Free State in the last resort, however grave the emergency might be', to which MacDonald replied that if de Valera declared a Republic, 'his next step in his present mood would be to endeavour to make a defensive alliance with the United Kingdom'.

It was only at this point that Inskip, now the Minister for Co-ordination of Defence, raised the question of the ports, saying that 'he imagined it was our intention to retain our hold on the defended ports . . .' Simon, who had said little during the meeting, suggested that the ports were militarily 'untenable' if they were attacked, and MacDonald, repeating the arguments of the Deputy Chiefs of Staff, said that if the Free State left the Commonwealth, 'we should only be able to maintain our position in the defended ports by force. Surely we would not contemplate that?'

For the second time in fifteen years, the role of the ports was being relegated to second, even third, place in British Government discussions on Anglo-Irish relations. This time, however, military doubts about the worth of the facilities, combined with the new confidence which Mac-Donald was trying to create with the Free State, were turning the harbours into a bargaining counter. That the great ports should be given away in order to be retained in war – on the grounds that their retention in peacetime might lead to their surrender – was an unquestioned equation; and at this stage, not one of MacDonald's Cabinet colleagues asked what would happen if de Valera opted for neutrality in the next war.

During the summer of 1936, the Chiefs of Staff deliberated over the ports, basing their judgements on MacDonald's determination that if the worst came to the worst, 'the Irish Free State should at least leave the Empire as a friend and not as an enemy.'[119] The Chiefs of Staff were encouraged to look upon the problem of the Irish defences in its constitutional context, although such political opinions as they expressed appear to have been reached by a robust military analysis; at a meeting chaired by Sir Ernle Chatfield, the First Sea Lord, on July 6, for instance, de Valera was uncharitably described as 'a fanatic by temperament'. But their military judgements contained the same ambiguities which had appeared in the February memorandum from the Deputy Chiefs of Staff. A 'most serious' strategical position would be created if the ports were denied to the navy in wartime since Ireland lay across Britain's trade routes. But:

> on the other hand, the usefulness of the ports to the Royal Navy, should the Irish Free State be hostile to us in war, was extremely doubtful. They were land-locked and impossible to use or maintain without the co-operation of the Irish, unless the whole country was conquered. The situation which might arise if we were at war, say, with Germany and if the Germans, by offering to leave Ireland completely independent, obtained their co-operation against us, would certainly be extremely serious. Nevertheless, doubt was expressed as to whether the Irish would be tempted even by this bribe; they might be even more suspicious of German domination than of British.[120]

Sir Edward Harding, MacDonald's Permanent Under Secretary who was attending part of this meeting, thought that Britain had two choices over the ports: 'One was to hold on to them as outposts in a foreign country, like Gibraltar. The other was to say to the Irish Free State that she could hold these ports as an independent Republic and guarantee us the use of them . . .' There was no doubt which of these two de Valera would prefer, although he would never agree with Harding that it was in the Irish Free State's interest to guarantee Britain the use of the ports.

A Joint Planning Sub-Committee was then asked for a report on defence matters relating to the Free State and later in July it produced a series of recommendations* which favoured an offensive–defensive alliance with Ireland rather than the maintenance of the harbours as British possessions, 'a series of "Gibraltars" scattered round the Irish coast'.[121] In September, Sir Warren Fisher wrote to Dulanty on behalf of the British Government, setting out the constitutional and defence questions which might be considered at formal discussions; he suggested a transfer of the ports to the Irish Free State on condition that the British should be guaranteed their use 'in time of war or strained relations'.[122]

Around the south Irish coast, the two British destroyers maintained their increasingly superfluous duties, keeping generally to Cobh and Berehaven after de Valera came to office. A proposed visit by a destroyer to Buncrana in 1935 was dropped after an objection by Dulanty in London.† The ports were in need of complete modernisation but the British, who estimated the cost of this at £276,000, decided that no further expense should be incurred since it was 'desirable' to transfer the harbours.[124] The debate on Irish defence now remained stalled for almost a year as de Valera, aware that no all-Ireland settlement would be forthcoming from the British, concentrating on his new national Constitution.‡

* It is a little disturbing to note that these provided for a war against France as well as Germany. In 1936, France was Britain's closest ally and was correlating her defence planning with the British. Whoever the war was to be fought against, the Sub-Committee added the Irish port of Dun Laoghaire east of Dublin to their list of required facilities.

† Two years later, the British still felt that the Irish would welcome their warships. Two Royal Navy vessels which called into Cobh after de Valera came to power had 'made themselves very popular', according to a Dominion Office paper in October 1937.[123] A hand-written note by an anonymous civil servant at the end of the same document, said: 'It seems clear that visits by ships of the R.N. wd [sic] generally be popular, but that the essential point is whether or not the F.S. [Free State] police can guarantee to prevent incidents which might be deliberately caused by a handful of irreconcilables . . .'

‡ Article 2 of the Constitution claimed all of Ireland to be the 'national territory' – Article 3 placed this in abeyance by accepting jurisdiction only over the 26 counties 'pending re-integration of the national territory'. The 'special position' of the Catholic Church was recognised but other churches were acknowledged and there were prohibitions against religious discrimination. Parliament was once again to have a second chamber, the prime minister (until then, the President of the Executive Council) was to be called 'Taoiseach' and the Constitution provided for an elected President as head of state, a post which further emphasised the nation's denial of the King's sovereignty. The name of the state was to be known in the Irish language as 'Eire' and in English as 'Ireland'. With this, the Irish Free State ceased to exist.

This did not, as MacDonald had feared, take the Free State out of the Commonwealth. It contained no reference to dominion status and the principle of external association was included only in the vaguest manner but it was left to the British Government to decide whether de Valera's state was still within the Empire. There was no mention of a Republic in the document; and on 29 December 1937, when the Constitution came into force, the British immediately declared that it did not affect membership of the Commonwealth.

Through the last six months of 1937, by which time the draft Constitution had been published, MacDonald's discussions with de Valera were therefore more or less confined to the economic war and defence. On October 4, the two men met again at the Grosvenor Hotel in London and de Valera repeated his country's refusal to pay the land annuities, a figure which MacDonald estimated at about £78 million.[125] MacDonald suggested a new financial agreement which would relieve the Irish Government of the annuity payments, requiring them instead to carry the cost of some pensions and small loans and to spend 'considerable sums' on the ports. The three defended harbours had now become an item in a financial deal between London and Dublin.

De Valera argued – as he was to do with Chamberlain, the new British Prime Minister, three months later – that the cost of the ports would be a heavy burden for his country and that an increase in the Free State's defence forces – necessitated, de Valera claimed, by the country's proximity to Britain – was likely to cost £1 million a year. He himself and 'strong Nationalists' would be glad if the Irish gained control of their own ports but he feared such a proposal would not be accepted if the Irish had to pay maintenance costs. MacDonald apparently did not contest this but asked how de Valera felt about a mutual defence agreement. 'He knew the importance which we attached to an assurance about the use of the ports in time of war,' MacDonald reported to the Cabinet. 'I knew that he felt it would be extremely difficult, if not impossible, to give that assurance.'

De Valera spoke of the possibility of making a request for British defence experts, a common defence plan and interchangeable equipment 'because our forces would co-operate together'. There was even talk of the construction of a munitions factory in the Free State. But de Valera said that the Irish people 'were nervous of being dragged into some Imperialist war' which Britain might wage:

They did not want to fight for India or other of our possessions far away. In the Irish Free State they really did not care about the Empire; they could not take the same pride in it which we in Britain did; they had not been so much concerned in the making of it, and had suffered a good deal at our Imperialist hands.[126]

This was as good a definition as any to explain why de Valera's Ireland could not be relied upon to stand by Britain in the approaching war. If MacDonald had been in any doubt as to the future neutrality of the Free State – or of Eire, as it was about to become known – such uncertainty could no longer be excused. In 1927, de Valera had claimed in the Dail that 'the right of maintaining our neutrality is the proper policy for this country' for he regarded this as the right of an independent state, irrespective of the prevailing diplomatic and strategic circumstances.[127] This policy did not change. In June 1936, he told the Dail: 'We want to be neutral';[128] Dulanty drafted a note of de Valera's attitude: 'If no common interest were at stake, our attitude that of benevolent neutrality.'[129] Eleven months later, de Valera emphasised in a Dail speech the importance for Irish neutrality of a transfer of the ports.[130]

By the end of 1937, political and strategic circumstances were grave indeed. European stability was collapsing as Germany cemented her ties with Mussolini and the Allied powers rearmed. Unknown to the Allies, Hitler was already planning the subjugation of Austria and Czechoslovakia and the civil war in Spain had garnered socialist or fascist sympathies in most European nations. Even Ireland had been peripherally involved when a contingent of Irish Blueshirts fought, rather unsuccessfully, for Franco. Since MacDonald had made it clear that Britain would make no concessions on partition, the British had no reason to assume that de Valera would recognise a 'common interest' or that a loyal Ireland was about to rally to her side.

When the British Cabinet's Irish Situation Committee met once more in the middle of December 1937, Chamberlain seemed resolved to accept any settlement with de Valera in the uncertain hope of cobbling up some form of defence agreement. 'Even an agreement which fell short of being completely satisfactory,' he told his colleagues, 'would be better than the insecurity of the present situation.'[131] The military, air and naval authorities continued to the end with their open counsel: insistence that the ports should be available in wartime tempered by a declared inability to defend them within an hostile Ireland. In January 1938, within days of the ultimate conference at Downing Street between de Valera and Chamberlain, the Chiefs of Staff – Lord Chatfield (Navy), Lord Gort (Army) and C.L. Newall (Air) – concluded that while the non-availability of the Irish ports might so increase Britain's difficulties that 'the life of the nation would be imperilled', it would need a British division together with anti-aircraft defences at *each* port to defend them from attack by the Irish Army. Then, in a final statement that sealed the fate of the Royal Navy's outposts along the western approaches, the Chiefs of Staff announced that although they agreed that Britain should insist on a complete assurance from Ireland on the wartime use of these ports, '. . . we consider that it would be preferable to waive insistence on a formal undertaking which might be politically impracticable for Mr de Valera to give, and which would not necessarily have any value in the event, if by so doing we could secure a satisfactory agreement with Ireland.'[132] What was in fact secured was Eire's neutrality in the Second World War, a publicly non-aligned independence that finally demonstrated the sovereignty of de Valera's state and her break with the Empire.

What had originally been intended by the British as a settlement to improve political and economic relations between Britain and one of her dominions was about to become a conference on Anglo-Irish relations in a future war. This was partly de Valera's doing. The Irish Cabinet's proposal for the Downing Street talks envisaged discussions 'in regard to economic and other measures to be adopted in time of war'. De Valera, who was now going to push harder for an end to partition, told his Cabinet in Dublin that 'he proposed to point out that such measures would depend fundamentally upon the relations existing between the two countries on the outbreak of war . . .'[133] The British were probably supposed to view this as an offer of wartime co-operation in return for an ending of partition or, at the least, the return of the ports and the cessation of the tariff war. The British records suggest that they were not so easily taken in, but when the conference began in London between Chamberlain and de Valera on 17 January 1938, this was the path along which the talks developed.

No progress was made on partition and so de Valera insisted on Irish control of the ports without a defence agreement. He maintained that there was no formula 'which would both hand the ports over to Ireland and yet lay it down that the United Kingdom had the right to use them in an emergency';[134] but there was a certain amount of sophistry in this. A defence agreement extending Article 6 of the 1921 Treaty – which allowed Ireland 'a share in her own coastal defence' in the future – could at that moment have been proposed. But de Valera would allow no conditions. MacDonald was to recall later that for de Valera, Irish control of the ports was 'not only a symbol of independence but an *establishment* of independence. He thought that any tiny qualification of a principle – in this case, sovereignty – was a denial of that principle.'[135] It must have been obvious to the British delegation that de Valera regarded the ports more as a political than a defence issue; British defence interests were represented at the Downing Street conference by Inskip but de Valera had left his Minister for Defence, Frank Aiken, in Dublin. De Valera himself dealt with the ports in his capacity as Taoiseach and Minister for External Affairs.

Less than twenty-four hours after the conference began, Chamberlain had conceded that he did not expect 'an assurance here and now' on the availability of the ports if they were transferred.[136] This was the policy of appeasement in operation, the satisfying of demands in advance of any request for political remuneration. Sure enough, the draft of a defence agreement was handed to de Valera on the following day and, with equal inevitability, de Valera announced that the powers of his delegation were limited and that he would have to take the draft to Dublin for his Cabinet to study. A month later, there were conference discussions of maintenance costs – during which de Valera temporarily contrived to represent the ports transfer as a heavy burden on Ireland* – and at one point Chamberlain said that the ports could not be handed back unless Eire made some form of trade concessions to Northern Ireland. But MacDonald urged that this condition be dropped.

As the weeks of negotiation passed, the prolonged conference caused apprehension outside the British Isles; towards the end of March, the Americans began to show an interest in the outcome. There was a discreet conversation between Chamberlain and Joseph P. Kennedy, the American Ambassador in London. The Americans were particularly concerned about the possible repercussions among Irish Americans of an Anglo-Irish diplomatic failure – there were to be mid-term elections to the United States House of Representatives later in the year – and Kennedy also visited Lord Halifax, the British Foreign Secretary, early in April with an idea which Halifax subsequently passed on to MacDonald. If the conference reached no agreement, Kennedy 'thought that it would be well worth while to get de Valera to make some statement commenting favourably upon the experienced sincerity of the British Government . . .'[138] In the event, de Valera was not called upon to make such statements about the quality of British diplomacy, for on April 25, British and Irish delegations signed an agreement which provided for a single Irish payment of £10 million to end the economic war and which gave Eire unconditional possession of the ports.

According to MacDonald, the ports were a very reluctant concession. 'We thought,' he said long afterwards, 'that if we tried to use the ports against the wishes of the Eire Government, this might drive Eire into the arms of our enemies. Also we hoped that if there was a war and if – or because – we had given up the ports, Eire could come in on our side.'[139] The calculations of the Chiefs of Staff undoubtedly played a decisive role in this argument but if their advice had not coincided with the policy of a government so determined to create a new understanding with a nation which was obviously passing outside any British control, the outcome might have been different. If there was a mistake in all this – and Churchill was among the first to regard the transfer of the ports as a colossal blunder – then it was a failure on the British side to appreciate that Irish policy towards Britain had not developed as fast or evolved in the same way as British policy towards Ireland over the past seventeen years. De Valera's resolve to establish the political independence of his country had remained unchanged since the Treaty signatories returned to Dublin in December 1921. Insofar as there was any movement in this resolve, it was his growing realisation that Irish possession of the ports was not just a symbol

---

* Chamberlain suggested with some sarcasm that it might therefore be better 'to spare Mr de Valera the embarrassment of having the Treaty ports offered to him'.[137]

but an essential physical requirement of an independent foreign policy in a European war.*

De Valera suggested this when he spoke in the Dail two days later. The handing over of the port defences, he said, 'recognizes and finally establishes Irish sovereignty over the Twenty-Six Counties . . .' It was unnecessary 'to stress to anybody who has desired the independence of this country the importance of that agreement from the point of view of Irish sovereignty.'[142] Cosgrave claimed that his Government could have secured the ports 'six or seven years ago' but had hesitated because of the expenditure which this would have imposed on the Free State. Aiken angrily interrupted Cosgrave, describing this assertion as 'absolutely untrue'.†

In the light of forthcoming events, the debate that took place in the House of Commons on May 5 was a good deal more memorable and historic. After summarising the economic settlement, which also included several mutually beneficial trade arrangements, Chamberlain explained the transfer of the harbours as a concession without any immediate advantage to Britain. 'After most careful consideration,' he said, '. . . we came to the conclusion that a friendly Ireland was worth far more to us both in peace and in war than these paper rights which could only be exercised at the risk of maintaining and perhaps increasing their sense of grievance . . .'[144] The transfer, said Chamberlain, had been 'an act of faith' conducive to good relations; de Valera had 'announced his intention to put those ports into a proper state of defence' so that he could implement his assurance that Irish territory would not be used as a base by any foreign power for an attack upon Britain.

Winston Churchill's speech was prophetic and pointedly malevolent in its references to de Valera. Churchill had held no office for nine years, and his warnings of German rearmament since 1934 had been regarded by

---

* In conversation with the author, MacDonald said that his original proposals in his talks with de Valera were different to the final agreement 'because of de Valera's toughness'. MacDonald was against any modification of Irish allegiance to the Crown. 'I was much too "wishful thinking" about the kind of agreement I could get with de Valera,' he said. 'This has always been one of my faults.'[140] He also tended to act upon intuition: the minutes of the 1936 Irish Situation Committee quote him as basing his assessment of de Valera's intentions 'more on instinct than on any direct evidence'.[141] Yet MacDonald's personal and political integrity helped to create the benevolence of Eire's future neutrality. For a detailed discussion of his pre-war negotiations with de Valera, see Deirdre McMahon's *Malcolm MacDonald and Anglo-Irish Relations 1935–8* (MA Thesis, University College Archives) Dublin 1975.

† Cosgrave said that his Minister for Defence, Desmond FitzGerald, had been told in London that the British 'looked forward' to handing over the ports but there is no record of an Irish approach to the British in 1930 or 1931. The Cosgrave Government had been told in 1926 that the British Cabinet 'was not prepared to discuss the handing over of the defences of the ports in Southern Ireland . . .'[143]

Baldwin and then by Chamberlain as irrational and alarmist. The Government's supporters could regard the former First Lord of the Admiralty as a man who had passed the peak of his political life; indeed, at that time the summit of his career was still framed by the 1921 Anglo-Irish Treaty and the foundation of the Irish Free State which, as Colonial Secretary, he had helped to build. Now he was witnessing the Government's participation in the destruction of the agreement to which he had lent his name, and at times the frustration which he felt at the public's acceptance of the new settlement with de Valera burst through in his speech. He was little interested in the economic *détente*, devoting himself almost exclusively to the question of British defence. He apologised for striking 'a jarring note' in the afternoon's proceedings then condemned the transfer of the ports with a combination of sarcasm and detailed strategic argument.

If the Royal Navy was denied the use of Lough Swilly and had to work from the Scottish port of Lamlash, he said, 200 miles would be struck from the effective radius of British flotillas; if the Navy was denied Berehaven and Queenstown and had to work from Pembroke Dock, 400 miles would be cut from their radius out and home.

These ports are, in fact, the sentinel towers of the western approaches, by which the 45,000,000 people in this Island so enormously depend on foreign food for their daily bread, and by which they can carry on their trade, which is equally important to their existence.

. . . Now we are to give them up, unconditionally, to an Irish Government led by men – I do not want to use hard words – whose rise to power has been proportionate to the animosity with which they have acted against this country, no doubt in pursuance of their own patriotic impulses, and whose present position in power is based upon the violation of solemn Treaty engagements.[145]

The Times, which supported Chamberlain's appeasement policies, had been unwise enough to refer to the defence of the Irish ports as an 'onerous and delicate task' from which Britain had been released. After quoting from the newspaper, Churchill drew his own conclusion. 'I dare say you could make arrangements with many countries to release us from a great many burdens of a similar kind,' he said. '. . . We are to sacrifice £4,000,000 revenue because this tiresome business of defence is taken out of our hands . . .' For Churchill, British defence priorities had not changed since 1921 – 'the primary purpose of holding these ports,' he said, 'is the defence of Britain' – and in one step he reached the climax of his argument: what guarantee did the British have that 'Southern Ireland' would not declare neutrality if Britain was engaged in war with a powerful nation?

> Under this Agreement, it seems to me more than probable . . . that Mr de Valera's Government will at some supreme moment of emergency demand the surrender of Ulster as an alternative to declaring neutrality.*

It would be an easy step for the Dublin Government to deny Britain the use of the ports in future:

> You hope in their place to have good will, strong enough to endure tribulation for your sake. Suppose you have it not. It will be no use saying, 'Then we will retake the ports.' You will have no right to do so. To violate Irish neutrality should it be declared at the moment of a great war may put you out of court in the opinion of the world, and may vitiate the cause by which you may be involved in war. If ever we have to fight again, we shall be fighting in the name of law, of respect for the rights of small countries . . .[146]

Churchill's speech, which did not pass without interruption, made no impression on the Government front bench.

By the autumn of 1938, when the two remaining ports of Berehaven and Lough Swilly were to be transferred to the Irish authorities, Hitler's demands for the Czech Sudetenland with its three million German-speaking population had taken Europe to the very edge of conflict. On September 15, eleven days before the Irish Army was scheduled to take over the forts on Bere Island, Chamberlain flew to Germany to appease Hitler by personally accepting the principle of the Sudetenland's incorporation into the Reich. On the 22nd – four days before the abandonment of the Royal Navy's westernmost defences – he returned to placate Hitler with a suggestion that the Sudetenland should be turned over to Germany without a plebiscite. But a new and unexpected demand from Hitler that Germany must occupy the area by October 1, was rejected by the Czech Government; Czechoslovakia's territorial integrity had been guaranteed by France and on September 25 Britain reluctantly decided that she would have to support her French ally if she became engaged in a war with Germany.

On the morning of September 26, in a corner of Europe far from these events, Second Lieutenant John Griffin, the 27-year-old artillery officer who had escorted de Valera across to Spike Island in July, was driven from Cobh to Castletownbere with a contingent of Irish troops. From the little town, which shelters at the foot of the Slieve Miskish mountains, they were taken by boat across Berehaven to the military pier on Bere Island

---

* When he spoke of de Valera – the man who had opposed almost every imperial connection in the 1921 Treaty – Churchill did so in terms that were certain to insult the Irish leader. British Ministers, Churchill told the House of Commons, had 'established pleasant relations with Mr de Valera. I understand that his view – a characteristically Irish view – stripped of its substratum of truth, is that the only way to unite the two islands is to dissolve every possible connexion between them.'

where they were met by a British lieutenant.[147] Brendan Murphy, whose family owned the grocery store beside the jetty and whose mother had draped a Tricolour from a bedroom window, remembers that only about twenty-five Irish soldiers disembarked from the first boat from the mainland.[148] British troops helped them to unload their equipment and the lieutenant took Griffin to the Officers' Mess opposite Rerrin Redoubt for lunch. Inside the white-painted wooden building, which looked like a cricket pavilion and was set back from the redoubt by a rose garden and a small lawn, the British had placed their regimental silver along the table.

But then a curious incident took place. The British troops, who had been loading their equipment onto two boats under the gaze of a small crowd of people who lived on Bere Island, were suddenly told to halt their task and to unload their bags back onto the jetty. The transfer of the port was suspended. Strangely, neither the British nor the Irish military records mention this episode* although the senior British officer on the island, Major Clarke, received an order on the afternoon of September 26 to stop the hand-over.[151] Even before the Irish arrived, British gun crews were manning the 6-inch artillery on Bere Island in a state of battle alert.[152]

Were the British, at this penultimate moment, having second thoughts about the transfer of the remaining ports? Developments on the Continent suggest that this could have been the case, for that afternoon Sir Horace Wilson, Chamberlain's confidential adviser, was on his way to Berlin with a letter to Hitler from the British Prime Minister which proposed a German–Czech conference to discuss the manner in which the Sudetenland should be given to Germany. It was a desperate endeavour by Chamberlain to avert a war which in many European capitals seemed only hours away. It appeared thus in Dublin, too. An Irish officer told Murphy on Bere Island later that as soon as the Irish Government received word of the delay in transferring the port defences, orders came from Dublin that the Union Jack was to be down by nightfall; and two hours after they suspended their evacuation, the British did recommence their embarkation preparations.

There was a short ceremony at Rerrin Redoubt, accompanied by the Irish Army band. But this time there were no Irish Government represen-

---

* Malcolm MacDonald remembers talk of a 'hitch' at Berehaven and recalls that the British authorities had 'forgotten something'.[149] Griffin, who does not recollect the delay, believes that MacDonald is referring to a later incident in January 1939, when the Irish Army discovered some old but still highly sensitive papers which the British had accidentally left behind in a cupboard on Bere Island in the confusion of their departure. Among the papers, Griffin found a 1920 British Army intelligence file, a relic of the Anglo-Irish war, containing the names of local Irish families who were 'actively pro-British'. It also included a list of IRA men who were to be arrested and whose property, the 1920 file suggested, should be burned in reprisal raids. The British asked for the return of these somewhat incriminating papers in 1939 but by then they had been sent to the Irish Army's command headquarters in Cork.[150]

tatives present. Not even the parish priest was invited[153] and there was no official photographer. The only picture taken of the occasion was a private snapshot. It shows the British and Irish troops presenting arms in the forecourt of the redoubt beneath an overcast sky. Silhouetted on the photograph are the Irish and British officers on the east wall, saluting as the Union Jack is lowered on the main flag staff. It fell to Griffin to raise the Tricolour while Second Lieutenant Bowles again took his band through 'The Soldier's Song'. The British, in an unexplained breach of imperial precedent, did not cut their flag staff and Griffin was given the Union Jack as a souvenir. The first boat-load of British soldiers then left the island and the remainder departed on September 30.* Before they did so, Griffin took charge of the Officers' Mess record book, a heavy volume bound in brown leather bearing the insignia of the Royal Artillery in gold on the front cover. He signed himself into the Mess, writing his name and unit in Irish.

When Lough Swilly was handed over the following week, Chamberlain had already been to Munich and agreed to Germany's military occupation of the Sudetenland. The threat of war had receded and there were no last-minute counter-orders when the Irish moved in above the lough where, one hundred and forty years ago almost to the day, Wolfe Tone had arrived in irons as a prisoner of the British navy. The departure of the last British troops from Eire merited only half a column in an inside page of the *Irish Independent* ;[155] in London, *The Times* devoted just one paragraph to the event and even then it got the date wrong.† There were, as the *Donegal Democrat* remarked, 'no fervent, national heroics'[157] although in the rain at Fort Dunree on October 3, there was one small feature of the ceremony which – though scarcely typical of the savage history of the two nations – at least symbolised a less painful consequence of the agonised embrace in which England and Ireland had been locked for so many centuries. For the British soldier who struck the Union Jack, Sergeant King of the Royal Artillery, and the Irish soldier who raised the Tricolour, Quartermaster-Sergeant McLaughlin, were brothers-in-law. There was no destroyer waiting in the lough to carry the British troops home. They simply climbed aboard a bus at 1330 hours[158] and travelled by road the twenty miles to the city of Londonderry, across Ireland's partition into the British-controlled six counties of Northern Ireland where the Union Jack seemed in no danger of coming down.

* Two British officers, one of them a Dubliner by birth, did in fact stay behind for several more days to complete the transfer of stores. At Cobh, 26 British soldiers remained for at least four months to act as a training cadre to the Irish troops. They were loaned by the British Government on condition that the Irish authorities offered the men a 'financial inducement'.[154]

† *The Times*, which had welcomed the British decision to give up the ports, apparently thought that the last British troops in Eire were those on Bere Island. It reported their final departure on September 30 under the headline 'Last British Troops Leave Eire', ten days before the British rear-party left Lough Swilly.[156]

Chapter 2

A Certain Consideration

> I have just read a speech by de Valera, the Irish Taoiseach, in which, strangely enough, and contrary to Mr Roosevelt's opinion, he does not charge Germany with oppressing Ireland but he reproaches England with subjecting Ireland to continuous aggression . . .
>
> Adolf Hitler *28 April 1939*

The forts had not long been evacuated when the War Office in London was asked by General Pollock, the GOC Western Command, whether British troops in Londonderry should be encouraged to play football with the Irish soldiers who had taken over at Lough Swilly and to make them honorary members of the British Mess. The main difficulty, the General explained, was 'the feeling in Derry itself, where a small Protestant majority has considerable difficulty in maintaining its present ascendency and might well resent this fraternisation'.[1] The Dominions Office debated this unfamiliar colonial problem for some time, at one point taking comfort from an inappropriate precedent set in Somaliland where British troops were fraternising with the Italian Army. After more heart-searching, the business was passed to the Home Office where Charles Markbreiter, an Assistant Secretary who dealt with Northern Ireland affairs, suggested that the General should approach the province's Prime Minister, Lord Craigavon, to secure his 'concurrence'.[2]

Under the 1920 Government of Ireland Act, to which Northern Ireland owed its reluctant birth, the British armed forces were an 'excepted' matter over which the Government in Belfast held no authority, but such inter-departmental discussions in London were indicative of the attention which was regularly paid to Unionist sensibilities. Londonderry, whose Protestant citizenry had defended their walls in 1688 against a three-month siege by the Catholic King James, occupied not only a strategic position above Lough Foyle but an almost sacred place in the hearts of Northern Ireland Protestants. Their determination to resist Catholic rule was palpably evident in the city, where the gloomy stone walls and ancient cannon still stood, lovingly preserved, over the harbour and the slums of

41

the Catholic Bogside. Of all things, the potent symbolism of the Maiden City could not be defiled.

In 1938, however, there was little sign that Londonderry had benefited from its seventeenth-century endurance or that it was about to find economic advantage and military prominence in a far more serious conflict. The city, cut off by the border from its natural hinterland in County Donegal, had watched its shirt-manufacturing industry languish through the depression years and by 1938 it shared with other parts of Northern Ireland an unemployment rate well in excess of 28 per cent;[3] in July of that year, almost 102,000 men and women were out of work in the six counties.[4] There were few people in the province who showed any appreciation of the importance that Londonderry might acquire now that the Treaty ports in Eire had been evacuated. Indeed, save for the efforts of the Northern Ireland Government to obtain more rearmament work for Belfast's ailing shipbuilding and engineering industries, and the statutory precautions which the authorities were required to take against possible air attack on the cities, the imminence of a European war had by the end of 1938 made very little impression upon the province.

Colonel Wilfrid Spender, the head of the Northern Ireland civil service, suggested that 'it does not make very much difference handing over Lough Swilly and Berehaven to the Eire Government', since the transfer of the ports was 'probably more satisfactory than to be relying upon a reed which was our own but might prove a broken one'.[5] Spender was far-sighted enough, however, to realise that Northern Ireland would not be immune from the effects of a war. 'It is clear,' he wrote in his diary in October 1938, 'that the fear of the operations of submarines on the east and south coasts of Great Britain may give to Belfast – and some other ports in Ulster – an importance which they have never before possessed as distributing centres to the United Kingdom. This does, therefore, make them more liable to some form of attack . . .'[6] A faintly similar idea had earlier made its appearance in the *Northern Whig*, a strongly Unionist Belfast daily newspaper which usually devoted its editorials to domestic politics and the border issue. The paper recalled how near Britain had come to starvation in the 1914–18 War when German U-boats were sinking British merchant ships in the Atlantic. 'The international situation today,' it said, 'is such that the possibility of a similar emergency has to be faced . . . Could Ulster feed itself if it were in the position of a beleaguered State?'[7]

Politically, however, developments in Europe had passed Northern Ireland by. European fascism had affected the province much less than it had influenced the rest of Ireland, where the Blueshirts had in 1933 represented a serious threat to law and order. There were two small Fascist clubs north of the border, one in Belfast and the other in Londonderry. Both were legal and law-abiding, and drew their membership from the province's Italian community; in Londonderry, the club was founded in 1930 by a local café proprietor whose fourteen black-shirted members paraded each Remembrance Sunday to the city's war memorial in the Diamond.[8] Such gatherings were scarcely large enough to broaden the international perspectives of the Unionist newspapers in Belfast whose leader-writers were generally more preoccupied with the supposed machinations of de Valera's Government than with Hitler's or Mussolini's intrigues.

As an integral part of the United Kingdom, Northern Ireland would, of course, be involved in any war which Britain fought. The provincial Parliament at Stormont, on the hills east of Belfast, could not legislate on peace or war. But under the 1920 Government of Ireland Act, it did have the power to vote Northern Ireland out of the United Kingdom – and thus out of any obligation to go to war. The Unionists would never have contemplated such a step but it is nonetheless significant that the comparative safety which a united Ireland might have afforded the six counties in a European war was never raised in this context by any party, even during the Stormont election campaign at the beginning of 1938.

Yet it was not unnatural that Unionists should take the possibility of a war in their stride or that they should still be concerned with issues which might be considered parochial elsewhere in Europe. The siege mentality which Northern Ireland Protestants and the Government had developed was not an historical anachronism but an understandable if exaggerated response to the threat of militant Catholic nationalism. Their young province, smaller in size than Yorkshire, had not been expected to survive – the Irish south of the border did not intend that it should survive – and from its inception in 1921, Northern Ireland had existed in a state of constant insecurity. Of the $1\frac{1}{4}$ million population, more than 33 per cent were Catholics[9] and since Catholicism was generally identified with nationalism (and vice versa), it followed that just over a third of the province's inhabitants repudiated Northern Ireland's right to exist. Nationalist MPs elected to the 52-member Stormont Parliament at first refused to take their seats, and from the start Catholics claimed that they were subject to discrimination.* The Northern Ireland House of Commons, which imitated in miniature form the ritual pomp and ceremony of Westminster, had in any case a permanent Unionist majority; the Government of Ireland Act had seen to this by withholding the three most Catholic of Ulster's nine counties from the embryo Northern Ireland. Inevitably, therefore, the province also had a permanent Unionist Government.

From its very first years, this administration found itself trying to control a land which was under regular assault, brought to life during a

---

* Sometimes, however, they discriminated against themselves. When Lord Londonderry, the Northern Ireland Minister of Education, introduced an Act in 1923 to provide mixed schooling – a law which could have initiated the breakdown of sectarian barriers – it was opposed by the Catholic clergy.

critical war between Irish nationalists and the British. So anarchic was the state of Ireland in 1921 that many documents needed by the new Government in Belfast had to be freighted up from Dublin Castle through the hostile countryside disguised as a load of waste paper.[10] For Protestants, the creation of Northern Ireland was 'no joyous occasion'.[11] Sir James Craig's brother Charles, who was a Unionist MP at Westminster, had told the House of Commons in London in 1920 that they would have much preferred 'to remain part and parcel of the United Kingdom'. They had not wanted a parliament of their own.[12] As the Unionists struggled to hold their territory, the IRA struck repeatedly across the border – in Belleek, County Fermanagh, British troops had to drive them out with mortar fire – and in Belfast, rioting and gun battles broke out between Protestants and Catholics. There were 232 dead in Northern Ireland in 1922 alone.[13]

The political turmoil in Europe in the 1930s consequently left the Unionists largely unmoved. Their province had been born into a state of war and for much of its existence it was to live in a condition of war, divided internally by its own population and intimidated – in Protestant eyes – by armed forces south of the border. Its efforts to survive were supported by harsh legislation. In 1922, Sir James Craig's Government had passed the Civil Authorities (Special Powers) Act, which set up a special court of summary jurisdiction and gave enormous powers to the Northern Ireland Minister of Home Affairs, including the right to introduce internment without trial.

Since the IRA was for the most part a product of Irish Catholic nationalism, it was the Catholic community that bore the brunt of the new regulations. A reorganised and armed police force, the Royal Ulster Constabulary, was established on the debris of its defunct all-Ireland predecessor, the Royal Irish Constabulary. One third of the RUC's membership was supposed to be Catholic but IRA intimidation and nationalist convictions prevented the attainment of this goal. The same non-partisan intentions cannot, however, be attributed to the Government's reorganisation of the Ulster Special Constabulary, an armed and exclusively Protestant gendarmerie which was placed under the control of Craig's Minister of Home Affairs, Richard Dawson Bates. The Specials were a direct continuation of the Ulster Volunteer Force which had been revived in 1920 as a Protestant defence organisation. Prominent in bringing about this revival was Sir Basil Brooke, a County Fermanagh landowner educated at Winchester and Sandhurst who had resigned his commission in the Hussars after a distinguished military career in the 1914–18 War. The UVF was at this time under the command of Lieutenant Colonel Wilfrid Spender, another Winchester-educated war veteran who had served at Lord Haig's headquarters in France before taking part in the Somme battle.

Craig himself was older, a tall, silver-haired Belfastman with a thick moustache, who, with his square head and slightly heavy features, resembled a farmer rather than a politician. He had served in the South African War and had, for fifteen years, represented East Down in the Westminster Parliament. A Presbyterian who cared more about *Ulster* unionism than the southern unionists who were left to fend for themselves after the creation of Northern Ireland,[14] he demonstrated at the start of his prime ministerial career a public determination to treat Catholics with justice in his corner of the United Kingdom, leading a Government that would be 'absolutely honest and fair in administering the law'.[15] In discussions with Churchill and Michael Collins in 1922, he had agreed to give Catholics a fairer representation in the RUC and to secure the return to work of Catholics who had been expelled from the Belfast shipyard.[16] But Lord Craigavon, as Sir James Craig became in 1927, was an avowedly Protestant leader and a member of the Orange Order, the one Loyalist society that could reach across class barriers in Northern Ireland. 'I have always said,' he told the Stormont House of Commons in 1934, 'that I am an Orangeman first and a politician and a member of this Parliament afterwards . . . All I boast is that we have a Protestant Parliament and a Protestant State.'[17] As an historian of the Unionist Party has pointed out, it was not really possible to create good community relations 'by constantly emphasising the domination of the majority religion, and by suggesting that the Orange Institution was more important than Parliament'.[18]

Craigavon's province in time developed a life of its own but it was not the prosperous, flourishing state that its founding fathers had envisaged. Its soaring unemployment rate, its diminishing internal revenues and its inability to maintain a standard of living equal to that in the rest of the United Kingdom meant that by the late 1930s, the population of the six counties was still blighted by ill health, poor housing, inadequate roads and indifferent education.[19] An imposing neo-classical structure had been erected at Stormont in 1934 to house the provincial Parliament but there had been no substantial building projects in Belfast for many years; the city had the grimy character of the British industrial north, a seedy Victorian environment dominated by the oppressive splendour of the City Hall in which Carson had signed the covenant against home rule. In 1939, a study of working-class conditions in Belfast showed that 36 per cent of those surveyed were living in absolute poverty, without sufficient food, clothing or fuel.[20]

Nor was there any end in sight to the political and religious divisions in Northern Ireland; in 1935, there had been further Protestant–Catholic rioting in Belfast in which eleven people died. The smallest alteration in the ratio of Protestants to Catholics in the province – the vital calculation that confirmed political power in Unionist hands – took on an almost sacred quality that outweighed every other issue. Thus in the summer of 1938, when most British and Irish daily newspapers were devoting their primary attention to the Sudeten crisis, the nationalist *Irish News* in

Belfast gave over its front page to a report of a fractional 0.8 per cent increase in the city's Catholic population.[21]

In the years before the Second World War, therefore, much of Northern Ireland had about it an air of dilapidation. Devolution had been a technical success because Craigavon had brought the institutions of government into being; but slightly more than a third of the population would not give his Government its allegiance. Furthermore, the Cabinet that was to lead the province into the war was elderly. It was in fact substantially the same as that which had governed Northern Ireland in the early 1920s. John M. Andrews, the Minister of Labour, Richard Dawson Bates, the Minister of Home Affairs, and Craigavon himself had held ministerial posts since the foundation of the state and three other ministers had been parliamentary secretaries in 1921. Some of the civil servants fell into a similar category. Lieutenant Colonel Sir Wilfrid Spender, who had commanded the UVF in 1920, was now Permanent Secretary at the Ministry of Finance and head of the Northern Ireland civil service. A new recruit to the service described him as 'a survivor from a bygone era of English colonial life . . . Remote, kindly, lisping, out of touch, hospitable, croquet-playing, correct, wary of political interference in civil service affairs . . .'[22] If the Cabinet in Dublin included men of the same generation, it might have seemed to a British minister that they were at least devoted to a more passionate cause. Northern Ireland's Government was struggling and defensive. Craigavon's initial victory had been remarkable but his achievement was less impressive.

Craigavon was to claim later that he had regularly given 'the most solemn warning' to British ministers on the dangers of surrendering the Treaty ports[23] but there is no evidence of this in the British or Northern Ireland Government records. When Malcolm MacDonald, the British Dominions Secretary, asked to see the Stormont Prime Minister to tell him of the forthcoming Anglo-Irish negotiations, Craigavon's reaction was unexpectedly mild. MacDonald, whose Lossiemouth-born father Ramsay had supported the establishment of the Boundary Commission against Unionist opposition, assured Craigavon that Britain would not 'give away' Northern Ireland. 'Craigavon was sitting there solemnly in Baldwin's room in the House of Commons,' MacDonald recalls. 'I told him that my private talks with de Valera were proceeding towards negotiations for an agreement. I said to Craigavon: "I suppose you think I'm out of my mind." But Craigavon smiled and said: "No, no. I just think you're another Lossiemouth sentimentalist." ' The conversation, MacDonald says, amounted to 'quite a pleasant talk'.[24]

If Craigavon surprised MacDonald by his tempered attitude towards the negotiations, he astonished his own ministers once the 1938 Anglo-Irish conference was well under way. The Northern Ireland Government was not entitled to participate in these discussions but Stormont ministers were informed by Neville Chamberlain, the British Prime Minister, that he was counting on some trade concessions to Northern Ireland from de Valera.[25] The Belfast Cabinet was led to believe that the province's goods, which had suffered an annual £6 million reduction in sales since partition, would have free trade in Eire.[26] Sir Samuel Hoare, the British Home Secretary and a strong Unionist supporter, told Sir Wilfrid Spender that if the Northern Ireland Cabinet stood firm for these privileges, 'a majority of his colleagues would see that Ulster was not let down'.[27] In January 1938, Craigavon sent John Andrews, Sir Basil Brooke – who had helped to revive the UVF in 1920 and was now Minister of Agriculture – and John Barbour, the Minister of Commerce, to London to obtain favourable terms for Northern Ireland. According to Spender, who accompanied the three ministers to Britain, the province might have gained its trade concessions; but in March, Craigavon himself came to London, breakfasted with Chamberlain 'and postponed the meetings which were to take place with our Ministers and officials so that we were kept very much in the dark as to what was going on behind the scenes'. Spender's account, written more than two years afterwards, describes how Craigavon then turned up late for a meeting with his ministers at which both Andrews and Brooke told him 'they would rather give up office than surrender the line that they had pursued throughout the negotiations . . .'

But Craigavon then contrived to exclude his own officials from a ministerial meeting attended by British civil servants, and accepted de Valera's refusal to grant trade privileges to Northern Ireland. Andrews and Brooke, who were present, were 'astounded at the new attitude adopted by Lord Craigavon who blessed the Eire Agreement and merely asked for certain special concessions for Northern Ireland'. Agricultural concessions were now to come not from Eire but from Britain; Andrews 'was exceedingly unhappy and considered very seriously whether it was possible for him to remain in office . . .' Hoare, noted Spender, 'felt that he and his Unionist supporters in the British Cabinet had been so let down by the volte face of the Ulster Government that he could no longer act as their protagonist in the future'.[28]

Why did Craigavon, at so decisive a moment, choose to acquiesce in such an agreement at the risk of fracturing his Stormont Cabinet? Was it because the eventual granting of trade concessions by de Valera might have encouraged hopes of Irish unity among British ministers? Or was it because he believed that Northern Ireland's constitutional subordination to the United Kingdom Government ruled out any question of realistic opposition to an Anglo-Irish settlement? Spender even wondered 'to what extent the personal relations between Lord Craigavon and Mr Chamberlain affected this issue', adding that 'it must be remembered that Mrs Chamberlain was staying with Lord Craigavon about this period'.[29]

Part of the answer lies in Craigavon's decision, two months earlier, to call a general election in Northern Ireland. According to his biographer, he resolved on this step on January 12 when he read in the morning newspapers that the partition issue was to be raised by the Anglo-Irish conference.[30]* It was necessary, he said the following day when he announced the election, 'to put the position of Ulster beyond doubt'.[32] It was also necessary, although Craigavon did not say so, to overcome the growing disenchantment among the Unionist rank and file with his Government's inability to lower the unemployment figures or acquire a larger share of Britain's rearmament programme for Northern Ireland's shipbuilding industry. Spender, who at this time assumed that Craigavon would oppose any suggestion of a deal between Chamberlain and de Valera that was disadvantageous to the province, thought the election decision 'exceedingly wise'. But he was under no illusion about the reasons behind it. 'Not only does it bring home to the British people the fact that these negotiations are regarded in Northern Ireland as a matter of vital importance,' he wrote, '. . . but it also enables the Prime Minister to spring a surprise upon his opponents over here, which I hope will prove very embarrassing to them. It is not unnatural that when a Government has been in power for seventeen years there should be tendencies of cleavage . . .'[33]

Craigavon, Northern Ireland's first and only Prime Minister, therefore fought his fifth and last election on the cardinal issue of partition. The Nationalists obligingly declared that they would stand on an exclusively anti-partition ticket in every constituency in which they had a majority. In vain did ten Progressive Unionist candidates campaign against the Government's economic neglect. Equally vainly did the province's diminutive Labour Party protest that the Government was attempting to escape economic problems 'by raising the Border cry'.[34] Craigavon was in ill health but it made no difference to the campaign. 'Instead of being a fight chiefly between the official Unionists and groups of Progressive and Independent Unionists on social and economic issues,' observed *The Times*, 'the contest has been converted overnight into a rally against the supposed danger of the compulsory inclusion of the Six Counties of Northern Ireland in what was the Irish Free State and is now called Eire.'[35] During January and February, the Northern Ireland press occasionally reflected the concern felt over world rearmament and the power of Nazi Germany; the *Northern Whig* condemned Italian and Japanese militarism,[36] berated President Roosevelt for his failure to cooperate with Britain in an effort 'to check the world drift towards anarchy'[37] and pondered the strength of German opposition to Hitler[38] but at no time was the threat of war mentioned in the candidates' speeches. Even the Nationalists ignored it. 'Do the Ulster people still value their birthright?' Craigavon had asked.[39] He won a landslide. The official Unionists took

* St John Ervine, whose life of the Northern Ireland premier is as much a eulogy as a biography, suggests incorrectly that Craigavon's perusal of the papers on the 12th was also the first he had heard of the conference – a mistake that has since been repeated in other accounts of the period.[31]

thirty-nine seats, the highest number since the 1921 election, while the Nationalists scored only eight and the Progressive Unionists captured not one seat. Craigavon had become 'the permanent figurehead of Ulster's ship of State', according to *The Sunday Times*, which went on to remark disconcertingly that 'Signor Mussolini and Ataturk are his only rivals in the post-war record of continuous office . . .'[40]

Having demonstrated that the majority of Northern Ireland's population wished to remain within the Union, the way was now open for Craigavon to consolidate this victory in monetary terms, not by insisting upon privileges from Eire but by making demands on the British Government which would further involve the province's economy with that of Britain. The British consequently received a long memorandum from the Northern Ireland Government in March, setting out the financial disadvantages from which the six counties would allegedly suffer because of the proposed treaty with Eire and suggesting that for the duration of this 'inequitable and indefensible' agreement, the United Kingdom should, among other concessions, pay a £400,000 annual grant towards Northern Ireland's industrial development 'which is already seriously handicapped by Eire trade barriers . . .'[41] At the end of the month, the Stormont Cabinet Office forwarded to Sir Alexander Maxwell, Permanent Under-Secretary of State at the Home Office, a second lengthy note, this time urging the British to allot more rearmament work to Northern Ireland.*

This document took the form of a survey of British Government contracts for naval vessels and arms factories in various parts of the United Kingdom. It showed – if the statistics were to be believed – that Northern Ireland had received much less than its fair share of orders. Of the five battleships, thirty destroyers and an unspecified number of submarines under construction, not one was being built in the Belfast shipyards and of the five aircraft carriers and fifteen cruisers which had been ordered by the Government in London, only one of each type of vessel was under construction in Northern Ireland. Of nineteen arms factories ordered in eighteen months, all were to be situated in mainland Britain. In view of the province's high industrialisation – the textile, shipbuilding and engineering trades were emphasised – together with the experience and facilities available there and its 'immunity from attack', the authors of the memorandum stated that a 'strong case' existed for the allocation of more naval contracts to Belfast and for the establishment of arms factories and two new military depots in Northern Ireland.[43]

What the memorandum did not say – but what was implicit in almost every line – was that the Stormont Government believed that the province

* A covering letter from Sir Charles Blackmore at the Stormont Cabinet Secretariat touched on Craigavon's political embarrassment in a revealing aside. 'As you are, doubtless, already aware,' he wrote, 'there has been very strong criticism not only in our House but in local circles generally of the relatively small share of the re-armament programme which has been allocated to Northern Ireland.'[42]

had a *right* to an equal share of the rearmament programme. It was this tacit emphasis on parity that lay at the heart of Northern Ireland's constitutional anxiety and which struck at much deeper issues than the transitory opportunities for increased employment afforded by Britain's military expansion. For the province's ability to maintain social and economic equality with the rest of the United Kingdom had been impaired since the state's inception. The system of taxation and financial control – whereby Northern Ireland made an 'imperial contribution' for the national benefits extended to it as part of the United Kingdom but possessed only limited powers of revenue collection[44] – had regularly thrown into doubt the province's claim to parity with Britain; and if this parity was questioned, as it was by a financial arbitration committee in 1924, then Northern Ireland's *de facto* status as part of the United Kingdom could no longer be taken for granted.

The demand for a fair distribution to Northern Ireland of the benefits of British citizenship was therefore of vital importance to every Unionist. If Craigavon's Government could not satisfy that demand – or if that demand was seen to be ignored – then the Government's own right to continue in office could not be guaranteed. As early as 1936, William Stewart, the Westminster Unionist MP for South Belfast, had demanded the resignation of Craigavon's Government because 'my blood boils when I see [arms] contracts given to every area in England and Scotland and nothing given to Northern Ireland'.[45] A parallel argument was developed in an editorial on the province's economic prospects which appeared in the *Northern Whig* just before the 1938 election. 'Her share of prosperity, due to the re-armament expenditure, has indeed been a lean one,' the paper commented, 'and it would be unjust that . . . she should still have to pay her full share of that expenditure in income tax.'[46] John Andrews, Craigavon's Minister of Labour, made the same point more diplomatically in a letter to Samuel Hoare; since the people of Northern Ireland would be contributing their share of the increased cost of the defence programme through higher taxation, he wrote, 'it seems only equitable . . . that they should share in the additional employment which will result from the expansion of the Defence Programme'.[47]

So anxious was the Stormont Government, however, to secure a larger portion of the United Kingdom's arms orders that it seriously misrepresented the amount of rearmament work already given to the province. The memorandum made no reference to a large number of contracts allocated to the Harland and Wolff shipyard, including the manufacture of fifty Cruiser tanks, more than sixty 3.7-inch tank mortars and the conversion of twenty-one 60-pounder guns. Nor did it mention a £210,000 purchase of stores and barrack accommodation. Inskip told an April meeting of the British Cabinet's Irish Situation Committee that the document also 'failed to do justice' to flying-boat contracts worth almost £2 million placed with the Short Harland Aircraft Works in Belfast, an allocation which he described as 'one of the largest individual orders placed up to the present by the Air Ministry'. The memorandum, Inskip observed sourly, 'overstated Northern Ireland's case and understated the volume and value of the Munition Orders . . .'[48]

By struggling to increase its share of Britain's arms production, the Northern Ireland Government was, of course, also turning the province into a potential target area in a war with Germany, a fact which drew a comforting conclusion from the authors of the Stormont memorandum. 'Enemy aircraft,' they said, 'apart from having to undertake the hazardous crossing of Great Britain itself, would still have the Irish Sea to negotiate, so affording valuable extra time for defensive preparations.'[49] This assessment was shared by both the civil and military authorities in London. Spender recorded some months later how Markbreiter, the Home Office Assistant Secretary, told him that 'the position of Northern Ireland was so sheltered that he did not think we need worry very much about war measures'. Spender noted in his diary that even Major General Sir Hastings Ismay, Deputy Secretary of the Committee of Imperial Defence, 'considered that there was very little likelihood of any attack being made upon us'.* But such conclusions were reached on the unquestioned assumption that hostilities would follow the same pattern as they did in the 1914–18 War; that the German Army could be checked in Continental Europe and would never reach the Channel coast. Spender, who had the foresight to recognise the possible dangers to the province, suggested that a Northern Ireland official should spend some days in Ismay's Committee to obtain guidance for the Stormont Government, an idea of which the General approved.[50]

Nonetheless, Northern Ireland's air-raid precautions left much to be desired. The public in the province was apathetic to the dangers, as it was elsewhere in the United Kingdom, and local authorities in the six counties were unwilling to undertake civil defence precautions until they were sure that they would receive financial assistance from the Northern Ireland Government.[51] Narrow trenches were dug in open ground throughout Belfast but the protective roofs placed over them would scarcely have withstood shrapnel let alone a near-hit by a bomb. Spender noticed a series of trenches beside the City Hall at the end of Royal Avenue and remarked that they 'would have been traps rather than shelters so poor was the design of the cover provided. There seems to have been a desire on the part of the public authorities . . . to do something to reassure public

---

* According to Spender, Ismay compared Northern Ireland to a Woolworth shop to which entrance could only be gained through Carrington's, the largest jeweller's in London. 'How, he said, could one imagine any burglar breaking into Carrington's and then out of Carrington's merely to pick up what he could in Woolworth's . . .' This woefully inadequate observation probably said as much about Ismay's regard for department stores as it did about Northern Ireland's strategic importance.

opinion that steps are being taken, quite irrespective of the adequacy of the steps taken.'[52]

The drive for a greater share of the rearmament programme, however, began to achieve its purpose, notwithstanding Inskip's pessimistic appraisal in April. There was, he himself said, a 'strong possibility' that a further aircraft carrier would be built in Belfast.[53] Within a few months, there were indeed further warship contracts, a new aircraft factory for Belfast and financial support for the airport at Newtownards and for a new airfield at Sydenham near the Belfast docks.[54] Orders arrived for the engineering firms which – as Northern Ireland's official war historian was to remind his readers – had provided Britain's imperial arms in the past: Fairbairn Lawson Combe Barbour had made shells for the Crimean War and sharpened the sabres of the 6th (Inniskilling) Dragoons who fought at Balaclava; James Mackie and Sons had manufactured grenades in the 1914–18 War and Sirocco had produced parts of aircraft and submarines for Lloyd George.[55] The increased allocation of contracts appears to have been in some measure due to Samuel Hoare who, despite his extreme disappointment with Craigavon's stand over the Anglo-Irish negotiations, still spoke on the province's behalf, arguing that although much of Northern Ireland's skilled labour had migrated to the Clyde because of the depression, Craigavon had assured him that trained men were still available for war work in the six counties.[56]

There was at least one other British political figure whom Craigavon identified as an influential ally of Northern Ireland, if not now then at some stage in the future when Chamberlain's Government might be replaced by more single-minded men of less forbearance. At Christmas, 1938, Craigavon sent a gift of an engraved silver cup to Winston Churchill. The two men had been friends for many years and Churchill's role in the 1925 Boundary Commission crisis – when as Chancellor of the Exchequer in Baldwin's Government he had produced a compromise that left the border intact – had assuaged any residual Unionist anger over his earlier encouragement of the Home Rulers. Ignored now by most of his parliamentary colleagues at Westminster, Churchill could hardly have remained unmoved by this gift from a politically courageous and old-fashioned patriot like Craigavon, 'one of the few who have it in their power to bestow judgements which I respect'.[57]

Upon the base of the cup were engraved a pen, paintbrush and sword, and beside them Craigavon had inscribed the words of three generations of Churchills, a gesture that was certain to appeal to a descendant of the Duke of Marlborough. The first of these inscriptions was Lord Randolph Churchill's declamatory statement, made in 1886, that 'Ulster will fight and Ulster will be right' while the third briefly quoted Winston's son Randolph who in 1922 proclaimed that Northern Ireland had 'often led the way for Empire'. The second – the longest of the three – was Winston Churchill's own commitment, which he expressed in Belfast a few months after partition had been sanctioned by the collapse of the Boundary Commission: 'Neither by threats or violence or by intrigues, nor yet by unfair economic pressure, shall the people of Ulster be compelled against their wish to sever the ties which bind them to the United Kingdom, or be forced, unless by their own free and unfettered choice, to join another system of Government.'[58]

For such family commitments to Unionism to be carved in silver and sent to Churchill was a very pointed way of reminding him of his personal undertaking to Northern Ireland. But Churchill saw nothing heavy-handed in this 'charming and beautiful gift' and sent to Craigavon an emotional note. 'Coming as it does,' he wrote, 'at this time of trouble and misunderstandings, in which I feel much alone, tho' constant, it is grateful to me beyond words. I shall stand by the declarations you have inscribed upon the cup . . .'[59]

Over the past decade, Churchill had shown little interest in Irish affairs. He sometimes still toyed with the idea of a united Ireland inside the Empire[60] but the Treaty had largely removed Dublin from the centre of British political life. The nationalist struggle in India, Soviet power and the economic depression in Britain were issues of more moment, especially for a Tory backbencher whose star appeared to be waning. De Valera's 1932 election victory, however, shook Churchill and he at once realised that the 1921 Anglo-Irish Agreement was in danger. When, therefore, the *Daily Mail* invited him in the early thirties to contribute a series of freelance articles on 'important questions of the day', it was only natural that he should turn his attention to the Irish Free State. And although there were times when clarity of thought was clearly expanded to meet the rewards of linage, three long articles – hitherto largely ignored by historians and biographers – provide a remarkable insight into Churchill's perception of de Valera's Ireland in the years before the Second World War.

Churchill's central theme was the legal inviolability of the 1921 Treaty, the 'solemn compact' whose two principal Irish signatories, Michael Collins and Arthur Griffith, had 'risked their lives in fulfilling it'. The British Parliament, Churchill wrote, had accepted that 'the Irishman's word was his bond. Michael Collins gave his life to prove that this was true.'[61] Yet de Valera's victory at the polls represented 'Irish hatred of England' and Churchill pondered on 'the strange contrariness of the Irish character' that had prompted this small nation to reject the economic advantages of the Empire in a tariff war:

Mr de Valera is unperturbed. Careless of the material deprivations which his people are bound to endure, he upholds the ideal of a self-contained Irish Free State. That is not a matter which need trouble us. We may be sorry for the

Irish; but if they choose that destiny, it is their right under the treaty . . . They will certainly be poor; but they may be happy. They cannot possibly be dangerous. Mr de Valera has signed the death warrant of Irish greatness and has broken the word of Ireland to do so.[62]

That Churchill should have equated greatness with military power said a good deal about his imperialist instincts but the apparent tolerance of his sentiments towards the Irish could be misleading. He did not believe Ireland had the right to repudiate the Oath of Allegiance, a 'hammer-blow' that raised 'supreme political issues not only in Great Britain but throughout the British Commonwealth'. If the Oath was abolished, then the Treaty would be broken 'and the Irish Free State will cease to exist as a political entity.' From that moment, 'Ireland would automatically revert to the status of a foreign country outside the Empire whose Government was unrecognised.'[63]

Thus Churchill began to question not just the morality of Ireland's possible secession but also the legality of such an act. In 1935, with an irony that bordered on sarcasm, he was condemning the 'shameful manner' in which the Treaty had been broken. By retreating from the Empire, he wrote, 'Irish nationalists have deprived themselves of two possessions which they treasured above all things. They have lost at one fell swoop both their Grievances and their Publicity. Hence their desperate efforts to manufacture grievances out of the shreds of association with the British Empire . . . Hence these complaints that they are denied their freedom, when their real trouble is that they have their freedom and that nobody cares.' Irish nationalism was now self-centred. 'Its strife takes place only within its own bosom . . . Some day perhaps, though we shall not live to see it, the genius of the Irish nation may emerge from its seclusion and play again its rightful part upon the world stage.'[64]

Hope was therefore not yet all lost that Ireland would recover her sense of purpose and return to the imperial fold. Churchill presented to his readers an elegiac but mocking portrait of the Irish:

The canvas is small, but it does not lack light and colour. We see a religious, agricultural community whose spiritual and material needs are self-contained. Culture is simple; riches they have not. Power has vanished. But a great deal of gaiety and Irish geniality remain. An atmosphere of old-world leisure and ancient controversy pervades the scene. The drip and drizzle of the Atlantic Ocean is often broken by gleams of sunshine which light the pastures of the Emerald Isle . . .

When a race so gifted with personal charm, so capable of producing in other generations poets, orators, soldiers, statesmen, and proconsuls elects to fall out of the busy modern world and to retire into a cool, damp cloister amid green bushes, their desires should be respected.[65]

For Churchill, the strange nature of this retreat seems to have been bound up with his suggestion that, because Collins and Griffith had been among de Valera's emissaries in 1921, de Valera had in fact originally agreed to the Treaty – which was untrue. Moreover, in none of the newspaper articles was there any direct reference to the civil war.

Here, then, was Churchill's assessment of a society that could be at once both charming and paradoxical, the spirit of whose two brave leaders – Collins and Griffith – had been inexplicably replaced by the 'wanton counsel' of de Valera. They were a people whose 'ancient controversy' should not, perhaps, be taken too seriously* and whose abstract ideals might be humoured so long as this did not impinge upon Britain's body politic. Such an influence, however, was not ruled out and there is, throughout Churchill's writing and speeches at this period, an ill-concealed impatience with the Irish that sometimes turns into contempt. Above all, there was his notion that by rejecting the Oath of Allegiance, de Valera's Ireland might somehow legally cease to exist. It was a very disturbing idea to have been gestating in the mind of a future British Prime Minister.

In contrast, of course, Northern Ireland had been an example of loyalty, a community which 'many people feared . . . would not be able to last as an entity over a long course of years' but which could now be seen as 'a going concern, unshakable in their attachment to Great Britain, unconquerable, except by a degree of good will which our generation will not experience'. Craigavon's men had kept faith and their 'wonderful tenacity and prudence,' wrote Churchill, 'deserves the gratitude not only of Britain but of the Empire.'[67] The Irish would 'not be allowed to drag Ulster down into the ditch with them,' he promised, and added a commitment whose terms, with slight variations, can still be found in the statements of politicians who support Northern Ireland today: 'England will defend Ulster as if it were Kent or Lancashire. We could no more allow hostile hands to be laid upon the liberties of the Protestant north than we could allow the Isle of Wight or the castles of Edinburgh or Carnarvon to fall into the hands of the Germans or the French.' Ulstermen should be of good cheer, for 'until they wish to abandon the British Empire, the British Empire will never abandon them.'[68]

Such an abandonment, however, was still very much in the mind of Eamon de Valera, whose failure to secure the unity of Ireland during the negotiations with Chamberlain had by no means deflected him from his ultimate political purpose. Indeed, his growing admiration and experience of Chamberlain had persuaded him that the British Prime Minister

---

* Churchill, whose first memories were of Dublin – his grandfather was the Lord-Lieutenant – recalled in his autobiographical *My Early Life* how his nurse had told him of her fears of the Fenians. 'I gathered these were wicked people,' he wrote with tongue-in-cheek concern, 'and there was no end to what they would do if they had their way.'[66]

was now personally in favour of unity but that his Conservative colleagues would not at present contemplate such an initiative. De Valera 'convinced the man but could not convince the leader,' noted Frank Gallagher, one of de Valera's closest advisers who was shortly to become his Director of Government Information.[69] De Valera also gathered encouragement from Chamberlain's appeasement of Hitler's territorial ambitions and reasoned that if Britain could accept the secession of the Czech Sudetenland, then she could also meet his own irredentist claims upon Northern Ireland.

In early September of 1938, some three weeks before Chamberlain finally bowed to Hitler's demands at Munich, de Valera raised the issue in these terms during a long meeting with Inskip, the British Minister for Co-ordination of Defence. According to Inskip's report of the conversation, de Valera spoke about the iniquities of partition and 'then made an illusion to the Sudeten Deutsch question and said they had their own Sudeten in Northern Ireland and he had even thought sometimes of the possibility of going over the boundary and pegging out the territory which was occupied by a population predominantly in sympathy with Eire and leaving Northern Ireland to deal with the situation.'[70]

Four days after the Munich agreement, de Valera met Chamberlain in London and 'after expressing his agreement with the action of H.M. Government in connection with Czechoslovakia, he went on to speak of the position in Ireland, and especially of the Southern Irish minority in Northern Ireland . . . Mr de Valera emphasised that the events in connection with the Sudeten Germans and other European minorities had stimulated the difficulties in the Northern Ireland minority problem also.'[71]

Immediately before his talk with Chamberlain, de Valera had received a visit from the Duke of Devonshire, one of Malcolm MacDonald's Under-Secretaries, to whom he expressed his feelings in stronger language. Devonshire, who called on de Valera in his London hotel, 'found him in a state of considerable excitement about Partition.' According to Devonshire's account, de Valera 'prefaced his remarks by saying that he thought the Prime Minister had done splendidly, but that there were other minorities to be considered. The Poles and the Hungarians were getting their just rights:* what about his minority who were denied all opportunities of self-government or of employment in the public service. He went on to say that there was a time when if he had felt strong enough he would have moved his troops up to the line to which he thought he was justly entitled, just as Hitler was doing . . .'†

* The question of the Polish and Hungarian minorities in Czechoslovakia was also to be settled under the Munich agreement. In the event, Poland and Hungary acquired several hundred square miles of Czech territory over the next six months.[72]
† De Valera added judiciously that he did not now intend to adopt this solution, partly because 'such a step would not solve the problem, for there would remain Belfast with its hundred thousand of Catholics [sic], and, anyhow, Ireland was one country and should never be divided.'[73]

The details of these discussions with Chamberlain, Inskip and Devonshire have until now remained generally unknown but there is no reason to doubt the accuracy of the British documents which record de Valera's conversations. At the time, the Munich settlement must have seemed to de Valera a tempting precedent with which to pursue his territorial demand. If the British Government could permit Hitler to occupy the Sudetenland, why could not the same British Government allow Eire her claim to Northern Ireland, or at least to those areas of the six counties which possessed a Catholic majority?

Yet the passing of time has not ameliorated the unhappy parallel which de Valera chose to draw between the political aspiration of his own nation and the territorial expansion of Nazi Germany. He understood the nature of Hitler's regime; in 1937, the Irish Government had let it be known that it did not favour the appointment of a Nazi Party member as the new German Minister in Dublin.[74] De Valera's biographers say rather forlornly that he 'felt that there was some justice in Hitler's claims' to Czech territory[75] but as President of the Assembly of the League of Nations, de Valera must have been aware that Hitler's pretension to the Sudetenland was historically fraudulent. The six counties of Northern Ireland had once been administered by an Irish Parliament in Dublin but the Czech Sudetenland had never been Germany territory – it had originally been part of Austria.[76]

It was a facile, even shameless argument to place before British ministers – even before members of a Government that had far more shamelessly connived at the destruction of Czech freedom – and today it is equally difficult to endow it with any moral justification. Czechoslovakia, like Eire, was a small, comparatively new state, a little country which in other circumstances might have engendered more compassion in de Valera.

Since 1932, when he took office as President of the Council of the League of Nations, he had supported the right of small nations to an equal voice in world affairs. The Irish Free State had demonstrated a measure of independence within the British Commonwealth by joining the League in 1923 and de Valera's Presidency of the Council nine years later conferred upon his country a status out of all proportion to her size. In theory, his high international office was proof that the views of small nations carried equal weight with the great world powers but, as he pointed out in his opening address at the height of the Sino-Japanese war, the League was being condemned for shelving or ignoring international problems. 'People are saying that the equality of States does not apply here in the things that matter,' he said, 'that the smaller States whilst being given a voice have little real influence in the final determination of League action . . .'[77]

Italy's invasion of Ethiopia in the autumn of 1935 established just how well-founded de Valera's pessimism had been. He spoke with despair when he addressed the League Assembly in Geneva that September.

'Today . . . the cynic is our teacher,' he said. 'He is whispering to each of us, telling us that man in the long run is only a beast, that his duty is determined and his destiny ruled by selfishness and passion, that force is his weapon, that victory rests with the most brutal, and that it is only the fool who credits such dreams as were uttered here.'[78] De Valera did not lack courage in his reaction to Italy's aggression. He supported the economic sanctions which the League applied against Italy, despite the uneasiness which this caused within the Catholic Church in Ireland[79] and despite the salient fact that Britain, with whom Eire was engaged in an economic war, was the chief protagonist of the sanctions policy. But he was prepared to go further than this.

A four-page memorandum was drawn up by the Irish Department of External Affairs, for which de Valera was also Minister, outlining his views on the Italian–Ethiopian crisis. It stated that if Article 16 of the League's Covenant was invoked – and if the League's Council approved the adoption of military measures by its members – then 'it would be contrary to the spirit of the Covenant for the member concerned to refuse to take part in the collective military action to be taken by the League . . .' This, according to de Valera, was 'what we would have to do in the most extreme circumstances.'[80] In other words, de Valera was in the last resort prepared to go to war against Italy under the League's banner in order to secure peace. It was not his fault that such collective action was never taken.

When civil war broke out in Spain in the following year, there was a good deal of Irish Catholic sympathy for Franco, particularly among members of Cosgrave's opposition party, which had now adopted the title of Fine Gael. The Irish hierarchy made a national appeal for prayers and aid for Nationalist Spain. Eoin O'Duffy, the former Blueshirt commander, expressed strong support for Franco, visited the Generalissimo in Spain and eventually raised a 700-strong Irish Brigade to join the Nationalists in what O'Duffy referred to as 'the fight against World Communism'.[81] Nevertheless, de Valera supported the League of Nations in its policy of non-intervention, refused to recognise Franco's Government until the defeat of the Republican forces and later enacted a Non-Intervention Pact which made participation in the war a punishable offence.*

By this time, however, the League's impotence was obvious. The organisation, de Valera told the Dail, 'does not command our confidence'[83] and he suggested that it should set itself 'an humbler task'[84] – in 1939 he was to refer to it as 'debris'.[85] The gradual disintegration of the League had driven him into the isolationist camp, a status that was best

---

* No such law had been in existence in 1935 when, according to reports in *The Irish Times*, up to seventy men, including Irish Army veterans, had attempted to enlist in the Italian Army for possible service in Ethiopia.[82]

expressed by a policy of non-intervention and neutrality. It also seems to have suggested to de Valera that international justice was a theoretical concept that could not be guaranteed just because nations stated their belief in its worth. 'We have been unable to bend our wills to sacrifice selfish advantage even when it conflicts with justice to others,' he told the League Assembly in Geneva. '. . . All history tells us that, in the long run, to be just is to be truly wise. But we seem unable to apply the lesson.'[86] Historians have largely disregarded the effect of the League's decline upon de Valera. His disappointment accentuated a pragmatic, almost ruthless sense of self-preservation which he applied to Irish Government policy from then on with ever-increasing severity. The failure of collective security brought about an introverted perspective which defined Eire's continued independence – and the future unity of Ireland – as the governing principles in all matters of foreign affairs.

In this lay the genesis of de Valera's insensitive analogy to the Sudetenland and of the hurried and occasionally dramatic meetings which he held with Chamberlain's ministers and officials in the autumn of 1938. His preoccupation with partition, his determination to maintain Irish neutrality and his readiness to accept military advice from the British Government – a relic of the defence agreement which the British had offered the previous spring – dominated these discussions.

His request for military information did not surprise the British. The Irish Army were taking over the Treaty ports and, as de Valera explained to Inskip on September 8, the Irish Government 'had been taking steps to put Eire in as good a state of preparation as possible for the event of war'. Eire was free to consult British defence experts, Inskip replied, and he suggested that rather than spend money on 9-inch guns for the ports, the Irish Army would probably do better to install booms and loops for anti-submarine defence. De Valera was also offered a copy of the War Book, the secret manual of instructions to be carried out by the military authorities in Britain on the outbreak of hostilities, but he was reluctant to accept this proposal, partly because the scope of the War Book was unnecessarily wide for Eire and partly because 'he was not very anxious to have a document which it was important to keep secret, because it was difficult to maintain secrecy all down the line.'

De Valera said that he was 'very much in the dark' about the best use Eire could make of the limited resources she had available for defence. 'If the United Kingdom became involved in war,' Inskip wrote later in his report of the conversation, de Valera 'felt sure the first desire of the Government of Eire would be to keep out of it. Just as we desire not to be involved in a European war over Czechoslovakia, although we might be caught up in it, so Eire would naturally wish to escape the disaster of war.' Inskip did not think that Irish neutrality would last very long because Eire's chief industry was agriculture and her nearest and biggest customer was the United Kingdom. '. . . If an enemy's object was to interfere as much as possible with our food supplies Eire could hardly escape scot free and sooner or later . . . they would realise that Eire depended on the protection given by the British Navy with command of sea and communications.' De Valera acknowledged that any suspension of Anglo-Irish trade would place Eire in 'a very serious position'.

Inskip took this opportunity of exploring the question of British use of the Treaty ports. It was 'most desirable from our point of view', he said, that Britain should have facilities for anti-submarine units in Lough Swilly and Cobh and 'the only alternative to our having the use of these ports was that the enemy should use them . . .' It was common ground between Eire and Britain, said Inskip, that this would not be with Eire's consent, so 'the enemy might take steps to occupy these ports as bases of operation against us.' But de Valera stated that he 'could give no undertaking at all that the ports would be available for the British Navy' – this was a repetition of his declaration to Chamberlain in the spring – and pointed out that he had 'to deal with people in Ireland who would immediately say that Eire was still under the heel of Britain . . .'

De Valera now turned to what Inskip called 'his familiar grievance about partition'. If partition could be got rid of, de Valera contended, then 'it would be comparatively easy for him to make a complete defensive alliance with the United Kingdom, providing for the availability of the ports.' When Inskip suggested that 'nothing was so likely to lead to a satisfactory arrangement between the two parts of Ireland as co-operation both in defence and in other matters', de Valera described this as 'putting the cart before the horse'. He then spoke 'with a good deal of indignation' about the case of a man called Donnelly from Armagh, who was in prison in Northern Ireland because he had refused to comply with a Deportation Order made against him fourteen years earlier. It was an incident, said de Valera, that 'had led to a recrudescence of the partition controversy and had inflamed feeling in Eire.' When he had heard that Donnelly intended to resist the Deportation Order, de Valera had approved because 'he himself had been treated in the same way by Northern Ireland even when he was a member of the Parliament of Northern Ireland elected by an overwhelming majority.'* This led de Valera to his conclusion that the Irish had 'their own Sudeten in Northern Ireland'. He spent some time 'deploring the consequences of partition and even discussed a possible constitution for a united Ireland which would he thought put the Unionist population in a very strong position.'

De Valera, who was accompanied by Dulanty, the Irish High Commissioner in London, reverted to what Inskip called 'more practical ques-

---

* De Valera won the South Down constituency as a Republican candidate in the 1921 Northern Ireland elections but he never took his seat. During the 1924 British election campaign, he travelled to Londonderry and was imprisoned for a month in Belfast because he had contravened an order signed by Dawson Bates which prohibited him from entering the province (with the exception of County Antrim).

tions', saying he thought the best use the Irish could make of their defence expenditure would be to have 'a few aeroplanes'. No preparation had been made against air attack on Irish cities, he admitted, and 'Dublin had not even considered any air raid precaution measures.' De Valera felt bound to keep his present limited army up to strength 'to deal with the internal situation as it was always possible in the event of a war, that a certain part of the population would take the opportunity of showing hostility to the United Kingdom.' Inskip then recorded that 'Mr de Valera in a rather curious aside, turned to Mr Dulanty and said: "Of course I am not suggesting they would do this from any improper motive; it would be a purely patriotic movement." ' When he eventually left to catch his train en route to Geneva, de Valera's last words to Inskip were: 'Now don't forget the partition question.'[87]

The British Government acted swiftly to meet de Valera's request for advice on the defence of the Treaty ports. Dulanty, a former British civil servant whose experience tended to be concealed by his deferential manner and humorous, almost puckish face, went to the Dominions Office on September 16 to make arrangements for the visit to London of Irish defence personnel. General Sir Hastings Ismay, who was present at the meeting, suggested that the forthcoming discussions could embrace not just the defence of the ports but censorship, supplies and other measures.[88] On the following day, however, Dulanty requested an urgent interview with MacDonald. According to Sir Edward Harding, the Dominions Permanent Under Secretary, Dulanty had that morning telephoned Sean T. O'Kelly, the Irish Tanaiste (Deputy Prime Minister) from whom 'he had derived the impression that there would be great difficulty in arranging for any further discussion on the question of the defended ports pending Mr de Valera's return . . .'[89] It looked as though the Irish Cabinet was not prepared to risk opprobrium at home by initiating defence discussions with the British in de Valera's absence.

As a result, Dulanty suggested that R.A. Butler, the British Foreign Office Under Secretary who was in Geneva, should seek de Valera's personal imprimatur for the start of defence talks.[90] But Butler found that de Valera was almost as perturbed as his Cabinet in Dublin at the possible effect on Irish opinion of the proposed discussions. 'He said that he must make it plain that the policy of Eire would be one of neutrality,' Butler reported in a memorandum to London. 'He would therefore not wish to sanction the taking, or even the discussion, of any special measures which public opinion in Eire could possibly consider as being part of a bargain . . . about which he had not told his own public.' De Valera concluded that he would prefer not to handle the matter from Geneva and – to Butler's surprise – added that 'he felt sure that our Foreign Office cypher must be known and that to use the telephone at this juncture was extremely dangerous.' Butler sent his memorandum to London in the diplomatic bag.[91]

De Valera was evidently a very worried man and his fears of an adverse domestic reaction suggest that he was not feigning concern when he told British ministers of the dangers that awaited him at home if he should be seen co-operating too closely with the British. But these were also decisive hours for Europe and de Valera did not lack resolve when it came to a different kind of initiative. With Germany on the point of invading Czechoslovakia, he even contemplated an appeal as Irish head of state to Hitler and Mussolini,[92] an idea that was only abandoned when Chamberlain travelled to Munich.

As a result, de Valera had to content himself with a lesser role. In a broadcast to the United States, he called for a European peace conference – he appears to have underestimated the strength of American isolationism[93] – and he mobilised support within the League of Nations Assembly for a unanimous resolution of 'concern'.[94] Butler expressed Chamberlain's gratitude for the broadcast[95] and de Valera, who had always believed in the policy of appeasement, sent the British Prime Minister a telegram of support, written in emotional language that took little account of the moral issues involved in Hitler's Sudeten demands:

> Let nothing daunt you or deflect you in your effort to secure peace. The tens of millions of innocent people on both sides who have no cause against each other but who are in danger of being hurled against each other with no alternative but mutual slaughter are praying that your efforts may find a way of saving them from this terrible doom.[96]

The telegram reflected de Valera's horror at the apparent inevitability of war, a circumstance that had also produced a temporary change in the Irish Government's attitude towards Anglo-Irish defence co-operation. Before de Valera returned from Geneva, the Irish authorities secretly dispatched two senior Irish Army officers to London for talks with their British counterparts. The discussions, which were largely the work of Dulanty and Joseph P. Walshe, the Irish External Affairs Secretary, were 'very satisfactory' according to the British, who noted that Major P. Maher, the Irish Director of Artillery, had asked for a detailed list and the estimated cost of the defences which should be instituted at the Treaty ports.[97] In Dublin, de Valera's Ministers also discussed air-raid precautions and agreed that ARP equipment should be purchased from what the Cabinet minutes delicately described as 'a source outside this country'.[98]*

But when de Valera arrived in London from Geneva, it was the partition issue which chiefly influenced his continued talks with the British. When the Duke of Devonshire went to see him, de Valera's first action had

---

* In their enthusiasm to buy British, however, Dublin Ministers did not neglect the interests of the Irish drapery trade. The Irish Cabinet minutes for November 7 record that the first item on the agenda was 'Contract for Army Underpants: Preference for Irish Manufacturers.'[99]

been to produce a shaded map showing those parts of Northern Ireland which possessed a Nationalist majority, together with a table of figures illustrating alleged gerrymandering of local government and parliamentary constituencies in the six counties. After remarking how he had once considered moving Irish troops over the border 'just as Hitler was doing', de Valera refused to accept Devonshire's argument that Britain, while she had no desire to see partition perpetuated, could not countenance its abolition without 'the complete goodwill of the people concerned'. Britain, said Devonshire, could not bring pressure on the people of Northern Ireland 'to induce them to throw in their lot with the South'.

De Valera 'replied that we had made "this ghastly mess" and it was for us to clear it up. We could at least withhold the "continual subsidies" which we made the North, which were strongly resented in the South and without which the North could scarcely continue to exist as a separate unit.' He repeated the suggestion he had made to Inskip – that he would be willing to come to an arrangement with Northern Ireland under which the six counties would continue to have a separate parliament with its present powers – and he maintained that the effect of joining both parts of Ireland together would be to strengthen the ties between Ireland as a whole and England. He had retained the Crown in his new Constitution 'in order that, when Northern Ireland came in, the contact with the Crown which they valued so highly should not be entirely severed.'

At this point, de Valera produced the same calculation that he had advanced to Inskip. Devonshire reported: 'In the event of war the attitude of Ireland would be very different if partition still existed from what it would be were Ireland one, and many of the steps which he would like to take in the event of our being at war would be impossible for him so long as partition lasted.' Then de Valera introduced a new equation. 'He contemplated that we should immediately introduce conscription if war broke out, but it would be morally wrong to apply conscription to Northern Ireland, and he would be almost bound to take some steps to protect his minority there should we attempt to do so. Public opinion in Eire would force his hand.'

Devonshire spoke of a more gradual approach to Irish unity but de Valera said that in the course of time he and his Fianna Fail Party 'would be superseded by something to the Left of them who would not be as patient and law-abiding as he had been . . .' He ended by observing that 'the contemplation of Europe had taught him how stubborn and difficult this minority problem was, and that it needed endless patience and goodwill to deal with it.'[100]

To Chamberlain a few minutes later, de Valera claimed that he had evidence of the way in which the Nationalist minority in Northern Ireland 'were deprived of representation in public offices and in other ways unfairly treated, and he felt that if a crisis arose such as might have arisen over recent European troubles, the existence of this minority with a grievance might become a positive danger.' Adopting a milder tone than he had in his conversation with Devonshire, de Valera urged that the minority in Northern Ireland 'should be given such safeguards as were being claimed for other minorities' although, as Chamberlain wrote in his account of the meeting, de Valera 'did not ask for autonomy or for cession of territory.' De Valera once more suggested that the Imperial Government's powers in Northern Ireland should be transferred to an all-Ireland Parliament, the conduct of local affairs being left to the six counties. He felt that 'some Conservative, having the necessary influence, ought to be deputed to take the matter up with Northern Ireland, who had hitherto preserved a completely intransigent attitude.'[101]

De Valera had presented the British with three interwoven ideas; the possibility of defence co-operation in wartime, the declared intention of Eire to remain neutral and the moral and political necessity of ending partition. The first of these considerations was contingent upon satisfaction of the third but the central theme of all three – the axis upon which all else turned – was de Valera's determination to keep Eire out of a European war.

In Ireland, there was nothing new or extraneous about the concept of neutrality. It had roots in the struggle of Irish nationalism; Irish opposition to the Boer War, in which two small Irish brigades fought against the British, manifested itself at home in anti-recruitment campaigns which played a part in separatist activity over the next two decades. Sir Roger Casement envisaged a form of Irish neutrality – admittedly under dubious German protection – in a 1913 magazine article[102] and the 1914–18 War gave a more powerful voice to those who believed that Britain had no right to expect Irishmen to fight in her wars. An Irish Neutrality League campaigned against recruitment in 1914 and the threat of conscription in 1918 prompted the Irish Party to withdraw from Westminster in protest. Irish nationalism – and Republicanism – had become associated with non-participation in war.

Nor was neutrality in any way a peculiar or exotic notion in an international context. In the 1930s, Belgium, Holland, Denmark, Norway, Sweden, Switzerland, Portugal and the United States were all following what was then regarded as a respectable and rational policy of neutrality. After the bellicose Chanak affair of 1922 – when the Australian and Canadian Governments were angered by Britain's apparent assumption that the Dominions would automatically send military assistance when requested to do so* – even the Commonwealth could no longer be counted upon to go to war on Britain's behalf. According to Cornelius Cremin,

---

* Britain had formally invited the Dominions to send contingents to reinforce a British division at Chanak on the Asiatic shore of the Dardanelles in order to repel a possible attack by Ataturk's army. The Dominions stated their readiness to do so but only after several governments had been angered by the release of a British press statement which appeared to take their assistance for granted.[103]

who was to become one of Eire's most experienced wartime diplomats, Chanak was a precedent that had not been forgotten inside the Irish Department of External Affairs.[104] The British themselves never suggested at this period that there was anything dishonourable or cowardly about Irish neutrality; only that it would prove to be an *impractical* policy for the Irish to pursue in wartime.

But Irish neutrality was not just an exercise in sovereignty, facilitated by the British evacuation of the Treaty ports. Since it had not yet been tested, it was also an experiment in independent foreign policy for Eire, as daring in its way as the experiment in devolved government that Sir James Craig had undertaken in Belfast almost two decades earlier. For sound historical reasons, neutrality had also come to be seen in Ireland as something intimately bound up with freedom from British rule. It was therefore inevitable that in wartime it would frequently be identified – on both sides of the Irish Sea – as essentially anti-British.

The impending war and the virtual collapse of the League of Nations, of whose influence de Valera had never been fully convinced, had now given neutrality a special urgency. It had hardened the determination of its principal Irish proponent, a man who instinctively refused to accept the simplified moralities of the great powers but who had for years allowed his own preoccupation with Ireland's domestic struggles to colour his vision of international affairs. He had felt able to draw on the advantageous results of the American civil war to demonstrate the unhappy and divisive outcome of Ireland's more recent civil strife.[105] Broadcasting to the United States, he had favourably compared the crippling German war reparations imposed by the Treaty of Versailles with the Irish annuity payments to Britain.* International disputes could illustrate Ireland's difficulties; and suitable examples from the crisis in Europe were selected to emphasise the evils of Irish partition. Thus the German-speakers of the Sudetenland were metamorphosed by de Valera into the Catholics of Northern Ireland. It was an exclusive form of introspection practised by a politician who had come to believe that only by standing outside the rivalry of the great powers could his small nation survive. 'Peace is dependent upon the will of the great states,' he had said. 'All the small states can do, if the statesmen of the greater states fail in their duty, is resolutely to determine that they will not become the tools of any great power, and that they will resist with whatever strength they may possess every attempt to force them into war against their will.'[107]

Such military strength as Eire possessed was diminutive enough. A secret memorandum prepared by the British Committee of Imperial Defence estimated that the Irish Army's strength amounted to only 6000

---

* According to de Valera's computation, Germany had to pay £20 in reparations for every £100 raised for governmental purposes although 'we have to find £24 for our payments to England.'[106]

regular troops, 6000 reservists and 16,000 Volunteers.[108] Even the latter figure was a gross exaggeration since by the outbreak of war in 1939, the number of Volunteers had hardly passed the 7000 mark.* The British document admitted that 'as there is not the normal interchange of military information with Eire, as is the case with other Dominions, our information cannot be regarded as reliable.' But it nonetheless presented a fairly accurate analysis of the regular Irish Army's organisation, which included five infantry battalions, a field battery of artillery, an armoured car squadron, a field company of engineers, three construction and maintenance companies of engineers, three signal companies, four motor transport companies, a horsed squadron and a cyclist squadron.[110]†

If Eire became involved in a European war – and if the strength of the old British garrison was maintained at the naval stations on a war footing – this meant that well over half of the country's regular troops would be committed to the defence of the three Treaty ports alone while the remainder of the Irish Army – scarcely 15,000 ill-equipped soldiers – would be left to guard about three thousand miles of coast-line and 250 miles of land frontier. There was no defence against parachute landings or air raids and, although the British memorandum mercifully neglected to assess Eire's supply of military transport, the Irish possessed only twenty-one armoured vehicles.[112] Thirteen of these were elderly Rolls-Royce light armoured cars which had first seen service under the British in 1920 and which could still occasionally be glimpsed trundling slowly along the main road between Kildare and the Curragh Camp with a single Vickers .303 machine gun in their rotating turrets. In all Eire, there were only two serviceable tanks – both were Swedish Landsverk L-60 light tanks attached to the Cavalry School[113] – with which to confront an invading army.

Eire's tiny air force – itself a branch of the Irish Army – was correspondingly powerless. The British memorandum again acknowledged its ignorance of details but concluded that just twenty-four military aircraft in Eire were fit for flying duty and that only ten of these were of modern design.[114] In fact by the autumn of 1939, the Irish Air Corps comprised four Gloster Gladiators, fifteen Miles Magisters, three Walrus amphibious aircraft, six Lysanders and an assortment of Vickers Vespas, Avro 636s, de Havilland Dragons and Avro Ansons.[115] Only the Gladiators could be regarded as fighter aircraft of any consequence. In conventional military terms, Eire was virtually defenceless.

There were also slight but ominous signs of unrest within the Irish

---

* On 2 September 1939, the Irish Army comprised a total strength of 19,783, of whom 7494 were Regulars, 5066 were A and B Reservists, and 7223 were Volunteers.[109]
† Not all the details in the memorandum were correct, however. The British credited the Irish with a searchlight company and a second horsed squadron which did not exist and overestimated the strength of a light artillery and an anti-aircraft battery and a survey company. The British also overlooked Eire's small tank squadron.[111]

Army Volunteer Force, some of whose members – seemingly unmoved by the international threat to their country – expressed resentment at the way in which they were allegedly refused promotion and extra allowances. In the archives of the Taoiseach's Department in Dublin, there are references during this period to disciplinary problems within the Force; some of the files appear to have been tampered with and pages have been torn from them, but several documents remain intact.

In July of 1938, for instance, the Irish military authorities intercepted two letters written by a Volunteer Force lieutenant to a fellow officer in the Curragh, complaining about cuts in allowances and suggesting that Volunteer officers should form an organisation to seek permanent posts for themselves in the newly-evacuated Treaty ports. One of the letters, sadly mis-spelt and ungrammatical, contained the flavour of disaffection:

> . . . We are just to remain 'week-end soldiers' and it is up to us to disillusion the powers that be. With that object in view I wish you would get the addresses of all the fellows on the course, together with their influence with other Vol. Officers, and their cooperation in organiziting [sic] all the Officers and have a show-down.
>
> The majority of them are a lousey [sic] bunch, who would leave us in the lurch – holding the baby, if we put too much on paper, and I suggest that a meeting of all Vol. Officers, in Dublin, on a date that is convenient for you fellows is indicated.
>
> . . .Keep all this under your hat, and *destroy this letter*, which is treason.[116]

There was nothing overtly political about this letter but such sentiments were of obvious concern to a Government whose national army, under a different administration, had mutinied only fourteen years earlier. The fact that commissions in the Volunteer Force had been given to ex-members of the IRA made evidence of this kind all the more disturbing.*

What the Irish military authorities required was a senior adviser, an experienced general who could define the country's defence priorities, organise the limited forces at Eire's disposal and help to inject a new sense of unity among all ranks of the Army. But it was now obvious that the British were not going to abandon partition in return for Irish defence co-operation and scarcely more than a week after his latest meeting with Chamberlain, de Valera made it clear that – for the present at least – he had no intention of placing Eire's Army under British tutelage. Frank Aiken was ill and de Valera, who had temporarily taken charge of the Irish Defence Department in his absence, came up with an unorthodox solution to his military needs.

On October 12, Dulanty and Walshe called at the Colonial Office to tell

---

* The lieutenant was dismissed for writing a letter 'calculated to cause disaffection among the officers of the Volunteer Force'.[117]

Malcolm MacDonald and Devonshire, his Under Secretary, that de Valera – 'extremely anxious to get the Irish defences into a good state, as he did not want to be "caught napping" if there were trouble in Europe' – planned to appoint a *French* General as principal military adviser to the Irish Army.

The Irish would accept any French officer whom the British suggested, MacDonald reported in a note to his Cabinet, and de Valera 'hoped that the plan would have our goodwill and that we would accept it as an indication that, since political expediency made the appointment of a British officer impossible, he had done the next best thing in securing a high military officer of our ally. The appointment of such an officer would be a clear indication to Germany and the world that Eire was on the side of the Western democracies.'

MacDonald could hardly have expected such a proposal. He and Devonshire, nonplussed by this sudden overture, thought it might be possible 'to get some experienced and really good officer in the British Army, who was an Irishman, to resign from the Army in order to offer his services to Eire'. It was in keeping with the unconventional tenor of this conversation that Dulanty should then have mentioned the name of General Sir Hubert Gough, the former Third Cavalry Brigade commander at the Curragh who had refused to order his troops into Ulster during the 1914 Home Rule crisis. Dulanty disclosed that Gough had privately told him on two or three occasions that 'his services were at the disposal of Mr de Valera' although Dulanty agreed that Gough's 'connection with the Curragh incident' presented difficulties. De Valera did not regard Gough as 'the right man for the post' but – no doubt attracted by the mutinous reputation of the unrepentant old General – nonetheless wanted 'very much . . . to discuss Eire's military problem with him'.[118]

MacDonald pointed out that de Valera's original proposal would mean that a French officer would be given access to secret British defence papers in the hands of the Eire Government – a difficulty which de Valera had himself foreseen – but promised to consult Inskip. Walshe once more emphasised de Valera's anxiety to press ahead with defence preparations.[119] On the face of it, this was hardly surprising because the British Chiefs of Staff – in response to the request for military recommendations made by Major Maher, the Irish Director of Artillery, during his recent visit to London – had prepared a memorandum of great length and complexity on the subject. The British were recommending the replacement of two 9.2-inch guns at Cobh, the procurement of four more 6-inch guns at Berehaven and the modernisation of Lough Swilly's heavy artillery. Further proposals for improvement of the port defences would take as long as nine years to implement.[120]

Somewhat inevitably, Inskip informed Dulanty eight days later that the Chiefs of Staff had convinced him that there were 'insuperable objections' to de Valera's plan. The British possessed 'certain devices and equipment,' he said, 'a large part of the value of which would be lost if it came to the knowledge of a potential enemy'. Inskip was almost certainly alluding to Britain's secret development of radar. There was no question, he said, about his country's willingness to communicate confidential information to the Eire Government but if a French officer was appointed then some of this information would be passed on to 'a foreigner'. To compound this unflattering reference to an officer in the armed forces of Britain's principal ally, Inskip added that 'the French are not in any case very good at keeping secrets . . .'

Dulanty expressed his disappointment and then made a strange admission. De Valera, he said, wanted to improve the port defences while Aiken was absent since he believed that the Minister for Defence would himself be unwilling to undertake the task; therefore 'it was important to get action taken while Mr Aiken was away.' Inskip asked if the Irish would consider a military adviser from one of the Dominions and suggested an Australian officer who was a Catholic but Dulanty again showed no enthusiasm. De Valera, he said, had already turned down a proposal to appoint a South African officer, General van Ryneveld, even though the South Africans had fought against Britain.

Dulanty explained that one of the reasons for de Valera's reluctance 'was due to the fact that Mr Aiken represents the IRA Organisation and Mr de Valera relies upon him to keep the IRA lot quiet and behind the government.' Dulanty 'did not think that any Dominion soldier or sailor would be agreeable to Mr Aiken.'[121]

The Irish High Commissioner had revealed what the British must have suspected for some months; that the political divisions in Eire over which de Valera was so exercised were also mirrored inside his own Fianna Fail Cabinet. Aiken, who deeply distrusted the British and who throughout the war was to regard Britain as a more serious military threat than Germany,[122] would never have countenanced a British or Dominions defence adviser and would probably have objected to the appointment of a Frenchman. There is moreover little doubt that, as a former IRA Chief of Staff during the civil war, he continued to carry some prestige and influence among the extreme republicans who had long ago lost faith in Fianna Fail.

Claims that Ireland was still 'a nation subject to a foreign King' – made, for example, by the IRA leader Sean Russell in 1936[123] – could still arouse much passion in Eire and it was essential for de Valera to use every means to keep these emotions in check. Irish Cabinet ministers nursed justified fears of an IRA resurgence. Dulanty's arguments accordingly reflected real pressures within the Eire Government, even if he outlined the circumstances of de Valera's position in rather over-dramatic detail in the hope of precipitating the British into hurried agreement with the defence plan. If they would still not consent to this, Dulanty had an alternative suggestion: would the British allow, say, 75 per cent of their defence information to be communicated to a French adviser and withhold the 25 per cent that might be too secret to divulge?[124]

This convoluted idea did not impress Inskip and the Chiefs of Staff subsequently made short work of it. The British had already furnished the Irish with secret equipment – including a Fortress range-finding device and a submarine indicator loop system operated by radar – which could not be revealed to a foreign national. 'It would be only natural for a French General . . . to pass on to his own country any information on our defence arrangements which might come his way,' the Chiefs of Staff said. 'Indeed this would be his duty as a French officer.'[125] Dulanty's plan of giving such an officer 75 per cent restricted access to military information was 'entirely unworkable' since defence plans could not be divided along such lines. If the Irish appointed a French General as their expert defence adviser, they concluded, 'all secret matters . . . should be withheld from the Government of Eire . . .'[126]

That was the end of de Valera's Francophile enthusiasm and the British heard no more about the French General.* As these latest talks were coming to an end, however, de Valera initiated a loud and well-orchestrated campaign for Irish unity, an attempt to gain by international publicity and political pressure what diplomacy and negotiation had failed to achieve. He set up an Irish Anti-Partition League, deploring in newspaper interviews the 'cruel wrong' of partition and advocating an All-Ireland Parliament that would for the time being permit Northern Ireland to retain her 'transferred' powers of limited revenue collection and domestic administration.[127] That de Valera should have launched his campaign at such a time – and when he had already refused to make any trade or economic concessions to the province – demonstrated how little he appreciated either the mood of the British Government or that of the majority in the six counties of Ireland to which Eire laid claim in her year-old Constitution.

Yet the campaign went some way in Eire to prove that Fianna Fail had not forgotten its national ideals and it was a measure of de Valera's influence – and of Britain's sensitivity on the subject – that the British Government decided to examine his complaints of anti-Catholic discrimination in Northern Ireland. Craigavon's Government in Belfast was asked to provide detailed replies to allegations of constituency gerrymandering, the misuse of Dawson Bates's Special Powers Act, and discrimination against Catholic employment in the civil service, police and local government. The Northern Ireland authorities submitted several documents to

---

* A number of retired Irish Army officers believed that the French defence adviser was to have been Charles de Gaulle, an appointment which might well have changed the course of French – indeed European – history. In 1938, de Gaulle was a lecturer on tank combat at the new centre for Higher Military Studies in Paris and the author of a book on mechanised warfare. But he was only a colonel at the time and there is no evidence in Irish or British archives that he was ever considered for a post in Eire.

the Home Office which subsequently used them as a basis for refuting de Valera's claims. In a long but generally uninspired memorandum, the Home Office stated that there seemed to be 'very little' in the allegation of constituency gerrymandering since 'the number of safe nationalist seats in Northern Ireland has been eleven . . . both before and after abolition of proportional representation.'* The document, which for the most part played down the more disturbing aspects of Stormont rule, admitted that 'there may be a grievance' over local government constituencies but claimed that 'the minority themselves are largely to blame for not having availed themselves of opportunities which were offered of making representations.'

Northern Ireland had, like Eire, found it 'necessary to make regulations abridging the ordinary safeguards of civilians in order to combat the subversive organisation of the IRA.' The Special Powers Act, said the memorandum, was 'in form exceedingly drastic' but 'in practice, the Regulations appear to be administered with great moderation.' The Home Office had heard of only two complaints in the last few years: the case of a boy 'not quite sixteen' who was sent to prison rather than borstal because the Northern Ireland Government believed 'he was being trained by the IRA to be one of their spies'; and the case of Mr Donnelly of Armagh – the man whose imprisonment had been specifically raised with Chamberlain by de Valera – who after contravening a 14-year-old Exclusion Order had been 'sent to prison for a month, having refused to pay a fine'.

So far as employment in the civil service and the police was concerned, there seemed to be 'a genuine desire on the part of the Government of Northern Ireland to admit the minority to such employment'.† There was 'no official information' about Catholic employment by local authorities; but with disarming candour, the memorandum added that 'there can be very little doubt that in those areas where there is a Protestant majority on the Council, in practice posts do not often go to Catholics.' On the wider

---

* This was an unconvincing argument. It was not the change from proportional representation to the direct vote in Stormont elections that provoked claims of gerrymandering; what nationalists chiefly disputed was the way in which constituency boundaries had been redrawn. The nationalist constituency of Londonderry, in which Catholics formed a majority of the electorate, had been split in two at the province's birth in order to provide a Unionist seat in the small Protestant district of the city.[128]

† This was probably true at the time. It was greatly to Wilfrid Spender's credit that he was steadfast in refusing to discriminate against Catholics in the Stormont civil service although his policy was frequently questioned. In his 1935 diary, for instance, he records how Sir Robert Lynn, the Stormont Unionist MP for North Antrim, came to discuss Catholic entry to the civil service: 'Sir Robert Lynn told me that he had had a great many representations from the Orange Order on the subject but had pointed out that I as Head of the Service could be trusted to ensure that no secret undermining of the Government was being carried on. I am afraid that this assurance did not give full satisfaction to his correspondents, who do not at all appreciate my decision that there is to be absolutely fair play amongst all ranks of our Service no matter what their religion may be.'[129]

financial issue, the authors of the document decided that the allegation that partition continued only because of subsidies from the British Government was 'quite seriously believed and at the same time quite unfounded'. Not surprisingly – since the pro-Unionist Samuel Hoare was Home Secretary – the Home Office adopted Craigavon's view of Northern Ireland and concluded that 'the British Government has taken more out of it than it has put in.'[130]

None of this, of course, made any difference to de Valera's anti-partition campaign, which continued to draw the wrath of Northern Ireland's Unionist population. Malcolm MacDonald believed that the campaign 'was bound to have the effect of stiffening people on all sides, and that it would do no good to his cause . . .'[131] Late in December, Dulanty told MacDonald that de Valera had little option because 'no man sitting in his chair could stand out of the partition campaign. If he did not enter into it and keep some sort of control over it it would get into unconstitutional hands.' Sean MacEntee, the Irish Minister for Finance, was 'strongly opposed' to the campaign, said Dulanty, but 'the rank and file in the party were feeling extremely bitter about partition, and the extremists would have got control of the movement if Mr de Valera had not intervened.'

The American President Franklin Roosevelt had asked de Valera to open Eire's pavilion at the 1939 New York World Fair and Dulanty chose this inauspicious moment to inform MacDonald that de Valera had accepted the invitation. 'Mr de Valera,' noted MacDonald with obvious irritation, 'will go on a tour in the States, visiting San Francisco, Chicago and various other places. I said that I supposed Mr de Valera would make some frightful speeches.'

Dulanty, in his familiar role of amiable factotum, replied that he himself had been afraid of this 'but that he understood that Mr de Valera's chief adviser in America – who had been his right-hand man on his last wildly successful tour – was warning him that he could not "raise the fiery cross" this time.'[132] The Dominions Office was clearly unmoved by this assurance. Their exasperation – not to say their capacity for wishful-thinking – was evidenced by a caustic note which was attached to Mac-Donald's account of his conversation with Dulanty. A civil servant with an illegible signature had written on it: 'I seem to remember that Mr de Valera is still liable in certain states of the USA to penalties with regard to his $10,000,000 Independence Loan of 1920. But he can be left to steer clear of these and other entanglements himself.'[133]*

De Valera's difficulties, however, arose much nearer to home. In

---

* De Valera had no need to be concerned on this score. The Dominions Office may not have realised that the legality of the bonds for the loan – much of which was later spent on the war against the British – was personally approved in 1919 by Roosevelt himself, who was then a partner in a New York law firm.[134]

January, 1939, the IRA sent an ultimatum to Chamberlain, the British Foreign Secretary Lord Halifax, the Stormont Government, Hitler and Mussolini, demanding a British withdrawal from Northern Ireland. Revived under Sean Russell's leadership after a dispute over the direction in which a new campaign should be fought, the IRA had renewed their link with the remaining Sinn Fein representatives of de Valera's Second Dail and therefore felt able to present themselves as 'the Government of the Irish Republic'. They called for a British declaration of withdrawal within four days; when this deadline was reached without any public response from the recipients of the ultimatum, six IRA officers – including Russell – signed a further demand for the departure of the British, summoning 'the people of all Ireland, at home and in exile' to compel this evacuation and, as something of an afterthought, invoking God's name in the enterprise as well.

Unfortunately for the IRA, the violent campaign which followed did not measure up to the tenor or the spiritual sentiment of the proclamations, although it might perhaps have seduced the attention of Irishmen who would otherwise have concentrated on de Valera's peaceful struggle against partition. In Britain, explosions damaged factories, power stations and telephone exchanges on January 16 and three days later – in what might have been an attempt to wreck the personal relationship between Chamberlain and de Valera – a small bomb was detonated outside a hotel in Tralee, County Kerry, where the British Prime Minister's son Francis was staying during an Irish shooting holiday.

The bombs were constructed and primed by a contingent of young Irishmen, some of whom – lonely and with only a vague notion of republican ideology – were recruited in London pubs.[135] Others, over-confident and possessing little technical skill, were sent to Britain by the IRA merely to be arrested within a few days by the police. Brendan Behan was put on the Liverpool ferry from Dublin at the age of sixteen with orders to blow up the Birkenhead shipyard of Cammell Laird but was detained shortly after his arrival. According to his own account of the incident in *Borstal Boy*, he told the police sergeant who arrested him that he had come to Britain to fight 'for the Irish Workers' and Small Farmers' Republic'.[136]

IRA recruits stored explosives in lavatories and carried bombs on trams[137] and bicycles; inevitably, the campaign – known to its authors as the 'S-Plan' – took on a sordid, bloody quality which discredited Russell's belief that casualties could be avoided.[138] A fish porter was killed in Manchester by a bomb concealed in a street main and in July, after about 120 explosions had occurred in various parts of Britain, there was another fatality when a bomb detonated in the left-luggage office at King's Cross railway station in London. On August 25, five people died in an explosion in Coventry; they included an 81-year-old man and a schoolboy.

The Irish preceded the British in passing legislation against the IRA's conspiracy. This was not surprising; the IRA may have been attacking Britain but they were also trying to usurp the authority of de Valera's Government. Throughout February, the Irish Cabinet was occupied with the Offences Against the State Bill[139] – it became law in mid-summer shortly before the Prevention of Violence Bill was enacted at Westminster – but de Valera must have realised that his own anti-partition campaign had been sabotaged. So far as Unionists in Northern Ireland were concerned, his campaign appeared to have provided incitement for the IRA attacks rather than a political channel through which republican passions might have been redirected in more peaceful form.

A new strain of anger became apparent within the Stormont Cabinet when Belfast ministers contemplated de Valera's imprecations against Unionism. Basil Brooke, addressing a meeting in Manchester under heavy police protection after threats from the IRA, compared de Valera's recent speeches with Hitler's territorial demands.* 'I imagine,' he said, 'that the Austrians or the Czechs must have felt the same way when they read in the German papers that their "unreasonable stubbornness" was preventing the realisation of the Pan-German Reich.'[141] Even before the bombings began in Britain, the Stormont Cabinet had complained that de Valera's Government was failing to control the IRA. In January, John Andrews – who was Acting Prime Minister in Belfast during Craigavon's absence on a Pacific cruise – told Malcolm MacDonald that 'he had evidence in his possession to show that . . . recent outrages in Northern Ireland were perpetrated by members of that organisation from Southern Ireland . . .'[142]

The Irish Government was certainly more interested in safeguarding its own state from subversion than in protecting Craigavon's province; and it would be unrealistic to imagine that there was not some latent sympathy within de Valera's party for Irishmen who, in however clumsy and brutal a manner, were asserting Ireland's right to national unity. The Dublin Cabinet was in a position to understand the personalities as well as the motives behind the bombings because several of its ministers knew the campaign's instigators personally. Russell had fought with Frank Aiken under de Valera's nominal leadership during the civil war and in 1935 Russell had met de Valera to talk over the possibility of 'co-operation' between the IRA and Fianna Fail; he was rebuffed.[143] Joseph McGarrity, who wrote the second IRA ultimatum to the British Government, had been a close associate of de Valera in the 1919–20 American fund-raising

* Brooke, of course, knew nothing of the favourable references which de Valera had made about the Sudetenland settlement in conversation with British ministers. But the parallel had never been difficult to draw. Nine months before de Valera's discussions in London, Inskip told the British Cabinet's Irish Situation Committee that de Valera's claim to Northern Ireland 'was not unlike the claim of Herr Hitler that there should be included within the German Reich those German communities outside the present political boundaries of Germany.'[140]

expedition and was a friend of Sean T. O'Kelly. James O'Donovan, who organised the 'S-Plan', had been Director of Chemicals in the IRA under Aiken's command in 1923.

De Valera's old friend Gerry Boland, who had accompanied him on the train to Cobh to raise the Tricolour on that historic July day the previous year, was among those Irish ministers who quickly realised the effect that this IRA resurgence could have on Anglo-Irish relations. Boland, whose republicanism had been 'bred in him' since childhood[144] and whose brother Harry had died for the republican side in the civil war, had formed an aversion to the more extreme elements in Fianna Fail who turned a blind eye towards IRA activity when it did not directly threaten them. He felt deeply over the predicament in which de Valera – 'the Chief' – found himself.

'Our name was mud in England,' Boland noted in the unpublished papers which he wrote a few years before his death in 1973. 'We could all feel proud of the attack on Chester Castle in 1867 and the rescue of Kelly and Deasy in Manchester* but this wanton murder was disgusting. There was great activity at home also by this organisation and there is little doubt that it had German backing. The IRA had a private Broadcasting Station and had regular broadcasts from April on . . . Joe McGarrity, a friend of Harry's and the Chief, Sean T. Etc. was the intermediary for supplying money for this campaign and made several journeys here . . .'[146]

To say that the Germans were backing the IRA was something of an exaggeration. They were certainly interested in the bombing campaign although at this stage they were not lending the IRA anything more than moral support. Indeed, for several months they had avoided any contact with the organisation. In the summer of 1938, Helmut Clissmann, a German exchange student at Trinity College in Dublin who had first come to Ireland in 1930 and had since married into an Irish republican family, heard rumours of the forthcoming IRA campaign. He was acquainted with Russell and other IRA leaders; but when he tried to pass on information to the German military intelligence authorities in Berlin, he was turned away.[147] The Abwehr II department – to whom Clissmann had vainly made his offer – was responsible for contacts with discontented foreign minorities[148] but had been expressly forbidden by the German Foreign Office to have any dealings with the IRA. Once the bombing campaign in Britain began, however, Abwehr II's Hamburg office over-ruled the Foreign Office's instruction and sent an agent to Dublin.

Oscar Carl Pfaus was an unlikely candidate for the assignment, a 38-year-old German adventurer who had spent much of the last twenty

---

* 'Colonel' Thomas Kelly and 'Captain' T. Deasy were Fenian organisers rescued from a prison van on their way to jail in Manchester in 1867. In fact, the dynamite war in which the American Fenians were involved some fifteen years later bore an uncanny resemblance to the IRA's 1939 campaign.[145]

years in the United States working as a lumberjack, cowboy and Chicago policeman while somehow also managing to edit a German-language newspaper which was highly critical of the Versailles Treaty.[149] He arrived off the English mailboat at Dun Laoghaire early in February and first approached Eoin O'Duffy in the hope that the former Blueshirt commander would introduce him to the IRA. It was an understandable error but Pfaus was clearly no student of Irish history; O'Duffy had admired Europe's New Order yet most of his recent years had been employed in vilifying the IRA. In the event, it was O'Duffy's secretary who introduced Pfaus to Maurice Twomey, Russell's predecessor as IRA Chief of Staff.

Twomey drove Pfaus to a house in the Dublin suburb of Clontarf where, after much suspicious questioning, he was politely welcomed by six members of the IRA's Army Council, including O'Donovan. As a result of this meeting, O'Donovan made three visits to Germany to discuss the possibility of acquiring German arms and wireless equipment for the IRA.[150] On his first trip, he spent half a night writing a long memorandum for the Abwehr on the IRA's organisation and objectives.[151]

But for the moment, this was as far as the Abwehr was prepared to go in its relations with the IRA. The German Foreign Office as well as military intelligence had, of course, maintained an interest in Irish affairs for several years already. German students had been sent to Ireland by the Abwehr to study Gaelic history and culture and on their return to Germany they reported to Berlin on the political situation in both parts of the country. Thus Jupp Hoven, a German anthropology student, found himself at Queen's University in Belfast in the early months of 1939, working on 'a sociological thesis on the Ulster problem'.[152] Information was also available from Nazis among Eire's small but closely-knit German-Austrian community; the leading Nazi Party official in Ireland at this time was Professor Adolph Mahr, the Director of the National Museum in Dublin,[153] whose journeys around Eire in search of antiquities seem to have included a good deal of photographic reconnaissance for the German military authorities. Clissmann, who was to work for the Abwehr during the war, believes that the German Foreign Office possessed 'a reasonable knowledge of Ireland' before 1939.

In a conversation with Eduard Hempel, the newly-appointed German Minister to Eire, Hitler himself displayed 'quite a knowledge of Ireland and its relationship to Great Britain'.[154] Hempel learnt several years later that Hitler was convinced that 'you cannot do anything in Ireland without or against de Valera.'[155] In public, Hitler – who understood nationalist sensitivities even if he did not respect them – always made a point of referring to de Valera by his Irish title of 'Taoiseach'.[156]

By late March of 1939, de Valera's attitude towards Hitler was less flattering, at least in private, although like the British Cabinet he still clung to the unrealistic belief that some form of European settlement was possible through Chamberlain's mediation. Hitler's troops entered Prague on March 15, finally destroying Czech sovereignty and by implication ridiculing the Sudeten concessions which Britain had made the previous September. Yet ten days later, de Valera was in Chamberlain's private study at Chequers, urging the British Prime Minister to continue with his policy of appeasement. Chamberlain later wrote a seven-page official report of their conversation in which his aggravation at de Valera's persistence over Irish partition occasionally surfaced. It was a curious and in its way an historic exchange since it also showed de Valera to be uncertain about the merits of Eire's self-induced alienation from the British Commonwealth.

He had arrived at Chequers with Dulanty who, ever the faithful major-domo, announced that it was his intention to 'take a walk in the garden' while the two prime ministers repaired to Chamberlain's oak-panelled study. De Valera began by commending Chamberlain's states-manship, saying that 'notwithstanding Hitler's recent actions, he had not changed his views that Munich was right and that in fact we had no other alternative but war. He said that he had maintained this thesis against all critics, but added that he hoped very much that what had happened would not deflect me from the policy of appeasement . . . In particular, he hoped that I should not be tempted to embark upon a preventive war.'

Chamberlain assured de Valera that Britain would not do this but warned that since Hitler had now demonstrated that his word could not be relied on, 'it was at present hopeless to engage in any negotiations with him or a settlement of grievances . . .' It was necessary, Chamberlain said, 'to see what steps could be taken to prevent his pursuing any further his policy of swallowing neighbouring small states'. With all this, de Valera agreed 'with deep regret and reluctance', but added that 'he much feared that we should find it impossible to stop Hitler's further advance in Eastern Europe since we should be faced with the crumbling of the resistance of the small states who would be so frightened that they would make agreements with Germany . . .' Chamberlain responded by talking of 'certain specific assurances' which Britain might be able to give to states which might otherwise become 'the next victims of German aggression'.

De Valera then raised the partition issue. 'Indeed,' noted Chamberlain, 'this was no doubt the real object of his visit.' De Valera spoke about the 'bad feeling' growing in Ireland over partition, a vague reference perhaps to the IRA's bombing campaign although it was the only one to be made during the meeting. 'Once again,' wrote Chamberlain, 'he dilated upon the alleged ill-treatment of the populations in the Southern part of the Northern area and he added that England was being blamed because she stood in the way and covered Northern Ireland with her protection, without which Eire would make short work of her.'

De Valera 'feared that, in the event of our being engaged in a European war, his position might rapidly come to resemble that of Mr Redmond in the Great War when the latter lost the support of the majority in Ireland through his loyalty to the Empire.' Chamberlain altered the course of de Valera's argument, reminding him that a year earlier the Irish Government had been urged by the British to make a gesture of good will towards Northern Ireland by offering special trade advantages. De Valera had turned down this opportunity, said Chamberlain, and:

> Since then . . . he had himself done and said many things which had embittered feeling in Northern Ireland and made things worse than ever; in fact, he had so conducted his affairs that he had not got a single friend in Northern Ireland.

Chamberlain wanted to know if de Valera could give any assurance to the province that Eire would not declare a Republic:

> I asked him to tell me honestly whether he thought the majority of people in Ireland wanted her to cut loose from the Empire, to which he replied that he thought they did because, mistakenly, they believed they would never have complete independence unless they were a separate Republic.

Chamberlain suggested with little enthusiasm that Britain might appeal to Northern Ireland to make some contribution to Irish unity by discussing issues of 'national safety' with Eire. De Valera 'gratefully accepted this promise' and there the conversation ended.[157]

It was to be the last meeting between the two prime ministers and Chamberlain's official report of their discussion provides ample evidence that de Valera was as intent as ever on pressing his case for Irish unity. It was also the last occasion on which de Valera admitted to any doubts about Eire's drift from Empire. But the resentment at Britain's continued support for Northern Ireland was still there and so was John Redmond's ghost, a spectre whose presence could only confirm de Valera's determination to avoid an alliance with Britain. In Eire, this preoccupation with partition could be interpreted as steadfastness of purpose, the unwavering policy of a man who, amid the breakdown of political morality abroad, did not forget his country's national objective. To the British, de Valera's attitude must have seemed a unique form of tunnel vision, the act of a mathematician pondering the formula to an insoluble problem as the world caved in around him.

This collapse affected Ireland almost immediately, as de Valera had realised it would. In April, Craigavon called for conscription to be introduced in the six counties. His decision provoked an explosion of anger south of the border, where Lloyd George's threats to conscript Irishmen into the British Army had been so vigorously opposed by Sinn Fein and the Irish Party in 1918. In Northern Ireland itself, the nationalists were equally bitter for it was not correct, as Chamberlain had impetuously claimed, that de Valera had not 'a single friend' in the province. This may have been true so far as the majority of Protestants were concerned but the Catholics of Northern Ireland, slightly more than a third of the population, looked to Dublin for their political leadership. Redmond's phantom, it seemed, had not frequented de Valera's conversation with Chamberlain by chance.

The British Government had foreseen the problems that might arise from the introduction of compulsory national service in Northern Ireland. At the time of the Munich crisis in September 1938 Sir Alexander Maxwell, Permanent Under Secretary at the Home Office, told Blackmore, the Stormont Cabinet Secretary, that 'the British Government deprecate any action which would seem to envisage the possibility that Roman Catholics would be less anxious to respond to the Nation's call than other religions.'[158] Blackmore subsequently told Wilfrid Spender that 'owing to the position of Eire, the British Government would be most anxious not to allow any action to be taken which could hurt the susceptibilities of that Government.'

John Andrews and Spender envisaged problems of a more practical nature. Andrews wished to find out 'whether there was any chance that those who respond loyally to the call would find their places taken in remunerative work by others who did not do so'. Spender thought there would be 'no difficulties with the loyalists' if conscription was fairly administered. But he shared Andrews' concern about conscripts returning home. He reminded Blackmore that when shipyard workers had returned to Belfast after serving in the 1914–18 War, they had found their places taken by others who had not joined up, a situation which had led to the expulsion of Catholics from the yards. Spender – who believed that conscription in Northern Ireland was 'not a religious question' – stated that he 'did not think our Government ought to allow the same circumstances to arise.'

If, however, a large number of Northern Ireland inhabitants were to cross the border into Eire in order to escape conscription, Spender warned that 'there would be a very bitter sentiment on the part of the men who joined up . . .' He felt that the Northern Ireland Government should be empowered to 'enforce severe penalties against those who evaded their responsibilities as citizens of our Province'. It was indicative of how seriously the authorities took this possibility that Spender actually discussed with Blackmore and two other colleagues penalties which included 'loss of citizenship and of unemployment assistance rights'.[159]

The Northern Ireland Cabinet had discussed conscription during Craigavon's absence in February 1939 but wisely postponed a decision until the Prime Minister's return.[160] It was Chamberlain's announcement on April 26 of the reintroduction of national service that finally moved Craigavon to act. The Compulsory Military Training Bill contained a clause which allowed conscription to be extended to Northern Ireland and Craigavon's Cabinet, which had no power over the implementation of national service, felt it should call at once for the extension of conscription to the province.

The condemnation which followed this decision was both widespread and inevitable although it is doubtful if even Craigavon – inured as he had become to nationalist criticism – expected such an outcry. Some of it was predictable. De Valera, who immediately cancelled his trip to New York, announced that since Eire claimed the whole of Ireland as her national territory, the conscription of Irishmen in the province would be 'an act of aggression'; he protested 'in the strongest terms' to the British Government.[161] The Irish Catholic hierarchy used almost identical words and Cardinal Joseph MacRory, the Primate of All Ireland, spoke of his people's 'moral right' to resist national service in the British Army.[162] Less expected was the reaction of Belfast trade union leaders, who also expressed their opposition.[163] In the United States, Roosevelt received cables from six Irish-American societies, insisting that the American Government 'use immediately all its influence to avert the threat to international peace' caused by Craigavon's demand.[164]

More ominously, the Irish protest provided considerable propaganda for Germany. Roosevelt had coincidentally sent an open letter to Hitler in April, appealing to him to give public assurances that he would not attack any of thirty-one specified countries, including Ireland.[165] The Reich Chancellor was aware of de Valera's statement that British conscription in Northern Ireland would be regarded as an act of 'aggression' and found good reason to take up the issue in his public reply to Roosevelt. In the course of a two-hour speech to the Reichstag on April 28, Hitler – who was, after all, now something of an expert on nationalist minorities – chose to point out 'one or two historical errors' to Roosevelt:

> He mentioned Ireland, for instance, and asks for a statement that Germany will not attack Ireland. Now, I have just read a speech by de Valera, the Irish Taoiseach, in which, strangely enough, and contrary to Mr Roosevelt's opinion, he does not charge Germany with oppressing Ireland but he reproaches England with subjecting Ireland to continuous aggression . . .[166]

Palestine was also 'occupied' not by German but by British troops, Hitler went on. It was a theme that Germany was to use repeatedly in its propaganda against Britain during the coming war: how could the British claim to be fighting for democracy in Europe when their soldiers were coercing Irish and other nationalist groups?

Hitler's words were taken into account by the British press which was in any case largely unfavourable towards Craigavon's demand. In a leading article on Northern Ireland conscription which appeared on the day after Hitler's Reichstag speech, the *Manchester Guardian* counselled its readers: 'Let us not forget that Herr Hitler, as he sarcastically reminded us yesterday, keeps a close eye on this rather vulnerable spot in our heel.'[167]

But it was a fear that the Irish unrest of 1918 would reappear in the province that underlay most editorial concern. 'Is it credible,' the *Daily Mirror* asked, 'that the British Government can even dream of repeating in 1939 the hideous blunder of 1918, and of forcing conscription in any part of Ireland?'[168] *The Times* advocated 'a reasonable settlement'[169] and the London *Evening Standard*, while it suggested that 'Britain can do nothing which might . . . undermine the authority of the Ulster administration', called for 'wise statesmanship'.[170] But there was also some distrust of Craigavon's motives. 'Lord Craigavon,' said the *Manchester Guardian*, 'could better show his statesmanship and justify the peculiar loyalty he claims by putting England to shame by the success of his voluntary methods.'[171] The only real editorial support for conscription in Northern Ireland came in the local press; the *Belfast Telegraph* – which was then an avowedly Unionist newspaper – announced that the opposition of Irish nationalists was 'nothing short of ignoble and contemptible', concluding that 'if men refuse national responsibilities they should be denied all political rights.'[172]*

The Unionists used strong language for there were more things at stake than the province's manpower contribution in a future war. Conscription was as vital to Craigavon's prestige as the prevention of it was to de Valera's. If the Irish leader had to defend his people on the northern side of that straggling, untidy frontier from unwilling service in the forces of the Crown, it was of equally momentous consequence to Craigavon to demonstrate that *his* people were prepared to take an equal share – and if necessary make an equal sacrifice – in the defence of the realm. Ulster's Solemn League and Covenant, signed by Craigavon, Carson and almost half a million others in 1912, had claimed 'equal citizenship' in the United Kingdom[174] and for nearly twenty years Craigavon had followed this pledge by demanding social and economic parity with the rest of the United Kingdom. Conscription was the first serious test of his province's loyalty to Britain. He could scarcely now accept that Northern Ireland's manhood, alone in all the United Kingdom, should be exempted from compulsory service in the British armed forces. Even less could he permit de Valera to exercise greater influence over Northern Ireland affairs than the province's own Unionist Government in Belfast. And if the British allowed any military exemption because of opposition from the Catholic nationalist minority, it would suggest that the consensus normally present

---

* It is worth noting that even the Unionist papers had in previous months shown no enthusiasm for conscription. When national service was first discussed in Britain in 1938, the *Northern Whig*, normally a supporter of Unionism and all its works, took the view that conscription had 'no place in Britain's peace-time policy . . .' The nation, it said, 'has reverted to the voluntary method, notwithstanding the presence of huge conscript armies abroad.'[173] The editorial, which pointed out that Northern Ireland topped the recruiting returns for the year ending May 1938, wilfully ignored the fact that conscription was being considered not as a peacetime policy but as a possible *war* measure.

in United Kingdom politics was somehow lacking in the six counties; that there was something innately wrong – distinctly *un-British* – about the British part of Ireland.

Chamberlain asked Craigavon to travel to London to give his advice in person and, in a state of some agitation, the Northern Ireland Prime Minister set off from Belfast on May 2. Two local newspaper reporters – David Kirk of the *News Letter* and William Irwin of the *Northern Whig* – tried to interview him at York Road railway station when he boarded the Larne boat train with Sir Robert Gransden, the Cabinet Deputy Secretary. 'We found him in his private coach,' Kirk recalled years later, 'and it was obvious that he was enraged. As he paced up and down he gave vent to his feelings in no uncertain language. Sir Robert Gransden . . . tried to calm him without much success. To us it was great copy – but as we left the coach Sir Robert followed us on to the platform and asked us to forget the scene on the train.'[175]

In her diary, Lady Craigavon left a vivid description of her husband's confrontation with Chamberlain a few hours later. 'The British Government,' she wrote, 'were frightened of the issue being complicated by de Valera kicking up a dust, though Ulster affairs have *nothing* to do with him. American opinion, as ever, had to be considered, too. The military authorities in Belfast also advised against it, on account of the trouble that might arise up the Falls Road when forcibly going to enlist people . . . J. was asked flat out by Chamberlain, "Is Ulster out to help Britain in her war effort?" to which, of course, he answered, "You know we are. I have offered personally all the resources at our disposal to help you, and we have passed resolutions in our Parliament to the same effect." Chamberlain then said, "If you really want to help us, *don't* press for conscription. It will only be an embarrassment." What else could J. do than say, "Very well, I won't!" '[176] Craigavon returned to Belfast, leaving Chamberlain to announce that conscription would not be extended to Northern Ireland because of 'special difficulties' in the province.[177]

The fact that national service lay outside the powers of the Stormont Government might in theory have proved a salvation for Craigavon who, having loyally requested that his province should be included in the conscription bill, could scarcely be blamed if the Imperial Government – for reasons of its own – turned the offer down. Craigavon, Chamberlain told the Westminster House of Commons, had been 'inspired by the purest kind of patriotism'.[178] But this did nothing to pacify Unionist opinion. Basil Brooke admitted to feeling 'resentment, anger and hurt pride'.[179] Craigavon had to endure the reproaches of Unionist rebels in the Stormont Parliament. Thomas Henderson, the vociferous Independent Unionist MP for Shankill, asked whether the Northern Ireland Prime Minister would resign now that Chamberlain had taken de Valera's advice rather than Craigavon's. 'The Prime Minister used to declare "not an inch",' he said. 'He has given away more than an inch now.'[180]

At Westminster, Samuel Hoare defended Chamberlain's decision on the grounds that the inclusion of Northern Ireland 'would have made a very deep division and would have had reactions in other parts of the world'.[181] In Belfast, the IRA claimed that they had 'made Britain withdraw the threat of conscription' and, in a proclamation read to two thousand sympathisers in the Falls Road area of the city, they urged the population to refuse all co-operation with the military authorities.[182] Brooke held a broader spectrum of nationalists responsible; the reason for Northern Ireland's exemption, he said, was that there was in the province 'a minority who, whilst prepared to share in the benefits of the Empire and trade with England, and to share in the benefits of their social services . . . were either afraid, or too despicable, to take a hand in the defence of the country which defended them.'[183] Brooke was at least acknowledging the strength of ethnic dissent in Northern Ireland, and there is no doubt that this would have been mobilised against the authorities if conscription had been introduced in 1939. As the war was soon to prove, however, it was not just the Catholic community which was unhappy at the prospect of bearing arms for the King.

For the present, Craigavon's Government had to content itself with the promise from Chamberlain that the British would constitute a new Northern Ireland tank section of the Royal Armoured Corps[184] – the North Irish Horse – to supplement the province's three infantry regiments and its territorial, air and naval reserves. Craigavon's efforts to win a greater share of the British rearmament programme, however, were yielding ever more positive results. In the next four months, Harland and Wolff were allocated the conversion and arming of seven liners, two auxiliaries and twenty-four trawlers.[185] Short and Harland were engaged in the manufacture of the Hereford bomber and had started preliminary work on the four-engined Stirling. A new ordnance factory was erected near the harbour and in May, shipwrights laid the keel of a 15,000 ton submarine depot ship.[186]

Belfast's importance as a wartime industrial centre was now visibly evident to anyone in the east of the city, where the rust-coloured hull of the aircraft-carrier *Formidable* loomed amid the gantries and cranes on Queen's Island. In August, Craigavon heard that the 10,000 ton cruiser *Belfast* was leaving the Lough and the old man walked down to the shore-line to watch the ship steaming for the open sea, her siren echoing twice against the mountain sides above the city.[187] It was an appropriate enough symbol of Craigavon's determination to involve his province in Britain's war even if his last display of patriotism had been rejected. In eight months, Northern Ireland's unemployment register had fallen by more than 30,000;[188] hundreds of extra workers – most of them Protestants – were being taken on in the shipyards. Now thrived the armourers.

A hundred miles to the south, the international emergency that had brought such sudden economic benefits to Belfast was inspiring a series of disturbing forecasts from de Valera's civil servants. In April, the Irish Department of Industry and Commerce presented a 19-page memorandum to the Taoiseach and his Ministers, outlining in harsh statistical detail the effect of a European war on Eire's economy. The document, which made little reference to the fact that practically all Eire's £200 million of foreign investments lay in British securities, pointed out that the United Kingdom provided 50 per cent of the country's imports and the market for no less than 90 per cent of Eire's exports. A high proportion of the imports consisted of 'essential supplies . . . which we cannot provide ourselves'.* Only five per cent of the shipping tonnage entering Irish ports in 1938 was Irish-owned; the British owned 64 per cent. Eire, the report continued, 'depends entirely on other countries for the shipping space necessary to carry our entire imports of wheat, maize, petroleum, timber, and any other "bulk" cargoes from abroad . . .' These facts, the memorandum bluntly concluded, 'make it clear that if war should break out we are very largely at the mercy of other countries, and particularly of the United Kingdom, in respect of our external trade, and that the economic activities of this country could in such circumstances be completely paralysed.'[189]

This was a crippling economic dependence for a neutral to owe to any nation involved in hostilities, let alone one that was likely to be among the principal belligerents. In September 1938, de Valera had drawn up a list of twelve matters requiring 'immediate attention' in the event of war and at the top of this inventory came food supplies and external trade, followed by censorship, counter-espionage and coast-watching. De Valera regarded these as 'probably the most urgent' issues to be considered and placed them higher in priority than military measures and air-raid precautions.[190] This was an authentic policy of neutrality, the desire to maintain the country's commercial life and safeguard its political integrity from external pressures, while taking only minimum defence precautions on the grounds that neutrality – if strictly adhered to – would obviate the need for enormous military expenditure.

Indeed, there is evidence that de Valera, having failed to reach agreement with the British over military co-operation, was ready to pare down even the limited defence scheme which he, Aiken and other ministers had prepared in case of war. There were plans for eight new rifle battalions, the creation of two field brigades, the provision of two anti-aircraft batteries – a total of sixteen guns – to defend Dublin and a new coastal patrol service.[191] The Department of Defence had ordered an additional

---

* A detailed analysis of the figures in the document showed, for example, that Britain provided all of Eire's coal, 84 per cent of her pig iron, 78 per cent of her aluminium manufactures, 94 per cent of iron piping, 51 per cent of the largest variety of cattle feeding stuffs and 74 per cent of copper plates and sheets. In 1937, Britain had purchased £18 million of Eire's goods out of an export total of £22½ million.

fourteen armoured cars from Sweden.[192] But Sean MacEntee, the Finance Minister, was worried about these 'heavy commitments'; by the end of September 1938, his Department had approved almost £1¼ million in defence expenditure and unless economies were made in other directions, he stated, 'fresh commitments must be financed by an increase in taxation.'[193] Warnings of this kind were taken so seriously that in February 1939 the Taoiseach's Department submitted a memorandum which suggested that arms for the rifle battalions might be reduced, that the coastal patrol service could be halved and that only one of the proposed new field brigades should be given artillery. Dublin might also have to make do with only one battery of eight guns to defend it from air attack.[194] The Swedish armoured car order was subsequently reduced from fourteen vehicles to six.

But it was Eire's economic dependence upon Britain which chiefly concerned de Valera. 'It is possible,' he told the Dail in February, 'that . . . if we desired and tried to carry on the trade which is essential to our economic life here, we would be regarded as a combatant, and our neutrality would not be respected.'[195] De Valera had little alternative but to explain to the Germans how much his country's economic survival depended upon Britain.

On August 31, only hours before Germany's invasion of Poland, Eduard Hempel, the German Minister in Dublin, called on de Valera at his office in Upper Merrion Street to ascertain the Irish Government's attitude in the event of war. On the instructions of Joachim von Ribbentrop, the German Foreign Minister, Hempel told de Valera that Germany would respect Eire's neutrality. According to Hempel, de Valera replied 'in his usual doctrinaire fashion', emphasising Ireland's desire for peace with all nations but also pointing out the vital importance of Eire's trade links with Britain. The Irish Government, said de Valera, would have to show 'a certain consideration' for Britain.[196] Hempel understood the message.

De Valera naturally hoped Germany would accept that this 'consideration' did not impugn Irish neutrality. It was a pragmatic appeal from a head of government who knew the limitations of his untried policy. It was also an admission of Eire's vulnerable diplomatic status. In the summer of 1939, de Valera still appeared confident that neutrality was the only coherent policy for Eire to adopt, although he was horrified that Hitler's latest demand – for the return to Germany of the Free City of Danzig – should provoke hostilities. For their part, the British had no excuse for any illusions about the attitude of Eire.

The British Government's archives for this period contain understandably few references to Ireland but we obtain one rare glimpse of Dublin in the last few weeks of peace from a British civil servant's report which found its way to the Foreign Office. Percivale Liesching, Assistant Under Secretary at the Dominions Office, paid a brief confidential visit to

Dublin in July to talk with officials of the Irish External Affairs Department. 'In all quarters,' he wrote, 'I found that the possibility of Danzig becoming a *casus belli* with Germany was regarded with horror. The Taoiseach himself during the six or seven minutes' conversation which I had with him spent his whole time deploring such a contingency . . . The numerous difficulties of the United Kingdom Government are appreciated, and there is much sympathy for them, but, nevertheless, so Mr de Valera assured me, it would be difficult, if not impossible, to convince ordinary people that a war should be allowed to take place over this issue.' Liesching heard no opinions 'which did not coincide with that expressed to me by Mr de Valera', adding that he had frequently been told that 'substantial' colonial concessions should be made by the United Kingdom. Whether this was an allusion to Northern Ireland or to British possessions in Africa which might be ceded to Germany, Liesching did not make clear. But his conclusion could not have been read with much warmth in London:

> My general impression was that it would not cause pain to anybody in Eire if, by entering into war of which Danzig was the immediate cause, or by refusing substantial concessions in the Colonial field, the United Kingdom should suffer, and should suffer to an extent which should teach her lessons which she has not learnt during a time of almost unchallenged ascendancy.[197]

Such was the mood among the rulers of the first nation to break with the Empire, as Eire prepared to watch her former colonial master go to war without her. It was also a watershed in the starved political relationship behween Dublin and Belfast. For the past seven years, Northern Ireland's struggle to maintain and strengthen her constitutional links with Britain had been paralleled south of the border by de Valera's equally strenuous effort to sever the imperial connection. Now both parts of Ireland were seeking to define their opposing territorial status within the context of the greatest European conflict in modern times; and the frontier which had been drawn in so hurried and arbitrary a fashion almost two decades before, would soon divide Ireland in a more fundamental and potentially more damaging way than its authors could ever have envisaged.

The last hours before the British declaration of war were redolent with the ambiguities of Anglo-Irish politics. In Berlin, where the British and Commonwealth envoys were burning their papers, Eire's young First Secretary William Warnock – a Dublin Protestant representing a nation that was still nominally a member of the Commonwealth – stayed on unperturbed in his small legation near the Tiergarten. 'The Germans,' he observed later, 'seemed happy enough at our neutrality.'[198] In Dublin, some necessary terminology was under construction. De Valera introduced legislation to amend Article 28 of the Irish Constitution, allowing the Dail to declare a state of emergency even though Eire was neutral.

Thus 'the Emergency' came into existence, a legally accurate but nonetheless euphemistic description for what, north of the border, was about to become the Second World War.

On the last night of peace, the black-out imposed by the British Government embraced all Northern Ireland and in the little village of Pettigo, where the border inconsiderately bisected the main street, the black-out curtains on the County Fermanagh side were dutifully pulled down. In the County Donegal half of the village – which came under the writ of the Eire Government – the lamps continued to cast their neutral glow over the streets.[199]

Northern Ireland's mobilisation in some respects followed the administrative pattern set in Britain. Stormont civil servants compiled a register of aliens in the province who would be interned on the outbreak of war – they included 200 Germans, 32 Austrians and 24 Czechs[200] – while Territorials and Royal Engineers guarded the coast defences. The 188 (Antrim) Heavy Battery of the Royal Artillery, a Territorial unit, joined the Antrim Fortress Company of the Royal Engineers manning the batteries at Grey Point and Kilroot at the mouth of Belfast Lough – the only one of the original four Irish Treaty ports still in British hands.

But most of the regular troops in Northern Ireland – far from protecting the province from any surprise German attack – were located 'entirely with a view to internal security'. For as Major General R.V. Pollok, commanding the British Army's Northern Ireland District, noted in his situation report for September 2, 'it is anticipated that if trouble comes to this country it will come from within the borders of Northern Ireland.'[201] Indeed on the same day, the RUC Inspector General, Lieutenant Colonel Charles Wickham, sent to Stormont Castle a secret report in which he warned that 'as the situation develops into war there is serious danger that the IRA may attempt a series of outrages . . . any moves by the IRA will immediately create a very dangerous situation which if not quickly controlled may well necessitate the use of troops.' Wickham advised that the 'B' Specials should be called out on patrol and that a proposed internment camp at Ballykinlar 'should be completed at an early date'.[202] At this critical moment, Northern Ireland was, as usual, preoccupied with essentially domestic fears.

Belfast's nationalist community was already making its protest against a war in which it did not wish to be included. From his home in the south Belfast suburb of Finaghy, Queen's University student Rodney Green noticed that the black-out was not being observed in the west of the city. From Divis Street up the Falls Road as far as Andersonstown, he could see lights shining in the windows of hundreds of Catholic homes.[203] The RUC discovered that more than just house lights had been turned on. Since the black-out had been imposed in Belfast on September 1, the police logged twelve incidents in forty-eight hours in nationalist areas of the city, including the lighting of street lamps and bonfires, the burning of gas masks and assaults on troops; a member of the Territorials was stripped of his uniform by six armed men in East Bridge Street on the afternoon of September 3 and another soldier was stripped by four men carrying guns in the Kashmir Road and had his uniform burned. A Reservist was shot in the abdomen at the end of Upper Library Street. Police patrols were stoned and on one occasion a crowd in Butler Street off the Falls Road shouted 'Up Hitler' when the RUC appeared.[204]

Informing Wickham of these events, RUC Commissioner R.D. Harrison reported that there was 'conclusive evidence of concerted action' behind the incidents. As proof of this, he listed the slogans which had been found painted – in almost identical wording – on the walls of streets in nine RUC sub-districts of Belfast:

> ARP for English slaves, IRA for the Irish.
>
> Damn your concessions England, we want our country.
>
> Join the IRA and serve Ireland.
>
> Remember 1916.
>
> England's difficulty is Ireland's opportunity . . .[205]

Chapter 3

The Weapons of Coercion

My friends in America say to me 'Why don't you take a leaf out of Hitler's book and work the Sudeten-Deutsch trick in Northern Ireland?

Eamon de Valera *14 September 1939*

About ten minutes after Chamberlain had announced Britain's declaration of war against Germany over the BBC on the morning of 3 September 1939, a four-engined RAF Sunderland flying-boat – short of fuel and buffeted by the storms that had raged all night over the Irish Sea – flew low over the holiday resort of Skerries, ten miles north of Dublin. The plane turned above Saint Patrick's Island and then touched down on the sea, just a few hundred yards from the Irish shore-line. By an odd coincidence, an Englishwoman witnessed this first, technical breach of Eire's wartime neutrality. Peggy Bristow, who was staying with friends in Skerries, had broken into tears when she heard Chamberlain's broadcast – she had two brothers in the British Army and another in the Royal Navy – and left the house to walk off her misery along the rain-swept beach. An amateur photographer, she had absent-mindedly carried her small box camera to the shore and was therefore able to take a photograph of the huge plane as it lay moored before the eyes of two astonished members of the Garda Siochana, Eire's police force. The air crew were brought ashore by dinghy and taken to the local Garda station while the Irish Government – which could scarcely have expected so hasty an intrusion into Eire's territory by the British – debated whether the RAF men should be interned. The authorities expediently decided to refuel the machine and within four hours Peggy Bristow was able to watch the aircraft lifting slowly into the air in a hail of spray in the direction of England.[1]

It was not the only practical question of Anglo-Irish relations confronting the Eire Government that day. All weekend, the mailboats from Britain had been crowded with passengers fleeing the war and the Irish Justice Department could not see its way to controlling the thousands of women and children disembarking at Dun Laoghaire and Rosslare.[2] By September 5, the numbers landing in Eire were so high that Dulanty anxiously telephoned the Dominions Office to find out what had happened to the British travel restrictions. He eventually spoke to the Chief Passport Officer in London who admitted that his travel permit system 'had virtually broken down so far as Ireland was concerned'. Indeed, the Great Western Railway had laid on an extra train to take yet more passengers from London to the Irish boat at Fishguard. In the chaos at the port, British immigration officials were reported to be turning back 'everybody who seemed to them to be of British nationality'[3] but the 'war-rush' – as Irish civil servants dubbed this unprecedented phenomenon[4] – went on almost unchecked for weeks.

More than 80 per cent of the original arrivals were Irish citizens returning home[5] and the Glasgow–Belfast ferries were packed with them as well. Basil Brooke, hurriedly travelling back to Belfast on September 1 after an ill-timed vacation in Scotland, noted unkindly in his diary: 'Passed evacuated children. Masses of Irish on Glasgow boat. Running away . . .'[6] But Britons also made the crossing to Eire to escape conscription.[7] Furthermore, the Department of Justice proposed to deport seventy Britons – classified as being 'without means' – if they did not return to England of their own accord. Mindful of the obligations of neutrality, however, the Department informed the Taoiseach's office that 'an exception is being made . . . in the case of Germans who have fled here from Britain. These people are not being told to leave, but the German Legation are being asked whether they can arrange for their repatriation through Holland.' The Department, which reported that eighteen such Germans had been traced by the police, also estimated that refugees arriving in Eire included 'a high proportion of Jews'.[8]

Accidental encroachments into Irish territorial waters and a flood of refugees from Britain were the natural burdens of neutrality and de Valera could not have been surprised by these events. Eire was the only British dominion to choose neutrality – the rest of the Commonwealth followed Chamberlain's lead by declaring war on Germany – and in the first week of hostilities, the British Government was too preoccupied with the débâcle in Poland and the difficulties of Anglo-French co-operation to worry unduly about de Valera's administrative problems. Besides, he had many times informed British ministers that Eire did not intend to participate in a European war while Ireland remained partitioned and there was nothing astonishing about his statement to that effect on September 2;[9] it is certainly untrue, as one historian has claimed, that the British Government was 'unaware of de Valera's intention' to be neutral.[10]

But it was appreciated at once in both London and Dublin that the absence of a British diplomatic representative in Eire could allow misunderstandings and distrust to arise between the two countries. Germany, Italy, Japan and other nations maintained envoys in Dublin but because of the constitutional complexities surrounding Eire's tenuous membership of the Commonwealth, the British had no diplomat in the Irish capital; the appointment of such an envoy would have amounted to British recognition of Eire's independence from the Commonwealth. Joseph Walshe consequently travelled to London to discuss the matter with Anthony Eden, who had just taken over from MacDonald as Dominions Secretary in Chamberlain's new War Cabinet.

'To guard against possible differences, I was convinced that we must have a diplomatic representative in Dublin,' Eden wrote later. 'A characteristic negotiation followed, Eire asking for an Ambassador and we declining anything so portentous for a country still in name a part of the British Commonwealth. Eventually a "Representative" was offered and accepted . . ."[11] The British suggested that his full title should be 'United Kingdom Representative in Eire', a nomenclature which de Valera ingeniously altered to his satisfaction by substituting 'to' for 'in'.[12]

Sir John Loader Maffey, the man chosen to fill this onerous role, had a record of colonial service that must initially have dismayed the Taoiseach's Department in Dublin, which dutifully copied out his curriculum vitae from the current edition of *Who's Who*.[13] A product of Rugby and Christ Church, Oxford, Maffey had acted as a political officer in Khyber, Peshawar and the North West Frontier of India before being appointed Governor General of the Sudan in 1925 and then Permanent Under Secretary for the Colonies in 1933. As holder of the 'Order of the Rising Sun', the Egyptian 'Order of Ismail' and the 'Grand Cordon Star of Ethiopia', he was not at first sight the kind of man who would appeal to the quieter, less imperial tastes of Eamon de Valera. Yet this tall, eloquent civil servant, whose high cheek-bones and precise manner suggested a colonial administrator as much as a diplomat of finesse and discretion, was to represent the British Government in Dublin throughout the Second World War.

Maffey's negotiating skills were to be tested almost immediately, for on September 12 – just two days before Maffey was due to meet de Valera for the first time – Dulanty arrived at the British Dominions Office bearing an unwelcome document for Eden. It was an *aide-mémoire* containing a list of restrictions which the Eire Government was about to impose, effectively prohibiting the Royal Navy's use of the three Treaty ports and banning any naval operations in Eire's territorial waters or RAF sorties in the country's air-space. The memorandum, which invoked the 1907 Hague Convention on the rights of neutral powers, was couched in formal language; Eire was to prohibit 'any belligerent vessel armed for war' from 'the right to sojourn within the territorial waters, ports or roadsteads of Ireland'.[14] The regulations would, of course, apply equally to Germany, France or any other warring nation. But the meaning was obvious. The prophecy which Churchill had made to a sceptical House of Commons fifteen months earlier was starting to be fulfilled.

At 10.15 on the morning of the 14th, Walshe conducted Maffey through the corridors of the grey-stone government buildings in Dublin to de Valera's austere and sparsely furnished room with its marble-top fireplace and heavy wooden desk. Before allowing any discussion to take place, de Valera began by pointing out his difficulties in accepting a 'United Kingdom Representative'. He asserted that this 'would be a battle cry for the IRA and Extremists'. It was clear that Maffey was to be given the full partition treatment complete with that familiar map.

De Valera, wrote Maffey in his report afterwards, 'spoke at some length of the difficulties of his position, his every action studied by men bitterly opposed to any sort of *rapprochement* with the United Kingdom, critical of any wavering from the strait path of neutrality. "All this happens because you maintain the principle of partition in this island!" He pointed to a map of Ireland hanging on the wall before him – Eire jet-black, Northern Ireland a leperous [sic] white.'

Maffey found that 'the subject of partition recurred again and again and we always performed a circle, the President [sic] saying that Eire could not consider any policy today except in the light of the crime of partition, while I said that the prospects of readjusting partition must be affected by the policy of Eire today.'

Maffey used this cue to raise the question of Dulanty's memorandum. '. . . I said that in the last hours before I left Whitehall a grave difficulty had been created by the presentation of an *aide-mémoire* on the subject of neutrality presented by the High Commissioner for Eire. It was fully understood that Eire had adopted a policy of neutrality and the emphasising of that policy in general terms must be expected. But this rigid *aide-mémoire*, dotting the "i's" and crossing the "t's" in the way of stringent rules affecting British ships and aircraft had been read with profound feelings of disappointment.'

De Valera assured Maffey that his intention was to be helpful, that he had wanted to oblige Britain by having strict rules about submarines. 'If he had an order about submarines his critics regarding that measure as entirely anti-German would at once ask what he had done about ships and aircraft. How could he escape from having rules as a guide in practice?' Maffey begged de Valera not to publish the memorandum and said that 'these restrictive rules in that crude form would excite much feeling in England, particularly in view of our action in surrendering the Irish ports so recently. It would be adding to Mr Chamberlain's difficulties. This argument evidently touched the President at once. He expressed the deepest admiration for and sympathy with the Prime Minister. He said "He has done everything that a man could do to prevent this tragedy".'

But de Valera made no commitment to withhold publication of the neutrality restrictions and he lost no time in raising the issue of the RAF's recent encroachment into Eire's territorial waters. He 'referred to an incident at Skerry [sic] when one of our military planes had come down. Its departure . . . had been allowed without interference and the news had been suppressed. But comment in Eire had been widespread. How could this continue? If he enforced rules against submarines what answer would he have to the Germans about our planes?'

This argument was emphasised with unexpected suddenness. 'By a strange coincidence,' wrote Maffey, 'the telephone rang and the President said "There you are! One of your planes is down in Ventry Bay. What am I to do?" He said that possibly something might be done in the way of transferring the ownership of the plane to Eire, but he would have to intern the crew . . . The President was greatly disturbed in mind and we were both much relieved when the telephone rang again an hour later to report that the plane had managed to get away – or rather had been allowed to get away. Clearly problems of this kind lie ahead of us.'

De Valera expatiated on Irish public opinion. Two thirds of his people were pro-British, he said – 'or at any rate anti-German . . .' Personally, he had great sympathy with England today but, though the cause of Poland was Britain's *casus belli* 'the reasons for the breach went deeper than that and motives which affected England could not affect Eire.'

Here again was that crucial distinction. Maffey saw the European war in broad terms of European morality but de Valera – who might once have viewed it in the same light – concentrated on his nation's destiny within a domestic framework far removed from the struggle against Nazi Germany. 'I said that England today had no war aims of a selfish character,' wrote Maffey. '. . . It had seemed to us that in this struggle at last there was an ideal for which England and Eire could stand together and that from that association a new chapter in our history would start.'

But de Valera wanted to talk of Redmond's failure; 'and thus,' reported Maffey, 'we travelled back to the Partition of Ireland. Why did not our Prime Minister put his foot down and stop the follies and oppressions of Northern Ireland? Look at what a picture we might have! A united, independent Ireland! Think of the effect in America where the Irish element had ruined and would ruin any possibility of Anglo-American understanding! Why could we not see where the flaw in our armour lay? It was not a matter of religion . . . The petty tyrannies and oppressions now going on in Northern Ireland must lead to disaster. "If I lived there", he exclaimed with heat, "I should say 'I'll be damned if I'll be ruled by these people' ". He went on to voice the fear that if the war went on for long the danger of a physical clash between the rival forces in Ireland could not be averted. He gave me to understand that he considered the rulers of Northern Ireland were seeking to provoke a conflict. "My friends in America say to me 'Why don't you take a leaf out of Hitler's book and work the Sudeten-Deutsch trick in Northern Ireland?' ".'

Maffey dismissed the idea of any trouble from Northern Ireland. 'I raised the question of submarines and the menace to Irish seaborne trade arising therefrom,' he wrote, 'but Mr de Valera evidently at present does not wish any consideration to obscure his vision of neutrality. The only line possible at present is to retain his goodwill and to render his neutrality as benevolent as possible.' De Valera said he 'could not deny the possibility of a German submarine receiving assistance but he would do his utmost to prevent it'. Maffey was unimpressed. 'This does not sound very reassuring,' he wrote.

De Valera seems to have been in a strangely wistful mood that morning. He told Maffey, for instance, that he 'could not believe that the outrages at Coventry were committed by Irishmen' and suggested that the explosion which killed five people there might have been caused by an aircraft accidentally dropping a bomb on the city.* He spoke of the British Empire in friendly terms. 'There was a time,' he said, 'when I would have done anything in my power to help destroy the British Empire. But now my position has changed. I can see that a united and independent Ireland might well find relationship with it.' De Valera talked about British royalty. Maffey reported him as saying: 'For some extraordinary reason or other Edward VIII was popular over here. If he had been King at the time of his abdication you would have had trouble in Ireland. Queen Victoria is very much disliked.'[16]

De Valera argued again about the title of 'Representative' – Maffey had not yet been officially assigned to Dublin – but he expressed his pleasure at Eden's appointment as Dominions Secretary. The two men had worked together at the League of Nations and Eden was later to record that he liked de Valera and that they 'were often of the same mind on international problems, always excluding, of course, the six counties of Ulster.'[17] Perhaps this personal friendship softened Eden's own reaction to the new restrictions contained in Dulanty's *aide-mémoire* for he informed the British War Cabinet on September 16 that 'it would hardly be possible to offer any serious criticism of the proposals set out in the memorandum.' He stated that 'it was essential in Eire's interests that the small but active and irresponsible minority who are implacably hostile to Great Britain should be given no loophole for creating difficulties.' Eden did not want to acquiesce in the Irish proposals 'without making an effort to see whether they could not be modified so as to be less embarrassing from our point of view' but throughout his appraisal there lay the constitutional anxiety that was to trouble the Dominions Office for many months to come.

A formal recognition of Eire's neutrality presented a serious difficulty, said Eden, because 'we do not want formally to recognise Eire as neutral while Eire remains a member of the British Commonwealth.' This would surrender the 'constitutional theory of the indivisibility of the Crown'. He did not, however, want to take the line that Eire was no longer a member of the Commonwealth. He favoured the acceptance of Eire's proposals with the proviso that Britain would reserve the right to 'deal' with German warships and submarines in Eire's territorial waters and to prevent them from using the ports as a base of attack on Britain.

* De Valera was wrong. Two men were hanged in February 1940 for the Coventry bombing. One of them, Frank McCormick, had declared himself to be a member of the IRA at his trial.[15]

'We could make effective use, in this connection,' wrote Eden, 'of Mr de Valera's own public declaration in the Dail on 19th May, 1937 that "it would be our duty to do everything in our power to see that no foreign country got a foothold on our soil . . . It is quite obvious that the people in Britain . . . would have to give us the assistance which we, for our own sakes, would be anxious to call for, provided it was clear that the whole object of it was to maintain the inviolability of our territory." '[18]

Maffey was dispatched back to Dublin on September 19 with a letter from Chamberlain in which the Prime Minister expressed Britain's anxiety over Eire's proposals. De Valera was handed the letter next day but his eyesight had now so deteriorated that he was unable to decipher the words and Maffey eventually had to read it to him. The discussion that followed was initially predictable. Maffey raised the question of coast-watching and the possible intrusion of German U-boats into Irish waters while de Valera ran through vaguely familiar arguments: he was 'known to be pro-British in sentiment on the question of the war' but already IRA members were in Berlin, stirring up opposition to this attitude. Maffey, however, was beginning to understand how to handle de Valera's introspection.

'He is a difficult man to interrupt,' Maffey noted. 'But interrupt him you must. He shows no resentment when this happens, and his nimble mind is soon lifted onto the new line you have started.' It emerged that de Valera was ready to consider a proposal that Royal Navy personnel of Irish origin should join the coast-watching service and that British aircraft which – in Maffey's words – 'may occasionally land like exhausted birds on Irish shores' should be repatriated. Information on a U-boat's presence would be wirelessed at once by the Irish authorities. 'Not to you especially,' de Valera told Maffey. 'Your Admiralty must pick it up. We shall wireless it to the world. I will tell the German Minister of our intention to do this.'[19]

Even at this early stage of the war, thousands of Irishmen were joining the British forces and de Valera, alive to the political embarrassment which they could cause, requested that they should wear civilian clothes when they returned to Eire on leave. 'You would help us and help yourselves,' he told Maffey, 'if the men did not come into Ireland in uniform.'[20] The British agreed to this request and dumps of civilian clothes were provided at Holyhead so that servicemen travelling home could change into them. 'This little device,' Eden wrote later, 'was endorsed by the Cabinet and worked smoothly through the war years.'[21]

Before the meeting ended, the Taoiseach produced his map again. De Valera, said Maffey, 'led me to his black map of Ireland with its white blemish on the north-east corner and said: "There's the real source of all our trouble." He could not let me go without that.'[22]

Maffey's report was forwarded to the Dominions Office, where the minutiae of Irish politics could have caused little excitement amid the news from Poland. A few hours earlier, Hitler had entered Danzig and the remnants of the Polish Army – fighting both German and Soviet troops – were on the point of collapse. The 'Bolshevik' attack on Catholic Poland on September 17 had received harsh condemnation in Irish editorial columns and Warsaw's resistance was chronicled in detail in the Dublin press. *The Irish Times*, whose Protestant editorship and Anglo-Irish sentiments remained unchanged throughout the war, described the Poles as fighting 'with a courage reminiscent of the defenders of Derry,'[23] a parallel that might have appealed more to the Poles than to the Protestants of Northern Ireland's second city. Short-wave radio listeners in Dublin were able to hear the sound of bombs and machine-gun fire from Warsaw over wireless station 'SB 48', a transmitter allegedly operated by Polish resistance fighters who mixed patriotic appeals with gramophone records of Chopin recitals. *The Irish Times* was able to carry long transcripts of these emotional broadcasts[24] before the Irish Controller of Censorship made full use of his powers and prevented such reports from appearing in print.

Warsaw radio was not the only short-wave broadcast to be picked up in Eire. On September 14, a retired wireless operator at Skibbereen in County Cork monitored a message which came in from the Atlantic: 'SOS from GPVR., lat 51.23 North, longitude 7.03 West. Sinking. Taken to boats. No receiver. Come rescue.'[25] The transmission was probably made from the British steamship *Vancouver City*, forty-one days at sea with a cargo of sugar bound for England, which was torpedoed and sunk off the coast of Eire on the 14th by a German submarine.[26] It was only the first of hundreds of similar radio distress calls from frightened, desperate seamen which were to be heard in neutral Eire over the coming years.

On the first night of the war, the British liner *Athenia*, carrying around 1400 passengers, had been torpedoed by the submarine U-30 north-west of Donegal with a loss of 112 lives. Some of the survivors were brought ashore in Galway.[27] Six days later, the 6000-ton *Olive Grove* was sunk south-west of the Cork coast by a barnacle-encrusted U-boat whose bearded young commander towed the ship's crew in gentlemanly fashion towards the Fastnet before submerging. The seamen, who included six Irishmen, were landed at Cobh from a neutral vessel.[28] That the German Navy recognised Ireland's strategic position beside Britain's trade routes to America was only too evident in the operations room of the RAF's 502 (Ulster) Bomber Squadron; as the British began to organise their first convoys, RAF air crews flying reconnaissance missions out of Aldergrove airfield eleven miles from Belfast noticed an ominous pattern developing around the east and north coasts of Ireland.

On September 10, the day after the *Olive Grove* was sunk, two German submarines were reported off Dundrum Bay and Larne. On the 11th, another U-boat was seen off Larne and on the 16th two more submarines were observed close to land off Strangford Peninsula. On the following day, a U-boat was reported to be near Tory Island, a craggy, wind-blown outcrop of rock in the Atlantic belonging to County Donegal in Eire. A 502 Squadron Anson flew a 15-mile radius around the island and although the pilot found no trace of a submarine, he recorded seeing a 'suspicious vessel', a small freighter lying stationary in a bay which mysteriously set course to the north-west when the RAF aircraft flew low over the sea to examine it. In the next forty-eight hours, three more submarines were reported near Northern Ireland; two were lying off the Ards Peninsula, the long strip of flat County Down farmland that curves southwards from Belfast, and a third off Rathlin Island, County Antrim.[29]

The U-boats were congregating around Ireland. Their devastating work along the sea lanes could sometimes even be seen from the coast. When the British steamer *Hazleside* came under shell-fire from a German submarine off Cork on September 25, for instance, people in the village of Schull were able to watch the sinking through binoculars. They could not have known that the first casualty on the ship was a fellow-countryman; an Irish crew member, Denis Treacy from Arklow, was decapitated when a shell hit him in the face.[30]

Nowhere, however, were the results of the U-boat war more vividly illustrated than in the statistics compiled at the Admiralty in London. The new First Lord of the Admiralty Winston Churchill informed the War Cabinet on September 17 that in the first two weeks of hostilities, U-boat attacks on British trade had produced a loss of 147,000 tons – a total of twenty-eight ships sunk – which equalled just over half the rate of tonnage lost during the peak period of the First World War in April 1917, when Britain faced starvation.[31]

No minister could be indifferent to so grave a threat to Britain's existence, least of all the new First Lord. So long excluded from Government, Churchill had returned to the British Admiralty after an absence of more than twenty years at the age of sixty-four, bringing with him an unrivalled knowledge of wartime administration, a determination to maintain the primacy of the Royal Navy and an unbridled enthusiasm for the prosecution of the war. Still smarting over the Anglo-Irish *rapprochement* of 1938, he also brought with him to the Admiralty his profound distrust of de Valera's young state.

If anything, Churchill's deep suspicion of Eire's intentions had hardened in the previous sixteen months. Attacking Chamberlain for his 'heart-to-heart settlement' with de Valera, Churchill had sharpened his criticism of the British Prime Minister in December 1938. 'I warned him, with my defective judgement,' he said then, 'that if we got into any great danger Mr de Valera would demand the surrender of Ulster as a price for any friendship or aid. This fell out exactly for Mr de Valera has recently declared that he cannot give us any help or friendship while any British troops remain to guard the Protestants of Northern Ireland . . .'[32] When the IRA opened their bombing campaign in Britain in January 1939, Churchill regarded it as 'the Irish trying to get hold of Ulster', commenting in a letter to his wife: 'How vain it was for Chamberlain to suppose he could make peace by giving everything away!'[33] Here, clearly, would be no friend of a neutral Eire.

So it was to turn out, for as Britain went to war against Germany, Churchill's contempt for Eire's political status surfaced almost at once. Only two days after the British declaration of war, he ordered Admiral of the Fleet Sir Dudley Pound, the First Sea Lord, to compile a special report 'upon the questions arising from the so-called neutrality of the so-called Eire'. Churchill asked: 'What does Intelligence say about possible succouring of U-boats by Irish malcontents in West of Ireland inlets? If they throw bombs in London, why should they not supply fuel to U-boats? Extreme vigilance should be practised.'[34] But it was the military outcome of the 1938 Agreement – 'the numbing loss of the Southern Irish ports'[35] – that occupied Churchill's mind when he looked at the map of the Western Approaches that hung on his Admiralty office wall.

He informed Pound that 'a study is required of the addition to the radius of our destroyers through not having the use of Berehaven or other South Irish anti-submarine bases; showing also the advantage to be gained by our having these facilities.' Churchill concluded by stating that 'the question of Eirish [sic] neutrality raises political issues which have not yet been faced, and which the First Lord is not certain he can solve.'[36]

It was, of course, no part of the First Lord's task to 'solve' the political issues of Irish neutrality, only to assess and advise on Britain's strategic requirements in Ireland. Even here, however, Churchill was encumbered by the original and ambiguous advice which the Chiefs of Staff had offered Chamberlain's Government in 1938: that while the loss of the Treaty ports might 'imperil' the life of the nation, Britain should not demand a formal undertaking from de Valera that the Royal Navy could use the harbours in time of war.

'It was incredible to me,' Churchill wrote later, 'that the Chiefs of Staff should have agreed to throw away this major security . . .'[37] Within the Admiralty, however, the uncertainty which had been generated by the Chiefs of Staff in 1938 still lingered on in the Local Defence Division, the naval department responsible for harbour protection. By the time war broke out, plans had already been formulated for British defence of the Irish ports – as if the Royal Navy was about to return to Eire. Boom vessels, indicator loops, stores and accommodation requirements for the Royal Navy at Cobh, Bérehaven and Lough Swilly were listed in a report by the naval Director of Local Defence in London.[38] On September 8, a hand-written Admiralty minute noted that 'up to the present the Government of Eire has shown every intention of remaining neutral' but that the British should be ready to sell the required defence material to the Irish authorities 'if, as seems not improbable, they make a request for the provision of port defence equipment'. The paper acknowledged that for the time being 'there can be no thought of putting it down ourselves'[39] yet just a week later, on September 15, the Admiralty went so far as to earmark a Royal Navy officer to command the harbour defences at Lough Swilly. Paymaster Lieutenant Commander O.W. McCutcheon, RNVR, was chosen for the job and the Admiralty took this contingency so seriously that McCutcheon was immediately appointed to the staff of the Royal Navy Flag Officer in command at Belfast in preparation for his new post in Donegal.[40] On the following day, the Director of Local Defence talked of protecting the Irish ports 'at short notice' and the construction of special boom vessels for the Irish harbours to prevent U-boat incursions was approved in London.[41]

But there was no word of encouragement from Dublin. Churchill's indignation at Eire's reluctance to assist Britain grew in almost direct proportion to the losses inflicted on British shipping by German submarines. His anger was to some extent shared by Inskip, now Lord Caldecote, who had become Lord Chancellor in the new Chamberlain Government. In his private diary, Inskip listed the recent attacks made on British merchant ships and on the Royal Navy. The aircraft-carrier *Courageous* – '22 years old and cranky . . .' – had been sunk on September 17 south-west of Ireland and five other ships, including an oil tanker, had been lost in a period of just two days. 'De Valera,' Inskip remarked, 'is making the usual play with partition as a ground for refusing facilities at Berehaven.'[42] On September 19, his diary entry stated laconically: 'It seems probable that the course of events will demand something more from Eire.'[43]

Eire, however, showed no sign of accepting the kind of responsibilities that Inskip had in mind, a fact which Maffey's unsatisfactory interview with de Valera next day made abundantly clear. The Taoiseach's anxiety over IRA plots and the hatred which he believed had been engendered by the partition of Ireland carried no weight with Churchill. 'Three quarters of the people of Southern Ireland are with us,' Churchill wrote in a secret memorandum to Pound and two of his subordinates, 'but the implacable, malignant minority can make so much trouble that De Valera dare not do anything to offend them. All this talk about partition and the bitterness that would be healed by a union of Northern and Southern Ireland will amount to nothing. They will not unite at the present time, and we cannot in any circumstances sell the loyalists of Northern Ireland. Will you kindly consider these observations as the basis upon which Admiralty dealings with Southern Ireland should proceed?'[44]

This extraordinary outburst – for the constitutional position of Northern Ireland scarcely had anything to do with the First Lord of the Admiralty – was followed by an even more alarming suggestion. 'If the U-boat campaign became more dangerous,' he wrote, 'we should coerce Southern Ireland both about coast watching and the use of Berehaven, etc.' This was the first indication that Churchill was considering some kind of military action against Eire and the rest of his memorandum to

Pound – which was marked 'for general guidance' – betrayed an unhealthy fixation with the idea that strong-arm tactics might be used against the Irish. If the U-boat attacks slackened off, he wrote, the Cabinet would not be inclined to face 'the serious issues which forcible measures would entail'. He would himself on occasion bring the Admiralty's grievances before the Cabinet. 'On no account,' he concluded, 'must we appear to acquiesce in, still less be contented with, the odious treatment we are receiving.'[45]

But the U-boat war did slacken off, while Hitler waited for peace overtures from Britain and France after the fall of Poland. In the third week of the war, British shipping losses amounted to just 12,750 tons – compared to 53,561 tons – and in the fourth week only 4646 tons were sunk.[46] German submarines were still being reported around Ireland at the end of September; on the 25th, the RAF's 502 Squadron at Aldergrove logged two U-boats on the surface off the west coast of Ireland and next day four more submarines were observed off Northern Ireland, two of them near the mouth of Belfast Lough. On October 1, a U-boat was sighted close to the Donegal coast but the RAF did not bother to investigate it. Then the 502 Squadron operations book also began to reflect the inactivity of the Germany Navy. In early October, there were so few reports of German submarines that the RAF controllers in Northern Ireland were not even putting their Ansons into the air.[47] In Dublin, *The Irish Times*, which sometimes exhibited more confidence in British victory than the British did themselves, predicted 'the failure of the U-boat campaign'.[48] The paper's leader-writer did not have to wait many days to see his sanguine forecast proved wrong.

During the course of a Reichstag speech on October 6, Hitler made an 'appeal for peace' to the allies but Britain was demanding a German withdrawal from Poland and Chamberlain effectively rejected any negotiations with Germany when he addressed the House of Commons six days later.[49] The Royal Navy was the first to bear the consequences of this rebuff. On October 14, the German submarine U-47, commanded by Oberleutnant Guenther Prien, made its way into the heavily-defended naval base at Scapa Flow in Scotland and sank the British battleship *Royal Oak* with a loss of 786 lives. After such a disaster, the Admiralty was bound to look for alternative harbours further to the west and it was equally inevitable that Churchill should once more have turned his attention to Ireland. He informed the Cabinet that the time had come to tell the Irish Government that the Royal Navy must have the use of the Treaty ports 'and intended in any case to use them';[50] then he ordered Rear Admiral Tom Phillips, his Deputy Chief of Naval Staff, to write a memorandum for the Cabinet explaining precisely why the British needed Berehaven as a base of operations.

Phillips' contribution to the debate took no account of political considerations. The Navy, he wrote, was short of convoy escorts and could not protect Britain's Atlantic convoys as far to the westward as it would wish. U-boats had recently realised this strategic weakness and had been operating further out into the Atlantic in order to attack ships when they were unescorted.

'It has now become imperative,' stated Phillips, 'that we should escort our convoys both inwards and outwards to and from a position further to the Westward; working as we are from Plymouth and Milford Haven it is impracticable to do this. Our destroyers and other escorting vessels have since the beginning of the war been running at their extreme capacity. Many of the vessels themselves are now beginning to show the signs of strain, and their crews are worked to the extremity of human endurance from lack of sleep and rest . . . There is one way in which this situation can be drastically and quickly relieved, and that is by the Eire Government giving the use of one or more of their ports to the Royal Navy and the Royal Air Force. Berehaven is the most suitable port.'

Flying-boats operating from Berehaven, noted Phillips, would be able to provide extra security for the convoys by driving U-boats beneath the surface very much further to the west. Good weather had reduced the toll of human life during the recent U-boat attacks but with the arrival of the winter months, the chances of survival for the passengers and crews of torpedoed ships would be 'very remote'. Battleships and cruisers were necessary to protect convoys against German surface raiders yet when these warships reached the U-boat area, they themselves needed an anti-submarine escort. If these ships could be oiled and turned round at Berehaven rather than Plymouth, 'a great deal of unnecessary steaming through submarine infested waters would be avoided . . .'* Phillips concluded his otherwise apolitical memorandum with the pointed observation that Atlantic convoys protected by the Navy carried 'Irish as well as British trade'.[52] It was a remark calculated to appeal to Churchill.

Lord Halifax, the Foreign Secretary, forwarded Phillips' memorandum to Sir William Malkin, the Foreign Office Legal Adviser, who in turn presented the Government with a shrewd ten-page report on the legal aspects of Irish neutrality and the Treaty ports. Eden, who had taken exception to Churchill's bellicose statement in the Cabinet on the 17th, admired the 'brilliant, modest and wholly likable' Malkin[53] and must have known that Malkin would adopt a cautious, more moderate approach towards British use of the Irish harbours, as indeed he did:

> If Eire is to be regarded as a neutral State which is bound by the obligations of neutrality, it is plain that for her to permit such use would be inconsistent with

---

* All this, of course, had been foreshadowed in that long and harmful appraisal by the Chiefs of Staff in 1938 which had warned that 'the non-availability of the ports in Ireland might so increase our difficulties in combating enemy submarine menace that our losses in merchant ships from that form of attack alone might reach an insupportable figure . . .'[51] Phillips wisely refrained from referring to this earlier memorandum which had so damagingly agreed to the surrender of the Treaty ports.

those obligations; and if Mr de Valera is determined to be really neutral there is from the legal point of view no more to be said.

This was as blunt an acknowledgement of Eire's juridical right to remain neutral as had yet come from a British Government official, although the document, classified 'secret', was naturally never disclosed to de Valera. Nor was it likely to be, for Malkin went on to define the complexities of Irish neutrality in a way that morally precluded any British action against Eire. Malkin framed his arguments cunningly; he set out the various choices open to the British Government, then proceeded to demolish each option with legal and political objections.

He thought, for example, that it might be possible for de Valera to adopt the attitude that 'while he was neutral in a sense, his neutrality was conditioned by his relationship to the King and the other members of the British Commonwealth of Nations.' Yet Malkin believed this would be 'inconsistent' with de Valera's maintenance of diplomatic relations with Germany. Furthermore, the idea was similar to a proposal put forward for the Simonstown naval base by the pro-neutral South African Prime Minister General Hertzog and it 'might create serious difficulties' for Hertzog's successor General Jan Smuts.*

Malkin wondered whether de Valera could allow the Royal Navy to use the ports 'by means of an extremely lax and indulgent application of the rules of neutrality' and reminded the Cabinet that Article 19 of the Thirteenth Hague Convention – which permitted belligerent ships to remain for only twenty-four hours in neutral ports – had never been ratified by Britain; but he added that 'too much importance should not be attached to this' because the Hague provisions represented 'generally accepted rules'. If the Irish were prepared to allow British warships to refuel regularly at the Treaty ports, if they would 'ignore, or wink at non-compliance with, the rule that a warship may not stay more than twenty-four hours in a neutral port' and if they would waive the penalties of internment, then Eire might be able 'to give us what we want while maintaining a rather ricketty [sic] facade of neutrality'. But the British would be using the ports as bases and 'the German Minister at Dublin

* With the diligence of an archivist, Malkin searched for precedents by which a British investment of the Irish Treaty ports might be historically justified. He came up with the British occupation of the Greek island of Lemnos prior to the Gallipoli campaign of 1915; on this occasion, the neutral Greeks allowed the British to take over the island on the pretext that the Turks still laid claim to Lemnos and that it could therefore legitimately be regarded as Turkish rather than Greek territory. When the compliant Greek Cabinet was replaced by a Government less amicable to British war aims after Gallipoli, the British refused to leave Salonika and the Greek island of Corfu on the grounds that they were honouring an earlier commitment to help the Serbian Army. Malkin illustrated these examples with long quotations from official histories and it could not have been lost on Chamberlain's Cabinet that the Minister whose demand for action against Eire had prompted Malkin's memorandum, had also been one of the most enthusiastic proponents of the catastrophic Gallipoli expedition – Churchill himself.

would find out fast enough.' Moreover, added Malkin, 'for us to induce such action by the Irish Government would be completely inconsistent with the attitude which we are taking in other neutral countries, where we are continually urging the local authorities to be strict as regards the use of their territories by . . . German raiders or submarines.'[54]

Eden, who regarded Malkin's paper as 'a very helpful, if ruthless, analysis', added to the document in his own hand: 'I fear that it becomes every day clearer that it is scarcely possible for "Dev" to square neutrality with the grant of the facilities for which the Admiralty ask. And at least 80% of the Irish people favour neutrality. Altogether a pretty problem.'[55]

Churchill, however, was in no mood to accept Malkin's troublesome conclusions. He read through the memorandum on October 20 then sent an angry letter to Halifax. Scribbled on official Admiralty note-paper in stunted, sometimes almost illegible handwriting, it revealed the extent of Churchill's disturbing obsession about Ireland:

So far as 'legality' counts, the question surely turns on whether 'Eire is to be regarded as a neutral state'. If this is conceded then the regular laws of neutrality apply. But is the neutrality which Mr Devalera [sic] has proclaimed a valid condition, and on all fours with the neutrality of, say, Holland or Switzerland?

It is to this point that attention should first be directed. What is the international juridical status of Southern Ireland? It is not a Dominion. They themselves repudiate this idea. It is certainly under the Crown. Nothing has been defined. Legally I believe they are 'At war but Skulking'. Perhaps Sir William would examine this thesis.[56]

Churchill was not just challenging Malkin. Nor was he merely throwing doubt on the international validity of Irish neutrality. He was questioning Eire's very right to exist as a separate and independent state. If he did not accept Eire's dominion status – because the Irish themselves denied such an affiliation – yet believed the country to be 'under the Crown', then Churchill had convinced himself that the twenty-six counties of Ireland which had left the United Kingdom in 1922 were in fact legally still British territory – and therefore in a state of hostilities with Germany. This was a harsh punishment to exact for the destruction of the Treaty which he had helped to negotiate with Collins, Griffith and the other four Irish representatives in 1921.

Halifax wrote a brief reply to Churchill, agreeing that 'the essential point is whether Eire is to be regarded as a neutral state', but he diplomatically avoided any further comment by sending a copy of the First Lord's emotional letter to Eden because 'this is in the first place a question for the Dominions Office.'[57]

Eden could not have been surprised by Churchill's extreme position on Ireland. It was the natural if not entirely logical development of that same frustration which had been fermenting since the early thirties when

Churchill first realised that de Valera intended to destroy the 1921 Treaty. In 1932, Churchill had said that the Irish Free State would 'cease to exist as a political entity' if the Oath of Allegiance was abolished and that accordingly 'Ireland would automatically revert to the status of a foreign country outside the Empire whose Government was unrecognised.'[58] This idea had reappeared in Churchill's denunciation of the 1938 Anglo-Irish agreement when he told the House of Commons that 'Southern Ireland is not a Dominion; it has never accepted that position. It is a State based upon a Treaty, which Treaty has been completely demolished. Southern Ireland, therefore, becomes a State which is an undefined and unclassified anomaly. No one knows what its juridical and international rights and status are.'[59]* Seventeen months later, Churchill had become possessed of the idea that Eire had no international rights at all.

His bitterness also served to emphasise the widely divergent views on Ireland within the British Cabinet. Whereas Churchill believed that three quarters of the Irish people were 'with' Britain – at least to the extent of supporting a British occupation of the Treaty ports – Eden was convinced that 80 per cent of the population of Eire favoured neutrality. That two senior Ministers could disagree so fundamentally on an issue of such potential consequence was an indication of the serious gulf which existed in the Cabinet over the Irish question.

The only hope of securing the ports for the Navy – let alone introducing some consensus on Ireland into the Cabinet – lay in a further approach to de Valera, and Maffey was immediately entrusted with this joyless undertaking. Eden's and Chamberlain's instructions to Maffey were a combination of the Admiralty's arguments – they included a slightly blander version of Phillips' memorandum – and an almost half-hearted appeal for fraternal assistance. Maffey was to tell de Valera that while the British 'fully appreciated' that the 1938 transfer of the ports was unconditional, there was 'nothing in the agreement to prevent the Government of Eire from according facilities to vessels of the Royal Navy to make use of Eire ports'. The United Kingdom Government had 'always felt . . . that in their view in a state of emergency circumstances might arise which rendered it imperative in the interests of both countries, that such facilities should be accorded. These circumstances have now arisen.' There was a reference to German U-boat attacks on neutral Scandinavian shipping but the instructions contained no inducement – no hint of an initiative over partition – which might have persuaded de Valera to reconsider his refusal to allow the British the use of the ports. To say – as Maffey's instructions stated – that 'it does not appear that any publicity need be given to an arrangement under which Royal Navy vessels would be

---

* Churchill had in fact made a curious qualification to these remarks later in the same speech. The Dublin Government, he said, would have the 'juridical right' to deny Britain the use of the Treaty ports. He made a quite different assessment in 1939.

authorised to make use of Berehaven . . .'[60] was not likely to tempt de Valera into risking his country's neutrality. 'Maffey returns to Dublin tonight to try his best,' Eden remarked without much hope to Malkin on October 20. 'He is fully briefed and we shall probably know by Monday how he has fared.'[61]

At 11.30 next morning, Maffey walked into de Valera's familiar office with its ascetic furnishings to request the use of Berehaven for the Royal Navy. De Valera knew what was coming. 'His uncompromising answer to every line of approach,' Maffey reported afterwards, 'was a categorical "non possumus". In this attitude there was nothing anti-British, though he indicated more than once that if we had paved the way to Irish unity, Ireland today might – only "might" – have been able to co-operate with us.' Maffey put forward the British arguments. 'Mr de Valera,' he wrote, 'listened with keen attention, but I was talking to a man whose mind had been made up.'

No Government could exist in Eire that departed from the principle of neutrality, de Valera told Maffey. The question of the ports was 'at the very nerve centre of public interest' and 'if a demand were made – he fully realised that no demand was being made – he would be forced at whatever cost to treat such a situation as a challenge, and his Parliament would endorse his measures.' Maffey faithfully recorded de Valera's personal feelings* and his explanation of Irish public opinion: 'He would greatly regret a German victory. His sympathies were with the Allies, but if there was on the whole, perhaps, a vague majority sentiment in favour of the Allies, any encroachment upon an Irish interest would create a swift swing over of opinion. Many people in Ireland were ready enough to acclaim a British defeat at any price, though that view might be based on ignorance. It had its roots in history.'

De Valera maintained that when the ports were transferred in 1938, 'there could have been no mental reservations on our side justifying any belief that Eire would adopt any particular course in the event of a world conflict . . .' Maffey said that 'nevertheless, such mental reservations had existed, and that the path of generosity had been followed as an act of faith and in the belief that in the hour of need the hand of friendship would be extended.' De Valera, reported Maffey, 'talked a good deal on this point indicating in sum that we had no right to expect to derive advantage from what was not ours. Such a view would justify encroachment by Germany on Holland or Belgium.'

At this point in the conversation, de Valera's telephone – which was developing a curious habit of interrupting his interviews with Maffey – rang with an enquiry from the French news agency Havas. A reporter

---

* When he read Maffey's report of this interview long after the war, de Valera apparently regarded it as accurate. De Valera's biographers say that he 'raised no objection to the gist of this account.'

asked about 'a rumour that facilities at the ports had been demanded'. De Valera denied the story. Maffey decided that 'this must have been a bit of quick guessing on the part of the press watching my recent movements.'

Maffey chose this moment to raise the partition issue with de Valera. 'The history of Ireland was one of lost opportunities,' Maffey told the Taoiseach. 'Today the opportunity lay with him. Who could see any hope for a united Ireland on the lines of our present conversation? What British Government would ever surrender the ports of the North after this experience?' But de Valera, who perhaps resented Maffey's maudlin and somewhat oversimplified view of Ireland's savage history, remained adamant; he even turned down the opportunity of discussing the ports with Chamberlain personally 'since it could not in any way alter matters.' De Valera regarded his policy as consistent, noted Maffey. 'His goal had been to maintain neutrality and to help us within the limits of that neutrality to the full extent possible.'

De Valera again stressed his admiration for Chamberlain and said that he was 'in full agreement' with everything Chamberlain had done. Maffey recorded de Valera's comments almost verbatim:

> 'England', said Mr de Valera, 'has a moral position today. Hitler might have his early successes, but the moral position would tell. Any action against the Irish ports would shake our* position of moral strength'. I said 'Not if help were voluntarily conceded'. He replied 'No, but that would stir up trouble which would quickly compromise your moral position'.
>   He spoke of the possibilities of peace and said that Hitler did not want war and that a reasonable solution embodying a partially restored Poland was to be had. I asked by what agency. He said that he thought Italy might act through Mussolini. That, today, seemed the only hope . . .

De Valera no longer regarded Roosevelt as a potential arbitrator in the conflict because of the American President's 'inept letter of appeal and remonstrance' to Hitler. But the Taoiseach appeared to be out of touch with the realities of the war. To have assumed that Hitler 'did not want war' and that a partial restoration of Poland would be acceptable to Germany or the Allies – let alone to Poland herself – was simplistic; England's 'moral position' was unlikely to decide the outcome of the struggle, however attractive this idea might be to de Valera. He had acknowledged that moral issues were at stake in the war but the integrity of Eire's sovereignty was still his chief concern.

Before leaving, Maffey told de Valera that his reply to Chamberlain's request 'would cause deep and natural disappointment'. Maffey's report ended with an intriguing observation on de Valera's intelligence network. It was noteworthy, Maffey wrote, that de Valera 'had evidently expected

---

* There appears to be a misprint in Maffey's official report. Since he was quoting de Valera, he almost certainly intended 'our' to read 'your'.

our request to be for facilities at Lough Swilly rather than Berehaven. Clearly he had up to date information on the recent movements of the Grand Fleet.'[62] It is in fact more likely that the Taoiseach assumed that after the sinking of the *Royal Oak* in Scapa Flow a week earlier, the Royal Navy would want to repeat its 1914–18 war tactic of withdrawing to Donegal waters.

Maffey had accurately assessed the British Government's reaction. When the War Cabinet considered Maffey's report three days later, Eden spoke of 'the rigid and unsatisfactory attitude adopted by Mr de Valera'. He felt that there were three options open to the Cabinet. They could seek further discussion with de Valera or they could acquiesce in de Valera's attitude and endeavour to secure what they could 'bit by bit'. The British could also 'make forcible use of the harbours'. If the third option was adopted, Eden did not think de Valera would oppose the British with military force 'but he would indict us before the world and rally his people against us. There would be serious repercussions in the United States and in the Dominions, and the passive support which we now received from great numbers of Irish people would be alienated. In addition, Eire might grant facilities to the enemy.'

This argument failed to make any impression on Churchill who was ruminating on the wider issues of Irish sovereignty. The Government should 'challenge the constitutional position of Eire's neutrality,' he said. 'We should not admit that her neutrality was compatible with her position under the crown. Unlike the other Dominions which were separated from us by thousands of miles, Eire was an integral part of the British Isles. She had in fact refused to accept Dominion status . . .' Churchill wanted to seek the support of the Dominions and then insist on the use of the Irish harbours, having made clear to the world that 'we were not committing a violation of neutrality.'

Eden, possibly aware that Churchill's fixation with Eire's constitutional status could prove troublesome, briskly announced that after consultation with the Dominions, the Government had decided not to take up the issue. 'Even if we could prove that Eire was not entitled to remain neutral and at the same time to remain a member of the British Commonwealth, the result would be, not to persuade Eire to abandon her neutrality, but that Eire would cease to be a member of the British Commonwealth.' But Churchill did not seem to care. Eire should be told that she was 'at the parting of the ways'; if she was declared a foreign power and expelled from the Commonwealth, 'we should insist on the return of the strategic points we required.'

Chamberlain, perhaps disturbed by the direction in which the discussion was going, conceded that Churchill had presented 'a powerful case' but said that seizure of the ports would be regarded as 'a high-handed and unwarranted action' in the United States and India. Britain would not be justified in taking the ports 'until the situation became much worse'.[63]

British losses in the North Atlantic had fallen and Churchill himself had told the Cabinet that British convoys had successfully avoided the German pocket battleship *Deutschland* that was still roaming the trade routes.[64] But he remained unconvinced by the moderation of Chamberlain and Eden. According to the Cabinet records, 'the First Lord of the Admiralty suggested that we should take stock of the weapons of coercion.'[65]

Churchill wanted Inskip, now Lord Caldecote, the Lord Chancellor, to examine the legality of terminating Eire's Commonwealth membership; two weeks later, the Law Lords presented a ten-page memorandum to the Cabinet which concluded – comfortingly for Chamberlain – that Eire's exclusion might create more problems for the British than existed already. If Britain expelled Eire without consultation, they said, 'such action might imperil the existence of the whole Commonwealth' if the other Dominions disagreed. De Valera's attitude had been 'consistently equivocal' and allegiance to the Crown in Eire had been 'whittled down almost until it can scarcely be said to exist'. But since the Treaty of Locarno, it had been recognised that 'it was entirely for a Dominion to decide whether it should or should not participate in a war.' If the ports were to be seized, it was true that this would be 'an act taken within territory of which His Majesty is at present King, and the inhabitants of which the United Kingdom Government can confidently maintain owe allegiance to him'; but any attempt to take the ports by force 'would be represented as a plain act of aggression'.[66]

Caldecote's conclusions were judicious although the very terminology employed in the memorandum suggested that the Law Lords might have been as out of touch with Irish national sentiment as de Valera was with the European war. That anyone could refer – eighteen years after a ferocious guerrilla war had won independence for the twenty-six counties of Ireland – to an Irish population that owed allegiance to the King, was a nonsense. It was probably inserted for the benefit of the First Sea Lord who still apparently believed that most Irishmen supported Britain. 'I hope you are fully conscious,' Churchill wrote to Eden two days after the Cabinet meeting, 'of the grave wrong that has been done to us and to our vital interests, and of the urgent need to repair it. If I were to let the public know the facts about how we are being hampered, there would be such a storm of wrath against de Valera and his adherents, not only in Great Britain but in Southern Ireland, as has never been seen. The British nation has a right to know who are the enemies who are hampering our efforts to feed them.'[67]

But who exactly were these enemies? To Churchill's political distrust of de Valera was added a more historical suspicion, the idea that Ireland might secretly provide assistance to Britain's antagonists along the fissured, gale-thrashed Atlantic coastline upon which French and Spanish armies had traditionally landed on their way to destroy England. 'What is the position on the West Coast of Ireland?' Churchill asked his Director of Naval Intelligence. 'Are there any signs of succouring U-boats in Irish creeks or inlets? It would seem that money should be spent to secure a trustworthy body of Irish agents to keep most vigilant watch. Has this been done? Please report.'[68]

Chapter 4

Any Sort of Stick to Beat Eire

> There seems to be a good deal of evidence, or at any rate suspicion, that the U-boats are being succoured from West of Ireland ports by the malignant section with whom de Valera dare not interfere.
>
> Winston Churchill *24 September 1939*

Just two weeks after the outbreak of war, Eden submitted to the British Cabinet a memorandum on Irish neutrality in which he referred to a curious and disturbing incident that had occurred on September 14, the very day on which Maffey had held his first meeting with de Valera. The Admiralty, wrote Eden, had received information that 'members of the rescued crew of a sunken German submarine have reported that they have recently landed in Eire, and purchased cigarettes there.'[1] Churchill commented cynically that this might prove to be 'a useful lever' for persuading the Irish Government to allow the British the use of Berehaven as a destroyer and flying-boat base;[2] and Caldecote noted in his diary that the U-boat's 23-man crew had been 'walking about in Eire'.[3]

If the report was true, then de Valera would indeed have reason to be embarrassed. How could he demand the rights of a neutral if his own security services were unable to prevent a German submarine crew from landing in Eire, casually buying cigarettes and sailing away unmolested? The German seamen were subsequently sent to London for 'special interrogation' but Eden seemed uncertain as to whether they had been ashore before or after the outbreak of war.[4] British newspapers gave considerable prominence to the report although the Irish Government denied that any Germans had landed in Eire and there are in fact no further references to the incident in the official British records. Nevertheless, the story gained credence in Britain where the idea of German U-boats nestling beside the Irish coastline had been popularly held ever since Roger Casement stepped ashore on Banna Strand, County Kerry, after being shipped to Ireland in a submarine. Nor had he been the only passenger carried to Ireland in this manner. In 1918, Corporal Robert Dowling of the Connaught Rangers, a colleague of Casement, was captured by the British after being landed by a U-boat on Crabb Island off the Clare coast.[5]

Could it be that the Germans were now repeating their naval tactics of the 1914–18 War by putting into Irish waters to refuel and perhaps even to land agents or saboteurs on the coast? The enquiry may seem trivial, irrelevant even if true; but the belief that Irishmen did refuel and service U-boats during the Battle of the Atlantic – submarines that were preying on the merchant ships that brought food and oil to Eire as well as Britain – was widely held in Britain and in Northern Ireland during the Second World War. It helped to poison Anglo-Irish relations and infected Churchill's own judgement of Eire's neutrality.

In 1939, the west coast of Ireland presented a bleak landscape of deprivation and economic decline, its rough villages decimated by almost a century of emigration and crippling poverty. Its cliffs and fiords and empty, rainswept roads were damp with a sea spray that crept five miles inland under the Atlantic gales, and in all the counties from Donegal to the south there survived the harsh skeletons of thousands of roofless cabins whose occupants died in the Famine of the late 1840s or abandoned their land for America. The memories of that gruesome decade remained vivid; children of those who had suffered in the Famine were still alive in Connaught and Munster, their recollections all the more poignant because they were expressed in Irish, the language that the English had once tried to suppress. Mingled with this bitterness was the antagonism of the War of Independence, a guerrilla conflict so savage that in 1919, Lord French placed Limerick, Kerry and Cork under martial law. The memorials along the laneways to the IRA men who had died in the hill-fields and villages after being trapped by Crown forces were scarcely fifteen years old.

The land and the off-shore islands, which had inspired Yeats and Synge, possessed a cruel beauty which its people understood and valued and which they captured in an almost Homeric idiom. On Great Blasket Island off the Dingle peninsula in Kerry, 'the storms of the sky and the wild sea beat without ceasing from end to end of the year and from generation to generation against the wrinkled rocks which stand above the waves that wash in and out of the coves where the seals make their homes.'[6] There was an epic quality to the sweep of land and sea off the Aran Islands where on a clear day in early spring, an islander could see 'Mount Brandon and the mouth of the Shannon along the Clare Coast to Black Head; the sand dunes near Salthill and along the Connemara shore to the Twelve Pins and Slyne Head . . . at night the lighthouses winked at us from Loop Head on the Shannon away to the south, from Inisheer, from Black Head to the north-east . . .'[7] It was a land associated with England's enemies for the past four hundred years. The Papal-Spanish expeditionary force had come ashore in Kerry in 1580 to be massacred in Walter Raleigh's presence; General Humbert's French Army had landed in Mayo in 1798. And the wrecks of the Spanish Armada lay beneath the strands and bays of Donegal, Sligo, Mayo, Galway, Clare and Kerry.[8]

But if the west of Ireland was rich in history, it was largely denied any material wealth. Virtually the only modern industrial development in the area was the Ardnacrusha power station near Limerick, built with German assistance in the late 1920s. Up in Donegal, 'a nakedly poor county', the Protestants – disowned by the Unionists of Northern Ireland – were as poor as their Catholic neighbours[9] in a district of mountains and lakes long cut off from its old market centre of Londonderry. The cultural roots of the west appeared to be dying. A £2 grant from de Valera's Government for every child who spoke Irish as a first language and lived in the Gaeltacht did little more than slow the gradual Anglicisation of the area[10] and many villages lost almost half their population in 1939 when the menfolk left for the only employment available to them, in the war industries of Britain. Those who stayed behind may have felt no particular warmth towards Germany but they had little reason to sympathise with England in her difficulties.

That U-boats were still operating close around Irish shores was obvious. The Operations Record Book of the RAF's 502 Squadron at Aldergrove reports a German submarine 'close to the coast in Donegal Bay' on October 1. Six days later, a U-boat was seen 'close to the South West coast of Ireland near the South end of the entrance to the Shannon'. On October 18, another submarine was reported in Donegal Bay and on the 20th a U-boat made its appearance off Valencia, County Kerry.[11] But on none of these occasions did the RAF mount an attack; and from the air, there was no way of knowing whether the submarines were sheltering from bad weather, surfacing to recharge their batteries or engaged in more sinister business.

Confronted by Churchill's atavistic memorandum, the Director of Naval Intelligence at the Admiralty was doing his best to find out the answers. British intelligence activities around Ireland were regarded as particularly sensitive during the war and even today many of the official records that would normally be open to historians are still closed without any time limit upon them. Memoranda by the naval staff dealing with Britain's intelligence organisation inside Eire are lodged at the Public Record Office in London but, according to the index, the relevant folios 'are not open to the public inspection and have not been filmed'.[12]

However, Admiralty records – and, in particular, the log-books of British submarines in the autumn of 1939 – provide an intriguing clue to the nature of a complex and potentially dangerous intelligence operation along the south and west coasts of Ireland upon which the Royal Navy embarked in its search for German U-boats. At 0300 hours on 10 October 1939, for example, His Majesty's Ship *H 33*, a twenty-year-old submarine under Lieutenant Commander H.J. Caldwell, can be found cruising on the surface past the Fastnet Light and, twelve hours later, passing Mizen Head at the south-western tip of Cork. At 1800 she stopped her port engine and, as the log records, at 2200 hours she 'rendezvoused [sic] with

Trawler in Position 245° Bull Light 5 miles.' The Bull is a small rock off Dursey Island at the end of the peninsula that forms the northern arm of Bantry Bay. Clearly, this was no routine sea patrol for *H 33*.

At midnight, she set off again, stopping six times before dawn when she dived and then surfaced not far from Loop Head at the mouth of the Shannon. For much of the day, *H 33* moved slowly northwards on the surface off the Kerry coast and not long after dark kept a second rendezvous with the mysterious trawler, following her astern into Blasket Sound between Great Blasket Island and the Dingle peninsula. Caldwell's submarine tied up to the trawler, took on provisions, and then set off alone once more through the Sound to the north east. Just over eighteen hours later, *H 33* met the trawler again, on this occasion plotting her position off Roundstone Bay on the Connemara coast. This strange nocturnal voyage recommenced at 0330 hours on October 14 when Caldwell took the *H 33* up past Slyne Head and 'Achille Point' – presumably Achill Head on Achill Island – and patrolled at periscope depth up to the Inishkea islands off north Mayo. Here, the log says, the crew 'kept listening on hydrophones'. The British submarine made its way across the mouth of Donegal Bay and secured alongside the trawler four miles off Rathlin O'Birne Island. Then she returned southwards, making a brief and final rendezvous with the fishing vessel off the Great Skellig rock before arriving back at Devonport on October 19.[13]

Here the log of the *H 33* ends, but the parallel set of records for her sister ship *H 43* commences just over two weeks later; and this time, they yield far more information. Attached to them is a memorandum to the Secretary of the Admiralty and the Director of Naval Intelligence, recording a voyage by *H 43* in company with HMS *Tamura*, an armed 'Q' ship crewed by Royal Navy personnel. The *Tamura*, under Lieutenant Commander W.R. Fell, was the anonymous vessel that appeared in the *H 33* log and her task was to masquerade as a trawler, fishing off the Irish coast and searching the small bays and harbours until she found a U-boat whose whereabouts she would then betray to her unseen but shadowing British submarine escort. Fell, who was later to develop one man submarines for the navy,[14] left Devonport for his second operation on November 9, towing the *H 43* behind the *Tamura* and apparently entering into the spirit of this typically Churchillian adventure, even if the start of the voyage proved somewhat inauspicious.

The men on the submarine fore-casing 'were continually being swept off their feet by the swell and it is thought that just before the weight of the tow was taken, the telephone cable fouled . . .' wrote Fell in his log. The *H 43* dived shortly afterwards and the phone link to the *Tamura* immediately failed. Next morning, an auxiliary armoured telephone cable to the submarine functioned for fifteen minutes only to be cut when the connection broke on *H 43*'s hull. Inside the submarine, however, Lieutenant Commander W.A.K.N. Cavaye comfortably recorded that the tow 'was very comfortable in spite of heavy swell'.

Fell steered the *Tamura* between two convoys of merchant ships and headed into a fresh south wind for Galley Head, County Cork. Here he slipped his tow with *H 43* and while Cavaye went off to prowl at periscope depth off the Old Head of Kinsale, Fell investigated the coastline and began innocently trawling within sight of a fishing fleet, handing his catch over to *H 43* later that evening. On Sunday, November 12, Fell searched 'all the bays between Galley Head and Fastnet including Glandour, Castle Haven, Toe Bay, Baltimore and Ocar Island' before keeping a rendezvous with Cavaye and towing the submarine into Castle Island Sound close off the entrance to Skull Harbour.

'This is a perfect anchorage for a "U-boat",' Fell recorded with some excitement. 'The entrance is well defined and comparatively free from rocks. Our windlass made enough noise to wake the dead and two lights appeared on the north shore about 1.5 miles East of Skull Harbour. The night was inky dark and the S/M [submarine] was certainly not seen or heard. She lay astern for two hours and then left . . .' Cavaye was not so happy. 'Suspicious light on Castle Island started to make Nos in morse,' he wrote in his own log, 'and another flashed on the Mainland. Thought I might have been seen entering so slipped and proceeded into Bay.' Fell kept watching the Irish shore-line. 'About 50 minutes later,' he recorded, 'a light appeared on Castle Island and flashed "Y's" and later "G's" towards the mainland at intervals of 2 or 3 minutes for an hour. The light came from a house on the summit of Castle Island and no one was seen replying.'

Half an hour before dawn next morning, *Tamura* put to sea, proceeding up Long Island Sound – 'a "U-boat" could not lie here without all the world knowing,' Fell noted – into a heavy swell and dense fog. Off Bantry Bay, he espied a foreign coaster and ordered *H 43* to shadow her. Then with the wind rising, he decided to search Dingle Bay for U-boats and steamed briefly up the Kenmare River. Here 'misty rain and intense darkness' made navigation difficult so Fell sailed to Coughlough Bay where his ship's cook, Stoker Lambert, 'was taken violently ill with great abdominal pain, vomiting and diarrhoea'.

This unpleasant development caused Fell some understandable concern. Already infringing Irish neutrality, he now faced the prospect of landing Stoker Lambert in Eire and the possible discovery of his operation by the Irish authorities. Next morning, Lambert was feeling a little better but was still in pain and 'unable to keep even spoonfuls of milk and brandy down'. The danger of putting the sick man ashore at Bantry or Valencia 'with the risk of internment', together with his slight improvement, convinced Fell that his wisest course of action was to steer into Valencia Roads and wait. Lambert's condition subsequently improved so Fell took the *Tamura* to the Blaskets and to Smerwick Harbour where, after dark on the 15th, *H 43* kept a rendezvous with him. The submarine took on fish, meat and stores from Fell's boat and then slipped her moorings. But shortly after *H 43* had left, Fell noticed lights flashing in the darkness once more, just as they had done at Castle Island Sound three days earlier. 'A light was seen on the East shore flashing "Y's" four times,' Fell recorded. 'This was replied to by four "G's" from West.'

The remainder of *Tamura*'s voyage was uneventful and among the Admiralty papers, one senses Fell's frustration. In the early hours of November 18, not far from Brandon Bay, 'three ships made "V's" which left me as much in the dark as ever.' He lost a rendezvous with *H 43* and ran into high seas off the Bull Light, taking shelter in Berehaven where two Irish boats came alongside 'wanting rope, coal, fish, anything'.[15] It could hardly be accounted a wildly successful operation although Admiral Sir Martin Dunbar-Nasmith, the C-in-C Western Approaches, in a 'Most Secret' dispatch to the Secretary of the Admiralty, praised Fell's 'resource and determination' and considered that 'valuable information' had been gained.[16] The Intelligence Division of the Naval Staff were interested in the signal lights that Fell had noticed on the Cork and Kerry coasts and in December they initiated an approach to the Irish Ministry of Defence in Dublin, reporting that 'a trawler' had seen suspicious lights and asking for an explanation.[17] From the records, it appears that none was forthcoming.

Yet de Valera's Government was well aware that U-boats were being observed inside Irish territorial waters. In the early days of the war, German naval commanders were in the chivalrous habit of rescuing the crews of the ships that they had torpedoed and depositing them on the nearest landfall. Thus on October 3, according to Irish military records in Dublin, the German submarine *U 35* sank the 8000-ton Greek freighter *Diamantes* forty miles west of the Skelligs and coolly sailed into Dingle Bay next day to put the rescued crew ashore.[18] The twenty-eight Greeks had been taken aboard the U-boat before the submarine fired three torpedoes at the *Diamantes*, which had been en route from South Africa to Barrow-in-Furness.[19]

According to the Greeks, *U 35* had 'cruised along for some time' off the Kerry coast 'seeking a deserted part to land its passengers'. Among the first to see the submarine after she entered Dingle Bay was an Irish customs officer, 'the only official in the immediate neighbourhood'. The U-boat lay on the surface 'some little distance from the shore' at Ventry while the rescued crew were rowed to the land four at a time by a German sailor in a small collapsible boat. Gardai patrolling the coast also caught sight of the U-boat after the survivors had been landed and 'rushed to the spot, but, while they were still some distance away the submarine moved off and submerged.'[20] De Valera's *Irish Press* emphasised that the Greek crew 'were treated with every courtesy and were given food and cigarettes' during their thirty hours aboard the submarine.[21]

But while Michael Long, the Lloyd's agent at Dingle, looked after the survivors, whose Captain publicly praised the gentlemanly conduct of the

Germans who had just sunk his ship, the Irish Government was experiencing some embarrassment. 'It was pointed out in Dublin circles,' the *Irish Press* reported, 'that the incursion of the submarine into Irish waters was exclusively for the purpose of landing a ship-wrecked crew.'[22] The *Diamantes* had not exactly been 'ship-wrecked' although it was perfectly true that the submarine commander had been acting from humanitarian motives. But the Germans were apparently so confident they would not be apprehended by the Irish authorities that they had cheerfully waved goodbye to the Greek survivors before they submerged at Ventry[23] and rumours began circulating in Dingle town that the U-boat's Captain had visited Kerry before the war and had consequently bid his Greek captives farewell with the rather startling adieu: 'Give my best wishes to Mickey Long.'[24]*

On this occasion, de Valera fulfilled his promise to Maffey by instructing the Irish authorities to wireless news of the U-boat's presence 'to the world' for the benefit of the British Admiralty. Maffey later noted the 'instant report of [a] German submarine in Dingle Bay' as an example of the Eire Government's helpfulness towards Britain.[26] On the morning of October 6, an RAF Coastal Command aircraft was ordered to 'locate and if possible attack' the U-boat. But the instruction also carried a warning to the British aircrew that 'EIRE territorial waters are NOT repeat NOT to be infringed.'[27] The Admiralty, however, seemed to have no such inhibitions when they sent Lieutenant Commander Fell to sea; and with not one U-boat sighted, let alone sunk, by *H 43* in the first three months of operations, it was probably inevitable that the British submarine and her faithful fishing smack would again be dispatched to their peregrinations on the high seas. On 11 January 1940, Dunbar-Nasmith once more ordered the two vessels 'to operate off the west coast of Ireland, with the object of destroying U-boats'. In his operational orders to *Tamura* and *H 43*, he also noted that the Irish Government had 'established a coast watching system for the purpose of coast protection', adding that 'no offensive action is to be taken in Irish Territorial Waters, which are only to be entered in case of distress or urgent necessity . . .'[28] The Admiral presumably had a sense of humour as well as a Nelsonian blind eye.

As usual, *Tamura* towed *H 43* into the Atlantic and, as usual, the telephone cable between the two vessels – reinforced now with a newly-secured clamp – broke apart. So did the auxiliary cable. 'Ship's company have almost all bad colds and coughs,' *H 43*'s log recorded as the submarine passed Fastnet in the early hours of January 13, 'and conditions are not conducive to rapid recovery.' *Tamura* occupied her time by making feint attacks on *H 43* as the two ships travelled up the Irish west coast, past

---

* The veracity of this will never be established. Michael Long died in Dingle shortly after the war ended. The submarine's Captain, together with his ship's papers, perished when *U 35* was sunk north-west of Bergen by three British destroyers two months after the landing at Dingle.[25]

Blacksod Bay to Eagle Island where Fell went off 'to investigate the inlets of Donegal Bay'. The submarine dived off Killybegs and observed two trawlers 'flagrantly poaching' east of Inishmurray before setting off on the surface through freezing snow storms to intercept a U-boat which had been reported by the Admiralty off Eagle Island.* It failed to materialise.

As the days went by, the submarine and her escort found it increasingly difficult to keep in communication with the Admiralty and with each other in the violent winter storms and heaving seas off Ireland; the wild and frozen coastline to the east seemed almost to mesmerize the crew of the *H 43*. When she surfaced on January 17 near Achill Head, County Mayo, the crew were 'surprised at the amount of daylight remaining, reflected in part by the snow clad mountains'. After a blinding snow storm next day, the log records that 'on coming to periscope depth an hour later every inch where snow could lie was covered and brilliant sunshine made a most wonderful sight.' *Tamura* put into the Mayo shore and 'found that the people in Blacksod knew nothing of any U-boat having been there. The Coast Watchers now wear uniforms. They were . . . most anxious to help in any way they could while having no suspicions as to *Tamura*'s function.'

But on the evening of January 22, *H 43* – submerged off Innishtearaght west of the Blaskets – thought she heard a U-boat's engines, diesel motors that were picked up to starboard by the submarine's amplified hydrophones. *H 43* surfaced but nothing could be seen in the gathering haze and she submerged two minutes later when 'diesel noises [were] now distinct and on the Port Plates'. She proceeded at full speed to close with the U-boat, surfacing as she did so and then zigzagging in the hope of catching the German vessel recharging her batteries. An Admiralty message confirmed a U-boat in the vicinity but *H 43* lost her quarry, ending her chase in an anti-climax of broken radio communication and mistaken identity. When she picked up the sound of diesel motors again, they turned out to belong to a trawler.[29]

Naval intelligence officers in London were understandably dispirited when they read through the record of *H 43*'s latest voyage. 'It was bad luck,' wrote one in the staff minutes on February 2, 'that *H 43* got so near to getting a contact with a U boat without actually seeing her.' But a colleague gave the report less credence. The *H 43*'s record of proceedings contained 'nothing of operational interest'. It was, he thought, 'rather a waste of paper . . .'[30]

There was, moreover, an ever-increasing chance that news of the Royal Navy's inquisitive patrolling up the Irish coast would eventually reach de Valera's ears. Indeed, some doubt exists as to whether the British Government were aware of Fell's travels in the company of *H 43*. In Sep-

---

* On several occasions, *H 43* and 502 Squadron RAF received specific details of U-boat movements. These could only have been obtained by the British Government's Code and Cypher School which had just begun to penetrate German naval codes at its new Bletchley headquarters. Royal Navy personnel and air crews on operations had no knowledge of this.

tember 1939, Eden had informed the War Cabinet in London that 'the Admiralty do not contemplate that British submarines should enter Eire territorial waters'[31] and the Irish *aide-mémoire* which had so vexed Maffey stated categorically that no 'vessels of war, whether surface or submarine craft' would be permitted to enter territorial waters unless they were in distress.[32] But neither the Royal Navy's patrols nor the erection by the Irish Marine and Coastwatching Service of eighty small concrete look-out posts on hill tops and mountain sides above the sea[33] prevented further intrusions by U-boats.

In early February, a German submarine arrived off the Irish coast with a spy on board, a man who made even Oscar Pfaus, the ex-cowboy and former Chicago policeman whom Abwehr II had sent to make contact with the IRA, look like a professional espionage agent. Doctor Ernst Weber-Drohl had been a wrestler and weight-lifter practising under the name of 'Atlas the Strong' before German Military Intelligence in Nuremberg took an interest in his connection with Ireland. Weber-Drohl had fathered two children on an Irish girl before the 1914–18 War and was apparently prepared to undergo a romantic reunion with her if Abwehr II wanted to ship him to Ireland. On January 28, Weber-Drohl, a short, muscular man with a shock of black hair on his forehead that gave him a faint facial resemblence to Hitler, stepped aboard *U 37*, under Lieutenant-Commander Hartmann, at Wilhelmshaven. He carried with him a bulky radio transmitter for the IRA. But off the coast of Ireland – probably near Sligo Bay – Hartmann encountered a strong westerly gale and when a sailor from the U-boat attempted to row Weber-Drohl ashore, their dinghy capsized in the Atlantic breakers. The sailor managed to right the boat and return to the submarine while Weber-Drohl staggered onto the beach, still carrying money and a set of wireless codes for the IRA but with his transmitter lost beneath the waves.[34]

There was, of course, no system – British or Irish – that could secure the hundreds of peninsulas and strands of the west coast against a U-boat landing, even one as farcical as this. Nor could German submarines be prevented from idling in the more remote bays at night before returning to hunt along the shipping lanes. But it should have been possible to discover if villagers along the coast were co-operating with U-boat crews by furnishing their submarines with fuel and food. In a third memorandum to the Director of Naval Intelligence, Churchill had said that there seemed to be 'a good deal of evidence, or at any rate suspicion, that the U-boats are being succoured from West of Ireland ports by the malignant section with whom de Valera dare not interfere'.[35] Yet evidence there appeared to be none.

On 27 February 1940, HMS *Tamura* – still masquerading as a Milford trawler but now graced with the inappropriate name of *Comet* – steamed out of Devonport into rough seas for yet another furtive patrol along the Irish coast. A force six wind and squalls of rain prevented *H 43* from taking her tow and it was a day later before the two vessels kept a rendezvous off the Scillies. Fell observed with customary resignation the failure of his telephone cable and began what was now a routine search for U-boats between the Old Head of Kinsale and Mizen Head. *Tamura* went trawling in Dingle Bay, sending across fish, meat and stores to *H 43* off Bray Head on Valencia Island. But while doing this, a basket slipped and knocked Able Seaman Morris's right arm between the hull of the submarine and the trawler, crushing his elbow. 'The wound looked nasty,' Fell recorded in his report to the Admiralty, 'and the man was in great pain and unable to move his fingers . . . administered one small square of morphia and decided that [the] man must have medical attention.'

Aware that the identity of his 'Q' ship might at last be revealed, Fell gingerly put into Valencia Harbour at midnight, turning down the offer of a pilot but accepting the loan of a small boat that took Morris ashore with the *Tamura*'s skipper and mate. 'They were well received and only usual questions asked . . .' Fell wrote. 'Morris was taken in [a] lady doctor's car to hospital and detained there with strict orders to divulge nothing and stick to the story that the falling topmast had hurt him and that he had recently joined this Milford ship.' An hour later, the Irish police arrived. 'Narrowly escaped detection,' Fell recorded, 'when Stoker Fahey recognised one of them as a friend of his.' The Gardai spent a long time inspecting the *Tamura*'s Lewis gun, 'curiously examining [it] and with no suspicion'.

At dawn, the *Tamura* slipped out of Valencia and, with her funnel disguised, headed for Long Island Bay about fifteen miles from Skibbereen. That night, the trawler 'steamed into Clonakilty darkened and lay under cliffs on [the] west side of [the] bay all night listening.' But not a sound came from the sea. The *Tamura*'s mission seemed no more successful than before. By now, it must have been clear to the British Admiralty that Fell and his crew were not only steering illegally through the neutral waters of Eire but were also navigating the wilder oceans of Churchill's own vivid imagination. In the bays around the south and west of Ireland, the First Lord of the Admiralty believed U-boats were being 'succoured'; but Fell had found only bad weather and destitute Irish fishermen begging for rope, food and coal.

At first light on March 5, Fell left Clonakilty for Baltimore, a tiny harbour in south west Cork sheltered from the Atlantic by a small headland and two flat, treeless islands. The *Tamura* entered the port at mid-morning and was:

. . . at once boarded by the most plausible scoundrels yet encountered. They begged or stole anything in reach from trouser buttons to the dregs of sauce bottles. One old man reputed to be worth thousands had his trousers patched with paper. All would commit any crime for a shilling. A so-called and most suspicious harbour master tried blackmail for harbour dues saying he would

119

not tell the owners if we paid him. It was like trading with the ancient Britons –
old bits of tin or junk being worth so many eggs. If the enemy are using Long
Island Bay then all Sherkin Island must be in 'the know'.[36]

Fell gained the impression that the local population were 'perfectly capable of anything'. He was told that a mine had recently exploded off
Sherkin Island, that another had been seen at Berehaven and that seven
gunshots had been heard in Baltimore two days earlier. 'The pseudo
harbour master seemed anxious to know what had happened last night as
regards sinkings and if we'd heard anything on the News about a ship
being sunk in [the] vicinity last night. When questioned he shut up
completely.' Another man asked Fell for news and remarked disconcertingly that 'he had seen a trawler like us yesterday bound east with a
different funnel.' Fell concluded that 'Sherkin is full of suspicion.'*

Yet it was unlikely that the villagers, so anxious to acquire the flotsam
off a trawler's decks, knew anything of interest to the crew of the *Tamura*
and Fell's Crusoe-like encounter with them somehow symbolises the
Royal Navy's operations along the Irish coast, seeking an unseen enemy
among an isolated and largely rural community that lived on rumours and
salvage and which possessed neither the money nor the ability to service a
fishing boat let alone a German submarine. Fell himself was a courageous
and a shrewd man even if his reports sometimes betray a distinct lack of
sympathy towards the Irish, but his efforts were for the most part wasted.
Tamura left Baltimore after two hours, with the barometer falling and a
stiff wind rising in the Atlantic. She developed engine trouble off Fastnet
and two of her crew were taken sick. The weather grew so bad that Fell
decided even a U-boat could not enter Clonakilty.[39] It was to be among the
Tamura's last patrols although the Admiralty records show that *H 43*
returned to the west of Ireland in late May 1940 in the company of a naval
trawler called *Manor*, searching vainly for U-boats which might have been
landing ammunition in Dingle Bay.[40] As late as June, the Royal Navy were
operating a patrol close to the west coast of Ireland, this time using a
warship, HMS *Orchy* under Commander Charles Jack, 'to engage and
destroy the enemy wherever he may be found'.[41] Jack stayed outside
territorial waters, incurring only the suspicion of two trawlers off the
Skelligs.[42] But the navy had not quite abandoned its 'Q' ship operations
in the area. Jack's sailing orders warned him that 'if your operations take
you to the West of Ireland, you may run across Submarine *H 43* accompanied by a trawler . . .'[43] Fell and his colleagues were still in business.

Churchill, however, was not yet satisfied that the Irishmen of Donegal

* The *Tamura*'s name does not appear in the Baltimore Harbour Commissioner's register
for March 1940.[37] The old pauper whom Fell met was Louis Nolan, the harbour master's
brother from Sherkin Island, although villagers in Baltimore claim today that it was his
shirt that was made of paper, not his trousers. Nolan is long dead but is still widely believed
in Baltimore to have been an immensely wealthy man.[38]

and Kerry were ignoring the opportunities afforded by England's difficulty. If the dispatches of Lieutenant Commander Fell had dampened the Admiralty's enthusiasm, Churchill, who had become Prime Minister of the British Coalition Government on May 11, now had his appetite for Irish intrigue sharpened by the reports of Sir Charles Augustus Tegart, graduate of Trinity College, Dublin, ex-Chief of the Bombay Police and former security adviser to the Palestine Police, whose 'firm, steady guidance' of the Calcutta gendarmerie had impressed Churchill almost a decade earlier.[44] Tegart was an Anglo-Irishman with an imperialist instinct and an abiding belief that Fifth Columnists constituted the front rank of an invading army; and a recent brief but energetic sojourn in Eire had convinced him that Germany was infiltrating hundreds of pro-Nazi Irishmen into Ireland by U-boat in preparation for the takeover of the Government in Dublin and an invasion of Britain.

It was an understandable emotion at the time. On April 9, Hitler's armies had landed in Norway and Denmark and just over a month later, the Wehrmacht overran neutral Holland and Belgium. As the British and French armies fell back across the battlefields of the 1914–18 War towards the Channel, the Germans dropped agents behind the Allied lines to confuse the retreating soldiers and to spread disaffection among the civilians. Prior to their attack on Norway, the Germans had organised the construction of a puppet government in Oslo under Vidkun Quisling, the leader of the Norwegian fascist party, the National Union. Experience therefore suggested that Hitler might be planning an identical political coup in other neutral countries. Now that Holland and Belgium had fallen, Eire could be high on his list of priorities and the notion that U-boats could be ferrying Fifth Columnists into Ireland seemed far from unrealistic.

Tegart was regarded as something of an expert in keeping insurgents away from British territory. In 1938, he had designed an eighteen-foot-wide barbed-wire entanglement with fortified police posts that ran the entire length of the Palestine–Syria border and which was intended to prevent Arab rebels from entering the British Mandate of Palestine. The 'Tegart Wall' did little more than irritate the Arabs – the frontier stayed open further south[45] – but it was the work of a man who identified problems boldly and attempted to solve them in an equally vigorous way. At the request of Colonel Valentine Vivian, a colleague from his days in the Indian police force, Tegart had been 'keeping an eye on events in Eire'[46] for the British Government and when he returned to London in the late spring of 1940 with apparently substantiated reports that German 'Gauleiters' were already in Eire preparing for the occupation of de Valera's twenty-six counties,[47] he was given an audience by Chamberlain, now the Lord President, and by Caldecote, who was Dominions Secretary in the new Government.[48] Tegart believed that 'the German plan to invade and conquer this country is set and ready and consists of the occupation of Eire, combined with heavy air attacks on the United Kingdom. Then an attempt to land on both coasts at once.' His narrative was so dramatic – it came as the last British and French troops were being evacuated from Dunkirk – that Desmond Morton, Churchill's personal intelligence adviser, sent a summary of it to the Prime Minister.

'Did you know,' wrote Morton with some consternation, 'that the German Gauleiters of Eire are already there, known by name and functioning in a certain way? The local Quisling is Sean Russell, who has been landed in Eire by a German U-Boat. The whole of his shadow Government has been formed as the Apostolic Successor of the 1916 Revolutionary Government, and exactly parallel to Quisling's effort, this Government is awaiting the signal to declare a revolution at the moment that German troops land.' According to Tegart, 'up to 2000 leaders have been landed in Eire from German U-Boats and by other methods since the outbreak of war.' Tegart said he had met 'the Gauleiter of Galway, who is a German called BECKE, introduced many months ago into the country, ostensibly to study Irish Folk Lore, under which cover he, and a number like him, have travelled all over the place, and in fact, have acquired a better topographical knowledge of Eire and its coast line than even the British Admiralty have got.' To substantiate this, Tegart said he had reported the movements of German U-boats in 'Dunbeg Bay'* to the Admiralty, only to be told by them that the water there was too shallow for submarines; so Tegart had been to Dunbeg to look for himself 'and found that there is an uncharted deep water channel leading between two bays and out into the Ocean'. Meanwhile, said Tegart, 'local Irishmen accept the visits of U-Boats with as common place an air as they accept sun rise on a fine day.'

Tegart also reported that the staff of the German Legation in Dublin – which was 'now nearly 300 persons' – had for the last year, with other Germans, 'been buying up estates on the West and South coasts, rooting up hedges, levelling suitable fields for landing grounds and . . . they are now ready for most things.' Tegart said that properties had been bought by Germans 'at Middleton [sic], Cork, Kerry, Scull [sic]† and a great many more places'. He pointed out that 'there is no secret about this at all locally.'[49] Morton informed Churchill that Tegart's information was being given 'deep consideration with a view to action'.[50] But the Prime Minister seemed just a trifle sceptical. 'I should be glad to know,' he scribbled on the bottom of Morton's covering note, 'what action is being taken, and whether the facts in Major Morton's letter are confirmed.'[51]

More than a month later, Churchill received a 20-page dispatch,

* Dunbeg is in County Kerry but it lies on a straight promontory above the sea. Tegart was probably referring to Bunbeg, south of Bloody Foreland in County Donegal, which would fit his later description.

† A strange combination of names. Cork and Kerry are both counties. Midleton and Skull are harbours in Cork.

marked 'Most Secret', parts of which had been unwittingly contributed by Captain Richard Pim, who had been on Craigavon's personal civil service staff in Belfast until 1939 and who was now in charge of the Prime Minister's Map Room at Downing Street. Pim was another Trinity College graduate, a former member of the old Royal Irish Constabulary who had served, too, in the Northern Ireland Ministry of Home Affairs under Dawson Bates. The new report on Eire contradicted Tegart's somewhat facile assessment in a number of damaging ways although it also raised some equally important questions of its own.* The statement that there were 2000 Germans in Eire was 'considered by the Crime Special Division of the Civic Guard to be without foundation'. There were, according to the Gardai, only 318 Germans and 149 Italians in Eire, and there was 'little confirmation of landings from U-Boats except in one or two instances at Dingle and Kerry and probable communication with the shore in Donegal Bay.' It was true, the report went on, that 'in some parts of Donegal, Limerick and Cork there is a small minority who would actively welcome the Germans on two grounds. First, that they would provide more employment and secondly, that they would reduce those who are better off to the same state of poverty as themselves under the Nazi system of Socialism.' This 'very small percentage' of the population, the document noted, 'is neither patriotic nor unpatriotic. It is purely communistic.' There was no confirmation that Sean Russell was in Dublin, and the intelligence paper quoted from a report by an officer in the Royal Ulster Constabulary, who had been informed by 'officers of high rank of the Civic Guard' in Eire that there was 'no truth in the rumour that Germans had bought estates on the Cork and Kerry coast.'† Some time ago, General O'Duffy's Blueshirts had made arrangements for the Italians to land arms in Eire but the idea had been abandoned when the IRA refused to give their support. It appeared that there had been an improvement in the Irish coast-watching service; telephones, the report noted, were now being installed in the watch houses. But 'the personnel . . . seemed anything but nautically minded and reports emanating from such personnel can hardly be relied on.'[52]

Having discredited Tegart's figures for U-boat landings, however, the dispatch was expanded by the addition of a very detailed intelligence report on the west coast of Ireland which seemed to give substance to some of Tegart's fears. From the British files at the Public Record Office in London, it is not clear who wrote this intelligence paper; the author might

---

* Pim says that while some of the information in this report appears to come from him, many of the military details were probably collated by a naval intelligence officer whom he escorted around Northern Ireland at this period. He did not write the 20-page document. 'Churchill never let me write a memo that was more than one page long,' Pim told the author in 1982.

† Although the manager of a beet factory at Mallow, County Cork, who was said to be a German, had 'bought a small place near Cork Harbour'.

have been a British diplomat in Dublin but a large number of Dominions Office files on Eire have been destroyed. These include, for example, all reports to London from British military attachés in Dublin between 12 December 1940 and 7 June 1941.[53] They are marked 'destroyed under statute'.* In any event, the annex to the dispatch was evidently the result of considerable effort, even if its conclusions were no more reliable than Tegart's.

On the west coast of Donegal, it said, a number of German hotel owners had established themselves, men who 'have become part of the people but have not lost their German sympathies'. Principal among them, according to the intelligence report, was:

> . . . Hemmersbach who runs the hotel at Inver and who is openly hostile to Britain, having had his property at Donaghadee, County Down, confiscated during the Great War. His hotel is the meeting place of many of the Germans in Eire and members of the German Consulate in Dublin frequent there, ostensibly for recreation . . . Hemmersbach was reported about a month ago to be buying up large quantities of eggs and butter for his hotel business, but it was suggested that the supplies were really required for submarine crews that came into Inver Bay in sailing and rowing boats. In this connection *U 29* and *U 33* are reported as having been at Inver during the past few months. About three months ago an unidentified trawler believed to be a German, as it showed no lights, was seen in Donegal Bay; Hemmersbach is alleged to have been greatly interested. He openly boasts that the war will be over in about eight weeks and that invasion of England is imminent.[54]

Wilhelm Hemersbach's old hotel still stands beside the bay at Inver, a white-painted two-storey building half hidden by trees, its lawns running down to the beach. It is a home for handicapped children today and Hemersbach died in 1956 but his two daughters, both married now, live within five miles of the former hotel. Regina Hemersbach can see the building from her home at Inver where she still keeps photographs of her father as a young man. Hemersbach – the British report spelt his name inaccurately – was a tall, distinguished-looking officer in the German Army of the 1900s; an early portrait shows him in military uniform wearing a flat army cap. Regina Hemersbach heard rumours during the war that her father was 'keeping German submarine officers in his cellar' but she says the stories were untrue.[55] His second daughter, Florence, believes that the British intelligence paper may have been written by a British agent who took lodgings for a few days in 1940 at Ardara, on the coast a dozen miles north of Inver. Her father had not supported the Nazis, although before the family left Germany his 14-year-old son Jim – Florence's brother – had been a member of a junior Nazi youth move-

---

* The Dominions Office was well known for its space-saving document destruction but it is noticeable that papers pertaining to other Commonwealth countries in the same series have not been so ruthlessly excised.

ment. 'My father never made any political comments,' Florence Hemersbach recalls, 'but in Germany he objected to Jim giving the Hitler salute. When we came here, Germans and British both visited our hotel. I remember my father saying "Treat everyone the same".'

Staff from the German legation in Dublin did stay at Inver during the war; the German Minister Eduard Hempel and his Counsellor Henning Thomsen spent several brief holidays at the hotel.* But Hemersbach's guests also included Lady Mountbatten, the wife of the commander of HMS *Kelly*, who regularly drove up from the family's castle in County Sligo for afternoon tea, and a host of British army and naval officers who crossed the border from Londonderry to go duck shooting at Drumbeg and Lough Eske; they included the young Lieutenant Philip Mountbatten – later Prince Philip, Duke of Edinburgh – who was said to be courting a girl who worked in a local post office. The mother of Major General Bernard Montgomery, 'Lady' Maud, who lived on the other side of Donegal, was an occasional guest. And so, according to Florence Hemersbach, was a certain Captain Richard Pim.

She says that she has no idea why the British intelligence paper should have suggested that Wilhelm Hemersbach gave food to U-boat crews. 'I lived in the hotel,' she recalls, 'and nothing strange ever occurred there. The only incident I can remember was when a dentist called McIvor from Lisburn in Northern Ireland became angry with Hempel. The Minister and his wife arrived for tea one day and the waitress took some plum pies from McIvor's table to give to the Hempels; McIvor objected vociferously that the pies should be given to them.'† But the British authorities clearly took a dislike to Hemersbach. His daughter Florence claims that when her first husband, a Donegal-born police inspector in the RAF, was killed in the London blitz, one of the British officers who used to stay at her father's hotel – not Pim – tried to prevent her receiving a widow's pension on the grounds that she was a German.[57] The Irish took a different view. Hemersbach's son James was later made an officer in the Irish Local Defence Force and patrolled the beach defences at Inver in 1942 to prevent a German or British landing.[58] Colonel Dan Bryan, who was later to become Chief Staff Officer of G2, the Irish Army's intelligence service, kept extensive lists of all German citizens who might have been working for their Government in Eire but he says that the authorities in Dublin 'never had anything on Hemersbach'.[59]

---

* Thomsen was at the hotel at Easter 1939, five months before the outbreak of war, when there was an unprecedented display of the aurora borealis, a pageant of blue, green and red lights across the night sky over the north of Ireland. 'There were colours in the sky everywhere,' Florence Hemersbach remembers. 'We were frightened because we had been told that when the Northern Lights shone like that, it meant there was going to be some kind of catastrophe. Thomsen assured us that nothing would happen.'

† Stuart McIvor still practises as a dental surgeon at Lisburn, County Antrim, although he recalls only that he argued with 'a German or a Free Stater' about the war. McIvor regarded Hemersbach as 'an old regular German officer'.[56]

The British intelligence file on Eire's German hotel owners, however, did not stop there. It remarked that 'a Mrs Cannon, also a German, and wife of an Ex-British Army officer whom she met in [the] USA runs the hotel at Glenties. She is also pro-Nazi . . .'[60] Cannon's hotel, with its pink portico, is now the Glenties post office but people in the village still remember Tom Cannon who would sing ribald songs every evening in the bar opposite his home. His wife Meta was 'very pro-German but not pro-Hitler' and she seems to have been an unlikely object for the attention of British intelligence. When she arrived in Donegal shortly before the war, she spoke no English and 'could often be seen in the street crying because she could not talk to anyone and was lonely'.[61] She had a sister who was a nun but all the family are now dead.

'Frick runs the hotel at Rossbeg,' the British report went on, 'and is rather a suave, reticent type . . . [he] is slow to discuss the war and bemoans the serious loss in trade. He is a very astute business man and in the way of supplying food and other requisites, sailing boats are believed to be the means of transport as they attract little or no notice.'[62] Colonel Bryan is certain that Frick, whose hotel overlooked the Atlantic beyond Dawros Head, was mentioned in an Irish intelligence file. Bryan was in any case observing not just suspicious Germans but potential British agents as well.

Tegart's 'public house stories' did not disturb him. He was more concerned with another former Indian police officer, who travelled around Eire generously distributing crystal wireless sets to Irishmen whom he considered sympathetic to Britain and asking them to give London advance warning of a German invasion of Ireland. The man was swiftly reported to Bryan.[63] So was Major E.Y. Byass, a British Army staff officer from Northern Ireland who was arrested with his wife by the Gardai at Mullingar, County Meath, while driving a car containing military plans and maps.[64] He was handed over to Maffey, the British Representative in Dublin, and dispatched hastily back to Belfast in July 1940. 'The Eire Government,' said the British intelligence file, 'object very strongly to espionage either by Germans etc or by what they term British Agents. They say there are a number of the latter and that each of them is under surveillance.' Another army major was named by the Gardai as a British agent – he travelled south of the border from Northern Ireland each week – and, added the British report, the Eire Government proposed to make arrests in the future 'as they are firmly decided to enforce neutrality in every respect.' The Gardai also held views 'on intelligence collected for Sir John Maffey's office'.[65]

The Irish Government were not trying to be particularly obstructive. When the British Government's RUC informant had enquired about the arrest of Major Byass, he was told by a Garda officer that 'if he'd only go to the Army, as you came to me, he'd be told anything he wanted, but we can't have them running round sketching the whole place.'[66] Yet the

British did not always follow this advice. Colonel Bryan, who had been closely involved in Irish counter-espionage since the first days of the war, was appointed head of G2 in 1941 and almost immediately found himself confronting an Englishman who had been detained in Wicklow after asking members of the local coast-watching service 'too many questions'.[67] In August 1941, another Briton, Geoffrey Jules Marcus, was arrested by the Gardai after carrying out a private inspection of military defences along the west coast of Ireland. Marcus contacted General Richard Mulcahy – Cosgrave's former Minister for Defence and now a senior member of the opposition Fine Gael party – and presented him with a memorandum claiming that German U-boats were making contact with villagers in Galway and Clare, and that the Irish coast-watching service in the area was not doing its job. Mulcahy, no doubt recognising the opportunity which this presented of embarrassing de Valera, forwarded Marcus's document to the Taoiseach's Department;[68] and it is a sign of just how seriously de Valera regarded such allegations that he immediately ordered Maurice Moynihan, the Secretary to the Government, to institute an enquiry into Marcus's claims.[69]

Chief Superintendent Carroll of the Garda Crime Branch subsequently reported to S.A. Roche, the Secretary to the Irish Department of Justice, that an investigation in Galway and Clare had not revealed 'any trace whatever of submarines in that area or any contact between these vessels and the land'. The only boats to put into port there had been British trawlers. Carroll said that Marcus had been 'a nuisance' to the naval authorities in Britain, who would pay no attention to anything he said, although 'it is quite possible that certain elements of the British press would be glad to avail of it'.[70]* Roche concluded that Marcus was 'a conceited busybody',[71] wrote him a polite note denying all his allegations[72] and, with some relief, told Moynihan that the young Englishman had left Dublin for Belfast with the intention of joining the Royal Navy.[73]

Whether Marcus was working for the British was not revealed but his case does raise questions about the co-operation that the British received from those politicians in Eire who were opposed to de Valera. In the summer of 1940 – when Tegart was composing his report for Churchill – Mulcahy was assembling his own dossier on German activities in Eire. On June 8, he wrote to Gerald Boland, the Minister for Justice in de Valera's Government, with information on 'Germans with hotels or other businesses on coast eg Frick Dawros Bay Hotel Rosbeg and Hammersback [sic] at Inver'. He urged Boland to 'note purchases (recent) of houses and land by Germans on South and South West Coasts – notably around Cork (Midleton etc) some of the purchasers are levelling the hedges and ditches (also at Scull?) Germans are known to be taking

---

* Carroll did admit that a coast-watcher on the south Aran island was not 'taking his appointment very seriously'.

soundings at Cobh harbour and in the Kerry bays.'[74] The content of this letter is so similar to that of Tegart's and the later reports – both of which were given a 'Most Secret' classification by the British Government – that it cannot have been coincidence. Mulcahy wrote to Boland three days before Tegart told Chamberlain about the exertions of German landowners in Eire but at least a month before the second British dispatch was submitted to Churchill. It is therefore unclear whether Mulcahy was feeding Boland with information that the British wanted Boland to receive in this way – the Minister for Justice was known to be anti-Nazi – or whether Mulcahy was privy to intelligence which he thought the British as well as his own government should be made aware of.

De Valera was by now convincing the British that he had no intention of wilfully ignoring assistance that might be given to U-boats on the west coast of Ireland. By December 1940 Maffey was 'quite sure that the Eire Government . . . would not countenance the giving of petrol to enemy submarines if they were made aware of it.' De Valera seemed ready 'to investigate any rumours' that Maffey brought to his notice.[75] But de Valera did not necessarily need British help, and when a U-boat arrived off the Dingle peninsula to land another incompetent spy in June 1940 Irish military intelligence had the man locked up within twelve hours. Walter Simon, alias Karl Anderson, was sent to Eire by the Abwehr on June 12, shortly before German troops entered Paris, with instructions to send weather reports and details of British convoy movements to Germany. He carried a wireless transmitter on which he was to contact the Abwehr daily, using lines from Schiller's *'Glocke'* as a code. He landed on the Kerry beach, buried his radio transmitter and set off for Dublin with a bag of counterfeit money in his pocket. But Simon aroused suspicion by waiting for a train at Dingle station, a railhead closed to passenger traffic for the past fourteen years; and when he did travel from Tralee to Dublin, he was accompanied on the train by G2 officers and met by more Irish intelligence men on his arrival at Kingsbridge station. Simon claimed that he had fallen out with a sister in Kerry and had left her home in the early hours of the morning to go to Dublin, a tale made less convincing by the amount of sand still visible on his boots.[76]

After June 1940, U-boats were sighted even more frequently around the north-west coast of Ireland. The fall of France had provided the Luftwaffe with French airbases from which their long-range Focke-Wulf aircraft could fly far out over the Atlantic, and German submarines were now able to operate from the ports of Brest and Lorient. The British were thus compelled to abandon their convoy route round the south of Ireland, sending their merchant ships instead through the North Channel and then westwards above Donegal. But British shipping losses – which in June stood at 282,560 tons – scarcely fell the following month.[77] British frustration was compounded by the RAF's lack of success in destroying German submarines around Ireland. In the first nine months of the war, only one attack was made on a U-boat by a 502 Squadron Anson; the aircraft dropped two bombs near a submarine off Fair Head, County Antrim, but was unable to confirm any damage to the vessel.[78] As more British ships were committed to the North Channel route to the Atlantic, British intelligence collected further reports of U-boats sheltering in the bays of Donegal. The second British intelligence report spoke of submarines that 'get sanctuary in the rocky islets off the extreme West coast from Bloody Foreland to Donegal Bay, but principally in the vicinity of Gola and Aran Islands'. Two submarines had been observed anchored off Gola and another on the surface off Owey Island.[79]

But still the British could not rid themselves of the suspicion that the people of the west of Ireland were somehow assisting the U-boats. Donegal fishermen, noted the report, 'often see submarines but are careful not to give away information as they get a ready market for fresh catches of fish . . . the natives [sic] on this coast were well accustomed to submarines in the last war, and apart from the anti-British feeling which is general in those parts, are undoubtedly open to turn to commercial account every opportunity of supplying requisites in the way of fish, food, fuel, etc.' The British intelligence paper referred to an unconfirmed report that German naval officers had landed at the fishing port of Killybegs and at Dunglow.[80]

No evidence of this was forthcoming. But there is no doubt that there *was* an anti-British sentiment in the west of Ireland that sometimes manifested itself in expressions of admiration for Germany and her military achievements. Nor can there be any doubt that Irish fishermen did sell their catch to U-boat crews. And on a few, very rare occasions during the war, individual Irishmen did give supplies of food to sailors who came ashore from German submarines. Frank Ward, who was a coast-watcher on Aranmore Island off Donegal, saw a German submarine surface next to a 400-ton Irish freighter off Green Island, south of Aranmore, in 1942. The U-boat remained alongside the ship for five minutes, took supplies aboard and then submerged. It was the only time Ward ever saw a submarine.[81] William Rose, a fisherman from Inver – the same village in which Hemersbach had his hotel – was sailing his 25-foot trawler to Buncrana in March 1942 when a German submarine with 'a sloping, brown-painted conning-tower' surfaced half a mile from his boat and travelled on a parallel course. Rose saw the periscope turn to observe him and assumed the crew would ask for fresh fish, but two Irish vessels – one of them apparently an Irish naval cutter – appeared on the horizon and the U-boat immediately submerged. Because another fisherman had been questioned repeatedly by the Irish Army and Gardai after seeing a submarine the previous week, Rose did not report the incident.[82]

There were closer contacts along the coast further south. Off Sheep's Head, County Cork, trawler-owners travelled out to sell fish to U-boats in 1941, even though the submarines were surfacing near the Irish Army's

Berehaven firing range.[83] In Dingle, County Kerry, Paddy Brosnan, the skipper of the 50-foot, 30-ton trawler *Elsie Mabel* was in 1942 told by men whom he assumed to be from the IRA that he should paint his boat blue and put to sea one evening to collect someone from a U-boat; but the project was abandoned when the 45-year-old fisherman discovered that a colleague was also setting sail in a newly-painted blue trawler. On another occasion, a U-boat surfaced close to Brosnan in Dingle Bay but he 'retreated quickly' because the *Elsie Mabel* bore a Grimsby registration and he feared she might be mistaken for a British boat and torpedoed. Nevertheless, Brosnan and his friends never hid their pro-German sympathies. They admired the U-boat commanders, especially after the *Royal Oak* was sunk by Prien at Scapa Flow. 'There were pictures of Prien in the newspapers,' Brosnan recalls. 'We cut them out and stuck them on our wheelhouse walls.'[84] Mort O'Leary, the harbour pilot at Fenit, on the other side of the peninsula, was also asked by 'the boys in Tralee' to keep a rendezvous with a U-boat in July 1942, but the submarine did not turn up.[85]*

Esteem for the Germans was not uncommon around Dingle town. Michael O'Sullivan found a photograph in an English magazine of Hitler in uniform and spent two shillings on a frame for the picture. 'My mother made me take it off the wall,' O'Sullivan remembers. 'I was only fourteen at the time but I did not forgive her for that. We were virulently pro-German. The Establishment people round here did not want Hitler to win because they thought their position in society would be reduced but the poor were for a German victory. We had an enormous admiration for the technical ability and sophistication of the Germans. If Ireland was going to be invaded, the poor wanted to see the Swastika.' O'Sullivan is one of the very few people in Ireland who admits giving food to a U-boat crew, albeit in a secondary role. In the spring of 1941, according to his account, he went with a man called Tomás Lynch to Brandon Creek on the northern side of the Dingle peninsula, a small rocky inlet with a concrete jetty that lies almost concealed immediately beneath Mount Brandon. They travelled from Dingle town:

> . . . with a donkey and cart which was loaded with food. There was a whole pig cut up into pieces, four bags of cabbages, four bags of potatoes and other things. When we got to the water, I could see a submarine on the surface just

---

* Age can sometimes distort time in the memory of those who have lived through more than one war. O'Leary recalled for the author an incident 'in 1940' when an American ship called *Seattle Spirit* entered Fenit where it was boarded by a party of British naval ratings; their officer produced a revolver 'and ordered the Captain to open a hatch with the words "You have guns hidden in there for the IRA — we have good sources of information".' O'Leary's memory was perfect in every detail, even down to the ship's tonnage, but the old Fenit Harbour log shows that the incident occurred not in 1940 but in 1920 — during the Irish War of Independence — when Fenit was a Royal Navy base and Ireland was still regarded by the British as part of the United Kingdom.

outside the creek and three crew members rowed in on a small boat and tied up to the jetty to collect the food. Each was wearing some sort of dark uniform and one had a badge on his jacket with an eagle on it. They had light-coloured scarves and naval caps with tapes at the back. They spoke in their own language but said 'Thank you' to us in English. We only saw them for a minute. No money changed hands. The business must have been arranged in Dublin.[86]

Lynch died soon after the war and O'Sullivan, who was only a boy at the time, says he has no idea who organised the contact with the U-boat crew. But his feelings about the Germans did not change even towards the end of the war. When Irish newspapers carried maps depicting the progress of the conflict in 1945, O'Sullivan 'saw that only a knife-edge of territory was left to the Germans but my friends and I still waited for the great break-out and a German victory.'[87]

Yet O'Sullivan's experience was an exceptional one. Others, who felt no particular sympathy for either side in the war, found little evidence of German activity along the Irish coast. William Glavin, who was on duty in nine posts from Clonakilty to Bantry for the Marine and Coastwatching Service in 1940, never saw a U-boat. Only in 1945, when he was a captain in the Irish Army, did he see a submarine but it was a British vessel that had been permitted to anchor off Kinsale for twenty-four hours to recharge her batteries.[88] Michael Brick, who was a coast-watcher at Sybil Head, eight miles from Brandon Creek, did not once catch sight of a U-boat although a torpedo – apparently fired by a submarine that mistook an outcrop of rock on the sea shore for a ship – still lies unexploded in Sás Creek on Dingle, the fins exposed to view at low tide. The *U 35*'s appearance at Ventry in 1939 prompted the Irish authorities to build a look-out post at Parkmore Point on the southern tip of the bay; but no further submarines were observed by the thirty-two men who later covered the nine posts in Dingle. Brick recalls no particularly pro-German sympathies in Brandon because 'for every man here, there were four men working in England and a lot of the young girls were in London as nurses.'[89] Hugh Wrenn, who from 1939 until 1944 was the district officer for the coastwatching service between Ballybunnion and Dingle – covering almost ninety miles of Kerry coastline – heard rumours of U-boat landings, particularly in Tralee, but thought that 'most of the submarines had been seen in pubs'.[90]

Nevertheless, it is not difficult to understand why Britain continued to feel uneasy about de Valera's assurances that submarines were not being welcomed into the little harbours of the south and west of Ireland. In May 1941, for instance, when British and Allied shipping losses amounted to more than 485,000 tons – a total of 120 ships sunk[91] – the British censorship authorities intercepted a letter from a Cork medical student to an American priest, the Reverend J.F. Murphy of Pensacola, Florida, in which the Irishman recorded that 'a few days ago some mines had to be exploded at Ballymecas. Jerome McCarthy . . . told me that he had a long chat with two German officers who came off a submarine which came up as far as the Eastern bridge!'[92] Later in the year, another correspondent referred in an intercepted letter to a Hull trawler that mysteriously gave away baskets of fish and tons of coal to 'pro-German villagers' at Crookhaven in County Cork.[93] Given the nature of the cruel struggle going on in the Atlantic, the mere suspicion that Irishmen were helping the Germans to sink Allied ships – in however indirect a way – was enough to ensure that the least circumstantial evidence for this presented itself as proof positive of treachery.

Long after the war, Frank Aiken, who was de Valera's Minister for the Co-ordination of Defensive Measures, said that 'no German U-boat landed on the Irish coast – if it had done, I think I would have heard about it.'[94] But the story of how Irishmen had refuelled German submarines at the height of the Battle of the Atlantic – helping the men who torpedoed the ships that kept Eire as well as Britain free – had already passed into passionate legend. Both during and after the war, Americans accused the Irish of harbouring German spies and servicing U-boats,[95] even though, for much of the war, diesel fuel and petrol was so scarce in the twenty-six counties that private motoring was banned. The accusation was, of course, an emotional one that could be used for political purposes, especially by those anxious to draw a distinction between the assumed loyalty of Northern Ireland and the apparent perfidy of Irish neutrality. It was therefore appropriate as well as inevitable that the last word on de Valera's 'malcontents' and their ubiquitous U-boats should have come from a Unionist member of the Westminster parliament, a Presbyterian minister with a reputation for strong anti-Catholic as well as anti-republican sentiments.

In March 1944, the Reverend Doctor James Little, MP for Down, forwarded to Herbert Morrison, the British Home Secretary, a letter from a Northern Ireland Protestant who had just visited Donegal. According to Little's anonymous correspondent, 'submarine crews from German Submarines come ashore in S. Donegal and are entertained lavishly by owners (Germans) of hotels there. Mr de Valera may deny that there is spying for Germany of any kind going on in Eire, but he knows that it is untrue. Two years ago I travelled in a bus from Tweedore [Gweedore]. Three people sitting behind me talked German all the way to Falcanagh [Falcarragh] where two of them left the bus. The one who stayed on said Heil Hitler to the other two when they were leaving. Surely something can be done to stop these spies.'[96]* The Admiralty subsequently wrote to Little, informing him that the First Lord had made enquiries 'about the

---

* Since west Donegal was a Gaeltacht area, the bus passengers were almost certainly speaking in Irish, which Little's Protestant correspondent would presumably not have understood. The 'Heil Hitler' may have been for his benefit.

alleged landing of German U-boat crews', adding however that 'similar reports have been received at intervals since the outbreak of war but after thorough investigation in no instance have they been discovered to have any foundation.'[97] What the Admiralty wisely refrained from telling Little was that the naval intelligence department in London regarded him as 'a rabid Orangeman, and a thorn in the side of the Security Service. He is always glad to get hold of any sort of stick with which to beat Eire.'[98] But Little's revelations had already found their way into the British press. De Valera personally condemned them as 'unscrupulous propaganda' but in resigned fashion concluded that 'the authors of such propaganda . . . are not deterred by denials which, even if published, do not catch up on the falsehood.'[99]

Even though these arguments were not irrelevant, they must have seemed remote along the west coast of Ireland where, month after month, the tide washed the war's human debris onto the beaches and estuaries of Kerry, Galway, Mayo and Donegal. The great ports of Berehaven, Lough Swilly and Cobh lay deserted, their desuetude confirmed by the partition of Ireland. A sack of cabbages or a catch of fresh fish for a U-boat crew could not tip that strategic imbalance any further. The bodies that came ashore were often buried beside the beaches, and the graves of British seamen – from the Royal Navy and the Merchant Service – can still be found on Clare Island, in the dunes above the Six Mile Strand and behind the bays of Donegal, 'direct payment', as Cecil Woodham-Smith wrote, for the Famine[100] and all that had gone before. Cycling through Donegal in July 1940 Rodney Green, a Belfast student, came across 'a row of very old taxis driving up the hill in the rain, each with a thin yellow box on its roof, tied down with string'.[101] The makeshift coffins contained the drowned passengers of the *Arandora Star*, a British liner carrying German and Italian internees to Canada, which had been torpedoed off Tory Island. That autumn, even as far inland as Glenties, the walls of the little Donegal cottages literally shook and vibrated each night to the blast of huge explosions from far out in the Atlantic, where the Royal Navy convoy escorts were fighting off the U-boat packs.[102] The war was getting nearer.

Chapter 5

Within the War Zone

> Neutrality is not like a simple mathematical formula which has only to be announced and demonstrated in order to be believed and respected . . . Instead of earning the respect and goodwill of both belligerents it is regarded by both with hatred and contempt, 'He who is not with me is against me'. In the modern total warfare it is not a condition of peace with both belligerents, but rather a condition of limited warfare with both . . .
>
> Frank Aiken, Irish Minister for
> the Coordination of Defensive Measures
> *23 January 1940*

Eduard Hempel, Envoy Extraordinary and Minister Plenipotentiary of the German Reich in Dublin, was a tall, polite, slightly balding diplomat with heavy, dark eyebrows and an inclination for flashy bow-ties. A 52-year-old former cavalry officer, his correct if undistinguished career in the German foreign service had taken him from India and the Far East to Norway and then to Eire in 1937. Unlike the rest of his staff in the Dublin legation, he was not a member of the Nazi party, a fact which de Valera apparently regarded with approval. The Irish Government had let it be known in Berlin that they did not favour the appointment of a National Socialist as German minister in Eire[1] and the Reich authorities presumably paid heed to this. Among the party men in the legation, the Counsellor, Henning Thomsen, was a member of the SS.

De Valera could scarcely have been displeased with Hempel's initial performance. From the first weeks of the war, the German minister followed a consistent and unbending policy of support for Irish neutrality, recognising that it was in Germany's interest to keep Eire out of the war and thus to prevent Britain from gaining the use of her airfields and ports. He advised Ribbentrop to give the British no pretext for invading Eire, to avoid 'any active interference in Irish internal conflicts' and to keep German submarines out of Eire's territorial waters.[2] His wisdom was sometimes appreciated more in Dublin than in Berlin, where the Abwehr did not always feel bound by the guidance of the German Foreign Office. But Hempel quickly grasped an essential element in Irish political life: that de Valera was 'the only recognised political leader of large stature who has the nationalists firmly in hand'. De Valera would 'maintain the line of friendly understanding with England as far as it is at all possible, on account of geographic and economic dependence . . . as well as [maintain] his democratic principles, even in face of the threatening danger of Ireland becoming involved in war.'[3] Hempel distrusted the IRA – occasionally regarded in Berlin as 'the natural ally of Germany'[4] – and urged his Foreign Office to exercise 'complete restraint' in their dealings with the organisation.[5] 'The IRA was a body that acted against the Government,' Hempel was to recall years later. 'I told Berlin that it would be the same as if another country backed Communists in National Socialist Germany. It would have been impossible.'[6]

Hempel viewed Irish neutrality and independence as 'a symptom of the loosening ties of the Empire';[7] and he was, after all, in a position to know. He was the only German diplomat accredited to a Commonwealth country during the war – his appointment had been recognised by the King[8] – and outside his legation at No.58 Northumberland Road, the Swastika flag of Nazi Germany flew each day. Maffey was not permitted to display the Union Jack.[9] A permanent watch, however, was kept on Hempel's red-brick Victorian offices on the south side of Dublin by four Gardai, 'picked to be "pickers" and they know every person who enters the Legation'.[10] Among the early visitors they identified was Lord Tavistock, later the Duke of Bedford, a former communist who subsequently decided that the disciplines of fascism were more attractive. Tavistock wanted to mediate between Britain and Germany, offering the latter peace in return for a withdrawal from Poland and Czechoslovakia. According to Hempel, Tavistock tried 'to intermediate [sic] with some people in Ireland. These people did not address me but Thomsen.' Hempel refused to see the Englishman because he had 'to remain in the background until I knew what would be the reaction in Berlin to Lord Tavistock's offer'. But he was sure that it stood no chance of acceptance because Hitler had no intention of returning Poland and Czechoslovakia.[11]

Hempel maintained after the war that he was never 'associated with any intrigue involving plots against the Irish Government and the country's neutrality'[12] and that his radio messages to Berlin were 'not military wires because I had nothing to report about military affairs, at least only very little'.[13] But this was not entirely true. He radioed the Foreign Office on 28 September 1939 that an American ship, the *Iroquois*, was due to leave Cobh for the United States in four days; and soon after its departure, the vessel was intercepted by the German navy and sunk.[14] In 1940, Hempel sent details of Eire's internal security forces to Berlin and informed the Foreign Office that the Irish Army Air Corps had increased its aircraft strength from 40 machines to 170, including 12 seaplanes. He described the defences of the Atlantic ports and outlined the lack of light weapons in the Irish Army.[15] As the war progressed, he also radioed a good deal of information (much of it inaccurate) about military developments in Britain and Northern Ireland.*

From their own agents – and from Maffey – the British were also making their assessments of Irish military preparedness. In July 1940, they estimated that Irish troop strength stood at 25,000 and that following large-scale commandeering of civilian lorries, the force was 'fairly mobile'. Its newly-appointed Chief of Staff, Lieutenant General Daniel McKenna, was, according to British intelligence, 'a good type of man who does not dabble in politics and will not allow politics to be discussed in the Army.'[17] It was a force, however, that was still trying to make up for the cuts in manpower that the Irish Government had imposed upon it shortly after the outbreak of war. After achieving a strength of 19,783 regulars, reservists and Volunteers by September 1939, de Valera's Cabinet had decided in December that for financial reasons the Army establishment 'should be based on the smallest number of troops necessary to garrison fixed positions'. Oscar Traynor, the Minister for Defence, was expected to reduce the figure to below 15,350.[18]

There had been no substantial improvements made to the defences of the Treaty ports and air-raid precautions – which even a neutral state had an obligation to take on behalf of its citizens – were negligible. Although the Irish Department of External Affairs had circulated British Home Office ARP pamphlets to government offices in Dublin[19] and the Defence Department acquired 300,000 British-made gas masks by the autumn of 1938,[20] intensive air-raid precautions were only in operation around the south and east coasts of Ireland when the war began.[21]† Colonel J.J. O'Connell – the former Chief of Staff whose kidnap in 1922 provoked the national army's attack on the Four Courts of Dublin – warned of the dangers of air attack on the capital in a 1938 magazine article, a copy of which was filed away in de Valera's department. O'Connell urged that 'black-out' procedures and evacuation schemes should be perfected in peacetime.[23]‡ Yet the Irish Cabinet only considered ARP for house-

---

* According to Carolle J. Carter, who undertook some formidable research into Hempel's activities, he reported on a Vauxhall tank factory thirty miles from London, on British and American troop strengths in Britain and Northern Ireland in 1942, and on the new B-24 Liberator bomber which the Americans were flying to Britain via Shannon. Berlin was also sent a message about the sinking of the *Queen Mary* off Belfast with a loss of 16,000 lives in July 1942; the report was false.[16]

† In 1938, *The Irish Times* had commented upon air-raid precautions in Belfast, comparing them favourably to the arrangements in Dublin: 'We have heard that there are gas masks in the city of Dublin. Where are they? If war should break out tomorrow . . . what would the citizens of Dublin be expected to do about it? Nobody knows.'[22]

‡ O'Connell regarded Dublin as the primary target in Ireland because it was 'a glaring example of a megacephalic capital city, with all the consequences that that entails'. Indeed.

holders in July 1939[24] and in November the Cabinet minutes recorded that expenditure on ARP training was to be 'reduced to the lowest practicable level'.[25] In the same month, a Cabinet memorandum maintained that there was no need for further lighting restrictions in Eire, that no air-raid shelters should be built outside Dublin, that fire-fighting equipment throughout the country was obsolete or non existent and that no further money should be spent on gas masks. The memorandum also suggested that the Government's attitude towards air-raid precautions 'lacked decisiveness',[26] which was something of an understatement.

It was only in May and June 1940, when the German advance to the French coast brought the war so much closer to Dublin, that the Irish Government belatedly awoke to the real necessities of national defence. Seven infantry battalions were placed on a war footing with an anti-aircraft brigade and two companies of engineers.[27] Twelve rifle battalions were to be raised, bringing the Army's total strength to 40,000.[28] The Cabinet gave orders for the immediate procurement of 492 Bren guns, 60 anti-aircraft guns, 100,000 rounds of ammunition, 16 3.7-inch guns, 20,000 steel helmets and 10,000 signal cartridges, together with what the Government records referred to – with a comforting lack of specific detail – as 'aircraft and spare parts'.[29] In August, the Government raised military strength to 42,000.[30] (Within a year, the Department of Defence would be recommending a figure of 50,000.[31]) The recruits – most of them wearing British-made but German-style coal-scuttle helmets – were forthcoming; but the arms were not. De Valera's persistent, occasionally frantic quest for weapons was to be a consistent theme of Irish foreign policy over the coming years, a search that was principally directed towards the belligerent powers and which was thus always rewarded by demands which would – if met – totally compromise Eire's neutrality. In return for guns, the British wanted the use of the Treaty ports, the Americans wanted Irish participation in the war, and the Germans – less ambitious because there was little else to be gained – wanted a closer relationship between Dublin and Berlin. Denuded of weapons, Eire's refusal to participate in the war was no longer just an assertion of sovereignty; from now on, the policy had to prove successful in keeping Eire out of the war.

The unity of a population that had less than twenty years earlier been embroiled in a civil war was now a prerequisite for such a success. When Hermann Goertz, an Abwehr agent, landed by parachute in County Meath in May 1940, Gerald Boland used the incident as a pretext to raise a 'Local Security Force', a form of paramilitary police based on the Gardai which could, if necessary, be used against the IRA.* This was not how the Irish Government presented the affair at the time; and Boland, in the

---

* Boland wrote later that 'the discovery [of Goertz] . . . made me decide after a talk with General Murphy to ask the Government to immediately set up a Local Security Force based on each Garda Barracks in the country.'[32]

private notes he wrote after the war, said that the LSF's task was 'to keep an eye out for parachutists or submarines in coastal areas and on suspicious looking strangers'.[33] But when de Valera's Government gave its official approval to the force, the Cabinet minutes specifically said that its duties were to assist the authorities in guarding against invasion and 'in dealing with subversive activities'.[34] Not only German agents were regarded as 'subversive' in Eire. By early June, more than 44,000 men had been enrolled, and within two months the figure climbed to 148,000.[35]

Less easy to bring together were the opposing political parties in the Dail. For years, there had been scarcely any contact between de Valera's ministers and the front bench members of Cosgrave's Fine Gael.[36] There were old, unpaid debts to settle. It had been Mulcahy's national army that had executed de Valera's captured irregulars. Mulcahy had once refused the imprisoned Boland parole when his Uncle Harry died and despite their official contacts now, Boland could still not bring himself to treat the General with more than a minimum of courtesy.[37] Deprived of power and smarting at the wound which their respect for the Commonwealth inflicted upon their nationalism, the loyal supporters of the old and desecrated Treaty could do little more than sneer at de Valera. Publicly, they could not afford to be too pro-British in outlook, for there was no doubt that a majority of the country favoured non-intervention in the war. So Cosgrave, Mulcahy and James Dillon, Fine Gael's deputy leader, adopted an attitude of scornful disdain towards de Valera, locked into his policy of neutrality yet anxious – sometimes recklessly so – to damage it. De Valera needed to engage their energies and he came up with an ingenious device. He offered Fine Gael three seats in a National Defence Conference, a forum in which the three Irish political parties could regularly offer advice on the problems arising from the war and defend Eire's neutrality. Fine Gael appointed Dillon, Mulcahy and T.F. O'Higgins to the conference. Aiken, Boland and Traynor represented Fianna Fail and William Norton, the Labour Party leader, and William Davin attended for Labour. The conference gave Fine Gael only a semblance of influence – de Valera was having no emergency coalition government – and Mulcahy did not hesitate to express his contempt at the way in which he and his colleagues were forced to grub for information, 'like hens scratching'.[38] But Boland thought that Fine Gael behaved well, especially in view of Aiken's 'extraordinary procedure' of refusing to discuss the minutes of previous meetings.[39]

De Valera opened his talks with Fine Gael on a solemn note. 'The German advance,' he told the party's delegation, 'has been very rapid. We are now well within the war zone.'[40] But Mulcahy's notes of the conference sessions make dismal reading. When de Valera first addressed the meeting, he obviously tried to capture Fine Gael's support, making it clear that he would count on British assistance in the event of a German invasion of Eire. 'Dev's idea,' wrote Mulcahy on 5 July 1940, 'is that the invasion of

Ireland will be a sort of side-show by the enemy. The main blow to fall on Britain; and that he will be able to resist the side-show long enough to enable British help to come in, namely, sufficient naval, military and air assistance as will be effective.' De Valera would do nothing until an invader arrived because 'a war declaration on his part would be opposed by perhaps more than half of his own party, one third of Fine Gael, and perhaps the whole of Labour . . .' [41] This may have been an accurate assessment; yet the information being given to Fine Gael was sometimes of a very questionable nature. On September 4, for example, when Britain hourly expected a German landing on her beaches, Mulcahy recorded that 'the Germans apparently had intended to invade Britain . . . whatever their plans were, they have been departed from and the German invasion is probably dropped.'[42]

Sensitive information was in any case a commodity of rare value in Eire and the state's policy of non-intervention in the war was underpinned by a system of censorship that remained the subject of controversy long after the European conflict had ended. The Irish Government's control over information was ostensibly exercised on behalf of neutrality. Newspapers and magazines were not permitted to publish 'statements or suggestions casting doubt on the reality of such neutrality' or 'expressions likely to cause offence to the peoples of friendly states whether applied to individuals or to the method or system of Governments or to the culture of the people of such States'.[43] In fact, the suppression of political opinion in Eire was such that it called into question the very nature of neutrality. If Eire's policy of non-intervention was intended to preserve the freedom and parliamentary democracy of the twenty-six county state, then how far could the Government go in restricting the democracy in order to safeguard its neutral shield? It was an issue that was to be argued not only in the Dail and on election platforms but in the censor's office itself. For censorship was not only intimately associated with the policy of non-intervention. It became neutrality's backbone and had to be defended as forcefully as neutrality itself.

When Joseph Connolly, the Chairman of the Board of Works, was asked by the Government to become Controller of Censorship in September 1939, he was told to work in cooperation with G2, the Irish Army's intelligence service.[44] But when he and Michael Knightly, the Chief Press Censor, settled into their office in the Upper Yard of Dublin Castle, their first duties were comparatively innocuous. They found that the Carlton cinema was still showing *The Spy in Black*, a film which had been running in Dublin before the outbreak of war but which they now felt would 'cause offence to Germans'. The film was cut.[45]* A few days after his appointment, however, Connolly sent de Valera a memorandum outlining the

---

* The Irish censors refused to permit Chaplin's *The Great Dictator* to be shown in Eire because 'it would have meant riots and bloodshed'. In 1942, 1661 films were presented to the censors; they passed 362 with cuts but totally rejected 82 of them.[46]

problems he foresaw in censoring the press, particularly the pro-British *Irish Times*. The censor's aim, he said, was to prevent publication of anything that would impair Irish neutrality 'but it is already evident that it is going to be difficult to keep out of . . . leaders and sub leaders the suggestions (a) that we are not really neutral, (b) that we cannot continue to be neutral, (c) that we are wrong in being neutral, (d) that the big majority of the people are opposed to the enemies of Britain.' Connolly noted that 'it seems likely that we will have definite difficulty in the case of certain papers such as *The Irish Times* in restraining them from tincturing all or most of their material with a definitely pro-British tinge and, particularly in their leading articles, getting them to follow a strictly neutral line of argument.' Connolly felt he had two options: to adopt a strict censorship that would prevent any comment that favoured the British, or to permit newspapers to argue 'for the support of the anti-German forces'. The first option, Connolly thought, might provoke 'an open breach with papers like *The Irish Times* where they may either refuse to obey our rulings or force us to take action up to the stage of fine or suppression or both'. This might be bad for 'a certain minority at home' and 'from the point of view of our position in Britain and abroad'. But many people watching would be 'quick to criticise anything that may seem to favour the British or pro-British tendencies and that will seem to "cut across" our avowed neutrality'. Connolly preferred a strict censorship,[47] and his office soon began to exercise its powers. It deleted a section from an official Government report on Irish exports[48] and took action against *The Irish Times* for ignoring an order prohibiting publication of an article. By the late autumn, the censor had begun to restrict press reporting of speeches by TDs – among them James Dillon – who spoke outside the Dail in support of the Allies.

The authority of the censor was ultimately vested in Frank Aiken, the Minister for the Coordination of Defensive Measures, whose unbending loyalty to his political leader embraced not only de Valera himself but also his philosophies. In response to the anger generated by the suppression of TDs' speeches in the newspapers, Aiken prepared an eight-page memorandum for the Irish Government in January 1940 justifying the strictness of his censorship.* It is worth quoting at length for it turned out to be perhaps the most forceful exposition of Irish neutrality made during the war, a self-confident assertion of Eire's right to be neutral and of the sacrifice which that neutrality entailed. The circulation of the memorandum was restricted to members of the Government and its existence has never previously been revealed.

Members of the Dail, Aiken wrote, might take the view that censorship was neither necessary nor democratic. They would claim that according to international law, people in a neutral state could think and say what they

---

* See Appendix 1.

pleased about belligerents, and that if democracy is to survive they must be allowed to do so. Aiken, however, recalled that the Irish parliament had showed unprecedented unanimity when it passed emergency legislation at the start of the war, legislation which included the powers of censorship. The Government was precluded from declaring war without the consent of the Dail and therefore it must use its executive power to preclude any of its citizens from provoking war. Aiken regarded propaganda as 'one of the most important weapons of war' and suggested rather rashly that Germany might have used more brain power on fostering propaganda than it had been employing on its U-boat campaign. 'In these days, therefore, no matter what the old and very much out of date international conventions contain, it behoves neutrals who want to remain at peace to walk warily in the zone of the propaganda war.' The freedom to advocate a declaration of war, Aiken went on, might have had some usefulness in former times but it would be 'positively dangerous' now. As a nation, he wrote:

> . . . we have a definite grievance against the nearest belligerent, but the Government have declared with general consent that we would be unwise, in the interests of the nation, to engage in war against this belligerent. Not all of our people approve this policy, and if a certain section were allowed to talk offensively about the morals of Germany in relation to its aggression in Poland and elsewhere, we can be quite sure that others would try to express in even more offensive terms their detestation of British morality. If we were a nation of Dillons words would only lead to words. But we are not . . . it might very well be that we would have a civil war to decide the question as to which of the European belligerents we should declare war upon. Consequently it would be the Government's duty, if it had not legal power to repress such activity, to seek that power immediately; and, as it has the power, it is its duty to use it.[49]

Aiken had sharper words for the 'self-styled democrats who would hold on to the peace time liberalistic trimmings of democracy while the fundamental basis of democracy was being swept from under their feet by the foreign or domestic enemies of their democratic State'. Wise men, he wrote, discarded these trimmings when necessary to maintain the citizens' right to choose their own government. Under Article 28 of the Irish Constitution, the Dail had given the Government power to legislate by Decree and 'thus the much loved trimming of discussion before legislation went by the board.' The Dail had the power 'to ask all questions and . . . to change the Government if they think it wise' but between meetings of the Dail, no representative had the right to say anything that might embroil Eire in war. Neutrality, wrote Aiken:

> . . . is not like a simple mathematical formula which has only to be announced and demonstrated in order to be believed and respected. It has in fact always been one of the difficult problems in human relationship. Instead of earning the respect and goodwill of both belligerents it is regarded by both with hatred

and contempt, 'He who is not with me is against me'. In the modern total warfare it is not a condition of peace with both belligerents, but rather a condition of limited warfare with both, a warfare whose limits, under the terrific and all prevailing force of modern total warfare, tend to expand to coincide with those of total warfare. In cold economic and military fact it is becoming more and more difficult to distinguish between the seriousness of the two emergencies called war and neutrality . . .'[50]

A neutral located near the belligerents, noted Aiken, may have to make more extensive use of censorship than a belligerent situated far from the theatre of war. If the Dail wished, it could withdraw the right of censorship from the Government but until it did so, the Government must use that power 'to maintain the neutrality of this democratic State'. If newspapers or citizens felt aggrieved, they could complain to their elected representatives but 'whoever says he is not satisfied with such a system of democracy in "time of war" is either a very foolish democrat or an *agent provocateur* for those who want to overthrow democracy or to embroil us in civil or foreign war.'[51]

Aiken's memorandum was a remarkable, indeed an historic document. There was, of course, a simplistic element in his analysis. Eire was not being physically attacked and her people were not being killed; thus the 'limited warfare' of neutrality could not possibly coincide with the condition of total war in which the belligerents existed. But there was a tough, pragmatic determination to Aiken's arguments. Contained within them was the fibre that would resist the pressures of Britain and America to participate in the war. Aiken not only defended neutrality; he raised it to a high, almost exalted plane. He described neutrality in an entirely new way, not as a symbol of national independence but as an active, decisive and coherent policy. It was – according to its own lights – honourable, even courageous. More to the point, it was realistic.

But Aiken's censorship did not impress Dillon who, having failed to get his pro-Allied views into the press, proposed to publish his speeches privately in pamphlets which he could distribute himself. The censorship office told him that he should not publish those passages in his speech which had already been suppressed in the newspapers. But the censors apparently had no power to stop Dillon printing his own statements and Connolly pointed this out to the Government. He asked for extra powers that would enable him to seize privately printed pamphlets at the publishers or in shops. The Department of External Affairs had already drawn attention to 'anti-German gramophone records' circulating in Eire, and Connolly even suggested that censorship might have to include 'effigies, dolls and toys'.[52] Connolly's extraordinary note seemed to worry Sean MacEntee, the Minister for Industry and Commerce, who – although there was no departmental reason why he should be drawn into the discussion – submitted to the Irish Cabinet an extract from a speech made in the House of Lords by the British Under Secretary of State for the

Colonies, the Marquess of Dufferin and Ava. In a debate on wartime censorship in Britain, the minister had remarked that 'if, every time an abuse of freedom is committed, we allow that to be an opportunity for further Government control, further censorship, further denial of liberty, then I do believe that you are going to erode in a very few years perhaps the whole rock of personal liberty.'[53] MacEntee made no comment on this statement but he obviously thought that things were getting out of hand at the Irish censor's office.

Connolly let the matter drop but raised it again six months later when James Larkin's *Irish Workers' Weekly* deliberately failed to submit its entire issue to the censor before publication. According to the censor's office, it had been 'publishing matter of an objectionable nature'. The offence was reported to the Chief State Solicitor but, as Connolly noted in a memorandum to the Government, 'the paper continues to offend in its weekly issues.' The new and more critical phase of the war had apparently persuaded him that 'there should be power to direct the seizure of any objectionable printed matter whether it be a newspaper or other periodical . . . a leaflet, book, pictorial representation, or any other document.'[54] It was a sign of Connolly's preoccupation with such matters that it was not until 1941 that he asked for powers to prevent foreign press correspondents from sending reports to London without first submitting their copy to the censor. His primary duty, of course, was to censor material of Irish origin – Eire could not be held responsible for the work of foreign journalists in Dublin – but in January 1941 an Associated Press correspondent filed a report over the telephone to his London office 'to the effect that German planes in force were bombing the city at the time he was speaking and that the German Minister had been given his passport'.[55] The report was untrue. Connolly wanted to make it a criminal offence for a correspondent to send a press message out of the country without first submitting it to the censor.

This in itself was understandable but the work of the censor's office was taking on increasingly political overtones. The authorities were deleting opinions from the newspapers which could not possibly have offended the belligerent powers but which were highly critical of Irish Government ministers. On 20 May 1941, for instance, Robert 'Bertie' Smyllie, the *Irish Times* editor, wanted to publish the text of a speech which Mulcahy had made in Dublin the previous day, criticising a visit which Aiken had made to the United States. The page proof was sent to the censor's office at Dublin Castle containing the following statement by Mulcahy:

They knew of no economic warfare by Great Britain against this country and it was appalling that an Irish Minister, going across to the United States, on a diplomatic mission, to get, by diplomatic means, ships, wheat, and other things, should go in for a class of soap-box diplomacy, and talk in such terms that he could hand himself over to be patronised by leading isolationist politicians.

Mulcahy's criticism could hardly be said to have called Irish neutrality into doubt or to have offended a belligerent power – the United States had not yet entered the war – but the newspaper proof came back from the censor's office with all but the first twelve words deleted.[56] Aiken, it appeared, was also being protected by the censor.

'It is damnably difficult for a newspaperman to deal with our friends in the Castle,' Smyllie later lamented in a letter to Mulcahy. 'It must be equally difficult for public representatives who have the moral courage to be critical. I have bitter experience of the whole hierarchy of Censors. I have found Knightly reasonable and even sympathetic, Coyne casuistically helpful, Joe Connolly a bitter Anglo-phobe, and Aiken unintelligently impossible! Whenever I have appealed to Caesar – and I have done so more than once – I have found the long fellow more than anxious to be fair.' Mulcahy partly agreed with these sentiments but could not accept Smyllie's compliment to de Valera. He replied:

> Your picture of the general combination is quite sound, up to a point – until you come to Caesar himself – you should be able to recognise by this that it is here that the whole hub and fount of dishonesty is. He has been the creator of all the disorder, division, dishonesty. He sits enthroned on his own creation, and after all, the equipment of any throne involves having a few smiles and gracious words and nice gestures to throw away. I don't suppose, in fact, that you ever got anything else . . .[57]

Despite Mulcahy's cynicism – a reflection of his impotence within the Defence Conference as well as the residual bitterness of the civil war – Aiken's censorship remained severe. Years after the war, he was prepared to take a gentler attitude towards the affair. 'I had a lot of fun with Smyllie,' he said. 'When he was censored, he would always write a letter about it. So I would sentence him to one or two pages of Coyne. We used to "hop off" each other.' It was not just in Eire, however, that Aiken's censorship was deeply resented. The British noticed that the Irish censor's definition of propaganda embraced even the most factual reports of documented Nazi atrocities.

Count Jan Balinski, who visited Eire in January 1941 for the Polish Research Centre – a branch of the exiled Polish Government in London – considered that Irish censorship was 'carried out with a severity which cannot be justified merely by a policy of neutrality. Nothing is allowed to appear in the Irish press on the subject of the ruthlessness of the Germans or even of the Soviets, either in Poland or in other European countries. Nothing is published which contains an appreciation of the magnificent spirit shown by the British people during the present struggle. Nor is anything published – though this would be natural in a Catholic country – regarding the Vatican broadcasts on the persecution of the Church in Germany and Poland.' Eire's attitude was bound to be commented upon unfavourably in the future, not only in Britain but in the United States, 'the country of most importance to the Irish'. Balinski, who sent a copy of his report on his visit to Eire to the British Foreign Office, felt that 'in this struggle against an inhuman adversary, even if neutrality in political matters must be maintained, a definite attitude should nevertheless be taken from the moral and Christian standpoint.'[58]

This was exactly Dillon's view. A conservative, deeply religious man with a ruthless integrity that led him down a tunnelled and lonely path away from his own people, he believed passionately in the moral rightness of the Allied cause, whatever the domestic implications of this may have been for Eire. He spoke out against neutrality again in July 1941 and on this occasion the censors, perhaps hoping to avoid another battle over Dillon's private pamphleteering, permitted the Dublin papers to report the speech in full. They even allowed a few inoffensive letters to appear in print from readers but, in Connolly's words, 'having, so to speak, given them all one "bite" on the subject in the editorial columns we then "closed down" on the matter.' Aiken refused to permit publication of 'all letters condemnatory or laudatory' of Dillon's views.[59] Dillon did decide to reprint his anti-neutrality speech anyway but only de Valera's personal decision prevented its suppression.[60] Connolly was now worried that excessive use of his powers might 'antagonise either the Dail or the public' and was concerned lest a series of bans on publications might be 'construed as an anti-British or anti-German gesture'.[61]

Dillon was forced to resign from his party in 1942 after telling Fine Gael's annual convention that 'whatever the sacrifice, whatever America may want from us to protect her from her enemies, she will get it for the asking.'[62] But standing as an Independent candidate in the following year's election, his speeches once again fell foul of the Censorship Board. This time, it was the turn of the Department of External Affairs to ponder the arguments of press censorship at a time when Eire's population was about to exercise its democratic franchise. In order to make any kind of a case for suppressing an election speech which was opposed to Eire's neutrality, said a memorandum from the Department, 'the Press Censor would have to resort to an argument that neutrality . . . assumed the sacrosanctity of a constitutional right' although no such case could be made under the Irish Constitution. Speeches, on the other hand, which advocated a declaration of war by Eire 'become inescapeably censorable' once they compromised Eire's position as a neutral state. Dillon himself, said the External Affairs memorandum, had pointed out that if the people did not know that a candidate wanted Eire to declare war, they could not elect him – or might vote unwittingly for him – and to resist this argument would be difficult 'without appearing grossly "undemocratic".' The most politic course might be 'to promise freedom of the Press during the election to all 100% inoffensive pro-war speeches. There will, in the nature of things, be very few such speeches, if any. Deputy Dillon is not a

145

political tight-rope walker – on the contrary!' But censorship in Eire, the memorandum concluded, had 'helped to unite the people on the policy of neutrality by withholding from them the bulk of belligerent propaganda' and the rules should not now be relaxed. A draft statement prepared for de Valera by the Department claimed that Eire was still at peace 'thanks largely to the wisdom shown by its Press Censorship' and insisted that no one 'by indiscreet or reckless utterances' would be allowed to imperil the country's position.[63] Dillon told the Dail that it was 'a fraud and a farce' to describe the election as free but Aiken refused to be moved. 'You cannot,' he said, 'throw up the policy of neutrality . . . like a balloon into the air and allow it to take care of itself . . . I am determined not to allow a few members of our community to use a propaganda campaign that might be a danger to the safety of the State.'[64]

The Department of External Affairs' memorandum was perhaps deliberately ambiguous. Since the Emergency Powers Act of 1939 had not specifically provided for the maintenance of neutrality – merely for the securing of public safety and 'the preservation of the State in time of war' – the censorship set up under these powers could not in theory suppress 'anti-neutral' statements. The Department, however, took the view that it would be 'contrary to all commonsense' to suggest that the 1939 Act did not relate almost entirely to the implementation of neutrality, even though the word 'neutrality' was not used. But to maintain as it did that censorship had helped to unite Eire by withholding from its people the propaganda of the belligerent powers, was incorrect. The primary purpose of Irish censorship was to suppress 'propaganda' that came from *within* Eire and which might compromise the state's neutrality in the eyes of the warring nations, not to prevent the flow of information coming into the country from outside; thus British newspapers continued to be sold in Dublin throughout the war and no attempt was made to jam BBC or German radio broadcasts, both of which could be clearly heard throughout Eire.

The most startling characteristic of the censorship debate, however, was the omission of almost any reference to partition. Only Aiken had touched on the issue in his 1940 memorandum, referring obliquely to 'a definite grievance against the nearest belligerent'. Surely anti-partitionist sentiment counted as propaganda against a belligerent nation? The answer is that it did not. Just as Germany was expected to demonstrate 'a certain consideration' for Eire's close economic and physical ties with Britain, so Britain had to accept that partition was a legitimate cause for complaint in Eire that could not be – and would not be – suppressed during the war. Censorship may have infringed personal liberty to an unacceptable degree in Eire but it ignored the one outstanding issue that remained, in de Valera's eyes, at the centre of Anglo-Irish relations. And it did so, no doubt, because within Eire, the injustice of partition – though not the means to destroy it – was a unifying rather than a divisive issue, a cause which for only two and a half years was superseded by the necessity of national defence. It was also regarded as an *internal* issue, unrelated to the world war except in so far as Eire felt she could identify herself with oppressed or divided nations. If Eire's neutrality was a result of her separation from the six counties of Northern Ireland, as de Valera had so strongly implied in his meetings with British ministers before the war, then it was inevitable that partition would remain a legitimate focus of public discussion. Even in July 1940 when Eire's attention might have been wholly diverted by the threat of foreign invasion, de Valera felt able to send a message to the New York World Fair in which he urged Americans 'to remember that the partition of Ireland is a headline for the unjust use of force everywhere by a strong Power against a weaker'.[65]

There was no reason to be surprised by de Valera's perspectives. His attitude had been the same on 10 May 1940, the very day that Germany invaded the three neutral states of Holland, Belgium and Luxemburg. As news of the attack came in, Sir John Maffey, without instructions from London, took it upon himself to call on de Valera and urge him now to join the Allies. 'It was indeed a fateful moment in the history of his country,' Maffey told the Taoiseach, 'and I trusted that we should find Ireland in her natural place, namely, no longer neutral in the cause of freedom.' Maffey sent his usual eloquent report of the meeting to the Dominions Office although this time a note of extreme irritation, even anger, can be found in his account. De Valera, he wrote, 'at once invoked the old bogey of Partition. If things had worked out according to his plan the nation would have been in a united Ireland and his freedom of action and the spirit of the people would be totally different . . .' As things stood, there was no disguising the fact that adherence to the British cause would create a grave situation. It was no use asking the people in Ireland to fight on behalf of freedom, de Valera said, 'when freedom was denied in a portion of Ireland owing to the influence of an uncompromising minority.' The talk on partition, recorded Maffey, 'ran its normal course and I will not repeat the arguments and counter-arguments for they are stale.' De Valera did not disagree that Britain had shown great generosity in her dealings with the twenty-six counties 'but said "I cannot understand why Mr Chamberlain does not tell Craigavon to fix up his difficulties with us and come in. That would solve the trouble". I said "If the Partition question were solved today would you automatically be our active Ally?" He replied "I feel convinced that that would probably be the consequence".' De Valera added that 'it was far from being his wish to exploit our difficulty to his own advantage', but Maffey complained that:

. . . his view on a grave crisis in world affairs was from too narrow an angle. Here was a maniacal force let loose in the world. It was not a time to talk of Anglo-Irish disputes which in the fullness of time would be peacefully liquidated. I might have come to him today with my French, Belgian and Dutch colleagues. He would know what they would have said. Where did Ireland stand today? Why not send an Irish Brigade to France? Surely the soul of Ireland would be stirred etc., etc., etc.

But we always travelled back to the old prejudice, to Partition, to the bitterness in the hearts of the active and extremist elements. I suggested that with clear leadership the adventurous spirits would respond to a better call. But Mr de Valera held to his narrow view. He seems incapable of courageous or original thought . . .[66]

Maffey suggested that 'the story of German intrigue and Quislingism in neutral countries had a lesson for him' but de Valera replied that if he took any action against the German legation, it would create grave internal difficulties for him. De Valera said that Eire was 'inadequately armed for the proper control of the subversive elements' but that Britain had blocked the sale of arms. Maffey claimed that Britain's own need for arms was now paramount although at the same time 'it was not very attractive to us to send weapons into a country where a German legation has facilities for intrigue.' The conversation did not last long and Maffey felt it had been unsatisfactory. De Valera, he wrote afterwards, was 'a physical and mental expression of the most narrow-minded and bigoted section of the country . . . Mr de Valera is not a strong man and his many critics here know that fact well. Nothing is more characteristic than his tendency to surrender always to the extremist view and to the extremist menace.' Temperamentally, thought Maffey, de Valera had 'a bias that way himself'.[67]

The German invasion of the Low Countries had elicited one sympathetic remark from de Valera. 'People would learn to realise what a German triumph would mean,' he had told Maffey, and two days later, at a Fianna Fail constituency meeting in Galway, de Valera did, uncharacteristically, give public utterance to his feelings on the subject. Perhaps the kinship of small and neutral nations which he had experienced personally at the League of Nations persuaded him to speak out. Here, after all, were two of the small states of which he had once spoken so emotionally, nations which should not become 'the tools of any great power' but which should 'resist with whatever strength they may possess every attempt to force them into a war against their will'. It had done them no good. De Valera told his audience in Galway:

I was at Geneva on many occasions. When I was there, I used to particularly seek out the representatives of small nations because their problems, I thought, were in many respects like our problems . . . the representatives of Belgium and the representatives of The Netherlands were people that I met frequently, because we cooperated not a little with the northern group of nations. Today these two small nations are fighting for their lives, and I think it would be unworthy of this small nation if, on an occasion like this, I did not utter our protest against the cruel wrong which has been done them.[68]

When he read a report of this distinctly un-neutral statement, Ribbentrop instructed Hempel to make an official protest to de Valera but Hempel had already visited F.H. Boland at the Department of External Affairs in Dublin. According to Hempel, Boland told him 'that Sweden and Ireland were the only two countries in Northern Europe to remain neutral and that Mr de Valera wanted to uphold the principle that small countries could refuse to be directly involved in the war.' Boland repeated de Valera's view that the invasion of Holland and Belgium had been a cruel wrong but Hempel claimed that de Valera was taking sides, that 'Germany's view was that taking sides was not permissible in neutral countries and that they should remain silent . . . Holland and Belgium had not adhered strictly to neutrality. And it was not in accordance with strict neutrality that Mr de Valera should have protested.'

When Hempel called on de Valera several days later, Holland and Belgium had already fallen and the British and French armies were retreating towards Dunkirk. According to Hempel, de Valera 'said that he wished, in view of the imminent and threatening danger, to clarify once more his point of view which was directed against any aggressor. If one of the big powers attacked a small power and he thought it was wrong he would say so.' If de Valera had not mentioned the German invasion, he would have been 'misunderstood by the Irish people'; it would have been interpreted as cowardice. Hempel repeated his objections but took the matter no further.[69] 'I had the impression,' he said years later, 'that the Irish Government did not want to have any doubts in Berlin about Irish neutrality. That was quite understandable at that particular time . . . Germany was having the most wonderful successes with her armies and the Irish Government had to be most careful to avoid any misunderstanding with Germany.'[70] But de Valera was evidently fearful that Germany might indeed be supporting Quislings among his own people. Five days after the invasion of the Low Countries, he called Maffey at a late hour and asked to see him. In the light of Holland's experience, Maffey informed the Dominions Office in an overnight telegram, de Valera 'viewed with great concern the prospect of similar contacts being made from Germany with the disaffected elements in Eire by air or otherwise.' As a matter of extreme urgency, de Valera wanted British weapons for his army, especially machine guns. Maffey now sympathised with his request, regarding an arms sale to Eire as 'a move against a common enemy'. There was no talk of partition this time. 'I can hardly overstress the importance of doing all that is possible without delay,' wrote Maffey.[71]

The relationship between the British Representative and the Taoiseach was now under considerable strain as the changing tone of Maffey's reports to London made clear. In his initial meetings, he appeared to draw some encouragement from his personal understanding of de Valera's domestic concerns but as the months went by – and as Britain's own military position became steadily more precarious – his patience turned to contempt; de Valera's concentration on partition, which had seemed natural at the beginning of the war – even if insular and unhelpful to

Britain – looked like a tiresome and callous self-absorption by May of 1940. Yet Maffey could not abandon the hope that de Valera might after all decide to throw in his lot with Britain. Nor was Maffey in any position to forget that within the constraints of his neutrality, de Valera exercised his 'certain consideration' towards Britain with less discretion than the Germans would have wished. In October 1939 he had privately agreed to accept a British naval attaché in Dublin who could travel around Eire and check the efficiency of the coast-watching service. He had held up, at Maffey's request, the series of emergency orders restricting the movements of warships in Irish waters which had been contained in Dulanty's *aide-mémoire*. De Valera allowed the British Admiralty to maintain an armed rescue tug at Cobh. He also specifically accepted the fact that British warships would 'pursue and attack hostile submarines in the territorial waters of Eire' whatever the regulations said to the contrary.* He did not include aircraft in the instructions to Irish coast-watchers. 'Our aircraft,' Maffey had told Eden in October 1939, 'are flying over the headlands of Eire, and even inland, and nothing is being said.'[72]

This official co-operation with Britain often went much deeper. When the Gardai discovered plans for a German–IRA attack on Northern Ireland – the so-called Plan Kathleen – in the home of Mrs Iseult Stuart in County Wicklow in May 1940, the Irish authorities promptly passed on photostats of the documents to MI5 in London who in turn forwarded them to the Royal Ulster Constabulary in Belfast.[73] Colonel Bryan twice visited MI5 operatives in London – in November 1941 and in the following year – and MI5 men came to Dublin to discuss with Bryan the proposals for seizing the German legation's radio transmitter.[74] Quite apart from strictly secret but mutually beneficial Anglo-Irish military co-operation in preparation for a German invasion, General McKenna, the Irish Army's Chief of Staff, regularly visited British officers in Belfast,[75] and twelve Irish officers travelled to Northern Ireland in 1942 to undergo commando training with British troops at Poyntzpass in County Armagh; a British General of Irish extraction wrote out their military passes at the border.[76] Irish assistance to Britain extended to humanitarian aid. In December 1940, the Government in Dublin agreed to look after hundreds of British women and children evacuated from London and south-east England during the Blitz.[77] They included more than two hundred children whose parents had been killed in German air raids.[78] More than two thousand Britons were subsequently evacuated to Eire.[79]†

---

* Warships, however, meant surface craft, not submarines. *H 33* and other British submarines were therefore excluded from this concession; Lieutenant Commander Fell's 'Q' ship would also have been quite unacceptable to de Valera.

† The British Government paid a food and clothing allowance for the refugees but the Irish authorities paid for part of the orphans' lodgings. A rather miserly attempt by Walshe at the Department of External Affairs to get the British to pay for refugees' hospital treatment in Eire was dropped when the request was 'unfavourably received' in London.[80]

Of much greater material value was the collusion between the Irish and British Governments over the Allied air crews whose planes crashed in Eire and who should, under the rules of neutrality, have been interned for the duration. At the start of the war, the Irish were by no means certain of their international obligations towards airmen and sailors of the belligerent powers who crash-landed in Eire or were rescued by Irish vessels. By October 1940, six Germans and one Briton had been imprisoned at the Irish Army's camp at the Curragh in County Kildare and a long report on their conditions was submitted to the Irish Cabinet by the Department of Defence. The German internees were accommodated in furnished bungalows in a cantonment surrounded by barbed wire while the lone Briton lived in the Irish Army's Ceannt Barracks, taking his meals in the officers' mess and exercising under military escort. The Germans were given playing cards and a set of chess and draughts and received a wireless set from Hempel. They were given facilities for gardening and basketball. 'Since it is the military duty of internees to escape, if possible,' the Defence Department's memorandum noted, 'they will not be permitted to leave the camp for the purpose of visiting their diplomatic representatives in Dublin . . . unless they give parole or their diplomatic representatives guarantee they will not escape.' The Germans and the Briton could receive an unlimited number of letters which were censored by the Camp Commandant. Hempel gave a 'field' allowance to the German airmen although the British had yet to decide how they would pay their internee. To prevent bribery of the camp guards, officers could carry with them no more than £3 and other ranks £1. There were, according to the Defence Department, 'no International Conventions specifically governing the treatment of belligerent internees and accordingly it appears open to neutral States . . . to prescribe conditions of internment in whatever manner they think fit.' But no complaints had been received from the British internee and the Germans had 'on several occasions expressed their appreciation of the kindness and consideration accorded to them'.[81] Internment in Eire was going to be an easy-going affair.

A year later, there were thirty-three Allied internees in the Curragh – including nine Canadians, a New Zealander and an American[82] – and the Irish grew increasingly sensitive about their presence. The Government in Dublin feared that Irishmen serving in the RAF might crash-land in Eire; the Department of Defence even undertook a long correspondence with the Irish Cabinet on the need for legislation that would prevent Irish citizens securing the release of sons or husbands from internment by initiating Habeas Corpus proceedings in the Irish courts.[83] The British prisoners were separated from the Germans by only an iron fence and some barbed wire; when German victories in north Africa had been announced on the radio, Allied internees had to listen to a Luftwaffe rendering of '*Deutschland Uber Alles*' but after the victory at El Alamein, the Allied airmen set off fireworks. It was, however, a congenial enough prison, more like a resort than an internment camp,[84] and internees of both sides were allowed to play golf, visit the Curragh races and dine out in Dublin on parole. A Canadian married his Irish girlfriend and even the escape attempts caused little friction. When all but one of the thirty-three internees tried a mass break-out in February 1942, Irish troops around the camp fired blank ammunition and used only wooden batons to force the men back into the prison. A gentleman's agreement with the British authorities meant that none of the Allied prisoners were permitted to break parole. When an American – Pilot Officer Wolfe from Nebraska – did use his parole to travel to Northern Ireland, he was promptly returned to Irish custody by the British.[85] Until 1942, it was not even a technical offence to aid the escape of an internee[86] and two Canadians reached Northern Ireland that year after being sheltered for eleven days by Irish friends. By October 1943, the Allied airmen had been moved away from the Germans and within a year all of them had been freed and permitted to return to Britain. The Germans remained at the Curragh.

It would be simplistic to suggest that this generosity was of a strictly altruistic nature. When de Valera first made his concessions to Maffey, the war was only six weeks old and there was every reason to think that Britain could emerge victorious. In 1940, when the German Army reached the French coast, British aircraft were no longer allowed to fly unhindered over the peninsulas of Eire. In December 1940, for instance, an RAF Hudson – probably from 502 Squadron – was fired on by anti-aircraft gunners at Buncrana in County Donegal, not far from the Treaty port of Lough Swilly, and the guns at Fort Lenan were directed towards the same plane shortly afterwards.[87] The restrictions on belligerent warships in Irish waters were in fact published in September 1940, with a specific list of the ports and anchorages which were forbidden to British and German vessels.[88] Attempts were also made by the authorities to prevent any private collections in Eire on behalf of the Allied forces. In October 1940, the Department of External Affairs objected to the raising of money in Dublin for a British 'Spitfire Fund', claiming that this would endanger Irish neutrality. 'Several private individuals,' said a note from the Department of Justice, 'are known to be collecting for the Fund and an organisation has been set up in Dublin known as the "Dublin Spitfire Circle". It is understood also that weekly collections are being made from the employees of some firms, including the Great Northern Railway Company, Guiness's, and the Swastika Laundry Company.'* Lord Beaverbrook, the British Minister of Aircraft Production, had personally acknowledged the help of the 'Dublin Spitfire Circle' in the London *Daily Express*. Gerald Boland, the Irish Minister for Justice, wanted to instruct

---

* The memorandum added that the collections were 'made by persons holding positions of authority in the firms, and reports have been made to the police that the employees are afraid to refuse to contribute to the collections'.[89]

the Gardai to stop all funds 'for the purchase of armament, equipment or comforts for the armed forces of any other State, but not to take any action against any collection . . . which may be organised to raise funds for the relief of civilian victims of air-raids in Great Britain . . .'[90]

Eire's assistance to Britain was thus of a very fragile kind. That help was given at all was surprising in view of the precise and legalistic nature of de Valera's neutrality. It demonstrated a desire for friendly relations between Eire and Britain but its significance should not be exaggerated. There was a cold, pragmatic quality about Eire's co-operation. Typical of this was the series of negotiations for an Anglo-Irish trade agreement in 1940. Sean Lemass, the Irish Minister for Supplies, and Dr James Ryan, the Minister for Agriculture, travelled to London in April for talks with Eden which were intended to produce a joint agreement on shipping and exports. Eden was anxious to ensure that Eire did not disregard her 1938 obligations on protective tariffs and that safeguards for British exports to Eire would be maintained.[91] Lemass and Ryan first claimed that the prices Britain wished to pay for butter, cheese and bacon were too low and the British then agreed to increase the price by effectively giving a subsidy of £500,000 on fat cattle imports. The proposals had also called for port, transhipment and repair facilities for British merchant vessels in Eire but only in November 1940, when all other issues were apparently resolved, did Eire reject the storage and transhipment arrangements on the grounds that they would impair Irish neutrality.[92] This new obstruction followed the fall of France and Britain's diminished fortunes in the war. Eire now feared that the Luftwaffe would attack her ports if British ships were berthed there; so the extent of Irish co-operation with Britain had been trimmed accordingly and the talks proved a failure. Not that the British were entirely open in their dealings with Eire; they were trying not only to secure a mutually advantageous trade agreement but also to ensure that Eire did not break free of her economic dependence on Britain. In a secret document on the forthcoming discussions sent to the Northern Ireland Government, the British Dominions Office had stated that 'it must be borne in mind that . . . undertakings should be avoided which would further force Eire in the direction of economic self-sufficiency.'[93]

If Eire and Britain adopted self-seeking attitudes towards the trade negotiations, so did Craigavon's Government in Northern Ireland, whose energies were now supposed to be harnessed to the war effort against Germany. On April 30 – the day on which the talks were to begin in London – the Stormont Cabinet decided to try to prevent Eire from 'receiving preferential treatment as compared with Northern Ireland and other parts of the United Kingdom'.[94] This was an understandable desire on the part of the Belfast Government but when John Andrews, the Northern Ireland Minister of Finance, wrote to Sir John Anderson, the British Home Secretary, to explain his Cabinet's views, he expressed himself in somewhat different terms. While he realised that 'the paramount consideration' in any discussions must be the successful conduct of the war, 'Eire is the only portion of the Empire which, by remaining neutral, has not rallied to the aid of the United Kingdom in the present emergency, and yet apparently desires the benefits to be derived from British protection without the restrictions and sacrifices inseparable from the conservation of foreign exchanges and the reduction of imports . . .' Eire had been free to import unlimited quantities of foodstuffs and fertilisers at a time when farmers in Great Britain and Northern Ireland had experienced great difficulty in securing supplies. 'Considerable criticism' had been voiced over the freedom with which tourists could obtain petrol in Eire. Andrews wanted to maintain a price preference for agricultural goods from Northern Ireland and to divert ship-repairing to Londonderry rather than Eire.[95] Anderson could not have expected this attack on Eire nor the demand that the ship-repair scheme should be based in the province. He replied indifferently to Andrews, stating that his points were 'being borne well in mind'.[96]

The British must have suspected that the Northern Ireland Government was trying to sabotage the trade discussions with Eire and a revealing letter from George Scott Robertson, the Permanent Secretary at the Northern Ireland Ministry of Agriculture, suggests that this was indeed the case. Robertson was attending British ministerial briefings before the Anglo-Irish talks opened each day. Writing to Robert Gransden, Craigavon's Personal Private Secretary, on May 6, he claimed that 'our "neutrals" have made very little progress in their negotiations – certainly not on the agricultural side, and I understand they had very long faces on Thursday . . . There was a disposition on Eden's part at the instigation of Maffey . . . to see if they could not give them something to prevent their going back empty handed. Butter was being explored and I had an opportunity of putting in a memo which will I hope stifle that effort.' The new British Minister of Food, Lord Woolton, had 'stood up to Eire like a man and unless he is overruled politically they will not get a single concession on the food side.' The Irish had not once mentioned partition, Robertson wrote, and British ministers 'kept stressing how pleasant Eire Ministers had been. The wine had I know been flowing and not only have Ministers entertained and been entertained but Eire has been entertaining all the British officials on a pretty lavish and all embracing scale.'[97] The letter was doubly cynical for while Robertson seemed almost gleefully happy at the prospect of a breakdown in the British trade talks with Eire, he ignored the fact that a Northern Ireland delegation had already been negotiating directly with Ryan in Dublin for flax for the Belfast linen industry, which was now cut off from its traditional source of supply in the Baltic states. In the course of these Dublin talks, Ryan had shown 'sympathetic understanding' of Northern Ireland's industrial problems.[98]

But there was nothing unique about Robertson's desire to damage Anglo-Irish relations. The fear that Eire might one day succeed in undermining the province's constitutional relationship with Britain coloured the attitudes of ministers in every Northern Ireland Government department. If Craigavon's Cabinet was not seeking parity with Britain – which it usually was – then it sought preference over Eire, and these preoccupations had not diminished on the outbreak of war. On the contrary, they spread hydra-like, affecting the most humble of governmental duties. Even the advent of censorship in Britain was greeted at Stormont with the observation that it had 'removed from the United Kingdom Press the insidious anti-Ulster propaganda which has been the subject of much discussion locally in recent months'.[99] When the Northern Ireland Government decided to appoint a publicity officer to the Cabinet Secretariat in November 1939, Gransden thought the new man's task should include the writing of newspaper articles about the province's industry and war effort. But he added that 'such articles should bring home to their readers in an unobtrusive, though none the less effective, manner the position that Northern Ireland occupies as part of the United Kingdom.' In London, Major General Sir James Cooke-Collis, the Ulster agent, worked now through the British Ministry of Information; but when he explained his new duties to John Andrews in November, he described how he was often 'correcting mistakes' about Northern Ireland's constitutional position. 'If evidence of pro-Eire propaganda activities is required,' he wrote, 'we need only point to the fact of the existence in Fleet Street of an Irish "news" agency run by James Whelan, and of the appointment of the Hon. Frank Pakenham as unpaid "Irish" propagandist in the Ministry of Information. Fortunately Pakenham is now no longer in the Ministry.' Cooke-Collis claimed that he countered 'anti-Ulster propaganda' by 'pushing forward the positive side of Ulster's recruiting and contribution to the general United Kingdom resources'.[100]

At that particular moment, however, Northern Ireland's recruiting record was not something that the Stormont Cabinet would have wanted to boast about too freely. In the spring of 1939, Chamberlain had refused Craigavon's request to introduce conscription in the province and it was left to the Northern Ireland Prime Minister to prove that his people were prepared to make an equal sacrifice in the defence of the realm. After the first two months of the war, it did not seem that they were. In October 1939, 2500 men in the province volunteered but after that, the monthly intake fell below one thousand.[101] This was despite an unemployment figure which reached an average of 19.4 per cent in 1940,[102] proving that the manpower of the six counties had not been absorbed by Craigavon's war production. It was claimed that Northern Ireland was only 'half in the war'[103] and it was difficult to dispute such an assertion. 'Some people believed it just hadn't happened, or that it would all be over in a few months,' Brooke wrote later. 'Others thought that, anyway, wars were for soldiers on distant battlefields and, as in the First War, the home population would be little affected at first. There was even a body of opinion at

Stormont, who were outraged at the idea that Northern Ireland should have food rationing . . .'[104] Craigavon's biographer spoke of 'the shallow optimism, amounting to apathy, of the working people who, though they were ready enough to cheer the Government's critics, acted as if they were certain that the Germans could do *them* no harm, and would not, therefore, participate adequately in their own protection.'[105]

The Lord Mayor of Belfast condemned the city's air-raid precautions as 'chaotic' and when the Germans picked up this information and broadcast it over Berlin Radio, Cooke-Collis assumed it must have been Hempel's doing. He wanted Craigavon to complain about this to the British Government. At a meeting with A.P. Waterfield, the Deputy Director General of the Ministry of Information in London, Cooke-Collis claimed 'that there seemed to be nothing to prevent the German Minister in Dublin or any of his representatives from going to Belfast and there getting information about United Kingdom activities. There was no closed frontier between the United Kingdom and the neutral country of Eire. There was no doubt that the German Minister had . . . his agents in Northern Ireland who could, for example, report to him movements of shipping in Belfast Lough and around the Northern Ireland coasts.'[106] Over the telephone, Cooke-Collis also urged Gransden to write a letter about the open border to Lord Macmillan, the British Minister of Information, who would bring it before Chamberlain's Cabinet. 'There is a strict censorship in Eire,' Cooke-Collis concluded over the phone, 'but you know what that means! We have a frontier in Northern Ireland contiguous with a neutral country and the present state of affairs cannot go on. Your letter to Lord Macmillan might state that you feel it is your duty to inform the British Government of what is going on.' Waterfield took the matter up with Dulanty who 'promised to do everything possible to prevent leakage of information'.[107]

The Northern Ireland Government had already taken its customary and energetic action against the IRA. On the first night of the war, Dawson Bates ordered the internment without trial of forty-five alleged members of the IRA[108] although there was far more lawlessness of a non-political kind along the border where, in the words of an RUC dispatch, 'a condition of affairs arose which shattered all preconceived ideas of smuggling.' As the RUC Inspector General Charles Wickham reported, 'ordinary consumers, speculators and syndicates commenced to export all classes of goods, including foodstuffs to Eire, and there was a danger that Northern Ireland would be denuded of much needed supplies which, in turn, would have a damaging effect on the war effort.' It took new legislation and several gun battles with the RUC before the smuggling was reduced.[109]

The IRA carried out a few desultory attacks in Northern Ireland in the first year of the war, bombing thirteen shops in Belfast and country towns and raiding a Royal Irish Fusiliers store at Ballykinlar in County Down.[110]

In April 1940, a report by a British Army regiment stationed in Northern Ireland said that the IRA could 'always rely on local assistance' and had found 'good places of refuge' in the Sperrin and Mourne Mountains, but it acknowledged that 'our sources of information about their intentions are few.'[111] Dawson Bates obviously believed he had better intelligence and in the following month he interned a further seventy-six suspected IRA men.[112] In July 1940, the IRA set fire to a large food depot in Belfast, leading a British Government intelligence officer to conclude that 'the IRA are more "vicious" in Northern Ireland than they are in Eire.'[113] Dawson Bates was meanwhile planning another seven hundred arrests and a prison ship was being sent from Britain to accommodate the latest internees.[114]

Craigavon could afford to take all this in his stride. The neutrality of Eire had provided him with proof to show Britain that Northern Ireland was loyal to the Crown and – more to the point – that her loyalty was likely to be of use to the Crown. He must have realised at an early stage that Londonderry – the westernmost port in the British Isles available to the Royal Navy – could soon become a strategic naval base. In February 1940 he had broadcast to the British people over the BBC. A photograph was taken of Craigavon as he sat in the radio studio, his greying, distinguished head turned slightly away, his large, dark eyes staring distrustfully at the camera. 'We are King's men,' he told his listeners, 'and we shall be with you to the end.'[115] In April, he gave an interview to a reporter from the London *Evening Standard* who asked him if the people of Northern Ireland were still loyal. 'You couldn't move them,' he replied. 'Union with Eire was always impossible. We consider ourselves part of the British Empire. They don't. How *can* there be union? For twenty years we have been misunderstood and criticised all over the world. Now the world can see the reason for our stand.'[116]

But still more than a third of his people did not accept this stand, and even the formation in May 1940 of the British Local Defence Volunteers – the Home Guard – gained a sectarian colour when it was translated into Northern Ireland. Craigavon told his Cabinet that 'there were grave objections . . . to the establishment here of a local Volunteer Defence Corps on the basis adopted in Britain' and suggested that the Ulster 'B' Special Constabulary was 'admirably suited for this work'.[117] The 'grave objections', of course, were the opportunities that a British-style Home Guard affiliated to the Army might have afforded republicans to join the force and carry arms. Catholics were thereby effectively excluded. It was agreed in Cabinet five days later that the 'B' Specials – the descendants of the Protestant Ulster Volunteer Force which Brooke had helped to revive in 1920 – would form 'a nucleus of the new Force'.[118] On May 23, Craigavon crossed to London to see his old acquaintance and new Prime Minister, Winston Churchill.

Churchill's appointment had been popular among Northern Ireland Unionists. 'Mr Churchill,' wrote Spender in his diary, 'is now a strong supporter of Northern Ireland and will, I think, resent anything in the nature of unpatriotic action in Southern Ireland or elsewhere more bitterly than his predecessor. On the other hand, the Labour influence is, of course, very amenable to Free State propaganda . . ."[119] Churchill was certainly conscious of Eire's military vulnerability. 'We have many reports of possible German parachute or airborne descents in Ireland,' he told Roosevelt in a message on May 15. 'The visit of a United States squadron to Irish ports, which might well be prolonged, would be invaluable.'[120] There is nothing to suggest that the British Prime Minister's meeting with Craigavon was anything but friendly and it is unlikely that Churchill – who confided to Richard Pim after Dunkirk that the 'B' Specials were the only properly armed and disciplined force left in the United Kingdom[121] – raised any objections to Northern Ireland's decidedly Protestant version of the Home Guard. Craigavon did suggest once more the introduction of conscription and Churchill rejected it.[122] On his return to Belfast, Craigavon told his Cabinet that the British Government recognised 'the voluntary effort which has been made in Ulster to keep the various Ulster units [of the Army] up to strength' and hoped shortly to inaugurate a recruiting campaign in the province. The British authorities had entrusted Craigavon's Government with the duty of raising a local defence corps.[123]

At least one British Cabinet minister, however, viewed Northern Ireland upon a wider horizon. The day after Craigavon left London, Halifax, the Foreign Secretary, wrote a personal note to Churchill on a matter of some urgency:

> My dear Winston,
> I do not know whether you have had a moment in which to give any further thought to the possibilities of securing any improvement in Eire on the political side by any *démarche* in the direction of Northern Ireland.
>
> I see that James Craig has just been over, and the whole business has been very much put forward in my thought by a report I was reading last night from the Joint Intelligence Sub-Committee on Eire, which will no doubt be now receiving consideration from the Chiefs of Staff and then I suppose coming forward to the Cabinet. The whole matter would seem to be one of the utmost urgency, and I doubt whether we shall make any effective progress with it unless we can make some really big change in the political background.
>
> I would therefore press upon your attention the importance of your placing yourself in a position, with the help of the Dominions Office and the Home Office, to take any action in this direction that may seem to offer even a faint hope of result.[124]

Just what this 'action' was to be, Craigavon would soon find out.

Chapter 6

An Offer of Unity and the Rule of 'Equal Holds'

> The present was the best opportunity that had yet offered itself of a union of the whole of Ireland being achieved. Such an opportunity might never return. If the North and the South could be united on the basis of their being joined together in the prosecution of a war in defence of the freedom of the whole of Ireland against the Nazi attack, then that union would not be broken afterwards. But if the leaders of Eire now stayed out of the war, and perhaps contributed to German strength by doing so, whilst the people of Northern Ireland and of the United Kingdom were joined in the supreme struggle against the Nazis, then none of us in Britain would be very concerned to create a united Ireland afterwards.
>
> Malcolm MacDonald *27 June 1940*

At any other time, Halifax's note might have provoked Churchill's disdain but the British War Cabinet was now so alarmed by the disastrous events on the Continent that the security of Ireland – the back door of Britain's defence and perhaps Hitler's next neutral target – began to dominate proceedings at Downing Street. On the day Craigavon visited London, the British Army was abandoning Boulogne under shellfire and the decision was taken to evacuate the encircled British Expeditionary Force from Dunkirk. German tanks had already passed Abbeville and now surrounded Calais. On May 15, the Cabinet had considered the possibility that German sympathisers – Fifth Columnists – might co-operate in a German invasion of Britain. On Churchill's instructions, Sir John Anderson, the Home Secretary, produced a memorandum on this apparent danger two days later. He and his colleagues spoke of 'the possibility of "Fifth Column" activities in Eire' and observed that there were 'unconfirmed reports that Germans are finding their way there by sea through ports on the West Coast of Ireland'. Anderson was worried that 'it might well be easier for the enemy to arrange for "Fifth Column" co-operation in Eire in the event of his intending to establish a footing there . . .'[1] De

Valera meanwhile followed up his late night meeting with Maffey and his request for British arms on May 16, by asking Britain to come to Eire's assistance if she was attacked by Germany.

Thus shortly after Craigavon left Downing Street on May 23, an unprecedented and highly secret meeting began at the Dominions Office less than half a mile away. Present at these discussions were the Secretary to the Irish Department of External Affairs, the Chief of Staff of the Irish Army's G2 intelligence service and a clutch of senior Dominions Office civil servants and British army, naval and air force officers. Sir Eric Machtig, the Permanent Under-Secretary of the Dominions Office, introduced Joseph Walshe and Colonel Liam Archer of G2 to the British officers* and referred to several messages which had been received from de Valera. Machtig understood that 'Eire would fight if attacked by Germany and would call in the assistance of the United Kingdom the moment it became necessary' but the political situation in Eire 'was such that there could be no question of the Eire Government inviting in United Kingdom Troops before an actual German descent, and before fighting between the German and Eire forces had begun.'[2] It was upon this regimen that the British were asked to help de Valera and it did not seem satisfactory to Churchill's War Cabinet.

On May 29, as the Royal Navy were evacuating British and French troops from the beaches of Dunkirk, Major General Sir Hastings Ismay, now Secretary to the War Cabinet, sent Churchill the minutes of this and subsequent secret meetings together with a letter which reported that 'information from secret sources points to the fact that the Germans have concerted detailed plans with the IRA and that everything is now ready for an immediate descent upon the country'.[3] A handwritten note in the margin of this letter observed that Chamberlain, the Lord President, would be looking at the matter 'in its political aspect'.[4] Next day, the Chiefs of Staff Committee reported to the War Cabinet that while military support should be given to Eire 'immediately it is called for', the arrangement would not secure Eire against the danger which threatened her. 'Until she abandons her attitude of neutrality she cannot fully safeguard herself against danger of enemy activities within her territory, nor obtain the full co-operation of our forces to anticipate and resist attack. Unless this security can be achieved, Eire will remain a serious weakness in the defence of these Islands.'[5] On June 3, the newly-formed Invasion Warning Sub-Committee at the Admiralty heard that 'German soldiers in civilian clothes are embarking at Naples for Spain, whence they will be sent from Cadiz for an attack on Ireland.' The Committee noted that 'young German male tourists' had been arriving in Galicia, some carrying uniforms with them.[6] This preposterous story was given some credence in

* It would be interesting to know exactly *how* Machtig introduced Walshe. The British minutes of the meeting describe Walshe as 'Minister for External Affairs' rather than Secretary to the Department, a serious error not least because de Valera was the Minister.

London. When Craigavon returned to the capital on June 5 – t
Dunkirk fell – the British Government was in no mood to let tl
isms of Northern Ireland interfere with the country's national d
was asked by Chamberlain 'to put forward some proposal whicl
helpful in inducing the Eire Government to take more effective
for the defence of the country against a German invasion'.[7]

It seems, however, to have been Tegart's whispering gallery of Irish
rumour that finally forced Chamberlain's hand. On June 12, the day after
Tegart had poured forth his warnings about Eire's 2000 Gauleiters,
Chamberlain wrote to Churchill to say that he was 'convinced' that
Tegart's picture was generally accurate and that he and Eden felt the only
course left was to urge de Valera and Craigavon to come to London as soon
as possible for a conference with himself and Caldecote.* 'At this conference,' he wrote, 'we should place the facts plainly before them and
endeavour to secure an adequate measure of co-operation in defence
preparations.'[9] Chamberlain had anyway become impatient at Craigavon's failure to respond to his request of June 5. 'I have been expecting to
hear from you since I saw you on Wednesday last,' he told the Northern
Ireland Prime Minister in a letter on June 12, '. . . however, I have not
received any communication from you.' In the past week, Chamberlain
wrote, fresh information had reached him which indicated that 'the German plans are all completed and only await the word to be put into
operation, when they would probably be carried out with lightning rapid-
ity and the assistance of considerable armed forces of the IRA.' It was clear
that 'the fullest cooperation' would be necessary between Eire and Northern Ireland, and Chamberlain wanted Craigavon to be present at his
meeting with de Valera.[10] Chamberlain's letter of invitation to de Valera,
sent the same day, was couched in slightly warmer tones and he was less
specific about the supposed German invasion plans. 'I have lately received
additional information of such a character as to cause me the most serious
anxiety,' he wrote, 'and I have come to the conclusion that the time has
arrived when a personal consultation is the only satisfactory way of dealing
with the situation.'[11]

Craigavon replied two days later, upset at the impatient note in Chamberlain's letter and perhaps suspicious that it foreshadowed some unpleasant suggestions from the British Government. 'I am *always* at your
disposal to cross at short notice,' he told Chamberlain. But his colleagues
were behind him 'in advising that harm rather than good would result
from any meeting between De Valera and myself until two vital points are
cleared up . . .' The British Government, he wrote, should first announce
to the public 'that De Valera has determined to drop neutrality and to
throw his weight with Great Britain and Northern Ireland' and,

---

* Churchill was not, it seems, prepared to meet de Valera himself. De Valera's biographers
suggest that 'perhaps it was felt that such a meeting could end explosively.'[8]

secondly, that de Valera had agreed that any conversation would be held 'putting aside all questions of a constitutional nature . . .' In fact, Craigavon had no right to stipulate to the Imperial Government the terms upon which it might discuss Britain's security with a Commonwealth state; indeed, from Craigavon's letter one might have been forgiven for thinking that it was Eire rather than Germany which was threatening to invade Britain. 'I have,' he told Chamberlain, 'long anticipated the serious situation which has arisen and have taken strong steps to safeguard this side of the Border.' He went on to enumerate Northern Ireland's defensive manpower – 3000 RUC men, 12,000 'B' Specials and a newly-enrolled 12,000 in the Ulster Defence Volunteers (the Home Guard) – and remarked that 'if De Valera takes similar steps with his Army and Civic Guards in defence of Eire against Germany and Italy there should be an effective instrument in both North and South for the protection of the territory against invasion.'[12] If Craigavon's reply was unhelpful, de Valera's was even more so. He thought that a visit to London would endanger Irish neutrality.[13] De Valera, Chamberlain told Craigavon, 'felt great difficulty in accepting the suggestion of a conference here and we are proceeding on another plan. Malcolm MacDonald is crossing to Ireland today to see De Valera and to do all he can to impress upon him the magnitude of the dangers that threaten.'[14] Craigavon could now do no more than await the outcome of this new initiative by the 'Lossiemouth sentimentalist' whom he had met in London two years before.

MacDonald was now Minister of Health in Churchill's wartime coalition Government although he considered his new ministerial position to be a tactical political measure on the Prime Minister's part rather than the result of any personal admiration Churchill might have felt towards him. 'A lot of Labour people were in his new Government,' MacDonald recalled years later, 'and Churchill probably thought it would help to maintain unity if a National Labour minister was kept on.'[15] MacDonald was being polite. According to Sir Alexander Cadogan, the Permanent Under-Secretary at the Foreign Office, Churchill regarded MacDonald 'as rat-poison on account of his connexion with [the] Eire ports'.[16]* But he

---

* MacDonald agreed that Churchill thought he was 'completely wrong' in ceding the Treaty harbours although his personal relationship with Churchill was not necessarily a hostile one. MacDonald recalled for the author how Churchill – a strong Zionist supporter – had angrily criticised him in 1938 for preventing Jewish immigration to Palestine. 'We had a terrific argument in the House of Commons and when we met in the Division Lobby afterwards, Churchill accused me of being pro-Arab. He said that Arabs were savages and that they ate nothing but camel dung. I could see that it was no good trying to persuade him to change his views. So I suddenly told him that I wished I had a son. He asked me why, and I said I was reading a book called *My Early Life* by Winston Churchill and that I would want any son of mine to live that life. At this point, tears appeared in Churchill's eyes and he put his arms around me, saying "Malcolm, Malcolm". Next day a package arrived for me from Churchill containing a signed copy of his latest volume of the life of Marlborough.'[17]

was certainly the most suitable candidate for the unenviable task of persuading de Valera to throw his neutrality aside, to invite British troops into Eire before the outbreak of hostilities and to permit the Royal Navy to return to the harbours on the south and west coasts of Ireland. The mutual friendship and admiration between MacDonald and de Valera had been largely responsible for the British evacuation of Cobh, Berehaven and Lough Swilly; and now the new Lord President, Chamberlain – who as Prime Minister had signed the agreement to hand over the Treaty ports – was dispatching MacDonald to Dublin. Churchill, who had condemned the surrender of the harbours with such rancour two years earlier, must have obtained some vexed satisfaction as he watched the 'appeasers' trying to regain what they had lost in their 'act of faith' in 1938.

MacDonald arrived at de Valera's office in the centre of Dublin on the evening of June 17 and the two men greeted each other warmly. They talked about the news from France – the Germans had entered Paris three days previously – but MacDonald noticed that this was not quite the same man whom he knew before the war. 'He was in one way the old de Valera,' he wrote in the first of his lengthy dispatches to the British War Cabinet. 'His mind is still set in the same hard, confined mould as of yore. But in another way he appeared to have changed. He made no long speeches; the whole procedure was much more in the nature of a sustained conversation between two people than used sometimes to be the case. He seemed depressed and tired, and I felt that he had neither the mental nor the physical vigour that he possessed two years ago.'

MacDonald embarked on a treatise about the morality of the war and the danger in which Ireland now found herself. De Valera must have been used to these arguments from Maffey but he apparently heard MacDonald out in silence. The war against Germany, MacDonald said, was a struggle in defence of the freedom of every European nation, great or small. Eire's freedom could not be exempted. A German invasion of Ireland might even precede an invasion of Britain. Documents that had been discovered on members of the IRA indicated that there was a plan for the invasion of Ireland; the experiences of Denmark, Norway, Holland and Belgium showed that the invasion of neutral countries was an accepted weapon for Germany. The secret talks between British and Irish officials in London had produced a plan for British troops to come down from Northern Ireland to help Eire resist an invader but they might arrive too late. Eire might be effectively overpowered, Dublin captured and an IRA government established within a few hours. The present plan did not go far enough. The wisest course for Eire, said MacDonald, 'would be the immediate abandonment of neutrality, and a joining with us in resistance to Germany so that from this moment onwards co-operation could be complete and we could put whatever naval and military forces were required at his disposal . . . We did not give this advice simply because it would help us; indeed, we gave it principally in the interests of Eire itself

. . .' MacDonald must have realised that this was less than the truth; in her greatest moment of peril since Napoleon planned an invasion across the Channel, Britain was not offering her troops to Eire for de Valera's benefit. MacDonald assumed that de Valera would not abandon neutrality but asked all the same whether it was possible 'for his Government, with the support of the Opposition, to invite our ships now to use the Irish ports, and our soldiers to come down and guard strategic points . . .'

De Valera 'emphatically rejected' any possibility of Eire abandoning her neutrality. He had already considered the idea of inviting the British into Eire before hostilities. 'But he was inclined to the view that the Germans would not attack Eire. They would invade Ulster, probably acting in areas where there was a Nationalist majority. In that case they would try to make out that they had come to end partition in Ireland.' MacDonald did not accept this. Germany did not commit aggression by halves, he said, and 'she would be anxious to clean up the business in Ireland quickly.' De Valera agreed that this was possible but said that he had received few arms from Britain and none from America with which Eire could be defended. He had hoped that by now he would have 50,000 well armed soldiers but he estimated he had only half that figure. His forces were inadequately prepared. 'Nevertheless, they would resist a German invasion with all their strength. He thought that his men would fight magnificently. The Germans would not find things easy, for the Irish were very skilful at guerilla warfare; they were very good hedge fighters and would fight the invader from hedge to hedge.' MacDonald, perhaps stunned by de Valera's lyrical approach to modern warfare, gently remarked that such tactics would be of no use against German tanks. It was essential that the Royal Navy should have the use of the ports if an invasion was to be strangled at birth before tanks could land.

If there had been a United Ireland, said de Valera, he 'might have been able to invite us in now. He wished that such a political change had been accomplished before the war. A United Ireland would have been a great strength to us. It is true that the country would (if he had had his way) have remained neutral at the outset of the war, but by now it might have been a belligerent . . .' But he had to reckon with public opinion in Eire and 'many of his supporters were inclined to say that Ireland had already been invaded, by the British in the North.' De Valera was ready to go as far as he could in co-operation with Britain at present, short of publicly compromising the country's neutrality. But MacDonald argued that the Irish should realise that if they waited for a German attack before calling in Britain, then British help would come too late. De Valera said 'that his people did not realise this. They knew too little of what had happened in the other small neutral countries. Their information service was not good. Moreover, as many Irishmen actually thought that the Germans would make them free. Prejudice against Britain was still strong, it would still take a long time to remove such an old sentiment.'

MacDonald then produced an idea that Chamberlain had proposed but which might have originated with Churchill. Supposing, he said:

> . . . that we were to establish a joint Defence Council, on which representatives of the North and of the South would sit and consult and take decisions together, that would be the first time for many years that any union between the Six Counties and the Twenty-Six Counties had been expressed. It might be only a first step to be followed by others. If the habit of co-operation on matters of common concern were once established, it would be difficult afterwards to break it down. We would be prepared to establish a Joint Defence Council for the whole of Ireland straight away.

This was the first reference that MacDonald had made to any kind of 'union' between Northern Ireland and Eire, and it was intended to appeal to de Valera. But it was disregarded. His supporters, de Valera said, 'would regard the creation of such a piece of machinery between neutral Eire and belligerent Ulster as itself prejudicing the former's neutrality. They would think it a provocation to Germany.' De Valera thought that the wisest step Britain could take 'would be to make an immediate announcement that Ireland was not only one country united for the purposes of defence, but united also henceforth for the whole business of government'. MacDonald said that such an announcement would be impossible. 'A great majority of Ulstermen would object strongly,' he said. 'At the moment when we expected them to put up the firmest possible resistance to an invader, we should be announcing a policy which was deeply offensive to their strongest feelings. It would take the heart out of their resistance.' It seemed to MacDonald that:

> . . . the best chance of Ireland eventually becoming united would be if the 26 Counties came fully into the war. Both parts of Ireland would then be fighting side by side; their union would be sealed by comradeship in arms. It would be very difficult to bring that unity to a sudden end at the close of the war. I knew the temper of my generation in British politics. We should not give any encouragement after the war to the revival of old, barren controversies.

But, said MacDonald, if those who had spoken so much about liberty shrank from liberty's defence in its supreme hour of danger while Ulster fought fully for that defence, 'then the differences between the 26 and the 6 Counties would certainly be aggravated and enlarged, and we politicians at Westminster who had gone through the fight would never agree to handing Ulster over to Eire against the former's will.'

MacDonald returned to Eire's military preparations against invasion. Would she invite troops from nations 'other than those of the old British enemy' to enter the country now – could French, Polish or Dominion troops be stationed in Eire? De Valera refused. He agreed that Hitler would try to defeat Britain at the earliest moment but he also 'asked

165

whether there was any prospect of our settling this business by negotiating peace. Hitler had always said that he wanted us to remain in possession of our Empire. Would we on this basis agree to his having a predominant role in Eastern Europe?'

Here was the old de Valera of the League of Nations who had supported Chamberlain's appeasement of Hitler. But now he was out of step with the times and MacDonald attempted to show him that this was the case. 'We should regard a Europe under Hitler's domination as intolerable,' said MacDonald. 'There would be no freedom for anyone on the Continent, and there would be no security for our two islands. Hitler's word could not be trusted.' MacDonald tried to impress de Valera with the potential strength of British resistance to Hitler. Dunkirk, he said, had proved that 'in a fairly confined space of sky our Air Force already had the mastery'. British production of aircraft had doubled in recent weeks and was now overhauling Germany's numerical superiority. American supplies would shortly be arriving in Britain. The Nazi regime might crack when the occupied nations resisted famine and oppression. British air raids on Germany had been extremely damaging to Germany's oil supplies. RAF fighters 'would do battle with the maximum of efficiency over our Island.'

De Valera listened to all this although he knew as well as MacDonald how desperate Britain's position had become. Dunkirk had not demonstrated any particular skill on the part of the RAF; on the contrary, it had proved the failure of British arms on the Continent and represented a crushing defeat for the United Kingdom. MacDonald's optimistic talk of increased aircraft production and German disaffection meant little when Great Britain was herself preparing for a German invasion. The fact that MacDonald's confidence in victory eventually proved well-founded – that the RAF did three months later 'do battle with the maximum of efficiency' over Britain – could scarcely have inspired de Valera then.

He did not attempt to contradict MacDonald. He merely asked for any weapons the British still had to spare. 'He wanted anti-tank guns and machine guns, rifles and ammunition,' wrote MacDonald. 'Could we not let him have more of these? He felt that Dublin was very vulnerable to attack by tanks . . . He would like to have a ring of anti-tank guns around the city.' De Valera asked for immediate help if the Germans landed in Eire. MacDonald replied that Britain needed all the weapons she could produce for a long time to come and had 'no inclination to send over equipment to Eire only to have it lost to the enemy'. Thus MacDonald reiterated to de Valera a now familiar and circular argument: that Eire needed prior British military support to counter a German invasion because she was too weak to defend herself – but that British weapons could not be given to Eire to rectify this since she would lose them to the Germans without British assistance. 'I could assure him,' wrote MacDonald, 'that we should not hesitate a moment in sending our forces to help. But he could hardly rely on our Air Force to protect him in Dublin.

We could not bomb Dublin without killing Irish civilians. I assumed that he did not want us to do that.' De Valera asked again for arms, promised that his people would resist a German invasion 'with all their might' and that he would then – and only then – 'take action against the German nationals who might help the enemy from within.'[18]

The meeting ended at midnight after three and a half hours. Mac-Donald did not seem surprised that de Valera had eschewed the idea of a joint defence council with Northern Ireland although de Valera himself must have sensed that the British might – given the extremity of their peril – offer something more tangible. Indeed, when MacDonald presented his report to the War Cabinet in London on June 20, British ministers were in a state of great emotion over the collapse of France. Chamberlain talked about the possibility of using force to seize the Irish Treaty ports and the Cabinet discussed a possible British declaration in favour of a united Ireland as a bait to bring Eire into the war. It was the first time that such a suggestion had even been considered by a British Government in three decades. Chamberlain argued that Craigavon would have to be approached and 'told that the interests of Northern Ireland could not be allowed to stand against the vital interests of the British Empire.'[19] Cadogan confided to his diary that this 'looked like coercion of N. Ireland'.[20] A curious reversal of roles was now apparent. Chamberlain, who had previously opposed the use of force against Eire, was now its chief proponent, while Churchill – whose belligerence towards 'Eirish neutrality' was well known to the Cabinet – tried to moderate the discussion. Perhaps he sensed the full implications for Northern Ireland. He made a 'passionate speech'[21] about 'the loyal province of Ulster' and suggested, rather surprisingly in view of all that had gone before, that the Germans should after all be allowed to make the first move against Eire and that the threat was anyway not as great as had been presented.[22] The idea of offering de Valera some kind of pledge of Irish unity – thought not yet formulated in any detail – seems to have come from Chamberlain although MacDonald recalled long after the war that it had been 'a definite proposal of Churchill'.[23]

MacDonald returned to Dublin on June 21. It was an inauspicious day. That afternoon, Hitler summoned the representatives of the French Government to sign an armistice at Compiègne. MacDonald had to tell de Valera that in view of the British Army's needs, it would be difficult to give him Bren guns, anti-tank guns and rifles, 'the very things of which we were short as a result of our losses in Belgium and France'. Britain felt, he said, that the danger of a quick success for a comparatively small invading force in Ireland was so real that she could not contemplate giving valuable equipment to de Valera. MacDonald asked again for the use of the ports and the conversation described the same weary circumference that it had done before. De Valera warned that the IRA would snipe at uninvited British troops in Eire but that his soldiers were 'good fighters' if only they had the arms to defend their country. The great majority of people in Eire wanted 'very friendly relations' with Britain. De Valera acknowledged that Britain had carried out her side of the 1938 Agreement 'in the letter and the spirit'. If only the question of partition had been settled then, 'there might have been an alliance between the two countries by now.' The Irish, said de Valera, were largely dependent upon Great Britain. 'This would be the case whether Britain won or lost the war. The destiny of Ireland must be closely linked with that of Britain. It was unthinkable that, so long as Britain did not interfere with Irish freedom, Ireland should give the slightest assistance to Britain's enemies.'

It was at this point that MacDonald, following his Cabinet's instructions, raised once more the question of joint defence, this time adding a more piquant political flavour to the proposal:

> The Prime Minister himself, as well as Mr Chamberlain and the others, had said that we should do nothing to discourage and everything that we could to encourage the unity of Ireland, so long as there was no coercion. The establishment of unity in war would almost certainly lead to the continuance of unity in peace. I therefore urged him to consider most seriously that by entering upon the war now he would not only be taking the most effective action in defence of the threatened freedom of Eire, but also the most effective action in the direction of union with the rest of Ireland.[24]

De Valera seemed pointedly to ignore this new line of approach. He did not share MacDonald's view that the Germans would invade Ireland. Presumably, he said – and here there was no gainsaying Eire's reliance upon Britain – 'the German ships and aircraft carrying troops would be subject to interference from our forces all the way.' MacDonald said that the odds were in favour of a German invasion and then asked de Valera 'whether there were any circumstances under which he would be prepared now, before a German invasion started, to invite our ships into his ports and our soldiers and aeroplanes into his territory, and to take vigorous action against the Fifth Column in his own country.' There then followed a long and cautious discussion of three options for a united Ireland, two of them from MacDonald and the other from de Valera. MacDonald stressed that his ideas were only exploratory; the British Government wished to have a clear picture of what was in de Valera's mind but MacDonald was making no formal proposals.

Nevertheless, it was to be the beginning of an historic dialogue between the British and Irish Governments that held out – in however fragile a form – the possibility of a final British withdrawal from Ireland after hundreds of years of repression and settlement. Had these discussions reached any kind of fruition, the history of Britain and Ireland in the second half of the twentieth century would have been changed irrevocably. Every word of MacDonald's initial and subsequent suggestions for the unity of Ireland – of such dark significance today – was underlined in his typewritten official report to the War Cabinet. His first alternative was:

> That there should be a declaration of a United Ireland in principle, the constitutional and other practical details of the Union to be worked out in due course; Ulster to remain a belligerent, Eire to remain neutral at any rate for the time being; if both parties desired it, a Joint Defence Council to be set up at once; at the same time, in order to secure Eire's neutrality against violation by Germany, British naval ships to be allowed into Eire ports, British troops and aeroplanes to be stationed at certain agreed points in the territory, the British Government to provide additional equipment for Eire's forces, and the Eire Government to take effective action against the Fifth Column.

De Valera rejected the suggestion. His people would regard the admission of British forces before a German invasion as an abandonment of strict neutrality, and national unity in the face of the German threat would be broken. There would be 'unfortunate skirmishes' between the Irish and the British. De Valera then proposed:

> That Eire and Ulster should be merged in a United Ireland, which should at once become neutral; its neutrality to be guaranteed by Great Britain and the United States of America; since Britain was a belligerent, its military and naval forces should not take any active part in guaranteeing that neutrality, but American ships should come into the Irish ports, and perhaps American troops into Ireland, to effect this guarantee.

De Valera thought that some of his colleagues might be critical of this proposal – the possibility that American ships and troops could protect Ireland's neutrality was his own idea – but that the only way in which mutual difficulties could be overcome would be by the establishment of a neutral United Ireland. This would consolidate national unity in Ireland and the majority in Ulster 'would only be a tiny minority of the whole population of the country'. It would kill the IRA organisation 'stone dead' and all of Ireland would be denied to Germany. The American guarantee would be an effective deterrent to would-be aggressors.

MacDonald thought this 'entirely impracticable'. There was, he said, no prospect that the people of Ulster would agree to desert Great Britain at the moment when her situation was more perilous than it had been for a century. The majority of the people in the North would feel 'deeply incensed' and the new state would be launched on its career under the worst possible circumstances. Britain could not now contemplate a neutral Ulster; vital war production was being carried on there. An American guarantee would be worthless without the presence of American troops and ships. MacDonald doubted whether the American Government would send these forces and neutrality was itself no defence against Germany. De Valera tried to counter these arguments, stating that

British forces would still be 'only just across the water' and could come to the aid of Ireland almost as quickly as if they had been stationed in Ulster.

MacDonald then threw out one more suggestion:

That there should be a declaration of a United Ireland in principle, the practical details of the union to be worked out in due course; this united Ireland to become at once a belligerent on the side of the Allies.

De Valera now seemed more interested. MacDonald wrote in his report to London that 'he answered that if there were not only a declaration of a United Ireland in principle, but also agreement upon its constitution, then the Government of Eire might agree to enter the war at once . . . But the constitution of a United Ireland would have to be fixed first.' De Valera thought this could be based upon the present constitution of Eire, keeping the 'external association' with the King. Within this constitution – and here de Valera was repeating a proposal that he had first made in 1938 – Ulster 'would enjoy a great deal of local autonomy in its own affairs. It would retain its Parliament to legislate on those affairs, and it would also send representatives to the Parliament of the United Ireland which would deal with all matters of common concern.'

MacDonald saw no chance of a constitution being prepared and agreed as rapidly as the war situation required. Britain could not hand Eire's constitution to the people of Ulster 'and tell them to take it or leave it'. There would have to be discussion, said MacDonald. 'There must be give and take, otherwise there would be violent ill-will.' All that could be expected from Britain was a declaration of union in principle and 'the immediate establishment of whatever machinery was immediately necessary to protect the vital interests of the new State born in the midst of a European war.' De Valera's condition that Eire only 'might' enter the war after a declaration of a united Ireland in principle was, MacDonald believed, a formidable objection. At this point, de Valera unwisely interrupted to emphasise that there would be 'a very big question mark after the "might" '. The British Government, MacDonald replied, would not even consider the suggestion of a united Ireland in return for a 'might'. De Valera maintained that his Government would not want to enter the war because 'their people were really almost completely unprepared for war. They had not a large equipped army, they had not guns to resist tanks and mechanised troops; Dublin was practically an undefended town . . . there were not even any air raid shelters in the city and the people had not got gas masks. They would be mercilessly exposed to the horrors of modern war, and he and his colleagues could not have it on their consciences that in this state of affairs they had taken the initiative in an action which so exposed them.' MacDonald promised that the British would give Eire sufficient weapons and equipment for her defence under the arrangement he had outlined, but de Valera 'only repeated his former argument with an emphasis which made me feel that one of the decisive factors in the whole situation is his country's nakedness of defence.'

If there had been proper defences for Dublin and sufficient equipment for the Irish Army, said de Valera, the situation might have been different. 'But as it was, some of his colleagues and advisers were almost in a state of panic.' There had been 'some talk which was thoroughly defeatist' at a meeting of the Irish Defence Council, de Valera told MacDonald, although he himself was not as pessimistic as some others. 'If there were a German invasion they would put up a stout fight . . . but, in the circumstances, he and his colleagues could not take a positive decision which exposed their people to war. If war were forced upon them, it would be another matter.'

MacDonald pressed de Valera again to take action against German nationals in Eire. 'I had heard of a man called Becker,' said MacDonald, 'and no doubt there were others who were under particular suspicion.' In his report to the War Cabinet, he concluded that de Valera would be influenced in his estimate of Britain's war prospects by the fate of the French fleet which Churchill was hoping – vainly as it turned out – to bring to British ports. If the fleet did not fall into Germany's hands, wrote MacDonald, de Valera 'holds the view that, provided we can withstand invasion in our island for the next two months, we shall defeat Hitler.'[25]

MacDonald's discussions had lasted two days and the British Government considered the results on June 25. Chamberlain presented the Cabinet with a memorandum summarising the talks and taking up Mac-Donald's hint that the Irish Government might be 'considerably influenced' by a promise of military equipment.[26] Chamberlain consulted the Chiefs of Staff, who drew up a list of arms that could be given to Eire.* He also listed the three tentative proposals that MacDonald had discussed in Dublin,† commenting that Maffey believed the third of these – a British

---

* They included 16 anti-aircraft guns, 18,200 rounds of anti-aircraft ammunition, twelve mechanised howitzers, twelve anti-tank guns, 17,800 rounds of 18-pounder ammunition, 80 anti-tank rifles, 30,000 signal cartridges, 19,000 steel helmets and 52 portable field cookers. In addition, the British were prepared to offer the Irish Army Air Corps eight Gloucester Gladiators, six Hawker Hurricane fighters, twelve Battle medium bombers, six Lysanders and a 'limited number' of Wellingtons. The Chiefs of Staff dropped some acid into this generosity by adding that the Irish would be unable to provide crews for the Wellingtons.[27]

† There was a strange omission in the first of these, which seriously misrepresented the substance of MacDonald's initial suggestion. He had proposed that British naval vessels should be allowed into the Treaty ports and that British troops and aircraft should be stationed in the country 'to secure Eire's neutrality against violation by Germany'. In Chamberlain's version, this reference to the protection of Irish neutrality had disappeared, giving the erroneous impression that the Royal Navy might be free to use the Irish ports for the prosecution of the war. It seems unlikely that so important an omission was a mistake by the War Cabinet clerks. Perhaps Chamberlain was exercising a little sleight of hand in the hope that Churchill would not realise the restrictions upon the Royal Navy inherent in MacDonald's suggestion.

declaration of a united Ireland in principle and the immediate entry into the war of the new state – might yet sway the Irish Cabinet.

Chamberlain then proposed that MacDonald should return to Dublin for a third visit, carrying with him this time a formal plan for the unification of Ireland and the entry of Eire into the war on the Allied side. British ministers did not view the prospects of success very highly. 'I am bound to say,' Chamberlain informed the Cabinet, 'that I hardly anticipate anything but a negative answer . . .'[28] Nevertheless, this was the first substantive offer of a united Ireland to be sent to de Valera, and the British Government promised that it would 'at once seek to obtain the assent . . . of the Government of Northern Ireland' if the plan was acceptable to the Irish Cabinet.[29] There were six clauses:

(i)   A declaration to be issued by the United Kingdom Government forthwith accepting the principle of a United Ireland.

(ii)   A joint body including representatives of the Government of Eire and the Government of Northern Ireland to be set up at once to work out the constitutional and other practical details of the Union of Ireland. The United Kingdom Government to give such assistance towards the work of this body as might be desired.

(iii)   A joint Defence Council representative of Eire and Northern Ireland to be set up immediately.

(iv)   Eire to enter the war on the side of the United Kingdom and her allies forthwith, and, for the purposes of the Defence of Eire, the Government of Eire to invite British naval vessels to have the use of ports in Eire and British troops and aeroplanes to co-operate with the Eire forces and to be stationed in such positions in Eire as may be agreed between the two Governments.

(v)   The Government of Eire to intern all German and Italian aliens in the country and to take any further steps necessary to suppress Fifth Column activities.

(vi)   The United Kingdom Government to provide military equipment at once to the Government of Eire . . .[30]

The decisive condition attached to this document, of course, was the acceptance of the plan – the 'assent' as Chamberlain had put it in his legalistic way – by Craigavon's Cabinet in Belfast. There can be little doubt that Chamberlain intended to put considerable pressure upon Craigavon if he opposed the scheme. 'I do not believe,' Chamberlain told the British Cabinet in disingenuous fashion, 'that the Ulster Government would refuse to play their part in bringing about so favourable a development.' Craigavon, who had not heard from Chamberlain for more than a week, was clearly suspicious of the British Government's silence, for on June 26 – the day upon which MacDonald returned again to Dublin – he wrote a nervous letter to Chamberlain. Craigavon wanted to tell him about a conversation which 'a friend' had held the previous day with de Valera. According to the Northern Ireland Prime Minister, de Valera had informed his anonymous confidant that 'it would be impossible for him to abrogate the position of neutrality on account of the strength of his "Fifth Column". My friend suggested that if he would declare himself as willing to come in with Britain I would be glad to meet him anywhere at any time to talk over mutual civil defence provided no "constitutional" questions were touched upon. Mr De Valera's answer was "quite impossible".' Craigavon did not name his informant – probably Sir Emerson Herdman, a Unionist Senator – and would reveal only that he was 'an absolutely reliable source'.[31] It was a sad attempt to counterbalance the reports which Craigavon must have known MacDonald was sending back from Dublin, and the letter – with its fulsome desire to be of assistance and its gloss of truth about de Valera – received no reply from Chamberlain.

In Dublin, MacDonald presented the British Government's offer of Irish unity to de Valera, reading the text of the six clauses aloud because de Valera's eyesight was now so bad that he could decipher the document only with great difficulty. The prospect of securing a united Ireland now, MacDonald told him, was better than it had ever been. But 'if the authorities in Eire missed this opportunity of reaching their great goal, the opportunity might never present itself again.' De Valera said that he realised the importance of the plan but that he could not give a favourable reply. There was no assurance that a united Ireland would actually materialise from the British proposals; he described the declaration of unity as 'a pious hope' and said that the joint conference on the constitution would not end in agreement. Eire was to enter the war but the establishment of a united Ireland was to be 'a deferred payment'.

MacDonald argued that the declaration, which would already have received the agreement of the Northern Ireland Government, would settle the issue. 'It would be most dishonourable,' he said, 'if that declaration of policy were broken afterwards; indeed, on the assumption that Eire had carried out its part of the plan and come into the war, it was unthinkable that the promise should be broken.' MacDonald believed that British representatives would have to be full members of the constitution-making body so that the work could be completed as rapidly as possible. But de Valera did not feel that a defence council or an organisation to devise a constitution would convince his people that the union of Ireland was really to come about. He wanted 'some more impressive demonstration' of the impending change. He suggested that the two parliaments that already existed in Ireland might be joined together and given sovereign powers. De Valera 'thought the junction of the two Parliaments might give a fair representation; there were about 140 members of the Dail and about 50 members of the Northern Parliament.' MacDonald assured him that the British Cabinet would be prepared to consider such a plan.

But de Valera was still deterred by the prospect of entering the war. MacDonald tried to soften this concern. Britain, he said, did not expect an Irish Expeditionary Force to go to the United Kingdom or fight outside

Ireland. Irish troops would be used solely for the defence of Ireland. Germany would no longer be tempted to invade Eire if Irish forces had been strengthened with the equipment Britain was offering. De Valera, however, 'thought it more likely that the Germans would wish to punish them savagely for presuming to enter the war against them. They would wish to make Eire a lesson from which other powers would learn not to intervene on the side of the United Kingdom. They would bomb Dublin.' MacDonald noted that at intervals during their discussion, de Valera:

> . . . wandered off into talk on the war situation in general. He was extremely gloomy about our prospects of winning the war – even more so than he had been in our previous talks, and I felt that this pessimism was having a considerable influence on his attitude to our plan. If he had thought our prospects of winning the war bright, he might well have been disposed to accept it. But . . . he was evidently very chary of throwing in his lot with us in these dark days.

De Valera had thought through MacDonald's arguments about Britain's increased aircraft production but now believed that Britain could not destroy the 'colossal machine' that the Germans would be able to build with the conscript workers of the occupied countries. 'I felt,' MacDonald reported to the British Cabinet, 'that one of the decisive influences on Mr de Valera's mind now is his view that we are likely to lose the war.'[32]

At the Irish Cabinet meeting next morning, de Valera told his ministers of the British proposals. MacDonald was to suggest later that de Valera did not pass the unity plan on to his colleagues with sufficient emphasis. In any event, the official Irish records show that the Cabinet decided that the proposals were 'not acceptable' and that this opinion should be communicated to MacDonald later in the day by de Valera, Aiken and Lemass.[33] The four men lunched together that afternoon and then went on to talk about the British plan. From MacDonald's report to the British Cabinet, it seems that he was at first unaware of how firmly de Valera's ministers had already rejected the proposals although this must have become clear to him as the day wore on.

De Valera remained largely silent, leaving his two fellow ministers to question MacDonald. Aiken – whose name MacDonald repeatedly misspelled as 'Aitken' in his dispatch to London – 'took it upon himself to do most of the talking, and was extremely rigid in his opposition to our plan. Mr Lemass seemed far more prepared to discuss our plan in a reasonable way, and to see whether there was any means of reaching some agreement which was mutually satisfactory. But whenever he began to develop at any length an argument which might have led to some compromise, one or other of his colleagues intervened with a fresh uncompromising statement of their views.' Lemass repeated de Valera's complaint of the previous day, that there was no guarantee that a united Ireland would come about; MacDonald suspected from this 'that Mr de Valera had not passed on with

full force to his colleagues the assurances on this which I had given him
. . .' MacDonald therefore reiterated his earlier promise that it was 'absolutely definite that if the plan were accepted as a whole, a united Ireland
would come into actual being within a comparatively short period of time
. . . I repeated that the establishment of a united Ireland was an integral
part of our plan, from which there would be no turning back.' Lemass,
reported MacDonald:

> . . . seemed impressed with this, and it also seemed to come as news to Mr
> Aitken, who began to discuss in greater detail constitutional points connected
> with the establishment of . . . a joint parliament. But he then launched out on a
> long exposition of Mr de Valera's favourite thesis that this new united Ireland
> should immediately declare its neutrality in the war . . . Nothing would shake
> Mr Aitken's conviction, and he proved even more persistent than Mr de Valera
> had been in advocating the establishment of a neutral united Ireland as the best
> means of denying the whole of Ireland to the enemy and so achieving security
> for us on our western flank.[34]

This was the first time that MacDonald had encountered Aiken's iron
philosophy of neutrality. He told him that it was 'a sheer waste of time' to
discuss proposals which were not practical, and Lemass attempted to
mediate in this discussion. From listening to MacDonald, Lemass said, he
had gathered that Britain was not so much concerned that Eire should
enter the war, as that the territory of Ireland should be secured against
German invasion. MacDonald agreed that this was so and then – apparently without any permission from the War Cabinet in London –
remarked that:

> . . . if we could feel assured by some other means that the enemy would not be
> able to accomplish a successful invasion of Eire, we should not wish to insist on
> Eire declaring war. If there was really an unsurmountable [sic] political
> difficulty to Eire entering the war at the present time, we should be content for
> Eire to remain non-belligerent if she invited our ships into her ports and our
> troops and aeroplanes into her territory to increase her security against sharing
> the fate which had befallen neutral Norway, Denmark, Holland, Belgium and
> Luxemburg . . .[35]

De Valera was unimpressed by this. He commented – not without good
reason – that to invite British troops into Eire would be 'tantamount to a
declaration of war on Germany'. What guarantee, he wanted to know, did
the British have that the Northern Ireland Government would agree, even
if they had accepted the plan in principle, to join in a united Ireland in
practice?
MacDonald said that Britain:

> . . . certainly would not coerce Northern Ireland. We would not and could not
> march troops into the six counties to force a policy upon their Government.

But if the Eire Government accepted the plan, we hoped to be able to persuade the Northern Ireland Government also to accept it . . . The United Kingdom Government would take full responsibility to the Eire Government for seeing that our obligations under the plan were carried out to the full.[36]

Aiken suggested that the British should point out to 'the Northern Irish leaders' that their security would be best served by a proclamation of neutrality over the whole of Ireland, but MacDonald claimed that his government could not do that because they did not believe it was true.

Then – perhaps for Aiken's benefit – MacDonald tried a personal approach once more:

I said that I would like to speak for a few moments not as a representative of the United Kingdom Government, but as a private individual whose sympathies were on the side of the establishment of a united Ireland, and who at the same time knew British politics and the British Parliament pretty well. The present was the best opportunity that had yet offered itself of a union of the whole of Ireland being achieved. Such an opportunity might never return. If the North and the South could be united on the basis of their being joined together in the prosecution of a war in defence of the freedom of the whole of Ireland against the Nazi attack, then that union would not be broken afterwards. But if the leaders of Eire now stayed out of the war, and perhaps contributed to German strength by doing so, whilst the people of Northern Ireland and of the United Kingdom were joined in the supreme struggle against the Nazis, then none of us in Britain would be very concerned to create a united Ireland afterwards. My private and sincere advice to them was to seize this opportunity, which might never recur.[37]

Aiken acknowledged that MacDonald's appeal had 'great force' and claimed that without the 1938 Anglo-Irish Agreement, the Irish would have been in the war against Britain. The Irish were now a friendly neutral and they wished to continue to be Britain's friends 'but the people of Eire would not support their Government in taking them into the war . . . without any actual provocation from Germany.' De Valera thought it no use pursuing the matter further 'at present' but MacDonald, sensing perhaps that history would exact its own retribution for a spurned offer of Irish unity, asked that the Eire Government's reply to the British proposals should be given in writing. In framing that reply, he said, they should remember that 'if the plan were accepted as a whole, the union of Ireland would definitely become an accomplished fact.' Furthermore, Eire could maintain her non-belligerency – MacDonald avoided the word 'neutrality' – if she permitted British forces to enter her territory to assist in her defence against German invasion. MacDonald undertook to prepare written amendments to the original British proposals to encompass these points.[38]

In a secret telegram to Churchill next day, MacDonald described his latest talks as 'most unsatisfactory' but urged the Prime Minister to reinforce Britain's offer of a united Ireland 'by insertion of words which would give specific assurance on this point'. When Churchill read Mac-Donald's telegram, he wrote in the margin next to this line: 'But all contingent upon Ulster agreeing & S. Ireland coming into the war.'[39] In his telegram, MacDonald failed to tell Churchill of the offer of non-belligerency; perhaps this was another sleight of hand.

Nothing, however, could have equalled the sense of treachery that Craigavon felt when he received details from Chamberlain of the Dublin negotiations. On June 26, Chamberlain had sent him the formal proposals for Irish unity which the British Government was offering to de Valera. 'You will observe,' he wrote, 'that the document takes the form of an enquiry only, because we have not felt it right to approach you officially with a request for your assent unless we had first a binding assurance from Eire that they would, if the assent were given, come into the war . . . If therefore they refuse the plan you are in no way committed, and if they accept you are still free to make your own comments or objections as you may think fit.'[40]

This was ominous indeed. Chamberlain was prepared to grant Craigavon the right to 'comment' or 'object' – but not to refuse. Craigavon was an old and sick man. In his seventieth year, he was already so unwell that he could do no more than an hour's concentrated work.[41] For nineteen years – almost to the very day – he had fought for the survival of his fractured province, only to find that its integrity could be sacrificed for de Valera. He had suspected that Northern Ireland might be in jeopardy and he had been proved right. So he fired off a cypher telegram to Chamberlain, a proud, impertinent, explosive message of a kind that no Northern Ireland minister had ever before sent to the Imperial Government or ever would again:

AM PROFOUNDLY SHOCKED AND DISGUSTED BY YOUR LETTER MAKING SUGGESTIONS SO FAR REACHING BEHIND MY BACK AND WITHOUT ANY PRE-CONSULTATION WITH ME. TO SUCH TREACHERY TO LOYAL ULSTER I WILL NEVER BE A PARTY.[42]

In his letter, Chamberlain had tried to mollify Craigavon, pointing out how unlikely it was that de Valera would accept the British offer. Now he was affronted by Craigavon's fury, and his response – preserved in the Public Record Office in London but curiously missing from the archives of the old Northern Ireland Government in Belfast – could only have strengthened Craigavon's conviction that the British Cabinet was prepared to destroy Northern Ireland's constitutional safeguards over the heads of its people. Chamberlain's wire back to Stormont was haughty and, in a subtle way, both patronising and insulting:

REGRET YOU SHOULD MAKE SUCH UNFAIR CHARGE AGAINST THIS
GOVERNMENT. SURELY YOU HAVE NOT PROPERLY APPRECIATED
PAGE TWO OF MY LETTER WHICH SHOWS THAT YOUR POSITION IS
ENTIRELY PROTECTED. MACDONALDS REPORT INDICATES LIT-
TLE LIKELIHOOD OF PROGRESS WITH EIRE BUT YOU CAN BE
ASSURED THAT YOU WILL HAVE EVERY OPPORTUNITY OF MAKING
YOUR VIEWS KNOWN BEFORE ANY DECISION AFFECTING ULSTER
IS TAKEN. MEANWHILE PLEASE REMEMBER THE SERIOUS NATURE
OF THE SITUATION WHICH REQUIRES THAT EVERY EFFORT BE
MADE TO MEET IT.[43]

This message, with its schoolmaster's reminder of Britain's peril, could
scarcely have quietened Craigavon's fears. How could Northern Ireland's
position be 'entirely protected' when all the British War Cabinet could
promise him was an opportunity of making his views known before a
decision was taken in London? It may have been this altercation that
prompted Churchill's reference to the pre-condition of Northern Ireland's
agreement in the margin of MacDonald's telegram. MacDonald himself
believed that the Irish Cabinet would reject an amended plan[44] and
when Chamberlain wrote to de Valera on the evening of June 28 with
revised proposals, he reminded him that the British Government 'cannot,
of course, give a guarantee that Northern Ireland will assent.'[45]

Churchill's War Cabinet, however, had moved forward in their prof-
fered commitments to Irish unity. The declaration accepting the principle
of a united Ireland was now strengthened by an additional clause specify-
ing that: '. . . This declaration would take the form of a solemn undertaking that the Union is to become at an early date an accomplished fact from
which there shall be no turning back.'[46]

Even more important – at least for de Valera – was a new clause in the
second British proposal which expanded the functions of the joint governmental body which would work out the constitution of a united Ireland. This work would now be intended: '. . . to establish at as early a date
as possible the whole machinery of Government of the Union.'[47]

Chamberlain's letter to de Valera also contained two crucial concessions. If the Irish Government wished to propose that the Parliaments of
Eire and Northern Ireland should meet together at once, then the British
Cabinet would 'gladly give it immediate consideration'. In addition,
Chamberlain did 'not think it would be necessary for our purpose that Eire
should issue a declaration of war.' All Britain wanted, he said, were
facilities for the Royal Navy and the British Army to guard Eire. The
reference to Eire's entry into the war on Britain's side was therefore
deleted from the original plan although Chamberlain was not prepared to
accept that a united Ireland should become neutral. This new and
expanded offer of unity* was first communicated to de Valera by telegram

* See Appendix II.

178

and then reaffirmed in a formal letter signed by Chamberlain.[48]

The world war had thus apparently brought about within the British Government a fundamental reappraisal of its relations with Eire and its commitment to Northern Ireland. With the German armies along the Channel coast and with Britain – and Ireland – awaiting invasion from the Continent, Britain devalued her obligations to Northern Ireland in the interests of her own national survival. By the same token, Eire was constrained to balance her outstanding political aspiration against her neutrality and the security which that seemed to offer. In constitutional terms, Eire could not regard herself as free until the remaining six British-held counties were united with the rest of Ireland. But she did at least hold undisputed sovereignty over the area of the twenty-six counties; to abandon neutrality – the very symbol as well as the protective shield of her new independence – in favour of a vulnerable 'non-belligerent' status and the promise of a united Ireland, could prove a deadly abrasion to the freedom Eire had already achieved.

For Britain, the surrender of Northern Ireland might be a necessary sacrifice to secure her own safety – to re-invest for a few years that 500-mile semi-circle of naval defence – and it was one which the British Government could propose in all seriousness in the summer of 1940. If Northern Ireland was a 'loyal province' to Churchill, it could appear to other ministers as a nineteen-year-old anachronism whose people would not 'refuse to play their part' in the unity of Ireland if this was in Britain's best interest.

In Northern Ireland itself, such considerations were unacceptable. Protestants who professed loyalty to the United Kingdom were in no mind to demonstrate this faithfulness by dismantling their government. Craigavon's ministers had directed their energies towards the survival of their province; to seek its demise with the assistance of another nation was, therefore, not just an act of infidelity on Britain's part, but 'treachery' as well. So when Britain warned her Irish province of the sacrifice she might demand in the cause of her war with Germany, Northern Ireland's primary concern was for itself – for the constitutional link which gave a surety of a Protestant majority and therefore of Protestant power – rather than for Britain. The logic of this reaction does not change the incontestable fact that Craigavon and his ageing Cabinet placed the survival of the six counties as a first priority when Nazi Germany was threatening to destroy Britain, the Crown and all that to which Northern Ireland was allegedly loyal.

Britain had reassumed her imperial eye, viewing Ireland as a bulwark against England's enemies. But that part of Ireland which had recently achieved its own independence did not care to put its achievements at risk at so dangerous a moment. Nor did Northern Ireland; her paradox, of course, was that her limited statehood and her loyalty existed only in so far as it was attached to the country which was now prepared to cast her off.

All three governments were acting from self-seeking motives, as governments tend to do, especially in time of war. The sacrifice which Britain offered might have been morally regrettable but it would hardly have caused any permanent damage to the state. But Eire's sacrifice was to have been certain involvement in the war, undertaken on the promise of a country which had occupied her land for hundreds of years. Northern Ireland's sacrifice would have been her own extinction. At so critical a moment and under such external threat, there could be no room for the creation of mutual political concessions that would be necessary to achieve a settlement in Ireland. Only months of negotiations in an atmosphere free of crisis could have prevented the intractability of history from exerting itself and when the British scheme for Irish unity failed in 1940 – as it was bound to – it did so with an element of melodrama and farce entirely appropriate to its conception.

On June 29, Neville Chamberlain received another astonishing message from the man who was expected to lead the six counties of Northern Ireland into Eire's embrace. Craigavon was responding to the Lord President's telegram which had advised him that there was 'little likelihood of progress' in MacDonald's Dublin talks. More militant than ever, Craigavon replied:

YOUR TELEGRAM ONLY CONFIRMS MY CONFIDENTIAL INFORMATION AND CONVICTION DE VALERA IS UNDER GERMAN DICTATION AND FAR PAST REASONING WITH FULL STOP HE MAY PURPOSELY PROTRACT NEGOTIATIONS TILL ENEMY HAS LANDED FULL STOP STRONGLY ADVOCATE IMMEDIATE NAVAL OCCUPATION OF HARBOURS AND MILITARY ADVANCE SOUTH.[49]

This insane and mischievous proposal was ignored by Chamberlain who must by now have despaired of conducting any form of serious discussion with Craigavon. Indeed a few days later, the Northern Ireland Prime Minister composed a sharp memorandum for Winston Churchill, setting out the terms upon which he would participate in an 'All Ireland Defence Force'. The document – once again missing from the Northern Ireland archives – urged the establishment of British martial law throughout the island. Its six points, which Craigavon signed with a beautifully executed and heavily underlined letter 'C', betrayed the ingenious attention to detail of a truly eccentric mind:

1. A Military Governor should be appointed over *all Ireland*, for the period of the war, without any consideration of the political border, with his headquarters in Dublin and a deputy in Belfast: a Scotch or Welsh Officer of high military rank, or Dill or Brooke (both Irishmen) would seem to be an appropriate choice for this position.
2. Subject to supreme control by the Military Governor civil administration to be carried on through the two Parliamentary institutions as at present.

3. To meet the susceptibilities of the South, the Defence Force might be composed chiefly of Scottish and Welsh Divisions, all ranks to be very specially warned of the strength of the IRA (Fifth columnists in Eire).

4. A few carefully selected Irish-speaking Officers should be attached to the Dublin headquarters of the Military Governor.

5. There should be disseminated throughout Eire very carefully prepared pamphlets in English and Irish, explaining that the military were there to defend the interests of the Irish people – no question of 're-conquering Ireland' etc – such pamphlets to be carried and distributed by the troops.

6. The American Ambassador should make the necessary representations to render impossible the export of munitions of war from the United States to *any* section of the Southern Irish.[50]

Churchill met Craigavon again in London on July 7. No record can be found of their conversation but the Northern Ireland Prime Minister's plan – though it would not have been out of temper with Churchill's feelings in September 1939 – was judiciously set aside. Craigavon had not visited the twenty-six counties since 1921, when at British instigation he had secretly met de Valera,[51] and he was now out of touch with events in Eire and with the mood of the people there. The idea that a British military governor could take office in Dublin was absurd. Nor could it have escaped Churchill's attention that the two officers whom Craigavon specifically suggested for this post – Field Marshal Sir John Dill and Field Marshal Viscount Alanbrooke – were both Northern Ireland Protestants. The defence plan was a curio, a symbol of the distance that now separated Belfast from Dublin. It held no attractions for the British although the spectacle of Welsh soldiers tramping around Eire under the command of Protestant Ulstermen while handing out pamphlets in Irish to potential Fifth Columnists would have proved to be one of the war's more enduring memories.

Craigavon had anyway done his best in public to blight MacDonald's efforts. He did so in more rational language than he used in his messages to Chamberlain and he implied that the initiative for Irish unity had come not from the British but from de Valera. When he addressed Unionists at Kirkistown in the Ards Peninsula south-east of Belfast on June 29, Craigavon claimed that de Valera was 'once again blackmailing the British Government to end Partition, and this, at the very moment when the enemy is at our gates. It is sinister evidence that something serious is afoot. I wish, therefore, to declare that I will be no party, directly, or indirectly, to any change in the constitution conferred upon Northern Ireland.' Craigavon said that he was prepared to enter into 'the closest co-operation' with de Valera on matters of defence, providing Eire joined the Allies, expelled the German and Italian diplomats in Dublin and did not raise any constitutional issues. 'If an All-Ireland Parliament had been in existence at the outbreak of hostilities,' he concluded, 'I am persuaded that Great Britain would have been faced with an All-Ireland neutrality today and British troops would have been unable to land on Irish soil except by force.'[52]

It must have been almost a relief for Chamberlain when Dulanty arrived at his office on July 5 with de Valera's curt and formal rejection of Britain's offer of Irish unity. The amended proposals for the union of Ireland had been considered by the Irish Government, wrote de Valera, but:

> We are unable to accept the plan outlined, which we note is purely tentative and has not been submitted to Lord Craigavon and his colleagues.
>
> The plan would involve our entry into the war. That is a course for which we could not accept responsibility. Our people would be quite unprepared for it, and Dail Eireann would certainly reject it.
>
> We are, of course, aware that the policy of neutrality has its dangers, but, on the other hand, departure from it would involve us in dangers greater still.
>
> The plan would commit us definitely to an immediate abandonment of our neutrality. On the other hand, it gives no guarantee that in the end we would have a united Ireland, unless indeed concessions were made to Lord Craigavon opposed to the sentiments and aspirations of the great majority of the Irish people.
>
> Our present Constitution represents the limit to which we believe our people are prepared to go to meet the sentiments of the Northern Unionists, but, on the plan proposed, Lord Craigavon and his colleagues could at any stage render the whole project nugatory and prevent the desired unification by demanding concessions to which the majority of the people could not agree. By such methods unity was prevented in the past, and it is obvious that under the plan outlined they could be used again. The only way in which the unity which is so needed can in our view be secured is, as I explained to Mr MacDonald, by the immediate establishment of a single sovereign all-Ireland Parliament, free to decide all matters of national policy, internal and external – the Government which it would elect being responsible for taking the most effective measures for national defence.
>
> It was in this connection that I suggested as a line to be explored the possibility of creating such a parliament by the entry into the parliament here of the present representatives in the parliament at Belfast.
>
> I regret that my proposal that the unity of Ireland should be established on the basis of the whole country becoming neutral is unacceptable to your Government. On the basis of unity and neutrality we could mobilise the whole of the manpower of this country for the national defence. That, with the high morale which could thus be secured and the support of the Irish race throughout the world, would constitute the most effective bulwark against attack, and would provide the surest guarantee against any part of our territory being used as a base for operations against Britain.
>
> The course suggested in your plan could only lead to internal weakness and eventual frustration.[53]

De Valera's rejection was pointed and contained within it not only a hint of Aiken's pragmatism but something which the Protestants of Northern

Ireland would immediately have identified as meanness of spirit. Before the war, Chamberlain had urged de Valera to make some concession toward the six counties, some token of generosity which might be reciprocated. But de Valera was standing by his Constitution, a document of strongly republican character that acknowledged the 'special position' of the Catholic Church and which had left in being only a tendril of allegiance to the King. De Valera regarded this as the limit to which his people were 'prepared to go to meet the sentiments of the Northern Unionists'. Craigavon's old slogan of 'Not an inch'[54] might have been de Valera's.

He did undoubtedly believe that Craigavon would try to sabotage the plan for Irish unity. MacDonald had emphasised that Eire would not be expected to fulfil her side of the British offer until Northern Ireland had agreed to the scheme. Yet it was an unusual feature of the plan that the pre-condition of Craigavon's assent was only attached to the proposals and not contained in writing *within* them. Craigavon and de Valera had found little common ground between them when they met nineteen years earlier, so could the British – who had gone back on their 1921 promise to renegotiate the border in favour of the twenty-six counties – be trusted to ensure Northern Ireland's co-operation in 1940, if necessary against the province's will?

There can be equally little doubt that de Valera was correct in his assumption that the British plan would have involved Eire in the war. Out of gratitude to Britain for the Home Rule Bill, Redmond had allowed thousands of young Irishmen to go to their deaths in the 1914–18 War. De Valera did not want a second generation of Irishmen to die in another European war for another illusory goal. It was scarcely ignoble of him to think that Britain was about to be defeated. If Britain had lost the war, Eire would inevitably have been occupied by German troops. And if Britain had won the war after securing de Valera's co-operation in 1940, would her enthusiasm for Irish unity have been maintained? Ironically, de Valera's suggestion of a united neutral Ireland under the protection of the United States – an idea so briskly turned down by MacDonald – might ultimately have provided Britain with what she wanted. If the Americans had agreed to safeguard the new Irish state by putting warships into the Treaty ports, they would almost certainly have taken Ireland into the war against Germany after the Japanese attack on Pearl Harbor in December 1941.

Years later, MacDonald disclosed that he actually went further in his proposals to de Valera than he revealed to the British Cabinet. According to MacDonald, 'Dev said that we were not offering a guarantee of a united Ireland, only an indefinite promise. I said to Dev: "Will you come into the war if we create a united Ireland straight away?" I'm pretty sure Dev's reply was: "If we have a united Ireland straight away, it will be neutral for at least twenty-four hours. We will then call a meeting of our assembly and

it will decide if we – as an independent nation – will come into the war."
Dev asked that this should not be put in my report.'[55] Mulcahy, who spoke
to de Valera on July 2 – five days after MacDonald's last meeting – records
that he asked de Valera 'if he would be prepared in . . . an All-Ireland
Parliament to advocate and support going into the war against Germany.
He stated that he would not.'[56]

MacDonald had an ally in Mulcahy, who told de Valera that Fine Gael
'would support the Government if they felt that changed circumstances
now suggested that they should go into the war as a United Ireland, and if
the Government were prepared to take such a decision.' But de Valera was
still ruminating on his own idea of a united neutral Ireland. 'He states that
he sees of course all kinds of difficulties in his own offer. The North of
Ireland having been at war with Germany, it might be difficult to disentangle them in the eyes of Germany . . . He had the idea that Irishmen in
the Canadian and British Army could be transferred as soldiers to the new
Irish Army . . .'[57] Mulcahy recorded on July 2 that 'MacDonald . . .
tendered a *plan* for an offer rather than an offer. At any rate, Dev does not
consider it to be what he would regard as a definite offer, or a thing to
which he would make formal counter-proposals . . .'[58]

MacDonald was particularly struck by Aiken's opposition to the British
proposals. 'Aiken felt fairly certain that there would be an Axis victory,' he
recalled. 'When he was on his own, Dev would say: "My Cabinet won't
agree with me." I think he meant Aiken, who was very strong in the belief
that Britain would lose.'[59] Aiken, who liked MacDonald and met him
again in Singapore after the war when the former British minister was
Commissioner General for South East Asia, says that he did not try to
persuade de Valera to reject the British offer because de Valera was 'quite
able to make the right judgement on his own'.[60] Aiken says he cannot
remember stating that the British would lose the war although Gerald
Boland, who viewed Aiken's influence with considerable jealousy,
recorded differently in the papers he left after his death:

> When France fell to the Germans, Frank was certain that Britain would fall in
> six weeks as were the principal officials of the Department of External Affairs. I
> was very much alarmed at this because Mr De Valera's sight was very bad at
> this time and he relied on Frank to keep him informed of what was happening.
> About the day after France fell, I went to the Taoiseac's office and warned the
> Taoiseac in Frank's presence of allowing himself to be persuaded that Britain
> would lose the war. Frank gave me the usual condescending smile with the
> 'God help you, you poor idiot' gesture – but I solemnly warned the Taoiseac to
> take no notice of what Frank said. I told him that the USA and Russia would
> eventually come into the war and that Britain was at that very moment
> preparing for the counter-attack . . . He did not laugh at me but Frank did;
> anyhow I left with this warning: if you base your policy and actions on the
> assumption that Britain will lose, may God help Ireland for we will certainly
> suffer for such folly. The Taoiseac never gave me the slightest idea of what his
> opinion was. He probably had none.[61]

Aiken, whom Boland regarded as 'a menace',[62] says that MacDonald's proposals were turned down because 'neutrality was a national policy – we weren't going to be dragged into any war by anybody. MacDonald was a decent fellah but the British offer was not practical and it was not logical.'[63] Some weeks after he had rejected the British proposals, de Valera told Maffey that 'it had gone hard with him to turn down any scheme which would bring about a united Ireland, the dream of his life. But in the present circumstances acceptance would have been impossible. It would have meant civil war.'[64] Years later, he compared the offer to the rule of 'equal holds' that small boys followed when swapping personal possessions. 'Each would have a firm grip on what he was to receive before he loosened his grip on that with which he was parting.' Churchill's offer did not give 'equal holds'.[65]

De Valera could not imagine how the British could ever obtain a firm grasp upon Craigavon, let alone thrust him towards Dublin. Ebullient as ever after the failure of MacDonald's mission, Craigavon flaunted a new self-confidence. 'We are closing the gates, as our ancestors did at Derry,' he announced triumphantly in the Northern Ireland House of Commons, 'and maintaining our position in the battle front.'[66] But Craigavon never opposed Irish unity as a concept. In 1922, he told Michael Collins that 'for the present an all-Ireland Parliament was out of the question, possibly in years to come – 10, 20, or 50 years – Ulster might be tempted to join with the South . . . He would do nothing to prevent an all-Ireland Parliament, and . . . if he were convinced it were in the interests of the people of Ulster, he would frankly tell them of his views, but should such an eventuality arise, he would not feel justified himself in taking part in an all-Ireland Parliament.'[67] Eighteen years later, Craigavon had said that he would not be a party to any union with Eire. But could he have opposed Churchill if the British Prime Minister had argued that Northern Ireland's presence in a united Ireland would strengthen the Commonwealth by preventing any further slide towards a republican state in the twenty-six counties?

Even if Craigavon refused to have any part in such a business, his ministers might have felt differently. Brooke said after the war that he had been worried that de Valera would offer the use of Irish ports and airfields to the British in return for the incorporation of Northern Ireland in Eire. 'In one deal, at a moment of crisis in the death struggle, Northern Ireland could have been sacrificed. I had an awful feeling that had we refused, we would have been blamed for whatever disasters had ensued . . . Thank goodness it did not arise.'[68] Brooke's son – the present Lord Brookeborough – remembers standing with his father near the little church on the family estate in County Fermanagh one Sunday morning in June of 1940:

My father told me that day that there were pressures upon the Northern

Ireland Government. He said that if he were faced with the choice of losing our civilisation or accepting the unification of Ireland, he would find it a very difficult decision. He regarded western civilisation as of greater worth than anything else, being absolutely convinced of the menace of Nazi Germany. It was my impression that day that in these circumstances, he would have to do his best to ensure Irish unity.[69]

Brooke was not alone in these considerations. John MacDermott, who became Northern Ireland's Minister of Public Security in June 1940, told John Andrews that Eire should enter the war on Britain's side and that 'if the price of this was to be a Council of Ireland, I would not oppose it, providing it was non-legislative.'[70] MacDermott recalled after the war that he would not have permitted a Council of Ireland to become a 'back-door way' to a united Ireland,[71] but in the circumstances that is precisely what Britain and Eire would have intended it to be.

Andrews told Wilfrid Spender, the head of the Northern Ireland civil service, that Craigavon's Cabinet would be 'thrown out' if it made such concessions. Spender thought that the Cabinet had been partly responsible for its own predicament because its 'complacency' toward the 1938 Anglo-Irish negotiations 'led Mr Neville Chamberlain to the belief that even on the question of Home Rule Ulster had no very strong views and that it was guided merely by political considerations. It was on this account that . . . he proposed that Northern Ireland should enter the Eire Parliament.'[72] In all probability, the Lord President merely found Craigavon irritating. But Chamberlain could be bullying as well as unsympathetic toward small communities who did not fall in with his grand designs, as the Czechs found out to their cost in 1938.*

Ultimately, however, Northern Ireland's fate would have depended upon Churchill. He it was who had promised the people of the province that they would never be compelled by threats or intrigue to sever their ties with Britain. His stated refusal in Cabinet to coerce Craigavon – not to mention his long-standing support for Unionism – suggest that he would never have turned Northern Ireland over to de Valera. Ulstermen should be of good cheer, he had proclaimed in that series of newspaper articles in the 1930s, for until they wish to abandon the British Empire, 'the British Empire will never abandon them'. The integrity of Northern Ireland's quarrel could nevertheless be overwhelmed by events of far greater moment.

* Chamberlain was joint author of a formal note sent to the Czech Government in September 1938 demanding that they agree to the secession of the Sudetenland to Germany. It said that 'both the French and British governments recognise how great is the sacrifice thus required of the Czechoslovak Government in the cause of peace. But because that cause is common both to Europe in general and in particular to Czechoslovakia herself they have felt it their duty . . . to set forth frankly the conditions essential to secure it.'[73] It is not difficult to imagine a communication of similar flavour and sentiment being framed for Craigavon.

In the emotional shock of June 1940 Churchill tried to withstand the effects of the European débâcle with visions of defiance and generosity. When France was collapsing under the German advance, he searched for some epic device with which to rally his broken ally; and on June 16, he offered France common citizenship with Britain, urging the French Government to proclaim the 'indissoluble union' of the two countries. British and French would become citizens of the same nation, protected by a joint defence organisation.[74] It was an audacious, breathtaking gesture whose ramifications were scarcely considered by the French, who in any case promptly turned it down. But it illustrated the extravagant way in which Churchill's mind was moving at that traumatic period. It was quite in keeping that he should, one day later, dispatch MacDonald to Dublin to seek a new ally with offers which also transcended the bonds of national loyalty.

For Churchill, a united Ireland at war with Germany would have produced advantages that extended far beyond the enormous strategic value of the Treaty ports. Her membership of the Commonwealth would be reinvigorated by the Protestants of the north who would still wish to show fealty to the Empire and who would inspire that 'majority' of Catholic Irishmen whom Churchill happily supposed to be on Britain's side. The 'illegality' of Eire and her policy of neutrality would disappear and the king might regain his place within the Constitution. The Irish Free State would be reborn; there would be – in Churchill's phrase of nineteen years before – 'dominion home rule'. And indeed, underlying the proposals which MacDonald took to Dublin – though he may not have appreciated this at the time – was the structure of the 1921 Treaty, the covenant which Churchill had signed, which had long been his supreme political achievement and which had so recently been destroyed. Ironically, the 1940 offer of unity seemed to hold out the very opposite rewards for de Valera. He sought in it the opportunity of a final break with the 1921 Treaty, the abrogation of partition, a united neutral Ireland with its own independent assembly, loyal only to itself. Northern Protestants might have been permitted to enjoy the status of Commonwealth citizens for a few extra years but de Valera would have little time for the King in Ireland's constitution.

Britain's offer of unity in 1940 represented, therefore, not so much a new departure in British policy towards Ireland but a re-negotiation by proxy of the old 1921 Treaty. De Valera, the absent signatory, was given a second chance to substantiate his dream while Churchill tried to rebuild the fabric of his triumph with Collins and Griffith. Churchill wanted to regain something that was lost but de Valera sought an independence that had been denied him; for this reason, his last rejection of Churchill's offer was even more dramatic than the proposals themselves.

Churchill and de Valera failed in their efforts, as middle-aged men usually do when they try to re-live the struggles of their youth. The

187

occasion was never to occur again. Within six months, both Craigavon and Chamberlain would be dead. MacDonald – thinking that 'perhaps Churchill wanted to get rid of me'[75] – was dispatched to Canada to become High Commissioner. Henceforth, Churchill and de Valera would face each other without intermediaries. The British Prime Minister did not immediately abandon his idea that Ireland might be united. In a letter to Roosevelt in December 1940 he was still speculating that 'if the Government of Eire would show its solidarity with the democracies of the English-speaking world . . . a Council for Defence of all Ireland could be set up out of which the unity of the island would probably in some form or other emerge after the war'.[76] But it was not to be. The border – the scar of partition for those who denied its legality – would remain, and the world war would now give it a new and enduring permanence that would permit it, thirty years later, to burst open upon Craigavon's descendants with a virulence of which neither Churchill nor de Valera could ever have conceived.

Chapter 7

Operation 'Green' and the 'W' Plan

> The occupation of Ireland might lead to the end of the war.
>
> Adolf Hitler *3 December 1941*

In the summer of 1940, few people outside Ireland could have had a more detailed knowledge of the border than the cartographers of the Wehrmacht's Department for War Maps and Surveys in Berlin. Their *Militärgeographische Angaben über Irland* – Military Geographical Data on Ireland – was produced for German invasion troops and contained relief maps and diagrams of the country's military bases, railway system, electrical grids, airfields, factories, gasworks, canals, rivers, mineral deposits, population density and townlands. It was a formidable piece of work, buttressed by an impressive volume of photographs and a 78-page green-covered booklet on Eire and Northern Ireland which described their frontier, sizc, historical background, industry, transport, administrative structure, vegetation, climate and weather. Seventeen pages carried thumb-nail sketches of 233 cities, towns and villages on both sides of the border and one map even outlined in black and grey shading those parts of the island that were Irish-speaking – *Keltische Sprachgebiet* – giving the Gaeltacht of Donegal, Mayo, Galway, Kerry and west Cork the distinction of more than 80 per cent native speakers.[1] On one of the larger maps, the Irish border was marked by a broken dark line that wandered south from Londonderry, passed 'Caslederg' (Castlederg), cut inconveniently through Upper Lough Erne and reached the sea on the east coast by way of 'Ready' (Keady) and the Dundalk tobacco factory in County Louth, represented on the map by a small drawing of a pipe. A mass of tiny illustrations – of aeroplanes, ships, cotton reels, oil lamps and gasometers – clustered around Belfast, generously symbolising the northern capital's aircraft, shipbuilding and textile industries, her refineries and power plants.[2] 'English brutality, which led to a decline in the Irish population, has constantly fed the flames of Irish hatred,' the authors of the booklet told their Wehrmacht readers. 'Even before the Great War, the Ulster people, English in their attitude, directed their attacks against the fanatical struggle for independence of the Catholic Irish in the Home Rule movement, which then led to the separation of Northern Ireland when the Free State was established . . ."[3]

The recipients of this brisk historical analysis were to be the men of the 4th and 7th German Army Corps under General Leonhard Kaupisch who in August 1940 was ordered to prepare detailed plans for an amphibious operation against Ireland. The idea's originator appears to have been the newly-promoted Field Marshal Feodor von Bock whose Army Group B, having distinguished itself in the attack on Poland the previous September, had just pushed the British and Belgian armies back to the Channel.[4] Army Group B was now entrusted with the western flank of Operation Sealion – the invasion of Britain – and given the task of securing a beach-head between Weymouth and Lyme Regis.[5] Kaupisch's offensive against Eire was to be an integral part of the attack on England.

The plans for the invasion of Ireland, classified 'Top Secret' and 'Very Urgent', were distributed in thirty-two copies by the German Army High Command on August 8, and at least one set of these instructions – still in its brown envelope bearing the wax seal of the German eagle and swastika – survived the war. It shows that the invasion of Ireland, code-named Operation 'Green'* – *Fall Grün* – was to have been a bold and extremely hazardous affair. From the French ports of Lorient, St Nazaire and Nantes, an initial force of 3900 troops were to be landed on an eighty-five mile front along the south-east coast of Ireland between Wexford and Dungarvan. Having captured the small harbours there – an enterprise which the High Command considered easy 'since no substantial resistance is expected in Ireland' – lightly-armed infantry and commando units were to fight their way up to thirty miles inland. Operation 'Green' proposed that the front line of this bridgehead would run from Gorey on the Wexford–Dublin road, across the 2610 foot height of Mount Leinster above Borris in County Carlow, through Thomastown, County Kilkenny, to the small market town of Clonmel in County Tipperary and thence to Dungarvan.[7]

Artillery and commando squadrons and a motorised infantry battalion were to take part in the first landings along the Irish coast. A bridge-building battalion, three anti-aircraft companies and several 'raiding patrols' – to probe any Irish military defences – were also to be included in the initial assault while reserves from the German 61st, 72nd and 290th Divisions were to take up occupation duties in the Gorey–Dungarvan

---

* The Germans made a practice of coding military operations by colours. Thus Operation 'Red' was a projected war on two fronts in 1940, 'Yellow' was the invasion of Holland and Belgium, 'Black' the occupation of Italy in 1943, and so forth. 'Green' does not appear to have been chosen for any symbolic reason. The Irish might have been disturbed to know that the same code name had already been used once before – for the projected invasion of Czechoslovakia in 1938.[6]

bridgehead once it had been established. A limited number of horses would also be carried aboard the invasion craft.*

But there was a fatalistic if not doomed quality about the invasion plans. The German naval officers who were to transport the troops from France to Ireland could not have been comforted by the instruction that 'preparations for landing in England must be given priority over the Ireland [Green] operation.' They were told that French vessels with French crews as well as local fishing boats, German naval tugs and ferries could be used for training the assault troops but that such ships were 'scarce'.[10] Indeed, when the German Navy began its search for suitable vessels around the ports of north-western France, they found only two steamships – the French *Versailles* and the German *Eule* – together with three small coasters, the *Mebillo*, *Clio* and *Franzine*. This was a poor start for an operation that would involve up to 50,000 men.[11] Nor could the instructions have given much confidence to the troops involved in the operation. The High Command anticipated that there would be communication difficulties between ships during the long crossing to Ireland and from ship to shore after the first invasion force had landed; they recommended the use of 'lamp-signals, signalling rods, megaphones, etc' while observing radio silence. Special life-saving equipment would be carried aboard the invasion craft and Kaupisch's planners were warned 'to avoid taking the crews of sinking vessels onto fully-manned ships, since this would place them in danger of capsizing'. Every vessel was to carry anti-aircraft weapons and constitute a self-contained fighting unit. Clearly the High Command expected the Royal Navy and the RAF to intercept its Irish invasion fleet.

Nor did they totally dismiss the possibility that the Irish Army would fight back on the invasion beaches. A revealing instruction to Kaupisch's equipment officers stated that 'an adequate number of weapons, especially automatic guns, should be installed in such a way that fire can be directed at the coast from the vessel itself.' The landing was to be made 'in as many places as possible simultaneously' and smaller invasion craft were to seek out 'free coastline' upon which to discharge their troops. Ramps, rafts and small boats were to be provided 'to enable the army to cover the distance between vessel and land as quickly as possible' but weapons and ammunition were to be water-proofed 'since in many cases, the landing troops will have to wade through shallow water'. The soldiers would be given 'ropes, rope-ladders and pulleys' for the cliffs above the beaches. However, 'as soon as resistance becomes evident, defence attack must commence from the vessels, even if this will have only a morale-boosting effect . . .'[12] German troops of the invasion force would be given cover by the Luft-

* In 1940, horses provided the only motive power with which the German Army could haul guns and limbers ashore from landing craft.[8] Operation 'Green' instructions insisted that 'the number of horses to be carried with the 1st Squadron must be restricted to a minimum'.[9]

waffe's West of France Air Command and – so far as sea defence was feasible – by warships of the German Navy from Brest. The plans for Operation 'Green' frankly admitted the possibility of failure, in which case 'landing at another point must be attempted'. Withdrawal should take place 'only in an extreme state of emergency'.

The indecisive nature of these instructions only confirms that the Irish expedition was to have been a diversionary one while the mass of German troops on the Channel coast crossed to England. Only three German divisions would take part in the first stages of the Irish invasion;[13] forty were scheduled to participate in Operation Sealion.[14] The planning for Operation 'Green' was to have been completed by the end of August and individual German army commands supervising the Irish venture were ordered to report on their final shipping requirements by September 5.[15] This was ten days before the preliminary date fixed for Sealion.[16] The German forces at Lorient and St Nazaire seemed to have fared only a little worse than their colleagues at the Channel ports who were advised to mount 6-inch guns on barges and rafts to provide a barrage against the British defences when the first commandos landed on the English beaches.[17] When the German 8th Division began its Sealion training on the French coast, they found only one steamer in which to practise their disembarkation techniques; many of the soldiers were struck by the contrast between their own modern weapons and the ancient craft that were supposed to transport them to Britain.[18]

It was not surprising, therefore, that the German commandos chosen to join the patchy armada on its voyage to Ireland – upon which officers were urged to travel by 'motor yacht' – should have been encouraged to regard their undertaking as a test of their military flexibility. The following advice from the 'technical operations' section of Operation 'Green', for example, would have aroused the suspicions of experienced troops aboard the ramshackle invasion fleet: 'The "Green" operation confronts us with an entirely new task. There is therefore no precedent from which we can work. In many cases, troops will have to look after themselves. Each commander must look for a way to achieve his individual objective. Everything depends on the extent of co-operation, on each individual's alertness and ability to take independent action. Confidence in the achievements of German Leadership and the German Soldier should be the foundation of this operation.'[19] This was not the sort of message calculated to instil confidence in the hearts of soldiers aboard ill-maintained French steamships as they prepared to wade ashore, loaded down with pulleys, ropes and water-proofed weapons, onto the isolated beaches of Wexford and Waterford, cut off from their comrades by communication 'difficulties' and aware that they might not be rescued if the Royal Navy should sink their boats.

It is possible that the German High Command never seriously intended to invade Ireland and there is evidence that they deliberately publicised

Operation 'Green' to stretch British defence preparations in advance of Sealion. Major General Walter Warlimont, Deputy Chief of the Wehrmacht High Command's Operations Staff, noted that on June 28 an instruction was issued 'to the effect that in order to mislead the enemy "all available information media" should spread the word that we were preparing a landing in Ireland to draw the net around England tighter and reinforce the "siege". '[20] But the extent of the planning and the distribution of the 'Green' documents suggest that the Germans were contemplating a real landing in the south-east of Ireland, if only to draw off British troops in Northern Ireland who might otherwise be sent to southern England to oppose Sealion. There can be little doubt that the Germans did eventually plan to occupy the entire British Isles, and when their newly-formed Military Economic Staff for England – *Wehrwirtschaftsstab ENGLAND* – met at the beginning of September 1940, they included Dublin among the six German administrative headquarters that were to have been set up in the two islands.[21]* Kaupisch continued his preparations for the Irish invasion throughout September, and only in mid-October – when Sealion had been postponed – was he allowed to slow the pace of his exercises, continuing them only as a pretence.[23]

In the following month, however, Hitler took a personal interest in an invasion of Ireland, prompted perhaps by an Abwehr interception of British radio traffic that suggested the British themselves were about to attack Eire.[24] On December 3, he ordered Admiral Raeder's naval staff to investigate the chances of occupying Ireland. According to the record of that day's Fuehrer conference, Hitler believed that 'a landing in Ireland can be attempted only if Ireland requests help. For the present our envoy must ascertain whether De Valera desires support and whether he wishes to have his military equipment supplemented by captured British war material (guns and ammunition), which could be sent to him in independent ships. Ireland is important to the Commander in Chief, Air, as a base for attacks on the north-west ports of Britain, although weather conditions must be investigated. The occupation of Ireland might lead to the end of the war.'[25]

Raeder, who had voiced enough doubts about Sealion, had little difficulty in disposing of this quixotic idea. German naval supremacy along the invasion routes, his staff reported, 'could never be attained by us in view of the vastly superior British Home Fleet, not even for the duration of one transport operation . . . The possibility of surprise is ruled out due to the necessity of starting from the French coast.' The geographical

---

* For unexplained reasons, the writer Peter Fleming concluded that this was part of a deception plan – presumably the same as that in which Warlimont was involved – and that the troop preparations at Lorient and St Nazaire were a feint. But he produced no proof to support this theory and was apparently unaware of the existence of the Operation 'Green' papers.[22]

position of Ireland was unfavourable because 'the coast of Wales and Cornwall extends like a wedge to our line of approach' and it would be impossible to maintain a defended supply line. 'Although the Irish might willingly open their ports to us,' Raeder's staff asserted, 'they would also be open to the enemy pursuing us.' There would be no time for the Germans to fortify the harbours and:

> To a defending force, cut off and left to its own devices, the topography of the country does not afford us much protection . . . without supplies and reinforcements they would soon feel the increasing pressure of a British expeditionary force brought over under the protection of British naval power; sooner or later our own troops would face a situation similar to Namsos or Dunkirk.[26]

There followed some familiar and gloomy prognostications about the Irish climate, a phenomenon characterised by 'a heavy rainfall and consequently low clouds and very frequent damp and foggy weather'. Airfields in Ireland would not meet German requirements and 'every attempt at transporting troops by Ju 52s would be in great danger from British fighters which are again increasing in numbers . . . Troops landed in Ireland without supplies of foodstuffs, weapons and ammunition would sooner or later be wiped out by an enemy whose supply routes are difficult to attack.' All Raeder's men could offer Hitler was the possibility that German blockade runners carrying weapons and ammunition might get through to Irish ports in the winter months 'as long as there is still no state of war between Britain and Ireland and as long as the Irish cooperate.'[27]

So Raeder, who had raised no alarums about Operation 'Green' four months earlier, now ruled out the occupation of Ireland. An attack on Eire was permissible, it seemed, if it coincided with – or became a diversion to – an invasion of Britain. But as a back door into Britain, as a tactic which 'might lead to the end of the war', it was out of the question. Irish neutrality was to be respected and a landing made there only at de Valera's request. Yet the idea was not yet dead. An attack on the island was to be considered on two more occasions, and throughout the rest of 1940 and the following two years German printers at the Institut Cartographique Militaire in Brussels produced thousands of copies of their maps and literature for German soldiers in Ireland. Whether or not this material ever reached the hands of combat troops is uncertain, but it was published with this end in mind and would have found its way to Wexford and Waterford in the landing barges of Operation 'Green' had the project ever been revived.

The Germans produced similar volumes for all those countries in which they thought their armies might have to fight – a parallel set for Britain was also published in 1940 – and their work represented a library of obsessive if dubious scholarship that sometimes revealed more about the anonymous authors in the German intelligence service than about the nations that formed the subject of each study. Military Geographical Data on Ireland presented a uniquely Teutonic view of Ireland with a mass of generally accurate but frequently useless facts and statistics and a characteristic interest in Irish racial stock. The Irish, it disclosed, were 'a mixture of western and Nordic components. Characteristic are a lively temperament, good nature, cheerfulness, a talent for music and dancing, education and social entertainments. The Irishman supports a community founded upon equality for all but associates with this an extraordinary personal need for independence which easily leads to indiscipline and pugnacity [*Streitsucht*] and makes large political power organisations more difficult. Unreliability and instability are also imputed to him. A profound piety characterises these people, who have defended their Catholic beliefs with fanaticism, and the authority of the priest – sprung from the ordinary people – is enormous.'[28]

Lest the German invaders should come to regard the people of the Gaeltacht as super-patriots, the booklet's authors warned that 'it should . . . be especially emphasised that Irish nationalist sentiments are by no means confined to those who speak Gaelic. More than anything else, religion is the distinguishing feature, in contrast to the inhabitants of the island who identify themselves with the British or English. These are, with the exception of some circles in Dublin, above all in Northern Ireland but they do not constitute a majority [sic]. They are mostly the descendants of English and Scottish colonists.'[29] In a separate section on north-eastern Ireland – the volume treated the island more or less as one country and rarely mentions the border – the German authors attempted to come to grips with the racial strain of Craigavon's citizens. 'The population consists to a great extent of so-called Iro-Scots [sic] and Anglo-Irish . . . in addition to that, there are still Anglicised Irish. A considerable part of the population is, however, Irish in character.'[30]

Readers were reminded that the Irish population decreased from 8,500,000 in 1846 to 4,223,000 in 1931 and that the population of Eire – which the authors always referred to as the Free State – now stood at 2,972,000. The mass of the population 'consists, even today, of small tenant farmers who often work quite insufficient allotments of land under very oppressive conditions . . . Hence, poverty was and still is a general thing . . . The houses, especially in the West, are often extremely primitive huts of broken stones with straw roofs and with a few badly aired and lighted rooms in which large families huddle. The possibilities for billeting troops are therefore, apart from the larger towns, to be described as bad . . .'

Military observations of this kind are scattered throughout the book and a special 'military appreciation' of each district of Ireland was drawn up for the German invasion troops. Landing places around the coastline were described as 'satisfactory to excellent' although the central eastern seaboard and the north-west coast around County Donegal 'which is all too rich in islands' was not recommended. Suggested beach-heads included the Waterford–Wexford sector – the planned landing point of Operation 'Green' – the estuary of the Shannon near Limerick, Galway Bay, Donegal Bay with Killala, Ballina and Sligo, Lough Foyle with London-derry, the 'Bay of Belfast with Belfast and forward harbours' and Cobh. Rather imprudently, the latter was recommended because it 'offers itself especially for . . . a peaceful or completely surprise landing, in which the considerable natural obstacle of the hinterland can be overcome before the development of any strong enemy counter-operation . . .' This was all very well providing the Irish troops on Spike Island and the two forts guarding the mouth of the port did not let loose on the German invasion fleet with their British 9.2-inch and 6-inch artillery, a possibility which the handbook's authors overlooked. Ireland, they claimed, was well suited for troop movements because of its 'excellent network of roads', a sentiment that might not have been shared by the Irish Army.* But if the roads were disregarded, the land appeared 'generally more unfavourable than the relief map suggests . . . In the central flat country, marshes, river-meadows and lakes severely restrict freedom of movement.' In the moun-tains, motorised troops would find it impossible to travel off the roads.

The authors were again pessimistic about troop billeting, referring once more to the lack of hygiene in 'the farmers' and fishermen's homesteads'. The Germany Army could 'count upon rather large quantities of butter, cheese, eggs, meat, oats and potatoes. The rather monotonous native food however will not always appeal to our soldiers. In the bog districts of the central depression attention should be paid to the supply of drinking water . . .' The area of Waterford was recommended for troop landings because of its road communications although the authors could not resist a glance at the district's pedigree. The area of Wexford and Waterford was 'strongly mixed with Norman, Anglo-Saxon and Dutch blood, but is, nevertheless, animated by strong Irish nationalist feeling . . .' As for the south-west, 'the Southern part of the natural land division of Kerry belongs politically to the county of Cork'† but Kerry was well suited for troop landings because of its sheltered harbours. Cork possessed 'a rocky, steep and cliff-like coast with deep estuary bays which form excellent natural ports' and numerous natural harbours would provide a landing place, but German troops would have to cross 'several natural zones of defence'.

A troop landing in Connemara and Sligo was discouraged because of the

---

* A complete set of these German documents found its way into the hands of the Irish intelligence service as early as 1942 – probably by way of the British – and Captain J.G. Healy of the Irish Army's G2 Branch later translated the booklets into English.[31]
† A comment which was unlikely to incline either Kerrymen or the inhabitants of Cork toward the German cause.

inland mountains and the 'countless rocky hillocks and . . . stagnant lakes'. The authors noted the existence of the Clifden Railway, an unhelpful observation since the line had been abandoned long before the war. Parts of this area were 'so windswept and subject to rain and mists that they are uninhabited and hardly used . . .' Donegal was also considered 'a specially barren and broken part' of the land although Enniskillen in County Fermanagh enjoyed 'a commanding and favourable position' in the region. Belfast and the area around Lough Neagh were described as 'a very good proposition from the point of view of troop movement . . . Prospects for provisioning and billeting are good.' In Dublin, there were many types of industry 'among which a great part is played by the brewery'. The countryside outside Dublin was 'the central field of operations in the island' and the German authors remarked that 'in the past Ireland has been conquered and ruled from it . . .'

The handbook also contained an extremely detailed description of the Ardnacrusha power station on the Shannon, together with a map and diagram that was presumably furnished by the German architects who designed the plant. The list of Irish cities and towns which the volume also included was an amalgam of population figures and industrial geography although it failed to mention important military details. Tiny villages like Ballyhaunis ('County Mayo, 1103 inhabitants') and Dalkey ('County Dublin, 4135 inhabitants, bathing and residential area on southside of Dublin Bay, station and garage') were awarded a place in the list although Castletownbere in Cork, the nearest mainland berth to the military harbour at Berehaven, was omitted. Long entries were given to Dublin ('390,000 inhabitants, capital of the Irish Free State, parliament (The Dail) in Leinster House, university, museum, schools, hospitals . . .') and the larger city of Belfast ('438,000 inhabitants, on the Lagan River near Belfast Lough, capital of Northern Ireland, parliament building on the edge of the city Newtownard's Road, city hall in Donegal [sic] Square . . .') but in neither is there any reference to the large Irish and British military bases in the cities. Some of the information was absurd. The German authors disclosed, for instance, that Magherafelt in County Londonderry was 'a town with a big rectangular market square in the centre from which roads go to the North, South, East and West directions', an observation that was unlikely to be of immediate use to a German tank commander under fire. Other facts were tantalising in their obscurity. In Dublin, for example, there was a 'project for a munitions factory, unknown if completed yet' in which a German officer would be more interested than the whereabouts of the Guinness brewery or the Jacob's biscuit factory.[32]

The separate volume of photographs that accompanied this booklet contained 120 illustrations, most of them copies of postcards or newspaper pictures. These may have given the German Army a general idea of the sort of country they were invading but would have been of little military use. Picture 19, for instance, shows a thatched cottage in the Kerry mountains outside of which a hen, two cows, an old woman in a long skirt, a small boy and a man in a bowler hat stare suspiciously at the camera. The caption announces: 'People and animals often live together in one or two-roomed huts when there is no stable.' Picture 74 is even less instructive. Captioned simply 'Bogland in County Roscommon', it depicts a moss-covered wall amid mud and puddles, all partially obscured by a downpour of heavy rain. None of this material was likely to commend itself to diligent members of the Wehrmacht. The photographs of Ireland's cities might have proved more useful. There is an aerial view of the centre of Belfast with the monumental façade of the City Hall dominating the surrounding rows of dark office blocks and the slums of the old Markets district. A picture of 'Stadt Cork, St Patrickstrasse' probably gave a fair enough impression of daily commercial life in Eire's second city, with automobiles and petrol buses driving between pavements crowded with shoppers and with a banner bearing the words 'Nathan the Tailor' flapping gaily above the awnings. But an illustration captioned 'Dublin, Stadtbild mit Liffeyfluss' would have been somewhat misleading. Apart from two electric trams negotiating the corner of O'Connell Bridge, the only vehicles to be seen are horse-drawn carriages. An elegant phaeton is approaching Bachelors Walk and the vessels moored in the fog opposite the Customs House down river are all sailing ships. The picture appears to have been taken at the end of the nineteenth century.[33]

An annex to the previous two volumes contained street maps of twenty-five cities and towns,* including street names, important buildings, hotels and petrol stations, the latter sometimes accompanied by the home addresses and telephone numbers of the garage owners.[34] The information for this booklet was taken largely from the first edition of the Automobile Association's Road Book of Ireland.† In a further two volumes for German invasion troops, published in May and October of 1941, similar use was made of information that had been freely available to the public before the war.[36] Maps were copied from the Irish Ordnance Survey; other sources included the Distribution of Peat Bogs and Coalfields of Ireland and John Bartholomew's 1891 map of Dublin. There were serious errors in the work. Two buildings in Dublin marked as hospitals – the Royal Military Infirmary at Parkgate Street and the Kilmainham Royal Hospital – were respectively the headquarters and G2 Intelligence Branch of the Irish Army and the headquarters of the Garda Siochana. A photo-

---

* Armagh, Athlone, Ballymena, Belfast, Carlow, Clonmel, Cobh, Coleraine, Cork, Drogheda, Dublin, Dundalk, Enniskillen, Galway, Killarney, Limerick, Londonderry, Navan, Newry, Portadown, Sligo, Tralee, Waterford, Westport and Wexford.
† In a long and witty article for the Irish Army's house magazine years after the war, Lieutenant Colonel Colm Cox also revealed that the index of towns in the first German volume was culled from Thom's Directory of Ireland, printed in 1939.[35]

graph of Dun Aengus fort on the Aran Islands, County Galway, was said to have been taken on Aran Island, County Donegal, a hundred miles to the north east.[37] The fourth booklet – *Von Mizen Head bis Malin Head* – attempted to furnish German troops with a pocket guide to the Irish language, a vocabulary of just ninety-eight words, translated with such woeful inaccuracy that it would have been useless even to the most academic *Feldwebel* unless perhaps he came across one of the Irish-language pamphlets that Craigavon wanted to distribute around Eire.* This adventure into Irish linguistics was probably the work of a German Gaelic scholar who may have been trying to phoneticise Irish into German.

Of far less innocent provenance, however, were the illustrations in these last two booklets. Photographs of the Irish coastline came from Luftwaffe photo-reconnaissance units and from snapshots apparently taken before the war by German tourists with an unerringly good eye for potential beach-heads. Three hundred and thirty-two photographs and coastal profiles were used to illustrate maps of a 1:250,000 scale, together with details of spring tides, geological formations and possible military routes inland from the beaches. Yet another series of pictures was published in 1942 by the Luftwaffe High Command in Berlin. The *Küsten-Beschreibung des Irischen Freistaates (Eires)* – Description of the Coasts of the Irish Free State (Eire) – in fact included the coastline of Northern Ireland as well as Eire and many of the photographs, taken at a height of about 30,000 feet, are of remarkably fine quality. A five-mile section of sea shore north of Bray Head is so sharply defined that individual trees as well as houses stand out beside the lanes and hills. Another picture, wrongly captioned 'Dalkey Island (Dublin Bay)', shows the shore of the bay from Dun Laoghaire to the entrance of Dublin port. A few clouds are drifting across the sea and over the north side of the city but every sandbank below Blackrock and Sandymount is clearly delineated. A train can even be seen entering Dun Laoghaire station, the smoke from the steam locomotive drifting over the mailboat pier.[39]

The Irish authorities were well aware that the Germans were photographing their coastline. On 29 December 1940, a Luftwaffe plane flew low over Dublin, coming under fire from Irish anti-aircraft batteries outside the city, and Mulcahy was later informed at the Defence Conference that the aircraft was 'definitely taking pictures'.[40] On another occasion, a German plane that crash-landed in Eire was found to have a photographer on board.[41] The Luftwaffe paid particular attention to possible invasion beaches; thus the Bray photograph included the sloping

---

* Nearly all the words were geographical – creek, cape, coast, shoal, mountain, etc. – and included neither verbs nor prepositions. Readers who speak Irish will appreciate the dire standard of the glossary from a few examples: fisherman's home *airidh*; hill *knowe*; bay *linsche*; clod *meall*; the *na, na la, nam, nan*; spring *tob*.[38]

strand below Killiney Hill and the picture of Dublin Bay showed the sands at low tide off Sandymount. A three-section photograph was also assembled of the lower half of Lough Foyle in Northern Ireland, a fold-out plate that covered the land and sea shore from the outskirts of Londonderry almost to Magilligan Point. The pictures showed the long, flat beaches north west of Limavady and two British military airfields – Eglinton and Ballykelly – as well as the Belfast–Londonderry railway line. Black lines had been superimposed on the airfields to emphasise the direction of the runways.

Several other photographs in this collection were of the Kerry coast. One illustration of the Blasket Islands was from a picture postcard, with magnetic north overprinted in the foreground. Several pages contained frames of Sybil Point and Slea Head on the Dingle peninsula; at least one of these photographs was taken from the sea, perhaps from a submarine, and five from the shore-line on a small camera. Nearly all showed the Blaskets, and some considerable attention was paid to the island of Inishvickillane. Drawings and sketches of the Blaskets were also included with mileage charts. These may have been the work of a German brass band which stayed in Cahirsiveen on the south side of Dingle Bay in 1937; local people remember the musicians 'drawing maps' as they relaxed in fields above the sea between performances.[42]

But while German intelligence work on Ireland was detailed, thorough and only occasionally careless, no attempt was made to conduct any serious analysis into the politics of the partitioned island. The Gestapo had prepared for themselves a 100-page handbook on Britain, *Informationsheft GB*, which contained an assessment of political groups and organisations in the country. There was a brief reference in it to the Communist Party of Eire but otherwise no mention of Ireland was made.[43] A separate 350-page *Sonderfahndungsliste GB* comprised a list of those people in public life who lived in Britain and who were to be arrested after the occupation. Churchill's Irish-born confidant Brendan Bracken – later to become British Minister of Information – was on the list and so was 'Claude [sic] Cockburn, 56 Jahr alt, Korrespondent'[44] but no other Irish name appears, not even Craigavon and his ministers in Belfast. Nor was a corresponding handbook published for the Gestapo on Eire or Northern Ireland. If Ireland was to be occupied, it would be as a means to the invasion of Britain, an object of military but not political attention. Doubtless the Gestapo would have arrived in Dublin and Belfast once the island was in German hands but it was important only as the back door of Britain's defences, a springboard for the final blow against Germany's only surviving European enemy.

This, of course, was precisely the scenario that the British and Irish Governments feared in the spring of 1940 and which led not only to Britain's offer of Irish unity in return for Eire's participation in the war but to the extremely secret military co-operation between the British and Irish

Armies to repel a German invasion of Eire. The meeting in London on May 24 between Joseph Walshe, Colonel Archer of G2 and British army, naval and air force officers explored almost every conceivable way in which the Germans might have been planning to attack Eire. After the invasion of neutral Holland and Belgium, the British seemed convinced that Ireland would be attacked from the air, and Major G.D.G. Heyman of the War Office suggested that up to 5000 German paratroops might be landed in Eire, closely followed by airborne troops in a fleet of Junkers 90s and Focke-Wulf 200s. So great had been the shock generated by German successes on the Continent that Heyman even raised the bizarre possibility of a U-boat invasion of Ireland, pointing out to Walshe and Archer that Germany might have 'as many as 100 submarines each capable of carrying 30 men'.

The British argument was calculated to persuade the Irish that British troops should be permitted to enter Eire before a German landing. Archer insisted that 'the Irish must take the first brunt of the attack' because the Irish public had to realise that the invasion was under way and that their own troops were engaging the Germans. Walshe wanted to know if the RAF could intercept the Luftwaffe's troop carriers while they were still in the air since 'the doctrine of hot pursuit in Irish territorial waters was already established.' He was told that interception could not be guaranteed at night. Archer confirmed that his government were considering a search of all vessels approaching Irish ports, although the British were not satisfied with Irish precautions against paratroop landings. The airfield at Rineanna on the Shannon was to be put out of commission with stakes and wire, and similar measures were being taken at the Irish military and civil airbases at Baldonnel and Collinstown. The airfield at Oranmore in County Galway was to be cratered. The British warned Walshe and Archer, however, that the Germans might land on roads, golf courses, race courses or parks and that it was essential that stocks of oil near possible landing grounds should be destroyed in the event of an attack.

Archer explained that Irish troops were already organised in mobile columns to deal with multiple parachute landings. But he agreed that some Irish ports did not even have permanent military guards and that there was a scarcity of anti-submarine defences in the harbours. Walshe was unwilling to discuss the issue of Fifth Columnists because 'the Government of Eire was satisfied with the position as it now stood.'[45] When the meeting resumed again next morning after both sides had consulted their governments, Heyman almost immediately expressed the War Office's anxiety over the IRA. Once more Walshe claimed that his government did not regard the organisation as a serious threat.

The War Office wanted direct liaison between the Irish military authorities in Dublin and the British General Officer Commanding in Belfast. Walshe and Archer therefore agreed to fly in secret to Belfast that afternoon in the company of Lieutenant Colonel Dudley Clarke, a staff

officer who had had practical experience of the Norwegian campaign.[46]*
The three men travelled to Northern Ireland in the twin-engined
Flamingo aircraft used by Churchill. After collecting two officers from the
British Army's headquarters staff in Belfast, Clarke – dressed in mufti at
Walshe's request – travelled on to Dublin by rail. His experience there
provided a surrealistic counter-point to the controlled panic of the War
Office in London. Clarke was picked up from the Shelbourne Hotel in
Dublin by Walshe and transported through a warren of underground
tunnels to a conference room beneath Government Buildings in Kildare
Street where he was confronted by a group of Irish Army officers. He
informed them that Lieutenant General Sir Hubert Huddleston, the
GOC Northern Ireland, already had a British mobile column awaiting
orders to travel south of the border to help the Irish Army if the Germans
invaded.[47]

Clarke underwent another underground tour next morning, starting at
the Irish National Gallery and walking beneath the Dail to a second
conference. Here he met General McKenna, the Irish Army Chief of
Staff, who disillusioned him of any preconception that the British would
be allowed into Eire before the Germans arrived. Clarke dined that night
with Frank Aiken and listened during the meal as the Minister for the
Coordination of Defensive Measures outlined 'a dozen new ideas for the
mechanical improvement of the war'. Walshe took Clarke to Phoenix Park
and then to Baldonnel airfield, which Clarke studied through binoculars
until a man on a bicycle somehow alarmed Walshe to such a degree that he
hustled his guest back to his hotel.[48]

The British adopted an especially secretive attitude towards this wartime co-operation with Eire, a sensitivity that has persisted to the present
day. As the Irish journalist Joseph Carroll discovered, Clarke wrote a
book about his exploits after the war only to be ordered under the Official
Secrets Act to delete all references to Dublin.[49] During my own
researches, the British Ministry of Defence refused to release five pages
from the war diaries of British Troops Northern Ireland, documents
which contain details of the military instructions for Huddleston's troops
to move south of the border.[50] However, from identical copies of the
BTNI papers lodged in Northern Ireland and from a mass of associated
files – some at the Public Record Office in London and others in Belfast –
it is possible to reconstruct almost in their entirety the secret plans that

* Before they left, Heyman mentioned that the British were 'interested in a rumour
concerning a ship said to contain 200,000 mauser rifles' that was reported to have arrived in
Holland just before the German invasion while ostensibly *en route* from America to
Rumania. The boat was now rumoured to be heading for an Irish port. Walshe, obviously
delighted at the prospect of receiving so many weapons free of charge, immediately
promised that his government would give 'urgent attention' to the seizure of the ship since
'the rifles and ammunition might well come in very useful for arming the Irish population.'
Unfortunately for Walshe, the phantom vessel never materialised.

would have enabled British and Irish soldiers to fight shoulder to shoulder against the Nazis in defence of Ireland.

Clarke returned to London on May 28 and reported to Machtig at the Dominions Office on his 'most encouraging' visit to Dublin. The Irish Army had given the British full details of their organisation and equipment 'without reservation' and had in return requested information on British troop strength in Northern Ireland.[51] Maffey was to be asked for his views on the appointment of military attachés to his office in Dublin. In the event of a German invasion, the Irish would call for assistance from Huddleston in Belfast who proposed that the British attachés in Dublin should then form 'the nucleus for a military mission' in Eire. Britain was already sending a primitive system of air alerts to Dublin, transmitting 'red' and 'yellow' warnings through GPO lines to the Irish Government whenever German aircraft passed over the midlands or west coast of Britain – even though the Germans were not actually flying to Ireland.[52] Since GPO lines would be cut in an invasion, the system was now to be augmented by an emergency military wireless link between Dublin and London, a radio network that would be hooked up through the GPO station at Seaforth in Lancashire. In their transmissions to London asking for help, the Irish Army were to use two code names – JOCKEY for the British War Office and KIOSK for the Air Ministry – and were to employ the call sign AGS when communicating to Britain.[53]

The British Army's advance from Northern Ireland into Eire – code-named the 'W' Plan – was a complex affair, fraught with administrative difficulties and political danger. The British suspected that the Germans would try to land in Cork because it was the nearest landfall in Ireland to the Luftwaffe fighter bases in north-western France. Northern Ireland was to serve as the base for the British expeditionary force that would move into Eire to repel the invaders, and troops of the 53rd Division in Belfast were held in readiness for the advance. Royal Marine units at Milford Haven were also prepared to seize a bridge-head in Eire the moment the Germans landed.[54] Officers at the headquarters of British Troops Northern Ireland, now ensconced at the new Thiepval Barracks at Lisburn in County Antrim, estimated that the Germans could embark five divisions by sea to Ireland although 'not more than 2–3 would reach land'. Up to 8000 German airborne troops could be flown into Eire, some of them by seaplanes which would land on the lakes. The British striking force of 53 Division, later augmented by the 5th Battalion, The Cheshire Regiment, were to concentrate on the west Down and Armagh borders, then drive across the frontier and race for Dublin along three main roads south – the Belfast–Dublin coastal route through Dundalk, Drogheda and Balbriggan, the inland road through Ardee and Slane, and the Castle-blancy–Carrickmacross–Navan road.[55] Before the German air force destroyed the bridges, all three British spearheads would try to cross the Boyne, thus bringing with them to Dublin not only the military assistance that de Valera would have requested but the impermeable dust of Anglo-Irish history as well.

By December 1940, the 'W' Plan had been extended. While the first British striking force headed for Dublin, the British 61st Division, in a quite separate operation, would move across the border into Donegal and secure the Treaty port of Lough Swilly for the Royal Navy, providing the British Government with a third of the naval defence requirements that they had been requesting from de Valera for more than a year. The BTNI war diary listed the Irish heavy armament at Fort Lenan and Fort Dunree – two 9.2-inch and two 6-inch guns – and mentioned that one heavy machine gun and eight light machine guns were positioned between the two forts. There were, the diary recorded, 278 Irish troops at Lough Swilly and only 976 Irish soldiers in the rest of Donegal, a specific detail that should have been superfluous if the British were arriving in Eire at the invitation of the Irish Government. A cryptic note at the bottom of the war diary in December 1940 observed: 'Close cooperation to be maintained with Eire forces including LSF if friendly.'[56]

That phrase 'if friendly' characterises many of the British military documents on the proposed advance into Eire. 'If Eire be hostile,' begins one instruction, 'it may be necessary for Royal Signals units to take over the civil telephone system . . .'[57] But why should Eire be 'hostile' if she had invited the British to help her? According to a restricted file prepared by the British Army's 'Q' Movements Transport control in Belfast, the British would not have crossed the border 'until invited to do so by the Eire Government'. But the document added that although most people in Eire would probably have helped the British Army, 'there would have been a small disaffected element capable of considerable guerrilla activities against us.'[58] The British were certainly worried that their operation would be opposed by Fifth Columnists, and a complicated system of radio codes was devised to prevent a premature advance. Maffey was to send the code word 'Pumpkins' – later replaced by 'Measure'* – to Northern Ireland to give Huddleston and General Sir Harold Franklyn, the BTNI commander, final permission to send the 53rd Division down to Dublin.[60] But was there any other reason why British troops might have expected opposition?

As British reinforcements made their way towards Dublin, the initial German invasion force – always supposing it had been obliging enough to land where the British and Irish expected it – would have been engaged by General Michael Joe Costello's 1st Irish Division from Cork, supported by General Hugo MacNeill's 2nd Division. The British would establish their railhead near the Fairyhouse race course[61] and be given billets at Lusk, Howth and Portmarnock north of Dublin.[62] Franklyn himself

---

* 'Measure' also appears to have been an Admiralty code for British naval action in the event of a German invasion of Eire.[59]

would be given a headquarters on the outskirts of the city.[63] Franklyn, a veteran of Dunkirk who had experienced the chaos on the roads of northern France as refugees blocked retreating military traffic, may have been responsible for the strict rules laid down for refugees in Northern Ireland and the border. All civilians fleeing from military action were to be kept away from the frontier and from military roads, from railway and bus stations, and would be given no emergency food outside Belfast and Londonderry. The Garda and the British military authorities co-operated to set up Garda Traffic Control Posts at points where refugee routes might cross priority military roads.[64]

To back up the British division fighting in Eire, elaborate plans were made in Belfast to supply the expeditionary force by rail with guns, ammunition, petrol and medical equipment. The British Army's marshalling yards at Balmoral, south of the city, were specially extended to take long ammunition and fuel trains that were loaded and ready on the new sidings. In addition, three ambulance trains were positioned around Belfast and an ambulance railhead was established on the outskirts to take the wounded returning from the south of Ireland. British soldiers stripped the sides from dozens of coal trucks, transforming them into flat cars for armoured vehicles and tanks that would be sent over the border.[65] Once the 53rd Division was committed in Eire, the British military authorities planned to run thirty-eight supply trains on the two railway lines to Dublin every day – thirty down the main line through Drogheda (if the viaduct over the Boyne was still intact) and the remainder along the track which cut through County Cavan. Belfast port would be handling 10,000 tons of stores a week and could receive up to 5000 troops every day for the battle-front.[66]

In London, considerable disquiet was expressed about the number of British troops that might be sucked into Ireland to deal with a diversionary German landing. Churchill, who was told that it would take ten days to transport a division across the Irish Sea, regarded the commitment of such precious resources as an 'undue risk' in June 1940 when British defences had to be concentrated in southern England. He told Ismay that 'schemes should be prepared to enable two or three lightly-equipped brigades to move at short notice, and in not more than three days, into Northern Ireland.' He did not think the Germans would make a naval descent on Eire and concluded that 'nothing that can happen in Ireland can be immediately decisive.'[67]

Churchill's conclusion was the product of desperate optimism rather than tactical judgement, for over the coming months, as Britain's military strength recovered from the débâcle in France, the RAF and the Royal Navy prepared sweeping – even drastic – contingency plans for a German invasion of Ireland. The RAF were to fly three Hurricane fighter squadrons into Baldonnel airfield south-west of Dublin and two bomber squadrons into Collinstown to attack German troops in Cork.[68] The British 1st

Heavy Anti-Aircraft Regiment was to be moved into Eire to defend the Drogheda viaduct, Collinstown and Baldonnel[69] while the Admiralty would issue instructions to sail all British and foreign ships from Irish ports, vessels in Londonderry to head for the Clyde and boats in Belfast for Holyhead and Liverpool. As many ships as possible would be cleared from Cork and Dublin, and taken to the Clyde, Holyhead and Fishguard. A 'most secret' Admiralty memorandum in January 1941 makes it clear that the Royal Navy would have their own officers in Dublin and Cork to direct this exodus. The embarkation of refugees was to be 'discouraged'.[70] British submarines were to patrol off Cork and the Shannon in readiness to attack the invasion fleet.[71] If the Germans landed, the Royal Navy would declare a 'sink on sight' zone in the Western Approaches and off the south and west coasts of Ireland. The RAF would also be given a free bombing zone on receipt of the code word 'Measure'.[72] In December 1940, submarine commanders were warned that the Germans would probably embark their invasion fleet from Brest, Bordeaux and Lorient and make simultaneous attacks in a number of places.[73] By April 1941, the new BTNI commander, General Sir Henry Pownall, spread the invasion area to cover fifty per cent of the entire Irish coastline. In order of preference, he thought the Germans would land in Cork, Limerick, Waterford, Westport and Galway, and Sligo and Donegal.[74]

The 'W' Plan was not without its lighter side. Journalists working in Belfast for Dublin newspapers were called to a British Army press conference in the autumn of 1940 and solemnly told by a major general that they would be permitted to accompany British troops into Eire as correspondents of a neutral nation.[75] British service personnel were not allowed to carry out first-hand reconnaissance in the twenty-six counties and the British Army's transport corps had little up-to-date information about the railway system south of the border. As a result, their officers 'frequently became apparently respectable citizens and would disappear for days at a time to return with bleary smut filled eyes but happily carrying in their heads much vital information.'[76] Fearful that their ammunition wagons would be lost on Eire's winding branch lines amid the confusion of battle, the British Army decided to equip their trains with carrier pigeons which could flutter off to advanced military headquarters with news of forthcoming arms supplies. A lieutenant colonel in charge of the War Office's first carrier pigeon section was actually summoned over to Belfast to explain his ornithological trade to the bemused men of 53 Division.[77] All British troops entering Eire were to be given Irish Tricolours in the hope that this would ensure them a friendly reception[78] although the proposed design of the expeditionary force's military motif, to be worn initially by the British Army's 6th Corps headquarters staff, caused some concern in June 1940. Anything remotely political or religious was banned, a prohibition which effectively excluded the colours blue, orange, green, roses, shamrocks and lilies. Officers considered using a picture of an Irish round tower, the conical stone medieval fortress common to both parts of Ireland. But this image was thought to be 'open to misrepresentation and acts of would-be humourists [sic]'. Avoiding such a phallic choice, the Army eventually chose an illustration of an Irish gate. This they regarded as a fitting symbol of their intention to bar the way of a German invader.[79]

The Irish Government did not doubt Britain's determination to push back a German invasion of Ireland but they never shook off the lingering doubt that British troops might cross the border uninvited, that the invasion of Eire might come from Northern Ireland rather than from France. Nor were their suspicions entirely misplaced. Quite apart from Churchill's threat to consider the 'weapons of coercion', the idea of reoccupying the twenty-six counties had been a topic of political conversation in Britain since the beginning of the war. 'We shall presently be attacked from the west, through Ireland, the British Finland,' George Bernard Shaw wrote to Lady Londonderry in January 1940, 'and shall have to re-occupy it and swallow all our virtuous indignation.'[80] Within the British Army, an attack on Ireland was being actively considered in the summer of 1940. In June of that year – the same month in which Malcolm MacDonald carried Britain's offer of Irish unity to Dublin – Major General Bernard Montgomery was busy planning the seizure of what he picturesquely referred to as 'Cork and Queenstown in Southern Ireland'. Cobh was to be attacked and captured by the British 3rd Division 'so that the harbour can be used as a naval base for the anti-submarine war in the Atlantic.'[81] The plan was dropped, much to Montgomery's relief.* But the following November, German army intelligence picked up a British radio signal which said: 'Fifty wireless operators (no Jews) are to be provided for transferring GHQ. Depart Carlisle November 22 1940 1300 hrs for operation Ireland. Starting point for operation Ireland is Rosslea in Ulster.'[83] This was enough to convince the German High Command that Britain was planning an invasion of Eire although it scarcely provided concrete proof. The radio traffic may have been intended for German ears – why else would it include so strange a reference to Jews? – or it may have been merely an exercise connected with the 'W' Plan.

But the 'W' Plan itself contained a number of inexplicable details which are hardly consistent with an advance into friendly territory to assist a new ally in repelling an invader. Why, for instance, did the British plan to send their 61st Division west into Donegal to take over the Treaty harbour of Lough Swilly when the German landing was expected in Cork, 250 miles to the south? They would certainly wish to prevent a German seizure of the port but it would scarcely have needed a division to reinforce the 278 Irish troops already defending Forts Lenan and Dunree when there was anyway little chance of an attack there by the Germans. The late inclusion

* 'I had already fought the Southern Irish once, in 1921 and 1922,' he wrote in his memoirs, 'and it looked as if this renewed contest might be quite a party – with only one division.'[82]

of Lough Swilly in the 'W' Plan also happened to coincide with mounting British shipping losses off Ireland and a speech by Churchill in the House of Commons, in which he referred to the 'most heavy and grievous burden' placed upon Britain by the Royal Navy's exclusion from the three Treaty ports.[84] This had been followed in London by a press campaign directed against Eire, in which even the *Economist* stated that Britain should seize the ports if they became 'a matter of life or death'.[85]

In these circumstances, it would not be surprising if Britain had intended – at the very least – to take advantage of an Irish call for assistance. Eire would be far too busy fending off a German invasion to stop British troops moving into the Lough Swilly forts. Perhaps, too, the British might have implemented the 'W' Plan after the Germans had landed but without waiting for de Valera's invitation if it seemed too long in coming. This would account for the references in the official documents to potential Irish Army opposition, to a 'hostile' country in which the British Army might have to run even the telephone system. But it is also just possible that they hoped that someone other than de Valera would invite them to enter Eire, and on 26 June 1940, a curious approach was made to Mulcahy by an Irish-born ex-British Army officer, a retired lieutenant colonel who was a county councillor in Eire and lived not far from the border. In a note marked 'Intelligence file', Mulcahy recorded that the ex-colonel:

> . . . called to say that 'the people in the North are prepared to make a military convention with this country without reference to the Northern Government' . . . He wanted someone to go up there from here unofficially, to speak to someone in authority and say how the land lay. In reply to questioning, he stated that the people he referred to were the British Army authorities in the North.[86]

The colonel confirmed that this was a proposal for a joint military command of Eire and Northern Ireland, and that 'the O.C. of the forces in the North was to be approached unofficially . . . by somebody with a view to bringing about the things he mentioned.' But Mulcahy, ever the constitutionalist, turned his visitor down. Such a proposal, he said, should be made by the British Government to the Irish Government. Besides, 'there was little use in thinking that any such arrangements could be made until the British and Northern Governments were prepared to say that the Border was wiped out, and Ireland became a unified state.' If this was conceded and the Irish Government approved of the idea, then Fine Gael would support the Irish Government in bringing about a unity of military control.[87] The colonel, a Protestant and veteran of the King's Royal Rifle Corps who had been wounded in the 1914–18 War,[88] took the matter no further. He had been 'stimulated' to seek his interview with Mulcahy, he said, after a discussion with 'important members of the British Army in the North of Ireland'.[89]

The identity of these British officers was not revealed and the 61-year-old colonel – who died shortly after the war – does not reappear in Mulcahy's papers. Could the British Army have been dabbling in politics, hoping at this critical moment after the fall of France to engineer some sort of Fine Gael coup in Eire that would permit them to reoccupy the country by means of a joint military control or an Anglo-Irish 'military convention'? The clumsy attempt to attract Mulcahy's interest by suggesting that Craigavon's government would be ignored – as Fine Gael might be persuaded to ignore de Valera's government – does not suggest the sophistication of a British cabinet minister. However, the colonel – though Mulcahy may not have known this – was a friend of Maffey; and what is remarkable is that he made his overtures to Mulcahy on the very day upon which MacDonald was handing de Valera the formal British proposals for the unification of Ireland, the third of which offered a joint defence council of Eire and Northern Ireland. Was this therefore a British attempt to put pressure on de Valera by obtaining the support of Mulcahy for the Irish unity proposals? Or were the British trying to chip away at Eire's all-party consensus in favour of neutrality? Six days after his meeting with the colonel, Mulcahy did tell de Valera that the Fine Gael front bench would support his government if they decided to enter the war as a 'United Ireland'.[90] But so far as is known, he never travelled to Northern Ireland to speak to British officers there; nor did any further intermediaries approach Fine Gael.

A Unionist member of the Northern Ireland Senate, Sir Emerson Herdman, did call to see de Valera at the end of June, presumably acting as an unofficial emissary for Craigavon. He wanted to know 'what could be done about Unity of Command' and asked if Eire would enter the war in return for an end to partition. De Valera repeated the same arguments he had been using on MacDonald; that Ireland should be united but that she could not participate in the European conflict without her people being 'split from top to bottom' in near-civil war. Even if Ireland was invaded, de Valera said, 'divisions of Canadian or Australian troops might be acceptable, but British troops would not be popular here.'* Herdman seems to have been testing the water of unity for Craigavon. Indeed, he is almost certainly the 'friend' whom Craigavon quoted in his letter to Chamberlain of June 26, in which he recorded a meeting between de Valera and 'an absolutely reliable source'. In any event, Herdman can only have been delighted by de Valera's reply. According to Mulcahy, he was amazed at de Valera's attitude and concluded that 'the only thing to do now for Britain is to send in powerful forces here, and prevent this country being seized, or prevent them [the British] having to use and lose large numbers of troops in putting the Germans out, if they got here.'[91]

---

* So much for the 'W' Plan and Franklyn's Tricolour-waving Tommies as they de-trained at Fairyhouse race course.

This view precisely echoed Craigavon's intemperate telegram to Chamberlain, urging a British advance south across the border. And if such a course of action had ever been contemplated – not at Craigavon's instigation but as a desperate measure by the Government in London – then by December 1940 there were enough British troops in Northern Ireland to fight their way through to one of the Treaty ports and to reach south, perhaps as far as the Irish capital. This raises one last intriguing possibility: that the 'W' Plan – while it was on one level fully intended to be the British response to an Irish call for assistance – was also the embryo plan for the British invasion of Eire, for the seizure of the ports and for the imposition from Franklyn's headquarters outside Dublin of a martial law not dissimilar to that advocated by Craigavon in June 1940. Ironically, the operational papers drawn up for the original 'W' Plan were all destroyed when the Luftwaffe bombed Belfast in 1941 and set fire to the British Army's Northern Ireland District headquarters in which the documents were kept.[92] Thus the only record of the scheme's development in 1940 remains the British Army war diaries, files which give us a detailed if incomplete record of the secret military plans for Eire, and which the British consider highly sensitive even to this day.

In 1940, of course, Irish officers were briefed by the British on the arrangements for reinforcing their troops. The Irish Army would certainly have needed help if the Germans had arrived. By October 1940, four more regular army brigades had been raised in Eire and the Irish Department of Defence felt confident enough to inform de Valera that 'the morale and *esprit de corps* of the Army is excellent' and that soon 'a force of very considerable striking power will be available for the defence of the country.'[93] This, however, was not entirely true. LSF recruiting figures were increasing and the regular army looked smarter in their new pale green uniforms and the rimmed British-style steel helmets which had now replaced the German coal-scuttle variety.[94] But the Irish had managed to obtain few arms for their new recruits, and their armour was mostly obsolete. Apart from their thirteen old Rolls-Royce light armoured cars and a total of sixteen medium armoured cars, the only additions were a series of armoured vehicles, constructed on Ford and Dodge chassis by Irish firms, which were purchased for the Cavalry Corps.[95]

The naval and air arms of the defence forces were even less impressive. The cadre squadron of four Gloster Gladiators – each sporting the Celtic design orange and green Air Corps insignia – still provided the only serious fighter defence in the country. In 1940, six Hawker Hinds were bought but even these were second-hand and used only as trainers. The remaining collection of Ansons, Lysanders, Walrus seaplanes and Magisters were of little or no use in a war. This was not the sort of air armada to put fear into the hearts of German or British invaders. Later in the war, the Irish repaired and cannibalised several Allied aircraft that had crash-landed in Eire, eventually putting into the air two former RAF Hurricanes, a Fairey Battle and an American Lockheed Hudson, complete with Irish insignia on their wings.[96]* The Naval Service, which probably left more to the imagination than it did to the sea, only acquired its first motor torpedo-boat in January 1940. There were to be six by 1942 but the only patrol vessels were the *Muirchu* and the *Fort Rannoch*, two former British gunboats, the first of which had the doubtful distinction – in British hands – of shelling Pearse and his colleagues in the Dublin Post Office in the Easter 1916 Rising. Together with a small training ship and a barge that was decorously called a 'mine planter', these vessels formed the total strength of the Irish Naval Service.[98]

The parlous condition of the defence forces did not improve. The Naval Service never acquired another ship throughout the war. The LSF was split into two, the 'A' force moving from police to military control and taking the new title of Local Defence Force. But there were few guns for this new auxiliary army. 'We have 100,000 LDF men with empty hands – as helpless as any civilians,' wrote Dr Thomas F. O'Higgins, one of the Fine Gael representatives on the Defence Conference, in March 1941. 'We have 20,000 LDF men with rifles of a bore that limits the supply of ammunition to less than 100 rounds or about a couple of hours service.' O'Higgins's views were naturally prejudiced but they reflected a reality that seemed only too obvious to the impotent Fine Gael leadership, which still wondered whether an alliance with Britain might not produce the best form of defence:

> We have an Army of about 20,000 fighters equipped with rifles, machine guns and some field artillery, most of this force would be required to deal with protective duties against internal forces. We have no aerial fighters worth mentioning and no anti-aircraft ground defences. Bombers could dominate the country at any time, so as to completely paralyse the Army, and force a very speedy surrender by the people. We are wide open to easy mass slaughter by any power who desires to wring concessions from us . . . I believe we should consider our territorial rights, our economic supplies, our defence equipment and that if we co-operate with Britain on those terms we may conceivably be increasing the danger of bombings but we are increasing our defence immeasurably.[99]

Down in Cork, Costello's 1st Division relied for its harassment techniques and mobility partly upon bicycle squadrons[100] although it boldly stitched a former southern brigade insignia of a thunderbolt onto its uniforms as if to emphasise its putative striking power should the Germans land.

Its problems were doubled by the Irish Government's fear that Eire's invaders could come from either of the two belligerent powers. MacNeill's 2nd Division, which might otherwise have been positioned with Costello's

* Only in 1947 did the Irish Army Air Corps obtain Spitfires, one of which was still in service in 1961.[97]

forces, was therefore facing north, and the Irish Army's Corps of Engineers spent weeks preparing two lines of defence against British invasion, placing explosives beneath bridges along rivers and canals from County Donegal to County Louth. The first line of defence, through Longford and Cavan, was centred on the Ballinamore–Ballyconnell canal. For their second line, the Irish chose King James's old and faithless rampart: the Boyne.[101] Lieutenant Kevin Boland – the son of de Valera's Justice Minister – laid some of the bridge demolition charges as a member of the Engineer Corps' 4th Field Company but regarded his work as a preparation for only a token resistance against the British. After a delaying action, a conventional static defence, the 2nd Division was to 'split up into smaller groups and start guerrilla resistance against the British.'[102] Irish military training to counter the British thrust, however, left something to be desired. When the 11th Infantry Battalion at Gormanston, County Meath, went on manoeuvres near the Boyne in December 1940, their artillery communication depended upon field telephones of 1914–18 War vintage and a senior battery subaltern discovered that gun ranges had to be calculated on an Ordnance Survey map of half an inch to the mile.[103] The battery commander in Longford, Second Lieutenant John Griffin, received invasion alarms on an average of two nights a week and on each occasion he dutifully took his guns to within thirty miles of the border, ready to open fire on the British.[104] According to Mulcahy, General McKenna later told the Defence Conference that the Irish Army could resist the British along a defensive line 'for two months'.[105] More realistically, Griffin thought that his unit could probably hold out for a maximum of two hours.[106]

Like many young officers at the time, Griffin thought it more likely that the Germans would invade and that the British 'would come in behind us in support.'[107] Costello's main line of defence against German attack was to be the River Blackwater, which runs in a conveniently straight line across County Cork. Bridges along this river were also mined. Artillery units and battalions under Costello's command were all trained to regroup in small units for guerrilla warfare.[108] General McKenna outlined the possibilities of a German invasion to the Defence Conference in April 1941, although his statistics were somewhat questionable if Mulcahy's record of the meeting is accurate. McKenna thought it unlikely that a German invasion fleet would come from Norway but said that in September 1940 there were '300,000 tons of shipping along the Brest coast capable of bringing to Waterford (320 miles), Cork (300 miles), Limerick (470 miles) a force of 75,000 men. It could be supported by troop-carrying aeroplanes . . . about 500 or 600 troop-carriers could be available, carrying 15 or 20 men. The total troop-carrying strength is about 10,000 planes . . .' This ludicrous figure may have impressed Mulcahy but he was considerably less overwhelmed by disposition maps which McKenna handed out to the conference upon which 'a final stand line was shown that could very easily be said to be nothing but an amateur strategist's drawing of a suitable line across a physical geography map. A line in which the whole strategic advantage would be on the side of the invader . . .'[109]

Despite the events that would have preceded it, a guerrilla war might have been more to the taste of the Irish Government and many of Eire's soldiers. De Valera's praise for his 'hedge fighters' was no mere rhetoric. Most of the Irish Cabinet had been guerrilla fighters against the British between 1916 and 1921; de Valera, Sean T. O'Kelly, Lemass, Boland, Traynor and Ryan had all participated in the Easter 1916 Rising, while Aiken, Sean MacEntee and Thomas Derrig (Minister for Education) had been active against the British after 1918. Among the Fine Gael leadership, both Cosgrave and Mulcahy had fought in the Dublin Rising, and within the Irish Army there were thousands of men who had experienced the war against the Black and Tans at first hand. Major General Joseph Sweeney, the GOC of the Irish Army's Western Command in 1940, had been in the GPO garrison with Pearse in 1916. Colonel Archer and Colonel Bryan of G2 fought the British in the War of Independence, and General MacNeill of the 2nd Division was the nephew of Eoin MacNeill, a former Chief of Staff of the Irish Volunteers and a founder of the Gaelic League.[110] Tom Barry, the legendary guerrilla leader who established the IRA's Flying Columns and attacked the British Army with devastating effect in 1920 and 1921, volunteered his services in 1939 and became Costello's operations officer in the 1st Division.*

Guerrilla warfare was in the blood of the men who might have to defend Irish neutrality. It was part of their young statehood, the reason for their national independence, and it was something they understood, particularly if it was directed against the British. Even the 1940 intelligence report to Churchill noted that members of the 'old IRA' who fought the British before 1922 had joined the LSF and that 'one example is that of Dan Breen, a notorious gunman of former days, who now . . . commands one of the Dublin Divisions of the Security Force with an ex-British officer as his second in command.'† These men would probably obey de Valera 'for the time being', the report said, adding that 'their one object is to prevent either British or Germans from entering Eire.'[113] It was not surprising, then, that British troops preparing the 'W' Plan saw fit to take seriously the possibility of Irish hostility. For how long the Irish guerrillas

---

* On Barry's death in 1980, Costello praised his 'shrewd judgement and remarkable insight into the capabilities and weaknesses of possible invaders.'[111] Costello's account was strangely contradicted by Seán Cronin, a former editor of the *United Irishman* and now Washington correspondent of *The Irish Times*, who claimed that the Army treated Barry 'like any other recruit' in 1939 and that the old IRA man 'packed his gear and returned home to Cork.'[112]

† Breen was co-planner of the Soloheadbeg, County Tipperary, ambush on the RIC in 1919, an attack that started the final war against the British. A reward of £10,000 was offered for his capture but it went unclaimed.

would have held together after an invasion is more questionable. Would they have continued to recognise de Valera's leadership if the country had fallen, or would they have broken up into civil war factions? Looking back on his days as Chief of Staff of the Irish Volunteers, Mulcahy once praised the discipline of his guerrillas and commended their 'anxiety to protect civilians and civilian property',[114] but different circumstances might have applied in 1940. If the British had invaded Eire and adopted the reprisal tactics of 1921, the struggle would have been ferocious enough, but the Germans are likely to have outdone the Black and Tans several times over. In the Soviet Union, Poland and France during the war, guerrilla attacks provoked indiscriminate revenge killings by the Germans, who sometimes massacred the entire population of villages. It was a practice that would almost certainly have been repeated in Ireland at the first sign of revolt. 'We believe,' wrote Mulcahy in November 1940, 'that a successful German invasion of this country would, after a successful war by Germany against Britain, result in the German occupation and domination of this country.'[115]

For obvious reasons, Fine Gael believed that the Germans were more likely to invade Eire than the British, and de Valera was of the same opinion in the summer of 1940. He had secretly requested British military co-operation and his fears had been expressed forcefully enough to Mac-Donald. James Dillon recalls de Valera explaining to him about this time that 'there was a danger facing us from the Germans. I said we could beat the Germans with British soldiers because there were 10,000 of them in Northern Ireland. De Valera said to me: "Mr Dillon, I wish to God there were – but the British have just withdrawn 8,000." '[116] If de Valera was worried, however, the Defence Conference appears to have been gripped by sheer panic. On June 14, Mulcahy was writing that:

> . . . the death and maiming of civilians will shake the morale of our people and the sufferings of women are likely to be of a character calculated to break their morale completely, with the consequent possibility of civilian collapse, to the possible fatal embarrassment of such armed forces as we could have in the field.
>
> To avert this suffering for our people and the possible collapse of morale (which if it touched the Army might degenerate into demoralisation) it appears to us that invasion must be prevented and that to do this, unified command for the defence of this whole island of 32 Counties is vital now . . .[117]

At this stage, Mulcahy envisaged Irish, British and French troops defending Eire and drawing supplies from the United States 'on the personal request of the Irish Government to President Roosevelt'. Next day, he thought that 'we might easily take here 100,000 French troops from a French evacuation.'[118] By the following month, a note of circumspection was evident:

There are two things about Partition: (1) The Northern Nationalists are pro-German (2) the section in the South who are pro-German would probably not be so but for Partition. Whoever came should understand that. They should have something definitely reassuring to say about Partition . . .[119]

Churchill's broadcast in September, warning Britain that she could expect invasion at any moment, set off another discussion in the Defence Conference in Dublin. Mulcahy apparently spoke to de Valera who 'stated that they were aware of all this about barges, and ships, and all that, weeks ago, but implied that there was no change in the situation.'[120] A German invasion was considered again at the Conference in October, when Mulcahy thought that the Germans might attack Ireland rather than Britain, coming ashore with five divisions between Kinsale and Rosslare.[121]

In November, when Churchill complained to the House of Commons about Eire's continued refusal to let the Royal Navy use the Treaty ports, the idea of a British invasion began to percolate through Fine Gael. 'It does seem clear,' wrote Cosgrave, 'that while it might be possible to resist German invasion with the help of the British and to preserve certain economic life here, the Germans could not help us to repel the British invasion and a British invasion resulting in hostilities would completely disorganise our economic life.'[122] The apparent threat from Britain had a strange effect upon Dillon. 'Any conflict with Great Britain seems to be something to be avoided almost at any cost,' he wrote, 'but while circumstances might be conceived in which we would be justified in facing such a conflict *provided that we had the support of our traditional ally, America* . . . no circumstances whatever could justify our permitting a situation to develop in which Ireland would be involved in war with Great Britain and the USA at the same time . . .' But if America and Britain were allied against Germany, Dillon argued, the Germans would not forbear from attacking the Irish ports if it suited them, so 'we lose nothing by launching ourselves openly on the side of our traditional ally.'[123]

De Valera paid no attention to these noisy suggestions. But on December 21, the Irish Army was mysteriously put on alert at four o'clock in the morning to repel an invader. Mulcahy, who found out about the incident three days later, noted that the Irish Government had received information that the Germans would invade Britain at five o'clock on the 21st and that Ireland could expect a subsidiary attack. Orders were given 'that the Army should stand-to from four o'clock, in full readiness to fight. That all aeroplanes should be fired at. Special importance was attached to Limerick . . . In Barracks B, General Absolution was given by the Chaplain . . . our patrols on the Border were removed, leaving unimpeded access . . . to any troops coming from the North.'[124] Mulcahy wrote to de Valera asking for an explanation,[125] and just after Christmas de Valera, together with Aiken and O'Kelly, met Mulcahy, Dillon and O'Higgins to try to assuage Fine Gael's concern. De Valera said that the Bishop of

Derry, Dr Farren, had sent a priest to tell him that 'the British intended attacking across the Border'. The Government, said de Valera, discounted this story but 'it was only one of the numerous rumours that came to them from time to time. The Army had to be always on the alert. He stated that he did not believe that General Absolution was given at any Barracks . . .'[126]

The alarm had in fact been real enough although controversy continues to this day in Ireland about the identity of the expected invaders. In the week before Christmas, Hempel, the German Minister, had told Frederick Boland at the Department of External Affairs that the Germans proposed to send extra staff to their legation in Dublin, flying them into Rinneana aerodrome on Christmas Eve. Boland told Hempel that the Irish Government would probably reject this request and when the German Minister visited O'Kelly, he received no satisfaction. De Valera was in hospital but when he was informed of the German proposal, he is said to have ordered the immediate arrest of the Germans if they landed at Rinneana.[127] General Costello was deputed to perform this task and General McKenna recalled after the war that a Luftwaffe aircraft did actually fly low over the airfield on Christmas Eve but flew away again.[128]

Long after the war, Colonel Dan Bryan disclosed that just prior to the German request, there had been an official 'alarm' along the border with Northern Ireland and that Irish troops had been moved from Dublin to take up positions near the frontier. When the much more serious threat of German action materialised a few days later, the Irish Army was stood ready to counter a German attack. Many officers who had been affected by the previous alert therefore erroneously assumed that the British were the potential invaders all along.[129] De Valera's closest associates still contend, however, that the real threat at Christmas 1940 came from the British, not the Germans. De Valera's youngest son Terry, who was an LSF Volunteer in 1940, claims that the British *were* threatening an invasion at that time and that his information came from 'a source even more senior and responsible than . . . the late General McKenna',[130] a coy euphemism for Eamon de Valera himself. But except for the Taoiseach's reference to the Bishop of Derry, there is no record in Mulcahy's notes of any further information about a British attack. Aiken recalled after the war that at Christmas 1940, 'there was a bit of a scare about the British marching on Dublin but we never knew the truth of it.' Aiken thought that 'Britain would be the most likely invader, with full American support.'[131] Even Colonel Bryan acknowledged that Britain did consider an invasion. Indeed, he received information from the brother of one of Churchill's ministers that the British had compiled an arrest list which included Joseph Walshe of the Department of External Affairs and Colonel Michael Hogan, an Irish Army officer.[132] In his traditional Christmas broadcast to the United States in 1940, de Valera referred to a publicity campaign in America which suggested the seizure of the ports. 'We are a small nation and we have no illusions about our strength,' he told his listeners. 'But should any attempt be made to put such a suggestion into execution we shall defend ourselves to the utmost of our power.'[133]

There was, however, one man other than de Valera who appeared to be convinced that Britain was about to invade Eire: General Hugo MacNeill, commander of the Irish Army's 2nd Division and the officer whose job was to contain a British attack across the border. MacNeill, a tall, bespectacled man with high cheekbones and a precise manner, did something rather extraordinary in December 1940; he went to discuss his fears with the Germans. He approached not Hempel but Henning Thomsen, the Counsellor at the German Legation in Northumberland Road. Thomsen, a member of the SS, was regarded in Dublin as a subversive agent, a reputation which Hempel claimed he did not deserve, although the German Minister took pains after the war to say that he had not been satisfied with the 'general outlook' of his young and aggressive counsellor.[134]* Thomsen was widely considered to be a 'strutting Nazi' and – whatever Hempel may have said to the contrary – he generally handled contacts with German agents in Eire, with the IRA and with any generally disaffected Irishmen.[136]

MacNeill's relationship with the German Legation remains obscure but it is clear that he discussed with Thomsen Irish military plans and the possibility of German assistance to Eire in the event of British invasion. General O'Duffy, the former Blueshirt leader, was present at some of these meetings in early December when MacNeill questioned Thomsen about Germany's ability to drop captured British anti-tank cannon and heavy machine guns to Irish troops by parachute, asking also whether they might be sent by ship.[137] MacNeill claimed that the Irish Army was expecting a British attack in the spring of 1941 and said that their most likely target would be the 'occupation of Lough Swilly, defence against which was useless'. He thought the British might, as a second preference, try to capture both Lough Swilly and Rinneana aerodrome.[138] MacNeill's suggestion that the invasion would be directed principally at Lough Swilly may have been no more than an inspired guess but it is interesting that only in December had the occupation of the northernmost Treaty port been included in the 'W' Plan.

MacNeill, who was a co-founder of the Irish Army's Military College and had been Director of Defence Plans, also wanted to contact Hermann Goertz, the Abwehr agent parachuted into Eire in May 1940. Bryan believes that MacNeill may actually have met Goertz and that MacNeill's intelligence officer did speak to the German spy. 'Hempel warned Berlin

---

* Thomsen was not quite the sinister figure that his SS membership would suggest. He had joined the Reiter SS – the mounted SS – when he was at the Brandenburg Gate riding school in Berlin after being told he had no chance of becoming a diplomatic attaché without some form of party affiliation. He said later that he had no contact with the military SS and was employed mainly as an escort at state functions.[135]

that the "head of Irish Intelligence" had contacted Goertz,' Bryan recalled thirty-eight years later, 'but I never saw Goertz until he was captured. Hempel must have mistaken MacNeill's intelligence officer for me.'[139] Hempel himself described MacNeill as 'typically Irish',[140] neglecting to mention what was obvious to all who met him, including Bryan; that he drank heavily. He was very anti-British and had a tendency, in the eyes of G2, to go 'rooting about on his own'.[141] MacNeill's young officers regarded him as a 'buccaneer'.[142] Perhaps because of his family's position in the pantheon of national independence, Irish Army officers are today still reluctant to criticise their former divisional commander, describing even a reference to his drinking habits as 'gratuitous'.[143] But MacNeill was fully aware of the British plans to assist Eire in the event of a German invasion and questions are now asked in the Dublin press as to whether Irish Army officers, 'including a general', passed information about the British Army to the Germans.[144]

It would be even more interesting to know whether MacNeill's apparently secret approaches to the Germans had any kind of official sanction. When the Irish Government feared a German invasion, they had asked the British for help. It would be quite in line with this policy if they had looked to the Germans for assistance when faced with the apparent threat of British intervention. Ribbentrop followed up the MacNeill initiative by asking Hempel if de Valera would accept German arms. He offered forty-six field guns, 550 machine guns, 10,000 rifles and 1000 anti-tank rifles, all of them British weapons captured at Dunkirk.[145] Hempel was told by Walshe that de Valera 'saw no possibility of shipping the weapons unnoticed to Ireland,' adding that 'if the English were to learn of the shipment, they would seize with both hands the welcome opportunity of asserting the existence of a German–Irish plot.'[146] When Hempel made the offer in person to de Valera, the Taoiseach 'said it was very kind and thanked me very much. He said he did not think it would be necessary. I said "but if you are attacked!" and he replied: "Oh, I don't think we have to make provisions now. Should it really happen, I think Germany is so efficient that they could find ways and means." '[147] And with this glossy charm, the Taoiseach brought the conversation to an end.

De Valera was still trying to obtain weapons from the British and their continued refusal to supply Eire with arms only fuelled his suspicions, as he explained to Mulcahy and Dillon in January 1941. De Valera 'had been endeavouring in every possible way to get the British to make a declaration that they did not intend to invade this country. He had said to them "If you don't intend to invade this country, why don't you supply us with the arms we want?" He took it that the non-supply of these arms meant that the British had in their minds to invade us.' If the British would promise not to attack Eire, said de Valera, 'it would help us to concentrate on any German danger in a more effective way – although even with such an assurance from the British, we could not put the danger from the British entirely out of our minds . . ."[148]* De Valera could not shake off the idea that Britain might have some long-term ambitions in Ireland, that 'they wanted to recover some of the ground they had lost in this country,'[150] and he developed this theme in May when conscription was once again proposed for Northern Ireland. 'He considered this was only a prelude to Britain coming in here,' wrote Mulcahy. 'He was of [the] opinion that Churchill's policy was to reabsorb this country.'[151] But Mulcahy thought that de Valera's anxieties had their roots nearer home. 'A lot of his fears that Britain wants to interfere with us here arise out of his own suspicious mind,' he wrote, 'and he has fed this fear like one would feed a fire with *brosna*, from the bits and scraps of conversations brought home by Civil Servants of odd suggestions made apparently in their contacts in London that things would be different if we gave facilities.'[152]

Under these real or imagined pressures, de Valera maintained the sort of hard-faced neutrality that Aiken espoused. O'Higgins wrote his own account of this policy, as it was outlined to him by de Valera's ministers in March, 1941:

Whoever comes first is our enemy. If America comes first we are determined to *shoot down the Americans*. If Britain comes first we will shoot them down with greater relish. If the Germans come first we will shoot them also. If Britain genuinely believing that she is forestalling a German invasion rushes her Northern troops down along our coast or her naval craft into our harbours, we are engaged immediately in bloody *war with England* . . . If the war ends in a negotiated peace we have made an enemy of Britain for many years to come and in my opinion we have made partition as permanent as British power can make it. Any future commonwealth conference will see our representatives begging for the scraps.
    If the war ends in a German victory I think this country will certainly become a German base.[153]

O'Higgins's bloodthirsty assessment may not have been quite what de Valera envisaged although the military alert at Christmas 1940 certainly showed that the Irish were prepared to try and 'shoot down' anyone infringing their neutrality. For several weeks after the alarm, Irish anti-aircraft guns blazed away harmlessly at aircraft rash enough to cross the Eire coast.† If this was meant to symbolise Eire's determination to fight, it was no more impressive than her anti-invasion measures on the ground. In August 1940, when the Germans seemed poised to invade Britain and

---

* At the same meeting, Dillon asked if it was not likely that Eire would find herself 'at war with the United States, Great Britain and Germany combined'. This amazing supposition was apparently taken quite seriously by de Valera who 'could see the danger of getting into that position'.[149]
† Mulcahy's Defence Conference notes record aircraft under fire from Irish ground defences at Ballyfermot in Dublin (December 29), Phoenix Park (January 3), Spike Island (January 4) and Fort Dunree, Lough Swilly (January 24).[154]

Ireland – and when German troops were actually in training for Operation 'Green' – the Irish Department of Defence decided that there was no point in placing obstructions along Merrion Strand, the 2500 acres of sand that emerged at low tide south-east of Sandymount in the Dublin suburbs, the very beach which the Luftwaffe were photographing so assiduously from the air. A memorandum from J.P. Candy, the Chief Engineer to the Office of Public Works, claimed that railway sleepers driven into the sand would be carried away by the tide, that fixing metal rails as 'spikes' would take too long and that strewing the beach with abandoned cars would be ineffective. He suggested building machine-gun posts along the coast road and on the old Martello tower – a relic of the Napoleonic period – which 'would be ideal for sweeping the area with machine gun fire'.[155] In the event, the Defence Department relied on the frequent tide, a lone anti-aircraft post at Ringsend Park and reinforcements that were 'conveniently available' more than a mile away at Ballsbridge to deter an airborne landing.[156] Only in July 1940 did the Irish Cabinet agree that Eire should manufacture mines to be laid in her ports and estuaries.[157]

But Eire's administrative preparations for invasion gathered momentum through the winter of 1940, and a mass of official documents in the Irish State Paper Office testifies to the thorough and sometimes ruthless measures which de Valera's Government intended to take in the event of attack. A scheme for the evacuation of 70,000 children from Dublin and Dun Laoghaire took shape in July 1940,[158]* and the Cabinet debated whether Irish doctors should be sent to England to gain experience of air raid casualties. Railway tunnels in Dublin were considered for air-raid shelters.[161] By 1942, the Government estimated that they could evacuate 160,000 people – almost half the entire population of the city – from the greater Dublin area in the event of a severe air attack. In the south-eastern district alone, the plan called for the evacuation of 41,000 people by rail while 5000 cyclists and 10,000 motorists would leave Dublin along the Bray road in just seventeen hours. The authorities rather unhappily called this a 'panic evacuation' – which it might well have turned out to be – but Irish troops were to cordon off every road out of Dublin, allowing refugees to leave only through specified exit routes. The Garda and the LSF were to supervise the transportation of 104,000 people to Meath, Westmeath, Longford, Leitrim and Roscommon, and 56,000 to Wicklow and Wexford.[162]

But the requirements of the Irish Army were to take preference over civilian safety. In Cork, local people proposed that a 'Citizens Committee' should supervise emergency evacuation[163] but de Valera turned the idea down.[164] The Army said that during an invasion around Cork, no trains

---

* This was not without its problems. O'Kelly accused Aiken of wrongly blaming him for a delay in implementing evacuation procedures.[159] Aiken's office was also worried that children from 'the poor and more congested areas' of Dublin might spread 'disease and epidemics' among the small homes of the Gaeltacht.[160]

would be available, private motorists would be 'debarred from using the roads or leaving the city' and that any evacuees would have to walk between six and fifteen miles before finding transport. Refugees might be attacked in order to cause panic and hinder Irish troops. General Costello, a Government memorandum stated, 'is concerned only to ensure that the evacuees do not interfere with military movements.'[165] The Northern Ireland Government had vainly attempted to evacuate women and children from Belfast in the months prior to the German bombing of the city in April 1941 and the 'complete failure' of their efforts had persuaded the Irish authorities that they would have to institute rapid evacuation of Eire's cities only after an air attack had begun.[166]

The Irish Government anticipated not only an invasion but an occupation of large parts of Eire by British or German troops. In the event of an attack, regional commissioners would exercise central government authority on a county basis. Extracts from the draft of a broadcast that de Valera was to have made after invasion had begun show that the population would have been expected to give their allegiance to these new leaders. 'I appeal with confidence to each member of the community,' de Valera was to have said, 'to co-operate to the best of his, or her, ability with the Commissioners, and to assist them in every way possible in discharging the heavy responsibilities with which they have been entrusted during the continuance of the present serious state of affairs.'[167] The Department of External Affairs produced an 11-page memorandum on the rights of civilians in occupied territory. If the Garda were to engage in hostilities, it said:

> . . . their uniform and disciplined behaviour might well secure for them complete recognition as belligerents, although their civilian character as police would be inevitably destroyed. On the other hand, if the LSF, wearing armlets and carrying small arms in their pockets, were to join in an action to repel invaders, the chances are that they would still be regarded as civilians and as such might be shot when captured or otherwise mistreated.[168]

Even if civilians drove a carload of soldiers, they might be regarded by the enemy as *franc-tireurs*, the memorandum went on. The Department of External Affairs ransacked the 1907 Hague Convention and Oppenheim's *International Law* for guidelines to the appropriate behaviour of civilians in enemy hands.[169] Instructions to be issued to the Irish population stated that 'if attacked, Eire will defend its territory with all its force. Nevertheless, in every war one must envisage the possibility that territory may be occupied by the enemy . . .'[170] At de Valera's request, Frank Gallagher, the head of the Government Information Bureau, drafted a newspaper article on the subject, stressing that 'the individual whose rights are most respected by an enemy in wartime is the soldier who fights against him.' If a civilian arms himself against the enemy, 'he can be treated very rigorously indeed.'[171] The gist of Gallagher's argument was that able-bodied

221

civilians would be safer if they joined the Army, a not altogether trustworthy piece of advice. But the article's assumption was that both soldiers and civilians would find themselves in enemy hands. In June 1944 – when Eire thought she might be invaded by American troops – the Taoiseach's Department was still investigating the rights of civilians under occupation, combing through the Swedish Government's instructions to its own neutral population, and discovering – disconcertingly perhaps – that Swedish civilians were expected to oppose their enemies more actively than their Irish counterparts, forming a free corps and taking up arms in unoccupied territory.[172]

Yet the powers of the Irish military authorities over the Irish population were to be Draconian if Eire was invaded. The Irish Constitution did not permit the introduction of martial law but equivalent rules could be instituted by the Government once an attack started.[173] The Defence Department in Dublin sent to its commanding officers an order headed 'Instructions as to the summary punishment of civilians for grave offences committed in time of invasion'. The document was marked 'Secret', as well it might have been. Each commanding officer of the rank of commandant or above was to appoint three commissioned officers to hold military trials of anyone accused of treason, murder, espionage, arson, sabotage or looting. If the accused man or woman was found guilty, the officer could order their execution.[174] A military court had been operating in Eire since August 1940, primarily to deal with the IRA, and there can be little doubt that the new instructions were aimed at the same organisation.

In January 1941, however, the list of crimes for which the Army would be able to impose the death penalty was radically extended to include such offences as 'unlawful assembly', 'unlawful drilling', 'being a member of an illegal organisation' (i.e. the IRA), and 'obtaining . . . information in a manner likely to prejudice public safety'. The punishment for those found guilty by the three-man military court was to have been 'the death penalty, by way of shooting'.[175] The crime of 'unlawful assembly' – which was intended to prevent the blocking of roads[176] – was later defined as 'an assembly of three or more persons . . . with intent to carry out any common purpose, lawful or unlawful, in such manner as to endanger the public peace.'[177] This was very rough justice indeed, and would have been open to a multitude of interpretations by the military judges. An additional and – in the circumstances – rather unusual paragraph in the Defence Department instructions added that violations of rules of warfare were only war crimes if they were committed without the order of a belligerent government. 'If members of the armed forces commit violations *by order* of their Government, they are not war criminals, and may not be punished by the enemy.'[178]

The Irish police were to remain at their posts even if their towns and villages were overrun by British or German forces, a decision that was only made after much debate and considerable delay by the Government.

Garda Commissioner Michael Kinnane discussed the issue with Roche of the Justice Department in January 1941, suggesting that the Garda should remain non-combatant, 'stay put' in their locality and continue to act as police 'as long as possible'.[179] Almost three weeks later, no decision had been taken by the Department and Kinnane sent a testy note to Roche complaining of the delay. His own inability to issue directions was 'bound . . . to have an unfortunate effect on my control of the Force,' he said. If the impression was to grow that the authorities were unable to agree on the duties of the police, 'the results might well prove disastrous to the maintenance of the discipline of the Force in the event of an invasion.'[180]

The delay was caused by the very kind of disagreement that Kinnane feared. General McKenna thought the idea of keeping the Garda out of the fighting was 'all wrong'. Roche explained to Moynihan of the Taoiseach's Department that even Kinnane:

> . . . thinks that some of the best of our Guard Officers will just not be kept out of the fighting – that when they see their fellow countrymen fighting all round them they will just ignore orders and refuse to go about as privileged persons, knowing quite well that however strongly they may be censured or punished officially their action will be openly approved by the ordinary Irishman and secretly admired even by those whose duty it is to reprove them . . . There is also the consideration that even if the enemy can be induced to respect the civil character of the police in these districts, there are some of our own people who will not respect it but will seize the opportunity to pay off old scores.[181]

Roche wanted to ask the police to volunteer for military service and then to turn isolated Garda stations into military posts, manned by policemen, the LDF and regular troops. He proposed that the rest of the Guards should be concentrated in the larger towns and cities and that the legislation for military courts should be brought into force immediately 'so as to discourage the IRA, etc., from taking advantage of the absence of regular police'. Roche even thought that a 'voluntary committee of public safety' could be set up in outlying districts, 'composed of the decentest elements of the local population' and able to administer justice to anyone whose crimes were not serious enough to come before the martial courts. De Valera discussed Roche's ideas with Moynihan but postponed any decision on them 'for the present'.[182] In the meantime, Kinnane sent out an order marked 'very secret' to Garda stations, informing the police that they were a non-combatant force and that they should remain at their posts if their area was occupied by the enemy. If an attack on their district appeared imminent, they were to hand over their weapons to the Irish Army and destroy any maps, cyphers or 'official documents dealing with aliens'. All members of the Garda were to 'continue to function as long as possible' in occupied territory unless ordered by the enemy 'to perform duties of an oppressive nature against the civilian population'.[183]

The only exception to these rules was to be the detective branch of the Garda who, it was proposed, 'should now be secretly attached to the Defence forces . . . and be called out for military service in the event of hostilities occurring.' The Department of Defence wanted the detectives to help military intelligence and pointed out that 'in view of their previous work in connection with unlawful organisations, they would run grave risk in remaining behind.' McKenna may have failed to enrol the police in the Army but he was at least trying to get the plain-clothes men to enlist. He was angered by the Government's insistence on the civilian role of the police and this may have accounted for a list of facetious questions which the Defence Department put to the Cabinet in April 1942. They included 'whether the Defence Forces should be enabled to use telephones in Garda Stations in unoccupied territory in the event of hostilities' and 'whether the Garda Siochana and Local Security Force in unoccupied territory should report belligerent aircraft movements to the military authorities'.[184]

The Irish were prepared for some small victories over their invaders. In December 1941, the Government decided that Portlaoise Prison and the County Home at Carlow would be used for incarcerating up to 350 prisoners of war.[185] Nine pages of legislation governing the treatment of POWs was drawn up by the authorities in Dublin[186] and the Irish Minister in Berne was instructed to pass on this information to the Swiss Federal Council – which safeguarded the Prisoners of War Convention – if Eire was invaded.[187] But de Valera's ministers spent far more time discussing the preparations for defeat. In October 1940, Lemass was so worried that Eire's broadcasting and power stations might be destroyed by air raids that he wrote to Moynihan suggesting a new form of co-operation with the British. Was it possible, he asked, for the British to broadcast the Irish Government's messages from transmitters in Britain or Northern Ireland if Eire was attacked? 'Should we approach the Northern Ireland authorities again with a view to linking up of our electrical distribution systems so as to provide against the destruction of generating stations in either area?'[188] There was no doubt whom Lemass thought the enemy would be. In the Department of Foreign Affairs, Walshe coldly informed Moynihan of the niceties of invasion protocol. His department's first task 'would be to make a protest to the Government of the country concerned and to inform the Governments of neutral countries, especially that of the United States, that our neutrality had been violated. The Government of the other belligerent power would also be informed, and, if our Government so decides, would be requested for aid against the invader.'[189]*

---

* In July 1940, de Valera's Cabinet decided that the Irish broadcasting station at Athlone should be destroyed the moment an invasion began, to prevent it falling into enemy hands.[190] Walshe wanted this instruction rescinded so that the Government could 'launch our protest to the world' over the transmitters.[191]

Walshe decided that his principal staff should remain at their posts in Dublin after an invasion 'in order to provide a channel for dealing with the invader when he arrives there and to do everything possible to lessen the harshness of the measures which he may wish to impose on the people. In any case, the Department must remain with the Representatives of foreign Governments and no purpose would be served by allowing these latter to leave the capital.'[192] So Maffey and Hempel were expected – or were to be forced – to stay behind to watch the occupation of Dublin. Not so the Irish Cabinet.

De Valera resolved that if the capital was attacked by invaders, he would try to run the government of the country from outside Dublin. If he was at home when the invasion began, he would immediately broadcast to the Irish people through a microphone that had been specially fitted in his residence at Cross Avenue, Blackrock, for this purpose. Giving a code word to identify himself to GPO staff in Dublin, de Valera would be hooked into the national radio system. If Dublin itself was under attack, he was to be taken outside the city where he could be connected with the Athlone transmitter by cable.[193] Then he would protest over the radio against the invasion and warn the population that only military forces were to participate in hostilities. He was to announce that regional commissioners had now been given powers to control their districts on behalf of the Irish Government and that 'allied assistance has been sought or obtained'.[194] Ireland would no longer be neutral.

De Valera and his ministers would then head for their secret government headquarters. In July 1940, in the early days of the invasion scare, six cars were to take the Taoiseach and his Cabinet out of Dublin.[195] Lemass, who was to be in the second car, was worried that government buildings in the city would be bombed and that the Department of Local Government staff in the Customs House by the Liffey – 'a very likely target for attack' – might be in danger. He wondered if civil servants should even remain in their offices.[196] Staff at the Department of Finance were to stay behind in occupied territory, following the practice of civil servants in Holland, Belgium and France, and Walshe – anxious as ever to accord with international precedent – produced as guidance a forgotten British parliamentary paper on the British military occupation of Samoa in 1914.[197] By November 1941, the Irish Government were debating whether the entire parliament might be moved outside Dublin if the country was invaded and the Department of Finance now suggested that a government staff of seventy-three people, including twelve shorthand typists, should accompany the Cabinet during their emergency evacuation.[198] A lorry driven by Garda officers would take their accumulated baggage to one of nine large houses which had been discreetly vetted by the Office of Public Works for emergency government headquarters. All the buildings were within fifty miles of Dublin and could accommodate the entire Cabinet.[199]*

Despite all these preparations, however, it at no time appears to have occurred to the Irish Government that the Germans might attack Northern Ireland, leaving Eire unoccupied and perhaps even presenting her with the chance of absorbing the six counties herself. Yet just such an attack was proposed in January 1941 by General Kurt Student, commander of the German 11th Airborne Corps, with whom Hitler discussed the plan at Obersalzberg on New Year's Day. Student, who was recovering from wounds received in the invasion of Holland, later wrote about this meeting, an account that naturally embellished his own personality but which also caught the frenetic enthusiasm for wild ventures to which Hitler was prone at this period. The Fuehrer was still considering an invasion of Britain, and it was in this context that Student suggested a diversionary paratroop attack on Northern Ireland to coincide with German landings on the south coast of England. In order to mislead the British, the air assault would have to be carried out by a strong force of paratroopers 'together with dummies which could be dropped by parachute'.[201] According to Student:

> . . . an even longer discussion followed on the question of the position of the Irish Free State. Hitler stated: 'Eire's neutrality must be respected. A neutral Irish Free State is of greater value to us than a hostile Ireland. We must be glad that Ireland has remained neutral up to the present. But we could not avoid trespassing on a small scale, through units losing their way, by emergency landings at night, by dropping in the wrong area . . .'[202]

Hitler counted on Eire's 'indirect and silent assistance' although he thought that the attack could still be successful even if Eire turned out to be hostile. With an astute eye for Irish nationalist history, he sharply suggested that the best date for the operation would be in April, on the 25th anniversary of the Easter 1916 Rising.

Student's plan was to drop 20,000 paratroopers and 12,000 airborne troops by night on two areas of Northern Ireland. The first and larger force would land in the triangle between the northern half of Lough Neagh and Divis Mountain above Belfast, capturing the RAF airfields at Aldergrove, Langford Lodge and Nutts Corner. At the same time, a second force of paratroopers would be dropped near Lisburn to destroy the planes on the Long Kesh airfield and cut the road and rail links between Belfast and the south. Student's dummies would be parachuted across the Mourne and Sperrin mountains to add to the confusion. Then at daybreak, Luftwaffe fighter squadrons would fly in from Brittany and land on the captured airfields.

* The houses from which de Valera could choose were: Hilltown, Drogheda; Balrath House, Duleek; Holmpatrick House, Skerries; Skryne Court, Tara; Emo Park, Portarlington; Ardcaen, Nass; Bert House, Athy; Inchinappa, Ashford; and Ballinpark, Rathnew.[200]

Writing after the war, Student claimed that the first phase of his operation would have been successful but that its further progress would have depended on the fate of the German landings in Britain. If British resistance in Northern Ireland proved too strong for Student's men, they would 'fight their way through to the Irish Free State and be disarmed there.'[203] De Valera would not have responded warmly to the prospect of interning the remnants of Student's army nor would the Irish Army have welcomed the German paratroopers who inconveniently 'trespassed on a small scale' along the border. If such an attack had ever come to pass, it is more than likely that the 'W' Plan would have been activated and that British and Irish forces would have found themselves fighting as allies before the Irish Government had time to realise that Eire was not Germany's intended target. Even if Hempel could have explained the true position, de Valera would not have been slow to see the opportunities afforded by the invasion to assist in the 'liberation' of the six counties from German aggression, an act that might ultimately have brought about the end of partition.

Perhaps, too, Hitler sensed the complexities of the affair for he moved on to discuss with Student the possible capture of Gibraltar and Malta, British islands of equally strategic significance to the Germans. Student travelled back to Berlin by rail the following evening with Reichsmarschall Hermann Goering, who was clearly unenthusiastic about the Irish enterprise. As they took their leave of each other at the Anhalter Station in the German capital, the Reichsmarschall tapped Student on the shoulder and said: 'Do not trouble yourself needlessly about Ulster. The Fuehrer does not wish to invade Great Britain. From now on Gibraltar will be the main task for you.'[204]

Student heard no more of Ireland although five months later his paratroopers stormed a more heavily-defended island – Crete – and overwhelmed the British garrison there. If he had known how poorly defended Northern Ireland had been for the previous six months, he might have pursued his ideas with Hitler in a more vigorous way. When military officials from London visited Belfast in July 1940 they discovered that the province was ill-equipped to deal with an invasion. The British 53rd Division had only thirty-six of its complement of seventy-two guns and only two-thirds of its anti-tank rifles, while the 61st Division, which was beginning to group in Northern Ireland, had no artillery at all, no engineers, and transport that was 'very deficient'. The reserve 148th Infantry Brigade had only three battalions. An anti-tank regiment arrived in July with only fourteen guns instead of forty-eight, and a machine-gun battalion newly attached to 53 Division had left all its ammunition in England. The only tanks in the province were a few light vehicles with the Fife and Forfar Yeomanry 'and ten serviceable old Rolls armoured cars with the North Irish Horse'.[205] This was little better than the Irish Army could muster although Craigavon's 12,000 'B' Specials and his newly-

227

formed 12,000 all-Protestant Volunteer Defence Corps strengthened the armed manpower of Northern Ireland. The Field Force that was to rush to de Valera's aid under the 'W' Plan – 53 Division less one brigade group – was 'of no use for any serious operation', according to the British military officials. ' Apart from being undersized it could only fight in 1918 style, not in the 1940 mechanised style, with air, tank, and artillery support.' The remaining forces, the British officers concluded, appeared 'too weak and too immobile to hold down Northern Ireland, and to meet any serious attack made in combination with IR A trouble'.

Naval vessels and at least thirty merchant ships were waiting for convoy in Belfast Lough but the city's anti-aircraft defences were 'very inadequate'; there were no searchlights, there was no balloon barrage, no anti-aircraft or army formation in the city and no defences for the RAF stations outside. The approved anti-aircraft defences for Belfast were twenty-four Bofors guns, of which there were only two, and twenty-four 3.7-inch guns of which there were just seven.[206] Like much of Britain in the summer of 1940, Northern Ireland almost invited invasion. Preparations for such an eventuality were – as befitted part of a belligerent state – somewhat more advanced than Eire's. Concrete blockhouses had been erected across the countryside, roads had been blocked and fields that might be used as landing-grounds were being spiked.[207] But even in the air, the province's defences were poor. To counter a German invasion, Air Commodore Carr, commander of British Air Force Ireland, would have four squadrons of old Battle bombers, one fighter squadron, some Lysanders and a squadron of Swordfish and Sharks from the Fleet Air Arm. Only the Lysanders and two squadrons of Battles were based in the province. This tiny force was evidently to become an integral part of the 'W' Plan in its early stages, for Carr was given a list of instructions about operations over Eire. 'British aircraft,' one order said, '*must not cross to Eire* till H M Representative in Dublin informs GOC in C of Eire Government's request for assistance.' Another recorded that the RAF was 'precluded from taking action against enemy forces in Eire unless Eire calls for assistance, which she might not do.' A separate instruction talks of the need 'to locate and destroy German troops and IRA Irregulars in cooperating [sic] with them . . .' Carr's orders also referred to the difficulties caused by political restrictions. One counselled 'discretion in attacking villages, likely to cause death of Irish civilians'.[208] Yet there was no suggestion at this stage that the RAF could operate over Eire without permission.

Craigavon's Government, of course, had no power over the armed forces of the Crown, and in the early summer of 1940, there was an especially parochial, almost cosy atmosphere about the deliberations of the Northern Ireland Cabinet. They decided that church bells – which were only to be used in Britain to warn of invasion – could still be rung above the province's presbyteries and chapels.[209] Craigavon thought that his Government should give guidance to the population about their duties in an invasion[210] but the Prime Minister was receiving plenty of advice himself in dozens of hand-written letters from members of the public that arrived at Stormont throughout May and June 1940. Samuel Hatty of Bushmills, for example, suggested that Northern Ireland's unemployed should be set to work laying underground telephone lines across the six counties so that German invaders could not interfere with communications. 'I live on a hill which enables one to see 5 miles all round,' he wrote, 'and would be pleased to have you send a lookout man who could phone you information at once.'[211] An ARP warden in Birkenhead claimed that Hempel would help to plan a German landing in Eire, including the capture of the Ardnacrusha power station, with the co-operation of 'Sinn Feiners and other unlawful persons'. He warned Craigavon: 'I *do* trust you have consulted the Government in London, having regard to your difficulties with the Eire authorities . . .'[212] Even old Fred Crawford, the irascible major who had smuggled more than 19,000 rifles to the UVF in 1914, bombarded Craigavon with soldierly advice. Why not defend Aldergrove with a force of 'B' Specials?[213] Why not issue the 'B' Specials with steel helmets?[214] 'Do bear & have a little patience in your very busy and trying time with such an "Old Dudd" as I,' he pleaded with the Prime Minister. 'I just wish to say when the 'B' men are mobilised against aircraft troops . . . they all ought to have "*bicycles*", if possible *motor* ones, so that tho' widespread in their posts they could concentrate at shortest notice where the aircraft troops are landing. Any bicycle is better than none. Yours as ever, Fred.'[215] Gransden replied kindly to each of these letters, aware that the elderly UVF man felt isolated from the struggle. 'I *do* wish I could be of more use just now,' Crawford had scribbled across the top of one of his notes.[216]

The Northern Ireland Government, however, still supervised the province's internal security. John MacDermott's Ministry of Public Security controlled civil defence, and during an invasion the Ministry could – under the 1939 Defence (General) Regulations – impose curfews and direct civilians to assist the Army. The Ministry of Home Affairs under Dawson Bates controlled the RUC and the 'B' Specials, a large number of whom would assume military status during a German attack. If an invasion began, the RUC – unlike the Garda in Eire – would not stay at their posts. According to the Northern Ireland Government's official guidance in 1940, the main body of the police were to 'withdraw, taking with them their arms: they should then place themselves at the disposal of the military authorities.'* The Home Affairs Ministry also arranged to set up war zone courts – with High Court or County Court judges as Presidents – for areas in which ordinary criminal justice could no longer be administered.[217]

---

* This instruction was later rescinded.

But what locked the Cabinet firmly into the military apparatus in Northern Ireland was the Ulster Defence Volunteers whom Craigavon created under the auspices of the 'B' Specials. Soon to be known as the Ulster Home Guard, their existence was to be a cause of legal as well as sectarian dispute in the coming years. The Council of the Ulster Unionist Party had originally urged Craigavon to rejuvenate the old UVF as a home defence force. The Council's Secretary, Wilson Hungerford, had written to the Prime Minister in May 1940 suggesting that 'we could select our own people in each area, who would have intimate knowledge of the districts . . . we could have a register of properly attested people who could be called upon at a moment's notice. Each group would have its own nursing corps, dispatch riding contingent [sic] and motor car and lorry register.'[218] The Unionist Council could therefore have found little to complain about in the system that Craigavon adopted, which placed the new Home Guard under the Special Constabulary – who were after all the paramilitary successors of the UVF.

By October 1940, however, MacDermott, who was a barrister by profession, was concerned at the constitutional issues raised by the existence of the Ulster Home Guard. Because the force had been recruited by the Northern Ireland Government, he told the Cabinet, it was not subject to discipline under the Army Act and had not obtained military status. The basis of recruitment through the 'B' Specials had 'always been criticised by anti-partitionists' but it had raised other issues as well. Home Guard members, said MacDermott, were asking themselves 'Why are we only "Specials" if our job is to fight the Germans?' Furthermore MacDermott, as minister responsible for the force, had to answer to the Northern Ireland Parliament for its activities yet he had to take guidance from the military authorities over whom he had no jurisdiction. The competence of Stormont to vote money for the Home Guard was in doubt and MacDermott therefore wanted responsibility for the force to be transferred to Westminster.[219]

The province's government was already coming under parliamentary criticism at Stormont, Jack Beattie, a Labour MP, asked if Craigavon would place the Ulster Home Guard under British military authority, and MacDermott – while strenuously denying that any sectarian motives lay behind its existence – fudged the answer by stating that the Northern Ireland Government was always ready to facilitate the wishes of the Imperial Government.[220] But the controversy was growing. Doubts about the Ulster Home Guard's constitutional position – and its sectarian make-up – had been put to Churchill in London, so Craigavon and MacDermott sought the advice of Major General Packenham-Walsh, the new Northern Ireland District GOC.[221] Packenham-Walsh thought it would be 'disastrous' if the Ulster Home Guard were separated from the 'B' Specials. The work of the Special Constabulary, he said, would be closely connected with the Home Guard if an emergency occurred. But something else was bothering the GOC:

> It is most important that the Army should not become involved in political differences. At the same time it is equally important that weapons should not get into the hands of undesirable elements, and that the latter should not get a foothold in our military machine. It is difficult for the Army to differentiate. At present it is best done for them by the Constabulary on the best information.[222]

Packenham-Walsh did not question the worth of that 'information' nor whether the Home Guard actually represented the population – Catholic as well as Protestant – which it was to defend. He wanted no change and suggested only that the British Government should provide battledress for the Ulster Home Guard and that an Order in Council be prepared – to be issued at the moment of emergency – to place both sections of the 'B' Specials under martial law.[223]

But MacDermott was still worried about the 'grave constitutional objections' to a situation in which the Northern Ireland Government raised a force whose role was not the maintenance of internal security but the defence of the realm against invasion by a foreign enemy. He told the Cabinet on December 3 that the Northern Ireland Government should ask the British authorities to assume responsibility for the force. If this was not possible, the British Government should 'devise some constitutional expedient' and 'give the necessary constitutional cover' to the Northern Ireland Government to raise an armed Home Guard.[224]

The archives of the Stormont Government shed no light on the number of Catholics who tried to join the Home Guard. Long after the war, MacDermott recalled that a few Catholics did enlist but that 'virtually all left because they hated the 'B' Specials'. According to MacDermott, 'the "B"s were only bad in parts – the Home Guard was quite sectarian but this was largely the fault of the minority for not joining.' Older members of the Cabinet, especially Craigavon, did not appreciate the constitutional difficulties and MacDermott was afraid that in an emergency there might be disputes between Stormont and the Army 'because the GOC didn't get on with Dawson Bates'. Under the 1920 Government of Ireland Act, he maintained, the Northern Ireland Government were not permitted to 'touch' anything like a Home Guard. 'In the agony of the moment in June 1940, nobody minded,' MacDermott recalled. 'But our authorities were out of step, they were legislating beyond their capability. It could have become a ledge on which the disloyal could stand. I was worried that there would be a constitutional crisis. I went to see Captain David Margesson, the Secretary of State for War, and told him that the Ulster Home Guard was a "concealed mine" for the Government in Belfast. But he said he could not enter into politics. I was told that things would remain as they were.'[225]

231

Sir Alexander Maxwell, Permanent Under-Secretary at the Home Office, gave formal notice of this in March 1941. In a letter to Gransden, he said that the British Government had decided it would be 'inexpedient' to make any change in the status of the Ulster Home Guard. 'The question,' said Maxwell, 'is not one which should be decided by legalistic considerations; it is a practical problem which must be settled in a practical way, having regard to wartime needs and to the importance of using all the available administrative machinery in the way which is most effective as a contribution to the war effort.' The Home Guard would therefore remain a branch of the Special Constabulary; an Order in Council giving them the status of the armed forces could not be made until they were placed under military control.[226] Thus the Imperial Government pressed exceptional – indeed unconstitutional – powers upon the Northern Ireland Government, at the same time strengthening the sectarian nature of the local security forces. MacDermott, who was opposing this for legal rather than moral reasons, remained dissatisfied. The British Government drafted a Defence Regulation that would have put the Ulster Home Guard under military control when an emergency arose but which officially denied the Home Guard's existence – except as Special Constabulary members – until that date. 'Either the Imperial Government does not need the Ulster Home Guard for the defence of Ulster, or it does,' MacDermott thundered vainly in a ministry memorandum a few days later. 'If it does not, then the force should be disbanded . . . the present proposals of the Imperial Government place the whole Parliamentary and constitutional responsibility for the force on the shoulders of the Government of Northern Ireland, while reserving to the Imperial Government the privilege of using the force during the existence of an urgent need.'[227]*

If that 'urgent need' arose, the military status of the Home Guard would have been among the GOC's first concerns. Northern Ireland, like Britain, was divided into administrative regions for an emergency, and civilian regional commissioners were appointed to control these zones. In the 'direst emergency', the Army would impose martial law, under which the province would be divided into three areas. The GOC British Troops Northern Ireland would become military governor to whom, as the draft martial law proclamation put it, 'all persons will render obedience . . . in all matters whatsoever.'[229]

The Army were especially worried that the IRA might stage an uprising to coincide with a German invasion although Sir Charles Wickham's confidence in his Protestant paramilitary police seemed to convince MI5

---

* In January 1942, almost all the 'B' Specials and the entire Home Guard were grouped in military regions, and arrangements were made for their officers to be given military commissions in the British Army when action stations were ordered. By February 1942, they constituted 29 battalions of about 38,000 men.[228] The force, which was by now totally Protestant, was stood down on 31 December 1944.

that the IRA could not take over the country on their own. According to the records of a visit by MI5 officers to Northern Ireland at the end of August 1940, Wickham thought there was little chance of an armed rising and 'pointed out that quite apart from the armed forces there was now in Northern Ireland a force of some 40,000 armed men, Protestants, who were included in the 'B' Specials and the Ulster Defence Volunteers. With this force available for duty, Sir C. Wickham's view was that the odds were too great for any subversive elements to meet with any success.'[230] By December, the British Army's 61st Division had been brought up to strength and an RAF Hurricane squadron was based at Aldergrove; over the next six months, two more brigades – the 71st and 72nd – were brought into Northern Ireland, together with the 6th Division.[231] By August of 1941, there were more than 100,000 British troops in the six counties[232] and seven RAF squadrons[233] – more than enough to fight off an attack by Student's paratroopers or plunge into Eire, with or without de Valera's permission.

If the Germans invaded the province, the 61st Division were to defend the Magilligan beaches along Lough Foyle, the strand in which the Luftwaffe photographers had taken such interest. If forced into a retreat by an attack in the west, the British Army were to form a defensive line along the River Bann that cuts north to south through the centre of Northern Ireland. That the province might be divided by a British withdrawal from Londonderry to the shores of Lough Neagh was not disclosed to the Stormont Government. MacDermott himself only found out about it when he visited the GOC and caught sight of a map on his wall upon which a thick blue line marked the course of the Bann.[234] If Belfast were attacked from the sea, the British would lay an artillery barrage along the coast roads from batteries of 4.2-inch howitzers positioned in the fields above the Lough.[235] Franklyn was worried that refugees would hamper his troops around the city and wrote to John Andrews, the new Northern Ireland Prime Minister, in June 1941 to say that he was 'most disturbed' at the evacuation machinery. He dispatched a map to Andrews showing the routes which refugees should take if 'active operations' began in Belfast, and offered to send along staff officers who had experience of refugee evacuations in France and Belgium.[236]* The Northern Ireland Home Defence Executive – a co-ordinating committee of Army officers and Stormont civil servants – decided not to order an evacuation of Belfast even if the city was attacked by German troops. Civilians were to be told to 'Stand firm'.[238] Secret reserves of food were stored across Northern Ireland in case of invasion[239] and a large supply of British currency had

---

* The Stormont authorities tended to be sceptical of military planning. In July 1940, they discovered that the Army were planning to flood an area near Downpatrick with sea water, an anti-invasion measure which would have inundated the town with sewage and made the land barren for ten years.[237]

been amassed in the province in case it was cut off from the rest of the United Kingdom.[240]

And in secret, trusted and carefully chosen members of the population – almost all of them Protestants – were instructed by the British Army in the techniques of guerrilla warfare. Men and women were taught how to manufacture booby-trap bombs and home-made grenades so that an underground movement could continue to fight the Germans in Belfast. The fact that this training took place – so ironic today, when identical methods of warfare are being used against the British Army in the same city – was never revealed to the Northern Ireland Government, few of whose members ever found out after the war that anything like it had been going on.[241] But if the Germans had occupied Ireland, they would have faced organised resistance groups on both sides of the border.

As American troops began to arrive in Northern Ireland in 1942, several British officials assumed that the defence of Ireland and the 'W' Plan would become a United States responsibility. 'The repelling of an invasion of Ireland will probably be an American Army Operation . . .' the Assistant Secretary to the Northern Ireland Cabinet remarked.[242] But the British maintained their own plans for the defence of the island. In August 1942, a revised directive to the GOC British Troops Northern Ireland stated that he was 'in operational control of all United States Army ground forces in Northern Ireland', and made it clear that a military advance into Eire would be a joint Anglo-American mission under British command. The GOC was told that if he was satisfied that a serious invasion of Eire had taken place which called for the intervention of his troops, he was 'authorised to take action forthwith, without obtaining authority from the War Office, provided that every effort has been made to obtain confirmation from the United Kingdom Representative in Dublin.'[243] This did not contain the safeguard of final corroboration from Maffey and there was, once again, a curious paragraph in the directive about Irish Army opposition:

It may be anticipated that the Eire Government and armed forces would be co-operating with us, but it would be unwise to rely upon the Eire forces to render any effective resistance. It is not inconceivable that the Eire Forces might actively oppose our operations. Although this is not regarded as likely, measures for such an eventuality should be included in your plans.[244]

It is unclear whether any measures of this kind were drawn up in 1942. But as the threat of invasion receded, so British operational planning for the defence of Ireland grew less important. Within a year, the Northern Ireland District GOC's directives comprised only ten paragraphs and no reference was made to Irish military opposition.[245] A few senior British naval officers still believed that the Germans might attack Eire, and in the spring of 1942 a long dispute began within the Admiralty between

Admiral Sir Percy Noble, Commander in Chief Western Approaches, and Admiral Sir Charles Forbes, Commander in Chief Plymouth. Noble was 'convinced that the menace of invasion of Eire remains very real' and said that there was insufficient co-ordination between the three services over the plans to defend Ireland from German attack. He also suggested that his own area of operations should be extended to cover the southern Irish coastline, excluding Forbes from any responsibility for repelling a German invasion of Eire.[246] Forbes, claiming that Eire 'cannot become the scene of the enemy's main invasion efforts', insisted that Plymouth should retain control of operations off the south of Ireland.[247] This sterile argument was never resolved.

The Admiralty engaged in more productive work in the autumn of 1942, when Eire agreed to accept advice from the British on her coast defences. General Franklyn had approached the Irish Army with the offer[248] and Maffey agreed that a party of British officers should secretly travel to Eire to make a tour of inspection as soon as possible. 'It is almost certain that there will be a general election here very early in the New Year,' Maffey informed the Dominions Office, 'and nobody can foretell what the front bench will look like if a new Government is formed.' He wanted the British military authorities to 'gain a more detailed knowledge of the essential features of the problems involved in co-operation'.[249] Thinking that Fine Gael might form the next Dublin administration, Maffey was obviously keen to prepare the ground for Irish involvement in the war. In December 1942, therefore, Lieutenant Commander E.S.D. Fremantle, a gunnery officer in the Western Approaches command, travelled to Eire with a British artillery officer and was escorted by General McKenna not just to the Treaty ports but to almost every prominent harbour around the coast, from Howth and Killiney Head outside Dublin to Donegal Bay. Fremantle reported to the Admiralty that McKenna and his colleagues – who included Captain Robert Childers, the son of Erskine Childers who was executed in the civil war – had given every possible help and that 'nothing was concealed or glossed over'.[250]

Fremantle secured from McKenna the Irish Army's plans for the demolition of the port of Cobh should it be about to fall into enemy hands. These papers, which remain classified in Dublin, can be found at the Public Record Office in London, still attached to Fremantle's Admiralty report, eight pages of preparations for the total destruction of the great forts and the anchorage which had for four years symbolised Eire's sovereignty. The garrisons, together with the 21st Battalion and the 47th Rifle Battalion of the LDF, were to fight off an invader until they had no more ammunition for their old British 9.2-inch and 6-inch guns. Then Forts Westmoreland, Carlisle, Camden and Templebreedy would be blown to pieces with dynamite. The oil refinery at Haulbowline would be set alight, the blockship *Owenabuee* would be sunk in the narrow channel between Camden and Carlisle, and explosive charges would be set off beneath the Atlantic quays. At the railhead, the station-master and his staff were under orders to destroy the remaining locomotives while engineers blew up the railway bridge.[251] This was the proposed end for the historic Royal Navy port of Queenstown which Churchill had so desperately wanted to keep in British hands. The Irish were going to make sure that no one took it from them.

Fremantle drew up a list of criticisms and recommendations – inadequate camouflage at Fort Templebreedy, inability on the part of Irish troops to understand the mechanism of a 6-inch gun at Ardmore Point, a shortage of artillery at Galway (where the Aran Island ferry was earmarked as a blockship) and a scarcity of mines in Cork harbour. Immobilisation of the ports had been 'well and thoroughly worked out'. Fremantle suggested that the Irish should be given two 6-inch and two 4.7-inch guns, two Bofors and four 60-pounders as well as mines for Cork and Waterford, explosives, barbed wire and searchlights.[252] But he had wasted his time. The Admiralty Director of Plans concluded that since the Cabinet believed 'that invasion is off for 1943 there is no justification for supplying any equipment additional to the mines for Cork harbour . . .'[253]

Eire, it seemed, was losing its strategic attraction for the belligerent powers. Germany and Britain had both been prepared to use Ireland as a battleground. Hitler thought its occupation might end the war, while Churchill was prepared to contemplate coercion, even to the point of sacrificing Northern Ireland, to gain the Atlantic ports. Kaupisch and Student considered their invasion plans with the same detachment as Montgomery, pondering the British occupation of Cobh as he awaited the German onslaught in southern England. Towards both belligerents, Eire adopted the same basic military doctrine: hostility towards any invader. But behind Eire's attitude lay a fundamental change. Irish neutrality was no longer just an expression of sovereignty, a reaction to the need for independence; it had become a serious and positive international policy, to be defended by force of arms if its own integrity failed to protect it. Throughout the critical years of the war, de Valera's attention was dominated by the exigencies of defence and national self-sufficiency. He stayed aloof from one of the few wars in modern times that really did involve the victory or the suppression of an evil creed, but he did so by adopting the same criteria of self-interest that governed the actions of the belligerents. It was to this unheroic but pragmatic idea that Aiken subscribed, although it was not as honourable or courageous as he liked to think. Frank Gallagher records how, late in 1941, de Valera had turned to him 'with a rueful smile' and said: 'I wish there was some way of knowing who will win this war. It would make decisions much easier.'[254] It was a narrow, constrained morality that determined Eire's affairs in the war years but its salvation was that Eire was ultimately prepared to use the language of the belligerents and fight for her freedom.

In fact, the Germans did once more consider an intervention in Ireland.

Clissmann, the former German exchange student in Dublin who now worked for the Abwehr in Berlin, remembers a meeting of about thirty German Foreign Office and military officials in a conference room at the Bentlerstrasse military headquarters in 1942 at which Ireland was discussed. Germany believed that Britain was again contemplating the seizure of the Treaty ports. 'There was a discussion about what we could do to stop this,' Clissmann recalls. 'Someone said that we could dispatch auxiliary forces by air but the Navy said they could not send anything worthwhile. An Army staff officer said that there was no General Staff plan for Ireland in Germany. So plans were drawn up in Berlin. But I was in Brest myself a fortnight later and I noticed no sign of preparations there.'[255]*

So Eire was not invaded and her willingness to fight if her neutrality was breached by the belligerents was never put to the test. It is easy to ask what might have been the outcome if events had developed differently, if the Germans had landed on the Irish coast or if the British had invaded. Indeed, it is always tempting to reflect upon decisions that were considered but not taken, upon the might-have-beens of history. It is a dangerous practice but we may be forgiven if we glance briefly in that direction, for in the summer of 1941 the British Army in Northern Ireland held a secret staff exercise, a 'war game' to find out what would happen if the Germans staged a mass assault on both parts of the island as well as on Britain. An official account of this imaginary invasion – 'J Day' – still survives:

At dawn on J.1 day, the Germans launched the attack on Great Britain. Some days prior to the attack aerodromes, centres of communications and industrial targets were heavily and continuously attacked. LONDON received its heaviest attacks of the war. In the second air battle of Britain the RAF took heavy toll of the Luftwaffe, but still the fight went on. The Royal Navy were busily engaged in a terrific chase of the TIRPITZ and DEUTCHLAND [sic] in the Atlantic.

The German attack was launched on a wide front extending from the SHETLAND ISLANDS to CORNWALL and included landings in EIRE.

The landings in EIRE took place at WATERFORD, CORK, LIMERICK and SHANNON ESTUARY, GALWAY and WESTPORT. A landing was reported in DONGEGALL [sic] BAY and gave rise to panic in the district, in actual fact no landing took place in this area.

In addition to the above sea-borne landings, strong forces of parachutists and other air-borne troops seized the aerodromes at COLLINSTOWN and BALDONNEL.

The invasion was preceded by heavy bombing attacks on CORK, DUBLIN and LIMERICK.

* Clissmann knew nothing about Operation 'Green' until long after the war when the author showed him the military plans. The German officer's claim that there were no plans for Ireland is inexplicable. According to the 'Green' documents, four copies were sent to Berlin.

EIRE troops fought well and gained some initial successes on J.1 day. Throughout J.2 day they were gradually forced back. On J.3 day a special meeting of Dail was summoned. An SOS was sent to H M Government.

Shortly after midday on J.3 day, the Field Force which had already completed its concentration in the South of the SIX COUNTIES crossed the border, in answer to the request received from the Government of EIRE. The situation in NORTHERN IRELAND was none too good at the time.

Commencing about midday on J.2 day the IRA started their activities over a wide area 'DERRY, LARNE, BELFAST, LISBURN, NEWRY and ENNISKILLEN. The railway bridge at DROGHEDA was seriously damaged. Serious acts of sabotage, aimed at military objectives and the disruption of communications, were also committed in ANTRIM, PORTADOWN, OMAGH, SESKINORE and SCARVA. On J.2 night BELFAST was heavily 'blitzed', and much damage was done to docks, harbour, electric light and power, gas works, water supply, bakeries and communications (telephone, road and rail). At first light on J.3 day DERRY was heavily 'blitzed' big fires were started and got out of control; parachutists and air-borne troops landed at LIMAVADY. Later in the morning the enemy appeared off McGILLIGAN [sic] and under cover of heavy bombardment succeeded in landing (It was just at this time that the GOC BTNI gave the order for the Field Force to cross the Border) . . .[256]

At this point, the exercise was interrupted. A copy of this military account, sent to Gransden and the Stormont Government's Home Defence Executive, contained the unconvincing assurance that on J.3 day, 'the situation at LIMAVADY and McGILLIGAN was well in hand before nightfall.' But during their war game, the British Army found that snipers were shooting at firemen and that organised looting occurred in many parts of the province. British troops were forced to take 'pretty drastic action' to keep military routes clear of refugees, 60,000 of whom crowded in panic around the Great Northern Railway terminus in Belfast. The exercise continued:

On J.4 day the enemy landed parachutists and air-borne troops behind the Field Force and marched on BELFAST. An infantry brigade had to be moved in a hurry from West of LOUGH NEAGH to BELFAST . . .[257]

On this nightmare note, the exercise mercifully ended, with reports of refugees crowding the blitzed Belfast docks. Comparable war games were also staged by the Irish Army in Eire. Official files on these paper exercises are still closed to the public but several Irish officers made copies of the maps and documents that they used during the war and these still exist, presenting a graphic account of the manoeuvres that General Costello and General MacNeill thought they might have to perform if the British or Germans invaded.

In 1940, the Irish Army had compiled a series of maps showing possible landing places which would be used by the British. In south-west

Donegal, for example, they anticipated landings in barges and small boats around Mountcharles, Inver, Rossnowlagh and Bundoran. They believed that the British could bring 'armoured fighting vehicles' ashore at all these points.[258] In 1942, German landings were expected at Waterford, Cork, Dublin, Shannon and possibly Galway. General Costello's forward line would run through Arklow, Carlow, Abbyleix, Roscrea and Athlone; he put his 1st and 3rd Brigades in Cork, holding the 2nd in reserve, left the 5th and 6th in Carlow and put the 9th Battalion in Waterford. Two reserve brigades were centred on Trim and Kells.[259] If and when these troops were overwhelmed, Irish troops outside Dublin were to form 'centres of resistance' around Castlebar, Ballina, Galway, Sligo, Boyle, Athlone and Mullingar.[260]

In Dublin, the Irish Army garrison would retreat slowly to the centre of the capital. De Valera wanted 'a ring of anti-tank guns around the city'.[261] An exercise for the defence of Dublin was held in June 1941, when Irish troops were to hold a perimeter line around the city that stretched from north of Raheny Strand, west to Phoenix Park, then south in a crooked line through the suburb of Terenure and east to Booterstown and Dublin Bay. Beaten back from these positions, the Irish Army withdrew to an inner perimeter that formed a 'box' between Mountjoy north of the Liffey, Kilmainham south of the river, and the bay. Then, no longer able to hold this line, Irish troops abandoned the north side of the city, leaving even the General Post Office – the shrine of republicanism – to the enemy, and formed a final citadel. This last stand by the Irish in their capital city was to have taken place between the Liffey, the Royal Hospital and Lower Leeson Street with troops defending the Castle, Trinity College and St Stephen's Green[262] where – twenty-five years before – the Citizen Army had dug their trenches in the lawns to fight the British.

Chapter 8

The Neutral Island in the Heart of Man

They saw Ireland safe under the British umbrella, fed by her convoys and protected by her airforce, her very neutrality guaranteed by the British armed forces . . . As they sailed past this smug coastline, past people who did not give a damn how the war went as long as they could live on in their fairy-tale world, they had time to ponder a new aspect of indecency. In the list of people you were prepared to like when the war was over, the man who stood by and watched while you were getting your throat cut could not figure very high.

Nicholas Monsarrat *The Cruel Sea*

We can only be a friendly neutral . . . Our circumstances, our history, the incompleteness of our national freedom through the partition of our country, made any other policy impracticable. Any other policy would have divided our people, and for a divided nation to fling itself into this war would be to commit suicide.

Eamon de Valera *14 December 1941*

In the late summer of 1940, Northern Ireland's new strategic importance was obvious to anyone who visited the north Antrim coast. Bruce Williamson, a 19-year-old Trinity College student from Belfast, spent much of his holidays that warm summer lying on the cliffs above Fair Head, 'watching the great convoys heading through the narrow passage of the North Channel between Northern Ireland and Scotland, then spreading out across miles of sea.'[1] All day and night, the British convoys from Liverpool and the Clyde moved slowly around the north of Ireland now that the south-western Approaches had been abandoned. The Royal Navy still thought they might obtain the Treaty ports; even before the last British troops had been taken off the Dunkirk beaches, the Chiefs of Staff were once more seeking the use of Berehaven, telling the British Cabinet that:

240

. . . the Western Approaches are our most vulnerable area for submarine attack on trade. With the Channel ports in German hands, the scale of attack is likely to increase if Germany and possibly Italy are able to make use of these ports as submarine bases. Our light forces are unable to operate from their present bases at Plymouth and Milford Haven further west than longitude 14°. Enemy submarines have operated in the focal area to the West of this long-itude, and it is imperative that our anti-submarine escorts should be extended further to the west. By the use of Berehaven we should be able to operate a further 180 miles west than is possible from bases in the United Kingdom.[2]

But Berehaven remained closed to Britain, and the Royal Navy there-fore looked further north for its Irish harbour. On August 23, the Director of Anti-Submarine Warfare sent a memorandum to the Admiralty that was ultimately to have enormous constitutional as well as military conse-quences for Northern Ireland. 'It is particularly desired to base A/S [Anti-Submarine] Striking Forces on the NORTH coast of Ireland as far to the westward as possible,' he wrote. '. . . FOIC [Flag Officer-in-Charge] Belfast reports that Free State authorities have raised no objec-tions to our using Londonderry and Lough Foyle as a base provided we go ahead and do so without referring the matter to the Free State authorities.'[3] The Irish Government's acquiescence in this proposal was necessary since the title to the waters of Lough Foyle was disputed between Eire and Northern Ireland. Maffey notified Walshe of the Royal Navy's intentions in early September[4] and the Irish Cabinet – no doubt thinking that this might soften British demands for the Treaty ports – made no objections. Two 6-inch guns were immediately installed on Magilligan Point as coastal protection[5] and a naval staff was established in Londonderry by mid-September.[6] Within six months, the Royal Navy's convoy escorts – destroyers, frigates and corvettes – were spread out across the broad waters of the Foyle, a spectacle greeted with silence by everyone in Eire except old 'Lady' Maud Montgomery, the Major Gen-eral's mother, who marked the passage of each British warship past her family home on the Eire side of the Lough by running to the shore-line and waving a huge Union Jack over her head.[7]

The navy went on to reinforce its trawler base at Belfast with anti-submarine and mine-sweeping trawlers while Belfast Lough was used as an ocean convoy assembly point.[8] In their anxiety to combat the U-boat packs in the Atlantic, the RAF also took a more serious interest in Northern Ireland's strategic potential, choosing seven new airfields in the province for Coastal Command aircraft and long-range bombers.[9]* Heavy industry in the six counties had turned into an arsenal. Throughout 1940 and 1941, the shipyards of Harland and Wolff were building 'Flower' class corvettes for the navy,[10] later switching to mine-sweepers, landing-craft, tankers and frigates.[11] In the course of the war, Northern Ireland was to

---

* This was in addition to a flying-boat base already being prepared on Lough Erne.

produce 140 warships, a tenth of the entire merchant shipping of the United Kingdom, guns, tanks, ammunition and aircraft, including 1500 heavy bombers.[12]

But it was at Londonderry that Northern Ireland's new status was most clearly defined. By February of 1942, more than eighty naval escort vessels were moored in the Foyle,[13] up which Captain Browning's *Mountjoy* had sailed in 1689 to relieve the besieged Protestants of the Maiden City. And in one sense, the Royal Navy's arrival in the Second World War represented an almost equally momentous delivery for the Protestants of Northern Ireland. Londonderry's strategic role meant that the six counties were now essential to the prosecution of the war and could no longer be used as a tempting bait for de Valera in return for the restricted use of the Treaty ports or the premature entry of British troops into Eire. De Valera's very refusal to hand back Eire's Atlantic harbours now served only to emphasise the loyalty of Northern Ireland's Unionist population whose six small and generally poor counties had become a defensive bridgehead to America. The province was now not just a willing armourer but a bastion in the Battle of the Atlantic. 'Here, by the grace of God,' Churchill later wrote, 'Ulster stood a faithful sentinel.'[14]

Craigavon would have approved of the sentiment although he thought that Britain's good fortune was owed to Unionist loyalty rather than divine intervention. He above most others realised in the autumn of 1940 that by a happy combination of Germany's victory on the Continent and de Valera's stubborn neutrality, Northern Ireland had been placed in a new and unprecedented relationship with Britain, one which apparently proved the intrinsic worth of his Protestant government in Belfast. Asked in November about de Valera's refusal to lend the Treaty ports to Britain, Craigavon replied that:

> . . . all the sacrifices Ulster has made in the past have been fully justified by having secured for His Majesty's Forces a *pied à terre* in Ireland from which they can successfully combat the dangers which confront us by land, sea and air. What has happened is a complete vindication of the Government of Northern Ireland since it took office.[15]

It was, in fact, nothing of the kind. The province's new role resulted from geographic chance as much as it did from the survival techniques of the government in Belfast. But Craigavon correctly interpreted the new mood in Britain. However deeply Eire's attitude might be deplored, he said:

> . . . no one who has studied closely each successive stage in the policy of Southern Ireland can be in the least surprised. It has been evident all along that Eire has been accepting concession after concession from Britain with the intention of giving nothing in return. In the midst of a war in which the Empire is fighting for its existence, Eire clings to her neutrality. Mr de Valera's

announcement that he would not allow Great Britain to use the ports marks the culminating point in the process which we in the North have foreseen for the past forty years.[16]

This was a view of Eire which the British could easily share, indeed it was a *British* view, one that cemented an identity of interest between Belfast and London, and Craigavon had de Valera to thank for it. Craigavon could sometimes adopt an attitude of paternalism towards Britain:

What people on the other side of the water apparently do not realise is the importance of having a solid English-speaking block from the East Coast of England to the West Coast of America. This is the greatest buffer against Hitler that we could have, and if you destroy the Ulster section of it, you create a gap that all the goodwill of America cannot bridge . . .[17]

But always there was the familiar reminder:

Ulster people will never divorce themselves from the Union Jack. We will not accept any status that takes us outside the British Empire. Ulster will stay where she is.[18]

In Britain, this sounded like a strong voice. But in Northern Ireland, Unionists had grown tired of the old rhetoric. The groundswell of Unionist dissatisfaction with their Government's handling of the province's high unemployment had not been assuaged after Craigavon's victory in the 1938 election. Younger men wanted a reconstruction of the Stormont Government and in May of 1940, two of Craigavon's ministers had resigned.[19] One of them, J.E. Warnock, the Parliamentary Secretary to the Ministry of Home Affairs, was appalled by Craigavon's inability to persuade the British Government that conscription should be imposed on the province. 'I have heard speeches about Ulster pulling her weight,' he said during a debate on the Home Guard, 'but they have never carried conviction . . .'[20] In September, Warnock actually moved a vote of censure against his elderly former colleagues, claiming that 'no limpet clings to a rock with the tenacity with which members of the Government have clung to their posts.'[21] Craigavon, it appears, could not even maintain a working relationship between his Government and the British Army GOC. 'There is no doubt in my mind,' Spender wrote in his diary in November, 'that General Huddleston was seriously contemplating the necessity of introducing martial law over here because of the unsatisfactory nature of his relations with our Government, more especially with the Ministry of Home Affairs.'[22]

Though frequently ill now, Craigavon maintained his interest in Northern Ireland's growing links with the navy. On November 21, he visited the Royal Navy's base in Belfast but he became tired during his inspection and developed a pain under his arm. His doctor gave him morphia and he seemed to have improved next day, sitting up in bed, smoking his pipe and reading a detective novel.[23] But at about seven o'clock in the evening, alone in his bedroom, he died.

Craigavon had lived just long enough to ensure that his province was secure within the United Kingdom, at least for a few more decades. In a telegram to the Governor of Northern Ireland, Lord Abercorn, Churchill mourned the loss of 'our old, tried and valiant friend, Craigavon . . . He reaped his reward in the splendid and vital contribution which Ulster is making to the British Commonwealth of Nations, and to the course of freedom at this turning point in world history.' But then Churchill added:

> He was the first to hold out the hand of comradeship to the South in the troubled times which followed the last war. This also will bear fruit in God's good time.[24]

Perhaps Churchill was still thinking of some distant union within the Empire, a united Ireland that would strengthen the Dominions rather than diminish the size of the United Kingdom. Craigavon would not have wanted to hear this. Andrews called him 'a great Ulsterman, a great Irishman, a great Imperialist'[25] but the last epithet was wrong. Craigavon's patriotism had its roots in Northern Ireland, not in the Empire. Spender, who *was* an imperialist and who regarded London rather than Belfast as his capital, understood this. 'There was always rather a difference in outlook on the Ulster question between Lord Craigavon and myself,' he wrote in his diary.

> Lord Craigavon was guided in his policy by his desire to ensure the prosperity of his province and its people, whereas I followed Lord Carson's line of thought in thinking far more of the general effect upon the Empire of any change in the Irish situation.[26]

Spender was pointing to the dichotomy that lay at the heart of Unionism in Northern Ireland. 'I have been at pains,' he went on, 'to emphasise the importance I have always attributed to the strategical importance of Northern Ireland to the British Empire since it has influenced my whole career.'[27]

Craigavon took quite the opposite view. He thought always of the strategic importance of the Empire to Northern Ireland. His decisions – even on national issues involving the war – were invariably based on local considerations. He showed little interest in the surrender of the Treaty ports until Northern Ireland found advantage in de Valera's neutrality. He pressed for conscription not because the Empire was in danger but because Northern Ireland, to prove her right to equal citizenship within the United Kingdom, had to be seen to share an equal sacrifice. His concern over the province's poor recruiting figures was prompted by the same anxiety. But where British practices did not square with Northern Ireland's necessities, the rules of parity were pushed aside. The Home Guard in Northern Ireland were distinctly un-British since they came from only one section of the community, a situation which Craigavon had brought about by insisting that the 'B' Specials should control them. When faced with the ultimate sacrifice – the end of partition as an inducement to bring Eire into the war on Britain's side – Craigavon talked of 'treachery', as if *his* was the imperial government, and followed this up by urging the invasion of a neighbouring Commonwealth country.

Until his death, therefore, Craigavon's first loyalty was to Northern Ireland* and this sense of priority continued to govern the decisions of the Stormont Cabinet throughout the war. Craigavon allegedly wanted Basil Brooke to be his successor,[30] perhaps believing that his family name would give the Northern Ireland Government some added prestige among British ministers. But John Andrews, the 70-year-old partially deaf Minister of Finance – 'a very good little man,' as Brooke contemptuously called him[31] – took over the premiership instead, emphasising as he did so the Cabinet's growing senility.

Craigavon was buried on a dark, foggy morning, his coffin drawn on a gun carriage and his funeral route lined with his faithful 'B' Specials and men of the Royal Ulster Rifles. The time of the funeral had not been announced for fear of a Luftwaffe air attack on the crowds who gathered to watch the cortège.[32] He was buried beside his Protestant parliament at Stormont, sealed into the ground by a massive memorial stone, a slab of Newry granite that had been specially chosen by his old Cabinet.[33] Craigavon had been regarded by some of his supporters as a Messiah but a historian of the Unionist Party would later refer to him as 'the Jonah of Ulster's political history', whose perpetuation of a Protestant state won by Protestants for Protestants ensured that the sins of the fathers would be visited upon the sons.[34] It did not look that way in late 1940 when – in British eyes – Craigavon's star was in the ascendant.

Not so de Valera's. After his rejection of Britain's offer of unity, Irish neutrality became the target of growing condemnation in the British press. In mid-July, he complained to Maffey about 'press propaganda'

---

* A Marxist interpretation of this period suggests that the province's Government might be divided into 'populists' and 'anti-populists' – Craigavon falling into the first category and Spender into the second[28] – but this fails to take account of the deep suspicions of British rule felt even by those whose primary allegiance was to Westminster. Spender, for instance, complained that 'the great weakness of English democratic government is that the political leaders concentrate on matters of the present or immediate future and take little interest in more remote questions even though they are of vital importance to the country since they know that their political powers may be short lived.' Spender was much exercised about the 'temperamental weaknesses' that Chamberlain showed in his dealings with de Valera and Hitler.[29]

directed against Eire, claiming it was so concerted 'that it suggested permission or connivance. America had come in on the same note . . . in Eire all this had been taken as British propaganda implying stronger measures to follow.' When the MacDonald negotiations failed, de Valera said, there was a feeling in Eire of strong resentment on Britain's part, and 'Craigavon's utterances had not been helpful.' Eire now believed that a British invasion was more likely than a German attack. He referred to Major Byass, the British officer who had been arrested by the Irish police in Mullingar with military maps and sketches of airfields in his car. 'We have shown these people everything,' Maffey quoted de Valera as saying. 'We have revealed our plans. But there is something more they want. What are we to think?'[35]

Maffey had already received a telegram from Caldecote explaining Byass's presence in Eire. The officer had been on leave but had been instructed by the British Army in Northern Ireland to collect information of military interest about roads in Eire. This was done without the permission of the Dominions Office although it was 'a genuine attempt to prepare ourselves for giving assistance to the Eire Government if they invited us to do so.'[36] Maffey read this telegram to de Valera, together with an official apology from Caldecote. 'This had a tremendous effect,' Maffey wrote in his report to London, 'and I felt the whole atmosphere change.'

De Valera then once again asked for arms. Britain's failure to help, he said, had 'lent colour to the idea that we wanted to come in and do the job ourselves.' He wanted 'a few anti-tank guns, a few fighter aeroplanes, a few anti-aircraft guns'. Dublin could not be declared an open town. It must be defended. De Valera's words – if Maffey's record of them is correct – did not sound as if they came from the leader of a neutral state:

Why will you not trust us? If you think we might attack the North I say with all emphasis we will never do that. No solution there can come by force. There we must now wait and let the solution come with time and patience.

If you think the IRA will get the arms, I can assure you that we have no fifth-column today. There is no danger in that quarter.

Give us help with arms and we will fight the Germans as only Irishmen in their own country can fight. There is no doubt on which side my sympathies lie. Nowadays some people joke about my becoming pro-British. The cause I am urging on you is in the best interest of my own country and that is what matters most to me.[37]

Maffey obviously appreciated the force of this statement for he told the Dominions Office that de Valera was 'insistent in his pleading for help' and that 'if we wish to get into a happier relationship a concession here would achieve wonders.'[38] Caldecote presented Maffey's report to the War Cabinet. 'I entirely agree with the view that the attitude of the Eire Government, in their rigid insistence on their policy of neutrality, is shortsighted and dangerous,' he wrote, 'and their suspicions are exasperating beyond words.' This qualifying remark may have been for Churchill's benefit, for Caldecote went on to warn that 'we are in grave danger not merely of not obtaining the participation of Eire in the war, but of losing such measures of friendly co-operation as the Government of Eire are prepared to afford . . . we might even jeopardise the secret understanding with them that in the event of a serious invasion they will resist the enemy and call upon us for aid.' For these reasons, Caldecote wanted to 'damp down' the British press campaign against Eire.* He also wanted Churchill to announce publicly 'that we have no intention of sending our forces into Eire without a request from the Government of Eire.' And he urged the Cabinet to release most of the weapons originally offered to Eire when MacDonald presented de Valera with Britain's plan for Irish unity. This would go a long way 'towards making Eire a friendly non-belligerent who would in case of invasion develop into an active ally.'[39]

Little came of Caldecote's memorandum. The British press campaign was temporarily halted but there was to be no guarantee from Churchill that the British would not invade Eire; and Eden, who was now Secretary of State for War, made only a desultory effort to accommodate de Valera's request for arms by producing a much reduced version of the list of weapons that had originally been offered to him.[40] Eden also explored an earlier British suggestion that de Valera might accept a brigade of troops from the London Irish. But he discovered that only 15½ per cent of the 1st Battalion and 9 per cent of the 2nd had actually been born in Eire,† and concluded that 'from the composition of these battalions, there seems no strong reason to suppose that they would prove more acceptable to Mr de Valera than other British units.'[41]

The threat of German invasion receded but U-boat attacks on British shipping in the Atlantic did not. Between July and October, 245 British vessels were lost and in November – the worst month of the year – a further 73 merchant ships, a total of 303,682 tons, were sunk, most of them in the Atlantic.[42] In the House of Commons on November 5, Churchill suggested that Irish neutrality was partly responsible for this carnage:

> The fact that we cannot use the south and west coasts of Ireland to refuel our
> flotillas and aircraft, and thus protect the trade by which Ireland as well as

---

* It was evidence of the degree of influence which the Government exercised over British newspapers during the war that Caldecote was able to record that Duff Cooper, the Minister of Information, had spoken to journalists 'on the line that the Press had fully ventilated the question and that the soft pedal might now reasonably be applied'. Caldecote hoped the press would 'respond to this hint'.

† Men from Northern Ireland constituted 12½ per cent of the 1st Battalion and 14 per cent of the 2nd although there was no breakdown of their religious denominations. The remainder of the troops were born 'elsewhere', presumably in Britain of Irish parentage.

> Great Britain lives, is a most heavy and grievous burden and one which should never have been placed on our shoulders, broad though they be.[43]

Churchill's statement touched off another violent press campaign in London in favour of a seizure of the ports. Replying to Churchill, de Valera told the Dail that:

> . . . there can be no question of the handing over of these ports so long as this State remains neutral. There can be no question of leasing these ports. They are ours. They are within our sovereignty, and there can be no question, as long as we remain neutral, of handing them over on any condition whatsoever.[44]

But the damage had been done. In Eire, public opinion, which had been alive to the dangers of German invasion, suddenly swung against Britain.

Cranborne received word of this from Elizabeth Bowen, the Anglo-Irish novelist, who during the war sent secret reports from Eire to the British Ministry of Information. Irish reaction to Churchill's remarks, she wrote, had been very unfavourable. Even were de Valera likely to be amenable:

> . . . he now clearly feels himself placed, with regard to public opinion in his own country, in a position of appalling difficulty.
>
> There seems – I have gathered from talk and the Irish papers – only one basis on which Eire would consider treating for the ports. That is, on some suggestion from the British side that the Partition question was at least likely to be reconsidered. It is felt here (I do not know how correctly) that the Six Counties' intransigence comes from British support.
>
> The flare-up of resentment and suspicion on this side . . . is all the more to be regretted because, since August, pro-British feeling and sympathy for the British cause had been steadily on the increase here. I was struck by this, and impressed by the change of atmosphere, when I arrived in Eire in the middle of last month . . .
>
> The childishness and obtuseness of this country cannot fail to be irritating to the English mind. In a war of this size and this desperate gravity Britain may well feel that Irish susceptibilities should go to the wall. But it must be seen (and no doubt is seen) that any hint of a violation of Eire may well be used to implement enemy propaganda and weaken the British case. Also, that aggravation of feeling in this country makes one more problem to settle after the war – or rather, is likely to make the settlement of an outstanding problem more difficult.[45]

But Churchill was concerned about Irish opinion on the other side of the Atlantic. 'We are denied the use of the ports or territory of Eire in which to organise our coastal patrols by air and sea,' he lamented to Roosevelt in December. '. . . if it were proclaimed an American interest that the resistance of Great Britain should be prolonged and the Atlantic

Top 11 July 1938. An advance party of Irish troops embarks at Cobh Harbour to take possession of Spike Island from the Royal Artillery. In the background, the Royal Navy destroyer *Acasta*. (Irish Army Artillery Officers' Mess, Kildare) *Bottom* The Union Jack is lowered at Rerrin Redoubt over the Royal Navy's harbour at Berehaven, County Cork, on 26 September 1938, as British troops (left) present arms beside soldiers of the Irish army (foreground). (Robert Murphy, Dean of Kerry)

A unit of Eire's 7500 regular soldiers marches down a quiet road near Dublin early in 1940. Their German-style helmets were made in Belgium but the British rarely lost an opportunity to ridicule what they regarded as a symbol of de Valera's pro-German policies. (EMI Films Ltd Pathé Film Library Reel 40/54 'Ireland, Outpost of Peace')

Irish Army mobile patrol crosses the Curragh in 1939, 'protected' by three Air Corps Lysanders. This picture – a 'still' from an Irish propaganda newsreel – was intended to boost public morale in the country's defence forces. (EMI Films Ltd, Pathé Film Library)

The Irish Army Cavalry Corps' 1st Armoured Squadron, stationed on the Curragh. The Swedish Landswerk vehicle (left) was obtained just before the outbreak of war but the Irish Army were so short of equipment that they had to build the six-wheel armoured car (centre) in their own workshops. (EMI Films Ltd, Pathé Film Library)

Top The guns of the Treaty Ports. A rare photograph of Irish troops test firing their 9.2-inch artillery from Fort Templebreedy across the approaches of the Royal Navy's former harbour at Cobh in 1941. (*Irish Press*) *Bottom* On a rainy morning in March 1941, Irish Army Air Corps pilots survey two of their six Lysander reconnaissance aircraft at Baldonnell airfield outside Dublin. In the background, two Miles Magister trainers stand on the tarmac. (Irish Department of Defence, Army Air Corps D 29/9)

NEUTRAL EIRE
NO REFUELLING BRITISH FLOTILLAS
& AIRCRAFT TO PROTECT THE TRADE
BY WHICH BRITAIN & EIRE LIVE

"GOD BLESS EIRE'S NEUTRALITY – UNTIL THE FÜHRER GETS THERE"

Top Eamon de Valera, Eire's leader in time of war, seen here in a previously unpublished photograph at a neutrality rally at College Green, Dublin, in 1940. (EMI Films Ltd, Pathé Film Library Reel 40/54 'Ireland Outpost of Peace') *Bottom* This cartoon by Low, which appeared in the New York magazine *The Nation* in January 1942, was typical of Britain's efforts to persuade Irish-Americans that de Valera's policies were harmful to the Allied cause.

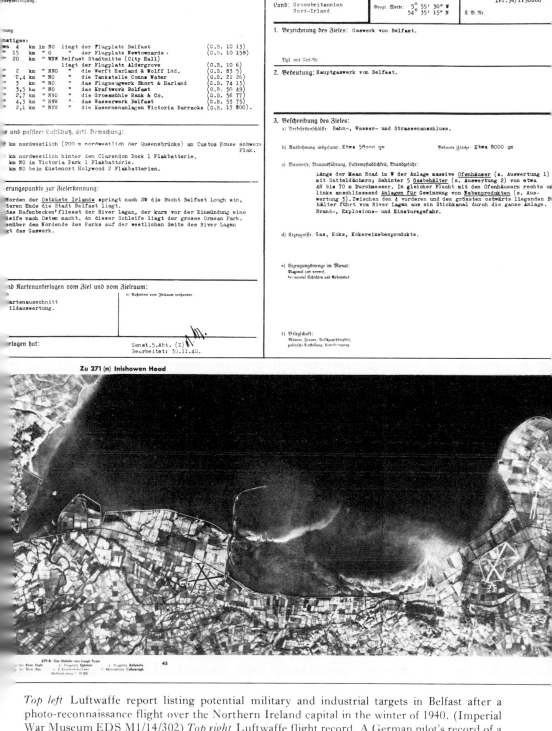

Top left part (report listing targets):

Ofenhaus (Koksbatterie) und Behälter (s. Auswertung 1 und 2).

...stoffversorgung:

...rung:
...nstiges:
...wa 4 km im NO liegt der Flugplatz Belfast   (G.B. 10 13)
"   15 km " O   "   der Flugplatz Newtownards   (G.B. 10 158)
"   20 km " WNW Belfast Stadtmitte (City Hall)
                   liegt der Flugplatz Aldergrove   (G.B. 10 6)
"   2 km " NNO "   die Werft Harland & Wolff Ltd.   (G.B. 83 5)
"   2,4 km " NO   "   die Tankstelle Conns Water   (G.B. 21 26)
"   3 km " NO   "   das Flugzeugwerk Short & Harland (G.B. 74 13)
"   3,5 km " NO   "   das Kraftwerk Belfast   (G.B. 50 49)
"   2,7 km " NNO "   die Grossmühle Rank & Co.   (G.B. 56 77)
"   4,3 km " NNW "   das Wasserwerk Belfast   (G.B. 53 75)
"   2,1 km " NNW "   die Kasernenanlagen Victoria Barracks (G.B. 13 800).

...r und passiver Luftschutz, örtl. Bewachung:

... km nordwestlich (200 m nordwestlich der Queensbrücke) am Custom House schwere Flak.
... km nordwestlich hinter dem Clarendon Dock 1 Flakbatterie.
... km NO im Victoria Park 1 Flakbatterie.
... km NO beim Küstenort Holywood 2 Flakbatterien.

...rungspunkte zur Zielerkennung:

...Norden der Ostküste Irlands springt nach SW die Bucht Belfast Lough ein,
...deren Ende die Stadt Belfast liegt.
...das Hafenbecken fliesst der River Lagan, der kurz vor der Einmündung eine
...eife nach Osten macht. An dieser Schleife liegt der grosse Ormeau Park.
...nüber dem Nordende des Parks auf der westlichen Seite des River Lagan
...gt das Gaswerk.

...nd Kartenunterlagen vom Ziel und vom Zielraum:
                                    b) Außerdem vom Zielraum vorhanden:
...artenausschnitt
...ildauswertung.

...rlagen hat: Genst.5.Abt. (Z)
                                    Bearbeitet: 30.11.40.

Top right part (Zielstammkarte):

Nur für den Dienstgebrauch

Zielstammkarte

Land: Grossbritannien
Nord-Irland

Ort: Belfast
(Nähere Lage):
800 m südwestlich
Stadtmitte (City Hall).

Geogr. Werte: 5° 55' 30" W
               54° 35' 15" N

Ziel-Nr. G.B. 52 49

Kartenbl.-Nr. Irl.5/1:126720
Irl.36/1:50000

E.B. Nr.

1. Bezeichnung des Zieles: Gaswerk von Belfast.

Vgl. mit Ziel-Nr.

2. Bedeutung: Hauptgaswerk von Belfast.

3. Beschreibung des Zieles:
a) Verkehrsanschlüsse: Bahn-, Wasser- und Strassenanschluss.

b) Ausdehnung insgesamt: Etwa 58000 qm   Behaute Fläche: Etwa 8000 qm

c) Bauweise, Bauausführung, Luftempfindlichkeit, Brandgefahr:
Längs der Mean Road im W der Anlage massive Ofenhäuser (s. Auswertung 1)
mit Satteldächern; dahinter 5 Gasbehälter (s. Auswertung 2) von etwa
48 bis 70 m Durchmesser. In gleicher Flucht mit den Ofenhäusern rechts u...
links anschliessend Anlagen für Gewinnung von Nebenprodukten (s. Auswertung 3). Zwischen den 4 vorderen und dem grössten ostwärts liegenden Be...
hälter führt vom River Lagan aus ein Stichkanal durch die ganze Anlage.
Brand-, Explosions- und Einsturzgefahr.

d) Erzeugnisse: Gas, Koks, Kokereinebenprodukte.

e) Erzeugungsmenge im Monat:
Maximal und normal,
bei wieviel Schichten und Arbeitern?

f) Belegschaft:
Männer, Frauen, Beschäftigungsbedürftigkeit,
politische Einstellung, Unterbringung,

Zu 271 (n) Inishowen Head

271 A Das Südufer von Lough Foyle   43

Bottom caption:

Top left Luftwaffe report listing potential military and industrial targets in Belfast after a photo-reconnaissance flight over the Northern Ireland capital in the winter of 1940. (Imperial War Museum EDS M1/14/302) *Top right* Luftwaffe flight record. A German pilot's record of a night reconnaissance mission over Belfast in the winter of 1940. Seeing the unprotected factories in the Northern Ireland capital, he notes that an attack on the city would produce 'fire, explosions and collapsing buildings'. (Imperial War Museum EDS M1/14/302) *Bottom* A 1942 Luftwaffe reconnaissance photograph of potential German invasion beach along Magilligan Strand in Northern Ireland. RAF airfields were clearly marked east of the Royal Navy's port of Londonderry (left). (Imperial War Museum EDS M1/14/302 Kusten-Beschreibung des Irischen Freistaates)

66. Dublin, Stadtbild mit Liffeyfluß.

19. Bauernhaus bei Killarney, Kerry.   4. Bergland

Ein- bis zweiräumige Hütten, in denen, wenn der Stall fehlt, nicht selten Mensch und Tier zusammen hausen.

Top Illustration from Wehrmacht booklet to be issued to German invasion troops in Ireland. Taken largely from pre-war magazines and postcards, photographs like this one would have been of little use to German soldiers. The picture, in which a phaeton approaches Bachelors Walk and in which the vessels moored in the fog downriver are all sailing ships, was clearly taken in the nineteenth century. (Imperial War Museum EDS M1/14/302 Militärgeographische Angaben über Irland) *Bottom* The same booklet contains this photograph of a thatched cottage in the Kerry mountains. The caption solemnly announces that 'people and animals often live together in one or two-roomed huts when there is no stable.' (Imperial War Museum EDS M1/14/302 Militärgeographische Angaben über Irland)

Above Survivors pick
their way through the
rubble of central Belfast
after the Luftwaffe raid of
15 April 1941. Worried
about low public morale,
British censors at first
refused to allow this
photograph to be
published in wartime
newspapers. (*Belfast
Telegraph*) *Right* 15 April
1941. At the run, Belfast
civil defence workers in
steel helmets carry
wounded civilians down
the residential Crumlin
Road past the inferno of
St Mary's Church.
(*Belfast Telegraph*)

Above Irish ARP workers salute as a dead body is carried from ruined buildings after a Luftwaffe air raid on Dublin's North Strand in May 1941. (EMI Films Ltd, Pathé Film Library, Reel 41/4 'Eire Bombed')
Left May 1941. De Valera (second from left, foreground) and beside him Frank Aiken (with hands clasped) examine a crater made by a German bomb in Dublin's North Strand. (*Irish Press*)

route kept open for the important armaments now being prepared for Great Britain in North America, the Irish in the United States might be willing to point out to the Government of Eire the dangers which its present policy is creating for the United States itself.'[46] Churchill even seems to have ruminated on the chances of setting up an American arms factory in Eire that would drive a wedge into Irish neutrality.*

But the most immediate result of Churchill's efforts was to convince his own and later the American public that Eire – because of her refusal to grant the Treaty ports to the Royal Navy – was primarily responsible for the deaths of thousands of British seamen whose ships were torpedoed in the Atlantic that icy winter and who might have been saved if the Royal Navy could have taken advantage of the extra 180 mile radius afforded by Berehaven. Statesmen and historians alike accepted this argument both during and after the war. Eden wrote in his memoirs that 'no minor contrivance could compensate for the loss of the Irish ports and of Berehaven in particular. The Agreement of April 25th, 1938, had surrendered their use, and the resultant toll in ships and lives was to be cruel and hard to bear. The same British convoys brought supplies to Eire, and this not unnaturally rankled, in particular with the Royal Navy. Small wonder that the seizure of the ports by force should have been considered by the Cabinet in October 1939, and only abandoned with reluctance by Mr Churchill . . .'[48]

Spender, who in 1938 had protested to Sir Samuel Hoare and other British Cabinet ministers about the transfer of the ports, noted in his diary in December 1940 that the surrender of the harbours 'has led to the loss, so I am told, of some hundreds of ships and some thousands of lives . . .'[49]† Liddell Hart, the British military historian, also maintained that Eire's refusal to allow the Allies the use of her western and southern coasts 'contributed immensely to the Allied losses in the Atlantic.'[52] Cyril Falls even stated after the war that the British abandoned the south western Approaches because they were 'hamstrung by the neutrality of the Irish Free State and the loss of the base at Queenstown . . .'[53] although it was the German occupation of the French coast which prompted the Admiralty's decision. In his memoirs, Ismay claimed that the ports had been denied to Britain by the Government of Eire 'in spite of the promises which they made when we handed them over in April 1938'.[54] But no such pledges had actually been made; Chamberlain had not insisted upon 'an assurance here and now' when he gave the ports back to de Valera.

---

* In November, Churchill had told Beaverbrook that 'it would be a very good thing if you started a factory in Cork or Dublin, which would afford cover for any visits you might wish to make. The first step I have in mind, however, is to try to interest Roosevelt in the business, and see how he reacts. I am quite sure we shall need to have these facilities.'[47]
† Spender referred to the transfer as a 'lamentable incident of weakness' on the part of the British Government.[50] He noted that *The Times*, which had supported Chamberlain's decision in 1938, was now 'at great pains to gloss over Mr Churchill's statement'.[51]

There was another factor which historians tended to ignore. For the first four years of the war, German intelligence had been able to break British naval codes and pin-point for Raeder's U-boat fleets the exact location of Allied convoys in the Atlantic. The German *Beobachter Dienst* – the Observation Service – penetrated the British and Allied Merchant Ship Code until 1943,[55] an appalling lapse in naval security and one that must take a large share of the blame for the loss of British ships in the Atlantic. On 30 August 1940, for example, the *B-Dienst* intercepted and read a British radio signal that Convoy SC2, outward bound from Sydney in Canada to the United Kingdom, would be at 57°00′ north latitude, 19°50′ west longitude at noon on September 6. The German Admiralty passed this information to its U-boats which sank five of the ships.[56]

And yet it remains undeniably true that a naval base at Berehaven *would* have given the British a wider radius of action for their anti-submarine operations in the Atlantic and provided the convoys with more regular and more frequent protection. The older, slower merchant ships which trailed behind the convoys could have been given a more consistent naval escort and the Royal Navy would have been able to reduce their turn-around time at the end of the Atlantic passage, refuelling in the west of Ireland rather than at Liverpool or the Clyde or – later – at Londonderry. The Irish Government could not escape the accusation – indeed should not have escaped the accusation – that dead British seamen were being washed up on Eire's shores because of her policy of neutrality.

De Valera never replied directly to this charge although his attitude was clear enough. Asked about the Treaty ports in November 1940, he said that 'this question is one that involves our national sovereignty and our people's will. It is also one that involves the safety of our people.'[57] Put in even simpler terms, de Valera would not risk the lives of his people for the lives of British seamen. Truly, neutrality was a form of warfare.

There were few in Britain who tried to explain why Eire was neutral. In 1940, Captain Henry Harrison, a former supporter of Parnell who had won the Military Cross while fighting as a British soldier in France in 1916, published in London a somewhat partisan account of the historical background to Irish neutrality. He emphasised that partition – 'an open wound that cannot be healed' – was largely responsible for Eire's non-participation in the war but contrived not to mention the Treaty ports.[58] For the most part, Irish neutrality engendered – particularly after Churchill's speech – feelings of disgust among the British, especially within the Royal Navy. This bitterness was experienced by a young RNVR lieutenant, Nicholas Monsarrat, who was to recall it in so savage and damaging a manner after the war in his novel *The Cruel Sea*:

> There are degrees of neutrality, just as there are degrees of unfaithfulness: one may forgive a woman an occasional cold spell, but not her continued and smiling repose in other men's arms. Even in the grossest betrayal, however,

whether of the marriage vow or the contract of humanity, there could be variations of guilt . . . But it was difficult to withhold one's contempt from a country such as Ireland, whose battle this was and whose chances of freedom and independence in the event of a German victory were nil. The fact that Ireland was standing aside from the conflict at this moment posed, from the naval angle, special problems which affected, sometimes mortally, all sailors engaged in the Atlantic, and earned their particular loathing.[59]

Monsarrat believed the rumours about the Nazi spies who were supposed to be thronging Eire. Dublin, he wrote, was 'an espionage centre, a window into Britain, which operated throughout the war and did incalculable harm to the Allied cause.' Nonsense though this was, his powerful assessment of Eire's denial of the Treaty ports no doubt reflected the fury and cynicism of his wartime colleagues:

> To compute how many men and how many ships this denial was costing, month after month, was hardly possible; but the total was substantial and tragic . . . from these bases, the Battle of the Atlantic might have been fought on something like equal terms. As it was, the bases were denied: escorts had to go 'the long way round' to get to the battlefield, and return to harbour at least two days earlier than would have been necessary: the cost, in men and ships, added months to the struggle, and ran up a score which Irish eyes a-smiling on the day of Allied victory were not going to cancel.[60]

Monsarrat acknowledged that Eire was within her rights 'from a narrow legal angle' but British sailors, 'counting the number of their friends who might have been alive instead of dead', saw things in simpler terms:

> They saw Ireland safe under the British umbrella, fed by her convoys and protected by her airforce, her very neutrality guaranteed by the British armed forces: they saw no return for this protection save a condoned sabotage of the Allied war effort; and they were angry – permanently angry. As they sailed past this smug coastline, past people who did not give a damn how the war went as long as they could live on in their fairy-tale world, they had time to ponder a new aspect of indecency. In the list of people you were prepared to like when the war was over, the man who stood by and watched while you were getting your throat cut could not figure very high.[61]

Monsarrat, of course, took no account of Irish history, nor of the thousands of Irishmen who were fighting on Britain's side, sometimes on the Atlantic convoys. It was supremely ironic that on the very day that Churchill made his Commons speech, an Irishman – Commander Fogarty Fegen from Ballinunty in County Tipperary – was steering the armed merchantman *Jervis Bay* in a suicide attack against the German pocket battleship *Admiral Scheer* in mid-Atlantic. His action saved almost all the forty-three ships on the convoy he was protecting. Fegen went down with the *Jervis Bay*, earning for himself a posthumous Victoria

Cross. But British anger was too deep to be deflected by such episodes. After a while it seemed as if the British found something anarchic about this demonstration of independence in the neighbouring island, a primordial and indifferent cruelty that Louis MacNeice, who was born in Belfast, captured in his poem 'Neutrality':

> The neutral island facing the Atlantic,
> The neutral island in the heart of man,
> Are bitterly soft reminders of the beginnings
> That ended before the end began.
>
> Look into your heart, you will find a County Sligo,
> A Knocknarea with for navel a cairn of stones,
> You will find the shadow and sheen of a moleskin mountain
> And a litter of chronicles and bones.
>
> Look into your heart, you will find fermenting rivers,
> Intricacies of gloom and glint,
> You will find such ducats of dream and great doubloons of ceremony
> As nobody today would mint.
>
> But then look eastward from your heart, there bulks
> A continent, close, dark, as archetypal sin,
> While to the west off your own shores the mackerel
> Are fat – on the flesh of your kin.[62]

Amid such passion, it was hardly surprising that the British would want to bring home to Eire the consequences of her neutrality and it was just as natural that one of the first suggestions as to how this should be done came from Northern Ireland. On November 9, Spender sent a personal and confidential letter to Lord Hankey, Chancellor of the Duchy of Lancaster, outlining a series of economic measures which he thought should be taken against Eire. 'It should be made clear to the Eire people,' he wrote, 'that the closure of the British ports [sic] will inevitably mean considerable hardships to themselves.' Spender wanted to see a tax on coal exported to Eire 'to raise an insurance fund to meet these unnecessary risks', a cessation of any arms supplies to the Irish military authorities, and a reduction in shipping facilities for Eire. He believed that 'for every British ship which is lost due to the closure of the Eire ports a ship intended to bring imports into Eire should be diverted to a British port.' During visits to Eire with his family, Spender said, he found it difficult to understand why 'we are able to get unlimited supplies of petrol and practically all other imports from Overseas whilst we in the United Kingdom are severely rationed.' He added a tough, schoolmasterly lecture to put backbone into his arguments:

> The Englishman usually begins a speech on Irish matters with an admission that the Irish were ill-treated in the past and that he wishes to make up for this

whereas in actual fact the Irishman has been the spoilt child of the British Government for the last 60 years. This policy of appeasement has had, I believe, the reversed effect to that which it was intended to achieve. All Irishmen, both North and South, respect a man who makes a hard bargain but have no use for one who is wheedled or blackmailed into giving too generous terms; it merely makes him wish that he had asked for more and determined to do so on the next occasion. Concessions which are wrung from weakness lead to contempt.[63]

Hankey circulated Spender's letter to colleagues in the British Government and wrote to him at the end of the month to say that his suggestions and comments – especially on the petrol supply in Eire – had met with a large measure of agreement 'in the most important quarter to which I sent it'. This may have been Churchill himself although Hankey would make only a final cryptic reference to the influence Spender's letter might have had: 'Do not ask me to say more in a written letter. I am afraid it is rather bare bones, but you may be able to read more between the lines than the uninitiated.'[64]

Spender could not resist a further note to Hankey, this time enclosing with it a copy of *The Irish Times* 'so that you may compare its 16 odd pages with the 6 small pages of *The Daily Telegraph*'. The Archbishop of Dublin's daughter, Spender wrote, had been staying with his family and had told him that 'she and a party of friends had just concluded a glorious tour in the south and west of Eire in four motors and also that her father had just bought a new Morris car. Although the import of English cars into Eire is forbidden, apparently . . . there is still no difficulty in getting British motor cars in Eire.' Thanks to the refugees arriving in the twenty-six counties, Spender concluded harshly, 'I am told that the tourist harvest in Eire is very good and that the brilliantly lighted towns which serve as such a useful landmark to the enemy areoplanes in their attacks on Liverpool and on our shipping prove a great attraction to those who have left the dimly lighted towns elsewhere.'[65]

Spender was advocating a programme of economic sanctions, and within days Churchill was demanding from his ministers – and receiving – advice on the financial and trade restrictions that could be placed upon Eire. There is no concrete evidence that Spender was behind this but he was to refer later to 'the new policy of firmness to Eire for which Lord Hankey, Lord Cranborne and Mr Churchill are responsible, following upon my note to the first . . .'[66] and it does seem as though his letter helped to inspire the Cabinet's new measures. On December 16, Sir Kingsley Wood, the Chancellor of the Exchequer, presented Churchill with two plans, the first of which envisaged restrictions on Eire's shipping space. To avoid unnecessary competition, Eire had in 1940 consented to charter ships through the British. It was an unwritten agreement of benefit to both countries but Wood proposed to terminate the arrangement, at the same time telling Greek and Norwegian ship-owners that they should not charter ships 'except to Allies or co-operators'. Eire would then receive only 25 per cent of her shipping needs 'if she were very lucky'. In addition to this, the British could also shut off the export to Eire of food, feeding stuffs and fertilisers, agricultural and other machinery, chemical and electrical goods, paper and cardboard. Britain could freeze Eire's balances of sterling and thus dislocate her remaining imports. If these measures were introduced, said Wood, the Irish population 'would probably begin to feel uncomfortable in a few weeks'. Under the second plan, Britain would withhold facilities for the insurance of ships going to Eire 'and this would mean that they would get no ships.' There would then be drastic shortages in Eire.[67]

At no point was it to be officially admitted that any of these restrictions were intended to be punitive. When asked about the measures, the British would explain – in Wood's words – 'that so long as we are subject to difficulties in the supply of certain things we cannot in present circumstances go on giving Eire the generous share of them that we have so far allowed her.'[68] In January, the British Cabinet duly went ahead and instituted the first plan and the effects were immediately felt in Eire, as they were meant to be. All over the country, petrol pumps ran dry after the Christmas holidays and subsequent rationing reduced private motorists' petrol allowance by 75 per cent. The two-ounce tea ration was halved and the absence of wheat imports meant the end of white bread.[69]

The Irish Government had already forwarded a memorandum to the British Government, complaining that they were finding it difficult to acquire shipping and claiming that the mutual arrangement to avoid competition 'imposed, at least by implication, an obligation on the British Ministry of Shipping to provide shipping for the reasonable requirements of Irish trade.'[70] The British Government refused to accept that such an obligation had been implied,* adding that 'they would be failing in their duty . . . if, while existing conditions continue, they did not give absolute priority to the urgent need of those engaged in the present war against aggression.'[71] The Irish Government retorted angrily that Britain's attitude was 'inconsistent' with remarks made by Eden in May 1940 when the then Dominions Secretary had promised 'to undertake, so far as reasonably practicable, to ensure the supply to Eire of the materials which she required to import from overseas.' It had never occurred to the Irish Government that Britain would use the shipping arrangements 'to secure control of all available neutral tonnage and then refuse the use of any portion of such tonnage for Irish requirements.'[72] The screw was being tightened.

On January 20, Maffey was summoned to an interview with de Valera.

---

* The British had claimed that the transfer of the Treaty ports had implied an obligation on Eire to let the Royal Navy use them in time of war. De Valera had rejected this idea and it was unlikely that the British were now going to entertain any notional debts allegedly owed to Eire.

Ostensibly, this was to confirm arrangements for RAF aircraft to fly west of Lough Erne over the neck of Irish territory that extended between the Northern Ireland border and the sea. But according to Maffey, the Taoiseach was 'in an exceedingly nagging mood'. Churchill's speech had caused a great change in Irish attitudes, de Valera said. 'Previously they had regarded Germany as the probable aggressor. Now they feared England. The campaign against Ireland in the English press had had the most serious consequences here . . . He hated the idea of a German victory, but we had been stupid. By getting involved in a sparring match about the ports, we had lost the substance for the shadow. The substance was very real, namely, an Ireland which was ready strenuously to oppose a German landing with its whole heart and soul, which only asked for arms to assist our cause in that way.' According to Maffey's report of the conversation:

Mr de Valera did not say a great deal about economic measures, but hinted that there seemed to be more in them than measures justifiable by our own urgent needs and therefore readily understood here. He was particularly bitter on one point, namely, the opportunity which had now occurred to acquire arms in America. The Purchasing Committee had, indeed, suggested that the transaction should be put through without delay. But the Treasury had refused to transfer funds for the transaction. Actions such as this would provoke violent anti-English feelings.[73]*

The British were playing cat and mouse with the Irish, and de Valera did not quite know how to react. Why would the Treasury have blocked funds for the arms transaction? He was not certain. Indeed, ten days later, he was telling the Fine Gael front bench that so far as supplies and trade were concerned, 'the British up to the present had been dealing with us with extraordinary generosity, that if he were in their place, he would look after his own country before anybody . . .'[75] But if Britain *was* deliberately initiating trade sanctions, it could be a preliminary step towards more serious measures. De Valera may well have had this in mind when he asked Maffey for an assurance that Britain would respect the neutrality of Eire and that there was no question of a British invasion or seizure of the ports. Maffey replied unsympathetically that 'nobody could foretell how the strategic factors of a world war would develop. It might well be to the advantage of Eire to grant us certain facilities.' He countered de Valera's demand for arms by pointing out that 'the worst impression had been created in London by his repeated and persistent refusal to consider any plans for anti-submarine measures in his western harbours.' Maffey was

* Maffey did not approve of strong economic sanctions against Eire, apparently fearing that de Valera would tell his people that the British were trying to squeeze them into the war. Spender, who was in London with Andrews in December 1940, noted that Maffey had been brought over from Dublin and that he 'evidently trotted out the usual "bug-bear" – the Anglo-American vote.'[74]

losing his patience with de Valera again, commenting contemptuously in his report to London that the Taoiseach:

> . . . did not show to advantage. It is sheer hypocrisy on his part to bring up the Prime Minister's speech, which he deliberately made use of here to inflame passions. I made it plain that I did not attach any weight to this line of argument. The fact is that Mr de Valera is more uneasy today than he has ever been at any stage of his non-stop political career. Ireland being Ireland, in the mass ignorant and responsive to old hatreds, he is still the chosen tribal leader for their feuds. But Mr de Valera hitherto has used this Irish fanaticism on a bigger stage than his platform of today. Through it he has achieved prestige in America, in England, and Geneva. He could stir world-wide interest in the soul of Ireland. But it is the soul of England which stirs the world today, and Eire is a bog with a petty leader raking over old muck heaps. He has in the past enjoyed world prestige, he is vain and ambitious, but the track he has followed without looking either to right or to left is now leading into insignificance.[76]

But de Valera's path was never quite that straight, and Maffey was aware that Irish American support for Eire still influenced Anglo-Irish relations. He noted that the American Institute of Public Opinion had announced that more than 63 per cent of Americans questioned in a recent poll wanted Eire to give up her neutrality and let the British use the Treaty ports. But in a special poll conducted among first and second generation Irish Americans, 52 per cent had opposed any abandonment of Irish neutrality. 'These Irish Americans,' wrote Maffey, 'are the pillars of Mr de Valera's temple. They created him, preserved him and endowed him. His feelings today when he hears the courageous speeches of President Roosevelt can be imagined. In his predicament he follows his old and only technique. He blames England.'[77]

Cranborne sent Maffey's dispatch to Churchill, adding in a separate memorandum of his own that Dulanty, the Irish High Commissioner, had also asked about the possibility of a formal British promise not to enter Eire unless requested to do so by the Irish Government. Cranborne had informed Dulanty that:

> . . . we had no present intention of occupying the ports . . . and the question was, to that extent, academic. But in a war like this it was impossible to foresee what might develop. A situation of life and death might arise in which it might be essential, in our view, to the survival of the liberties of Britain and of Southern Ireland too that we should have the use of the ports. I devoutly hoped that such a situation would never arise. But if it did, and we had made a public statement such as he suggested, we should be widely accused in Southern Ireland of a breach of faith . . .[78]

But Cranborne was inclined to support de Valera's request for arms, 'especially as he seems to regard our acceptance or refusal of his request as, in some sense, the touchstone of our goodwill.' De Valera was now permitting British civil aircraft to use the flying-boat base at Foynes for their service to Lisbon and West Africa, in addition to allowing RAF flying-boats a corridor over Irish territory beside Lough Erne. Cranborne thought that the Taoiseach: '. . . might naturally expect some gesture in return. But at present we are, in the economic sphere, tightening the screw against him. His request for arms seems to afford us an opportunity of showing that our economic measures are not a sign of hostility against Southern Ireland, but are genuinely the result of difficulties created for us by shipping losses.'[79]

Churchill was in a less tolerant frame of mind. As he read through Maffey's dispatch and Cranborne's covering note, he scribbled monosyllabic comments in the margins of the documents. Where Cranborne and Maffey had raised the question of arms supplies to Eire, he had written a large and decisive 'No' on the side of the paper and had drawn a thick and approving black line next to Maffey's description of de Valera as 'a petty leader raking over old muck heaps'. This was language that Churchill approved of. His old animosity towards de Valera and the Taoiseach's legally dubious twenty-six county state had been reawakened. There were going to be no deals with Eire now, as Churchill's personal reply to Cranborne next day made clear:

> I agree with the general line of your talk. I could in no circumstances give the guarantee asked for, and for the reasons you state.
>
> About arms. If we were assured that it was Southern Ireland's intention to enter the war, we would of course if possible beforehand share our anti-aircraft weapons with them, and make secretly with them all possible necessary arrangements for their defence. Until we are so satisfied, we do not wish them to have further arms, and certainly will not give them ourselves.
>
> The concession about Lough Swilly is important and shows the way things are moving.* No attempt should be made to conceal from Mr De Valera the depth and intensity of feeling against the policy of Irish neutrality. We have tolerated and acquiesced in it, but juridically we have never recognised that Southern Ireland is an independent Sovereign State, and she herself has repudiated Dominion Status. Her international status is undefined and anomalous. Should the present situation last till the end of the war, which is unlikely, a gulf will have opened between Northern and Southern Ireland, which it will be impossible to bridge in this generation.
>
> Let me have a further report on economic pressure.[80]

Here was all the old Churchillian malevolence, the hatred of de Valera's neutrality and that familiar suspicion that Eire – despite her irritating political freedom – might not have the constitutional right to exist. He still sought to destroy Irish neutrality – though by economic means rather than

---

* Churchill meant Lough Erne; a curious error since he had made a similar mistake during the discussions which preceded the 1921 Anglo-Irish Treaty, thinking that Lough Seilly was in Northern Ireland (see page 17).

military coercion – and he was more anxious than ever that de Valera should comprehend his anger. But there had been a change. Churchill now acknowledged that Britain was tolerating this 'anomaly'; and he must have realised that British acquiescence represented a grudging acceptance of Eire's independent status. He spoke now of the future, of the gulf that might open wider between the two parts of Ireland. Amid the responsibilities of wartime leadership, Churchill would have had little time to consider the implications of all this but he was beginning to understand what neutrality meant to the Irish and to grasp with painful accuracy the effect that this phenomenon would have upon post-war Ireland.

Yet neither Churchill nor his ministers had abandoned the idea that Eire might after all be cajoled or intimidated into the war, and they were encouraged to think that she might be by America's steadily increasing support for the Allies. With Roosevelt safely re-elected, the British thought that de Valera's Irish American support would now carry less weight. In February, David Gray, the United States Minister in Dublin, urged Cranborne to visit Eire and the Dominions Secretary informed Churchill that he thought such a trip might now be opportune. Britain's economic measures, he told Churchill: '. . . have at last brought home to the Irish people the fact that they cannot insulate themselves from the war. They have been shaken out of their complacency. They realise too that they cannot turn to America for sympathy . . . On the other hand, there are signs that Mr de Valera is beginning to take steps to turn the situation to his own advantage. He is throwing out hints that our action is a deliberate attempt by Great Britain to squeeze Ireland . . .'[81]

Cranborne would speak not only to de Valera but to his colleagues and supporters, explaining the reasons for Britain's trade restrictions and 'drumming into them the fact that the interests of Ireland and Great Britain are inevitably linked, and that shipping losses are bound to hit them just as hard or harder than they hit us.' Maffey had supplied Cranborne with some notes for his visit, a document which claimed from the outset that America held 'the key of the Irish position in the war' and went on to describe the apparent change of mood in Eire:

> . . . as manifestations of American sympathy with Britain have recently developed in unequivocal and unmistakeable strength the effect upon Irish opinion is a matter of deep and immediate interest.
>> 'Humanity with all its fears,
>> With all its hopes for future years
>> Hangs breathless on thy fate.'
> The note breathed by President Roosevelt and echoed so resoundingly by the Prime Minister has shaken the self-satisfaction of Irishmen in their homeland. Against the world background De Valera's creed looks mean and parochial. To re-assert himself he turns to his one and only technique – the working up of feeling against England. He is not pro-German, but you cannot teach an old dog new tricks . . . The trade restrictions we have imposed have

served and are serving a very useful purpose. The Fools' Paradise has come to an abrupt end. There is every reason why the policy should not be relaxed. But unless we keep it going on the right note it will be used by Mr de Valera to excite the old passions and to strengthen his own difficult position.[82]

Maffey suggested that Cranborne should 'concede nothing but would talk on the text that the losses to our convoys involve immense difficulties and hardships. If our convoys were better protected there would be more commodities available. Eire can help powerfully in the matter of protection. Her neutrality hampers protection, etc, etc.'

Churchill felt uneasy about the project. He asked Cranborne if he would not find difficulties:

. . . in repelling the charge that our action was 'a deliberate attempt by Great Britain to squeeze Ireland'? I have a great dislike myself of dealing in humbug especially with a nation like the Irish. You might easily have to make some inconvenient admissions or else say what is not true. You would leave behind you a trail of courtesies, comforts and reassurances which ill-consorts with the hard policy which it is our duty to pursue. I do not see what you could learn that you do not know already, only too well. We always make the mistake of not following through a policy. What can you say that would alter the situation?[83]

Churchill's dislike of humbug was somewhat at variance with the British Government's whole policy of economic sanctions, which was officially explained away as the consequence of convoy losses in the Atlantic but which was in fact deliberately designed to cause hardship in Eire. Cranborne would only have been saying in Eire what British officials were already telling Irish representatives in London. But Cranborne's visit was postponed and de Valera was left – in Churchill's words – to 'stew in his own juice for a while'.[84] He did not do so. He had warned the Dail in mid-January that food shortages were likely and an immediate order was made extending compulsory tillage to bring one fifth of Eire's arable land under the plough.[85] If Britain had turned to economic warfare, Eire would strive for self-sufficiency.

Churchill's baleful warnings of the previous November, however, had not been ignored in Dublin. At the Defence Conference, ministers and Fine Gael leaders pored over charts of the northern Atlantic which Aiken brought to the meetings, discussing interminably the convoy losses and the tactics which the RAF might have employed against the Luftwaffe and the U-boats if the British had been using airfields in Eire. When the Conference met in late December, Mulcahy recorded that 'a large number of sinkings are taking place close up around Malin Head. This apparently is the main stream of traffic. The next largest is in a widespread area about 200 miles off the Mayo coast.' Aiken pointed out that some of the heaviest losses took place 'within easy reach from plane bases in Derry. He implied from this that no assistance from Ireland would be of any use.'[86]

But, as Mulcahy noted the following month, the Luftwaffe had adopted a new tactic, flying their long-range Focke-Wulf Condor bombers from French airfields around Brest up the west coast of Ireland to attack British shipping and then, with their tanks low on fuel, continuing on to airbases at Stavanger in German-occupied Norway. 'The manoeuvreability of these bombers is not high,' Mulcahy wrote after an interview with de Valera in late January. 'Nests for fighters jumping off the West Coast of Ireland could be very destructive, and could practically stop any great volume of this.'[87] This may not have been an exaggeration. Although it was true, as Aiken said, that attacks on shipping were taking place close to Donegal, the Focke-Wulfs were able to conserve fuel by flying close to land around the south-west coast of Ireland. At the deserted port of Berehaven, local people watched the big four-engined Condors flying over them every morning *en route* to the Atlantic convoy lanes, undisturbed by British fighters or anti-aircraft fire.[88] In February, seventy-nine British ships were sunk, the highest losses in the war so far.[89]

To his concern at this tragedy in the Atlantic, James Dillon added his own special moral anguish. 'The Anglo-American alliance is placed in danger of defeat by the Brest–Stavanger tactics,' he told his front bench colleagues in March, but:

> . . . fighter(s) from Ireland would break this patrol. A German victory would result in this country being infiltrated with Naziism. A position would be brought about in which children would never be allowed to hear the Word of God . . . religious persecution would show itself here on an unprecedented scale . . .[90]

Mulcahy noted briefly that Dillon 'wants to go into the war in the cause of democracy.'[91]

The British took a special interest in Dillon. As American influence failed to bring about the desired shift in Irish public opinion, so they came to believe that Dillon might prove to be the instrument of political change that would bring Eire into the war on the Allied side. Maffey, who was on 'very friendly terms' with Dillon and saw him constantly,[92] wrote to Machtig, the Dominions Office Permanent Under-Secretary, in March in a state of some excitement about Dillon's activities. At the Fine Gael party meeting in February, he reported, Dillon 'made a sensational speech advocating the abandonment of neutrality. He did this without the approval of Mr Cosgrave, and the interesting fact was that his sentiments were received with applause by a majority of the delegates.' Dillon had been pleased with this response and had become more active, 'his line of attack against the neutrality of Eire being that the only way in which Ireland can preserve her soul is to join in with those who are fighting the battle of civilisation.' Maffey took encouragement from this, telling Machtig that: '. . . it has always been a matter of considerable surprise to me that the voice of America should hitherto have had so little apparent effect on public opinion, but, here, at last, we are getting some evidence of the leaven working. It is all highly distasteful to Mr de Valera, who continues firmly set in his tramlines . . .'[93]

Dillon's speech to Fine Gael delegates at the Mansion House in Dublin certainly contained few of the ambiguities that the British usually identified in de Valera's statements. Indeed, Dillon appeared to be wholeheartedly behind the Allied cause, arguing for religious rather than political reasons that Eire should abandon neutrality:

> We do not meet today as if things were normal or as if there were no world crisis. We are living under a Sword of Damocles that might fall to destroy freedom and man's right to adore God. All decent things are being assailed by the most formidable combination that ever existed to destroy worship of God. It may be policy of this Government to stand neutral, but I am not neutral. The issue at stake means whether I want to live or to die. I pray Germany and its rulers may be smashed by the Anglo-American alliance. I also pray that the day will dawn when a United Irish People will play their part in helping to smash Germany.[94]

This was music to the ears of the British War Cabinet who in April 1941 even considered inviting Dillon over to London.[95] But he did not follow up his initial speech. 'His intention is as firm as ever,' Maffey told Machtig three days later, 'but it is a question of the timing of his effort. At the present moment if he were to come out with an open attack, the leader of his Party would have to disown him and that would not help matters.'[96] The truth of course was that Dillon in no way represented a transformation of Irish political opinion. The British hoped that he did because he said what they wanted to hear but Dillon had no serious popular following. There had been massive public demonstrations in Dublin in favour of neutrality in 1940, rallies that had been attended not only by Irish ministers but by Cosgrave and Norton who stood together with de Valera to show their solidarity with the Government's policy. Dillon could not break this public unity despite the private doubts about neutrality held by many Fine Gael TDs. And as Maffey commented in a revealing aside to Machtig, 'it is difficult to conceive of this country carrying on at all if the reins fall from Mr de Valera's hands.'[97]

Dillon might just have acquired the prestige to effect some change in public opinion if the British had given him what they refused de Valera: a pledge that they would on no account violate Irish neutrality. Dillon had asked for such a promise in January but Churchill turned him down. 'I could not . . . give the assurance suggested by Mr Dillon that in no circumstances should we "violate Irish neutrality",' Churchill told Cranborne. '. . . Should the danger to our war effort through the denial of the Irish bases threaten to become mortal, which is not the case at present, we should have to act in accordance with our own self-preservation and that of our Cause.'[98]

This was Churchill's consistent reply to all such appeals and when he heard that Duff Cooper, the Minister of Information, had contradicted his policy in a speech in May 1941, he immediately called him to account. Duff Cooper had been rash enough to state that however deeply and disastrously Britain suffered from Irish neutrality, 'we respect the independence of Eire and allow them to remain neutral while we are fighting for our lives. That shows that Great Britain abides by her word . . .'[99] This was too much for Churchill who wrote angrily to his minister:

> I am very sorry you committed yourself to this statement, which is contrary to the policy of HMG and differs widely from my own views. Eire has repudiated the status of a Dominion. We have not recognised in any Statutory or formal manner its present position, which is anomalous and undefined. You have heard me in Cabinet repeatedly refuse to give any guarantee to Mr De Valera's Government that we shall not take the ports by force in certain eventualities. On the contrary I have often said that if it became a matter of life and death, we should do this. It may well be that force will have to be used. This principle was accepted even by the Chamberlain Government . . .[100]

But Churchill knew that force was now a most unlikely option. Refusing to give guarantees to Eire was just another way of making de Valera feel uneasy.* Maffey had helped this policy along in March when in the course of a conversation with Joseph Walshe at the Department of External Affairs, he mentioned that Britain could give no assurances about Eire's neutrality because 'strategic factors' might override them. The Government of Eire, he added ominously, 'must keep that possibility in view and frame their policy accordingly with human understanding of our difficulties.' Maffey's task was now almost wholly devoted to 'educating' de Valera's Government in the realities of the war and his meeting with Walshe was characterised by a new and grim cynicism. Maffey claimed that Hitler was 'using Eire as cover for the deadliest attack upon us' by concentrating his efforts against England in the Western Approaches. Did the Government of Eire have a policy, or were they content to leave everything to chance? Did the Department of External Affairs realise the risk they ran of being suddenly stampeded into rash decisions? 'I said that perhaps Eire had decided to accept Hitler's New Order – if it ever came!

---

* Lord Bradbury, a former Joint Permanent Secretary at the Treasury, had written to Churchill in June 1940 suggesting that the United States should guarantee Eire's neutrality and place her warships in Irish ports.[101] The Dominion Office thought it was 'very doubtful whether Mr de Valera and his government would welcome a suggestion that they should put themselves under United States protection',[102] although this was the very proposal that de Valera was to put to MacDonald a few days later. The British were not interested in giving Eire this security when they thought she should be fighting on their side.

That would be a policy. But if they felt that Eire's proper place was in association with the Anglo-American and democratic group they had better start moving or they would find themselves nowhere.'

Walshe said that partition had been the factor which had counted against Britain but Maffey suggested that the Irish Government had forgotten the 'generous approach' to a solution made by MacDonald in 1940. According to Maffey, Walshe explained that the rejection of the unity offer had been 'due to distrust of the proposals which envisaged a "Committee after the war" and therefore re-erected a familiar bugbear in the long history of Irish disappointments.' Maffey retorted sharply that de Valera 'had made no criticism or suggestion to assist a solution', adding sarcastically that he:

> . . . understood the attitude of the Eire Government at that time. France had just fallen and the Government of Eire firmly believed that England was down and out. Walshe demurred to this unheroic suggestion (which is the true one) and said that certainly our chances looked poor then, much poorer than they do today. I said that today we were on the road to Victory and I could detect – he surely could detect – great uneasiness in this country in regard to the policy of the de Valera Government. Neutrality was the accepted and enforced policy. But censorship had prevented the people from understanding the moral issue.[103]

Maffey recorded that Walshe got 'rather heated' about the moral issue and said the Irish resented being told that it was their duty to get into the war. England was fighting for herself, for her life, and nothing else. America was thinking of nothing but her own interests. Ireland would fight for herself and for nobody else. Maffey did not disagree 'since it was obvious that England was fighting for everything that Ireland stood for in song and story' but he appreciated the 'tragic dilemma' in which Eire's policies had placed Britain. 'On the physical side the possession of facilities in Eire might become a matter of life and death to us. On the moral side the principle of respecting the rights of small liberty loving nations was a matter of life and death to us.'

Walshe had not liked the suggestion that Eire might incline towards Hitler's New Order. He wanted Maffey to know that de Valera was 'at heart a sincere friend of Britain. He hates the German policy of aggression. When the German Minister rings up with a request to see him I always try to put him off as Mr de Valera detests having interviews with him.' Walshe also took exception to the American Minister, David Gray, who 'brandished the big stick too much', but Maffey defended his colleague who, he said, 'spoke the language of America'.[104] He did not realise then that it was Gray rather than Hempel whom de Valera detested meeting.

At no point did Maffey refer to Britain's trade and shipping restrictions – this lesson to the Irish was supposed to be a silent one – but Cranborne was telling the War Cabinet three days later that 'the bubble of Irish complacency has effectively and we may hope finally been pricked. The Southern Irish now know that England is not dependent on them and that on the contrary, it is Ireland that is dependent on England.' Cranborne – who persisted in referring to Eire as 'Southern Ireland' – believed that life in the twenty-six counties was 'very uncomfortable' and was going to become progressively more so. 'But for this she is not able to blame us. The blame rests, first on Germany and secondly on herself. It is a direct result of her policy of neutrality.'[105]

De Valera was certainly anxious. In February, he decided to send one of his ministers to the United States to seek the arms and ships which Britain was so reluctant to furnish. According to Maffey, David Gray first suggested the idea because he thought that an Irish envoy would find the trip 'educational' while the mission was unlikely to accomplish any of its objectives.[106] Aiken claimed many years after the war that he proposed the visit after Churchill's Commons speech in November, telling de Valera that 'somebody will have to go to America and counter Roosevelt's attitude.' Aiken recalled that he was sent on the mission because Sean T. O'Kelly refused to go.[107] Maffey urged the British authorities to facilitate his journey by air through Lisbon because Aiken's visit to the United States would 'help to dispel the idea that our economic measures are punitive' and because his contact with outside opinion would do immense good in Eire 'where views are narrow and insular'. Maffey himself had little time for Aiken – an attitude shared by Gray – and described him as 'anti-British but certainly not pro-German. He is not impressive and rather stupid.'[108]

Aiken was certainly no intellectual. A tall, outwardly diffident man, he often concealed his shyness by adopting a gruff manner that was easily mistaken for rudeness. He was deeply suspicious of the British – he had been burnt out of his boyhood home in County Armagh – and his republicanism still had the rough edges of a man who had been forced to experience defeat.* He provided the muscle for de Valera's nationalism, the firm if not always comprehending Samson upon whom de Valera could lean in his physical infirmity. In Dublin, unkind hearts called Aiken 'the iron man with the wooden head'[110] and he would not have objected to the first of these metaphors. His strength lay in his absolute loyalty to his political leader – even today a life-size bronze bust of de Valera stares short-sightedly down from the sitting-room mantelpiece at Aiken's Dublin home – and this faithfulness could generate a stubborn political resolution that occasionally had more in common with the British than Aiken would have cared to imagine.

The arduous journey to the United States by flying-boat via Portugal,

---

* As IRA Chief of Staff in the civil war, Aiken had given the order to lay down arms although he later wanted to initiate a hunger strike among the imprisoned Irregulars.[109]

West Africa and the Amazon, and the crowded schedule that was to follow did not require a Socrates, merely a prosaic, hard-headed man who would have the stamina to espouse de Valera's increasingly unpopular policies in an increasingly distrustful America. But dealing with United States Government officials also required a responsiveness towards American domestic politics and an understanding of the great shift away from isolationism that was taking place there. Aiken had the stamina for the trip, but whether he had the sensitivity was another matter. In December, Roosevelt had scoffed at Eire's neutrality. Could Ireland hold out if Britain was defeated, he had asked. 'Would Irish freedom be permitted as an amazing exception in an unfree world?'[111] Aiken was not the sort of man to whom Roosevelt was likely to warm.

Several accounts have been written of Aiken's visit to the United States – that of Robert Brennan, the Irish Minister in Washington, being the best known – but Aiken's own memories provide the flavour of the aggressive way in which he approached his mission. Many years after the war, he recalled for the author how he landed at New York in March 1941 after a turbulent flight in the flying-boat from Latin America to be confronted almost immediately by a large and hostile corps of newspapermen. He had been the only one of the thirty passengers who was not sick on the flight into New York but he did not feel well. He had wanted to put in an official request to see Roosevelt but:

> . . . the press people invited me to meet them first. I was taken to a large room in a hotel choc-a-bloc with reporters, principally American and British. One man said 'You're pro-German'. I said 'We're not pro-German or pro-British – we're pro-Irish.' This was not well received but if they had any wit they must have known we were anti-fascist. I was doing my best to state our case.[112]

Aiken met Dean Acheson, the Assistant Secretary of State, on April 2 and asked for arms. He dismissed the value of the ports to Britain on the grounds that the convoy routes were around the north of Ireland and not around the south as they had been in the 1914–18 War.[113] This was not unlike the argument he had put before the Defence Conference in Dublin: that the convoy sinkings were in easy range of RAF bases in Northern Ireland and therefore could not have been avoided by the use of airfields further south.

Roosevelt granted Aiken an audience five days later. Aiken says that the American President was 'very antagonistic' towards him from the start of their meeting[114] and Brennan's account bears this out. According to Brennan, Roosevelt began by charging Aiken with having said that Ireland had nothing to fear from a German victory. Aiken denied this and Roosevelt launched into an oration about Britain's need for Irish help. But the Irish envoy had hardly spoken when a presidential aide arrived to signal the end of the discussion.[115] Not to be put off, Aiken asked for supplies of arms to protect Ireland from invasion but Roosevelt sarcastically wanted to know what Eire would do if she was attacked. Aiken remembers that:

> . . . Roosevelt was asking 'How could you defend yourselves?' and I said our defences were very high. I said something like 'You'd need a good horse to get over them'. Roosevelt was very much annoyed. An aide had been laying lunch things on a table and Roosevelt grabbed the table-cloth and pulled it and I suddenly saw knives and forks flying all over the room. Roosevelt knew what we were up to – trying to maintain our independence as best we could and he didn't like this.[116]

Brennan's account is somewhat different. He does not mention Aiken's facile joke but says that the President's anger was caused by Aiken's insistence that the invasion of Ireland might come from Britain rather than Germany. Roosevelt disagreed and Aiken asked why in that case the British refused to promise that they would not violate Irish neutrality. 'What you have to fear is German aggression,' the President said. 'Or British aggression,' Aiken replied. At that, Roosevelt shouted 'I have never heard anything so preposterous in all my life' and sent the cutlery flying.[117] Brennan's version of events sounds more plausible – Roosevelt was more likely to be infuriated by Aiken's suspicions of Britain than by his poor sense of humour. But the meeting was a disaster. Aiken realised that Roosevelt did not intend to be reasonable and thought he knew why. 'Churchill had been at him to put the screw on us.'[118]

In fact it was Halifax, now the British Ambassador in Washington, who had got to Roosevelt just a few hours before Aiken arrived at the White House. He had apparently told the President that secret British Foreign Office sources indicated Aiken was not only anti-British but positively wished for a German victory.[119] This was the origin of Roosevelt's opening attack. The rest of Aiken's visit went almost as badly. He wrote out a speech on Irish neutrality and travelled across the country, reading it to audiences in dozens of halls and hotels. 'It was terribly wearying,' Aiken recalls. 'I was always afraid that people would twist what I said so I gave out copies of the speeches everywhere I went.'[120] The address was not particularly inspiring; indeed it was remarkably similar to those speeches which de Valera had made at the League of Nations before the war. Small nations and their leaders, Aiken told his listeners, had little influence over the outbreak of war and the best that Eire could do was 'to defend in relation to our own soil and people in the territory over which we have control the principles and aims which are set out so clearly in our Constitution.'[121] This was not going to sway the mind of America. If he could have defended neutrality with the same fire he had used in 1940 when he wrote his secret memorandum on censorship for the Irish Cabinet, Aiken might at least have obtained the respect of the American administration. But his anti-British remarks – he talked about Eire as 'the free portion of Ireland'[122] – lost him any residual sympathy within Roosevelt's entourage and he compounded his sins by mixing frequently with Irish Americans who actively opposed the President's aid to Britain.[123] Aiken could not shake off the idea that American officials despised him. 'They took Brennan and myself round some arms factories,' he recalls. 'I felt they were regarding me as a big buck nigger. They took me to their firing ground and pumped up a few shells from their guns. It was meant to impress me – but it impressed me to the contrary.'[124] There was no way that the American Government could do business with Aiken and he went home almost empty-handed. When Roosevelt made his only concession at the end of the month – the sale of two ships to Eire – the State Department told Gray that the transfer of the vessels could be negotiated with de Valera but not with Aiken.[125]

De Valera identified David Gray as the man chiefly responsible for Aiken's failure – it was an accurate enough guess – and Brennan, who thought that Gray was behind United States press reports of German espionage in Ireland, went so far as to recommend that de Valera should demand the American Minister's recall.[126] The Taoiseach might have been tempted to accept Brennan's advice. When Gray had complained to him about a speech he had made claiming that Eire was being blockaded by both sides in the war, de Valera had 'flushed angrily and shouted that it was impertinent to question the statements of a head of state.'[127] In mid-May, Maffey wrote to Machtig to inform him that de Valera 'appears to be starting a campaign against Mr Gray. Last week he went out of his way to impress upon the Kenneth Clarkes [sic] that Mr Gray was little less than a disaster as a representative of his country and was doing infinite harm here . . .' Maffey regarded Gray as 'a splendid representative of his great country' and thought that the American Ambassador in London and Halifax in Washington should be told of what was going on because 'I should hate to feel his reputation was damaged by intrigues originating in the de Valera–Aiken group.'[128]

De Valera's Government was now on poor terms with both the United States and Britain. In April, Cranborne had suggested that de Valera should be invited to London but Maffey thought that the Taoiseach would find it impossible to accept such an invitation. When Cranborne drafted a note to this effect, Churchill wrote 'Good' in the margin.[129] Neither he nor de Valera wanted to see each other. In one way, this political estrangement had its advantages for it afforded both sides the opportunity of co-operating without publicity or political acrimony. Thus in May 1941 the British quietly gave Eire ten Hector training aircraft, some military wireless sets and 20,000 gas masks. In November, Britain sent across to Eire twelve 3.7-inch anti-aircraft guns, four 18-pounders, twelve 75-millimeter guns with trailers, 100,000 grenades, a quarter of a million rounds of .303 ammunition, spare parts and armour plating. In the following month, two 6-inch guns arrived in Eire from Britain for the defence of the Shannon.[130] These weapons were shipped with Churchill's personal approval. In July 1942 the War Cabinet agreed that Irish Army officers could attend the British Battle Training School in Northern Ireland.[131]*

These transactions were kept secret even from the Americans and when Gray advocated a well-publicised gift of Allied war material to Eire – primarily to embarrass de Valera – the British opposed the idea.[132] Churchill was adamant that the United States should not interfere. In February, 1942, he wrote to Eden:

> No arms for de Valera till he comes in (except a few trifles by the RAF in return for conveniences).
>
> We request most incessantly that *no arms be supplied by the United States*. This would spoil the whole market. If necessary I will telegraph to the President personally.[133]

The 'trifles' included equipment for the Irish Army Air Corps whose disbandment, the Chiefs of Staff believed, 'would not be in our interests'.[134]

But Churchill no longer wanted to concern himself with Eire and came to regard the issue of military supplies as a distraction. In February 1942 Clement Attlee, who had just become Dominions Secretary, was agitated that the Germans might after all stage an invasion of Ireland and proposed to Churchill that the British should check that the Irish Army was still in a position to hold off an initial German attack and provide airfields for RAF reinforcements. He added that 'if, in order to secure all that we want on this last head, we have to make some military supplies available to the Irish, I suggest that this would be well justified.'[135] Churchill agreed that the Chiefs of Staff should examine the position but Ismay reported to the Prime Minister that they could hardly expect the Irish to construct new airfields without adequate defence supplies from Britain. 'I had hoped this might rest for a little while,' Churchill wrote wearily at the end of Ismay's letter. 'This is a bad moment for British bargaining with anyone.'[136] Attlee sent a note back to Churchill. 'I do not want any bargaining or change of policy,' he stated. 'I wanted a purely military appreciation from the Chiefs of Staff to ascertain if there was anything that should be done in our own interest . . .' Churchill remained dissatisfied. 'I am afraid of getting on the slippery slope,' he wrote on the bottom of this latest letter.[137] In June 1942 Churchill would not even consider such representations from Attlee. 'Very large United States forces are coming into Ireland,' he wrote. 'The Germans are deeply involved in the Eastern Front. It is *we* who are making preparations now to invade the Continent. There is therefore very little likelihood of the weapons which it is now proposed to give to

---

* It was a sign of the British Government's new respect for Northern Ireland that the War Cabinet first sought the views of the Stormont authorities which they were not constitutionally obliged to do.

Southern Ireland being used against anybody but ourselves, in case we have need of these bases.'[138]

The Irish duly accepted what they could get from the British and their appreciation was generally expressed privately by the Irish Army officers who were the immediate recipients. In October 1941, the Irish Cabinet had decided to send Irish soldiers to Britain in groups of two or three at a time to receive bomb-disposal training[139] but no reference was ever made to this in Britain or Eire. It was a decision that should have been taken long before. Indeed, one of the ironies of Aiken's visit to the United States was that General Costello had travelled to Washington in the spring of 1939 to buy arms and could have purchased them had it not been for the reluctance of the Irish Government which regarded the price of the weapons as exorbitant.[140]* But by mid-1941, the Irish Cabinet was absorbed by the problems of the country's economic survival. It was a situation for which Irish Government ministers were themselves once again partly to blame, for in the days before the war – when neutrality raised political rather than military issues – neither de Valera nor his Cabinet had taken any precautions against the future possibility of economic isolation. In 1935, a memorandum drawn up by de Valera's own department had stated that in a war, 'the stoppage or serious curtailment of supplies . . . of petrol and other fuel and lubricating oils would practically bring road transport in this country to a standstill in a short time.' The same would apply to coal for rail traffic, and the document urged the Government to investigate the use of wood or peat-burning transport engines and the construction of a factory to make spare parts for engines. Supplies of raw materials, it said, would also be 'critical' during a war.[142] The prediction that the Irish transport system might collapse through shortage of fuel was almost fulfilled in 1943, but de Valera had not bothered to follow up this early warning.

In 1940, an Irish Government inter-departmental committee had estimated that more than a quarter of a million men and women would be made idle in Eire if the country was isolated for a long period[143] but the Cabinet was almost totally unprepared for the British economic sanctions when they came. Some of these restrictions were enormous. In 1940, for instance, Eire had taken 74,000 tons of fertilizers from Britain but in 1941

* According to American archives, Costello assured Joseph C. Green of the Department of State Division of Controls that American guns would never be used against Northern Ireland. According to Green, Costello 'explained that his Government had entered into a secret agreement with the British Government to support Great Britain to the fullest extent in case of a war with Germany. He went into some detail as to the terms of that agreement, which envisaged the fullest military and naval co-operation and the use of all the Irish armed forces. He said that, for political reasons, the very existence of this agreement could not at present be made known to the Irish people.'[141] Costello may have been exaggerating the pre-war Anglo-Irish defence talks – but no such agreement ever existed.

this figure was down to only 7000 tons, and none at all in 1942. Well over five million tons of feeding stuffs had been imported in 1940 but less than one million arrived in 1941 and none in the following three years.[144] Before the war, Eire had been prepared in an emergency to cut loose from sterling if the British pound deteriorated seriously[145] but in 1941 the Irish found that their difficulty was in purchasing dollars from the British Treasury to buy ships to replace the tonnage which Britain would no longer grant to Eire.[146] To prevent starvation, de Valera asked Irish farmers to double their acreage of wheat in 1941[147] and a year later threatened that 'penalties' would be imposed on farmers who planted alternative crops.[148] James Dillon, who was himself a farmer, suggested to de Valera that the Irish Government should enter a new barter agreement with Britain, offering 600,000 tons of Irish-grown oats and barley in return for 400,000 tons of wheat, which did not grow so easily in Eire.[149] But the authorities had learned their lesson and the Department of Supplies duly told de Valera that Dillon's proposal exhibited 'a child-like faith' since it would put Eire at the mercy of the British who could cut off the wheat supply whenever they chose.[150]

By the spring of 1942, the British War Cabinet's Committee on Economic Policy towards Eire was being told that exports of gas coal to the Dublin Gas Company had fallen from 3500 tons a week to 1600 tons and that the company was now considering a total shutdown of all gas supplies in the Irish capital.[151] The British Board of Trade proposed further cuts in May 1942 – providing Eire with less than 34 per cent of the goods she received in 1940 – although Attlee, who chaired the War Cabinet's committee, claimed that 'any policy of putting economic pressure on Eire with a view to securing political concessions was most unlikely to prove successful.' British policy, said Attlee, should be based solely on Britain's economic interests. This was unlikely to find much favour with Churchill, who at one stage had contemplated cutting off 'subsidies' on Irish farm produce under the mistaken impression that the British paid such grants.[152] In August, Lord Selborne, the Minister for Economic Warfare, wanted to prevent Eire from acquiring more than her minimum needs of raw materials. He thought she might obtain supplies from more than one source and therefore recommended that the British Government should 'withdraw' a promise given by Cranborne in 1941 that the British navicert system of shipping control would not be used to interfere with Irish trade. The navicert was a ship's warrant which the British issued for the ostensible purpose of denying neutral vessels to the Germans. Under this system, all Irish ships sailing on international sea routes were obliged to call at a British port for examination; without the warrant, they would be stopped by Allied naval patrols and refused bunkering and repair facilities at Allied ports. Attlee's committee subsequently decided that navicert papers for Irish ships due to carry commodities in short supply from neutral countries should be subject to 'delay'.[153]

When the British reduced Eire's allowance of petrol – already half of the 1940 shipments – by a further 25 per cent in 1942, Dulanty angrily informed Attlee that this would cause 'individual hardship on a wide scale' in Eire and have 'the gravest consequences on the economic life of the nation'. He told the Dominions Secretary that as a result of British restrictions, Irish householders no longer received domestic coal, railway services had been seriously disrupted and gas supplies in Dublin were now available for only just over six hours a day. The Irish Government regarded the latest fuel cuts as 'harsh and inequitable' and insisted upon the return to the Irish register of seven tankers which had been transferred to British control at the beginning of the war.[154] The demand was ignored and the Irish never got their ships.

In the summer of 1943, the Irish Department of Supplies submitted a 10-page memorandum to de Valera's Cabinet on the effects of what they now officially regarded as sanctions. According to this document, the British had been using their navicert system to prevent Eire from obtaining supplies from neutral countries; the Department had found that warrants were no longer being issued for the shipment to Eire of vegetable oil and seeds, castor oil, animal fats, rice and leather. 'The British attempt to justify their action by saying that these commodities are in short supply,' the memorandum contended. 'The result is that the navicert system is being turned into an economic weapon to squeeze us out of obtaining these supplies in neutral countries.' The Irish had similarly allowed themselves to become trapped by an agreement with the British over tea. In 1940, Britain had requested Eire to purchase all her tea through the United Kingdom to avoid competition that would raise prices; but at the end of the year, Britain unilaterally ended the arrangement leaving Eire still dependent on the United Kingdom for her supplies. The Irish tea ration was now only three quarters of an ounce a week compared to two ounces in Britain. Similarly, the 1938 trade agreement had given the British a monopoly on coal supplies to Eire but while British households still used coal in 1943, there was none available for Irish homes and even peat was now rationed to half a ton a month per household. Only one train a day ran in each direction on the Irish Great Southern Railways in 1943, bus services in Dublin stopped in mid-evening for lack of fuel and no petrol was available for private motorists.[155]

The Irish complaint was that the British had undertaken trade agreements with Eire but had then reneged upon them while leaving Eire still locked into the original agreements. And when Hugh Dalton, the President of the British Board of Trade, told the House of Commons that 'in view of her neutrality, Eire cannot expect the same consideration as those who are at war with the common enemy', the Irish Department of Supplies not unnaturally concluded that this 'quite clearly indicates that because of our neutrality we are being subjected to a "squeeze".'[156]

They were right, and one had to look no further than Britain's treatment

271

of Eire's shipping demands for proof. Early in 1941, the Irish Government decided to buy its own ocean-going ships in order to offset the severe restriction on British tonnage available to them. But since these ships would also need a navicert, the Irish Government were obliged to approach the British Ministry of War Transport for a warrant every time their newly-formed company, Irish Shipping Limited, wanted to purchase a vessel. And as the Department of Supplies memorandum pointed out, 'there have been a number of neutral ships on offer which Irish Shipping Limited could have acquired were it not that the British authorities refused to give warrants.' In some cases, the British were prepared to issue navicerts only on condition that half or more of the Irish ships' voyages were on British service. 'The British,' the Department maintained, 'have failed to observe an informal arrangement to provide for our minimum requirements of tonnage; and they have prevented us, by use of the warrant system, from acquiring more than a fraction of the tonnage necessary to import our minimum requirements from abroad.'[157]

If the British were morally entitled to levy economic sanctions against a neutral nation that chose to stand aside from the war, this particular restriction was questionable to say the least. In December 1940, Churchill told Roosevelt that 'our merchant seamen, as well as public opinion generally, take it much amiss that we should have to carry Irish supplies through air and U-boat attacks . . . when de Valera is quite content to sit happy and see us strangled.'[158] Yet when the Irish proposed to send their own ships to sea with Irish crews on board, the British did their best to sabotage the scheme. Indeed, the Irish Government discovered that when the British did grant navicerts to Irish vessels they sometimes stipulated that the ships should travel on routes that added up to 1300 miles to their voyage.[159]

But again the Irish had started out at a disadvantage because of de Valera's lack of foresight. Despite the warnings of economic isolation, no attempt was made before the war to establish an ocean-going Irish merchant fleet and in September 1939 only fifty-six ships – including three lightship tenders and a schooner built in 1859 – remained to serve Eire.[160] Only in December 1940 did an Irish Government committee finally advise that Eire should charter additional shipping to safeguard her supplies.[161] Irish Shipping Limited was formed in March 1941 and bought its first vessel, *Irish Poplar*, within a few weeks. Built in 1912, she had already been attacked by a German bomber in the Bay of Biscay while sailing under a Greek flag, and her Irish crew had to travel to Spain to collect her from a salvage company.[162]

Irish ownership, however, proved no firm defence against attack by either of the belligerents. In February 1940, the passenger ferry *Munster*, on charter to the Belfast Steamship Company but flying the Tricolour, was mined in Liverpool Bay. Then in August, the *Kerry Head*, a Limerick collier, was subjected to a more deliberate assault and attacked by an unidentified aircraft off the Old Head of Kinsale. Several bombs fell around her but the crew were unhurt. In the same month, another mine destroyed the Irish livestock carrier *Meath*. All Irish vessels sailed under their neutral flag. Up to four huge Tricolours were painted on the sides of each ship together with the word EIRE in letters twenty feet high, but Allied and Axis aircraft and submarines sometimes mistook Irish ships for French, British or German vessels and the crews suffered accordingly. In September 1940, for example, the cement carrier *Luimneach*, which had already been damaged by bombs at Valencia during the Spanish Civil War, was stopped by a German submarine in the Bay of Biscay while on her way to Drogheda. Despite the name EIRE on the *Luimneach*'s hull, the U-boat's captain ordered the crew into their boats and then sank the vessel by gunfire.[163] For several months afterwards, the Irish Government believed that the submarine was Italian[164] although it was in fact *U 46* commanded by Oberleutnant Engelbert Endrass who recorded dismissively in his war diary that the *Luimneach* had been flying a 'British or Irish flag'.[165]

In October, the *Kerry Head* was sunk after being attacked by an aircraft off Cape Clear, County Cork. Her destruction, with the loss of her twelve crew, was watched by several people on Clear Island although to this day the nationality of the plane that attacked her is unknown. An eye-witness said long after the war that a German plane dropped a stick of bombs on the vessel at around two o'clock in the afternoon, that the *Kerry Head* exploded in a sheet of flame and that the blast from the explosion brought down the aircraft which crashed in the sea. A trawler was moored off Cape Clear but did not have sufficient fuel to reach the scene of the attack. An Irish launch was only taken out from Berehaven at eight o'clock in the evening because the authorities were not at first convinced that there had been a sinking. Some of those who watched the attack from Clear Island claimed later that they saw survivors clinging to wreckage after the explosion.[166] Two months later, another unidentified aircraft bombed the Irish lightship tender *Isolda*, whose captain had been third officer on the *Lusitania* when she was torpedoed and sunk off Kinsale in 1915. The bombs that hit the *Isolda* started a fire in which six of the crew were killed.[167]

Fine Gael was not slow to appreciate the political significance of those attacks which were known to have been carried out by German aircraft. In February 1941, James Dillon asked in the Dail whether de Valera was prepared to install guns on Irish ships since Irish seamen had been 'machine-gunned when trying to escape in their boats by German aeroplanes'. De Valera replied that seven of the ten attacks on Irish ships to that date had been made from the air and that:

. . . in two of the seven cases the vessel concerned was machine-gunned as well as bombed. I have received no specific charge that in any case the crew were

273

machine-gunned while actually in their boats escaping from the ship, but in one case the Master of the vessel reported that four machine-gun attacks were made on his ship and one of these took place after the order to take to the boats had been given and while the crew were carrying it out. In all but one of these seven air attacks, the markings of the attacking aircraft were identified as German. It is right to say, however, that I have also received reports of cases in which German aircraft have circled and examined Irish ships at sea without attacking them.[168]

The question of putting guns aboard Irish ships was a particularly sensitive one since not only Dillon but the crews were demanding that this should be done. Even on short voyages to Britain, they were now coming under regular air attack. Typical of the reports that were forwarded by the shipping companies to the Irish Government at this time was that of Captain C. Waldren of the *Glencullen*, a collier owned by the Dublin Gas Company. At 10.45 a.m. on March 21, his ship was outward bound from Barry Docks when a German aircraft:

. . . came from right astern and flew very close over the ship. A new ensign was flying and flags on vessel's sides and on top of wheelhouse could easily be seen. Deck was machine-gunned, no damage to crew and slight damage to vessel . . .[169]

At 7.0 p.m., when the *Glencullen* was three miles west of the St Govens Light Vessel, a second attack started when:

. . . an aircraft came from right ahead and flew very close over the ship. The attack was much heavier than the first and an explosion was seen close to the stern as if a bomb was dropped, no damage to crew and considerable damage to deck work of vessel . . .[170]

At exactly the same time, the *Glencullen*'s sister ship *Glencree* was also being attacked about three miles away by a German aircraft. Next day, the Department of Industry and Commerce reported to the Irish Government that the men on both ships 'have gone on strike, one of their grievances being that the trips to Cardiff average about 16 hours . . . They ask for extra hands to be employed and claim protection. In this connection the men ask that their ships be armed . . .'[171] In late March, the collier *The Lady Belle* was attacked by a German aircraft off Milford Haven. The captain reported a direct hit and then, according to the vessel's Dungarvan owners, 'when the plane found he had no gun on board they came down and riddled the ship with machine gun bullets.'[172] Two weeks later, the ship-owners wrote to tell the Irish Government that *The Lady Belle*'s crew refused to return to sea unless they had armaments on board.[173]

On March 27, three German aircraft attacked the Irish collier *Edenvale*, *en route* from Cardiff to Rosslare, straddling her with bombs, scoring one hit on the starboard quarter and strafing her with machine-gun fire.[174] The crew then refused to sail in daylight and the *Edenvale*'s owners, the Wexford Steamships Company, pleaded with the Irish Department of Defence to be given a gun for the ship. According to the company, the crews:

> . . . realise that the defensive armament may not be of much avail but state at least they are afforded the satisfaction of fighting back if attacked, and their minds are occupied instead of just waiting during the attack for the hit, or the possibility of some of them being killed by machine-gun fire. Would it not be possible to issue each ship with even a few rifles and some ammunition . . .[175]

The Government solved the strike of the Dublin Gas Company crews by putting three firemen on board their ships although they were less than sympathetic about the behaviour of the seamen. 'The men's nerves are gone,' Sean MacEntee recorded laconically.[176] But the Irish authorities decided that 'the arming of neutral vessels would be contrary to the interests of the country's neutrality . . . a neutral merchant vessel which opens fire on a belligerent aircraft or submarine, from which it apprehends an attack, commits an act of piracy if the gun and gun crews are provided by the owners of the vessel without official approval.' They would be committing 'an act of war' if the guns were provided *with* official approval. Sweden and Switzerland, the Government noted, informed both belligerents of their sailings beforehand; Sweden – which co-operated with Germany – had four ships sunk but Switzerland had lost none.[177] But the Irish could not adopt this practice since their ships sometimes sailed with British convoys and they could therefore not tell the Germans of such voyages. So Irish crews continued to go to sea without arms of any kind, undefended in the interests of neutrality.

When German aircraft or U-boats were clearly identified as responsible for attacks on Irish shipping – upon the *Glencullen* and *Glencree*, for example – the Irish Government instructed William Warnock, their First Secretary in Berlin, to complain to the German Government. But not all the aircraft involved were German. In October 1943, two Mosquitoes of the RAF's 307 (Polish) Squadron attacked the Irish diesel coaster *Kerlogue* in the Bay of Biscay after confusing her flag with the French Tricolour. The two planes strafed the ship for twenty minutes, destroying the bridge, compass, radio transmitter and lifeboats, and wounding Captain Desmond Fortune, two of his officers and an able seaman.[178] With water pouring into the engine room, the *Kerlogue* reached Cobh where the Irish Naval Service put a doctor on board.* The ship had been off course and the British therefore refused to take responsibility for the attack but made *ex gratia* payments to the wounded men.[179]

---

* The *Kerlogue*'s Tricolour, shredded by RAF gunfire, hangs today in the Irish National Maritime Museum at Dun Laoghaire.

The *Kerlogue*, however, took her own peculiar revenge two months later when, steaming from Lisbon to Dublin, she was circled by a German bomber which requested her to steer on a new course in the Bay of Biscay. The *Kerlogue* did as she was asked and found herself in the aftermath of a sea battle, the waters around her littered with men on rafts and the wreckage of German warships. The Irish crew did not know the nationality of the men in the water until one of them recognised the German naval hat ribbons. They spent ten hours pulling men out of the water and then, with 168 survivors on board, the *Kerlogue* headed for Cork, ignoring British radio signals to observe the terms of her navicert by putting into Fishguard. Her new captain had pulled out the plugs of his radio receiver after requesting medical aid in Cork harbour.[180] The Irish too, it seemed, could turn a Nelsonian blind eye towards instructions that they did not wish to obey. Unable to interrogate and imprison the German survivors, the British angrily delayed the *Kerlogue* when she next called at Milford Haven for her warrant. The captain claimed that he had sailed straight to Cork because of the poor condition of some of the German seamen but the British closely questioned the *Kerlogue*'s crew, discovering that only two of the Germans had been able to speak English 'and little new information about the action in the Bay was obtained.'[181] Maffey told the Irish Government that although humanitarian considerations were 'an excuse for unusual procedure in this case', the British Admiralty's confidence had been 'shaken'.[182]*

Throughout the war, Irish ships rescued 521 seamen of all nationalities. In August 1942, the *Irish Pine* picked up survivors from the British freighter *Richmond Castle* who were drifting in the Atlantic in lifeboats and less than two weeks later the *Irish Willow*, in passage from St John to Waterford, took aboard forty-seven British crew from the torpedoed freighter *Empire Breeze*.[184] Sometimes, in mid-ocean, the old ambiguities of Anglo-Irish history reasserted themselves. When the Irish schooner *Mary B Mitchell* under Captain Arthur Dowds was sailing to Lisburn in 1943, a British corvette stopped her for examination in the Bay of Biscay; but the RNVR officer who climbed aboard the schooner turned out to be from Cork and was an ex-pupil of Dowds, who had been principal of the Irish Nautical College.[185] A less sanguine collision with history occurred when the Irish steamship *Kyleclare* under Captain Frank Dawson found a raft with a figure lying on it drifting eighty-three miles from the Fastnet. There was no response when Dawson blew the ship's whistle and he ordered his Chief Officer Diarmuid de Burca to row across to the raft. Its young occupant was dead, his face blackened by the sun. Frank Forde,

---

* Irish confidence in British procedures was itself not very high. In February 1942, British police took the Irish diplomatic bag – destined for the Minister in Lisbon – off an Irish vessel awaiting a navicert and returned it later with the seals broken. Another diplomatic bag was taken off an Irish ship at Barry the following month and only returned four days later.[183]

who wrote the history of the Irish merchant service, described how de Burca found a Royal Navy identity disc on the body and:

> . . . gazing at it, he experienced a new emotion, for the name was distinctively Irish – F. O'Rourke – and the letters RC after a number indicated the religion of the youth. What journey had brought him to this dreadful end, to die alone, on a raft, in the Atlantic. Was he the grandson of a famine emigrant, dead in the service of the King he was born under? Or a native Irishman, enlisted in the Royal Navy for adventure or from a sense of duty? . . . Such were de Burca's thoughts as he prepared to bury him. He removed the lifejacket and recited the prayers for the dead, the boat's crew alongside making the responses, then reverently the body was eased over the side and sank into the clear sea . . .[186]*

Irish shipping companies did their best to protect their crews. Their vessels were degaussed to protect them from magnetic mines, and Hempel was given details of all Irish vessels for him to pass on to the German Admiralty and the Luftwaffe. German naval and air crews were instructed to check their targets but inside the blockade zone around Britain they did not always have to do so. The Irish only learnt of this in the last months of the war after an extraordinary incident in which a U-boat scuttled itself off Cork. The crew had put their ship's documents into two metal canisters and thrown them overboard before rowing ashore and being taken into custody at Collins Barracks in Cork. But the canisters later floated onto the beach and were retrieved by an old man who had the good sense to put them on his horse-drawn cart and take them to General Costello's head-quarters.[188] The twenty crew members of the submarine were installed at the barracks, singing German songs as they made their way to and from their meals,[189] unaware that Colonel Bryan of G2 had sent Douglas Gageby, one of his young intelligence officers, down to Cork to examine the canisters.

Inside them, he found ship's papers, a series of photographs of an air attack on a small trawler and a copy of the submarine's Standing War Orders signed by Grand Admiral Karl Dönitz, the former Flag Officer U-boats and now Commander in Chief of the German Navy. Supplement 3 of this document, printed on water soluble red paper, stated that:

> . . . basically Irish ships also come under the neutrality regulations . . . In addition, for political reasons, Irish ships and also at times Irish convoys are not to be attacked within the blockade zone if they are seen to be such. However, there is *no special obligation* to determine neutrality in the blockade zone.[190]†

* Able Seaman Francis O'Rourke died on 18 June 1942 when the British destroyer *Wild Swan* was bombed and sunk by German aircraft in the Western Approaches.[187]
† The documents also included an order, dated 1 January 1942 stating that 'Ireland forbids the entry of warships into her territorial waters under penalty of internment. This prohibition must be strictly observed in order to maintain her neutrality.'[191] U-boats which landed spies on the Irish coast and sheltered in the bays at night were deliberately flouting this instruction.

Irish ships were still permitted to sail with British vessels under Royal Navy escort but after Irish seamen had observed at first hand the carnage on two British convoys in 1941, they preferred to travel alone, trusting to their neutral flag and their country's name on the hull. This trust was sometimes misplaced because Dönitz's instructions – while they were usually obeyed – were sometimes disregarded even outside the blockade zone. The freighter *Irish Oak* – one of the two ships which Roosevelt had released to de Valera after Aiken's trip to the United States – was sunk by *U 607* under Oberleutnant Wolf Jeschonnek 700 miles west of Ireland in May 1943. Before the attack, he saw the neutrality markings but could not find the ship's name in his Standing War Orders.[192] The *Irish Oak*'s survivors were all rescued by another Irish freighter but the *Kyleclare*'s eighteen crew members were all killed when she was torpedoed by *U 456* while on her way home to Ireland from Lisbon in February 1943. The submarine captain, Kapitänleutnant Max Teichert, said later that he had not seen the *Kyleclare*'s neutrality markings because she was low in the water and his periscope was awash. Only when he had fired a fan of three torpedoes did his U-boat rise higher in the water and he saw the 'EIRE' on the ship's side. Seconds later, the *Kyleclare* exploded.[193]

Neutral nations generally pay special honour to the merchant seamen who died maintaining their trade routes in the Second World War. In Malmo in southern Sweden, a model of a fully-rigged sailing ship hangs suspended over the south aisle of St Peter's Church in memory of the Swedish seamen who were killed in the war[194] but until recently no attempt was made to honour the 135 Irishmen who perished on Eire's neutral ships, save for a yearly church service. It was a strange omission, occasioned perhaps by a general reluctance on the part of the Irish immediately after the war to contemplate their much-criticised neutrality. Perhaps, too, the dead Irish seamen were too sharp a reminder of those other bodies that drifted ashore on the Irish west coast, of the British sailors who died amid the desolation of the Atlantic and who might have lived had the Treaty ports been open to the Royal Navy. Only in 1978 was it decided that the streets in a new Dublin housing estate should be named after the sixteen Irish ships lost during the war.[195] They were a brave enough symbol of the neutrality that de Valera would not break, even when the country to which he looked for his traditional support – the United States – entered the war in 1941.

Churchill did not understand de Valera's persistence. In his exuberance after Pearl Harbor, knowing that America would at last join Britain in her struggle against Germany, Churchill sent an excited wire to the Taoiseach:

> Most Immediate. Prime Minister to Mr de Valera. Personal, Private and Secret. Now is your chance. Now or never. 'A Nation once again'. Am very ready to meet you at any time. Ends.[196]

It was a startling telegram, all the more remarkable because it was the first personal message that Churchill had sent to de Valera since the war began. But its dramatic emphasis did not appeal to the less emotional de Valera, nor could Churchill's use of the song that was once the 'national anthem' of the Irish parliamentary party have captured the spirit of a man who was desperate to avoid Redmond's mistakes. And the dispatch of the telegram was attended not by decisions of great moment but by farce. When Walshe told the Taoiseach at 1.30 a.m. on December 8 that Maffey had a message for him from Churchill, de Valera assumed it was an ultimatum and immediately called General McKenna, instructing him to order the Irish Army to their agreed defensive positions.[197] Maffey called at de Valera's Blackrock home at 2.0 a.m. to deliver his Prime Minister's message personally. De Valera recorded later that Maffey seemed 'rather surprised' at the telegram which he regarded as 'Churchillian'. After being informed that it was an invitation to go to London, de Valera said that it would be unwise for him to travel to England because 'it would probably be misunderstood by our people and regarded to have a significance beyond anything which it would in reality have.'[198] Maffey handed the text of the message to de Valera who – in his own words – concluded:

> . . . that it was Mr Churchill's way of intimating 'now is the chance for taking action which could ultimately lead to the unification of the country'. I indicated to Sir John Maffey that I did not see the thing in that light. I saw no opportunity at the moment of securing unity, that our people were determined on their attitude of neutrality . . .[199]

According to Maffey's account of the meeting, de Valera was 'evidently nervous of meeting and apprehensive as to its outcome'. De Valera stated:

> . . . that the country has achieved unity on the policy of neutrality and that neither he nor anybody else would have a mandate for entering the war on a deal over partition. His sympathies lay with us in the war, but the best help he could give would be to keep the position in Eire secure for us and to enter the fight if attacked . . . Meanwhile wild rumours of secret understandings would unsettle the country and strengthen the extremists.[200]

What had happened, of course, was that de Valera – in company, it seems, with Maffey – had misinterpreted Churchill's cryptic message. He thought that the British were suggesting another version of the unity offer which MacDonald had brought to Dublin eighteen months earlier, an offer which de Valera rejected and which he was now rejecting again. Churchill, in his enthusiasm after Pearl Harbor, was merely hoping that America's entry into the war would persuade Eire to join the Allies. There was no intention of offering the unity of Ireland in return. Cranborne, who had approved Churchill's original message,[201] was the first to spot this ludicrous misunderstanding and immediately brought it to the Prime

Minister's attention. He had taken Churchill's quotation of 'A Nation once Again' to mean that:

> . . . by coming into the war, Ireland would regain her soul. Mr de Valera seems to have read it quite differently to mean that Northern and Southern Ireland should be reunited . . . Ought we to leave him under this misapprehension? His Cabinet, on reconsideration, might accept your invitation on this basis, and then feel that we had led them up the garden path.[202]

Churchill confirmed Cranborne's doubts. 'I certainly contemplated no deal over partition,' he scribbled at the foot of Cranborne's note. 'That could only come by consent arising out of war comradeship between North and South.'[203]

This business-like sentiment was communicated to de Valera who waited two days before replying to the British Prime Minister. In a private message to Churchill on December 10, he proposed that a visit to Dublin by Cranborne 'would be the best way towards a fuller understanding of our position here.'[204] Churchill agreed although his response to de Valera's suggestion referred to the need for 'a fuller *explanation*' of the Irish position, a subtle change of emphasis that could not have been lost on the Taoiseach.[205] Cranborne's journey to Dublin was to be made in secret – at the desire of both governments – for security reasons and to avoid what the Dominions Office referred to as 'embarrassing Press speculations'.[206] It was not, in the event, a very fruitful visit.

De Valera noted that Cranborne found Churchill's original message 'vague' but that the Dominions Secretary thought it possible for Eire to enter the war on the Allied side. 'I said there was considerable goodwill for Britain here,' de Valera wrote afterwards, 'but of course there was a section who, on account of our history and the existence of partition, were still strongly opposed.' De Valera resurrected his old suggestion of a local parliament for the north of Ireland 'having the powers of the existing parliament and the same boundary, with the Westminster powers transferred to an all-Ireland parliament.'[207] Cranborne wrote his own account of the meeting for Churchill. He found de Valera 'extremely friendly' but told him that if Eire remained neutral until the end of the war, 'the solution of the partition problem would be postponed indefinitely.' Neither Northern Ireland nor Britain could in such conditions hand over the northern ports which had proved essential to their survival.[208]

De Valera remained unmoved. These conversations with Maffey, with MacDonald and now with Cranborne had become almost theatrical. They had a ritual quality about them, each side rehearsing virtually the same lines with only slight differences in the text to take account of developments in the war. The British would come, sometimes appealing to de Valera on moral grounds, at other times bearing a conditional offer of Irish unity, a poisoned chalice from which de Valera would not sip. Occasionally they would threaten him with potential demands or warn him of the impending contempt of the post-war world. And de Valera, still the mathematician searching for a formula to his unique conundrum, courteous, implacable, suspicious and dogmatic, would concentrate upon the past and future objective, seeking a solution of such algebraic purity that no mind would be able to withstand its force; or so he thought. But the British politicians who used to admire this personality – Chamberlain and MacDonald – had gone. In their place stood figures who saw in de Valera's single-mindedness only a meanness, 'a petty leader raking over old muck heaps', as Maffey had described him.

Thus de Valera's own demands came to be disregarded almost before they had been made. To Cranborne he once more appealed for arms. With British weapons in Irish hands, Cranborne quoted him as saying, Britain and Eire would – in fact if not in appearance – 'be standing side by side in a common cause'. But Cranborne was not convinced. De Valera, he noted, 'was throughout extremely forthcoming in his manner and outspokenly sympathetic to our cause; he said that he had now come to the conclusion that we should win the war. His difficulty in rallying to the Allied cause came not from lack of sympathy but because, he said, in existing circumstances any attempt to bring a united Southern Ireland into the war at our side would be doomed to failure.'[209] Churchill's midnight telegram, with its touch of Lloyd George ambiguity, had had no effect.

Cranborne went on to talk to David Gray who 'had reached the conclusion that it was impracticable to bring Southern Ireland into the war on the Allied side for the moment at any rate.' Gray was advocating his idea for making a token supply of arms available to Eire[210] but Churchill, in conference with Roosevelt at a secret mid-Atlantic rendezvous, was unimpressed. 'We must give time for American pressure to work,' he wrote back to Cranborne in a cypher telegram from his battleship. 'If as I hope, US arrive Northern Ireland in near future this will be a potential factor. Meanwhile do not give any arms.'[211] De Valera knew what this American 'pressure' meant, for he had already formed his own opinions of David Gray's pushy, forthright, bullying personality. America had supported Ireland's struggle for freedom and now Ireland would be expected to support America. On December 14, de Valera spoke at Cork about the United States' entry into the war. It would be unnatural, he said, if Ireland with her ties of blood and friendship did not sympathise with Americans 'in all the anxieties and trials which this war must bring upon them.' But:

> . . . the policy of the State remains unchanged. We can only be a friendly neutral. From the moment this war began, there was for this State only one policy possible – neutrality. Our circumstances, our history, the incompleteness of our national freedom through the partition of our country, made any other policy impracticable. Any other policy would have divided our people,

and for a divided nation to fling itself into this war would be to commit suicide.[212]

De Valera's 'friendly neutrality' was in effect his concession to America's entry into the war. More to the point, it was a gesture of his realisation that the United States would help to win the war for the Allies. It is difficult to fix the moment when friendly neutrality became benevolent neutrality but its most obvious manifestation was the policy that developed in 1942 of releasing Allied air crews who crash-landed in Eire. Instead of being interned in the Curragh, they were sent straight to Northern Ireland – sometimes with their aircraft – in an operation about which the Irish and British authorities are both still very reticent. A few incidents became public knowledge shortly after the war but Irish military documents on this officially sanctioned breach of Irish neutrality – all of them filed by the G2 intelligence branch – have never been released in Dublin. Nor can any British records of these transactions be found in the old Air Ministry files at the Public Record Office in London.

But, once again, Irish officers made copies of their official reports on the crash-landing of Allied aircraft and these private papers are still extant. Furthermore, Northern Ireland's official war historian was given access to Air Ministry records in London before the war ended; several of these documents contained details of Allied planes which came down in Eire and copies of the Ministry papers – laboriously typed out in 1944, sometimes in summary form – still survive in Belfast. In a few instances, it is even possible to collate both sets of records to give a comprehensive view of a most extraordinary and highly secret arrangement between the Allied powers and neutral Eire. On 5 December 1942, for example, an Irish officer sent the following report to G2 headquarters at Parkgate in Dublin: 'Mullaghmore, Co. Sligo (American). Total Crew: 5. No Killed: Nil. No Injured: Nil. Landed undamaged – 4 taken to N.I. by car on 7.12.42; 1 by a/c on 22.12.42. a/c developed engine trouble and had to remain until new engine and fittings were brought from N.I. Repairs completed and a/c took off for N.I. on 22.12.42.'[213] This note is complemented by a British file, apparently culled from a civil defence record, where an entry for 1942 says: 'On 5th December . . . a Flying Fortress with a crew of five Americans made a forced landing on the beach at Mullaghmore, Co. Sligo. An Eire Army official reported the facts next day to the RUC at Beelleek [sic] and . . . RAF mechanics then crossed the border and made their way to the scene of the crash. Meanwhile the crew (less one mechanic) were escorted to the border by Eire military and crossed into Northern Ireland.'[214] In the same month, an American P-51 aircraft crash-landed in Eire and a replacement pilot was sent down from Northern Ireland to pick it up.[215]

On 15 January 1943, the British records stated that 'an American aircraft crashed at Athenry, Co. Galway. An Eireann Army Officer contacted the RUC at Belleek and arrangements were made to have the crew sent there. Two Eireann Officers escorted the crew to Belleek where the party was met by representatives of the American Army.'[216] What this report did not say was that the plane, a B-17, was carrying General Jacob Devers, commanding general of the United States armoured forces, who was on his way from the Middle East to Portugal. His pilot had flown far off course over the Atlantic and Devers ordered him to bring the plane down on the nearest landfall. The local Irish Army commander took Devers to an Athenry hotel where he was given an impromptu banquet by the people of the town before travelling to Northern Ireland. It had needed David Gray to secure his safe passage north.[217] Hempel found out about the Devers crash from Hans Becker – the same 'Becke' whom Tegart had met and described as the 'Gauleiter of Galway' in his report to British intelligence – who happened to be travelling by rail from Galway to Dublin and saw the badly damaged plane from his carriage window. Becker was indeed an agent; he conducted German classes in Galway and the Nazi party instructed him to stay on in Eire when war broke out.[218] But his monthly £12 retainer from Hempel suggested that he did not qualify for the seniority that Tegart had ascribed to him. At the Department of External Affairs, Frederick Boland told Hempel that the crashed aircraft had merely been flying from Canada to Britain.[219]

Nor did the Irish Government change their policy over releasing Allied aircrews. In March 1943, an RAF aircraft made a forced landing near Clonmeny, County Donegal, and the British records noted that 'the crew of seven were conveyed to Londonderry in an Eireann Army vehicle.' On the same day, an RAF pilot baled out of his plane over County Cavan just south of the border, parachuted to the ground and crossed the frontier to Northern Ireland.[220] In mid-April, a Flying Fortress was actually refuelled outside Dublin and permitted to continue its journey.[221] Two months later, an American officer and the RUC Head Constable at Belleek were allowed to inspect the wreckage of a Fortress that had made a forced landing on the sands at Bundoran, County Donegal. The crew of ten were 'passed into Northern Ireland' while the officer 'stripped the machine of the principal parts and secret equipment'.[222] Before the year ended, a Sunderland flying-boat crashed on the side of Mount Brandon in County Kerry with several RAF men on board, one of them an Irishman from Limerick; the Irishman was allowed to visit his home before the crew were sent to Northern Ireland.[223]

The Irish transported crews across the border regularly until the middle of 1944 when crash-landings became much rarer. British and Irish records report the safe passage to Northern Ireland of American, British and Canadian crews from a Fortress and a Mitchell bomber that came down at Benmullet in County Mayo, from a Sunderland at Ballybofey, County Donegal, from a Fortress that crashed in the sea off Killybegs and from a Liberator that landed in a bog near Foxford, County Mayo. In their reports, the British had by now adopted the uniform phrase 'the crew made their way to Northern Ireland' in order to avoid any mention of un-neutral Irish behaviour. By June 1944, Irish records were confined only to a few words. 'Elly Bay, Co. Mayo,' stated one, 'British Aircraft Forced Landing. Aircraft and crew of three permitted to leave.'[224] From those who witnessed the crash-landings, it is evident that many of the Allied aircrews were hopelessly lost. When Captain Thomas of the United States Air Force brought his Flying Fortress down at Clonakilty, County Cork, he told Lieutenant Colonel Jack O'Connell, the Irish officer sent to interrogate him, that he had thought he was landing in occupied Norway. Thomas, whose plane bore the name *T'aint-a-bird* painted in large letters at the front of the fuselage, telephoned Gray, drew £200 from a local bank and bought drinks at a bar for 'just about everyone in Clonakilty'.[225] Other pilots knew only too well where they had landed. Second Lieutenant John Griffin of the Irish Army found that many of the Canadian crews were 'dossers', men who had been sent on bombing missions over Europe but who had flown towards the Atlantic and deliberately landed in Eire in the hope of escaping from the war in the presumed comfort of an Irish internment camp. They usually claimed that they had been in combat against German aircraft but Irish troops invariably found that their canvas gun covers had not been torn open.[226]

The Irish Government agreed to release the crews of crashed planes on condition they were not on 'operational flights',[227] all Allied airmen being ordered to preserve the trimmings of Irish neutrality by claiming – however fraudulently – that they were on training missions. In April 1942, the British Air Attaché in Dublin had advised the RAF that crews flying near Ireland should be briefed 'to tell the following story if they crash-landed in Eire: "That the aircraft was engaged in Air-Sea Rescue operations in response to an SOS from an unidentified aircraft believed to be German".'[228] De Valera accepted these dubious conceits with the same equanimity as he had once signed the oath of allegiance to enter the Dail. Retrospectively, these British excuses provided reason for the release of the forty-six Allied aircrew who by 1943 were imprisoned in the Curragh. The 260 Germans in the camp, including the seamen rescued by the *Kerlogue*, were told that the British had been moved to Gormanston, County Meath, when in fact they had been driven across the Northern Ireland border in cars.[229] The British and Irish co-operated in trying to avoid navigational errors by Allied aircrews; in 1942, the Irish authorities painted the word 'EIRE' in giant, bold letters upon every cape and peninsula in the country and General McKenna flew round the coast with British and American officers to familiarise them with the terrain. Each cape was given a number that was then printed on RAF and USAF maps.[230]

This, however, could not help the crews of aircraft too damaged by gunfire or too low on fuel to choose a landing place. There are still mountain sides in Ireland upon which the burnt-out engines and wings of crashed Allied aircraft can be found. British and Irish records are filled with reports of aircrews who were burnt alive in their planes or killed by the impact of their crash-landing in Ireland. In September 1941, an RAF Hudson *en route* from Newfoundland to Prestwick ran short of fuel over the Atlantic and landed at Baldonnel outside Dublin. America had not then entered the war and this was one of the first occasions on which the Irish agreed to release an Allied aircraft. They refuelled the machine and it took off for Northern Ireland but then crashed into a mountain-side just south of the border. The crew – a Briton and two Canadians – were killed and their bodies handed over to the British at Newry, County Down.[231] Irish soldiers remembered these incidents vividly, probably because the crashes brought home to them the horror and sadness of the war they had been spared. Just six months later, a Liberator flying from Egypt to Britain hit the same mountain side at Slieve na Gloic near Jenkinstown, County Louth, and burst into flames. Lieutenant Colonel Niall Harrington, the officer commanding G2 Branch in the Irish Army's Eastern Command, reported to his headquarters in Dublin that the plane had crashed in mountain bogland. 'The tail, body and fore-part were spread over a distance of about 50 yards and the fore-part which enclosed the Pilots cabin had apparently burnt out . . . the whole area was strewn with bodies, baggage and debris. The fire had burnt itself out and mist made it intensely cold for the few survivors . . .' Fifteen of the nineteen crew died. The maps found on the plane were handed over to G2 in Dublin while Harrington sorted through the personal possessions, trying to relate them to the bodies. One small parcel that he could not identify with any of the corpses carried a label which said: 'To the dearest girl in the world, on her third Birthday.'[232]

The Irish Army brought each consignment of dead aircrew to the Northern Ireland border, handing their gloomy cargoes over to the RUC. On 23 August 1943, they arrived at Belleek with the corpses of eight RAF crew members who died when their aircraft crashed at Brandon Head, County Kerry. Another nine bodies – including two more from the Brandon crash – were sent up on August 30. Seven more RAF crew were killed when their Halifax blew up at Tuam, County Galway, as it tried to make a forced landing; the plane's bomb load had exploded on impact. On December 21, an RAF Wellington crashed into Mount Brandon, killing its six-man crew. Michael Brick had just finished his turn at coast-watching duty and recalls that the plane was still burning when he reached the wreckage. Bombs and bullets were exploding in the fire, sending pieces of metal ricocheting off the rocks on the mountain side. Six bodies were found scattered among the gorse bushes.[233] There were so many crashes at Brandon – a German Focke-Wulf had also come down there in 1940 – that the Irish Army Air Corps conducted tests over the mountain later in the war at the request of the Allies because aircrews suspected that the hillsides there contained some kind of magnetic force that distorted aircraft navigational equipment.[234] In January 1944, another Halifax crashed near Bundoran, County Donegal; the plane struck a cliff top by the seashore and broke in half, scattering the dead crew across the beach and in the sea.[235] In some cases, RAF crews were buried in Eire at the request of their families and the Irish were able to watch the British grieve for their dead. At one such funeral at Baltinglass, County Wicklow, a wreath arrived bearing a label which read: 'Winston and Clemmie.'[236] In all, 163 British, American and German aircraft crashed in Eire with 830 crew aboard; of these, 223 died.[237]

No politician in Eire felt the loss of Allied lives more keenly than James Dillon whose public support for Britain – and equally public condemnation of Hitler – regularly angered the Dail. 'I could never forget,' he recalled long afterwards:

> . . . that the west coast of Ireland was littered with the bodies of dead English seamen who had been bringing supplies to us. In 1941, the Germans were flying the Cherbourg–Stavanger route up our coasts and dropping magnetic mines into the Atlantic. Britain was at a hair's breadth of being cut off from America. The British had no tanks, no oil, no means of bringing US troops to Europe. I felt the time had come to take a moral stand. I spoke against Hitler in the Dail. Mr Cosgrave came up to me afterwards – he was a very correct man – and said: 'Mr Dillon, your speech in Dail Eireann was extremely embarrassing to us. But we recognise you had a special moral obligation to say what you did and if that's the end of it, we'll forget about it.'[238]

However it was not the end of Dillon's campaign. In February 1942, he told the annual Fine Gael conference that 'whatever the sacrifice, whatever America may want from us to protect her from her enemies, she will get it for the asking.' Even Gray thought the speech was ill-timed.[239] After the conference, Cosgrave, Mulcahy and two other senior Fine Gael TDs met Dillon at the party's headquarters in Merrion Square. As Dillon recalled, 'they preferred that I should resign rather than be asked to go.' So the most outspoken and the most isolated of Britain's supporters in the Dail became an Independent, able to speak with more freedom and even less influence. Not long afterwards, he opposed neutrality at a student debate at University College Dublin, arguing against Sean MacEntee, the Minister for Industry and Commerce. Dillon condemned Nazi Germany on moral and religious grounds, and remembers that after the debate, MacEntee turned to him and said quietly: 'I wish I had had your freedom to speak my mind tonight.'[240] It was a moot point. De Valera could express his support for Britain in a confidential discussion with Cranborne, and secretly order the release of Allied aircrews; Fine Gael could talk among themselves about an alliance with Britain. To be un-neutral in private was one thing, however. To oppose neutrality in public was quite another.

Chapter 9

The 'Natural' Ally

> As long as Ireland conducts herself in a neutral fashion it can be counted on with absolute certainty that Germany will respect her neutrality unconditionally . . .
>
> Joachim von Ribbentrop *11 July 1940*

> After England was finally crushed by us, Ireland could then expect in an entirely altered situation to be able to realise her national goals.
>
> Ernst von Weizsäcker, State Secretary at the German Foreign Ministry *13 November 1940*

> Hitler would have sold the Irish down the river. I would have told the Irish that their freedom was coming. I would have been a Lawrence of Arabia. It happened to several friends of mine, with the Bretons and the Walloons. Their freedom was promised but then, when the Germans had what they wanted, the separatist groups were abandoned. Northern Ireland would have been given to a 'Vichy'-type government in London. Hitler did not want to harm the British Empire.
>
> Helmut Clissmann, former Abwehr agent

From the very first days of the war, Eduard Hempel had realised that Irish neutrality was widely supported in Eire and that it was in Germany's interest to help maintain de Valera's policy. He had few illusions about the strength of the IRA and feared only that British pressure on Eire might ultimately bring the country into the war against Germany. Just a month after the war began, he noted in a radio telegram to the Foreign Ministry in Berlin that neutrality had 'visibly strengthened Irish national self-consciousness'. The IRA, he said, was generally confining its activities to the Irish in America; neutrality had caused the organisation 'to reconsider the danger of premature activity and to stand by inactive for the time being, although supposedly determined to intervene if the neutral attitude is abandoned . . . The arrest of nearly 100 of its members in Ireland went off without incident.'[1]

Hempel's dispatches to Berlin were in sharp, cold contrast to the eloquent and occasionally emotional memoranda that Maffey sent back to the Dominions Office. There was an element of hearsay and caution about Hempel's reports which probably said more about the regime for which he worked than about the situation in Eire. The absence of any historical relationship between Germany and Ireland made it difficult for him to grasp the complexities of Anglo-Irish history, and his simplified if generally accurate account of developments and public opinion in the country sometimes gave the impression that he was reporting from a Balkan dictatorship rather than a democratic and newly independent nation. The Irish Army, he told Berlin:

> . . . is supposedly ready to defend neutrality in all directions, in spite of the presence of pro-British elements. The feeling with reference to our pact with Russia, especially in view of the sympathy for Catholic Poland which has had a similar fate to Ireland's, is to a large extent anti-German but at the same time strongly anti-British; certain pro-German trends exist particularly in the country, where the German radio is especially effective. The Irish press is strictly controlled, but the British press gets through. The Catholic Church is obeying the Government's appeal for a neutral stand. The personal attitude of the Government towards me is definitely friendly.[2]

There was a certain innocence about Hempel's understanding of Irish history. 'Previous bad experience on the part of the British in British–Irish conflicts,' he solemnly told the Foreign Ministry, 'as well as regard for America and the Dominions, may impede the consideration of possible steps against Ireland.' Hempel noted that Maffey, whom the Irish Government wished to see appointed as British Minister rather than representative, had been partly educated in Germany. Irish neutrality, he went on: '. . . is said to be watched very closely in the United States of America; conversely, a possible abandoning of American neutrality would constitute a threat to Irish neutrality. We should continue to support consolidation of Irish neutrality and independence on a broad national basis . . .'[3]

Hempel advised that there should be no 'active interference' in Irish internal conflicts and that U-boats should not make incursions into Irish territorial waters. Consideration should be shown for Irish trade problems and great care exercised in propaganda. Over the German radio, he said, 'only facts should be given without direct exploitation for propaganda against England. It should be borne in mind that Ireland strictly rejects belonging to the Empire and recognises only a loose connection with it in matters of foreign policy.'[4]

Three weeks later, another dispatch reached Berlin, not from Hempel this time but from Jim O'Donovan, the organiser of the IRA's abortive bombing campaign in Britain. Back in Ireland after his three trips to Germany, he transmitted a brief message to Abwehr II, the German intelligence division under Lieutenant Colonel Erwin von Lahousen which maintained contacts with discontented minority groups in foreign countries and prepared sabotage operations. According to the Abwehr II War Diary, O'Donovan – generously referred to as 'the chief agent in Ireland' – asked for arms and other equipment. But the War Diary added that 'his message gives no indication . . . as to what supply route is now possible.'[5] There were apparently no further transmissions for a month when on November 28 the Abwehr papers recorded: 'Order received to enter into discussions with Naval Operations Division in order to find out whether it is possible to land saboteurs in Ireland by means of U-boats.'[6] The Abwehr wanted to send agents to Eire to strengthen relations with the IRA, many of whose leaders – as Hempel had faithfully recorded – were now behind bars. The agents were to approach the IRA on the basis of Germany's desire to see Ireland united and persuade the organisation to abandon political activities in favour of military action.[7]

Unfortunately for the Abwehr, most of the operatives they had maintained in Ireland before the war were attending the Nuremberg rally in Germany when Hitler invaded Poland, and could not return.[8] They included Professor Adolph Mahr, the Director of the Irish National Museum, whose drawings and photographs of the Irish west coast were soon to be of use in the compilation of the German Army's guidebook to Ireland. He was already well known to both the British and Irish intelligence services. Tegart noted in his intelligence report to the British Government that Mahr had been appointed to his post by W.T. Cosgrave although there was 'no suggestion that Cosgrave knew what he was doing'. According to the former Indian police officer, Mahr had 'worked his people in to similar archeological and research posts all over Eire.' Tegart also stated – wrongly – that 'the paymaster of the IRA is one of Mahr's men named Klissmann [sic], who lives in Mount Street, Dublin, opposite the Police Headquarters.'[9] Colonel Dan Bryan was well aware of the Nazi sympathies of Adolph Mahr, 'an aggressive and arrogant man',[10] although Tegart's report – written in the summer of 1940 – was somewhat invalidated by the fact that neither of the two Germans had been in Dublin for almost a year.

Mahr had been prominent in the German Association, a German–Austrian group that used to meet regularly for oysters, beer and cigars at the Red Bank Restaurant in D'Olier Street near the Liffey in central Dublin. Members of this organisation – which became avowedly Nazi in 1938 – included a junior Nazi party official called Stumpff who was a radiologist at the Baggott Street hospital, and Heinz Mecking, who was head of the Nazi Party's Dublin Group.[11] Mecking, a 36-year-old married man from Oldenburg, was Chief Engineer for the Irish Turf Development Board and had been transferred to Eire in 1936 to work at £50 a month as a 'turf expert'. Mecking hurriedly returned to Germany on September 9.[12] Before the war, Irish friends of the Association used to be invited to German nights at the Red Bank at which a Swastika flag was draped ceremoniously over a table at the top of the dining room. There were tourist excursions for members of the Association to a large hotel in Wicklow whose wealthy owner – a man named Budina – visited Hempel at the outbreak of war and developed a sudden and mysterious desire to travel to Germany. He left his affairs in the hands of a Dublin lawyer, his car still parked in a Dublin street, and departed for the Dun Laoghaire mailboat in shirt-sleeves. He reached Germany, broadcast over German radio to Ireland and in 1941 joined the Wehrmacht and was sent to the eastern front where he was later taken prisoner by the Soviet Army. Helmut Clissmann, who was the representative of the German Academic Exchange Board in Dublin and had married Elisabeth Mulcahy, an Irishwoman from a prominent republican family, left with her for Germany when the war started.[13]

The Abwehr was therefore in some ignorance of the IRA's condition at the very moment when they most wanted to maintain contact. In April 1939, Sean Russell had left for America to publicise the IRA's British bombing campaign, appointing Stephen Hayes, a Wexford County Council official who was IRA Adjutant General, as acting Chief of Staff. Hayes, who drank heavily, now led the IRA but rarely called meetings of the organisation's Army Council. The disillusion that followed the failure of the campaign in Britain swiftly destroyed any continuity in the movement. The Cork and Kerry IRA broke away from Hayes's command while members in Belfast lost patience with leaders in the south. New men in the Army Council – Michael Traynor, Tony D'Arcy, Jack McNeela and Donald Adams – realised there was little hope of overthrowing even de Valera's Government without a move away from the ostentatious military parades and confusion that had marked the IRA's record south of the border.[14] As a result, there was a growing number of violent incidents in Dublin. In October 1939, a gelignite bomb was detonated outside the wall of Mountjoy prison in an unsuccessful attempt to free four IRA inmates. Bomb-making apparatus was discovered at Killiney Castle outside Dublin, and in November two armed robberies in the city emphasised the IRA's increasing strength despite the imprisonment of a hundred of their members. The Abwehr took note of these events, apparently without realising that the Irish Cabinet was almost as anxious to crush the organisation as the British were in Northern Ireland. De Valera's new Justice Minister, Gerald Boland, was attempting to uphold the Government's right to intern IRA men. One of them, Seamus Burke from Mayo, claimed in the Dublin High Court that part of the Offences Against the State Act of 1939 was in conflict with the Irish Constitution and was therefore invalid. He appealed for his own release on grounds of Habeas Corpus. Mr Justice Gavin Duffy ordered him to be freed – 'as was to be expected', Boland noted with disgust – although the Supreme Court overturned the decision.[15] Boland – who thought the IRA was 'very strong' in 1939, chiefly because of their bombing campaign in Britain and the existence of an illegal broadcasting station – suggested German involvement.[16]

Hempel was concerned that this might be true and in November he expressed his fears to Paul Woermann, the Director of the German Foreign Ministry's Political Division. Rumours of German support for the IRA, he wrote:

> . . . lead me to point out that in my opinion complete restraint continues to be advisable for us. According to my observation the Government is in control of the situation so far, in spite of the increased danger of unrest of late because of the refusal to release the political prisoners engaged in a hunger strike. The IRA is hardly strong enough for action with promise of success or involving appreciable damage to England and is probably also lacking in a leader of any stature . . . Sensible adherents of the radical nationalist movement, correctly sizing up the situation and the dangers, are opposed to coming out into the open at the present time; they also recognise, in agreement with the over-whelming majority of the population, the determination to maintain neutrality which the Government has shown so far in spite of difficult circumstances. Interference on our part would, even in their opinion, prematurely endanger the whole nationalist movement including groups which are not radical because the latter would accuse the IRA of making national interests dependent on Germany.[17]

Hempel was worried that Germany might try to land agents in Eire by submarine – in his dispatch he mentioned 'the lessons drawn from the Casement case' – and thought that German interference would give the British a welcome pretext for intervening. He saw 'the rise of an active nationalist movement on a broad basis, perhaps inclusive of the Government' if Irish neutrality was violated or if the weakening of England made the prospects of regaining Northern Ireland appear more favourable. Hempel had heard it said that 'in case of a suitable development of the situation we would at the proper time promise Ireland our support for the return of Northern Ireland, to be made good at the conclusion of peace, and thereby assure ourselves the friendship of all Irishmen.' Hempel's enthusiasm was meanwhile directed towards the English-language radio broadcasts from Berlin which could be heard in Eire, describing them as 'the best of propaganda'. He added one prim word of caution. 'However, I hear time and again that sharp attacks on Churchill which extend even to his most intimate personal affairs achieve the opposite of the intended effect, especially in England.'[18]

In December, Hempel again warned Woermann of the consequences of German interference in Ireland, noting that Oscar Pfaus, the agent who had made contact with the IRA in Dublin before the war, had been sending propaganda material to 'radical Irish-nationalist personalities'. The British, who controlled mail into Eire, had allowed Pfaus's propaganda to pass through untouched, presumably so that they could expose the recipients 'at a given time to point to German connections with subversive Irish elements and to a breach of neutrality'. Walshe had approached Hempel about the pro-Nazi pamphlets which were being sent into Eire by the *Fichtebund*, the German propaganda organisation, and said that the Irish Government intended 'to put a stop to the propaganda of both sides'. Hempel had complained about 'a number of gross insults to Germany' in the British newspapers which were still on sale in Dublin. In the future, Hempel told Woermann, 'the greatest caution' should be exercised over *Fichtebund* material.[19]*

The Abwehr, however, were unlikely to allow Hempel's sensitivities to deflect their interest in the IRA, whose fortunes changed from day to day. The Irish Cabinet, conscious that it might have acted unconstitutionally in ordering the imprisonment of a hundred IRA men, released fifty-three of their internees. The police did manage to seize the transmitter on which O'Donovan had been broadcasting subversive and sometimes anti-semitic propaganda.[21] But at about the same time, Tom Doyle, a civil servant in the Irish Department of Defence, proposed to the IRA that they should raid the Irish Army's Magazine Fort in Phoenix Park on the western side of Dublin. The Army Council accepted the idea and two days before Christmas, IRA men overpowered the garrison – an officer, two NCOs and ten soldiers armed with rifles and a Lewis gun – and escaped with more than a million rounds of ammunition in thirteen lorries.[22] Boland was appalled. 'The place was very lightly guarded – if at all – and the OC was a permanent resident, a ridiculous position which should never have been allowed,' he wrote later. He protested at the dismissal of the fort's commanding officer on the grounds that 'if anyone was to be dismissed it was those in charge of the Army who had allowed this system to be established.'[23] The Government decided that an Army captain at the fort should be dismissed, four officers censured and three soldiers – two corporals and a Volunteer – court-martialled.[24] Most of the ammunition was recovered but the most immediate result of the raid was an overwhelming vote in the Dail to set up detention camps for the IRA at the Curragh. Within a few days, the Special Branch arrested most of the leading IRA men in both parts of Ireland as they gathered at the Meath Hotel in Dublin to discuss plans for an attack on Northern Ireland.[25]

Russell, who had been campaigning in the United States with Joseph McGarrity, talking to crowds who included Clann na Gael members, Nazis, communists and American Government agents,[26] now decided to make contact with Germany. He wanted to return to Ireland but the direct

---

* The British were well aware of the German propaganda that passed through their postal system. In June 1940, the British Ministry of Economic Warfare identified Otto W. Fritzsche, the Havana agent of the York Street Flax Spinning Company in Belfast, as a *Fichtebund* operative and ordered his employers to fire him. Fritzsche, who was hard up for money, was said by the British Ministry to be 'a most objectionable person . . . he is actively engaged in disseminating enemy propaganda, the receipt from Germany of which we have definite evidence.'[20]

steamship route was closed and he risked arrest if he travelled via England. Through John McCarthy, a steward on the American liner *George Washington*, he sent a message to the German Government, requesting permission to go to Berlin. McCarthy duly turned up with Russell's message at the German Consulate in Genoa. The resident diplomat immediately sent a report to the Foreign Ministry in Berlin to say that 'the delegate of the Irish movement, John McCarthy, who has arrived from New York, asked today whether the German Government was prepared to take to Ireland John [sic] Russell, the Chief of Staff of the Irish movement, who is still in New York without the knowledge of the American Government.' If so, Russell would arrive in Genoa by boat under an assumed name.[27]

The Germans were delighted. Eager to re-establish contact with the IRA, they had suddenly been presented, at his own invitation, with the Chief of Staff. Woermann sent a memorandum to Ribbentrop, outlining the republican aims of the IRA and the Irish Government but obviously anxious that Russell should not be used to upset the delicate balance of Irish neutrality. The IRA, he told Ribbentrop:

> . . . is a secret militant society which fights for the union of Northern Ireland with the Irish Republic and the complete separation of Ireland from the British Empire. This is also the ultimate objective of the present Irish Government. The difference between the Government and the IRA lies mainly in the method. The Government hopes to attain its objective by legal political means while the IRA tries to achieve success by terrorist means. Most of the members of the present Irish Government formerly belonged also to the IRA.[28]

Even Churchill would not have objected to this crisp analysis. But then Woermann added a single sentence that summarised the folly in which the Germans were about to indulge. 'By reason of its militant attitude towards England,' Woermann wrote, 'the IRA is a natural ally of Germany.' For a regime which had used the German minorities in Czechoslovakia and Poland to advance its policy of territorial expansion, the sentiment was understandable. But to encourage the German Foreign Minister to believe that a serious alliance could be considered between the angry, divided men of the IRA and the Reich was also extremely dangerous. Hempel opposed the idea of dispatching Russell to Ireland, informing Woermann that 'the IRA in Ireland does not have enough striking power to bring about success.' He feared that Russell's arrival and Germany's part in bringing him to Eire would 'lead to a further discrediting of the IRA, and that England will profit therefrom in the end. Thus an incident would be created that would be parallel to the landing of Sir Roger Casement by a German submarine in the World War.'[29]

Russell was himself mindful of Germany's earlier help to Irish republicans. When he was in New York in 1936, he had written to the German

Ambassador in Washington, apologising for the Irish Government's refusal to grant Germany a seaplane base in Galway Bay but thanking the Germans for their assistance in 1916 'in a fight calculated to rid our country of foreign rule'. He 'awaited the day' when this assistance could be repeated.[30] His letter had been sent at the instigation of McGarrity, the Tyrone-born leader of Clann na Gael who had helped de Valera during his fund-raising journeys to New York but who – unlike de Valera – never made the transition from a philosophy of physical force to one of political struggle. McGarrity's influence on Russell was considerable and when the IRA suffered one of its periodic ideological splits in 1938 – between those who wanted to press their campaign forward on a basis of social and economic change and those who preferred to struggle only through violence – McGarrity, who remained in the United States, was partly responsible. It was he who had written the second ultimatum to the British Government in 1939 and who had – as Gerald Boland realised – acted as a financial intermediary for the bombing campaign in England. The ethics of neutrality and the symbols of twenty-six county sovereignty left these men unmoved and the Abwehr's interest in them therefore contradicted the German Foreign Ministry's enthusiasm to maintain Eire's non-belligerency. Woermann realised this when he told Ribbentrop that 'if it learned of Russell's arrival, the Irish Government would in all probability have him arrested and, if German complicity became known, as could be expected, it would have to take the necessary steps with reference to us. Irish neutrality would thereby be jeopardised.'[31]

He supported Hempel's view that Russell should not immediately be sent to Ireland although he conceded that the Abwehr should 'for the time being' maintain contact with McCarthy without any interference from the Foreign Ministry.[32] Russell arrived in Genoa on 1 May 1940, and was taken to Germany where he was installed in the house of a bank director outside Berlin at the expense of the Foreign Ministry.[33] He studied sabotage techniques under the authority of Dr Edmund Veesenmayer, the Ministry's special adviser to Ireland who had distinguished himself over a year earlier by encouraging the minority Slovak community to secede from Czechoslovakia. Russell, who was allowed to watch German commandos of the Brandenburg Regiment training with explosives, impressed the Germans. Ribbentrop thought him the only 'decent' revolutionary leader in the IRA.[34] Clissmann, who was himself in the Brandenburg Regiment at the time, recalls that 'Russell made an excellent impression in Berlin; he was a munitions man and he knew what he was about. We thought then that the IRA was a fairly coherent organisation and had no inkling that anything was wrong with it.'[35]

The Germans were to be reinforced in this view when the Abwehr brought about an extraordinary reunion between Russell and one of the many former IRA men who had left the organisation's ranks to form a revolutionary workers' party in the mid-1930s: Frank Ryan. It was Ryan who had talked in 1932 of forbidding free speech to 'traitors', but in the years that followed his republican, socialist ideals took him to Spain where he fought with great courage in the International Brigade during the civil war. After fourteen months, he had been captured by Franco's forces and spent more than a year under sentence of death at Burgos Prison. The Irish Minister in Madrid, Leopold Kerney, hired a Spanish lawyer who was a friend of Franco to try to secure his release while de Valera appealed for Ryan's life to be spared in a telegram to the Generalissimo. Kerney visited Ryan regularly and the two men became close friends but it was Jupp Hoven, the Abwehr agent who had studied at Queen's University in Belfast before the war, who eventually secured Ryan's release.[36] Both Hoven and Clissmann knew Ryan well from their days in Ireland and, through his commanding officer in the Brandenburg Regiment, Hoven interested Admiral Wilhelm Canaris, the head of the Abwehr, in the Irishman's case. Wolfgang Blaum, the senior German intelligence officer in Madrid, interceded with Franco and on July 14 Blaum escorted Ryan across the frontier to France. Clissmann met his old friend in Paris six days later and brought him to Berlin in early August. Here Ryan met Veesenmayer who in turn, without warning, confronted him with Russell. The Germans watched the encounter closely as Russell threw an arm around Ryan's shoulders and said: 'I'm going to Ireland tomorrow, Frank. Will you come with me?' Ryan immediately agreed.[37]

The two men were to be landed at Smerwick Bay on the Dingle peninsula on August 15 – both knew the area well – and Russell was to carry a wireless set with which he could communicate with Berlin. The Foreign Ministry code-named the plan 'Operation Dove' although Russell was given no specific task, merely 'the chance to make use of Ireland's opportunity'.[38] It was hoped that he might start some kind of action in Ireland when the Germans began their invasion of Britain, possibly by arrangement with Hempel's Legation in Dublin where a red flower-pot might be placed in a specified window as a signal to Russell. Hempel, who was not informed of Russell's impending arrival, was instructed to buy flower-pots which he could put on the Legation window sills 'if a big scale invasion had been started against England'. According to Hempel:

. . . it was never intended by Germany to start a rebellion against Mr de Valera's Government. In sending Russell to Ireland they wanted in some way to support the IRA with a man they could trust. They took a poor view of Stephen Hayes as an IRA leader. What the High Command had in mind was what would happen west of England, meaning Ireland, if England had been invaded or if an invasion was being launched. The High Command wanted to create unity between Mr de Valera and the IRA, in the event of British or American aggression in Ireland. We did not want a rebellion against Mr de Valera but to come to terms with him . . .[39]

Russell and Ryan, who was only a passenger on the submarine, left Wilhelmshaven on August 8 in a U-boat commanded by Korvetten-Kapitan Hans-Jerrit von Stockhausen. The noise of the submarine's engines and Ryan's partial deafness prevented any conversation on the voyage but Russell began to suffer bouts of vomiting and stomach pains. He was given laxatives but the pain grew worse and on August 14, the day before the two men were to land in Ireland, Russell died in Ryan's arms. The IRA Chief of Staff was buried in the Atlantic, only a hundred miles west of Galway.[40] Von Stockhausen wanted Ryan to land on his own but he refused. He had no idea of Russell's mission – the two men had never discussed 'Operation Dove' – and resigned himself to return to Germany. So the U-boat continued its regular business, torpedoing Allied merchant ships in the Atlantic, until mechanical trouble forced her to sail to the German-held French port of Lorient for repairs. Two doctors concluded that Russell had died of a perforated duodenal ulcer although for years afterwards there were rumours that Ryan had assassinated the IRA leader; Ryan was contemptuous of the stories. Veesenmayer travelled to Lorient to collect Ryan who now deeply regretted that he had not after all taken the opportunity of landing in Ireland. Hempel knew nothing of this; and the British – or at least Tegart – thought that Russell, 'the local Quisling', had already landed.

In Russell's absence, the IRA had been enduring one of its less flamboyant periods. In Mountjoy, the men arrested in January were treated as ordinary prisoners and they claimed – as IRA men have done since – that they should be given political status. Some of them threatened to follow the example of Terence MacSwiney, the Lord Mayor of Cork who starved himself to death in Brixton Prison in 1920. They went on hunger strike to support their demand. Three prisoners had already used the hunger strike as a successful weapon to gain their release in 1939 and de Valera had at first refused to submit to their demands. He had told the Dail that there were no means by which the Irish Government could secure the public's safety other than by arresting and detaining those who could 'bring this country to disaster'. The policy of the hunger strike, he said, 'is aimed at taking away these means from the Government, and once these means are taken away, what is to happen is obvious. You are going to have organisation to such an extent that the only way in which ultimately the supremacy of the people can be established is by arms.' Everyone knew that there was 'a body in this country with arms at its disposal', de Valera said, and that:

> . . . in the last year, its activities have taken a new turn, that the body has definitely proclaimed itself as entitled to exercise the powers of government here, to act in the name of our people, even to commit our people to war. Now, we are in a time of peril. We have a war being waged around us, the outcome of which no man can tell. We have seen already in this war nations, comparatively large nations, losing their freedom. Is the Government of this country to be

deprived of the only power that it has to prevent things taking place here which are going, I firmly believe, if not prevented, to rob us of the independence which has been got so far as this part of the country is concerned . . .[41]

It was a strong stand that de Valera made, accusing the hunger strikers of deliberately forcing the Government to choose 'the alternative of two evils'. He had decided that 'the lesser evil is to see men die rather than that the safety of the whole community should be endangered.'[42]

But the Irish Cabinet understood the historical precedents of the hunger strike and if the ghost of Redmond appeared to de Valera when he rejected British requests to abandon neutrality, the infinitely more wraith-like figure of MacSwiney now tormented the Government. All three prisoners gained their release. On 25 February 1940, therefore, the seven IRA men who went on hunger strike assumed that they too would win concessions. They demanded the right to walk around the jail freely without being confined to their cells at four in the afternoon. The prisoners included John McNeela and Jack Plunkett, who had been running the IRA's propaganda radio station, Tony D'Arcy and Michael Traynor who had refused to answer questions about the raid on the Meath Hotel, Thomas MacCurtain, awaiting trail for the murder of a Garda officer in Cork, and Thomas Grogan, who had been charged in connection with the Magazine Fort robbery. One of the seven, John Lyons, took food after less than two weeks but the remainder held out.[43] De Valera now felt the personal venom of those who believed he had betrayed the republican cause. At a memorial ceremony at Arbour Hill prison, on Easter Sunday 1940, de Valera laid wreaths on the graves of the men the British shot in 1916 but the solemnity of the occasion was broken by Philomena Plunkett, the sister of Joseph Plunkett, one of the 1916 dead, and also of Jack Plunkett who was at that moment on hunger strike. She screamed abuse at de Valera, calling him a traitor.[44] D'Arcy died first in Saint Bricin's Hospital and then McNeela. At this point, Hayes sent word to the four surviving prisoners that concessions had been granted, a statement that later proved to be untrue.

De Valera had won the struggle although Boland had to defend the Government at the inquest on D'Arcy and McNeela, a gruelling experience in which he was shouted down by IRA sympathisers in the court and subjected to a fierce cross-examination by Sean MacBride. MacBride, the barrister son of John MacBride who was executed in 1916, had been the IRA's Chief of Staff in 1936 but had broken with Russell in the same year because he believed the organisation should take on an international character in its struggle for a republic. This in no way tempered his treatment of Boland who later described his appearance in the witness box as 'one of the worst experiences I have ever had'. Boland never forgot how MacBride asked him if he realised 'that the whole country was against the Government for letting these men die.' Boland had replied that the results of a forthcoming by-election in Galway – the home of one of the dead hunger strikers – would prove otherwise. He told MacBride 'that the Government had done retreating before hunger-strikers, that we had retreated much further than I thought wise already.' If the Government had given way to the prisoners, Boland wrote later, it would have had 'to abdicate and allow chaos to destroy the country'. Fine Gael obviously agreed, for they did not put up a candidate at Galway, allowing Fianna Fail to win with a handsome majority. Boland was proving to be as ruthless as some of the IRA leaders, partly because he thought the Government should resign if they made concessions to the hunger strikers.[45]

But the phantoms of the Anglo-Irish war did not disappear. On 13 June 1940, MacCurtain – the son of another Lord Mayor of Cork who had been murdered by the Black and Tans in 1920 – was himself convicted of the murder of the police officer in Cork. MacCurtain, who was commander of the Cork IRA's First Brigade, refused to recognise the Special Criminal Court but stated before the death sentence was passed on him that 'it is a proud moment for me to know that I can face my death knowing that I have done my duty to the army to which I belong and to Ireland.' He also claimed that the *Irish Press* had published a letter about his case and that Aiken's press censor had later compounded this contempt of court by forbidding newspapers to print parts of a statement MacCurtain had delivered to the President of the tribunal.[46] The trial ended with MacCurtain unrepentant as ever, as the record of the proceedings – which was sent to de Valera – made clear:

THE ACCUSED: . . . I am happy to die and I can assure you that I die a soldier.
THE PRESIDENT: . . . And may the Lord have mercy on your soul.
THE ACCUSED: May the Lord have mercy on your souls.[47]

This was the face of the stubborn, courageous and brutal opposition which de Valera was trying to crush. It was the great flaw in the republican movement, the fissure which opened again and again – between those who used violence for the republic and then renounced it, and those who continued to believe in physical force and felt betrayed by their former comrades. The republican movement would go on splintering, torn apart with the same permanence as the border that divided Ireland.

It was this division that de Valera also talked of when he warned Maffey, MacDonald and Cranborne that the country would be 'split from top to bottom' if Eire was to enter the war. These were the pressures that lay upon him as he struggled to maintain neutrality. He was being 'squeezed' by more than the belligerents, and his anxiety was increased by his Government's inability to destroy the movement from which his own authority had sprung. As one political scientist was to observe, de Valera's suppression of the IRA was partly an ironic function of power; 'like Creon in *Antigone*, de Valera had learnt the logic of necessity.'[48] Yet he was also trapped by the campaign he had undertaken against the IRA, temporarily successful in destroying their capacity to cause violence but constantly troubled by his failure to crush the movement. Malcolm MacDonald had witnessed this nervousness in June 1940 when de Valera told him he had taken 'severe action' against the IRA and that he:

> . . . thought that all the leaders outside Dublin were under detention. The difficulty was the organisation in Dublin itself. The authorities could not lay their hands on all the leaders there. There was an underworld in Dublin into which these people disappeared. They simply could not be found. His Government took action against them whenever they got the slightest chance, but he had to confess that some of the Dublin leaders were still at large . . .[49]

MacCurtain's hanging was fixed for July 5 and de Valera's Cabinet was to consider the sentence a week before the execution date. A confidential Garda report forwarded to the Cabinet by the Ministry of Justice revealed that after the trial had ended, one of MacCurtain's sisters said to the Garda officer who had helped to convict him: 'You will remember the MacCurtains as long as you live, and I hope that won't be long . . .' The Garda document noted that his grandfather was an epileptic and had been committed to Cork Mental Hospital, his uncle was committed to the same institution and his aunt died in hospital after suffering from 'Mania'.[50] The Cabinet postponed its decision[51] then delayed the execution and de Valera finally commuted the sentence to penal servitude for life, apparently following an appeal by Cardinal MacRory, the Catholic Primate.[52]

But de Valera's clemency towards MacCurtain may have been prompted by more than compassion. When an RUC officer arrived in Dublin in July 1940, he found his senior but unnamed Garda contact – who had actually been in charge of the preparations for MacCurtain's execution – upset at the reprieve. The RUC officer recorded how he had:

> . . . started my conversation by reminding my host that on my previous visit he was very busy . . . making arrangements for what he then described as 'a hanging match'. To this indirect question he replied, 'Sure, I had the grave dug and all, and Pierpoint in the gaol forby'. It was quite obvious he felt somewhat hurt at McCurtain's [sic] reprieve, and seeing this I saw an opportunity to develop the subject. After some preliminary sparring I hinted that perhaps the IRA and De Valera had made a bargain about McCurtain, but this was denied 'so far as I know'. He told me that the Church and public opinion and 'chiefly politics which has always been the curse of this country' was responsible for obtaining the reprieve.
> My host then passed into a different view of thought, and explained that there had been a material benefit to them, as Police, by the cancelling of McCurtain's execution. He said that the Government had let it be known throughout the Defence Corps that in repayment for this act of grace, they

expected all Volunteers who were in illegal possession of firearms or ammunition, or knew where such weapons were, to at once surrender them to the police. A promise was given that any person so doing within one week after McCurtain's reprieve, would be free from prosecution. The response was good. My host informed me that hundreds of arms and quantities of ammunition had been handed in, which had greatly assisted in arming the new Defence Corps.[53]

Despite the RUC man's imaginative version of the southern Irish dialect, it was clear that the Garda officer – who consoled himself with the remark that MacCurtain 'would have been a far bigger man dead, than he'll be alive'[54] – thought that de Valera had turned the affair to advantage. But it was one of the Taoiseach's last acts of mercy during the war. When two of the hunger strikers who had been released in 1939 were convicted of the murder of two detective officers in August 1940, de Valera allowed their executions to go ahead. They were put before a firing squad at Mountjoy.

The Dublin IRA had meanwhile been making contact once more with the Germans. They had already been visited by the physically impressive but intellectually dull ex-weight lifter Weber-Drohl who had stumbled ashore in Eire from *U 37* in early February 1940. He had faithfully delivered money and a radio code to O'Donovan but had been arrested in March while staying at a hotel in Westland Row. He succeeded all the same in convincing Irish intelligence that he had been put ashore from an Antwerp steamer at Waterford in order to seek his long-lost sons. The court fined him £3 for violating the Aliens Act.[55] In April, the IRA – unaware of Veesenmayer's plans for Russell – had sent Stephen Carroll Held to Berlin as an emissary. Held, the illegitimate son of an Irish mother and an adoptive German father, was a middle-class businessman who sympathised with the IRA. He travelled through Britain to neutral Belgium and then across the German frontier, carrying with him what became known as 'Plan Kathleen'. This scheme, which had been concocted by an IRA man called Liam Gaynor, proposed a German attack on Northern Ireland. It suggested that German paratroopers should be dropped around Divis Mountain and Lisburn outside Belfast and that simultaneous landings should be made from the sea at Lough Swilly and Magilligan Point.[56] The IRA would assist the Germans by attacking across the border from the south.

The plan bore an uncanny resemblance to the proposal that General Kurt Student was to put to Hitler less than a year later and an even more astonishing similarity to the 'war game' which the British Army carried out in Northern Ireland the following year. Since notes of 'Plan Kathleen' were later seized by the Garda in Eire, photocopied and sent to MI5 and then sent on once more to the RUC in Northern Ireland, Gaynor's plan may well have been used by the British Army for its paper exercise in the summer of 1941. But it had been the work of only one man. There had been no concerted planning among IRA members and Sonderführer Kurt Haller, an Abwehr agent who had been involved in Ryan's release from Spain, claimed later that it was so amateurish that the German authorities at first thought Held was double-crossing them as a British agent.[57] The plan had been approved by Stephen Hayes, who apparently also sent an invitation for a German officer to go to Ireland.

Unknown to Held, he was observed by the German officer who was coincidentally about to take up Hayes's invitation. Dr Hermann Goertz, a 50-year-old lawyer, was the agent already selected by Abwehr II for a mission to Ireland. Born in Lubeck, he had won the Iron Cross as a soldier in the 1914–18 War before being wounded and transferred to the Air Force. Discontented with a lawyer's life in Germany, he travelled to America and on his return placed himself at the disposal of the Luftwaffe. They sent him to collect information on RAF airfields in southern England but he was arrested when he went back to Britain to collect some notes he had left in a Kentish boarding house. He spent three years in Maidstone prison and only got back to Germany in February 1939. According to Goertz's own account, he then suggested to the Abwehr that they should use IRA men in England as saboteurs. Goertz had met McGarrity during his stay in America and had come into contact with several Irishmen while in Britain. His ideas sufficiently impressed the Abwehr who transferred him to Army headquarters[58] and in the spring of 1940 selected him for operations in Ireland. Goertz was trained in sabotage techniques and hand-to-hand fighting at the newly-formed commando school near Brandenburg, the same unit with which Russell trained and to which Helmut Clissmann and Jupp Hoven belonged. He was also introduced to Francis Stuart, an Irish writer who lectured at Berlin University and who had been attracted by the Nazis' determination to destroy the old capitalist economic system in Europe. Stuart told Goertz that he could in emergency contact his wife Iseult who lived in County Wicklow. Goertz was given two objectives in Ireland; to gain the IRA's help during a possible German invasion of Britain and their assistance in cutting off Eire's connections with the United Kingdom. Germany wanted Eire to remain neutral and Goertz was ordered to avoid involving the Irish Government in his plans. He was to try and persuade the IRA to direct their enthusiasm into intelligence work against the British rather than against de Valera's administration.[59]

On May 5, Goertz left Germany aboard a Heinkel aircraft at the start of what the Abwehr had code-named 'Operation Mainau'. Goertz would later try to convince his Irish Army captors that he had intended to make his parachute drop over County Tyrone in Northern Ireland but in fact his plane flew across England and circled about thirty miles north of Dublin over County Meath. The Irish Army records show that ground observers logged an unidentified aircraft as it described a figure of eight over Balbriggan on the coast at 23.59 hours on May 5 and then disappeared north of Gormanston at 01.10 hours on the 6th.[60] At some point within the space of those seventy-one minutes, Goertz jumped from the Heinkel but a second parachute carrying his radio disappeared into the night and he could not find it on landing. He hid his own parachute under a hedge and trudged off southwards in his jackboots, with a black beret on his head, 20,000 American dollars in his jacket and a pocketful of his 1914–18 war medals. He also claimed later that he swam the River Boyne, destroying a pad of invisible ink that had been sewn into the shoulder of his jacket. On the fourth day of his journey, he reached Iseult Stuart's home at Laragh in County Wicklow. She bought clothes for him and called O'Donovan who took the German to his own home at Shankill south of Dublin[61] and then to Konstanz, Stephen Held's house. Goertz spent two weeks with Held and was visited by Hayes with whom he discussed 'Plan Kathleen'. The IRA also found his parachute and brought it to him although they never recovered his missing radio transmitter.

One of Held's domestic servants, however, became suspicious of the visitors to Konstanz and told the police, who raided the house on May 24, arresting Held but failing to discover Goertz who hid behind a garden wall. The Garda found Goertz's parachute, Luftwaffe insignia, military cap, coded messages and some rough plans which he had made for shipping German guns into Dingle Bay by submarine. Held ingeniously invented 'Heinrich Brandy', an imaginary German relative of a dead Irish friend, who had supposedly stayed at Konstanz but had left shortly before the police arrived. Held claimed that the 20,000 dollars – which the police discovered in a wall vault – belonged to 'Brandy'.[62]

Hempel, ignorant of Goertz's identity or his arrival in Eire, reported to the German Foreign Ministry next day that the Irish state radio had given a detailed account of Held's arrest and of the apparent presence in Held's house of a German named 'Brandy'. Hempel innocently thought that Held had been the victim of a British *agent provocateur* called Hamilton and that the British might be using the latter to instigate trouble against the German Legation. He decided to adopt this theory in his conversations with the Irish Department of External Affairs and informed Berlin that he would tell Frederick Boland he was suspicious of 'renewed provocation by the English . . . and, if necessary, I shall express the firm expectation of a satisfactory attitude on the part of the Irish Government.' Hempel reported that numerous German homes in Eire had been searched by the police and he asked the Foreign Ministry for 'very detailed instructions as soon as possible in order that I may regulate my attitude accordingly.'[63]

His interview with Boland next day was not an easy one. Iseult Stuart had now also been arrested, thus upsetting Hempel's theory of British intrigue. He told the Foreign Ministry that his conversation with Boland:

. . . revealed a most serious view, especially of the support of subversive activity against the Irish Government. I now fear a critical undermining of our position here, which is indicated among other things by an unsparing, though objective publication of all details. Since Stuart had friendly relations with us . . . my personal position is also seriously involved. I fear indiscreet statements in Stuart's letters. Exploitation in England and the USA is inevitable. Brandy has apparently not been apprehended as yet.[64]

This was the first that either the German Foreign Ministry or the Abwehr knew of Goertz's escape from the police and on June 1, Woermann revealed to Hempel that 'Brandy' was 'entrusted with special missions directed exclusively against England and was to make use of personal connections with the Irish.' Woermann stressed that any activity against the Irish Government had been expressly forbidden and that although 'certain Irish personalities' had frequently submitted to Germany 'subversive plans against the Irish Government', these were always rejected.[65]

The Irish police were not at first as certain of German involvement as Frederick Boland originally made out to Hempel. When the RUC's emissary to the Garda Siochana met his contact shortly after the raid on Held's house, he found the Irish police officer 'was of the opinion that this case was an IRA affair. He doubted the story of a parachutist having been dropped in County Meath, and finding his way, carrying his parachute, German airman's hat, Iron Cross, etc, etc, to Co. Wicklow. He said "Germans are not such fools as that, and the parachute had not even a piece of mud, hay or grass on it".' But when the RUC man returned to Dublin some days later, he reported that 'the HELD–STEWART [sic] file was shown me. My host was inclined to take a different view to that already expounded on my first visit. He believes that a man was parachuted; that HELD was an IRA Treasurer, and that probably the money found came from Germany.'[66]

Faced with the embarrassment of the arrests of Held and Stuart, Woermann authorised Hempel, in a message marked 'Top Secret' and 'Most Urgent', to make a confidential approach to the Irish Government before the trials started; Hempel was to tell them that:

The Irish Government must be clearly aware that the struggle between the German Reich and England was now entering upon its decisive stage. We were conscious of the fact that the measures we had to take for carrying out this struggle against England which had been forced upon us might also affect Irish interests. Just because of this, however, we considered it important to inform the Irish Government once again that our sole objective in the struggle was England. We believed that Ireland, whose enemy through history was known to be England, was fully aware that the outcome of this struggle would also be of decisive importance for the Irish nation and the final realisation of its national demands. Given this situation, we believed that we could also count on the greatest possible understanding from the Irish Government, despite its neutral attitude, even if Ireland might in some ways be affected by our measures.[67]

If Hempel's approach met with a satisfactory response, said Woermann, he should suggest that matters such as the Held trial 'should be treated in a correspondingly careful manner by the Irish Government, and above all, in the press.'[68]

Woermann need not have worried himself unduly. On June 15, the Germans had entered Paris and when Hempel went to pass on the German Foreign Ministry's message to the Irish Government two days later, Joseph Walshe was in no mood to complain to a victorious Reich about the German parachutist's arrival. Hempel reported back to Berlin that:

> . . . the conversation, in which Walshe expressed great admiration for the German achievements, went off in a very friendly way. I started out by saying that I had reported on the Held affair and the reaction here, especially the increasing Irish fear of Germany. Walshe here interrupted and said that immediately after his return from London he had urged cautious handling of the affair . . . W thinks that, in general, it ought to be discussed as little as possible.[69]

Walshe was concerned about the possibility of a German landing which would, he said, be 'a great misfortune'. He wanted Germany to declare that she would not stage a landing in Ireland. Hempel replied that such a declaration was 'impossible in the present military situation' – which was precisely Churchill's response when the Irish made a similar appeal to the British – and added that Germany 'expected complete and realistically wise understanding on the part of Ireland, in case of any collision between Irish interests and our measures.' According to Hempel, Walshe thereupon relaxed 'and added that they were cognizant of the possible difficulties which Ireland had to expect with a more vigorous prosecution of the war against England – for example, as a result of blockade, and drew the correct conclusions.' Walshe remarked that fears of England occupied first place in the Irish Government's mind and that '90 per cent of the people' were behind de Valera. He was, however, worried about a statement that Hitler had made to the effect that Germany did not intend to destroy the British Empire. Walshe hoped that this did not mean 'the abandonment of Ireland'. Hempel assured him that it did not. He reported to Berlin that Walshe was especially interested in 'what I had told him about the importance of the outcome of the war for the final realisation of Irish national demands.'[70]

Germany was now injecting two new and fundamentally important elements into her policy towards Eire. She would continue to respect Irish neutrality but would now also expect Eire to show consideration for German war aims by displaying a 'complete and realistically wise understanding' of any potentially embarrassing incidents involving Germany.

De Valera had sought 'a certain consideration' from Germany before the war; now the Reich was asking for the same appreciation in return. Added to this was the growing assurance that Eire's irredentist claims on Northern Ireland were respected in Berlin and would be satisfied after a German victory. Ironically, on the very day on which Hempel spoke to Walshe, Malcolm MacDonald was in conclave with de Valera, starting his own negotiations towards a British offer of Irish unity. Both Britain and Germany were now using the possible fulfilment of Eire's domestic ambitions to persuade her to bend or break her neutrality.

On June 20, de Valera himself summoned Hempel for a lengthy conversation that was held 'in a forthright and pleasant manner' in Walshe's presence. 'As to the case of Held,' Hempel reported, 'I had the opportunity of expressing, without displaying too great an interest and keeping to the line pursued heretofore, our wishes for careful treatment, especially in public, which Walshe readily supported.' De Valera listened to this 'with interest' but attached principal importance to assuring Hempel of Eire's continued adherence to strict neutrality. According to Hempel's report to Berlin, de Valera:

> . . . explained that at the beginning of the war anxiety about English intervention had been uppermost in his mind but Irish neutrality had so far been respected by the English. This could, of course, change. Without any reference to the case of Held, he admitted that with Germany's closer approach anxiety had increased, as was understandable, concerning possible German intentions to use Ireland as a base for attacks on England by exploiting 'the weak minority which was working against the Government's policy.' He had repeatedly declared publicly, and had only in that way succeeded in obtaining the return of Irish ports from England, that Ireland would not become a point of departure for an attack against England. To this he would adhere . . .[71]

De Valera explained that except for Eire's economic dependence on Britain and 'the minimum of loose connection with the British Empire', his country stood in exactly the same position towards Germany as she did towards Britain. 'With regard to the solution of the Northern Irish question,' Hempel observed, 'he must in view of the English–Irish power relationship, adhere to a peaceful solution, as only so could a permanent and tenable position be reached. If it came to an invasion then Ireland would inevitably become a battlefield for the belligerents.' If the English invaded, Hempel wrote:

> . . . we would fight with Irishmen against the English, in a German invasion the English would fight along with the Irish. He was carrying out a completely realistic policy and regarded determination to resist any attacker to the uttermost as the only possibility to reduce danger.[72]

This was almost exactly the way in which de Valera had set forth his policy to the British although he had not talked about German military assistance in the event of a British invasion when he spoke to Maffey and Mac-Donald. Nor did de Valera appear to 'detest' his meetings with Hempel in quite the way that Walshe was later to make out to Maffey.

Hempel found out about MacDonald's overtures on the following day when Frederick Boland told him 'in strict confidence that English pressure for the abandonment of Irish neutrality – apparently accompanied by the bait of future concessions in respect of Northern Ireland – had recently increased again, but that de Valera had rejected all advances "most vehemently".'[73] It seems likely that de Valera wanted Hempel to learn of MacDonald's approach so as to elicit some further assurance of German respect for Irish neutrality. Hempel himself realised that de Valera was quite able to use information in his own interests. He also suspected that it was 'very possible that de Valera is, in his usual clever way, exploiting incidents such as the case of Held which brought out the German danger, so as to be better armed also against English intentions and to strengthen his position against the largely anti-German Cosgrave opposition.' Hempel observed, however, that there was 'a growing realisation, at any rate on the part of Walshe and Boland, of the great and decisive importance to Ireland of the changed situation in world affairs and of the obvious weakness of the democracies.' Hempel did not think there would be a *rapprochement* with Northern Ireland, especially since Craigavon, 'whose position is under attack by his own rank and file', had himself reportedly rejected any such settlement. From all this, Hempel concluded that: '. . . in view of German strength, it seems to me that the idea of possible German action for the return of Northern Ireland would now also find ready acceptance in nonradical nationalist circles, among others allegedly with the far-seeing influential Irish Cardinal MacRory.'[74]

Hempel had himself first urged the adoption of this policy a month earlier, telling Berlin that 'any German assistance, especially a simultaneous proclamation of the liberation of Northern Ireland as a German war aim, a matter in which . . . there is, in my opinion, no German interest, would probably give the anti-English nationalist movement a powerful impetus.'[75] But Hempel could never, it seems, quite make up his mind whether Germany should give encouragement to the 'anti-English nationalist movement' – which included the IRA – or to the Irish Government. He still believed that IRA disturbances could be crushed by de Valera and that the Irish Army – save for Volunteer members who might be 'permeated with elements in close contact with the IRA' – would on the whole prove to be 'a reliable tool in the hand of the Government and would obey its orders'.[76] Ideally, of course, the Germans wanted the IRA to settle their differences with de Valera's Government so that such striking power as they possessed could be engaged exclusively against Germany's enemy. British policy, on the other hand, was directed towards the suppression of the IRA by de Valera's Government.

On June 27, Held was sentenced to five years' imprisonment after being found guilty of aiding persons unknown and possessing a radio transmitter. Hempel reported this to Berlin without comment the following day, adding that the 20,000 dollars which the police had found at Konstanz remained confiscated.[77] Four days later, he informed the Foreign Ministry in a message marked 'Urgent' and 'Secret' that as a result of the Held affair, the Irish Government were still suspicious that the Germans might attempt a landing. At the same time, he wrote, the British: '. . . are again exerting increasingly powerful pressure on de Valera to bring about the end of Irish neutrality through a dangerous playing on the question of Northern Ireland, in which the American Minister here is apparently assisting. De Valera declares, as I have reported, that he does not intend to give in . . .'[78]

In order to 'restore the confidence of de Valera, which has been shattered as a result of the Held and Stuart cases, and thereby to strengthen his power of resistance to British threats', Hempel urged the Foreign Ministry to declare that Germany was not trying to form 'a fifth column in preparation for future use of Ireland as a military base against England'.[79] Hempel's recommendation was for once accepted and Joachim von Ribbentrop, the German Foreign Minister, subsequently wired Hempel, instructing him to tell the Irish Government: '. . . that in connection with Ireland we have exclusively the single interest that her neutrality be maintained. As long as Ireland conducts herself in a neutral fashion it can be counted on with absolute certainty that Germany will respect her neutrality unconditionally . . .'[80]

Ribbentrop added with cloying innocence that it was 'an utterly unreasonable suspicion that we might have the intention to prepare to use Ireland as a military base against England through a so-called "fifth column", which besides does not exist.' In view of the preparations for Operation 'Green' which were soon to be initiated – not to mention the fate of other neutral countries in Europe – this was not a very worthwhile reassurance. De Valera, however, might well have agreed with Ribbentrop's assessment that a British offer of Irish unity was 'only a sham, which is only engaged in for the purpose of manoeuvering Ireland out of her neutrality and drawing her into the war.'[81]

The man who was the immediate cause of the Irish Government's anxiety had meanwhile sought refuge near Dublin. After wandering around County Wicklow for a week in a state of semi-starvation, Hermann Goertz arrived at Iseult Stuart's house only to discover that she too had been arrested. He made his way to Dublin and was hidden by two elderly women, first in Dun Laoghaire and then at a rented house in Dalkey, eleven miles south-east of Dublin. He paid occasional night-time visits to Stephen Hayes's house but was already deeply disillusioned with the IRA. 'You know how to die for Ireland,' he told one of their members, 'but have not the slightest idea how to fight for it.'[82] The organisation, he wrote later, 'was rotten at its roots'.[83] Goertz's mission was already a failure. He had lost his radio transmitter even before he had set foot in Eire and the organisation with which he was to make contact had turned out to be an occasionally willing but generally unreliable guerrilla movement that caused more concern to the Irish Government than it did to the British. The disturbingly simple equation elucidated by Woermann – that the IRA and the Irish Government shared the same 'ultimate objective' – had taken no account of the fear and sense of betrayal that each side felt about the other. It was therefore not surprising that Goertz wanted to return to Germany. He made contact with Hempel who informed Berlin that the Abwehr's spy was still on the run.

The German Minister was unhappy at the idea of acting as an intermediary between the Abwehr and its agent in Ireland[84] and was even more disenchanted by Goertz's continued presence in Eire. In the autumn of 1940, he decided to take the risk of meeting Goertz to tell him of the damage which he was causing to the diplomatic relations between Germany and Eire. With much trepidation, Hempel arranged to hold a reception at the Legation for the forty or so German nationals in Dublin. He then instructed Goertz to enter the building undisguised with the other guests under the eyes of the Irish Special Branch men who were watching the building. Once inside, he was to ask the cook for directions to the lavatory and would be taken to the seclusion of the drawing room. Goertz turned up at the party and was immediately ushered into the private room. Hempel confronted him there, telling him that his activities were harming relations between the two countries. When Hempel was asked about this meeting after the war, he gave a dramatic account of his conversation with Goertz, a narration in which he somewhat predictably cast himself in the favourable light of an honest diplomat who was only trying to ensure the integrity of his Legation and its contacts with the Irish Government:

> I told him that I had heard repeatedly that he was the liaison officer between the German High Command and the IRA and I wanted to know what all this was about. I told him that I had requested information from Berlin but had been ignored. I told him that I objected strongly to his activities because they were anti-de Valera and could destroy Ireland's neutrality . . .[85]

Hempel claimed that Goertz was 'astonished' when he explained that it was nonsense for the IRA to call de Valera a traitor.[86] It is unlikely that Goertz, an intelligent man who had visited Ireland as a tourist in 1927,[87] would really have been so amazed at Hempel's political analysis. But there can be no doubt that Hempel wanted Goertz out of Ireland. So presumably did the Irish Government although it remains a mystery how the most wanted man in Eire could have entered and freely left the German Legation in Dublin at a time when the Irish Special Branch, who allegedly knew the identity of everyone who entered the building, would have been more alert than usual. Even more remarkable was the way in which Goertz, after repeated attempts to leave Ireland by boat, eventually succeeded in meeting O'Duffy and probably General MacNeill, as well as a Fianna Fail politician,[88] without being discovered by the authorities. According to his own exaggerated account, he met several Irish Army officers who asked him what help Germany could give Eire if the British invaded, offering to put an aircraft at Goertz's disposal so that he could fly to France to put their questions to the German High Command.[89] When he was finally arrested, in November 1941, it was more by accident than design; the police were raiding a house in Blackheath Park, Dublin, and became suspicious when they saw a woman watching them from a neigh-bouring doorway. They found Goertz inside her home.[90] Carolle Carter, in her long and exhaustive study of German spies in Ireland, discloses no proof that Goertz was at large with the tacit approval of the Irish Govern-ment. But their failure to arrest him for nineteen months in a small country in which the police had already penetrated the organisation with which Goertz wished to co-operate, remains one of the most intriguing features of wartime espionage in Ireland. The Irish Army's G2 Intellig-ence Branch monitored radio transmissions and knew that the spy was unable to make regular broadcasts to Germany. As long as he did not attempt to enter Northern Ireland, all he was likely to discover in Eire was the intrinsic worthlessness of the IRA as a serious guerrilla movement; and it remains true that if the Irish Government wished to dissuade the Germans from using the organisation, they could have devised no better way of doing this than by allowing Goertz free contact with Stephen Hayes and his suspicious associates.

For suspicion was one of the characteristics of the IRA, as Goertz realised. He was not alone in thinking that there might be traitors within the organisation and on 30 June 1941 a number of IRA men from Belfast kidnapped Hayes when he arrived for a routine meeting in Dublin, accusing him of betraying the IRA to the Irish Government. He was court-martialled and interrogated at secret locations in the Wicklow mountains and in Dublin, then condemned to death on the authority of a newly-formed and enlarged IRA Army Council. In an effort to prolong his life, Hayes agreed to write a 'confession', a fanciful document of prodigious length that claimed among other things that James Ryan, the Irish Agriculture Minister, had tried to put General MacNeill in touch with Goertz. Hayes subsequently escaped from his captors, sought the refuge of the nearest police station and turned state's evidence, thus confirming in the IRA's eyes what they had until then wrongly believed to be true; namely, that Hayes was working for the Irish authorities. Hayes's 'confession' also described how an IRA man, Michael Devereux, had been allegedly framed by the Government. The IRA ordered his execution and two men – George Plant and Joseph O'Connor – were charged with

Devereux's murder. When the case collapsed because witnesses were intimidated, the Irish Government manipulated the law with the Emergency Powers Order of 30 December 1941, permitting the Special Criminal Court to accept written statements with or without the presence of witnesses. Plant was put on trial again and found guilty. He was sentenced to death and executed at Portlaoise prison in March 1942.[91] A final grim twist was added to the struggle between de Valera and the IRA by the Irish Government's decision to employ the English hangman Albert Pierpoint to dispatch those upon whom the Taoiseach visited no mercy.

It was not surprising, then, that Hempel frowned upon any contact between Goertz and the IRA. His warnings to Berlin, however, had not been sufficient to dampen the enthusiasm of the Abwehr who in March 1941 had sent another spy to Ireland. Gunther Schütz, a Silesian who had operated as an intelligence agent in Britain before the war, was originally to have entered Eire with a passport containing an Irish visa. He was issued by the Abwehr with identity papers in the name of Jüdel Robemensch, a Jew who had been sent to a concentration camp. Schütz was taken by Professor Ludwig Mulhausen, a Gaelic scholar at Berlin University, to the Irish Legation near the Tiergarten where he presented his documents to William Warnock, the Irish First Secretary, explaining that he was a half-Jew anxious to leave Germany and seek asylum in Eire.[92] Suspecting that his visitor was not genuine, Warnock turned him down on the grounds that visas could not be issued until the Irish knew the route which the applicant intended to take to Eire; a German would not have been permitted to travel on British or American airlines to Ireland. The Abwehr therefore gave Schütz a forged South African passport in the name of Hans Marschner.

His task in Ireland was to send daily weather reports for the Luftwaffe, to observe British convoy movements and to report on Belfast's war industries.[93] He was trained in explosives and radio procedures by the Abwehr but he was also confused about the politics of Ireland. He was led to believe that the IRA and the Irish Army were one and the same organisation and was told that Goertz could 'walk around freely' because Eire was neutral; Schütz later claimed that this was not a misunderstanding on the part of the Abwehr but a deliberate lie which was intended to encourage him in his mission to Ireland and make him less suspicious once he arrived there.[94]

It did him little good. With £1000, invisible ink powder, a microdot code, a list of contacts, a sausage and a bottle of cognac, Schütz set off from Amsterdam in a Heinkel 111 on the evening of March 12 bound for Ireland.[95] He jumped from the plane in darkness over what he hoped was County Kildare although it was only after a night spent sleeping under a hedge that he realised he had landed sixty miles to the south in County Wexford. Two policemen, alerted by a suspicious schoolboy, stopped

Schütz as he was walking along the Wexford Road, asked him to open his bag and found his radio transmitter. They also discovered the microscope with which he was supposed to read his microdot instructions, which were disguised as punctuation marks in an English novel.[96] Schütz spent almost a year in prison but escaped from Mountjoy in February 1942, seeking refuge in the homes of IRA men and eventually making his way to the Rathmines house of Caitlín Brugha, the widow of Cathal Brugha who had been Minister for Defence in the separatist republican government set up by the Dail in 1919. According to Schütz, it was Mrs Brugha, who had also helped Goertz, who finally disillusioned him about the connections between the IRA and the Irish Army. It was not the only mistake she clarified. Schütz had seen pro-Irish propaganda films in Berlin cinemas before the war, films in which the Irish were shown as a repressed people under the heel of an English enemy, but he thought that there was little difference between the Irish and the Scots, and at one point angered Caitlín Brugha by referring to 'your King' in a conversation about the British monarchy.[97] Berlin learned of Schütz's escape from Hempel who sent the spy £80 and hoped that he, like Goertz, would try to leave Ireland. The Abwehr wanted Schütz to stay, and a complex system of communication was established between the Legation and the escaped German, using an intermediary who had apparently helped Weber-Drohl.[98] But Schütz was arrested at Caitlín Brugha's home on April 30, apparently betrayed by the IRA, as he waited to be taken to Bray for transportation home to Germany.[99] When the police entered the Brugha house, they found Schütz dressed as a woman and wearing dark glasses.

Hempel's own position remained a delicate one throughout the war, at first because of the compromising activities of the Abwehr's agents and then because of Allied pressure upon de Valera to expel both the German and the Italian ministers. In the summer of 1940, however, Hempel worried too much about the effect of Goertz's arrival. With the German armies poised to invade England, he was an invaluable conduit to Germany through which the Irish Government could express their hopes and fears about Eire's position in the aftermath of a British defeat. Hempel had informed Berlin in July 1940 that from his talks with Walshe and Boland:

> . . . I assume that the Irish Government may be placing hope in future German interest in the maintenance and completion of an entirely independent United Irish state. They express this rather in a negative fashion by saying that they hope that in a future peace settlement we will not sacrifice Ireland to England . . . Their particular anxiety is that England immediately following a defeat might be inclined to reduce Ireland to her old position of dependence since Irish neutrality is regarded as a severe blow to the prestige of the British Empire.[100]

The Germans did their best to reassure Eire, attempting at the same time to show goodwill by giving 'special consideration' to Irish ships in the dangerous waters within the German blockade zone around Britain.[101] De Valera had asked MacDonald about the prospects for a peace with Germany, and Walshe obviously thought that some kind of ceasefire between Britain and Germany was possible in July 1940 for Hempel reported to Berlin that the impression in the Irish External Affairs Department was that 'a speedy conclusion of peace on reasonably tolerable terms on the basis of conditions brought about by the German success to date would be favoured in general by Chamberlain, Halifax, Simon, and Hoare . . . also conservative circles (the Astors, Londonderry, etc.), high officialdom (Wilson), the city, the *Times*. Prospects for continuation of the war are generally regarded with pessimism.'[102]

The Irish Government was keen to manipulate Irish-American opinion against a British attack on Eire, and was also prepared to co-operate with the Axis powers in such an enterprise. In a report to the German Foreign Ministry on July 31, Hempel noted that de Valera had instructed Brennan in Washington:

> . . . to make contact with Senators of Irish origin who are friendly to Germany, in order to take steps against the agitation against Irish neutrality . . . Walshe indicated to me further that closer cooperation between the Irish element in the United States and the German element there, and also with the Italians, might be in the general interest, and he had also stated something like that to the Italian Minister. The Irish Government apparently believes that if the Irish element in the United States is properly used, it could constitute a powerful influence in our favour, likewise the Irish-American press. By other channels I heard that perhaps something could be accomplished along this line also in the Hearst press. The difficulty is, as Walshe, too, pointed out, that if any German participation became known outside, it could easily lead to an undesirable effect in the opposite direction. I assume that the Irish Government because of well-justified anxiety about a possible unfavourable British reaction against Ireland must also avoid the appearance of cooperation with us.[103]

The Germans maintained their interest in Irish-American opinion after Roosevelt's re-election. In January 1941, Ribbentrop asked Hans Thomsen, the German Chargé d'Affaires in Washington, to report on what Irish-Americans thought the Irish Government would do in the event of a British seizure of the Treaty ports.[104] Thomsen thought that 'the hatred of the Irish-Americans for England has not diminished' but that 'the Irish Catholics incline, under the influence of their clergy, to join in the propaganda against National Socialism for ideological reasons.' If America entered the war:

> . . . the opposition of the Irish to this can play only a minor role. In the mass hysteria that is then to be expected, the majority of the Irish-Americans will probably, partly under pressure, partly from conviction, take a stand against us, although not in favour of England. Nor would this be changed much on the

surface by the fact that England previously, by resort to force, took possession of the Irish ports. The press here has for considerable time been preparing the American public for the need for such an act of violence . . .[105]

The Irish in America believed that Ireland would defend herself against an English act of violence, wrote Thomsen, adding that he had been cultivating relations with the Irish-American press. The German Embassy in Washington had spent 'considerable sums' from its War Press Fund in order to 'make use of the Irish-American newspaper *The New York Enquirer*, whose circulation . . . we have in various ways greatly increased.' Thomsen pointed out that he was 'personally in touch with the well-known champion of the Irish freedom movement in Congress, Senator Murray of Montana.'[106]

Churchill's Commons speech in November 1940 at last provided Germany with an opportunity of partially assuaging Irish fears that an Axis victory might place Eire under increased dependence to Britain. Hempel reported to Ribbentrop that Walshe thought the speech was 'probably to be interpreted less as an indication of British intentions to attack Irish ports in the near future than as an internal political diversionary manoeuvre on account of British shipping losses through German submarines.' Hempel himself felt that 'the actual value to England of the possession of the Irish ports in view of the lack of strong fortifications (particularly Berehaven), and their vulnerability to German air attacks from the French coast, was disproportionate to the advantages to be expected . . .'[107] But when Hempel mentioned that he expected to have de Valera as his luncheon guest just over a week later, he received a telegram from Ernst von Weizsäcker, the State Secretary at the German Foreign Ministry, telling him that 'if there is a suitable opportunity at the social meeting with de Valera which you mention, there is no objection to your saying in the course of a conversation that the determined resistance, which we definitely assume that Ireland would offer to any attempt by the English to violate her neutrality, would naturally lead to Ireland's being in a front with us. After England was finally crushed by us, Ireland could then expect in an entirely altered situation to be able to realise her national goals.'[108]

This, of course, fell some way short of promising Ireland her national unity in the event of a German victory; it appeared to carry the condition that Eire would have to have resisted an invasion herself and participated in the war on Germany's side before she could expect German consideration of her 'national goals'. This would have sounded familiar to de Valera who had received parallel overtures from the British four months earlier. The German Army's latest assessment of the military situation in Eire in the event of a British invasion, however, was far from hopeful. General Walter Warlimont concluded in mid-November that the only assistance Germany could give Eire if the British attacked would be a concentration of U-boats around the newly-occupied Treaty ports and an extension of Luftwaffe attacks on the harbours. The use of airborne troops was 'out of the question'.[109] Nevertheless, Ribbentrop – after discussing the matter with Hitler – urged Hempel to see de Valera again, 'cautiously and without letting on that you are acting on instructions', and to suggest that if the British attacked, then 'the Reich Government would be in a position to give Ireland vigorous support and would be inclined to do so.'[110] This help, it quickly transpired, could only take the form of arms supplies shipped into Eire. General Alfred Jodl, the German Army's Chief of Operations, wondered if captured British war material might be carried to Ireland in Irish ships from the French coast.[111]

At his luncheon, Hempel had had no opportunity to speak to de Valera about Germany's views on a British invasion of Ireland. He had spoken to Walshe, however, who had said that 'there were many voices in Ireland expressing anxiety that Germany might sacrifice Ireland to England at the eventual conclusion of a peace.' There was also anxiety that Britain 'would attach special importance to having possession of Ireland when the future new order is established' in view of the impending loss of their position in Europe and the Mediterranean. Hempel, who reported that there was opposition within the British Cabinet to any policy of force in Ireland, thought that Irish resistance 'would be conducted with every available resource of total warfare by the nationalist elements, known to be ready for any sacrifice. The Army, including the recently incorporated armed security forces, is now approximately 150,000 strong. The Irish feel very confident, despite a lack of sufficient heavy weapons, that they would be able at first to hold their own even against superior British forces by guerrilla warfare or by operations with mobile columns which would probably launch simultaneous attacks on Northern Ireland.' The Army, he went on, expected 'effective action by the German Luftwaffe if the British should attack'. Hempel assumed that such an assault would be made across the border from Northern Ireland and at unfortified ports on the east and south-east coasts.

But Goertz's influence appeared to be spreading and Hempel – in an evident attempt to warn the Foreign Ministry of the damage which the Abwehr could cause – added that:

> . . . it is persistently asserted in IRA circles . . . that Germany would attack Northern Ireland in March or April; that despite the opposing view held by the Foreign Ministry, the German High Command would then also attack the Irish Free State and support Ireland (the IRA) in order to overthrow de Valera; that Ireland (the IRA) knew all this through its continuous contact with the German High Command. Since the Irish Government is also likely to be aware of these assertions, it is to be expected that while it is convinced of the Foreign Ministry's intention to respect Ireland's neutrality, it may question that this assumption applies to the High Command and react with the appropriate apprehension and distrust.[112]

Ribbentrop responded to this report by ignoring Hempel's concern about the damaging rumours of German–IRA collaboration and instructing him instead to raise with de Valera the possibility of English intervention in Ireland. In a message marked 'Top Secret Exclusively for the Minister Personally', Ribbentrop told Hempel to claim that he had received information from Germany on the subject of a British invasion:

> . . . to the effect that the German Government was naturally interested in strengthening Ireland's power to resist such an event. At the conclusion of the campaign in France, Germany had come into possession of large quantities of English arms. You considered it not unlikely, circumstances permitting, that the Reich Government was prepared and in a position to give the Irish Government free of charge a considerable quantity of these weapons, the kind and calibre, etc, which were identical with those of the weapons in use in the Irish Army.[113]

It was now that Ribbentrop's offer and General MacNeill's initiative in seeking talks with Hempel's Counsellor, Henning Thomsen, coincided. Ribbentrop thought that the captured British weapons could be shipped to Ireland 'under special camouflage' and visualised their transportation in ships which 'would be directed by us towards the Atlantic, and then, coming from there from the west, camouflaged as transports from the United States, they would sail on the familiar navigation lanes to Ireland under the Irish flag.'[114] This was the idea ultimately rejected by Walshe and de Valera who saw no possibility of shipping the weapons unnoticed.

The Irish were still worried about Germany's intentions towards Ireland after a British defeat and Hempel reported this to Berlin again at the beginning of December. 'They are afraid that we might disinterest ourselves in Ireland,' he wrote, 'or, for considerations of *Lebensraum*, abandon her to England at the conclusion of peace.' The moment had now come, Hempel thought, for an assurance that Germany would remain interested in an independent Ireland. Neither de Valera nor any Irish Government official had ever mentioned to him the possibility of recovering Northern Ireland with German help but he believed that it would have a favourable effect on Irish public opinion 'if restoration of Irish unity were at the appropriate time accomplished with visible German participation'. It would be premature to indicate such intentions to the Irish Government now but Hempel wanted to give 'a hint' that Germany actively desired the restoration of Ireland's unity.[115]

But before such opportunities arose, Germany advanced her demand for an increase in Hempel's Legation staff. Warlimont seems to have started this off in November, recalling that some German meteorologists were supposed to have been sent to Ireland and asking whether 'an official or officer experienced in military reconnaissance' might be sent to Dublin.[116] Both the Luftwaffe and the German Admiralty wanted advance weather reports from Ireland, especially now that Allied convoys were

315

sailing around the north of the island; the proposal therefore represented an obvious threat to de Valera's neutrality. Hempel's Legation staff numbered only eight, including two female secretaries – not the '300 persons' whom Tegart fondly imagined to be installed at 58 Northumberland Road – but the addition of any new members, particularly men trained in meteorology, would be an immediate provocation to the British. Frederick Boland and Sean T. O'Kelly had stalled over the proposal when de Valera was in hospital for his eye operation but Hempel renewed the German pressure immediately the Taoiseach was back in his office. Two days after Christmas, Hempel went to see de Valera and pointed out 'the gravity of the situation' brought about by his failure to allow Germany to increase her Legation staff. De Valera seems to have acknowledged that there was an 'international obligation' upon Eire to accede to this request but insisted that neutrality had to be applied according to a nation's individual circumstances. According to Hempel, de Valera argued that:

> . . . it had been recognised as a piece of boldness for Ireland, in the particular political, economic, and geographic situation of this country with respect to England, to have dared to make a neutrality declaration at the beginning of the war . . . Neutrality could not, in such circumstances, be administered as a schematic concept of uniform applicability to all countries. It was a matter of having a general policy that could give none of the belligerents even as much as a pretext for intervention.[117]

In the context of 'this policy of prudence', de Valera had refused to comply with England's various demands which might have brought about vigorous German intervention. From the same standpoint, he regarded the sending of a German aircraft with new Legation personnel as 'a serious danger'. It was de Valera's duty, Hempel reported, 'to request us urgently to refrain from pursuing our plan further'.

Hempel appears to have been sympathetic to de Valera's arguments. He told Berlin that he had 'vigorously disputed' the Taoiseach's thesis but added that if Germany 'pursued the matter further, possibly even in the form of an ultimatum, he will adhere to his position, with all the consequences which might result.' Hempel concluded that the Irish Cabinet and the Dail would support de Valera, and that the end of Eire's neutrality would give 'the greatest satisfaction' to Britain and her Empire.[118] Six days later, Hempel was instructed to inform de Valera that while the German Government regarded Eire's attitude as 'incomprehensible', it was withdrawing its proposal to send an aircraft to Ireland with the additional personnel. New Legation staff would instead travel by 'ordinary transportation facilities'.[119] Since American ships no longer sailed to Ireland, and Irish ships had to call at British ports under the navicert system, it was in fact impossible for the Germans to carry out this plan.

But before Hempel delivered this last anti-climactic message, German aircraft dropped bombs in various parts of the east coast of Eire, killing three people in the village of Borris, County Carlow, and injuring twenty-four near the South Circular Road in Dublin. The Germans at first denied responsibility for the bombings, and Karl Heinz Petersen, the German News Agency's reporter in Dublin, spread the word that the British were to blame. Several Irish Army officers, however, believed that the bombings were a consequence of de Valera's refusal to permit the extra German Legation staff into Eire.[120] The Carlow deaths and the destruction in Dublin formed the subject of a long discussion in the Defence Conference at which James Dillon demanded an Irish Government statement that the bombs were German 'in order to combat propaganda that they were British, being circulated by Petersen and his connections'. Dillon claimed that an American diplomat had found that 'seven out of ten people' on the South Circular Road believed the bombings to have been the work of the British. Infuriated by this suggestion, which presumably emanated from David Gray, Aiken asked Dillon: 'Do you think that there is one person in the country who does not know that the Government believe that the bombs were German?' Aiken said that he had not 'the slightest doubt' that the bombs were German. This gave rise to another of the Defence Conference's interminable debates on the possibilities of invasion, with Aiken acknowledging that there was a danger of a German attack but confiding that he did not 'exclude the other fellows'. Aiken thought the Germans might attack Ireland as a diversion, as a subsidiary assault while they landed in Britain or as a 'special invasion' to break up Britain's sea communications. He said that he feared an attack from both Britain and Germany, and that 'his mind switched from one to the other from day to day.'[121] Mulcahy, who recorded this alarming flexibility on Aiken's part, had suggested at the Defence Conference the previous year that if there was a night or two of German bombings in Eire, 'Hempel might get a brick through his windows.' Gerald Boland agreed and confirmed that he had already 'put an escort car on Hempel.'[122]

Germans living in Eire suffered no restriction on their movements although the Irish Army's G2 intelligence branch kept a list of German nationals whom they regarded as unreliable.[123] So did Mulcahy. Quite apart from the German-born hotel owners whose names he gave to Gerald Boland, he also forwarded to the Minister for Justice some suitably enigmatic details about six individuals whom he thought particularly suspicious:

Blunck 8 Dungar Terrace, Sandycove. (gets large remittances from abroad)
Hans Menhausen His headquarters is in Youghal – ostensibly there for his health. Travels all over south coast.
Capt Little Solicitor, Middleton (ex-British Army) is working with him and other Germans (Menhausen). Little's wife's sister is married to a German, believed to be in Dublin.

H. *Martin* (or Markin?) – a German on 2nd floor at No ? [sic] South Mall, Cork. He has a pedicure business on 2nd floor from which he is very frequently absent.
Graham Picton-Hughes is apparently from Cardiff and stays at Casey's Hotel, Glengarriff. Associate of *Father Huhn*, ostensibly a refugee from Germany, but apparently a 5th Columnist.
Maiskey (only phonetic rendering) German Works Manager at Haulbowline steel works. He has a motor boat. Please note proximity of petrol storage tanks. This man is important.[124]

There is no indication whether Mulcahy's list contained accurate information nor whether Boland bothered to investigate the mysterious Blunck's payments or Cork's absentee pedicure. Nor is it clear if the details came from Irish or British sources although both countries seem to have kept an eye on a German schoolteacher. He appeared on a G2 file[125] and was then investigated in 1944 by the British Admiralty after the Reverend James Little, the Northern Ireland Westminster MP, had informed Herbert Morrison that the German gave up a well-paid job as a teacher to become the proprietor of an island hotel off the west coast.[126] Little's reputation for inaccuracy did not suggest that the man had much to fear from the security authorities. Petersen was routinely watched by G2 and was distrusted by almost everyone with whom he came into contact, including Hempel who thought he drank too much and gossiped indiscreetly.[127] Off-duty British officers who had homes in Ireland sometimes asked to be introduced to him by Smyllie, the editor of *The Irish Times*, 'just so we could say we'd met a German with the name of Carl Heinz Petersen'.[128]

Hempel relied on his Legation's radio transmitter for his communications with Berlin but after 1941 he reduced his messages because he was concerned that the Irish might take his set away. G2 monitored the signals but could not break his code. The British, however, regularly deciphered the transmissions and passed on the contents to Dublin. Bryan discovered that after 1942, the transmissions were being made from outside Dublin and G2's direction-finding equipment later tracked the signals to Bettystown in County Meath, on the coast thirty miles north of Dublin.[129] When the Allies were preparing for D-Day, they insisted that the Irish Government should take possession of Hempel's transmitter; it was handed over to one of Bryan's junior officers in early January 1944 and placed in a safe at the Munster and Leinster Bank in Dublin.[130] Hempel and his staff were then effectively cut off from Germany. It is doubtful if he could have radioed much information on the D-Day preparations although he would probably have tried to do so since he had earlier in the war transmitted to Berlin details of British and American troop strengths as well as reported sinkings.

William Warnock, the Irish First Secretary in Germany, had even less opportunity to communicate with Dublin than Hempel did with Berlin.

He had no radio and when the war started, he was cut off from the Department of External Affairs for a week[131] and thereafter sent mail to Eire via Lisbon. Warnock was an Irish-speaking Dublin Protestant who had first visited Germany in 1934 and spent the following year hiking around the Eifel mountains. A slim, courteous and quietly-spoken man, he had virtually no commercial work to do during the war since trade relations between Eire and Germany were at a standstill but he repeatedly expounded the policy of Irish neutrality to German Foreign Ministry officials who dined at the Legation.[132] Irishmen who spent the war in Germany claimed later that Warnock curried favour with the Germans and provided better food for Nazi dignitaries than he did for Irish guests.[133] Warnock says that he had no love for Nazi Germany, which he regarded as 'an oppressive and objectionable regime,' and never tried to curry favour with the Germans, but that if he had to entertain Foreign Ministry officials, he regarded it as his duty 'to make sure they had a good meal'. Warnock thinks that he 'might have expressed anti-British sentiments' to German diplomats but says that his prime concern was the protection of Irish neutrality. 'The Germans,' he recalled long after the war, 'expressed their appreciation that Ireland had managed to assert and hold on to its neutrality. Any fear they might have had would have been of Ireland's invasion by Britain.'[134]

Warnock complained to the Foreign Ministry when German aircraft attacked Irish ships or bombed Eire and also apologised for the speech which de Valera made at Galway in May 1940 protesting at the German invasion of Holland and Belgium. Woermann, the Political Department Director at the German Foreign Ministry, recorded at the time that Warnock 'expressed himself in a similarly apologetic manner as the deputy of the Irish Foreign Minister had done to our Minister. Warnock added the remark that Ireland wished to maintain neutrality towards all Powers and said personally that Ireland, in the last war against England, had struck too early. This mistake would not be repeated. In view of the German successes the question, however, was whether Ireland would not come too late.' Woermann did not explain the meaning of this last cryptic comment.[135]

Warnock knew most of the Germans who had travelled to Ireland before the war, including Professor Mulhausen and Dr Hans Hartmann – 'a pleasant man' – who had been one of Adolph Mahr's former acolytes at the Irish National Museum. Hartmann, whose wife had once been a typist at the German Legation in Dublin, was now running a propaganda department in the German broadcasting service specialising in Irish affairs. Warnock also kept in touch with the small Irish community resident in Berlin although he had, perhaps wisely, few social friends among them. Most of the Irish in Berlin were assisting the German war effort in one way or another and Warnock pointedly refused to renew Francis Stuart's Irish passport when it expired. Stuart had dined at the

319

Legation on several occasions but Warnock was unhappy at the nature of Stuart's later propaganda broadcasts to Ireland over the German radio. The Irish Minister was briefly introduced to the wife of the Irish-born broadcaster William Joyce and once caught sight of Frank Ryan at the Leipzigerplatz press club but did not speak to him. When he travelled back to Dublin, de Valera asked to see him but Warnock says that he has forgotten their conversation. He was offered a lift to Killarney in de Valera's railway carriage and recalls only that the Taoiseach 'wanted to know about everyday life in Germany.'[136]

Everyday life had in fact become extremely dangerous, not least for Warnock who was in the Irish Legation in November 1943 when the building was set on fire during an RAF incendiary raid on Berlin. He had ignored the air-raid warning at eight o'clock in the evening and was working on his accounts in an upstairs room when a bomb set fire to the lower floor and walls. Warnock's files and archives were destroyed and he just had time to see the Legation's grand piano go up in flames before hurriedly leaving the building as the roof collapsed. He then set up a temporary Irish diplomatic mission in the potent confines of a stud farm at Staffelde outside Berlin.[137]

The Legation building was therefore already in ruins when Cornelius Cremin arrived in the city a few days later to take over from Warnock as Chargé d'Affaires.* Cremin had already developed a distaste for Nazi Germany. As a student, he had gone to Munich to learn German in 1932 and sat only two rows behind Hitler at a rally in the Munich sports field. He had come away with the impression that Hitler was 'a tremendous demagogue'. But Cremin was a firm supporter of the League of Nations and later watched at first hand the effect of the German victories in Europe in 1940. As Counsellor at the Irish Legation in Paris, he left the city with the fleeing French Government just three days in advance of the German Army's arrival. By contrast, his journey through the French countryside was almost exotic. The French authorities at first gave him an ornate château – the home of a banker – from which to conduct his business, but Cremin was unhappy at working amid such opulence and moved to Ascain then to Baarboule in the Massif Central where he set up his Legation under what had become the Vichy regime. On his appointment to Germany, Cremin took the train to Berlin through Paris where he read in a newspaper of the destruction of the Legation. Allied air raids were already disrupting communications in Germany and Cremin's train terminated at Potsdam outside Berlin. At the local police headquarters, he obtained a car that took him to the gutted Legation building where he

---

* The Irish had originally wanted to send Thomas Kiernan, a former High Commissioner in London, as Minister in Berlin with ambassadorial rank but such an appointment still needed King George VI's signature. Joseph Walshe was prudent enough not to risk British apoplexy by requesting the King's consent.

learnt of Warnock's new address. Cremin had little enough to do. He processed several claims against the Germans for attacks on Irish ships and received only irregular supplies of mail from the External Affairs Department in Dublin. He also discovered that three Irish citizens – two men and a woman – were awaiting execution in Gestapo prisons for allegedly spying for the Allies; one of the men and the woman, who was being held in Paris, were freed, but the third prisoner died in an Allied air raid before Cremin could secure his release.[138]

Unknown to Warnock and Cremin, however, Frank Ryan was also keeping open a diplomatic link with Dublin through Leopold Kerney, the Irish Minister in Madrid. In a series of carefully written letters, Ryan told his friend of Russell's death and of his own predicament now that he was back in Berlin with no way of returning home. The Germans were aware of most of his correspondence with Kerney and sometimes used Ryan's letters to pass on Germany's views of de Valera's policy. In November 1941, for instance, Ryan told Kerney that:

> . . . so far as I can judge, things stand thus: There is a very definite hands-off policy with regard to the little island. The Foreign Office chokes off everybody who tries to interfere there. On two occasions to my knowledge in 1940 things were done behind their backs, & there was hell to pay, as a result. The office is apparently dominated by the fear that Sam or John would find an excuse to step in there. (The gentleman who is at large there at the moment is not a representative of the office, and was in fact sent there without their knowledge.) The office appears very satisfied with your Boss' unyielding attitude towards Sam and John. They look upon him as a future potential friend . . .[139]

Kerney, of course, realised that 'Sam' was the United States, that 'John' was Britain and – more important – that 'the gentleman who is at large' referred to Hermann Goertz. This information was sent back to Dublin by Kerney who also met both Clissmann and Veesenmayer.

Ryan's own position, however, remained paradoxical and almost tragic. Having risked his life to fight fascism in Spain, he had no desire to aid Nazi Germany; but he could not return to Ireland without German assistance. Almost ten years earlier, Ryan had reviled the Cumann na nGaedheal leaders as traitors yet now these men and their political opponents were ready to defend Ireland from British or German attack while he was living as an official – and privileged – guest of the German Reich. He kept a close circle of friends, among them Francis Stuart and Helmut Clissmann, but his deafness and inactivity depressed him. Clissmann remembers Ryan as 'a likeable, clever, clear man who could not be bribed'[140] but Ryan must have realised that his mere presence in Germany now compromised him more seriously than any inducement of a material kind. His belief in Irish neutrality was genuine enough. He spent Christmas of 1943 with the Clissmanns in Copenhagen, and they remember how Ryan, sitting by the fireside with a glass of wine in his hand, composed an emotional but imaginary telegram to de Valera urging him to keep up his policy of non-belligerency.[141] But to support Irish neutrality in Germany was to fall in line with Germany's own policies towards Ireland.

Ryan had been given one last opportunity of returning home in the late summer of 1941 when Veesenmayer proposed to reactivate the supposedly dormant strength of the IRA and direct it against Britain. The project was to be code-named 'Operation Sea Eagle'. Veesenmayer planned to send Clissmann and Ryan – together with a German radio operator called Reiger – to Eire to make contact with the IRA, distribute funds and organise guerrilla resistance in case the British invaded. Reiger would send back reports on the weather and on convoy movements while Ryan was supposed to address himself to the chimera of a truce between the IRA and de Valera's Government. The three men were to be landed by seaplane on Lough Key in County Roscommon just south of the Northern Ireland border. Clissmann chose the lake himself because he thought it far enough away from any town to enable them to land undetected. 'Both Ryan and myself had friends and connections whom we hoped would help us,' Clissmann recalled after the war. 'I was to tell the IRA that a German victory would at last bring about the unity of Ireland.'[142]

But the war in Russia sapped German interest in the plan, and Ryan's subsequent ill health caused the abandonment of 'Sea Eagle'. Ireland was once more of only peripheral concern to the Abwehr. Indeed, their poorly prepared and often absurd attempts to set up agents in the country seemed always to be symptomatic of an ignorant enthusiasm; the spies who parachuted from aircraft over Eire or who clambered ashore on the west coast were entering the penumbra of one of Europe's darkest political conflicts, a domestic struggle of infinite and inbred proportions that overwhelmed them in almost the same way as it could blind de Valera to the international significance of the world war. Sometimes the agents were simply inept. Willy Preetz, who was married to an Irishwoman, landed from a U-boat in Dingle Bay in June 1940, reached Dublin and began sending weather reports from a rented house in Westland Row. But he gave himself away by mentioning the presence of an Irish friend during one of his transmissions, and the police then followed the Irishman home from work to Preetz's rooms.[143] Walter Simon had been arrested within twelve hours of his landing at Dingle after waiting for a non-existent train on a deserted branch line. The Abwehr also chose agents whose appearance was bound to give them away. In early July 1940, they arranged to land two South Africans and an Indian – Dieter Gartner, Herbert Tributh and Henry Obed – from a yacht near Baltimore but the three men had not even been given forged residence papers and were almost immediately arrested. Obed had blessed his mission by setting off along the coast road in County Cork dressed in a bright silk Indian suit and a straw hat, and the local Garda sensibly refused to believe his claim that he was a student. G2 were then advised by the nearest police station that 'two whites and a nigger have appeared from nowhere'.[144]*

The Abwehr also dispatched three Irishmen to Eire to spy for them. Two of the men had been captured in the Channel Islands in 1940, and one of them, called Lenihan, used the offer of a flight to Ireland as a trip home. He parachuted into County Meath and handed himself over to the British in Northern Ireland.[146] John Francis O'Reilly had worked for German radio in Berlin, broadcasting to Britain and Ireland under the pen name of Pat O'Brien. After enduring a thousand-bomber raid on Hamburg in 1943, he induced the Germans to send him to Ireland and bailed out of a Luftwaffe plane near the airport at Foynes together with a radio transmitter, a code and £300. He was picked up at once, imprisoned at Arbour Hill and escaped. Then he too became caught up in the toils of history. He returned home to Clare where his father promptly handed him back to the police and collected a £500 reward which he diligently invested for his son. O'Reilly senior turned out to be the ex-policeman who had arrested Roger Casement when he landed from a U-boat in 1916.[147] John Kenny, a friend of O'Reilly's, also parachuted into Ireland in late 1943 and was swiftly jailed.

But the burden of imprisonment fell hardest upon Goertz. He had in a curious anthropomorphic way, fallen in love with Ireland and the failure of his mission there obsessed him. As Germany's borders shrank towards the end of the war, he was tormented by self-doubt and self-pity, the conduct of his operation becoming ever more important to him as the war news made it ever more irrelevant. He translated the poems of W.B. Yeats into German and wrote a rambling essay entitled 'Germany Speaks to Ireland' in which he compared his affection for Ireland to that of an unrequited lover. 'Although I have nowhere abroad found better friends than in Ireland,' he wrote, 'I have sometimes had the feeling that I might perhaps have carried out my task better if I had by chance been born a Catholic.'[148] It was a strange irony that Goertz and his idealist counterpart Ryan should have become trapped in each other's respective countries, although Ryan at least remained rational to the end of his life. Goertz was a haunted man. He wrote about death and claimed that his fellow prisoners had told the prison authorities about an escape tunnel.[149] Schütz, who was still known by his false name of Marschner, was himself accused of being an informer. Goertz turned to him one day and screamed: 'I am afraid there is a traitor among us – Marschner!' Whereupon he attacked Schütz with his fists. When he later discovered that Schütz had been listening to the BBC, he condemned him to death and announced that he would arrange for the execution when they returned to Germany.[150]

---

* Since all three men were Commonwealth citizens, the Irish at first suspected that they had captured three British spies.[145] Hempel was originally of the same opinion.

Goertz aroused different emotions in different people. To Hempel, he was 'a vivid, impressive character'. The German Minister remembered him as 'a fine type, alert and intelligent. He was nearly six feet tall, with a fine military bearing, with strong features and good-looking.'[151] To Francis Stuart, Goertz was 'an idealist who was completely inefficient'. Stuart thought that 'if the Germans really needed someone for his job, they couldn't have chosen a worse man.'[152] Schütz was less generous. 'He was a tragic figure because he always failed,' he observed after the war. 'He failed as a lawyer; he failed as an agent in England; he failed as an agent in Ireland. He even failed to escape. Between fifty and a hundred people were arrested in Ireland because of his activities. He was also a fanatic and a Nazi. He was not particularly anti-semitic but he believed in Hitler's New Order.'[153] Goertz was now a sick man, imprisoned mentally as well as physically. His state of mind was evident in a long and disturbing play he wrote about Stephen Hayes in which he depicted the hunted IRA leader sitting in the garret of a Dublin house, terrified of discovery, smoking, drinking and watching the street outside through a mirror so that no one could see him.[154] Clissmann, however, thought that Goertz was racked by more understandable fears, that he was frightened of being handed over to the British and of being tortured to betray the names of agents in Northern Ireland.[155]

Goertz had falsely claimed to Irish intelligence that he had originally intended to parachute into County Tyrone but he also mentioned a radio in Northern Ireland, code-named 'Ulrike', which allegedly transmitted to Germany. Were there German spies in the six counties whom Goertz was fearful of betraying? According to the province's official war historian, 'only two enemy agents were known to be active in Northern Ireland during the summer preceding war.'[156] He does not identify either, although one was presumably Jupp Hoven who had been studying at Queen's University. The Northern Ireland authorities often talked of the possibility that German agents crossed the border from Eire but little evidence of espionage in the province ever came to light. Several incidents reported to the Stormont Government were certainly suspicious. On 27 July 1940, for example, Rear Admiral Richard King, the Flag Officer in Charge at Belfast, reported to Major William Iliff, the Secretary to the Ministry of Public Security, that on the 26th:

> . . . one enemy plane passed over the Lough about midnight and was fired at by one of our ships in the Lough, but not hit . . . She then flew up towards the Twins and signalled in the direction of the Zoological Gardens, and her signal was answered.
>
> A second plane flew in over the Lough about 1.45 a.m. and was again fired at, but not hit . . . She flew up over the town and also signalled in the direction of the Zoological Gardens and her signal was again answered.
>
> Fighters were sent up from Aldergrove, but I understand saw nothing.[157]

Incidents like this were extremely rare but there was no doubt that the IRA in Belfast attempted to collect military information, which was passed on to Dublin. In 1940, an IRA intelligence officer called Maguire – later believed to be an informer – arrived in the Northern Ireland capital and gave instructions to local IRA units to make lists of Belfast's ground defences. Paddy Devlin, who was a teenage IRA volunteer in the west of the city, remembers that Maguire was collecting intelligence from all over the six counties to take back to the south. 'He made out that the whole thing was some kind of an exercise,' Devlin recalls. 'But each IRA battalion logged the gun positions around the city and the details were then given to battalion intelligence officers.'[158] Devlin never found out what happened to that information.

In fact, the IRA in Belfast knew very little about the war or the way in which it might affect Ireland. When the Germans accidentally bombed Eire, Terence Healy, the Secretary of the Gaelic League in Dublin, wrote a pamphlet which named the 'British agents' supposedly responsible for the destruction, and this mendacious document was peddled around Belfast by the IRA as proof that Britain wanted to invade the south.[159] Gas masks were burnt as public demonstrations of anti-British sentiment but despite the pro-Nazi slogans sometimes shouted in Catholic districts and the provocative graffiti on the walls, there was little to suggest that Germans were in personal contact with IRA members in Belfast. Basil Brooke, who rarely lost an opportunity of emphasising the machinations of Hempel's Legation in Dublin, claimed that after the bombing of Belfast by the Luftwaffe in the spring of 1941, he 'was told on good authority that the Air Attaché from the Nazi Embassy visited the city to see the damage and report via Dublin to Berlin.'[160] In reality, there never was an air attaché at the Dublin Legation and it seems highly unlikely that a German would have risked the journey across the border into Northern Ireland to observe the effects of the blitz on Belfast when Dublin was thronged with refugees from the city who could give graphic and accurate descriptions of what had happened there.

Alive to the dangers of collaboration between the IRA and the Germans, the British authorities fully supported the Northern Ireland Government's policy of internment without trial. By 1942, 802 men had been interned, 450 of them in the Crumlin Road jail in Belfast and the remainder on the prison ship in Strangford Lough. Ex-IRA men still talk of the conditions on this floating hulk, of the fighting on board and of the tuberculosis that was rampant among the prisoners there.[161] The IRA's Northern Command under Hugh McAteer, however, was still able to organise a new campaign against the police in 1942. With 20,000 rounds of ammunition from the 1940 raid on the Magazine Fort in Dublin, and more than £4000 robbed from a Northern Ireland civil defence headquarters,[162] they attacked RUC personnel in Dungannon and Belfast.

Six IRA men were arrested in April after the killing of Constable

Patrick Murphy in Cawnpore Street in the Falls area of west Belfast, and all were tried and condemned to death. Five of the sentences were commuted after appeals to the British Government from de Valera and, privately, from the United States Government. But the Stormont Cabinet decided that Thomas Williams, a nineteen-year-old IRA Volunteer who had been wounded in the shooting and admitted the murder in court, should be hanged. The archives of the Northern Ireland Government still contain a list of petitions calling for Williams's reprieve that came from a disparate mixture of individual Catholics and pro-nationalist groups. They included 'the Wardens of "D" Group Civil Defence, Londonderry', members of the Dublin Fire Brigade, the Communist Party of Ireland, 'the people of Achill', the residents of Cawnpore Street, the Lord Mayor of Dublin and the 'Aid To Ireland' organisation of Times Square, New York.[163] Williams's solicitor wrote to the Northern Ireland Governor, Lord Abercorn, pointing out that the evidence of an RUC witness to Constable Murphy's murder strongly suggested that the condemned man had not fired the fatal shots.[164] The day before the hanging, however, the Prime Minister, John Andrews, wrote to Abercorn to inform him that the Northern Ireland Cabinet had decided that there were 'no grounds for the exercise of the prerogative'. Abercorn wrote 'I agree' on the top of the letter[165] and Williams was hanged next morning.

Catholic crowds had gathered outside the prison on the morning of the execution and an outbreak of violence followed Williams's death. An RUC man and a 'B' Special constable were shot dead in County Tyrone and gun battles broke out in nationalist areas of Belfast, prompting the Stormont Government to impose a curfew. IRA men were arraigned not only on specific charges but also for 'treason felony', an offence created by the 1848 Treason Felony Act which John MacDermott, the Minister of Public Security, felt applicable to 'the present time when the interests of the Nation as well as the protection of our own State require that those who sustain the [IRA] movement should, on conviction, receive sentences of an exemplary nature.'[166] Yet IRA men were never charged with spying for the Germans. Indeed, the only remotely pro-German gesture MacDermott could remember after the war, was a letter written by an old man in Enniskillen to 'a hot-headed priest', asking for advice on what to do when the Germans took control of Northern Ireland.[167] The letter had been intercepted by the censor and the priest was briefly interned.

Nationalist sentiment in Northern Ireland was anti-British rather than pro-German. Catholics in Belfast regularly listened to William Joyce – 'Lord Haw Haw' – on the radio, and sometimes turned up their receivers when RUC patrols passed their homes;[168] they were stirred, however, not by German victories but by IRA successes. When Hugh McAteer broke out of the Crumlin Road jail with three other men and when a further twenty-one IRA members escaped from Londonderry prison, the IRA's stock soared in Catholic areas of Northern Ireland. McAteer crowned this success by appearing on the stage of the Broadway cinema on the Falls Road during a film show on Easter Saturday to read a statement of IRA policy and to call for a minute's silence in memory of the 1916 dead. Several IRA men expressed sympathy with the Germans – Devlin recalls that one IRA officer from Hannahstown was a self-proclaimed Nazi – but as the war progressed, the internees at Crumlin Road 'began to understand what the Germans represented – that the Nazis were a different colour from us.'[169] The old Belfast Fascist movement was itself long dead; its founder member – an Italian who was interned as an alien – drowned on the *Arandora Star*.[170]

If Germany's connections with Northern Ireland appeared to be nonexistent during the war, however, Jupp Hoven still had contacts in the province. Under interrogation by the British in 1945, he threw himself from a third-floor window, preferring to commit suicide rather than reveal the names of people he knew in Northern Ireland.[171] His life was saved by wire netting which the British had thoughtfully hung beneath the windows of the interrogation centre. But Goertz, faced with the prospect of similar questioning, was later to be successful in his suicide attempt. The irony for the German agents and for their potential nationalist allies was that throughout the war they encouraged nothing more than an illusion. Clissmann, who was to have gone to Eire to train the IRA for its fight against the British and to tell the Irish that Germany would restore Ireland's unity after England's defeat, realised later that his promises would have been lies. It was quite clear, he said after the war, that:

> . . . Hitler would have sold the Irish down the river. I would have told the Irish that their freedom was coming. I would have been a Lawrence of Arabia. It happened to several friends of mine, with the Bretons and the Walloons. Their freedom was promised but then, when the Germans had what they wanted, the separatist groups were abandoned. Northern Ireland would have been given to a 'Vichy'-type government in London. Hitler did not want to harm the British Empire.[172]

Chapter 10

Today I Spoke of
Liam Lynch . . .

When we read of the sinking of British vessels by German
submarines, let us remember the battering in of little cottages
in Donegal by the English, and the turning of poor Irish
families out onto the roadside.

German radio broadcast to Ireland
18 November 1942

The time has come to say to Eire: 'Forget your trouble with
England – at least till after the war.' Eire like the rest of
us will go under if the Nazis win. Don't let history say that
de Valera unknowingly helped Hitler to fill the bloodbath of
the New Order.

'Ireland – The Plain Issue' made by Paramount Films
London 1942

Francis Stuart's first sight of Hitler was in Berlin one night in the early
summer of 1939. 'There was a blue light on his Mercedes as it came down
the Unter den Linden,' Stuart recalled after the war. 'He was a small,
stocky, very wooden-like figure in a comparatively simple uniform surrounded by ostentatious Foreign Ministry dignitaries and SS men. No
reaction to Hitler could be objective. I felt that somehow the system in
Europe needed completely destroying and for me Hitler was a kind of
Samson pulling everything down.' Stuart was not a fascist – not at least in
the racist, anti-communist sense of the word – but he felt a powerful
attraction towards the new Germany that was preparing to overthrow the
old capitalist order. He regarded Hitler as 'a super-dissident' and it was
entirely in keeping with this frame of mind that he could also admire de
Valera, who had defied the conventions of Commonwealth statehood by
declaring neutrality and refusing to support Britain. In Stuart's eyes, Irish
neutrality was 'a gesture that would consolidate independence, an act of
sovereignty similar to Pearse's occupation of the Post Office yet on a far
larger, wider scene.'[1] Perhaps somewhere between Dublin and Berlin,

Pearse's theories of blood sacrifice became entangled with a more sinister cult of martyrdom.

Stuart was an unusual man. The son of County Antrim Protestants, he was born in Australia, educated at Rugby and Trinity College, Dublin, fought on the republican side in the civil war and married Maud Gonne's daughter Iseult after converting to Catholicism. He wrote several intro-spective and distinguished novels, and was briefly praised as 'an Irish Dostoyevsky'[2] before his growing literary distinction took him to Ger-many for a series of lectures that culminated in the offer of a post at Berlin University. Stuart accepted the lectureship, partly because his marriage to Iseult Gonne was breaking up and also because the new job was well paid. War had already broken out when he returned to Berlin, travelling through Britain to neutral Belgium armed with a bogus medical certificate announcing that he required treatment for tuberculosis in Switzerland. His old friend Helmut Clissmann was instrumental in securing his return to Germany.[3]

Although Stuart was drawn towards the Nazis because he 'had the idea that the war might end in everything collapsing, and this was always my dream',[4] he was also a political innocent, contemplating a visit to Moscow until advised against it by some White Russian friends, and realising only after a year that Hitler − far from being a dissident − was an ultra-conservative. He says that he used to see Jews in the streets wearing yellow Stars of David and 'wondered what happened to them' until he heard about the extermination camps a few months before the end of the war. Ryan, who became a close friend after his arrival in Germany from Spain, tried to disillusion Stuart about the nature of the regime but there can be no doubt that the Irish writer was seduced by what he found in Nazi Germany, by the order and cleanliness of the place and by the sheer invincibility with which the German Army seemed to be invested. He remembers feeling 'exhilarated' after the German victories of 1940 but admits that he 'could not help feeling sympathy for the British at the time of Dunkirk.'[5] He was to feel equally emotional about the German defeat at Stalingrad.

Yet in 1942, long after he had begun to have serious doubts about the morality of Nazi Germany, he agreed to broadcast to Ireland over German radio. It was, even for Stuart, an extraordinary decision since his reputa-tion as a writer would be irretrievably compromised the moment his voice was heard on the air. He had already written several scripts for William Joyce, whom he regarded as 'a heavy drinker and very anti-Irish', but he hesitated before broadcasting himself. He remembers that:

. . . a nice old German in the Foreign Ministry advised me very much against broadcasting. He said that it would be guaranteed to stop publication of my books in English. But somehow I felt the necessity to broadcast. I could never be a writer in the bosom of society. Being in Germany was one thing, lecturing at Berlin University was bad enough – but going over to the other side of the street, slinking down a street, was something a writer could not do in peacetime. I had the opportunity of doing something that would cut me off from all the *bien pensants* in society. I did not regret it. I don't stand over what I did but I don't regret the consequences, though they were painful. Without them I could not have become the writer I am now. There was one aim I did have; I had the idea that I could help to counteract the flood of Allied and American propaganda. I disliked the Allied sanctimoniousness about fighting a Christian crusade against evil. I think I did have some idea of a new Europe in which Ireland would be involved although I didn't know how this would happen. I was very confused . . .[6]

Confused – dangerously confused – Stuart undoubtedly was. But he prepared his first script early in 1942 and on March 17 – Saint Patrick's Day – the monitors at the BBC's receiving station at Caversham in England, who listened to all Axis transmissions from the Continent, heard a German voice announce that 'the well-known Irish writer Francis Stuart' would broadcast that night to Ireland. The British monitors duly tuned in to the Zeesen and Oslo transmitters of German radio on long and short waves at 9.45 p.m. to listen to Stuart, confident but cautious, expounding on 'Ireland's place in the new Europe'. He was clearly conscious of the step he was taking and anxious from the very start to refute the accusations which he knew would be levelled at him. 'I am not trying to make propaganda,' he began:

. . . had I wanted to make propaganda I could have done so during my two years in Germany. I only want to put forward my idea of Ireland's place in the world and her future, which I am perhaps able to view with greater clarity from a distance. What a blessing it is that we are celebrating this day at peace, not having escaped war by dishonourable and cowardly means but by refusing – as far as lay within our power – to waver from a strict and fearless neutrality. As an Ulsterman it is galling to me that a large number of foreign troops are today occupying that corner of our country. But though we have escaped the war, and I hope may be able to do so until the end without sacrificing anything of our national integrity, we cannot nor do we desire to escape taking our share in building the new Europe . . .[7]

Stuart did not criticise de Valera's neutrality; like the Germans, he supported it. And his condemnation of the presence of 'foreign troops' in Northern Ireland – which specifically referred to the American soldiers who had arrived in the province two months earlier – only echoed a protest that de Valera had made about the arrival of United States units in the six counties. But his references to a 'new Europe' were vague and ambiguous. After the war, he said:

. . . there will be no such thing as complete isolation, political, economic or cultural, Nations will have to live as members of a group or family, with as much individual freedom as members of a family have but with certain duties and responsibilities towards the family. We do not fall clearly to any group, but I believe it is of the utmost importance that we follow our early tradition and turn towards Europe. I believe we can rebuild our country only by belonging to the great European tree, and neither to the British Commonwealth nor to the American sphere . . . Whether we turn to England or the United States we see the god of money, and in the case of America we were sometimes forced to appeal to this god, but all the same it was and always will be an alien god to us . . . Ireland belongs to Europe and England does not belong to it.[8]

Stuart's arboreal comity of nations and his prim disgust at the evils of capitalism did not clarify what this new European system would be like. But the references to 'family', 'duty' and 'responsibility' – key words in the litany of fascism – suggested that he had something more in mind than a mere economic common market. Just over two weeks later, Stuart expatiated to his Irish audience once more, this time on the new 'world Revolution' in which Ireland would be involved. Europeans to whom he had spoken did not want 'the old Europe' back again, he said. They did not want:

. . . another League of Nations, in whose Assemblies one of the few honest speeches ever heard was delivered by Mr de Valera when President. Nor do they want to return to a system whereby international financiers hold sway. We want no more fine-sounding speeches about liberty, equality and fraternity, but warm hearted realism. We want to live at peace under our leaders . . . We must be part of the European whole and learn to see that our good is bound up with the European good.[9]

Stuart was careful to exonerate de Valera in this outburst but he could have left no one in any doubt that the system of government he was expounding was the National Socialist one. The cause he espoused – to 'Irish Nationalists,' as he put it, 'in this hour of crisis' – was anti-democratic.

But Stuart's broadcasts were unexceptionable compared to most of the material about Ireland which emanated from Germany. Throughout the war, the Axis powers and German-controlled radio stations in occupied Europe devoted hundreds of hours of air time to propaganda broadcasts about Ireland. A regular transmission was beamed to Eire in both the English and Irish languages while broadcasts to Britain often contained material directed specifically at the Catholic population of Northern Ireland. In dozens of German broadcasts beamed overseas – to Latin America, South Africa and particularly to India – Eire's neutrality was depicted as a courageous stand against British imperialism, while the efforts of the Northern Ireland Government to crush the IRA were portrayed on the German Home Service and in occupied countries as a graphic example of British ruthlessness and repression. The Stormont authorities were worried that information used in German broadcasts might have been sent by Axis agents in the province, so each week the BBC Monitoring Service furnished Robert Gransden, the Northern Ireland Cabinet Secretary, with transcripts of several dozen transmissions to or about Ireland which originated in Germany, Italy or their satellite stations. Although by 1942 the British had found that there was 'no occasion on which information had been included in the German broadcasts when it was possible to establish the source as an enemy agent',[10] the Stormont Government retained the transcripts, documents which now provide an invaluable index of the propaganda that Germany derived from Ireland's partition.

To Eire, Germany's air waves usually carried a homely blend of encouragement for the country's neutrality, admiration for Gaelic culture, and political commentaries on international events occasionally laced with stern warnings about the evils of communism. The Irish service of German radio was run by Hans Hartmann, the Celtic scholar who had worked under Adolph Mahr in Dublin before the war and who had travelled extensively in Irish-speaking areas of Donegal. Hartmann, who vainly tried to recruit Frank Ryan to his *Redaktion*,[11] was harassed by his superiors – including Mahr – who did not think that his programmes were sufficiently aggressive; Stuart remembers him as 'a gentle, ineffective man' who always claimed that his job involved 'walking on eggs'.[12] Hartmann's broadcasts had a dull, heavy flavour about them together with an unhealthy fixation on the Teutonic purity of Irish racial stock. It was difficult, he told his Irish listeners in June 1943, to think of any two nations with less in common than Ireland and England. The English had:

> . . . never had the slightest regard for the Irish. They never made any attempt to understand the Irish mind; or if they did make the attempt, they never succeeded. England's only object was to establish and maintain her domination over Ireland, and the results for Ireland were misery and subjection . . . On the other hand understanding is possible between Ireland and the continent. The Celtic races came originally from the south of Germany, and although the English came too from the north of Germany, and left the continent to settle in the British Isles much later than the Celts, the Celts, and especially the Irish remained in many ways more faithful to the spirit and traditions of Europe than did the English.[13]

Hartmann, who spoke Irish fluently, tried to inject some hearthside warmth into his transmissions, telling his listeners in November 1943, for instance, that he had 'come to love the Irish people and to have a deep admiration for their ancient Gaelic culture' while staying in the Donegal and Galway villages of Gweedore and Carna. But he felt it necessary to warn the Irish people that 'Bolshevik ideas . . . might find a fertile breeding ground among the Irish workers now in England whose poor living conditions rendered them very susceptible.' Such people, said Hartmann, 'could do grave harm to the native culture on their return.'[14] When Alfred Rosenberg, the Nazi 'philosopher' who was turning eastern Europe into German *Lebensraum*, decreed that property in the occupied Soviet Ukraine should be given to the Russian farmers who had allegedly worked on the land, Hartmann thought that 'you in Ireland will more than any other people be interested in such measures, for it reminds you of the slavery endured by your ancestors on the lands stolen from them by the landlords.'[15]

When the people of the Gaeltacht were not being warned of the ideological contamination of their relatives in Britain or urged to admire the social changes brought about by Dr Rosenberg, they were treated to cultural lectures on Ireland of a peculiarly Germanic kind. 'There is an old custom in Ireland,' Hartmann informed his audience on 5 April 1942:

> . . . to climb to the top of the hills on Easter Sunday to watch the rising of the sun, and the day is still sometimes called the 'Sunday of the Sun'. For many centuries, they no doubt associated the rising of the Easter sun with the coming freedom of Ireland and the banishing of the foreigner from their land. They certainly kept the spirit of freedom alive, although it nearly died under English oppression, and in 1916, on the morning of Easter Sunday, or the 'Sunday of the Sun', they attempted to break the bitter darkness of English tyranny and to reach the light of the sun . . .[16]

This extraordinary passage – Wagner grafted onto Celtic mythology and modern Irish history – was followed by a reading of Pearse's 1916 Proclamation of the Republic. Hartmann had been preceded by Stuart who had talked less rhetorically about the 1916 Rising but had nevertheless drawn the appropriate – and by now familiar – political conclusions. 'Had those few men not thrown down the gauntlet in Dublin,' he said, 'Ireland's position would be very different today . . . The spirit of Easter Week is the one thing which will bring us safely through this crisis. Please God, we shall remain neutral to the end, but if we were to fight it would certainly not be for any so-called ideal. We have had enough of these to make us sick.' For the Irish, said Stuart, there was only one reality: 'our own life on our own soil, freed from the tyranny of money.' The end of the war would restore Ireland's unity, and the country's isolation would 'give way to our taking our place in the great organic European family.'[17]

Germany's appeal to Ireland to join Hitler's New Order was based largely on Ireland's known Catholic hostility to communism. In August 1941 – two months after Germany's invasion of the Soviet Union – a transmission to Eire invited Ireland to fight under a 'common banner' in the war against Bolshevism, a battle in which Ireland – 'the last bulwark of Europe' – could not remain indifferent. Germany was fighting for a spiritual ideal which had been 'for all time a link between Ireland and

Germany'. The broadcaster – it was not Stuart – pointed out that Germans had co-operated on the Shannon hydro-electric scheme and that 'thousands of Irish students came to German colleges and universities'; Ireland's history marked her place 'in the Europe of tomorrow'.[18] An earlier broadcast – probably by Hartmann for it was in the Irish language – announced that 'the Celtic race will come into its own again if England collapses.' The Irish could be rich in a new Europe and: '. . . share the wealth of the world instead of being in constant danger from an English attack for the purposes of regaining the ports. Everyone willing to collaborate in the foundation of the New Order which is at present being set up will be heartily welcomed. This Order means the freeing of Europe from the tyranny of England . . .'[19]

The destruction of Germany, the Irish were told, would mean the spread of Bolshevism 'through Europe and throughout Ireland'.[20] The German struggle on the eastern front was also presented in these terms and when Field Marshal Friedrich Paulus's Sixth Army was annihilated at Stalingrad in January 1943 Hartmann asked the Irish to admire the German 'heroes of Stalingrad' because 'the bravery of these men was saving Europe from Bolshevism'.[21] Francis Stuart was moved to tell his listeners that:

> . . . if I were a German I would be proud to belong to a nation which could produce such men. As it is, I am glad to be among them . . . Besides speaking to Ireland about Germany, I speak to Berlin University students every week about Ireland. Today I spoke of Liam Lynch and Cathal Brugha, of Yeats and Synge and Pearse, for a nation's soul is revealed in its soldiers and poets. I would refer again to Stalingrad. The Irish would understand what the German people felt. This has moved Germany more than any other event of the war, for while such victories as the fall of Paris might be attributed to the perfection of the German war machine, this is a triumph of flesh and blood.[22]

Stuart's statement was military nonsense; Stalingrad was a German disaster by any reckoning, not a triumph. But it was not by chance that Pearse's name was linked – in however remote a way – with the slaughter in Russia. For Stuart's statement contained within it the notion of victory through defeat, of the blood sacrifice, of a redemption through 'flesh and blood' that Irish republicans would immediately understand. Nor was Stuart being hypocritical in his sympathy for Germany. He recalled after the war that he 'hated the insufferable attitude of Germans when they were on top but a defeat like Stalingrad often aroused emotion in me.'[23]

Hartmann's talks were less in tune with Irish republican ideology or indeed with Irish emotions. He attacked the British but he also lauded Japanese victories over the United States, successes which many Irish men and women – with their Irish-American family ties – would not have admired. In January 1942, for example, Hartmann – speaking in Irish – described how 'Japanese aeroplanes swooped down from the skies' over

Pearl Harbor, and 'before the American soldiers knew what was happening, the greatest part of the American navy had already been destroyed.'[24] Hartmann was apparently forced by his superiors to include these references to Japanese prowess[25] which probably accounts for the fact that he never spoke of American defeats without mentioning British setbacks as well. He ended such commentaries with the invocation: 'God bless and save Ireland.'[26] Less important talks were sometimes given by 'Pat O'Brien', the pen name of John Francis O'Reilly who was to parachute into Eire in 1943. His Irish accent was obviously preferable to a German voice but his scripts lacked both Hartmann's confidence and Stuart's emotion. In early 1942, 'O'Brien' spoke of Allied pressure on neutral Portugal but forgot to draw any parallel between Portugal and Eire.[27]

Britain was regularly condemned by all the Irish service broadcasters. They constantly recalled England's history of repression in Ireland and frequently alluded to Britain's supposed spiritual bankruptcy, a destitution which was, of course, unfavourably compared to the flowering of Gaelic culture on the other side of the Irish Sea. 'Civilisation as boasted of by the Anglo-Saxon powers,' German radio told its Irish listeners in April 1942, 'is typified by hire purchase, tinned foods and wireless sets.' This odd assertion – which was a little hard on the Irish who after all needed a wireless themselves to listen to Messrs Hartmann and Stuart – was followed by the claim that 'present-day Englishmen have forgotten their sweet singers of past centuries.'[28] Irishmen, needless to say, had not. Hartmann's *Redaktion* often resorted to nightly readings from Wolfe Tone's diaries; another popular feature was Tone's speech to the military court in which he proclaimed that the bond between England and Ireland was detrimental to Irish prosperity.[29] More frequently still, the Irish service of German radio transmitted details of British killings in the Irish War of Independence. Typical of these was a transmission in November, 1941, which began:

> Flashback to British terrorism in Ireland. Exactly 21 years ago, British Crown forces waging war against the civil population of Ireland shot dead a six-year old Irish girl, Annie O'Neill of Charlemont Avenue, Dublin City. Black and Tans patrolling the city in lorries shot and fired indiscriminately . . .[30]

These items were broadcast daily for weeks at a time, each referring to different incidents but all ending with the same formula:

> Twenty-one years ago, the British were prepared to stoop to the lowest forms of brutality. They did not care because they thought they were triumphant. Today, they would rather have these atrocities forgotten, because they are now being beaten and fear retribution.[31]

The 'flashbacks' were discontinued in 1944, presumably because no one any longer thought that the British were being beaten, let alone fearing retribution. They were obviously intended to counter any sympathy the Irish may have felt for Britain's struggle against Germany, a theme which ran through many of the programmes put out by Hartmann's service. 'When we read of the sinking of British vessels by German submarines,' the Irish were told at the end of 1942, 'let us remember the battering in of little cottages in the mountains of Donegal by the English, and the turning of poor Irish families out onto the roadside.'[32]

The Germans always emphasised the threat of a British seizure of the Treaty ports, suggesting after the American entry into the war in December 1941 that Churchill might use the United States to occupy the harbours. It was a shrewd piece of propaganda made no less credible by the fact that it contained a considerable layer of truth. England, the German radio announced:

> . . . would actually prefer that one of her allies should do the dirty work. What ally would do England's dirty work in this case? England remembers that the USA has a large Irish population, who were forced to emigrate there owing to the criminal effects of English policy. England now thinks that were America to occupy Southern Ireland, the native Irish would not object because of their relatives in the States . . . It is all part of the neutrality game as played by England. Were the Irish to object to this skilful procedure, they would, of course, be in the wrong, since anyone not participating in England's war is immoral and suicidal . . . The only question that remains, therefore, is whether the neutral states concerned in Mr Churchill's and Mr Roosevelt's plans prefer to regard their neutrality as the wholesome and holy thing it is, or whether they take the English view and regard themselves as immoral and suicidal.[33]

For their part, the British did not at first regard Irish neutrality as particularly immoral, and Britain's own propaganda was initially at pains to portray Eire as a small neutral like Holland or Belgium, ready to defend herself against German aggression. The nearest equivalent of Hartmann's organisation was not the BBC, which avoided the kind of crude propaganda in which the German radio indulged, but the newsreels which were produced twice a week to accompany feature films at United Kingdom cinemas. The archives of Pathé News demonstrate clearly that until 1941 – when the Treaty ports had become of critical importance in the Battle of the Atlantic – Eire was generally represented as a nation which was behaving with wisdom and common sense. British newsreels of the time adopted a patronising attitude towards almost every country which was not an ally in the war but it was obviously hoped that as time went on, Eire would take her place in the fight against Germany. In June 1940, for example, Pathé produced a 50-second newsreel on the pro-neutrality rally addressed by the three Irish party leaders at College Green in Dublin; but the film's commentary implied that the crowds were supporting Irish Government defence measures against Germany.[34] Footage of de Valera,

Cosgrave and Norton taking their seats on the rostrum in front of the old Irish Parliament building was accompanied by a script which stated that: '. . . this is the symbol of Eire's unity as she faces the danger of aggression. Britain and Eire may not always have seen eye to eye in the past, but today all that is forgotten in the common danger.'[35]

Cinema audiences were told that de Valera had called 'on the manhood of Eire to join in her defence' and that Cosgrave appealed for unity 'for the lives of our people and the liberties they enjoy'.[36] But at no point in the film was it pointed out that the rally was supporting *neutrality* and that Eire's defence was directed against British as well as German invasion. Two weeks later, Pathé produced another newsreel which gave an equally distorted picture of Irish defence policy. The film showed Irish troops manning the guns of the Treaty ports, and an Irish Army Air Corps Hudson flying over Howth Head; but the commentary maintained the pretence that this was part of Eire's preparations to defend herself solely against Germany:

> Eire is on guard. The Nazi press has started an attack on Eire, accusing her of not observing strict neutrality. Eire is not being fooled. So she is redoubling her defensive measures . . . Eire is ready with her military answer if the Germans attempt any sort of aggression against her. Eire is on guard.[37]

But Pathé News at least showed no hostility towards Eire in 1940. The company produced a 60-second film later in the year which commented approvingly on the work of the Irish Naval Service in mining Dublin Bay.[38] When German aircraft bombed the Irish capital in January 1941, Pathé was ready with a 35-second newsreel that showed damage in Rathdown Park, Dublin; the commentary spoke of how 'Nazi raiders deliberately unloaded their bombs on these houses in Eire' and asked: 'Is this another case of Germany seeking to threaten Nazi "protection" to our neutral state?'[39] The fact that several officers in the Irish Army believed that the bombs *were* dropped intentionally did not mitigate the illusion that the British felt they could regard Eire as 'their' neutral state. But this was nothing compared to what was to come.

The British Government's desperation at the shipping losses in the Atlantic and its impatience at Eire's continued neutrality percolated through to the newsreel companies a few weeks later. So when the Germans again bombed Dublin in May 1941 Pathé News not only used the incident to emphasise German bestiality but also to point an accusing and derogatory finger at Eire herself. Over film of dozens of wrecked houses in Dublin's North Strand and of a corpse being carried from the rubble, cinema audiences were told that:

> The Germans respect nothing. Latest evidence of this is their bombing of – neutral Eire! Nazi planes dropped their loads of death over a wide area of

Dublin, killing and injuring more than a hundred people. This is not the first Nazi air raid on Eire. There were three such 'incidents' in January but not so serious. The Eire Government has protested to Berlin against the wanton attack on their professed neutrality – but unfortunately protests will not bring back the dead or heal the wounds of the injured! Maybe this is the price that Eire has to pay for – sitting on the fence![40]

The logic of this 45-second film was somewhat questionable. If the price of neutrality was to be bombed by Germany, the cost of joining the war on the Allied side was surely not going to be lower. But the gratuitous tone of the commentator's script was deliberately offensive, with its suggestion that Eire had adopted her policy of neutrality – 'sitting on the fence' – out of cowardice rather than necessity. This was not an accusation that the newsreels had made about Eire in 1940 when her neutrality seemed ready to dissolve in Britain's favour.

Infinitely more damaging, however, was a 10-minute news film made by Paramount in 1942 that sounded – and looked – as if it was intended to prepare the British public for an Allied invasion of Eire. Its theme was the Royal Navy's need for the Treaty ports but it contained some of the most prejudiced material used about Ireland and the Irish in any film of the period. As propaganda, it was powerful and dangerous. The newsreel opened with footage of a British convoy in the Atlantic, over which an English voice announced that 'Atlantic convoys entering the high danger zone often pay a terrible price for the centuries' old Anglo-Irish quarrel. Eire, remaining inflexibly neutral, reaffirms that British men-of-war shall not use the Irish bases in the Battle of the Atlantic.' The commentary outlined the strategic advantages of the Treaty ports and introduced Captain Bernard Ackworth, a naval writer who warned that 'while the loss of the use of the southern Irish ports is a severe handicap to the Navy in its ceaseless life-and-death struggle in the Atlantic, their acquisition by Germany would be a disaster. Indeed, we could never tolerate the presence of German warships – or aircraft – working from these advanced Atlantic bases . . .' Ackworth's assessment was a fair enough reflection of British Government policy but the film then reverted to a rather astonishing commentary:

Speaking from Dublin, with such popularity as makes him virtually a dictator – not only in the Dail but throughout the country – Prime Minister de Valera is unmoved by British persuasion. Take good stock of this man de Valera – never did any man's speeches more faithfully reflect his character. He has what the Irish prize more than other peoples – a long memory. Merely to look at him is to see that more vividly than most of us recall yesterday. He remembers Cromwell, who put his countrymen to the sword – a mere three hundred years ago. Equally, he remembers that after the 1916 rebellion, he was England's prisoner – under sentence of death! Though he escaped that penalty, de Valera took no part in the 1920 settlement with the hereditary enemy, England. Not till those other Irishmen who did negotiate the Treaty were removed from the political stage – Griffiths [sic], O'Higgins, Michael Collins, the last named by assassination – did de Valera return.[41]

This was an extraordinary passage; to accuse de Valera of being a dictator because he was popular was to deny the validity of the democratic system by which he was elected. To talk about the 'long memory' of the Irish may have had considerable justification, but even a short memory should have advised the film's makers that the Anglo-Irish Treaty was signed in 1921 – not 1920 – that Kevin O'Higgins was not one of the Treaty negotiators, that the chairman of the Treaty delegation was named Griffith and not 'Griffiths', and that Collins was not the only one of the three Irishmen mentioned to be assassinated; O'Higgins was shot dead in Dublin in 1927. The newsreel commentary continued with little more respect for accuracy than it had already shown. Since de Valera came to power, it said:

> . . . the peasants are with him to a man. This very green and lovely land breeds a race as different from the English as Englishmen differ from Italians. Most of Eire's three millions wrest from the soil a living which would be poverty this side the Irish Sea. But, unlike the English, they do not generally want more than they have. In many ways, the Irish peasants – sharing their cottage with the pig, living on potatoes – are freer than the English artisan. The Irish outlook is less material . . . The Irishman is little interested in what the rest of the world calls progress. Offer him the material things of life and you may leave him unmoved. Appeal to his imagination, his soul, his sense of injustice – and he is your man! By temperament, he is the born Roman Catholic – no country is more firmly attached to this religion. And as the Vatican seldom frowns on those who dislike Protestant England, the priest in Ireland is wholeheartedly behind de Valera.[42]

Eire was a poor country and there were still cottagers in the far west of the country who kept farm animals in their homes, but to imply that the majority of Irish were 'peasants' who lived in these circumstances – as the German Army's pictorial invasion guidebook had also coincidentally suggested – was particularly insulting. The sectarian remarks about the Vatican were also surprising since it was scarcely in Britain's interest to foster hatred towards Catholics either in Ireland or Britain. But at least the commentary did acknowledge, in however grudging a way, that most of Eire's population did support de Valera's neutrality policy by being 'with him to a man'. Nor would de Valera himself have objected to the idea that the Irish were less materialistic than the English. But the film then proceeded to show its contempt for the Irish Army:

> Even Eire's pocket army – 7,000 strong – reflects anti-English bias. Their drill is nine-tenths American. Their higher officers learned the art of war in US

339

military academies. Though equipment was bought in Britain when unobtainable elsewhere, the German-style helmet saves them from the embarrassment of looking British. The gallant 7,000 have read that there's a war on. Eire, they declare, will be defended against whoever attacks her – no names, no parachutes. The IRA – a body not always helpful to the de Valera Government – and other volunteers are doing Home Guard duty; less to stop two million Nazis dropping from the sky than to raise Cain should a British destroyer stray within territorial limits.[43]

This kind of misrepresentation bordered on the absurd. The figure of 7000 represented the strength of the Irish Army in 1939; by 1942 – when Paramount made their film – Irish regular and volunteer troops numbered around 250,000[44] and their German-style helmets, with which Britain's Norwegian allies also happened to be equipped, had long ago been replaced by helmets of a British model. The LDF certainly included members of the old IRA – so did the regular Army – but it was ridiculous to suggest that the embittered young men of Stephen Hayes's movement were involved in the Irish 'Home Guard'.

If it was true, however, that 'no Irishman who had visions of Dublin blasted overnight into a Coventry or Rotterdam opposed the Government's desire to keep its head in the sand,' the film found that Northern Ireland was 'one hundred per cent in the war'. The commentary assured cinema audiences that the province was making:

> . . . a fine contribution to the Allied effort. The famous linen industry is also working far beyond its peacetime maximum capacity. Because Ulstermen are wealthier than the southern Irish, more enterprising, better businessmen, they refuse to be governed by Dublin. Ulster will not allow the economic tail to wag the dog. Eire, with its population of little more than three millions, not only turns a blind eye and a deaf ear to the world war but is apparently indifferent to what might happen to her if the Germans won.[45]

How Northern Ireland could be 'one hundred per cent in the war' when its population had not been conscripted was something that the film did not explain; and it totally ignored the fact that one third of the province – the Catholic, largely nationalist population – looked to Dublin rather than Belfast as its capital, and had no particular desire to be in the war at all. The film, with its patronising, 'English' attitude towards Ireland, concluded by declaring that:

> . . . the time has come to say to Eire: 'Forget your trouble with England – at least till after the war.' Eire like the rest of us will go under if the Nazis win. Don't let history say that de Valera unknowingly helped Hitler to fill the bloodbath of the New Order.[46]

Paramount must have been well aware how objectionable this newsreel would be to the people of Eire, many thousands of whom were fighting in the British services. Its grotesque caricature of the Irish was little different in attitude or substance to those cartoons which appeared in nineteenth-century England, portraying the Catholics of Ireland as dissolute and ignorant. Indeed, when the commentary compared the 'enterprising' businessmen of Northern Ireland with their counterparts in Eire, the film showed children playing amid rubbish beside a block of tenements in a poor district of Dublin. It propagated the idea that the Irish were unclean, weak, idle and cowardly, that their religion was demeaning and their political motives naïve and selfish. The script's cynical – almost racial – abuse had something in common with the propaganda of the Nazis; it was both provocative and deeply disturbing.

Nothing like this appeared again although newsreels continued to berate Eire for her neutrality and to repeat the rumours that Dublin was a German espionage centre. When the British stopped all communication between Eire and the rest of the world before the D-Day landings, Pathé News told its audiences that 'Mr de Valera's neutrality permits German agents to establish themselves in an easy position for the collecting of vital information.' In March 1944, a newsreel showed RUC men checking the identity of passengers on the Dublin–Belfast train because, according to the commentary, 'Germany and Japan are no respecters of neutrality – slipping their spies over the border was far too easy.' The idea that Japanese agents had been able to enter Northern Ireland without anyone observing their rather foreign appearance was a new one, but the film was apparently convinced that the new checks on Eire would 'put an end to the situation where we work while others peep.'[47]

The Northern Ireland Government took what opportunity it could in the newsreels to endorse the province's loyalty to Britain although it did not always do so with much confidence. 'As you know,' Basil Brooke reminded his audiences in one early newsreel, 'we are part of the United Kingdom.' He described how Northern Ireland's engineering and textile industries were helping the war effort, and commented that 'Ulstermen, I'm glad to say, have played a distinguished part in the fighting in [sic] the sea, on land and in the air. But we are conscious of room for expansion . . .'[48] Late in 1943, the Stormont authorities collaborated in making a film for the British Ministry of Supply which was to show the province's factories turning out guns, ammunition, parachutes and military clothing. But the completed film – *Ulster at Arms* – began with footage of the Stormont Parliament building and the statue of Carson in front of it, prompting the commentator to refer to the loyalty of the province, a loyalty which he said was 'more freely expressed here than in any other part of the British Commonwealth'.[49] Once again, no indication was given that approximately one third of the population did not share this senti-ment. But it was significant that at this stage of the war, the British authorities chose to cut from the film a reference to Irish neutrality and the

Treaty ports which, in the words of a Northern Ireland civil servant, 'rather startled everyone, as it was quite unexpected.'[50]

Needless to say, the Axis nations did not exercise much sensitivity towards Northern Ireland. When Thomas Williams was hanged in September 1942, the Germans broadcast news of the subsequent violence to most European countries, including the Soviet Union. Russian listeners were told that a gun battle between the IRA and 'Anglo-American forces' had cost so many Allied lives that British and American troops had been withdrawn from the Irish border.[51] French listeners were informed that the British authorities in Belfast had declared 'a state of siege' in Northern Ireland[52] while Spaniards who tuned to Radio Rome's Spanish service heard a commentary by Hugo Andrea on the alleged iniquities of British rule in the six counties. It was not surprising, he said, 'if some Irish patriots will not bow to the idea of a subjugated Ireland . . . Is it such a crime to be a lover of liberty and fight for it? What about the Maltese, the Egyptians, the Arabs, the Indians and so on? They are told that they are fighting for their liberty.'[53] Italians were informed by Rome's Home Service that the RUC had batoned Catholic women as they recited prayers for Williams.[54] 'The picture of the Irish capital in mourning,' Radio Paris told its audience in occupied France, 'constitutes a moving protest against the execution of the young nationalist Thomas Williams.'[55] The German Home Service put out daily reports on the battles supposedly going on in Northern Ireland between 'Irish freedom fighters and British police'[56] as a result of the execution of 'the young hero'.[57] According to the Finnish Home Service, British tanks 'cruised the streets' of Belfast dispersing crowds.[58]

The Axis powers displayed no parallel sympathy for IRA men executed in Eire on the orders of de Valera's Government, and when a Garda officer was shot dead by the IRA in Dublin in September 1942, Italian Radio attributed his murder to 'British espionage agents'.[59] De Valera himself was never criticised. On his sixtieth birthday in 1942, the Germans told their English listeners that his policy was 'characterised by the determination and skill of a great personality'[60] while German Radio's American audience was informed that 'all Europe recalled . . . how this great Irishman warned the world against the menace of Bolshevism in 1934, at the time when the Soviet Union was taken into the dying League of Nations.'[61] Although he had no control over them, these broadcasts could hardly have endeared de Valera to the Allies. He could not have welcomed a Japanese radio transmission in March 1944 in which Subhas Chandra Bose, the leader of the anti-British Indian National Army that was fighting in alliance with the Japanese in Burma, communicated his 'profound admiration for the hard fight of President de Valera and the Irish Government for the maintenance of neutrality'. Bose, a Bengali educated at Calcutta and Cambridge, had proclaimed the 'Provisional Government of Free India' in 1943, and declared that 'in the history of our fight against

British imperialism, there is perhaps no other struggle which influenced us so much, and for which we have had so much sympathy, as that of the brave Irish nation for their birthright of liberty. Having been a close student of Irish history, and having been in Eire myself, I know that this sympathy is fully reciprocated on the Irish side . . .' Bose noted that the Dail had discussed the possible recognition of his provisional government. 'I know for a fact,' he said, 'that the symapthy of the entire Irish nation is with us in our struggle against our common foe and, having had the privilege of knowing President de Valera and his Cabinet Ministers personally, I am fully aware that in their attitude toward India there is no difference whatsoever between the Government and the people of Eire.'[62]*

The obvious parallels between nationalist resistance to British rule in India and Irish demands for a British withdrawal from Northern Ireland were not lost on the Germans. Their 'Free India Radio', broadcasting in English to the Indian sub-continent, regularly referred to events in Ireland and drew comparisons between the anti-British struggle in the two countries. 'Just as the Indian princes are the greatest allies of British imperialism,' Indian listeners were told in 1944, 'so in Ireland, Ulster is the best ally of Britain.'[64] Since Britain was trying to regain control over the small Irish nation, 'Free India Radio' reported in December 1943, 'it is not surprising that Churchill is trying to force Eire also into slavery, not satisfied with exploiting Northern Ireland for the British imperialist war.'[65] The British blockade of Eire in April 1944 was considered a 'piece of characteristic arrogance' on the part of a nation which claimed it was 'fighting for democracy and the freedom of small nations'.[66] Broadcasting in Parsee, 'Free India Radio' spoke of de Valera's protests at British claims that U-boats had been refuelled in Eire. 'Similarly in India,' said the radio, 'British propaganda makes a desperate attempt to convert neutral states into belligerent nations.'[67]† But if German broadcasts to India could employ the Irish anti-partition struggle as proof of British perfidy, so India's experiences of British rule could be deplored in transmissions to Eire. This palindrome technique was frequently applied by German radio. 'Ireland and India are akin in their relations to England,' 'Pat O'Brien' told his Irish listeners in 1941. 'Both have been robbed and have fought desperately and persistently for independence. In the eighteenth

---

* When Robert Gransden, the Northern Ireland Cabinet Secretary, read the transcript of this broadcast, he informed two of his colleagues that they might find it 'interesting and perhaps useful!'[63] Bose thought he could follow the Irish example of setting up a provisional government in opposition to British rule but it did him little good; his Indian National Army lost every battle it fought against the British. Bose died in an air crash in August 1945.

† This was presumably a reference to Afghanistan which had declared its neutrality at the start of the war but had been forced by Allied pressure in 1941 to expel all Axis nationals who did not have diplomatic status.[68]

343

century, the Ulster wool industry was ruined. Identical measures were taken in India to stifle her industries . . . Recurrent famines followed. Ireland was turned into a charnel house during the artificially created famine of 1845–1848 . . . India was subject to terrible periodical famines which swept away millions of the population.'[69]

Anti-Catholic discrimination in Northern Ireland provided a focus for almost all the Axis radio stations that spoke to or about Ireland. A programme beamed to Eire by Rome Radio in 1942, ostensibly celebrating the 350th anniversary of the Salamanca Royal College of Irish Noblemen, remarked that religious discrimination was still alive in 'the British-occupied part of Ireland' and that 'the actions of the Orangist mobs in Belfast against the Catholics show that the fundamental outlook of the British bigots has not changed.'[70] Hartmann's radio service could be more specific and occasionally directed its programmes at Northern Ireland's Catholic population, although it sometimes chose to do so in such 'pucka' English that its effect must have been blunted. When Sir Knox Cunningham was defeated as Unionist candidate in the 1943 West Belfast by-election, for example, German radio's Irish service addressed nationalists in the city:

> Good for West Belfast! It is a heartening thing to observe the crushing defeat of the Unionist candidate . . . Coming as it does at a time when the cocks of the North are preening their gold braid and brass buttons in that inimitable manner that only a buck jingo will have, it is good to see one of them come a cropper . . .[71]

Whether the Catholics of west Belfast appreciated this remarkable mixture of public school slang and cricket commentary enthusiasm is a moot point. But the remainder of the programme included a fairly accurate catalogue of nationalist grievances. The radio claimed that among the factors that had contributed to Knox Cunningham's defeat was:

> . . . the demonstrative [sic] execution of a young man called Williams . . . There have been numberless arrests and house searches. The gaols are overflowing with republican prisoners, many of them held without charge. There was the arrest and internment for many months of the Nationalist member of the Northern Parliament, Mr Cahir Healy.* There was the attempt to introduce compulsory conscription . . .[72]

Since it emanated from a nation which practised mass murder on an unprecedented scale and in which imprisonment without trial was a mild form of punishment, the broadcast – which also stated that the RUC had

---

* Healy, who represented South Fermanagh, was arrested in 1941 and interned at Brixton for two years. Axis radio stations gave wide publicity to the nationalist demonstrations held to protest his imprisonment.

committed 'acts of indescribable terrorism and butchery' – was a piece of pre-eminent hypocrisy. But it was aimed at a volatile and discontented minority whose members – emotionally and sometimes physically antagonistic towards the Northern Ireland authorities – might well be responsive to its message.

The renewed proposal to introduce conscription in the province in 1941 provided the Germans with some of their most potent propaganda. A speech by Frank Aiken was given wide publicity on German radio, which quoted him as saying that the enforced enlistment of the six counties' population would be 'an unheard-of crime'.[73] In a broadcast to Asia and Northern America, the Germans said that Aiken had called the proposal 'a monstrous scandal'.[74] African listeners were told of anti-conscription demonstrations in Belfast,[75] and when the London *News Chronicle* called the idea 'frivolous', Axis stations trumpeted this over the air to France, Holland and Turkey.[76] Hartmann pronounced personally on the issue, telling followers of his Irish programme that he hoped Irishmen would 'have their reward for their bravery and steadfastness.'[77] Infinitely more sinister was a transmission to Ireland that urged Irish conscripts to desert the British Army and cross to the German lines if they were sent to the war. Catholic listeners were told that the British 'cannot make you fight for the continued occupation of your own corner of Ireland.' If conscription was introduced:

> . . . you have only to wait for a suitable opportunity and go over to the Germans . . . you have simply to wait patiently until you are actually at the Front and then, having arranged a suitable plan amongst yourselves, even if you only happen to be two or three – for you will probably be split up among different regiments – you can go over to the Germans or the Italians. And I can promise you that you will be received as friends as soon as you have explained who you are, for the case of the Six Counties is well known here in Germany . . .[76]

Potential deserters were assured that they would be 'treated with every consideration both during the war and as long after it as you would have to remain away from your homes.' The programme ended with a final reminder that if conscription was enforced, 'you have still the power to do as much harm to those who coerce you as by actual fighting in the streets of Belfast . . . If the so-called Northern Government think they can turn Ulster nationalists into British soldiers, they will certainly be shown their mistake.'[79]

Robert Gransden, who scrupulously read his way through the hundreds of transcripts that were sent to the Stormont Cabinet, placed a cross beside this passage, as he did with all material that seemed to be damaging or suspicious. At the beginning of the war, the Northern Ireland Government wanted to reply over the BBC to German broadcasts which they thought particularly misleading. Gransden was told by one of his civil servants that a transmission from Hamburg on 5 March 1940 had quoted an article in the *Irish Press* which contained 'complete misrepresentations of matters affecting Ulster' and that the Northern Ireland Government had not been given the opportunity to respond to this.[80] But the Cabinet Secretary decided that 'the *Irish Press* would only continue their attacks with still more venom if they found we were getting a reply over and the result would be a continuance "ad nauseam" of the arguments from Eire of which we have heard so much. I think we should keep an eye on developments.'[81] When Italian Radio claimed in April 1940 that the RUC had fired on nationalists in Belfast and that the Craigavon Bridge in Londonderry had been blown up, the Stormont authorities complained that the BBC Monitoring Service had failed to record the broadcasts, which had been heard in Belfast and Dublin.[82] Many of the German news reports were distilled from Swedish newspapers whose correspondents sometimes reported from Northern Ireland, and Gransden concluded in 1942 that several recent German broadcasts had 'all the appearance of having emanated from the visiting journalists of the Foreign Press Association.'[83]

Had he realised how ramshackle an organisation Hartmann's Irish service really was, Gransden might have spent less time considering the origin of the German reports. When the radio studios were moved from Berlin to Luxemburg later in the war, Helmut Clissmann's wife Elisabeth was called in to advise on a 'black' Irish broadcasting station which the Germans were proposing to open. The announcers would pretend that they were transmitting from within Eire, in much the same way as the German 'New British Broadcasting Station' claimed that it was operating from inside Britain. Elisabeth Clissmann dismissed the idea as ludicrous but at the same time discovered that the German studios had almost no up to date information on Ireland. The girl who was supposed to monitor Radio Eireann, the Irish state broadcasting service, told her that since no one bothered to read her reports, she usually marked her reception chart 'poor' and failed to record the contents of the Irish news bulletins. When Elisabeth Clissmann was asked for the location of the Bishop of Kilmore's diocese, she found that the studio staff did not even possess a map of Ireland.[84] Hartmann's *Redaktion* was paid occasional visits by Dr Hans Otto Wagner, an Abwehr functionary who had originally specialised in Flemish and Breton minority questions.[85] When the grievances of these two communities were no longer of any use to the Reich, Wagner was transferred to the French Canadian section of German radio where he condemned the evils of Britain's involvement in Ireland to a minority that was far enough away to avoid Germany's influence.[86] William Joyce, the best-known of all the Irish-born broadcasters in Germany, used to put out his programmes to Britain from studios one floor above Hartmann's section but he so disliked the Irish that he never came into their offices. He worked almost exclusively in the English section and rarely referred to

Ireland, although he was remembered in Eire for some disparaging remarks about the Irish Naval Service's old gunboat *Muirchu*.[87]

But Eire was never deliberately insulted by Axis propaganda outlets. Whenever de Valera restated his country's determination to remain neutral, German radio reported this without comment.[88] If Irish actions could be interpreted as anti-communist, all well and good. Thus Radio Paris quoted the right-wing and very Catholic Dublin newspaper *The Standard* when the journal warned of 'the catastrophic consequences which an Anglo-Bolshevik victory would entail for Europe'.[89] By the same token Belgian transmissions praised Eire's 'truly courageous and independent attitude' in refusing to hand over to the Soviet Union several ships belonging to the Baltic States which were in Irish ports when the Russians absorbed Latvia, Estonia and Lithuania in 1940; by her action, Eire had 'adhered, to a certain extent, to the anti-Bolshevik front'.[90] Sympathy was extended to Eire when the United States refused to supply her with arms; 'in the eyes of Roosevelt,' Italians were told by their national radio, 'Eire is not considered as a democracy on the same level as the robber government of Chiang-Kai-shek [sic] or Stalin's Bolshevik regime.'[91]

The Germans were shrewd enough to realise that when strikes broke out in the Belfast shipyards in early 1944 – during the build-up to the Allied invasion of Europe – appeals to the largely Protestant workforce should be addressed through the English rather than the Irish section of German radio. But they totally failed to comprehend that the shipyard men – while they were led by trade unionists – were mostly Orangemen with an ingrained distrust of left-wing or communist propaganda. So after announcing that 'twenty thousand workers' had downed tools in Belfast after the strike spread to the aircraft industry,[92] the Germans handed their propaganda campaign over to one of their 'black' stations, 'Workers Challenge Radio', which pretended that it was run by communists and broadcasting secretly from within the United Kingdom. 'The trouble in Belfast shipyards and factories came at the right moment, but there must be many more such strikes,' the 'Workers Challenge Weekly Newsreel' urged its supposedly revolutionary Protestants at Harland and Wolff. 'The chance to set up a socialist government is here, workers. Decision action [sic] is all that is needed to smash the already tottering capitalists. And don't you think about those stinking lies which the bosses' propaganda has been putting up . . .'[93] This ineffective nonsense was taken up two weeks later by 'Radio National', another German 'black' radio, which also mischievously warned that German agents had been able to 'pass on the whole of the invasion plans' by telephone from Belfast to Dublin.[94]

The Belfast strike broadcasts were in many ways typical of German propaganda about Ireland; they caught hold of some popular grievance and played on it, but they generally failed to take account of the underlying prejudices and feelings of Irish men and women on both sides of the border. The radio propaganda reflected what the Germans wanted to see in Ireland rather than the reality. Thus the IRA – which Goertz's experiences had already proved to be weak and unreliable – was credited with enormous feats of arms against British and American troops. Catholic nationalist opposition to the Stormont Government was rightly regarded as a source of disaffection but its power was grossly exaggerated; British tanks never cruised the streets of Belfast because the RUC were perfectly capable of breaking up uncoordinated riots in the city. Appreciating the anti-British sentiments of many people in Eire, the Germans spoke of English moral collapse, disregarding Hempel's advice to avoid anti-English propaganda on the radio. Broadcasting to a neutral country which had many thousands of its nationals working in Britain or serving in her armed forces required a defter hand than this.

To some extent, the Germans – or, more specifically, the Nazis – grafted their own world-view onto Irish politics, and it was in this context that they felt free to indulge their anti-semitic instincts in front of the Irish. In 1943, for instance, Hartmann's Irish service claimed that Harry Midgley – MacDermott's successor as Northern Ireland Minister of Public Security – was 'concerned about the well-being of alien Jews who have infiltrated from England.' So far, the radio said:

> . . . the people of the Six Counties just don't like the Jews who have come to live among them and on them, during the past five or six years. They experience a healthy instinct of repulsion every time they see one. Up to now, they have not sought to link up the Jews with the inexplicable shortage of certain commodities which forces the people of the Six Counties to patronise the black market – nor have they realised that the black market is a Jewish-run racket which thrives on sometimes real and sometimes artificial shortages . . .[95]

This poisonous broadcast was directed to listeners in Eire who were told that since their own country was neutral and therefore suffered fewer shortages than Belfast, it held out 'little attraction for Britain's swarming refugee Jews'.[96] Anti-semitism and racialist propaganda was an essential part of most German broadcasts in Europe although it had previously been restrained in transmissions to Ireland.* But an almost equally nauseous bulletin on the German radio's English service in 1944 announced that 'a company has been founded in Belfast for the exploitation of unoccupied house property. Its promoters are Jews who prefer the climate of North England [sic] to that of South England . . . The Jews in the UK are

---

* German home stations had allowed themselves an outburst of racialist abuse when American troops arrived in Northern Ireland in 1942. A programme from the German studios in Luxemburg commented that a Jewish rabbi among the US Army chaplains in the six counties 'was seen proudly strutting about in his uniform with a Star of David on his sleeve.'[97] A radio bulletin for German troops in occupied Norway reported in July 1942 that 'further detachments of Roosevelt's Upholders of Culture in the form of nigger troops have landed in Northern Ireland, which is still oppressed by Britain.'[98]

successfully endeavouring to turn war conditions to their own financial advantage.'[99] What effect this sort of race hatred was supposed to have on the Protestant burghers of Belfast is unclear, but the city had never experienced an outbreak of anti-semitism against its small Jewish community either before or during the war.

This kind of propaganda never came from the Irish broadcasters although Stuart continued to work for Hartmann's *Redaktion* until 1944. He had himself belatedly discerned the truth about the Nazi regime but it took the arrest and execution of two personal friends to teach him that the 'super-dissident' he had once admired in fact controlled a ruthless police state. Stuart had befriended Harold and Libertas Schulze-Boysen, an aristocratic and rather Bohemian couple who rejected both Nazism and communism. Unknown to Stuart, Harold Schulze-Boysen was a leader of the *Rote Kapelle* – the Red Orchestra – which controlled a vast Russian espionage network within the German military establishment and Government ministries. When Stuart heard that both Schulze-Boysen and his wife had disappeared and had later been murdered in the Gestapo headquarters in Berlin, he was deeply shocked. The Gestapo found his own home telephone number in one of Schulze-Boysen's notebooks and turned up at his flat one morning to question him about the couple but they left satisfied that he knew nothing about the *Rote Kapelle*.[100]

Stuart had already seen evidence of the Nazi system in operation when he travelled to occupied Poland with Clissmann and Hoven, who were visiting prisoner-of-war camps to find Irish-born soldiers who would join a German-sponsored Irish Brigade. He saw German officials bullying Poles at road checkpoints, screaming abuse at them as they demanded identity papers. Although these 'petty persecutions' did not even begin to reflect the atrocious treatment which the Nazis meted out to the Poles, they nevertheless left a strong impression on Stuart. Back in Berlin, he was asked to write anti-Russian speeches for Hartmann's *Redaktion* which he refused to do; then his telephone began to ring at odd hours of the night and anonymous voices at the other end of the line threatened him with being 'sent to a camp'.[101]

Yet Stuart continued to broadcast. His early, passionate style of monologue had gone. In 1942, he had felt able to talk of Germany's 'revolt' against unemployment and capitalism. 'Because Germany demanded the restoration of Danzig,' he had told his Irish listeners, 'Irishmen can now visualise the return of Belfast to Ireland.'[102] But by 1943, Stuart sounded maudlin and sentimental, announcing on Saint Patrick's Day that he would like to forget the war at a hurley match at Dublin's Croke Park or at the races at Baldoyle. 'One day we will have a great hurley match, or a great race meeting to celebrate peace,' he said, 'and we will hold it outside Belfast to celebrate the return of the Six Counties!'[103] In one of his last broadcasts, in January 1944, he condemned capitalism but no longer talked of Ireland's place in the new Europe or of Germany's courage. He

349

spoke instead about the effort needed to secure Irish unity in a post-war world. 'What do you want to become after the war?' he asked. 'It is not enough to talk about freedom and nationalism.' Stuart was in a melancholy mood, still hoping for the overthrow of materialism but raising new questions about the future of Ireland:

> It is of no importance at all that the Tricolour should fly from the City Hall in Belfast instead of the Union Jack if Belfast workers are to find it as hard to live and support their families as before. Such freedom is merely illusion and such nationalism a farce and a danger . . . The first thing to do is to face the truth. Until Dublin becomes a much better place for the average working family to live in than Belfast we lose more than half the force of our claim to Belfast. This may not be a very palatable statement, but I think that to most of you it is quite obvious.[104]

This was a strange message to come over the airwaves from Nazi Germany. The idea that Ireland could not be united until Eire made herself more acceptable to the six counties was one which the British had urged upon de Valera, although Stuart thought that only by breaking with Britain's 'financial and social traditions' could Eire achieve this new status.[105] The broadcast was a generous epilogue to the self-induced misery of Stuart's compromised existence in wartime Germany. Like Ezra Pound, his literary confrère on the Italian radio, his career would now always bear the stigma of his Axis collaboration. In September 1944, he left Berlin for Munich where he saw Ireland's oldest enemy fire-bomb the city by day; at night, he would sit at his apartment window and watch the RAF Mosquitoes caught in the German searchlights as they laid flare paths for the British bombers. With a German girl who was later to become his second wife, Stuart made his way to an Austrian village and he was there when the war ended, having rarely contemplated what would have happened if the Allies had lost. 'If I had really asked myself in a sober way in 1940 whether I wanted a German domination of all Europe,' he said later, 'I don't think I would have desired that.'[106]

He was imprisoned by the French who locked him in a cell with French and Belgian collaborators but who lost interest in him after a few months. He never regarded himself as a Nazi sympathiser and when, long after the war, he reviewed a new work by the Irish-born playwright Samuel Beckett – who had worked for the French resistance against the Nazis – Stuart mentioned that he had been imprisoned only for 'alleged' collaboration.[107] Since Germany had not been at war with Eire, there was in one sense no more reason to call Stuart a collaborator than there was to make the same imputation against the Irishmen who worked and fought for the British. The stigma stayed with him, however, as he knew it would; even thirty-three years after the war, he could still be publicly reviled in Dublin as 'that dreadful political reprobate'.[108] Whether his wartime influence on the Irish was as dramatic as the alienation which he deliberately brought upon himself is open to question. Even at the height of the war, there were fewer than 200,000 wireless sets in Eire,[109] and those Irish listeners who tuned in to Germany generally recall only Joyce's 'thin and drawling' voice on the English service.[110] Off the west coast of Ireland, the Aran islanders remembered that a German broadcaster – presumably Hartmann – 'spoke to us in Irish every week'.[111] But when Stuart eventually returned to Dublin, he discovered that the details of his Berlin broadcasts were not only forgotten but almost unknown. 'I hardly ever met anyone who heard me,' he said later. 'I don't think anyone really listened.'[112]

Chapter 11

Plato's Cave

> Eire . . . sees her neutrality as positive, not merely negative.
> She has invested her self-respect in it. It is typical of
> her intense and narrow view of herself that she cannot see
> that her attitude must appear to England an affair of
> blindness, egotism, escapism or sheer funk.
>
> Elizabeth Bowen, in a secret report to the
> British Government 9 November 1940

There were those who believed that wartime Dublin was one of the whispering-galleries of Europe, 'a natural centre for intrigue and spying of every kind'.[1] But the old imperial city, in which the flaking statue of Queen Victoria still sat – tiara'd and sceptre in hand – outside Leinster House, had neither the flamboyance of neutral Lisbon nor the forced gaiety of post-war Vienna. It was a dull, grimy place of soot-encrusted Georgian façades and decaying tenements, whose poverty grew more obvious as the war outside Eire cut into the thin fabric of the country's economy. The city was still gracious but no longer graceful, 'a faded eighteenth-century beauty in greatly reduced circumstances',[2] a metropolis once renowned for its public displays of wealth but whose deprivations were now partly brought about by the nation that had once made it rich. To the Irish poet Patrick Kavanagh, who arrived there in 1939 from the soft countryside of Monaghan, Dublin was 'malignant'.[3] A visiting girl factory worker from Belfast could remember it long afterwards as a dirty, squalid city 'overcrowded with poor people and beggars and barefoot children who grabbed at your coat to ask for pennies'.[4] When the Irish Government were considering the evacuation of Dublin, they found themselves forced to discuss 'the problem of large numbers of children infested with lice or suffering from contagious skin diseases'.[5]

Yet the war which had left Dublin physically untouched, also failed to transform the violent social contrasts that had been a feature of the rest of Europe in the 1930s. Thus the British journalist Kingsley Martin, comfortably ensconced at Maffey's residence one weekend in the early summer of 1940, could talk of 'the familiar, easy atmosphere of Dublin' in which he found not poverty but 'lavish hospitality, good food and drink and endless talk'.[6] The Anglo-Irish novelist Elizabeth Bowen was not so deceived by this surface, middle-class normality; in November of the same year, she reported to the British Ministry of Information that Dublin 'seemed to be suffering from claustrophobia and restlessness . . . socially and culturally speaking, the virtual closing of the Irish Channel is equivalent, for the more intelligent and Europeanly-minded [sic] people in Dublin and throughout Ireland, to a closing of the Burma Road. An increasing threat of parochialism in Dublin talk, interests, artistic outlook and social amenities is being recognised, and deplored . . .' Bowen found that 'there is still, among people of any means, a good deal of good living' but that there was also 'a general wish to escape, in society, from the general sense of oppression, or depression, caused by the war'.[7]

The British Government had already been apprised of the physical and cultural isolation which the Irish were experiencing, not only by Maffey's reports but by a whole series of confidential dispatches that found their way to the Foreign Office and the Ministry of Information in London from British and Anglo-Irish informants. Long ago filed away – and for the most part forgotten – in the British archives, these documents provide for us today a vivid, impressionistic image of de Valera's state and of the personalities which dominated Eire's affairs during the war. For the most part, the writers were sympathetic to Eire but firmly committed to the Allied cause, and their historical perspective was thus often questionable; so, too, was their rule-of-thumb judgement on Irish public opinion.

As early as October 1939, R.A. Butler, the Foreign Office Under-Secretary, received a seven-page memorandum on 'Irish Opinion and the War' from Frank Pakenham, now Lord Longford. Writing after a visit to both parts of Ireland, Pakenham – a lecturer and historian who had already incurred the wrath of Major General Sir James Cooke-Collis, the Ulster agent in London, for his allegedly 'propagandist' views – advised the British Government to respect Irish neutrality since public opinion in the twenty-six counties rested 'in a state of precarious equilibrium'. Approximately eight out of ten people supported neutrality, he claimed, one out of ten was 'sympathetic to Irish intervention on the British side' and an equal number favoured intervention against Britain. However, Pakenham believed that 'this mild preference for the Allies . . . while serving to promote a benevolent interpretation of neutrality, is utterly trivial compared with the kind of feeling that would be required to bring Ireland into a War on the Allies' side . . . it would vanish overnight if either Germany or England deliberately violated Irish neutrality.' Neutrality, Pakenham wrote:

> . . . dominates the foreground of Irish thought. Partition and its corollary, alleged discrimination in Northern Ireland against the Nationalist Minority, form the permanent background. So long as Partition remains, England, however superior her internal regime, is placed qua *international aggressor* on

the same level, in Irish eyes, as Germany. 'The Crime of Partition' is felt to be every bit as fresh as Germany's rape of Poland.[8]

Pakenham's memorandum referred to Eire's 'absorbing economic anxieties' and to the 'psychological detachment' of the 400,000 Northern Ireland nationalists who 'would prefer to be included in the South'. Any plan of bringing Eire into the war on the British side should be renounced, Pakenham wrote. British interference 'would for *certain* bring a substantially united Ireland, led by Mr De Valera, into the war against England, in precisely the same spirit as prompted Belgium to resist Germany in 1914.' All British and even Allied propaganda should be avoided. 'To achieve any serious effect, it would have to be organised; the fact of its organisation would be straight away detected and resented . . . the Editor of the [Anglo-Irish] *Irish Times* and Sir John Maffey vie with one another in deprecating any attempt whether blatant or subtly camouflaged to "put over" the Allied Case in Ireland.'

Pakenham's own bias was evident enough. 'Let it be repeated *ad nauseam*,' he wrote:

> . . . that the Irish mentality towards the war could be transformed . . . if England 'undid' Partition. Failing that, an immense impression would be made if the British Government announced officially that they regarded it as a British interest that the North should see their way to enter a united Ireland. Failing even that, an attack might be made on the regrettable consciousness of being not only an imprisoned but an oppressed minority that distinguishes Northern Nationalists and makes them definitely anti-British, in a way that is no longer true of the South. The easiest and most obvious step would be to remove some of the restrictions on freedom of speech in the six counties. Still more effective would be an improvement in Catholic chances of gaining employment not only in Governmental, but also in large private concerns.[9]

If this undisguised reference to anti-Catholic discrimination in Northern Ireland did not achieve the desired effect, Pakenham clearly hoped that more strategic reasons would persuade the British Government to adopt a moderate policy towards Eire. 'Mr De Valera's Government is desperately anxious to make Irish neutrality effective,' he wrote. 'At present, Ireland lacks the military and naval equipment to carry out the main task involved – the exclusion of German submarines from Irish territorial waters and coasts.' Pakenham urged the British authorities to supply de Valera with 'fast anti-submarine craft – six if possible, also guns for coastal defence purposes, and a number of aeroplanes' and recommended that the British should adopt 'an accommodating spirit regarding finance'. The British Admiralty might 'hanker after keeping open the possibility of cancelling, in extreme circumstances, the *de facto* neutrality that this country at present accords Ireland,' he concluded, but: '. . . if the British Government ever let itself be led into an organised violation of

Irish neutrality it would be opposed immediately by an Irish Government, whose armed enmity would be solidly supported throughout the twenty-six counties, and throughout at least one third of the remaining six.'[10]

The Ministry of Information, which also circulated Pakenham's report to the Dominions Office, forwarded it to Butler with the observation that 'any failure on our part to solve the problem of Irish neutrality by a method equally satisfactory to ourselves and to the Irish Free State [sic] might have disastrous results abroad . . .'[11] Butler wrote 'Good' on the top of the memorandum but took the matter no further.[12] Pakenham's occasional lapse into political rhetoric may well have detracted from the impact of his report. He tended to furnish the British Government with advice rather than information, and the fact that de Valera would have agreed with almost every sentiment Pakenham expressed would not have added to the writer's credibility in London.

The same could not be said of the novelist Elizabeth Bowen, whose gentle, sensitive dispatches from Eire are still a delight to read, a pen portrait of a nation and its people desperate to avoid involvement in a war that was not of their making. So astute was a report she wrote for the British Government in November of 1940 – just after Churchill had spoken in the House of Commons about the 'grievous burden' which the loss of the Treaty ports had imposed upon Britain – that Lord Cranborne immediately sent it to the Foreign Office for Halifax's personal attention, commending Bowen's 'shrewd appreciation' of the situation in Ireland.[13] 'It may be felt in England,' she wrote:

> . . . that Eire is making a fetish of her neutrality. But this assertion of her neutrality is Eire's first *free* self-assertion: as such alone it would mean a great deal to her. Eire (and I think rightly) sees her neutrality as positive, not merely negative. She has invested her self-respect in it. It is typical of her intense and narrow view of herself that she cannot see that her attitude must appear to England an affair of blindness, egotism, escapism or sheer funk.[14]

It would be 'sheer disaster' for Eire, in its growing stages and with its uncertain morale, to be involved in war, wrote Bowen. 'That Eire might lease her ports *without* being involved in war is a notion the popular mind here cannot grasp . . . "being involved in war" now conjures up only one picture – a bombing of Eire. The panic caused by this is intense: it is like England before Munich, twenty times more. People say, "*We* could never stand it," and they are right. One air raid on an Irish city would produce a chaos with which, in the long run, England would have to cope.'

Bowen had already experienced the London blitz at first hand – it was to form the background to several of her finest novels – and she did not try to hide her contempt for Irish men and women whose reactions to the war seemed either unheroic or ambivalent. She recorded some typical Dublin comments from 'the anti-British, or swivellers':

What right have the British to keep denouncing the Nazis?

Haven't they been Nazis to us for centuries, and aren't they trying to be Nazis again now?

Churchill timed his speech very cleverly; he waited till he was certain he would get Roosevelt in.[15]

The 'swivellers' – a peculiarly English expression – received little sympathy from Elizabeth Bowen but she made some austere, disciplined judgements about both Britain and Ireland:

I could wish some factions in England showed less anti-Irish feeling. I have noticed an I suppose inevitable increase of this in England during the last year. The charge of 'disloyalty' against the Irish has always, given the plain facts of history, irritated me. I could wish that the English kept history in mind more, that the Irish kept it in mind less.[16]

Dublin society held fewer attractions for Bowen now that Eire had become isolated by the war. From the small flat she occupied on St Stephen's Green, she made forays around the city to meet old friends 'over tea or sherry', and discovered that a lethargy – a sense of escapism – had beset the middle classes among whom she had previously felt at home. 'At some of the less inspired parties that I attended,' she wrote, 'this deliberate escapism produced a rather dreary effect. But on the whole I was struck, in all circles, by the intelligence (if not always the wisdom) and the animation of the talk. The stereotyped, or completely conditioned, mind seemed to me rarer in Dublin than in London . . . Public opinion in Dublin is almost dangerously fluid. It is, at the same time, less homogenous than in any English city I have known.' Bowen found among individuals 'a great deal of bigotry'.[17]

A slightly different form of social hypochondria was diagnosed by Herbert Shaw, a former southern Irish Unionist MP, a Protestant who had been Secretary to Lord French when he was Lord Lieutenant of Ireland in the closing days of British rule. Visiting Dublin just a month after Bowen, Shaw noted in a report for the British Government that he had found 'an increased introversion of the Irish mind'. He observed that 'Ireland, always inclined to be a *malade imaginaire*, is now more than ever confined by the walls of her sickroom, and outside events are of little interest unless they seem likely to enter and disturb it . . . The Irish, though they still chase shadows, have lost much of the idealism of a quarter of a century ago. The old literary and conversational brilliance is dying out, and I am forced to the conclusion that much of it came from the sparks struck from the age-long friction between Ireland and Great Britain . . .' This had its bearing on the Irish attitude towards the war; the majority of the Irish people, wrote Shaw:

. . . are by nature and religion opposed to Hitlerism; and yet the wrongs the Fuhrer has inflicted on small nations seem to stir, in the great majority of intelligent Irishmen, little more than an academic condemnation . . . Nothing indeed impressed me more than the unanimity of Southern Irish support for the policy of neutrality as defined by Mr de Valera. I had expected to find it in the ranks of his supporters, and to a lesser extent in those of the Cosgrave Party. I was surprised, however, to discover that even former Unionists, who were prepared without hesitation to send their sons into the British Army, held no other policy to be possible.[18]

Deep in the consciousness of some Irishmen, wrote Shaw – repeating in less kind a fashion an observation of Bowen's – 'there is realisation of the fact that they and their fellow countrymen would not stand up to bombing as the English, possessed of a strength of character which has so long tended to inflame Irish jealousy, have done.'[19]

If this was an unfair reflection on the stamina of a people who had, after all, defeated a far more powerful nation in a guerrilla war less than twenty years earlier, Shaw's assessment of the support for Irish neutrality was independently confirmed in a two-page report to the Foreign Office by Percy Loraine, who was also in Dublin in December of 1940. Eire, he wrote, was more pro-British than at any time since the 1914–18 War and 'there is a certain feeling, maybe a slightly guilty feeling, in some quarters and certainly among the pro-British elements, that Ireland ought to be fighting in this war with Britain. But even so there is a disposition to think that De Valera may be right in insisting on Irish neutrality on account of Eire's defencelessness against German air power . . .'[20]

This sense of vulnerability made a powerful impression on Count Jan Balinski when he visited Eire on behalf of the Polish Research Centre in London. He arrived in Dublin in January 1941, only a few days after the Luftwaffe had dropped bombs on the south of the city. 'The general feeling among the better informed circles,' Balinski confided to the British Ministry of Information:

> . . . is that they were dropped to intimidate the Irish and show them what would happen to them, should they make concessions to England such as the grant of naval bases. It is commonly said: 'We have no anti-aircraft defences, no shelters, no balloon barrage, no aeroplanes: Dublin could be smashed by German bombardment with great loss of life. Britain is wealthy enough to rebuild London and other cities, but Ireland is poor and would not be helped by Britain when the time came to rebuild the country.' In my opinion, for what it is worth, if the Germans intended to intimidate the Irish by the bombing, they have achieved their purpose.[21]

In reality, it was not just German bombing but the war itself which the Irish wished to avoid. 'Among the small nations of western Europe,' began the commentary of a Pathé newsreel specially made for the Irish Government in the summer of 1940, 'there are very few which have so far avoided being drawn into the maelstrom of war. But one at least has so far succeeded in maintaining her national integrity. Ireland, the romantic green isle of the west, is still at peace; but she has no illusions about the security of her position.'[22] In fact, Eire had precious little security about which to hold any illusions. The anxiety that Bowen, Shaw, Loraine and Balinski noticed during their visits to Dublin had been demonstrated at the Defence Conference in June of 1940 when Mulcahy anticipated the complete breakdown of Irish morale if Eire became involved in the war. De Valera had expressed to Maffey and MacDonald his fear that – quite apart from the destruction that would be visited upon Dublin – his country would break apart in renewed civil war if the population was asked to choose which of the belligerents it wished to support. Neutrality represented the unity of the state, and de Valera was able to tell Herbert Shaw during an hour's private interview in December 1940 that 'the cause of Irish neutrality was one in which . . . he felt justified in asking Irishmen to lay down their lives.'[23]

Eire thus clung tenaciously to a policy which Professor Michael Tierney, a Fine Gael Senator and admirer of Italian fascism, had described – not without some truth – as 'sacred egoism'.[24] The twenty-six counties of Ireland progressively sealed themselves off from the outside world, shutting out the war, the conflicting ideals and moralities – indeed, the very history – of a rapidly changing and violent world. Professor Lyons has described Eire's condition of almost total isolation from the rest of mankind in a memorable passage:

> It was as if an entire people had been condemned to live in Plato's cave, with their backs to the fire of life and deriving their only knowledge of what went on outside from the flickering shadows thrown on the wall before their eyes by the men and women who passed to and fro behind them.[25]

But the prisoners in Plato's cave had been incarcerated in darkness since childhood. Eire's isolation began when the state was already eighteen years old; and the effect of this self-imposed quarantine was not ignorance but stagnation, a sudden suspension of the political and social life of the nation, in which its people continued to obey the principles and follow the ideals of a world that had collapsed for the rest of Europe in 1939. The national preoccupations of pre-war Eire – partition, economic self-sufficiency, the Irish language – were maintained, and the war only served to throw them into sharper focus. Even foreign policy occasionally seemed to take little account of the war. In the 1930s, de Valera had placed his faith in the League of Nations, and it was entirely in keeping with Eire's pre-war priorities that in March 1941 – as the Battle of the Atlantic was fought off Ireland's west coast and as Germany prepared to invade the Balkans – de Valera's ministers would solemnly debate, over the course of several days, whether or not their country should pay its annual contribution to the League, which was by now – to quote an Irish Government memorandum – in 'a state of virtual disintegration'.[26]*

Just as neutrality was an assertion of sovereignty, so the wartime emergency provided Eire with new opportunities to enlarge her sense of cultural identity and nationhood. Thomas Derrig, de Valera's Minister for Education, saw in the formation of a junior division of the Local Security Force a chance to rejuvenate the Irish language. From his departmental correspondence – most of it in Irish – it is clear that Derrig and his civil servants regarded the war as of only secondary importance in the creation of this 'Local Youth Corps' (*An Macra Áitiúil*), who were supposed to be used as ARP messengers. In December 1941, Pádraig Ó Cochláin, the head of the Technical Branch at the Department of Education, announced to the somewhat sceptical Garda Commissioner, Major General W.R.E. Murphy, that 'this was a wonderful chance (*seans bhreágh*) to establish a movement that would greatly advance the interests of Irish.'[31] The emergency, Ó Cochláin told his minister, 'provides an opportunity to establish the foundations of a Gaelic movement for youth – something permanent for the benefit of the youth and the nation after the war.'[32]† But few LSF members were fluent in Irish and the Guards who spoke the language were based largely in the west of Ireland. The British meanwhile took a mischievous interest in the difficulties which Irish troops allegedly faced when given orders in their native tongue; a British intelligence report spoke of confusion among soldiers 'as to whether they are ordered to pile arms or open fire'.[34]

If there seemed to be a naïvety about Eire's response to the war, some of this must be put down to inexperience. When de Valera attended an ARP conference in June 1941, for instance, he was confronted by a departmental memorandum that asked, among other questions: 'Should sirens be sounded on approach of belligerent aircraft?'[35] But there was also an innocence – a dangerous one but nonetheless genuine – in de Valera's behaviour. As the war continued and the Irish economy showed signs of fragmentation, the search for self-sufficiency coalesced with a more inti-

---

* The Irish Cabinet were concerned lest the predominantly Commonwealth and 'refugee' nation membership of the League had identified it with 'the Allied cause in the war'.[27] In the event, Eire made her £10,670 payment; the British, who now claimed that the moribund League was 'a symbol of the cooperation of free nations', also contributed their share.[28] In his study of Irish foreign policy issues, Patrick Keatinge described Eire's decision to maintain her payments in these last years as 'a striking example of a government's concern with the world beyond its immediate and obvious interests'[29] but it was probably unwise to gift the Irish Government with such altruistic motives. In a note to de Valera in 1941, J.P. Walshe, the Secretary to the Department of External Affairs, warned that non-payment by Eire 'might be quoted against us as a breach of faith' in the American and British press.[30]

† The Department's enthusiasm for the scheme was not shared by General Murphy who, though once interested in the Irish language, now thought that there was 'a great deal of hypocrisy (*a lán cur i n-iúl*) associated with the Irish language question'.[33]

mate quest for cultural revival, an introspection to which de Valera gave unqualified encouragement. On Saint Patrick's Day 1943, we find him celebrating the fiftieth anniversary of the Gaelic League by envisaging an 'ideal Ireland', a land: '. . . whose countryside would be bright with cosy homesteads, whose fields and villages would be joyous with the sounds of industry, with the romping of sturdy children, the contests of athletic youths and the laughter of comely maidens, whose firesides would be forums for the wisdom of serene old age.'[36]

At a time when the Allies were already planning a second front in Europe and when the war in the Soviet Union was entering a decisive phase after the German catastrophe at Stalingrad, this was a unique form of escapism, a world of fantasy – de Valera actually talked of 'that Ireland which we dreamed of' – which was totally divorced not only from the realities of the war but from the hard facts of Irish life now that food was strictly rationed, fuel and raw materials were running out and private transport had ceased to exist. There was, too, something disturbing about de Valera's enthusiasm. It was as if he welcomed the emergency for the necessities of self-sufficiency that it imposed upon his people and for the path – rural, folk-loric, almost mystical – down which the pressures of the outside world now propelled them.

This cultural revival was immediately noticed by Elizabeth Bowen, who found a Gaelic festival in progress at the Dublin Mansion House when she arrived in the city in late 1940. 'Enthusiasm for the teaching, use and general cult of the Irish language seems to be on the increase,' she wrote. 'Mr de Valera gives the movement every support. Even *The Irish Times* now prints part of itself in Irish . . .' Bowen noted that 'plays, singing and conferences appeared to compose the programme' at the festival, adding rather sadly: 'I say "appeared" because all reports were printed in Irish, which I cannot read.' Irish 'national dress' was evident in the Dublin streets and no political interest appeared to be attached to the events although Bowen quickly realised that 'the Gaelic movement goes with a cult of *Heimkunst* ['home-art'] that certainly is not negligible. It is the source of considerable, if limited, sentiment. The German Minister and his wife are said to be liked in Gaelic circles . . .'[37]

Maffey was among those who suspected that de Valera gained some satisfaction from Eire's isolation. The Taoiseach, he told Sir Wilfrid Spender during an encounter in London that same December, 'was a man who lived in "blinkers" ' and who 'would like to segregate Ireland from all outside influences and all contacts with the world and to live a simple contented life delving into Gaelic literature . . .' When Spender registered his surprise that de Valera 'had given the British Government so little support in upholding the rights of the smaller Powers for whom he had previously expressed so great a concern,' Maffey replied bleakly that 'Mr De Valera was a man of very simple tastes.'

Yet de Valera exercised a fascination for the British. Perhaps they unconsciously admired his individuality, his very refusal to fall in line with the ideals ostensibly held by either side in the war. Even Maffey was constrained to admit to Spender that he 'respected Mr De Valera who though very narrow was quite upright.'[38] Shaw noted that he 'was, although a rebel, once a soldier of valour';[39] and it was arguable that de Valera's personal history of resistance to British rule in 1916 and the years that followed – his very contemporaneity with the early Churchill – gave him a moral authority that the British did not usually acknowledge. Infuriating he could always be; on the great issues of the war, he could make no public statement and if he ever felt bitterly opposed to the Nazis and their cruel world, the circumspection of neutrality never permitted him to display such animosity. There are few clues to de Valera's real feelings at this time although an occasional private note, a paragraph or two in a diplomatic report – even the elderly memories of a former political colleague – provide the faint outline of a man who wanted to see the downfall of the Nazis.

In the summer of 1940, he had told Maffey that 'there is no doubt on which side my sympathies lie. Nowadays some people joke about my becoming pro-British.'[40] Walshe had attempted to persuade Maffey that de Valera detested his interviews with the German Minister, Hempel. Such partisan expressions, however, could be expected in private diplomatic discussions; they cost nothing and required no subsequent confirmation. Herbert Shaw recorded after his meeting with the Taoiseach in December 1940 that 'Mr de Valera left on me the impression that in his heart he desired the decisive defeat of Germany; but was unable to see how Great Britain, in view of her huge and far-spread commitments, could well secure it.'[41] In conclave with Balinski, de Valera questioned the aristocratic Pole at length about 'the effects of the German/ and, to a lesser extent, the Soviet/occupation of Poland . . . he remarked that a peace dictated by a completely victorious side would always contain a seed of danger in the way of future reactions. From the way he worded this remark I had the impression that he regarded a negotiated peace as the best solution.'[42] The damage that the Versailles treaty had inflicted upon German society seems to have obscured from de Valera the essential characteristic of this new and more terrible war. He had also talked to MacDonald about the possibility of a negotiated settlement, as if unaware that the latest conflict in Europe was an ideological as well as a military struggle. De Valera's abhorrence of war had led him in January 1939 to tell Hempel that he 'had been seriously considering appealing both to the Fuhrer . . . and to Mussolini and making an effort for the preservation of peace' in his capacity as Taoiseach.[43] But by the summer of 1940, only Hitler was contemplating peace negotiations with Britain. When the German armies were overrunning the Low Countries, de Valera did briefly speak out against this 'cruel wrong'; there his criticism abruptly ended.

Did de Valera understand what the Nazis represented? Did he know – or care – about the fate of the millions of Jews who were being massacred in the concentration camps during the second half of the war? Aiken claimed years later that both he and de Valera 'thought Hitler was a madman' although he did not expand on this. 'What was going on in the camps was pretty well known to us early on,' Aiken said. 'But the Russians were as bad – you only have to look at what happened in the Katyn forest. There are photographs to prove that.'[44]* There is, however, no wartime evidence – save his speech condemning the German invasion of Holland and Belgium – that de Valera ever uttered any reproof or condemnation of German atrocities in occupied Europe. Indeed, the only surviving document of the period to record any reference by de Valera to the Jews is a memorandum – written just before the war but largely ignored by historians – which was sent by Hempel to the German Foreign Ministry on 3 January 1939, at a time when the Nazi persecution of German Jews was at its height. Reporting on a discussion with the Taoiseach, Hempel stated that:

> When the question of Jewry in Germany was briefly touched upon and I said that National Socialist Germany's procedure against the Jews must primarily be explained by the behaviour of the Jews after the [1914–18] war, Mr de Valera merely answered briefly that he was fully aware of this.[45]

If Hempel's report was accurate, de Valera could scarcely be said to have made a ringing denunciation of Nazi anti-semitism.

By the time the war started, he had narrowed his vision to one imperative: the territorial integrity of his country. The larger moral issues of the war, the acts and policies of the belligerent nations, assumed relevance only when they touched upon Eire's independence. Concentrating exclusively upon this priority, de Valera could be puzzled by the motives and intentions of his nearest neighbour. 'I was astonished,' wrote Shaw, 'to find that he was in considerable perplexity as to what Great Britain actually wanted. He could not believe that it was the ports alone . . .' De Valera's bewilderment bred suspicion, and produced in him a kind of loneliness. Shaw believed that, 'blind and conscious perhaps of the grave disadvantages of his position, [he] felt himself out of touch and deprived of the sympathy of Mr Chamberlain.' De Valera passed no criticism of the

---

* In 1943, the Germans found the bodies of 12,000 Polish officers buried in the Katyn forest near the Soviet city of Smolensk. The Nazis immediately recognised the propaganda value of their discovery and announced to the world what was evidently the truth: that the Polish soldiers had been prisoners of the Russians after the Soviet invasion of Poland and had subsequently been murdered by their captors.

new British leadership but spoke warmly of Chamberlain's 'rectitude and goodwill', lamenting to Shaw: 'He understood my mind.'[46]

It was not difficult to see how Chamberlain's successor failed to understand de Valera's apparent contradictions. The Taoiseach's wartime policies could lack definition, and his aversion to putting his ideas down on paper may have been prompted by more than security. In a letter to Richard Mulcahy in early 1941, he explained that 'so greatly is the Government impressed with the dangers inherent in multiplying documents . . . that they themselves rely in the main on oral reports made by the responsible Ministers, and written records on military affairs, external relations and internal security are restricted to a minimum.'[47] Years after the war, however, de Valera confided to an Irish Army officer that 'the Irish like to act intuitively not cerebrally. As for myself there is nothing I hate so much as having to put in writing something that is difficult to express.'[48] De Valera would sometimes depend upon repetition rather than disciplined argument to persuade others of the validity of his policies. Sean Lemass recalled that at Cabinet meetings, the Taoiseach 'relied upon the force of physical exhaustion to get agreement . . .'[49] But this practice did not have the same effect on the British, who felt that the partition issue had become an almost necessary distraction for de Valera. Shaw noted that 'in his references to Partition his mind dwelt on the past rather than the future. I wondered indeed whether he, in fact, regarded a United Ireland as more than an academic ideal, and I feared that the most cruel of all partitions lay in Mr de Valera's own mind.'[50]

In London, de Valera's inflexibility was often regarded as a sign of stupidity – Balinski deprecated a British newspaper cartoon that portrayed the Taoiseach as a donkey[51] – but few who visited him emerged from his offices in Merrion Street with so low an opinion of his character. Kingsley Martin found him 'by no means the doctrinaire and humourless monster commonly depicted in the English press',[52] while to Shaw he was 'frank, courteous and occasionally humorous, speaking now and then as if he were thinking aloud . . . The Irish Prime Minister is indeed a difficult, narrow and suspicious man bound by a rigorous consistency to his own earlier beliefs and utterances. Nevertheless, he tends to become Conservative . . .'[53] It was an epithet that begged questions, for de Valera's orthodox nationalism had a less reassuring side to it. He was not an aggressive man, but he had a brutal, perhaps slightly fascistic faith in his own judgement, as if he believed himself to be the exclusive oracle of his people's desires. He might not have wished to forge the uncreated conscience of his race but two decades earlier he had felt able to inform the Dail that 'whenever I wanted to know what the Irish people wanted, I had only to examine my own heart and it told me straight off what the Irish people wanted.'[54] De Valera's pastoral, chauvinistic dream of Ireland – with its Spartan youths and passive women and its almost Germanic interest in physical fitness – was in line with this sentiment: de Valera, the

Philosopher King, telling his people of the halcyon future that was in store for them.*

His unshakeable conviction in his own judgements was supported by a censorship which excluded from the press any serious criticism of his wartime policies. Political opposition could easily be interpreted as treachery. James Dillon remembers this darker side of de Valera:

> He could get up in the morning desiring to do something he knew to be wrong. But he never did anything which at the time of doing he believed to be wrong. When he acted, he would act ruthlessly and inflexibly and never look back. He would talk to you interminably but if he realised you were not persuaded, he was then like an owl. There would drop over his eyes a kind of film and from that moment onwards he was convinced that you were not only erroneous but in bad faith.[56]

De Valera's personal isolation was matched by an equal if self-induced loneliness within Dillon; sensing this perhaps, visitors to Dublin inevitably gravitated towards the small, bespectacled Fine Gael deputy leader to find a contrast to the Taoiseach as well as to hear some of the most pro-British views in Eire. A proud, incorruptible man with a theological intensity that amounted at times to a form of intimidation, Dillon's monastic personality was just as dominating as de Valera's, if not more so. When Elizabeth Bowen met him privately for tea one afternoon in November of 1940 – by which time his speeches in support of the Allies had already endeared him to the British – she found that:

> . . . in talk he is equable, rational and shows the kind of intellect that can make fullest use of any experience. He is less parochial in outlook than most Irishmen: in fact, not parochial at all. His personality is at once monkish and worldly. Superficially, Mr Dillon would be (from the English point of view) a very much easier man to deal with than Mr de Valera. I say superficially, because while Mr de Valera's fanaticism is on the surface, Mr Dillon's, which exists quite as strongly, is deep-down: it exploded once or twice towards the end of our talk – religious fanaticism of the purest kind I have met.[57]

The 'fanaticism' that Bowen detected in Dillon was no transitory phenomenon. In his occupation as a Mayo farmer and in his political career, Dillon's behaviour was governed by an unbending religious conviction that stayed with him all his life. Many years after the war, he told

---

* 'Chauvinistic' was not a word that would have been used of de Valera at the time. But Countess Markievicz's role in the struggle for Irish independence had not convinced him that women should take an equal place alongside their men. When the Irish Cabinet considered the creation of a 'Women's Auxiliary LSF' in December 1942, de Valera placed double quotation marks around the title and disparagingly appended the phrase ' – so-called' in his own hand.[55]

the author of this book that 'the ownership of land has about it a mystical quality. It is one of the only occupations a man can have for which he is responsible to no one on this earth but to God.' Dillon claimed that 'governments are answerable to God for the use they make of their authority.' He saw the war as 'a battle against evil rather than against a political danger.'[58]

Bowen believed that the religious 'streak' in Dillon might be felt in Eire if he ever came into power. 'If the de Valera Government were to fall,' she reported, '. . . I have no doubt that Mr Dillon would emerge as leader of the so-called Cosgravites. Mr Cosgrave seems (these days) to be negligible. Mr Dillon is said to be the ablest speaker (in fact, the only orator) in the Dail.' Bowen thought him to be 'the ablest, and at the same time, least spectacular, figure in Irish politics . . . he is very much disliked, and I must say that, though liking him very much personally, I see why. He holds some views which even I distrust, and which are abhorrent to many Irish people whose integrity I respect.' With a novelist's penetrating eye, Bowen noted that she 'could gather Mr Dillon's own strong feeling for power from his speaking to me of his distrust of it.' Materially, he was 'well off . . . and shows a contempt for "society". His nature seemed to be concentrated, and his intellect powerful and precise.' Bowen regarded him as 'important now, if only as a counterpoise to Mr de Valera. In any dealings with Eire he is a man with whom one would have to reckon; he might become the man with whom one would have to deal. He may, on the other hand, be a man who is better in Opposition.'[59]

Dillon's reputation for political integrity was such that, in December 1940, Herbert Shaw sought his advice on ways to improve relations between the British and Irish Governments; Dillon unhesitatingly confirmed that de Valera 'could be trusted to keep secret information to himself' if a British minister took the Taoiseach into his confidence. He warned, however, that 'an essential preliminary to any discussions would be an official assurance from Mr Winston Churchill that he intended strictly to observe Irish neutrality.'[60]* It was in character for Dillon to speak so freely and so fairly of de Valera for he distrusted party barriers, regarding politics as a philosophy rather than a system. He told Bowen that:

> . . . his fear for the world was, that we should be left, at the bitter end of this war, with the idea ('fallacy', Mr Dillon called it) that it was the *form* of government that mattered. Forms of government (said Mr Dillon) do not matter: all forms of government amount, in effect, to the same. What matters, what determines the state of a country, what makes in the long run for good or bad legislation is the good or evil in men's hearts. Mr Dillon then explained to

---

* Such an assurance, of course, Churchill was not prepared to make, a refusal which Dillon would describe years later as 'understandable and honest'.[61]

me what he felt to be the constitutional importance of the spiritual-moral. So far as I could see, Mr Dillon believes in government by Divine inspiration.[62]*

Dillon made enemies easily. Aiken never took him seriously and still describes how the Fine Gael deputy leader, in moments of impassioned oratory, 'would swing his arms about in the Dail.' He says now that Maffey – far from respecting Dillon – 'was cute enough to size up our friend.'[64] Dillon maintains that Aiken admired Nazi Germany and – together with Dan Breen, the former IRA guerrilla leader and Fianna Fail TD, and Patrick Little, de Valera's Minister for Posts and Telegraphs – 'used to canvas in the Dail corridors to find TDs who would accept social invitations to the German Legation.'[65] Gerald Boland claimed that Aiken adopted a 'pro-Nazi attitude which he held almost to the last days of the war'.[66] Aiken vehemently denies both allegations, saying that during the war he was 'anti-fascist like the rest of the Government'.[67]

Suspicion that Irish ministers and their civil servants were sympathetic to Hitler's Germany found a natural receptacle in British minds. Maffey told Spender that Sean MacEntee, the Minister for Industry and Commerce, was 'a strong Anglophobe'[68] although Shaw, who talked to the Irish minister in December 1940 came to the conclusion that MacEntee was 'an honest man, who would like to see Hitler defeated'.[69]† J.P. Walshe, whom Hempel reported as expressing 'great admiration for the German achievements' in the summer of 1940, incurred the particular displeasure of the British, who had perhaps got wind of the External Affairs Secretary's friendly conversations with the German Minister. Bowen, who met Walshe twice, noted that he was 'not popular and seemed to be out of contact with any of the other people I met. He struck me as having a good intellect (he is a 'spolit' Jesuit) and he has a personality you could cut with a knife. His judgement might well be questionable. His person is uncouth and his past (apparently) sinister. I was frequently told he was a pro-German. It would have interested me to discover if this were really the case, and, if so, why.'[71] Shaw formed a kinder impression. He

---

* Dillon had no idea that Bowen reported to the British Government on their conversation until the author of this book showed him a copy of her secret memorandum in 1979. Now aged 77, Dillon read it carefully; it was typical of him that he expressed no anger at Bowen's unflattering references to him, only at the way she had abused his hospitality in 1940 by breaking the confidentiality of their meeting. Of Bowen's remarks about his 'religious fanaticism', he commented: 'Poor woman – you can see her unhappy agnosticism.' He explained that above nations, 'the power of God is fundamental. If you don't stand for something, you don't have the right to be a nation.' Dillon quoted Acton's proverb about the corrupting nature of power to justify his contention that governments were 'answerable to God', adding that he was 'a passionate believer in parliamentary democracy.'[63] He could apparently see no contradiction in these last two statements.
† Spender also reported Maffey as holding a low opinion of Sean Lemass, commenting enigmatically that 'Sir John admitted . . . that some of the rumours which had reached us about his dealings might be true, especially as he had a strong taste for gambling.'[70]

thought Walshe was 'highly intelligent and well-informed of European and world affairs' but had 'a suspicious and somewhat scholastic mind'. His chief ambition, Shaw was given to understand, was to be Irish representative at the Vatican. Walshe declared himself 'a true Republican' but Shaw did not believe he was 'necessarily past praying for, especially in an undefeated England' and assumed that 'through the Irish missions abroad, Mr Walshe has sources of information, which, under happier conditions, might well have supplemented those of our own Government.' But he had clearly irritated his opposite number in London. Next to the line in which Shaw referred to Walshe's intelligence, Sir Alexander Cadogan, the Foreign Office Permanent Under-Secretary, had written in the margin: 'Unfortunately small – and narrow – minded.' Shaw himself felt uneasy about Walshe, upon whom de Valera relied so much for information about the war. 'In his company and remembering my talk with Mr de Valera,' wrote Shaw, 'I recalled the blind Polyphemus feeling the reassuring backs of his sheep, though all unconscious of the lithe and crafty Greeks who hung by the wool of their bellies.'[72] Dillon felt that this applied to Walshe, who was 'a very decent personality but completely under de Valera's thrall'.[73] Given the extent of British anger at Eire's neutrality, it was probably too much to expect politicians in Whitehall to regard Irish diplomats with anything approaching impartiality. Dulanty, the Irish High Commissioner in London, who according to Dillon 'became a passionate admirer of de Valera',[74] had worked under Churchill in the British Ministry of Munitions in the 1914–18 War. But Churchill, who thought him 'highly friendly to England', cynically described Dulanty in 1939 as 'a general smoother, representing everything Irish in the most favourable light.'[75]

Even among their friends in Ireland, the British seemed able to detect something potentially demagogic, although Bowen was careful to qualify such observations:

> I have heard Mr Dillon labelled a Fascist – which is I am afraid at least partly true. I have also heard him accused of pro-Germanism – which is, I think, 'wild'. He showed a truer sense than most Irishmen of the British mentality: his attitude towards England struck me as guarded, calculating, satirical-respectful, not hostile in even the oblique sense. In his almost morbid interest in Hitler's personality he struck me as following a private bent of his own . . .[76]

Dillon's career had already been marked by his association with General O'Duffy's Blueshirts, the militant offspring of the Army Comrades Association which had been formed as a reaction to the IRA's renaissance in 1932. Whether the Blueshirts were an essentially fascist organisation or merely 'a final instalment of the Civil War saga'[77] is still a point of some contention in Ireland. A man of limited intelligence but undoubted organisational ability, O'Duffy – who had been Garda Commissioner under Cosgrave's Government but was dismissed by de Valera in 1932 – claimed within weeks to control a force of 30,000, and their subsequent adoption of a uniform of blue shirts, black berets and buttons formed a natural parallel to the fascist movements that were growing in influence on the Continent. O'Duffy admired Mussolini and later praised Hitler[78] although his movement did not share all the characteristics of Italian fascism or German National Socialism. It was violently anti-communist but there is no evidence that it was anti-semitic or irredentist, except insofar as it demanded, like all Irish nationalist groups, an end to partition.[79] The Blueshirts, however, espoused a corporate state,[80] and when O'Duffy threatened to parade the National Guard – the new title of the Army Comrades Association – into Dublin in August 1933, ostensibly to honour the memory of Arthur Griffith, Michael Collins and Kevin O'Higgins, his plan bore an unhealthy resemblance to Mussolini's march on Rome eleven years earlier. De Valera banned the parade and outlawed the National Guard, an event which prompted not O'Duffy's eclipse but the amalgamation of his movement with Fianna Fail's political opponents, Cosgrave's Cumann na nGaedheal and Frank MacDermott's National Centre Party, a farmers' organisation to which Dillon belonged. Their new party – Fine Gael – was led by O'Duffy, with Cosgrave, Dillon and MacDermott as vice-presidents. It was a serious error of judgement for these three orthodox politicians to have accepted O'Duffy's leadership; however dictatorial de Valera's Government appeared to be, they had given the General a cloak of constitutional propriety that overnight made the Blueshirts far more formidable in the politics of Ireland than Oswald Mosley's Blackshirts ever became in Britain.

Exactly how men like Dillon could ally themselves with the para-fascist histrionics of Eoin O'Duffy revealed a good deal about the hatred which still existed between the old civil war antagonists, an animosity that did not fade away with the advent of the national emergency in 1939. Dillon himself first saw the Blueshirts when he was addressing a public meeting in Macroom, County Cork, as a leader of the National Centre Party. He was being shouted down by 'IRA people' when a Blueshirt officer approached him and 'asked for five minutes to clean these fellahs out'. When the hecklers had been driven over a wall, the Blueshirt returned to tell Dillon to continue his speech. Fianna Fail, says Dillon:

> . . . were carrying out a campaign to forbid the platform to anyone who wanted to criticise Mr de Valera. But for the Blueshirts, Fianna Fail would have put an end to the right of public meeting in this country. Then Cumann na nGaedheal, the Centre Party and the ACA met in a Dublin house and decided to combine to provide the people with an alternative to de Valera's administration. Tom O'Higgins was then the leader of the ACA. O'Higgins and Ernest Blythe of Cumann na nGaedheal urged that we should act on this proposal and said that the man with dynamism for the new party was Eoin O'Duffy. Cosgrave gave his assent to this. So did Frank MacDermott, who thought it

would be only a short time before he became the leader. O'Duffy was politically courageous and he was extremely wise and prudent for the first twelve months or so, committing his speeches to manuscript. He was a very effective public speaker.

Then one day in west Cork, I was standing behind him on a balcony when he addressed a rally of several thousand young Blueshirts. He was speaking very rapidly. It dawned on me that they were hanging on his words in a kind of obsessed way and I suddenly realised that he was speaking without any verbs. It had no discernible meaning. It dawned on me that if this fellah told them to go and burn the town, they'd do it. I thought: 'We've got to get rid of this man — he could be dangerous.' I remembered Hitler.[81]

Dillon and Cosgrave 'told O'Duffy to prepare his speeches, to stick to the approved text and to stop shooting his mouth off on platforms.'[82]* Amid much acrimony, he resigned the leadership of Fine Gael in September 1934.

O'Duffy turned out to be no führer. 'Whether for reasons of euphony or of irony,' Professor Lyons has charmingly remarked, 'the chant of "Hail O'Duffy" seemed somehow to lack the hypnotic effect of "Heil Hitler".'[84] His demise ultimately came about because Dillon and Cosgrave valued parliamentary democracy more than they did the possibility of overthrowing de Valera. Their realisation five years before the war that O'Duffy represented something alien to the Irish political tradition undoubtedly helped to temper any attraction Hitler might have held for the more right-wing members of Fine Gael, while Irishmen who regarded England as their first enemy had been given a glimpse of just how ugly fascism could be. Aiken, whom Dillon so disliked, insisted years later that it was the 'Night of the Long Knives' — when Hitler liquidated hundreds of his own Nazi Brownshirts in June 1934 — that 'turned Irish people against fascism.' Even so, Aiken said, 'Ernie Blythe and a lot of Fine Gael TDs eulogised the dictatorial *principe* — they were quite enamoured of this thing.' Aiken recalled travelling home to Dublin from a public meeting in Donegal one night in 1934 and seeing 'Blueshirts standing at every crossroads along the 150-mile journey, patrols of them every few hundred yards.' It did not take much imagination to realise how such an organisation could be mobilised for a putsch. Aiken claims that he 'had to fire a number of Army people who might have been nosing around with these boys.'[85]

Yet it would be a mistake to underestimate the influence that O'Duffy exerted over otherwise rational people. Professor James Hogan of University College, Dublin, and Professor Tierney, the Fine Gael Senator, lent a

---

* Talking to Bowen in 1940, Dillon gave a similar account of his disillusionment with O'Duffy, claiming that he 'decided to get rid of O'Duffy when . . . he heard the General passing over into Hitlerian convulsions of speech.' He felt that 'something dangerous was getting loose.'[83]

semblance of intellectual respectability to the Blueshirts; their corporate state ideology owed as much to the Christian corporatism of Pope Pius XI's *Quadragesimo Anno* as it did to Mussolini[86] although O'Duffy probably failed to appreciate this. At this stage, Irish fascism was of the Italian rather than the German variety, and in the early thirties those fascists who had taken power in Europe – Mussolini, Dollfuss and Salazar – were widely regarded as respectable Catholic national leaders. O'Duffy's demand for order in an increasingly lawless country also attracted the 68-year-old W.B. Yeats, who wrote several marching songs for the Blueshirts and noted that he found himself 'constantly urging the despotic rule of the educated classes as the only end to our troubles'.[87] Yeats's rather silly flirtation with fascism apparently ended after meeting O'Duffy, whom he found to be 'an uneducated lunatic'.[88] Yeats supported de Valera's neutrality policy and urged that the Irish Army should be supplied with modern weapons to 'throw back from our shores the disciplined uneducated masses of the commercial nations'.[89] De Valera's dismantlement of the Treaty, however, produced a truly absurd comment from the poet. 'You are right in comparing de Valera to Mussolini or Hitler,' he wrote to Olivia Shakespeare in 1933. 'All three have exactly the same aim so far as I can judge.'[90]*

Fascism as a mass movement had already collapsed in Ireland by the outbreak of the Second World War. Its last manifestation appeared in 1936 when seven hundred Irishmen left to fight an undistinguished campaign for Franco's Nationalist forces in Spain. It had capitalised on a sentiment that was to outlive it by many years: a constant and mainly Catholic propensity for anti-communist causes. The Irish Church had shown its sympathy for fascist Spain, and even those who regarded Hitler as insane believed that Stalin's Russia represented an equally grave threat to Christian Europe. 'In my view,' Gerald Boland wrote years later, 'Russia was as much responsible as Germany for starting the war. Mad as Hitler was, he would never have started a war on two fronts and by a pact with Stalin each marched in to Poland and grabbed [a] portion. The Russians still have their part and will probably hold on to it.'[93] When the Soviet Union invaded Finland in November 1939, a number of Irish volunteers, soldiers and firemen joined the Finnish Army to fight the Russians; several of them stayed on when the Finns continued their war against the Soviets in 1941 with German assistance.[94] In 1943 – by which time O'Duffy had already been mischievously involved with the Abwehr

---

* Yeats's admiration for fascism was many years later the subject of a tiresome debate between Dr Elisabeth Cullingford, an English lecturer at Lancaster University, and Dr Conor Cruise O'Brien, the former Irish Government minister and journalist, who claimed that in 1938 'when Yeats's nationalism is most manic . . . what comes through is a wish for the defeat of Britain by the Fascist powers.'[91] Cullingford took the view that Yeats 'turned briefly to fascism as a new political philosophy which might unite and harmonize both Irish society and his own diverse beliefs.'[92]

agent Hermann Goertz – word reached the German Foreign Ministry that the indefatigable Blueshirt General was now ready to raise an Irish 'Green Division' to support German troops on the Eastern Front 'in the fight against Bolshevism'. The Wehrmacht showed no interest in the idea since it would be impossible to transport an Irish volunteer force from Eire to the Continent, but the Germans wanted to encourage O'Duffy so that they 'could utilize, for propaganda purposes, the fact that Irishmen have declared themselves willing to fight against Bolshevism.'[95]

The struggle against communism became for some Catholics almost a spiritual crusade; and when Germany invaded the Soviet Union in 1941, Britain's hurriedly arranged alliance with Russia became proof positive for many people in Eire that the war was not after all being fought – as the British had hitherto claimed – on behalf of democracy. There could be, it seemed, no ideals in such an ungodly struggle. Eire's neutrality suddenly appeared puritanical by comparison. Even before 1941, Elizabeth Bowen sensed a certain Catholic self-satisfaction about Eire's wartime neutrality:

> I find a great readiness, in talkers of all classes, to stress the 'spirituality' of Eire's attitude towards world affairs. At the root, this is not bogus: that this country *is* religious in temperament and disposition as well as practice is, I take it, an accepted fact. Unhappily, religion is used to cover or bolster up a number of bad practices. I . . . still see a threat of Catholic-Fascism. And officially the Irish R.C. Church is opposed to progress, as not good for the people.
> The most disagreeable aspect of this official 'spirituality' is its smugness, even phariseeism. I have heard it said (and have heard of it constantly being said) that 'the bombing is a punishment on England for her materialism.'[96]

The better side of this 'spirituality', wrote Bowen, was that 'it can breed a very genuine charity, that it makes the people capable of imaginative pity and distress.' But, she added:

> The theory that England is ungodly *is* dangerous: it might be worked upon. Possibilities of an English alliance with 'atheistical' Russia are very unfavourably seen. The idea of a Catholic-Latin block does not seem to have caught on here in the intellectual sense as much as I should have expected. But I believe it to be a latent emotional wish. Sympathy for Petainist France (idea of spiritual re-birth) if not in the increase since last summer is certainly not on the decrease. The equally reconstructive side of the Free French programme seems to be overlooked. And there is still admiration for Franco's Spain . . . The effect of religious opinion in this country (Protestant as well as Catholic) seems still to be, a heavy trend to the Right.[97]

Bowen remarked on one symptom of this rightward trend, more disturbing and potentially more dangerous than religious fanaticism, though not unconnected with it. 'I noticed that anti-Semitism in Eire is considerably on the increase,' she reported to London. 'It is said to arise from business jealousy – plus the inevitable results of campaigns abroad. It has ugly manifestations in the business world.'[98]

A small Jewish community had lived peacefully in Ireland since the seventeenth century and only once had it been a victim of persecution. In 1904, Father John Creagh, a Redemptorist priest in Limerick, persuaded his parishioners to boycott the Jews of the city, eighty of whom were eventually driven from their homes. The chief victim, a trader of Lithuanian origin, was later to complain that his customers 'all of a sudden, like a thunderstorm, spoke hatred and animosity against the Jews, how they crucified Lord Jesus, how they martyred St Simon . . .'[99] Creagh's superiors later disowned him, concluding that 'religious persecution had no place in Ireland.'[100] The Jewish faith was officially 'recognised' in de Valera's 1937 Constitution, but just before the war the Irish Government refused a Vatican request to give temporary refuge to a number of Jewish doctors; the Papal Nuncio in Dublin told the Vatican that the committee trying to organise the refugee status of the doctors had been discouraged by the amount of anti-Jewish feeling that had been encountered. Another committee, however, did help to settle several Jewish intellectuals in Ireland.[101]* In the early part of the war, anti-semitic, pro-German pamphlets, published by Sinn Fein, began to circulate in Dublin – one of them warning that a *coup d'état* might come from Robert Briscoe, a Fianna Fail TD who was a member of the city's Jewish community[103] – and Jews were ostracised at several golf clubs.[104] There is no evidence that they felt themselves to be under any immediate threat although they might have felt less confident had they known that figures presented to the Nazi conference at Wannsee in January 1942 included the number of Jews to be liquidated in countries not yet overrun by Germany, estimating that 4000 Jews in Ireland would have to be murdered.[105]

In 1943, Oliver Flanagan, who had just been elected a TD on a monetary reform ticket, asked in the Dail – on the basis of 'Christian principles' – why the Irish Government's Emergency Orders had not been:

> . . . directed against the Jews, who crucified Our Saviour nineteen hundred years ago and who are crucifying us every day in the week? . . . There is one thing that Germany did, and that was to rout the Jews out of their country. Until we rout the Jews out of this country it does not matter what Orders you make. Where the bees are there is the honey, and where the Jews are there is the money.[106]†

* Official Irish Government records do not give details of Jewish immigrants during the war; aliens statistics drawn up for the Taoiseach's Department in early October 1939 list 326 German nationals and 27 Poles, of whom a proportion were almost certainly Jews. The documents also refer to four 'Palestinian' citizens who were presumably Jewish.[102]

† Flanagan, now a Fine Gael TD and the longest serving member of the Dail, apologised years later for his outburst.[107] Anti-semitism remained a sensitive issue in Ireland; when in 1979, Radio Telefis Eireann, the Irish state broadcasting service, produced a 45-minute radio documentary on the 1904 anti-Jewish campaign in Limerick, the city's mayor demanded its cancellation on the grounds that 'this is the kind of programme that Limerick must be protected against . . . the documentary can only do damage to the image of Limerick . . .'[108]

Gestures of support for Germany came in many forms. When the Irish Army commandeered Killiney Castle, a Gothic pile twelve miles from Dublin, at the start of the war, the owner of the keep – a violently anti-British civil servant – would emerge from the basement and run the Irish Tricolour up the flag mast every time the Germans announced a military victory.[109] Similar sentiments afflicted J.J. Walsh, who had been Cosgrave's Minister for Posts and Telegraphs in the twenties and who now usually travelled into Dublin from Foxrock on the same tram as Colonel Dan Bryan of the Irish Army's G2 intelligence branch. Bryan recalls that when reports of German successes appeared in the Dublin press in 1940, 'Walsh would look up at me from his morning paper and say: "I see we are still winning." '[110] In fact, Walsh's admiration for the Germans took a more sinister form, as Gerald Boland discovered. After a heavy air raid on Belfast in 1941, the Irish security officials responsible for tapping the telephones at the German Legation heard Walsh's voice on the line talking to diplomats in the building. Walsh 'told them it was Enniskillen they should bomb and not Belfast,' Boland wrote later. 'The idiot never suspected that his message was recorded.'[111]

Infinitely more worrying than Walsh's blundering enthusiasm, however, was the case of Alec McCabe, who had distinguished himself in the guerrilla conflict against the British, entered the Dail as a Cumann na nGaedheal TD and then broken with the party because of his sympathy with the 1924 Irish Army mutiny. In the notes he left after his death, Boland claimed that McCabe was 'actively engaged helping, as far as he could, the Germans' and that for this reason he was interned. Mysteriously, Boland did not enlarge – even in his private papers – on the nature of this assistance, although he records that Richard Mulcahy called on the Department of Justice to protest at McCabe's detention. Boland lent Mulcahy the confidential police file on McCabe 'and told him to see Mr Cosgrave and other ex-Ministers and if they said I should release McCabe I would do so.'[112]

Boland knew only too well that after reading the file, Mulcahy would no longer attempt to secure McCabe's release. For – although the Justice Minister never disclosed the fact in his personal notes – the dossier contained a series of reports by a police intelligence agent who had penetrated a secret Irish Nazi movement that was preparing for the arrival of a German invasion force. McCabe was only one of the leading figures in this anti-semitic group, which also included General O'Duffy, a number of Fianna Fail party workers and apparently several police officers. Unknown to Boland, however, Mulcahy made a private copy of the confidential Garda reports, which thus survived the war years and today provide a chilling if unintentionally sardonic picture of the fixated, grubby neo-Nazi underworld that awaited the Germans in Dublin. Written by an anonymous Garda officer, who insinuated his way into the movement by posing as a St Vincent de Paul charity worker, the reports are disjointed and occasionally ungrammatical but Boland and his fellow ministers could not have failed to grasp their significance.

'On Friday, May 31st, 1940,' the first report began:

> . . . I meet Mr White and Mr Holden, two prominent members of the Fianna Fail Organisation . . . They opened the conversation by asking me what progress I was making in disposing of the tickets for the Fianna Fail outing in Kilmacurra Park on Sunday next the 9th June. I informed them that I found it very hard to dispose of the tickets but that I was going to the outing myself. Mr Holden then started speaking of the Jews and Freemasonry and the poverty in Dublin brought about by the hands of the Jews, I answered him by stating that I had no time for the Jews and he then invited me to a meeting to be held in the Red Bank Restaurant on that night (Friday) at 8.0 pm . . . He (Mr Holden) then stated that this was the only Organisation that was going to do away with Jews, turning the lapel of his coat and showing me a badge in the shape of a wing and the Swastika on the centre of the badge . . .[113]

The Red Bank, on the east side of D'Olier Street a few hundred yards from the Liffey, was the restaurant in which Adolph Mahr and other members of the German Association used to meet before the war. The Garda agent duly turned up to the meeting which was held in a locked room. In the constabulary language of his report:

> . . . About 50 persons were present and they were seated around tables, they were all partaking of refreshments in the nature of minerals, whiskey and stout . . . When I entered a Mr Griffin . . . was addressing the meeting. He pointed out that the propaganda regarding the German cruelties and the persecution of the Catholics were nothing but a fabrication of lies and that it was the jews [sic] that were responsible for the circulation of such stories, the time has now come when this organisation must take definite action. He stated that there were at present 27,000 jews in the country . . . and before the termination of the war a further 27,000 would be hear [sic] if action was not taken. He further stated that we were not getting the truth about Germany here, and from what he knew Hitler was the only man whose policy in the extermination of the jews lead [sic] to the Success of National Socialism.[114]

Two men identified as Dublin solicitors moved a vote of thanks to Griffin for this unpleasant little speech while the Garda agent noted that among those present at the meeting were '(Chairman) Alec McCabe also Holden and Capt Liam Walsh.' When Holden's turn came to speak, he:

> . . . stated that they were being called the 5th colum [sic] but this was not the case, that it was the Jews they were after and everything must be done to make their lot miserable and to get rid of them out of the country. He finished by stating that they did not wish to embarras [sic] Mr De Valera . . .[115]

At this point, 'a young lady went to the piano and played the Irish National

Anthem and also the German Anthem at which some members rose [sic] their hands in salute.' When the police agent asked Holden if he was worried that the meeting might be raided by the security authorities, Holden replied that he was not because 'a number of the Garda were members of the Organisation'. This inside help was not much use to Holden who, with McCabe, Liam Walsh and three other men – O'Connor, O'Gorman and a German called Hand – were arrested a few days later, presumably given away by the author of the Garda intelligence report. If this was the case, other members of the neo-Nazi group did not suspect him; he was told that a meeting scheduled for the Red Bank had been hurriedly cancelled and that he should travel instead to an address in a south-west Dublin suburb. In the company of a Dublin grocer called Hurley, the police officer was taken to a house where he found fourteen people, including Griffin and Captain Walsh's wife, all of them much exercised over the recent arrests. Hurley claimed that he had made contact through a third party with Richard Mulcahy who 'was going to take the matter up with the Minister of [sic] Justice, to secure the release of Alec McCabe'; Boland would have enjoyed Mulcahy's embarrassment at reading this disclosure. Holden, said Hurley, might be freed because he was a member of Fianna Fail and 'a political string could be pulled'.

It is clear that members of the People's National Party – as the police agent later discovered its name to be – had little idea of security. But there could be no doubt that they understood something of National Socialist ideology and wanted to help Nazi Germany. Mrs Walsh suggested to the meeting that they should 'offer their services' to Hempel. Hurley announced that 'a friend in the British War Office' had given him details of British troop movements and that he had since passed this information to the German Legation in Dublin. Hurley and Griffin also expressed the curious belief that 'Mr Dillon was the person that was now running the Government of the country, that De Valera was only a second figure . . .'*

There did appear to be some contact between the Irish Nazis and Germany. Griffin told the meeting that among the papers found on Holden at the time of his arrest were 'letters from Capt Liam Walsh, dealing with the proposed landing of German troops on the Wicklow Coast'. A week later, Griffin told a party gathering at the Swiss Chalet Restaurant in Dublin that the movement's founders were 'General O'Duffy, Liam Walsh, Seamus Bourke and a Mr O'Callaghan . . . who published the German War News.' According to O'Connor, who had just been released from custody, the People's National Party was: '. . . approved by the German Government, run on National Socialist Party

---

* Hurley appears to have been responsible for giving the party the alternative title of the 'Anti-Christian Association', a name that was not on the face of it likely to attract much support among Eire's devoutly Catholic population.

lines. Offices would soon be open in Dublin . . . From information he had, the German Army would invade England by the 14th July. The Germans would be in this country by the 15th of July. They had their groups ready to facilitate the German Army in every respect. The meeting was told to hold themselves in readiness . . .[116]

By assiduously cultivating Griffin's trust, the Garda agent was able to lay hands on a copy of the party's policy document, a manifesto of predictable authoritarianism and considerable length which the policeman dutifully summarised:

1. Control of Finance.
2. All property of aliens to be confiscated without any compensation.
3. That all persons who took up residence here since 1916 to be expelled from the Country.
4. All charity to be discontinued and work found for all unemployed persons.
5. The training of the Youth of the Country.[117]

On July 1, Boland's Garda informant returned to the house in southwest Dublin where the wife of this would-be gauleiter made him feel at home. 'Mrs Griffin then served tea,' the police officer reported with courtroom grace, 'and I was requested to partake of same which I did.' He discovered that a Guard had attended a recent party meeting although he could not find out which station he was attached to. He watched Mrs Griffin tune her radio in to the New British Broadcasting Corporation, one of the 'black' German stations transmitting from occupied France. The announcer reported the arrest of the British Fascist leader Sir Oswald Mosley, at which Griffin got up from his seat, opened a file and 'pointed a document to his wife stating "I was right". I think he was referring to the remark of the announcer regarding the arrests.'[118]

At this point, the police agent's intriguing reports abruptly come to an end. There are no further references in Mulcahy's papers – and none at all in the archives of the State Paper Office in Dublin – to this strange episode and its shadowy figures. All those named by the Garda agent are now dead. The Irish authorities had successfully infiltrated the embryo Irish Nazi movement, and their agent had listened to the muddled, violent but authentic voice of national socialism, much as it must have been heard in capitals all over Europe in 1940 before the arrival of the German Army. Mulcahy returned Boland's police file after a few hours and informed the Justice Minister that he and his party colleagues were 'satisfied' with McCabe's internment.[119] There was a surprising codicil to this story some weeks later when J.J. Walsh turned up at Boland's office to request McCabe's release. Exactly what Walsh's connection with McCabe and his racist neo-Nazi party was remains obscure although Boland evidently had some incriminating evidence against the former Cumann na nGaedheal minister. He told Walsh that he was 'thinking of interning him as well as

McCabe' and had 'heard his statements that the IRA were our commandos
. . .' But the immediate threat of invasion had passed, and Boland said
that if McCabe promised to 'leave Foreign Affairs in the Government's
hands till the war was over', he would be released. Walsh visited McCabe
in Cork prison where the internee readily agreed to Boland's request. The
Justice Minister thereupon helped him to return to his previous employment as a schoolteacher.[120]

If McCabe's organisation believed that reports of German brutality
were propaganda, it seems to have shared this view with at least a section
of the Catholic clergy in Eire. 'As a Catholic and a Pole,' wrote Balinski, 'I
gathered from many accounts given to me by Irish Catholic friends that
the rural clergy is extremely insular and not interested in what is going on
in Europe, even as regards the persecution of the Church. Many of the
parish priests have visited Germany in the past on the invitation of
German Catholic monasteries, seminaries, etc, and they cannot believe
the reports of German persecutions . . .' This did not apply to the Jesuits,
who had 'very decided pro-British feelings', or to the hierarchy. Balinski
was very much struck by the views of the new Archbishop of Dublin, 'a
man of great intelligence and personal charm', as well as by those of the
Papal Nuncio, both of whom were well acquainted with the facts of the
religious persecution carried on by the Germans and Russians.'[121] Shaw
was less enamoured with the Nuncio's understanding of international
events. Though 'at heart friendly to our cause', he thought that Monsignor
Robinson, the Papal envoy to Dublin, 'viewed Ireland and her squabbles
from an Olympian, or rather a celestial height.'[122]

British intelligence believed that Monsignor Robinson directed Cardinal Joseph MacRory, the Catholic Primate of All Ireland, 'to meet the
Italian consul for conversation' in 1940. MacRory reportedly did so at a
convent near the Irish border town of Dundalk in County Louth, apparently 'pressing the Italian representative to use his influence to ensure that
Eire . . . should not be invaded.'[123] In 1941, the Foreign Office in London
took exception to Monsignor Robinson's behaviour after receiving a
report from the Secretary to the French Legation in Dublin that the
Nuncio 'had been telling everybody that it was very sad that the Italians
would certainly overrun Egypt, that subsequently they would capture
Malta, and that British power in the Mediterranean was inevitably
doomed.' The British were at the time growing increasingly weary of the
Vatican's toleration of fascism, and there is a note of impatience in a
minute about the Nuncio which Victor Cavendish-Bentinck, the head of
the Foreign Office's Dominions Intelligence Department, circulated to
his colleagues on 17 February 1941. 'It might have been expected,' he
wrote, 'that General Wavell's successful operations would have caused
this eminent prelate to change his tune, but he now says that General
Wavell's successful operations in Cyrenaica are of no real importance and
that our statement that we have taken more than 100,000 prisoners must

be incorrect as Marshal Graziani had not got a force of this size in that area. This tends to confirm the strong pro-Italian attitude of the Vatican . . . Perhaps this attitude may be dictated by a fear that the fall of Fascism might be succeeded by a measure of anti-clericalism with resultant decrease in Peter's Pence from Italy?'[124] A.W.G. Randall of the Foreign Office disagreed. The Nuncio, he wrote, was 'ill and in any case old and feeble. But he has always been very friendly . . . So I think his attitude must for the most part be ascribed to general pessimism and susceptibility to the stories which I have no doubt the German and Italian Ministers in Dublin pour into his ears.' The official suggested that the British Ministry of Information should try to counteract the propaganda of the Axis ministers in Dublin.[125] But Cavendish-Bentinck was unconsoled. The BBC could be heard in Dublin without the slightest difficulty and English newspapers arrived there regularly, he observed. 'There are none so deaf as those who do not wish to hear.' Foreign Office counsel continued to be divided. Another departmental official regarded Monsignor Robinson as 'about the most pro-British Irishman I have ever met.'[126] This may have been nearer the truth, for Sir Shane Leslie, a relative of Churchill's, had spoken to the Nuncio in October 1939 and been informed by him that Irish Catholic opinion was '95% with us in the present war and has been made even stronger than before by the destruction of Poland . . .'[127]

Fear of communism inevitably played its part in any discussion on religion in Eire. Elizabeth Bowen discovered that 'the word "revolutionary", in whatever context, has a purely sinister connotation here. I found that to say that we younger people in Britain are fighting this as a revolutionary war produced an unhappy effect: hearers' minds seemed to turn immediately to chaos, red flags and barricades. I find "reconstructive" better . . .' The English idea of world betterment through social reform was dismissed as 'materialistic', Bowen noted. 'Good regard towards individual English statesmen seems to be meted out according to whether they are felt to be "Christian" or not . . . It is remarkable that, though the Tory party in England have seldom shown themselves sympathetic to Irish claims, they are respected, at present, here as being *Christian*. Whereas the Labour Party and the intelligentsia are suspect, as being "red" (or godless).' Where one met the conditioned mind in Ireland, 'the conditioning has been done by religion', but Bowen continued to hear among those Catholics whom she considered enlightened, 'considerable criticism of the R.C. Church for its failure to take up a more positive attitude in this world crisis. This ranges from criticism of the parish priests for their lack of outlook, their ambiguous and teetering attitude . . . to criticisms of the Vatican's political feebleness.'[128]

Balinski was angered by the parallels drawn between previous British repression in Ireland and German persecution in occupied Europe. The work of the Folklore Commission at the national universities at Dublin and Cork – which he considered 'quite unique and conducted on very scientific lines' – seemed to keep Irish sufferings fresh in the minds of intellectual leaders. 'Sometimes,' wrote Balinski, 'when I spoke of the persecution of Poles, I was told by Irishmen that they know by experience what persecution meant. I reacted with some heat to such assertions . . .'[129] The Irish universities held different lessons for Bowen. She recorded the view of Dr George O'Brien, Professor of Economics at the National University of Dublin, that a large number of students graduating in Eire no longer found the employment to which their education entitled them, a wartime phenomenon which O'Brien feared might 'breed discontent, spread depression and . . . political mischievousness.'

At Trinity College, Dublin – traditionally an outpost of the Anglo-Irish ascendancy – Bowen noted that 'TCD's most extreme move to the Left appears to be the existence of a Fabian Society.' The university seemed to feel 'a certain Protestant-Unionist isolation' and many of the students refused to join the LSF for fear of 'having to fight England'. Bowen spent an evening with three Trinity undergraduates who proclaimed themselves distressed about their future because 'the British Empire has always supplied us with jobs, and what will we do if the British Empire breaks down?'[130] Britain's wartime struggle was certainly followed in Trinity College with considerable emotion. A British scientist recruiting Irish students for work on military scientific projects in Britain, was dining at Trinity on the night Singapore fell to the Japanese in 1942 'and there were as many drawn faces that evening among the Irish as there would have been in London.'[131] It was interesting, Bowen noted, 'that the worst defeatism, on behalf of Britain, that I have met . . . in this country has been among the Protestant Anglo-Irish. A far more optimistic view of "England's chances" is taken by the Irish-Irish.' The Anglo-Irish, Bowen decided, 'would be doing much better service to both England and Eire if they would not so zealously represent themselves as England's stronghold here . . . If the Anglo-Irish would merge their interests with Eire's, they could make – from the point of view of England – a very much more solid and *possible* Eire, with which to deal.'[132]

Bowen regarded the two Dublin universities, the medical and legal professions 'and some of the more popular and socially-minded of the Senators' as the nucleus of 'the most distinctive Dublin society'. Their traditions were in the British favour. Outside these circles, however, 'political figures are very little met. Thus there is very little infiltration of ideas between the theorists and the practitioners in politics.' In the same way:

> . . . the literary people sequester themselves, or are sequestered. With the
> death of Mr Yeats and the departure of Dr Gogarty* Dublin seems to have lost

* Oliver St John Gogarty, poet, surgeon and former Senator, had moved to America in 1939 after losing a libel action in Dublin. A close friend of James Joyce, Augustus John and W.B. Yeats, he loathed de Valera and the conservative Ireland which he thought the Taoiseach represented.

her only two social-literary figures. No view expressed by any Irish writer (novelist or poet) on the European situation, on Irish politics, seemed to be much listened to, or cut much ice. In fact, Dublin in general holds the Platonic view of the poet. The writer as propagandist in any sense seems to be ineffective in this country.[133]

Bowen did not have the opportunity to explore that one institution in Eire that was growing faster and more important by the week: the Irish Army. Balinski, however, met several senior military officers, including General Brennan, the former Chief of Staff, and General Hugo MacNeill (whose name he mis-spelt as 'O'Neill'). 'I had a very clear impression,' Balinski recorded, 'that they have a deep admiration for the behaviour of the British nation in this war. The name of General O'Connor, one of the chiefs of the army in Africa, was mentioned to me with pride as that of an Irishman . . . My strong impression is that the army people whom I met were very pro-British.' Balinski found among the Irish officers 'a feeling of sympathy for the British Army as distinct from British policy and politicians'.[134] This emotion was, of course, sometimes translated into real assistance for the British military authorities. Colonel Bryan of G2, whose work was in theory far too sensitive to allow him any political sympathies, admitted long after the war that 'people say I was pro-British and so in a way I suppose I was.'[135]

Within the ranks of the Irish security forces, however, conditions were such that soldiers might have been forgiven if any latent bias was visited against their own Government. As late as 1942, at an LDF and LSF parade in Arklow, Oscar Traynor, the Minister for Defence, was promising to put 'a weapon of one kind or another into the hands of every trained man'. This bald admission that Eire's part-time soldiers were still not properly armed actually found its way into a Government-sponsored newsreel.[136] By March 1943, a memorandum to the Taoiseach's Department from the Garda Siochana revealed that more than half the 63,000 members of the LSF still had no uniforms. 'Discontent in the LSF,' the document warned, '. . . is rapidly coming to a head.'[137]* The Irish Army refused to give its soldiers a marriage allowance until they were aged twenty-three; in 1943, Traynor was pleading vainly with Sean T. O'Kelly in his capacity as Minister for Finance, to lower the age limit because army families had been forced to seek help from the Public Assistance.[138]

Anglo-Irish observers might cast a jaundiced eye across the institutions of the Irish state, but they would speak no evil of Sir John Maffey. Shaw reported that he 'heard on all sides the warmest praise of Sir John's tact,

* Nostalgia for Eire's 'Home Guard' continued in the post-war years, much as it did for the British variety on the other side of the Irish Sea. It was not by chance that the BBC television series 'Dad's Army' – which presented a farcical version of the British Local Defence Volunteers' preparations for a German invasion – was also extremely popular when it was shown in the Irish Republic.

competence and understanding', [139] and it is true that the British representative – who regularly fielded a cricket eleven in Trinity College Park with
the Irish poet Patrick Kavanagh in his team[140] – acquired a reputation for
political integrity. This may not have been due solely to his practice of
speaking plainly to those with whom he disagreed; Maffey's offices in
Dublin – unlike several British visitors to Eire during the war – were never
associated with espionage activities. Rumours still persist in Ireland that
the English poet John Betjeman, who was attached to Maffey's department, was a British spy tasked with the mission of courting the staff of the
right-wing Catholic newspaper *The Tablet* 'away from their alleged Nazi
sympathies'.[141] In fact, Betjeman – far from being anything so preposterous as a spy – was a cultural attaché in whom even Colonel Bryan could
find nothing more suspicious than an interest in Gaelic poetry and a
predisposition 'to go around calling himself "Sean" Betjeman'.[142]*

No such innocence could apply to the German Legation staff in Northumberland Road, whose activities were constantly monitored by the Irish
authorities. In late 1941, two Irish Army officers accidentally discovered
that Hempel was transmitting radio messages to Germany from his Legation car as he toured the by-roads of County Wicklow,[144] but Dublin was
already alive with gossip to the effect that the German diplomats in the
city were all spies. Rodney Green, the Queen's University undergraduate
who had watched the bodies of the *Arandora Star* victims being brought
across Donegal in the summer of 1940, attended a party in Dublin at
which Karl Heinz Petersen, the German news agency reporter who also
worked for Hempel, turned up with an accordion. According to Green,
the function – at the home of an Irish-American only a few hundred yards
from the German Legation – had scarcely got under way when a Dublin
student named Conor Cruise O'Brien wandered up to the German guest,
and asked: 'Tell me, Petersen, what does it feel like to be a spy?' Petersen
stared at his questioner for some seconds. 'Can I play you a tune on my
accordion?' he asked.[145]

The institution of government in Eire was never seriously questioned
during the war – except by the IRA – although de Valera's political
leadership did not look as secure at the time as it was to appear in
retrospect. His near-blindness caused the British to speculate on his
possible successors. Herbert Shaw ventured the names of Lemass and
O'Kelly, adding that 'certain Cosgravites told me they believed a coalition
Government might well follow in a few months.' This was probably
wishful-thinking, for even Shaw realised that Cosgrave lived 'deep in the
wilderness of opposition'. De Valera's personality, on the other hand,

---

* According to the Soviet spy Kim Philby, the British double agent Guy Burgess, who
made a habit of brawling with his professional colleagues, 'had been in trouble in Dublin' in
the 1940s or early 1950s.[143] But Philby did not make it clear if Burgess had at any time been
in contact with Maffey. He certainly did not know Betjeman.

provided 'a rallying point in time of anxiety and danger. True, his followers may feel he has nothing left to give as largess, and that there is no obvious or general enthusiasm for him, but there is certainly no apparent rival to him.'[146] There were reports that de Valera was in physical danger. In December 1940, Percy Loraine told the British Government that the Taoiseach 'is a much threatened man and has to go about heavily guarded.'[147] Shaw thought that 'if Mr de Valera conceded the ports he might well be shot.' But it was an inner political flaw that Shaw distinguished as a ground for concern about the future of Fianna Fail. He believed it was:

> . . . Mr de Valera's weakness that he chooses 'yes-men' in his entourage, and his party, as a result, may not long survive him.
>
> It was indeed suggested to me that the usefulness of both the existing Irish parties is exhausting itself, and that, after the war, even Ireland may find herself obliged to turn from political to economic problems. If so, something in the nature of a Christian agriculture labour party might conceivably emerge.[148]

Shaw, like so many unionists and British politicians, had underestimated the importance of partition in Irish politics. Fianna Fail was not to die.* The party itself did not, it seems, always support neutrality with the unanimity that de Valera might have wished. Mulcahy – who was by no stretch of the imagination an impartial observer – noted in the summer of 1940 that Fianna Fail would not accept 'the wiping out of Partition on a condition of going into the war on the British side'. A party meeting on June 27 agreed that this would 'split the country from top to bottom . . .' According to Mulcahy, the 'general belief was expressed that the Germans did not mean any mischief here. That they would leave us after they had driven out the British. That if the Germans were occupying the Shannon and the British occupying the Liffey against them, they (some Fianna Fail members) considered that we should take side-line seats and let the Germans and the British fight it out between them.'[149] This complacent, box-office view of the war seems to have diminished over the following months, for in early 1941 Sean MacEoin, one of Mulcahy's front bench colleagues, was recording discontent among Fianna Fail party members in his own constituency of Longford-Westmeath in the Irish midlands. 'Strong Fianna Fail supporters,' he claimed, 'have put up the view that "neutrality is damn little use to us, if everything that we have is going to be lost. Today, they had to sell off their pigs and hens because there were no feeding stuffs. If that was the price of neutrality, it was no damn good. The difference between disaster that way, and disaster from bombing, is nothing" . . . If a bargain was made with the British, any step the Government would take would get support . . .'

* Although it was prescient of Shaw to foretell de Valera's electoral defeat in 1948 at the hands of a coalition that included a farmers' party (Clann na Talmhan).

Fine Gael considered taking advantage of the serious economic effect of the emergency to persuade the electorate that their living standards would improve if Eire joined the war on Britain's side. As Thomas O'Higgins told a front bench meeting of Fine Gael in March, 1941:

> You cannot go out empty-handed. Empty handed in Leix-Offaly I would not get ten per cent of the votes. But if I told them that that industry here, and that industry there, is closed because you have no raw materials, emphasise the position of the farmers, that war or peace was no good to them if they were in poverty, and was able to say 'But here is an offer – great supplies – Ulster restored – defence to meet attack' I would at least guarantee in Leix-Offaly to hold as many seats as Fine Gael has at the moment, and would put a lot of money that I would double it . . .[150]

MacEoin enthusiastically supported this idea. 'Every nation in Europe is bargaining today,' he said. 'It can be done in a perfectly diplomatic way. What the Irish people condemned Redmond for, was that he failed to make a bargain. He gave Britain what Dillon would give now, without making a bargain. If we changed our policy, it must be because of some advantage which will satisfy the people.'[151]

But neutrality was not something that could be the subject of Fine Gael huckstering. Neither they nor the British seem to have realised how attentive, even obsessive, de Valera's Government was towards the minutiae of non-belligerence. Foreign precedents were sought for controversial decisions; in the censorship debate alone, the Government called upon examples of electoral and press restrictions in Switzerland, Sweden, Norway, Denmark and Holland to justify their actions.[152] Even Sir John Maffey believed that the Irish newspapers 'took a pride in publishing the German and British records on even terms and that they were very proud of their strict impartiality.'[153] Anxious not to offend the British – or support the IRA – by giving publicity to militant republicans in Northern Ireland, de Valera's Cabinet refused in 1941 to grant air time on Radio Eireann to a charity supported by Dr McQuaid, the Archbishop of Dublin, that wished to appeal for funds for internees in the six counties.[154] The Government could be equally unhelpful to other, less politically-motivated charity movements. When Jim Larkin, the Irish labour leader, proposed bringing up to 2000 British evacuee children to live with Irish workers' families in Dublin in 1940, Walshe of External Affairs opposed the idea because 'there seem to be many difficulties, and not only of a social and religious character, connected with an uncontrolled scheme of this kind.'[155] Even on matters of trifling importance, de Valera and his ministers could spend hours deliberating. In early 1941, the Cabinet were asked if regimental badges should be engraved on the headstones of the dead British servicemen whose bodies were being washed ashore around the coast of Eire. A long discussion ensued, enlivened by a four-page memorandum from the Department of External Affairs which advised de Valera that 'no such badges should appear on the headstones.'[156] The Taoiseach could see no reason in principle why the regimental insignia should not be engraved, but he then postponed a decision 'until after the war' – partly out of deference to the previous objections of local authorities in County Sligo and County Clare.[157]

There were times when the Irish spoke as if they were actually participating in the war. 'Yes, it's been a hard year,' an Irish newsreel concluded smugly at the end of 1942. 'Sacrifices have been made by rich and poor alike. Nobody has minded that. No sacrifice, no hardship can ever be too great when the reward is our own homeland . . .'[158] But life was not lived amid such heroic emotions. It was, in many ways, a slow as well as an isolated world into which Eire locked herself. As fuel grew scarcer and the transport system gradually collapsed, the railway authorities recorded that one train took twenty-three hours to travel the 210 miles from Killarney to Dublin and another three hours to make the seven-mile journey from Dun Laoghaire to the capital, the passengers collecting timber beside the track to fuel the locomotive. A train from Dublin to Athlone was twice overtaken by a sailing barge on the Royal Canal.[159] Across Eire, the Automobile Association's familiar yellow signposts were taken down, leaving only directions in the Irish language for the population to follow. 'The presumption must be,' a British intelligence report observed with cynicism in 1940, 'that the Germans or English who may land will not be able to understand the Irish language any more than the Irish do.'[160]

To the British, it seemed a small world. In his semi-autobiographical novel *Woodbrook*, David Thomson, a young Englishman who spent the war years in Eire, recalled the day in 1940 on which he heard of the German victory that led to the fall of France and Dunkirk:

It had been a showery month of May and the day was dark and glaring by turns. We were working in the field near the gate-lodge, and Trevor-Roper and I had come back early after dinner and were sitting with our backs to a huge elm tree that grew inside the fence near the bottom of the avenue, waiting for the others. Tom was the next to arrive, and when he saw us he almost ran . . . When he drew near he said 'England's finished' and told us what had happened. 'Hitler's taken France,' he said, 'and in a few days he'll take England.' It was a horrible shock to us. Trevor-Roper said 'Don't be stupid!' . . . I stood up and walked towards where we had been working, overwhelmed by patriotic emotions that I thought I had discarded at the age of fourteen . . .

Charlie bought one of the few wireless sets obtainable in Carrick, an ornate and heavy box that might have done for a dog's coffin, and when its batteries were strong it blared out the news two or three times a day. I am told that the news was more censored in Ireland than in England. No one but Charlie listened to it unless they happened to be in the room, but all through the war years he would switch it on and sit by it; then, even after listening to the most dreadful and dramatic events, would switch if off with a sigh and exclaim, 'No news.'[161]

Eire's physical detachment from the war was nowhere more vividly symbolised than in the small ports around her shores that once maintained a flourishing coastal trade. The harbour master's log at Fenit records that thirty-nine ships put into the harbour in the first four months of 1940. From then on, only the occasional Irish gunboat – the *Muirchu*, *Fort Rannoch* or an old tank-landing barge – visited Fenit until 1943, when all shipping stopped.[162] Not one vessel entered Wexford during the entire war; the pilot boat was used for fishing off the harbour mouth.[163] The only maritime traffic that still operated on a regular basis was the cross-channel ferry service, carrying the unemployed of Eire to work for Britain in her war with Germany. It was a journey filled with the folk memory of emigration. Donal Foley, who was later to become a distinguished journalist on *The Irish Times*, was among those hired to work on the railways in London; he travelled up to Dublin for the Holyhead boat from his home town of Waterford in 1944 on 'a silent expectant train'. His initial passage from Plato's cave was not into light but into darkness:

> The British Railways ship on which we travelled was like a travelling Irish town, moving slowly and darkly across the water. Only the voices of the people, the shouts of command of the sailors and constant gurgling of the channel disturbed the eerie silence of the night. All the lights were blacked out, the first grim reminder that we were travelling to a country at war.
>   . . . In the darkness a young clear singing Cork voice pierced the silence like a rapier. 'Boys like Barry are not cowards . . . British soldiers tortured Barry just because he would not tell.' A primitive feeling of fellowship with that young defiant voice welled up in my breast. The song was taken up by hundreds and when our ship landed at Holyhead, that strange chorus filled the dark air . . .[164]

Chapter 12

A Pied à Terre in Ireland

> Before 1939 Ulster was too often in the position of reminding
> Great Britain that she also was one of the great family of the
> British Commonwealth and Empire. During this war Great
> Britain and the Allies have had reason to be grateful for our
> insistence on remaining in the family group . . . We have
> never doubted that you are necessary to us. We hope that
> you now realise that we are necessary to you.
>
> Sir Basil Brooke *27 April 1944*

When the British Army's Royal Corps of Transport was completing its
wartime duties in Northern Ireland, it produced a 25-page document that
purported to tell soldiers something of the character of the province. 'The
Northern Irish,' its readers were informed, 'have little in common with
the people of Eire and are very largely descended from the Scots. They are
very loyal to the Crown, which is only natural as practically all their raw
material (including all their coal) and much of their manufactured goods,
have to be imported from Great Britain. They have an intense and much
expressed dislike of the people of Eire, which is heartily reciprocated.'
The anonymous authors of this simplistic monograph had, like so many
wartime British visitors to Northern Ireland, ignored the one third of the
population that was neither loyal nor expressed any particular dislike of
Eire. If the Army document presented a cruelly selfish reason for the
province's unique allegiance to King and Empire, however, it was equally
ruthless when it did choose to comment on the conflicting nature of
Christian belief in the six counties. 'Religion has a large influence on the
life of the people and is a subject best left alone by the stranger,' it
announced with disarming frankness. 'Catholics about equal Protestants
in number, but the franchise is so arranged that the Protestants are the
dominant community. Many of the advertisements in the daily papers for
lodgings, vacant situations etc are followed by the words "Protestant" or "no
Catholics" in brackets.' No ethical comment was offered on this discrimination save for a reference to the difficulties encountered by military
transport officers who discovered the existence of 'two separate Dockers
Unions, one Protestant and one Catholic'.[1]

386

There were two separate Belfasts as well. Although not so clinically delineated as they were to become thirty years later, the Shankill Road was the fiefdom of Protestant unionism just as the Falls Road, running almost parallel across the west of the city and then turning symbolically southwards, was the home of Catholic nationalism. There were many impoverished streets between these two religious canyons in which Catholics and Protestants still lived together as neighbours. Catholics held jobs – mostly as barmen – in the Shankill, while the Protestants were employed in the glass factory off the Springfield Road and occasionally went drinking in the Falls.[2] Catholics worked mainly in the flax and textile mills; the Protestants controlled heavy industry, including Mackie's engineering works on the Falls, where only six Catholics were able to contribute to the firm's output of armour-piercing shells.[3] In war work as in what passed for peace, the two communities demonstrated their respective political persuasion with sometimes startling ostentation. When Herbert Morrison, the British Home Secretary, toured a Portadown factory that was producing tailplanes for the Sterling bomber, he found the shop floor decorated with Union Jacks and bunting, and the girls wearing orange lilies in their hair. Basil Brooke had to explain to the astonished minister that this was 'intended for neither you nor I but for the late King William III.'[4] If there was one distinguishing mark by which a wartime stranger might identify nationalist Belfast, it was the rows of wooden shutters which Catholics had placed over their windows to protect them from police batons in the 1930s and which now served as makeshift black-out curtains when the occupants chose to obey the ARP regulations.[5]

One of the few British visitors who bothered to consider the Catholic minority was Frank Pakenham, who predictably and shrewdly commented upon their apparent docility in 1939. 'Their mood,' he told the British Ministry of Information, 'is one of suspicious tranquillity, their role that of a neglected Achilles heel.'[6] Travelling to the province a year later, Herbert Shaw – himself an enthusiastic Unionist – was struck not by Catholic disenchantment but by 'the admirable relations between the majority of the inhabitants and the huge garrison which now throngs the six counties. Ulster's ideal loyalty to Great Britain has been translated into a real and lively friendliness towards individuals of the British Navy, Army and Air Force.'[7] This amity was not always appreciated by the servicemen themselves. In both Belfast and Londonderry, troops found that the Protestant churches opposed Sunday entertainment for the forces on the grounds that they 'greviously wound the spiritual sensitiveness of the Christian community.'[8] The war diary of British Troops Northern Ireland noted in 1942 that the rate of venereal disease among servicemen in the province was the highest in the United Kingdom because the men were far from home and had 'few entertainments'. Between forty and fifty new VD cases were recorded each week, two thirds of them from the

100,000-strong Army garrison.[9] In the spring of 1943, a confidential dispatch from the Royal Navy in Londonderry to the Commander-in-Chief, Western Approaches, complained that most naval officers in the city lived in 'conditions of squalor and discomfort', and that 'Americans raise the prices to get what they want, the British must follow or go without and profiteering is rampant.' The port was by then the base for 140 British and American warships and 19,000 service personnel[10] but the Navy was unimpressed by its surroundings. 'No bombing occurs to remove the useless civilian or to stimulate the useful one,' said the report. 'An uninspiring level of complacent prosperity has settled on Londonderry City, situated beyond the calls of conscription.'[11]

The image of the 'useless civilian' – unconscripted and unemployed – plagued the Northern Ireland Government. In May 1940 Craigavon had expressed himself 'very concerned' about what he called 'the unsatisfactory position in regard to recruiting in Northern Ireland' and told the British Government that his Cabinet 'would be happy to co-operate in any recruiting "drive" that might be made.'[12] John MacDermott, the Minister of Public Security in Belfast, suggested that the Cabinet should place advertisements in the local papers calling upon civilians to enlist. 'We put an "ad" in one of the Belfast dailies,' he recalled after the war, 'and there was quite a turn-up in William Street in response. Then the figures tailed off again.'[13] A Belfast Protestant girl – a stitcher in a clothing factory off the Shankill Road – remembers how 'some Army lorries turned up in Dover Street and an officer gave a speech about "King and Country". But only three fellahs volunteered and they were village-idiot types. No-one wanted to be sent away from Northern Ireland.'[14] MacDermott put this down to a natural fear that the slaughter of the 36th (Ulster) Division on the Somme would be repeated, and that the Protestant survivors would return home to find their jobs filled by Catholics or citizens of Eire. 'I thought the moral issues for joining-up were the same as in 1914,' he said. 'We had to stop the Germans, and I didn't think we could live on the same planet as Hitler. But there was this memory of the First War. On July 1st, 1916, there were some Belfast streets with blinds down in the windows of thirty houses or more because so many men had died. There was no encouragement to enlist again.'[15] MacDermott admitted that 'Northern Ireland in World War II had fallen below its rigorous enthusiasm for World War I.'[16]

To make matters worse, two dozen Irish and Anglo-Irish notables, most of them ex-British officers and all of them fervently pro-British in outlook, mounted a political campaign against Craigavon's Ulster Defence Volunteers – the only proof that the province's manhood was prepared to defend its country in strength – alleging that the organisation was sectarian in content and by design. In September 1940, Churchill received a four-page memorial signed by his own relative, Shane Leslie, old General Sir Hubert de la Poer Gough of Curragh 'mutiny' fame,

Colonel James FitzMaurice, co-pilot of the first east–west flight across the Atlantic, and a host of retired and serving British Army and Royal Navy officers of Irish extraction, all claiming that the UDV's embodiment in the 'B' Specials had identified it 'with all the most bitter sectarian and political differences which have long divided Northern Ireland opinion'. Its enrolment, they said, 'has been largely governed by considerations of religion and politics which would naturally be absent if it had been conducted on normal lines by the British War Office . . . It has thus incurred the odium attaching to a political police force of a type familiar on the Continent of Europe . . .' Believing in the 'struggle against the treacherous, violent and rapacious aggression of Nazidom', the memorialists regarded the enrolment of defence volunteers in the 'B' Specials as 'pregnant with many evil consequences'.[17] Faced with so patriotic a declaration, Churchill took the matter up personally. In October, Charles Markbreiter, the Home Office Assistant Secretary who dealt with Northern Ireland, wrote to Gransden, the Stormont Cabinet Secretary, to tell him that 'Mr Churchill has asked not only what reply is to be sent to the Memorialists, but what can be done.' Markbreiter, who never forgot the sensitivities of Craigavon's Cabinet, thought that 'it could be explained to Mr Churchill that whereas in England a force could be created at very short notice . . . this was not so in Northern Ireland, and would not have been so in any part of Ireland, since, unless one was to make use of a body which was already accepted as of proved loyalty, it would be necessary to vet each individual application . . .'[18]

In Northern Ireland too, the sectarian colour of the local 'Home Guard' had become a political issue. MacDermott was in the Stormont Parliament when local MPs raised General Gough's objection to the force; he was relieved when 'Craigavon lumbered to his feet, got hold of the dispatch box and said: "Mr Speaker, Sir – General Gough has gone off." There was not a single supplementary.'[19] Unionist MPs, however, received letters from several Protestant constituents who disagreed with the apparent parochialism of Craigavon's Government. Major George Panter, the Stormont Unionist MP for Mourne, who had lost an arm fighting on the Somme in 1916, was told by one constituent that 'the Prime Minister of Northern Ireland is – I think – the only one in the whole world who in speech after speech since the outbreak of war, has stressed – not what united but divides the people he governs – the name of "King"!' In her letter, Charlotte Warner, a Protestant living in Newcastle, County Down, told Panter that 'the breed of the men of Narvik and Dunkirk and of numbers in the merchant fleet are to be denied the elementary right of guarding their own homes. But they are given a grievance – yet one more – and, in this country, to be given a grievance is to get a gun.' Warner wondered why 'in the week when here in this district every two citizens that met were for Churchill, the four members of the Imperial Parliament voted for Chamberlain. All were for the party and none was for the state.'[20]

She wanted the oath of allegiance to be made to 'neighbours' – along the lines of the first Swiss Confederates – rather than to the King. 'God save him from his friends,' Warner remarked. 'They do him more harm in N.I. than all the IRA, old, new, dead and alive.'[21] But the Northern Ireland Government was not impressed by such arguments. 'I know you will appreciate,' Gransden told Panter after reading Warner's letters, 'that the greatest possible care must be exercised in the enrolment of volunteers who will be issued with lethal weapons . . . it is one thing to enrol a large body of volunteers regardless of the requirements of the area in which they live, and another to build up more steadily, but certainly more surely, an organisation, the members of which are of proven loyalty . . .'[22]

By November of 1940, Spender was again advocating conscription. 'At present,' he told Lord Hankey, 'the Ulsterman is in the unfair position that he is earning quite unjustly the contempt of the men of the Welsh and the Midland Division who cannot understand why they should be sent over to protect a Province whose young men fail to respond to the Country's Call. However, it would have a very salutary effect upon our unemployment situation.'[23] Here lay the other embarrassment of the Stormont Government. If Northern Ireland's manpower could not be forcibly enlisted or voluntarily recruited, why could it not be fully mobilised in civilian labour for the war effort?

Between August 1939 and November 1940, the number of men and women out of work in the province had increased by more than 8000, bringing the overall percentage unemployment figure to 21.7%. In the same period, unemployment had fallen in the rest of the United Kingdom from about one and a quarter million to 791,000.[24] The extent of Northern Ireland's economic failure at this time was dramatically illustrated in a detailed report on the province's contribution to the war effort prepared by Harold Wilson, who was then Joint Secretary of the British War Cabinet's Manpower Requirements Committee. In December 1940, Wilson – who was to become British Prime Minister more than twenty years later – noted that 'at the end of fifteen months of war . . . Ulster, far from becoming an important centre of munitions production, has become a depressed area. While other areas of similar size and industrial population have played an increasing part in war production, Ulster has not seen the construction of a single new factory. At the same time orders placed with existing firms (shipbuilding yards excepted) have been on an exceedingly meagre scale.' Northern Ireland's unemployment figures were 'roughly equal to the percentage unemployment in Great Britain in 1932 . . . the worst year of the great depression. It would be difficult to find a more striking index of depression than this.'

At least 20,000 of the unemployed – most of them women – came from the linen industry, which had collapsed when the war cut off the supply of flax from the Soviet Union, the Baltic states and the Low Countries. Even with a surplus of 50,000 employable workers, however, Northern Ireland's contribution to the economic war effort had been negligible. Ship-building activity had increased appreciably but employment in the engineering and allied industries had increased since the outbreak of war by only a little over 4000. There was no employment at all in explosives or chemical industries, and less than 20,000 men and women were engaged on directly productive war work. Wilson reported that:

> . . . among the more tragic results of the neglect of Ulster in the war effort is the disappointment and disillusionment of several thousand workers and others keen to do war work. The exhortations of English politicians to work harder and longer have been a positive embarrassment to the Northern Ireland Government. It is on record that when a batch of 'Go To It' posters arrived in Ulster a deputation of employers petitioned for their suppression on the ground that they would only cause discontent, owing to the absence of any-thing to which a loyal and willing population might go.[25]

Wilson concluded that 'so far as can be seen there is little or no economic co-ordination between Great Britain and Northern Ireland.'[26] When Wilson's report was shown to him, Lindsay Keir, the Vice-Chancellor of Queen's University, Belfast, more than agreed with some of its claims. Morale, he wrote in the draft of a letter to Wilson, seemed to be getting worse. 'Those who are loyal are, as you say, disheartened and disillusioned by there being nothing to "go to". Among the other, extremism of all kinds, eg communism and the IRA, are flourishing on industrial depres-sion. I have even been told of young Protestants being attracted into membership of illegal organisations.' The situation, said Lindsay Keir, 'gives the greatest concern to those who care most for the Province and its people.'[27]

So it should have done, for the desire of the Northern Ireland Govern-ment to 'keep in step' with Britain was now failing at both national and provincial level. The Stormont Cabinet could neither demonstrate the presumed desire of the six counties to make an equal sacrifice – militarily or economically – in the British war effort, nor could it give its own people prospects of employment equal to those in the rest of the United King-dom. Unemployment figures were to fall later in the war; the province's Government tried to absorb its labour market by sending workers to Britain – 30,000 in two years alone – but by February of 1942, there were still 29,000 out of work in the six counties.[28] Even in August 1944, one in twenty of the insured population in Northern Ireland were unemployed, compared to only one in two hundred in Britain.[29] When the province did secure war work, the British Government often expressed dissatisfaction with the results. In March of 1941, Churchill was insisting that the construction of airfields in the province should be completed more quickly – the Northern Ireland Government promised to use their 'full resources' to accelerate the work[30] – but in May came a further, more impatient demand. 'I think I ought to let you know,' Herbert Morrison wrote to

John Andrews, Craigavon's successor in Belfast, 'that Mr Churchill has recently sent me a personal note expressing his concern about the limited extent of Northern Ireland's contribution to the nation's industrial war effort.' What progress, Morrison wanted to know, had Andrews' Cabinet made in alleviating the shortage of machine tools and in building a new power station to supplement the vulnerable electricity plant at Belfast harbour?[31] Some months later, Lord Beaverbrook, now Churchill's Minister of Supply, was castigating Basil Brooke, the Northern Ireland Minister of Commerce, for delays in supplying electricity to vital war industries. 'Without adequate supplies,' Beaverbrook wrote, 'we cannot place orders in Northern Ireland. And the production on which we rely in Russia, Libya and at home will be less than we expect and need.'[32]

John Andrews' reaction to these problems was to blame the British. 'There is a very strong general complaint,' he told Beaverbrook in February 1942, 'that Northern Ireland is not being helped to anything like the extent it should be as regards war work, and that it is quite wrong that Northern Ireland capacity to produce for war requirements is not being fully utilised.'[33] Brooke supported Andrews' requests for further contracts but was more circumspect in his approach to the British Government. He had developed a caustic but far from unfriendly relationship with Beaverbrook, whom he regarded as 'a man of very strong and unshakeable opinions' although 'rather theatrical in discussion'. When Beaverbrook, who had 'his finger in the pie of Irish politics', refused to send aircraft contracts to Short Brothers and Harland because of 'the unstable political situation', Brooke threatened to tell the Stormont Parliament that 'we are being refused permission to help in the war effort because you feel we are too dangerous a risk.' According to Brooke's version of their conversation, the Supply Minister relented and awarded the contracts to Shorts.[34] But the two men connived together to put pressure on the Northern Ireland Government over delays in war production. Beaverbrook, it transpires, was prevailed upon to write his critical letter on the province's electricity supply by Brooke himself, who let the British minister know that he 'would welcome it as strengthening his hands.'[35]

Brooke, of course, had been Craigavon's choice as successor. As a Minister in Andrews' elderly Government, his abilities far outshone those of his Cabinet colleagues. Visiting Stormont in December of 1940, Herbert Shaw reported that Andrews was 'a much lesser man than his predecessor, and does not enjoy anything like the same veneration among the Ulster Unionists. He is head, moreover, of a weak Cabinet in which Sir Basil Brooke seems to be the only really effective minister.'[36] Andrews was indeed an unimpressive man. Seventy years old and so hard of hearing that his ministers sometimes had to shout in order that he should hear their advice,[37] he led a Cabinet that could be as cantankerous as it was old. Even in Craigavon's time, there had been rivalry between Government departments and the British Army, whose potential powers were regarded by ministers with some suspicion. So concerned were the British about this deteriorating relationship that when Andrews paid a formal visit to Buckingham Palace a month after Craigavon's death, the King found it necessary to question the Northern Ireland Prime Minister 'as to whether the Civil Government was working amicably with the Military Authorities'.[38] Wilfrid Spender feared his Government was unwilling to share responsibility with the Army in the event of hostilities, and thought 'that unless they do so we shall be involved in martial law and . . . the Civil Service will have to take over the responsibility of Ministers, which will be a grave reflection upon our form of Government.'[39] Not that the province's civil service was unaffected by ministerial rivalry. Brooke, who liked the Army officers with whom he came into contact in Northern Ireland, told Gransden that he was 'much perturbed at the rather flippant manner of the discussions of the Civil Servants' at the first meeting of the Home Defence Executive in 1941, and regretted 'that such a lamentable exhibition had been given to the Service members.'[40]

No member of the Government, however, was more obtuse than Dawson Bates, the Minister of Home Affairs, a small man with a thick black moustache and a reputation for anti-Catholic discrimination and drunkenness.[41] Shaw noted that Andrews' relations with the minister 'though outwardly friendly, are, I am told, in fact by no means so.'[42] This was putting it mildly. General Sir Harold Franklyn came to see Spender when he took over the British Army's Northern Ireland District in 1941 and confided that 'there was one Minister, Sir Dawson Bates, who seemed to behave in an extraordinary way and who did not even have the courtesy to acknowledge his letters.' Spender admitted to the General that 'the Ministry of Home Affairs was the one Ministry which caused me great anxiety at the present time.'[43] Dawson Bates not only failed to answer letters from the Army; on one occasion – in February 1941 – he had even neglected to turn up for a Cabinet meeting at Stormont, claiming later that he had not found the paper notifying him of the appointment.[44]

The unwieldy, largely ineffective government over which Andrews presided gradually lost the support of its own Unionist Party MPs at Stormont. Shaw had noted in 1940 that 'for some time past there has been murmuring on the Unionist back benches, though no attempts at revolt could survive Lord Craigavon's frown. Now, however, the back benches might conceivably carry a vote of censure, without perhaps realising how heavy would be the responsibility they would thus assume . . . If this revolt did occur, the task of the Northern Civil Service would become arduous indeed; but it is possible that one result might be an increased susceptibility to British control and pressure.'[45] The revolt that Shaw predicted took more than two years to gestate; and when it came, it did not impose quite so serious a burden upon the province's administrative life as Shaw supposed. A general discontent among backbenchers and among the Protestant population as a whole, both at the continued high rate of unemployment and the poor economic contribution that Northern Ireland was making to the war effort, helped to lose three Unionist seats at by-elections. Andrews was unwilling to bring younger men into senior Cabinet posts,[46] and Brooke, who was also Deputy Prime Minister, refused to stay in the Government when it was clearly so unpopular with the Unionist parliamentary party. On his own evidence, Brooke 'frequently disagreed' with Andrews and 'had occasion several times to tell him so', but he insisted that 'at no time had I any contact with those in the back benches who were organising the "revolt" . . .'[47] Andrews did for a time believe that Brooke had manoeuvred against him, and Brooke's motive in offering to resign – to quote an historian of the Unionist Party – 'must remain open to question'.[48]

Andrews' resignation in April 1943 marked the end of Craigavon's Government; for the Cabinet ministers that served under Andrews were essentially the same ones who had worked for Northern Ireland's first Prime Minister. The war did not in itself bring about this change in government but it precipitated the transition. Younger men would now guide Northern Ireland's affairs. But the war did not alter the spirit of Unionist government; if it contained more energy than its predecessor, Brooke's administration nevertheless adhered to Craigavon's old principle of a Protestant Parliament and a Protestant State. When Brooke chose to follow the example of the British War Cabinet and provide some semblance of party coalition in his Government, he mimicked rather than copied Churchill's system of wartime rule. Ignoring the opposition Catholic Nationalist MPs, he appointed Harry Midgley, a member of the Northern Ireland Labour Party's breakaway 'Commonwealth' faction, to be his Minister of Public Security. Brooke was later to explain that:

> . . . I knew that I could not invite the Nationalist Party to run in double harness with the Unionists. At that time they were entirely non-cooperative especially with regard to any effort during the whole war. Indeed one of the Nationalist MPs of the day went so far as writing to the German Ambassador in Dublin asking that if Germany won the war, would they unite the two parts of Ireland.[49]

Brooke therefore sought out Midgley who was 'as loyal to the fundamental principles of union with Great Britain as I was'.[50] There is evidence that Midgley's appointment did gain grudging acceptance among some sections of the trade union movement* but his presence in the Cabinet presented only the façade of coalition.

---

* A month after Brooke became Prime Minister, the British censorship authorities monitored a private telephone call between a Belfast trade unionist and the offices of the Communist *Daily Worker* newspaper in London; a transcript of the conversation was sent to the Northern Ireland authorities, who noted with approval the following passage:
BELFAST We cannot encourage anything that will develop into personal enmity against
Midgley. The new Cabinet is a big improvement. I admit it is unfortunate that he is

The Catholics of Northern Ireland thus remained unrepresented in Brooke's wartime administration, their political views influencing the authorities only in so far as they represented – or were thought to represent – a threat to the province's security. After two decades of sectarian violence, they were – in the words of one of Dawson Bates' internees – 'almost totally submissive, hating the police rather than the Germans'.[52] Spender told Lord Hankey that when the war broke out, he 'had hoped that there might be an opportunity to bring together the different political parties in Northern Ireland and we endeavoured to secure co-operation of our Roman Catholic citizens in regard to the War Savings Campaign.' Why Spender should have imagined that Catholic nationalists – who could neither co-operate in the government of the province nor in its volunteer defence force – would want to participate in a war savings campaign is not easy to understand. In any event, when the Lord Chief Justice of Northern Ireland approached Cardinal MacRory on the matter, he received 'a very discourteous refusal'. Spender took a comfortable view of the affair. 'It is solely due to the attitude of their leaders,' he wrote, 'that this part of our population is making little or no contribution to the war effort which is very disappointing, especially in view of the magnificent response made by the English Roman Catholics . . . I still believe that if this part of our population were taken outside Ireland and away from this local influence they would be found as ready to support our Cause as were the men of the 10th Division in the last war.'[53]

The unreality of Spender's assessment was matched by Shaw, who also felt that the nationalist community was 'badly led'. Although they had 'a blackmail influence on Irish sentiment,' he reported, 'they seem incapable of using it effectively. Cardinal MacRory, and other Roman Catholic prelates, exploit the grievances of the Catholic minority to the full . . . I formed, however, the general opinion that the grievances of the minority are not as grave as they protest.' Shaw's Protestant Unionist background coloured his vision of Northern Ireland and of MacRory; in his memorandum, he did not give the impression that he had allowed many Catholics to help him shape his 'general opinion'. Shane Leslie had met MacRory in the late autumn of 1939 and formed a more moderate view of his activities. 'He lives in Armagh . . . and is therefore mostly surrounded by Protestants,' a Dominions Office official wrote of the Cardinal after talking to Leslie. 'He feels that he is rather cut off from information and contact with

---

included and we made that point about the Trade Unions to show that Midgley does not represent the Trade Unions and the Labour Movement.

LONDON . . . I can see a possibility that Midgley is the way that Sir Basil Brooke intends to get around the question of Labour representation. It makes it very awkward for us and for the Labour Party.

BELFAST I know. But our job is to get the public to view the new Cabinet solely in the interests of the war effort . . .[51]

governmental authorities. The rulers of Ulster do not see anything of him socially or consult him on matters in which he is deeply interested, such as education. I dare say they are afraid of their own Orangemen, but it would certainly be a good thing if they could establish a little closer contact with him.'[54]

In some ways, the Catholic community of the six counties was more isolated than the people of Eire. Shaw thought they were 'somewhat despised in the South',[55] which may have been partly true, and certainly young Catholics in Belfast were able to nurse curious illusions about the nascent republic across the border. Languishing in the Crumlin Road jail in 1942, Paddy Devlin, the teenage republican from the Falls, who was later to become a respected Catholic politician, wondered why IRA men were executed in Eire. 'In Belfast, we thought de Valera was a Messianic figure, almost a god, a saviour of Ireland,' Devlin recalled years later. 'We knew that IRA men died in the South at the hands of the Government there. But we believed that "Dev" was too great a man to permit this to happen, that the hangings and firing squads must have been going on behind his back and he didn't realise what was happening.'[56] This was a world away from the grim records of Dublin Cabinet discussions on the death sentences. When Irish ministers decided against a stay of execution for an IRA man, the minutes would always conclude: 'It was decided that the law must take its course'; and these words would invariably be followed by the small, neat signature 'Edev' in de Valera's own hand.[57]

The internees were originally guarded by warders and 'B' Specials but the possibility of German invasion in July of 1940 forced the Northern Ireland Government to consider handing their prisoners over to the British Army, a step which would place them under the control of the British Home Office. The secret files of the province's Home Defence Executive show that the idea was strenuously opposed by Stormont civil servants. Adrian Robinson, the Secretary to Dawson Bates' Ministry of Home Affairs, for instance, argued that if internees were transferred to the Home Office, 'there would be a grave danger of their being very soon released since the Government of Eire would undoubtedly bring pressure to bear on the Imperial Authorities through the Dominions Office.' E.W. Scales, the Secretary to the Ministry of Public Security, however, ventured a more revealing reason for not allowing the British to take control of the 155 men who had by then been interned. He pointed out that the British Home Secretary 'would not agree to the internment of British subjects unless there were very firm grounds for doing so . . .' Then – in a passage which was later deleted from the official minutes – Scales added that the Home Office 'would probably decide to release most of the internees on the evidence available on the Ministry of Home Affairs files.'[58]

There can be no doubt that IRA officers were numbered among the prisoners. Even the young Devlin, a lowly volunteer in the IRA's 'D'

Company, admitted years later that he 'threw bombs and fired shots at the police' before his internment in 1942.[59] But the wartime internee records of the Ministry of Home Affairs have never been opened to the public. They would make interesting reading. Why, for example, was Cahir Healy, the Stormont Nationalist MP for South Fermanagh, arrested in 1941 and interned at Brixton prison, in south London? Since Healy, a distinguished parliamentarian who had also been interned by the Northern Ireland Government in 1922, was transferred to Britain, the United Kingdom authorities must have approved of his imprisonment. Was he the Nationalist MP whom Brooke claimed had written to the German Minister in Dublin? Or had he, as the Irish journalist James Kelly believed at the time, sent a letter to a Catholic priest in the village of Newtownbutler about the chances of Irish unity after a German invasion? Nationalists in the province immediately wanted to know why – if Healy was to be imprisoned – the Northern Ireland authorities had not also arrested Lord Londonderry, Churchill's cousin whose pre-war friendship with Goering and Ribbentrop was still remembered in the six counties.[60]

Londonderry, the former Stormont Minister of Education and British Air Minister, had been excluded from Churchill's Government, apparently because of his pre-war attitude to Nazi Germany.[61] In 1936, Londonderry and his family had been entertained with lavish hospitality by Hitler himself as well as by Goering and other Luftwaffe leaders during a visit to Germany;[62] Ribbentrop, the German Ambassador in London – later to become Hitler's Foreign Minister – was invited to Mount Stewart, Londonderry's family seat in Northern Ireland. James Kelly, based in Belfast for the Dublin *Irish Independent*, remembers Ribbentrop's visit to County Down and Londonderry's 'real Tory praise for Germany' at the time.[63] The former minister had in fact passed to British officials all the information he gleaned in Germany, but there can be little question of his admiration for the enthusiasm which ordinary Germans displayed towards Hitler. He was to condemn the Nazis once the war started, and became Northern Ireland Commandant of the Air Training Corps. But the damage had been done. He became convinced that his mail was being subjected to special scrutiny by the censors because of his alleged pro-German sympathies before the war.[64] Thomas Henderson, an Independent Unionist MP from the Shankill, spread the word that Londonderry had invited him to a private room at the Grand Central Hotel in Belfast to discuss Germany.[65] Even in 1941, Hitler was able to refer to Londonderry and to Lord Rothermere as 'leading pro-Germans'.[66]

The Northern Ireland authorities, however, were much more interested in Victor Fiorentini, the Italian-born former secretary of the Fascist party in Londonderry. Fiorentini owned a restaurant in Strand Road not far from the city's harbour and before the war had been a fairly zealous supporter of Mussolini's regime in Italy. In 1934, he had been invited to Rome to meet the Duce but on his return to Londonderry had

been forced to resign from the party by jealous colleagues.* Fiorentini
says that an RUC Chief Constable warned him that he would be interned
if Italy declared war, so when Mussolini did decide to ally himself with
Hitler in 1940, Fiorentini escaped by car across the border to Muff in
County Donegal. Even today, he breaks down in tears when he recalls how
he had to leave his Irish wife behind in Londonderry and go into 'three
years exile'.[68] The British placed a different construction upon his hurried
departure. Fiorentini, noted an intelligence report to the British Government, 'is strongly anti-British. He is married to a Donegal woman whose
father, James O'Donnell, is one of the pilots employed by the Londonderry Harbour Board. The Pilot Station is situated at Shrove, Greencas-
tle, Eire, on Lough Foyle. The pilots send telephone messages to Londonderry re the approach of ships and receive instructions, some of a
confidential nature, from the SNO [Senior Naval Officer] Derry. Fiorentini . . . no doubt has access to these instructions. As he is in the Free State
the Northern Ireland authorities cannot touch him but are unhappy about
the situation.'[69] Fiorentini says that he 'heard rumours that I ran out to
spy' but denies that he ever contemplated espionage. He arrived at his
father-in-law's house at Shrove on 8 July 1940, 'excited, pale and crying',
and spent three years there, helping to gather corn on the Inishowen
peninsula each summer and worrying about his young wife – against
whom there was no suspicion and who stayed to run the restaurant – when
he heard reports that the Germans had bombed Londonderry.[70]†

The Northern Ireland Government remained convinced – publicly, at
any rate – that Eire was somehow involved in a conspiracy with Germany.
It was in the interests of Unionists to project this idea to a British
Government already exasperated by de Valera's neutrality. But it would
be a mistake to imagine that Northern Ireland Protestants did not
genuinely believe the rumours of Nazi sympathies within the Dublin
Cabinet. In May 1941, Spender commented in his private diary that
recent Dail debates proved that the Irish Government's policy 'had been
definitely pro-Nazi. They have prevented their people from hearing the
Vatican's pronouncement against the Nazis and have deliberately stopped
the explanations given by the British Government of some of the Nazi
attacks . . . I am afraid that certain members of the Eire Government who
have lately received great accession in their personal wealth must be

* According to Fiorentini, Mussolini showed some interest in Ireland. 'When I told him
where I was from, he said: "Oh Londonderry – that's in Northern Ireland",' Fiorentini
recalled. 'I told Mussolini that we were the smallest Fascist club in the United Kingdom,
and he replied: "Then grow!" '[67] This was something of a tall order in the Maiden City.
† The British were themselves satisfied with Fiorentini's innocence after he travelled to
Dublin in 1943 and told Maffey that he would 'rather hang than be a spy.' The British
Representative arranged for him to return to Londonderry, where a police officer welcomed him back with the information that his had been the sixth name on the RUC's arrest
list when Italy declared war; Fiorentini was to have been put aboard the doomed liner
Arandora Star with the aliens.[71]

obtaining it from hostile sources.'[72]

It was this sort of suspicion that made any British suggestion of Irish unity – in whatever circumstances – doubly unthinkable to men like Spender. Maffey had suggested to him in 1940 that 'if the British Empire were defeated in this war . . . it would be very greatly to the advantage of Northern Ireland to join up with Eire and that the British Government would advise Ulster to do so.' Spender had been horrified. 'I replied,' he wrote, 'that this was a contingency which I refused to visualise and that I did not think it merited any thought or further discussion.'[73] Yet if Northern Ireland Protestants could not see themselves as Irishmen – even *in extremis* – did they really regard themselves as part of a country at war, as earnest in their desire to defeat Hitler's Germany as the British were? MacDermott believed that 'there was a certain self-interest about our patriotism in the Second World War – there was more in it commercially for Northern Ireland.'[74] The province did show more support for the 1914–18 War than it did in 1939, he believed, but 'one had to remember that, compared with 1914–18, the enthusiasm for the conflict was naturally lower on *both* sides of the North Channel.'[75]

And yet there was a fundamental difference in attitude and temper between the men from Northern Ireland and their counterparts in Britain, as they fought their war against Germany. Servicemen from the province sometimes noticed this at moments of great stress. Sam McAughtry, a Protestant from the Tiger's Bay district of Belfast, was an RAF Coastal Command navigator who held more or less the same views about the conflict as MacDermott, 'that there was no choice but to put an end to Nazism.' But there was on occasions an emotional distance between McAughtry and his British officers. 'I used to come back from convoy and harbour strikes wound up to hell's gates,' he afterwards recalled, 'only to be reduced to silence by the Wing Commander's level stare. I felt distinctly un-British. The element in the British character that glorifies ice-cold acceptance of duty is missing in me . . .'[76] McAughtry illustrated this frame of mind years after the war in a book he wrote about his merchant seaman brother, who died when the German pocket battleship *Admiral Scheer* attacked the British convoy IIX 84 in the Atlantic in November 1940. It was the same engagement in which Fogarty Fegen of the RNVR won a posthumous VC 'in the classical situation so dear to the hearts of the British,' as McAughtry cynically remarked, '– on the receiving end in a naval slaughtering match.'[77] The British, McAughtry observed, 'will never let go of the belief that thirty-two ships' crews owed their safety to the fact that Fegen and 189 of his men laid down their lives for them.' The truth, he decided, was that the rest of the convoy were saved by the stupidity of the German naval commander.[78] 'The British like the figures in their legends to wear uniforms,' McAughtry wrote later, 'so . . . the 206 merchant seamen whose lives were lost didn't crop up in the legend.'[79]

Northern Ireland servicemen could at least claim to be making an equal contribution to the British war effort. The same could not necessarily be said of the workers and management in the province's armaments factories. Throughout the war, the censorship authorities provided civil servants in Belfast with a unique source of information which proved beyond a shadow of doubt that British ministers had good reason to be angry at the delays and inefficiency in Northern Ireland's wartime industrial production. Extracts from hundreds of private letters, written by unsuspecting workers to their relatives and containing evidence of idleness, wastage and sometimes sheer dishonesty in the large factories producing aircraft and guns for the British forces, flooded onto the desks of Stormont Cabinet officials. Many of these letters were from Eire citizens who had travelled north for the new jobs available in wartime industry; they provide damaging proof that Catholics from the twenty-six counties were often little interested in the war effort, and that Northern Ireland ministers who tried to restrict the immigration of Eire workers were not acting totally without reason. But other letters came from Protestants in the province – even from Americans – and the story they told was the same: of big industrial concerns paying high wages for little work, of mismanagement and slackness and low morale.

'It makes my blood boil,' wrote a Protestant from County Londonderry to a friend in Cheshire in early 1942, 'to see men on Nissen Huts construction – one man working and six or seven looking on. No wonder camps are still in the making which were supposed to be completed for the winter, now nearly over. At this rate there is no earthly chance of our winning the war when so many only concern themselves over what they can make out of it without much effort.'[80] An American woman who worked in a Belfast ammunition factory, voiced similar sentiments to her husband in New York at about the same time. 'If only the people would all put their hearts into the job of winning the war,' she wrote, 'there would be less setbacks. Honestly John, there are some folk who don't care a dam [sic] about the war. In the firm I work the men earn swell money but they will not work for it . . . sometimes we waste hours doing nothing waiting for a man to fix our machines, jobs that we could do ourselves but dare not.'[81]

Workers in the aircraft factories and shipyards of Belfast seemed to be among the worst offenders. A Catholic employed in an aviation works told his father in Dublin in 1942 that 'most of the employees are loafers who do not want to work but always are sure to be around on Friday when the pay envelopes are being handed out. I was amazed at the amount of idleness that is tolerated by the foreman . . . I will sum up by saying that the War effort in this particular factory is disgraceful.'[82] The same man wrote to a friend in Dublin two days later, telling her that 'when a man is doing an honest day's work somebody is bound to come along and tell him to get wise to himself which means that he should slow up and have a rest every few minutes.'[83] Another Catholic worker in an aircraft factory told a friend in County Louth that 'it is quite clear you don't have to work at all. Well I mean to say I work hard – I drilled 4 one-eighth holes for my days work on Wednesday after all I don't want to strain myself that would never do . . .'[84]

Similar accounts came from those who worked in Belfast harbour. 'It is like a holiday going around the docks,' an Irish Catholic informed his brother in Cork in August 1942. 'The three of us are in the Aircraft carrier. We are to be on the flight deck before 8.20 in the morning and they all sit down and talk until about 10 o'clock. At 12.40 we go to the canteen about 2 minutes walk from the carrier and get all the grub you want for 1/- . . . Then we have to be back about 1.45 & they don't start work until 3.0 o'clock . . . So you see its a gift of a job. Every part of the docks is the same for all trades men.'[85] Another Eire citizen employed in the harbour remarked in a letter to his sister that 'there is a joke on this boat that there's supposed to be sleeping sickness on board. You would trip over fellows asleep even the foreman have [sic] to wake them up sometimes.'[86] A fitter in the shipyard claimed that the hardest job he had was 'killing time';[87] so did a Londonderry Catholic engaged on building military huts.[88] Slackness in war industries spread even to the men repairing blitzed houses in Belfast. A building labourer wrote in 1941 that 'this is a great life out in the Belfast hills every morning . . . for the first 2 weeks we got paid for getting up in the morning and then going to the office on Friday to draw our pay . . .'[89]

Reading through the mass of censorship intercepts, Robinson, the Secretary to the Ministry of Home Affairs, commented gloomily that 'it certainly looks as if there was a considerable waste of public money and that the war effort is not running much of a horse in Northern Ireland.'[90] The authorities occasionally followed up reports of slackness but, rather remarkably, the Secretary to the Ministry of Commerce acknowledged much later in the war – when the intercepts had 'assumed "Gone with the Wind" proportions' that he could 'not honestly say that the information conveyed was of high value or that it materially affected our actions.'[91] Perhaps the Stormont civil service thought that the task of investigating each report – to which the names of the relevant factories were usually attached – would be more trouble than it was worth, that the constant exposure of industrial inefficiency might even prove embarrassing.

For a number of the letters related not to work-shy employees but to bad management. A private letter sent by a staff official at Short and Harland's aircraft works alleged that 'the management seem to be taking advantage of the present emergency to build up the place for peacetime production and don't seem to give a damn about war time production. I could write a book of examples of inefficiency and bad management and leadership . . .'[92] A Protestant woman whose husband worked as a welfare officer at the same aircraft company alleged in a letter to a friend in Scotland that 'S & H don't give a damn about welfare. Their idea of a welfare officer is a

401

kind of dummy who will listen to the men's complaints and then shelve them.'[93] The same woman wrote later to another friend, recording her husband's frustration. 'It made him wild feeling that our young AIRMEN were losing their lives every day while other people wouldn't – to save themselves trouble and inconvenience – allow him even to carry out his duties properly.'[94] A letter addressed to Admiral Sir Roger Keyes, the Westminster MP, referred to wastage of petrol by Belfast managements. 'Although there are trams,' it noted, 'the businessmen go back to lunch and return to their offices every day – 4 trips – and drive large cars . . . home sitting alone in their glory; they've never been known to offer anybody a lift.'[95] A Belfast Protestant working in an armaments factory complained to his daughter in December 1942 that he was being victimised by the management 'for being honest and exposing the hold-ups as being artificial, being engineered in Manager [sic] office for the specific purpose of retarding production. Unfortunately the workers' position in Ulster is next to hopeless, he has no one to appeal to that would give him a sympathetic hearing, that is in any real authority . . .' The writer described how the management of his factory forced employees to work slowly – by constantly switching them to new jobs with which they were unfamiliar – so that the company would not have to pay a production bonus. 'From the charge hands up to the manager,' he concluded: '. . . none of them seems desirous of the war ending soon – knowing the sooner it ends, the sooner they loose [sic] a good job. They don't care about the atrocities in Europe, or how many Ally fighters lose their lives so long as they keep their jobs.'[96]

It should not have come as a shock to the Stormont authorities when industrial unrest began to have a serious effect on war production. In 1941, a strike of carters at the docks held up material for the Royal Navy. Unused to dealing with labour discontent of this kind but anxious not to provoke the strikers, the Northern Ireland Government were at first reluctant to permit service personnel into the docks to collect essential military equipment.[97] A year later, however, eighteen thousand shipyard, aircraft and engineering workers walked out in a prolonged pay dispute that caused disquiet in Whitehall. Churchill wrote personally to Andrews to express the British War Cabinet's 'shock' at the scale of the strike, adding with frosty sympathy that it was 'very hard on Northern Ireland to have to carry such a burden.'[98] According to RUC records, most of the 260 strikes in the province during the war years were illegal because 'the strikers did not take advantage of the machinery provided by the law for the settlement of grievances.'[99] Trade union correspondence in the files of the Northern Ireland Government, however, gives some idea of why industrial negotiating machinery was not always used. According to the Belfast branch of the Amalgamated Engineering Union in 1943, for example, the Chairman of the Joint Production Committee at Harland and Wolff's Aircraft Department – which was then producing Stirling bombers and Sunderland flying-boats for the RAF – 'continuously reminded us that he did not want increased Production, repeatedly saying, Production was being maintained, the men were making time and a half bonus and the factory was ahead of Schedule . . . in many cases [he] tells our representatives their complaints, concerning obstructions, hold-up, etc, are groundless. When we insist they are well founded and get so far as to prove them, he becomes infuriated, Hells, Dams [sic], turns and twists in chair, throws pencil on table, so that logical reasoning on a point is out of question . . .'[100]

The Stormont Cabinet tried to break the strikes by sending the instigators to prison. The RUC records reveal that as many as 6000 men were prosecuted in this way during the war.[101] Sometimes the strikers reacted defiantly; dockers' trade union leaders burnt their summonses in Corporation Street off the Falls[102] – there were, of course, two dockers' unions, divided on sectarian lines – but Paddy Devlin remembers the five shop stewards who were held responsible for a one-month aircraft and shipyard strike in 1944 'arriving at the Crumlin Road jail and looking around them, very cowed and tranquillised, not speaking to the other prisoners.'[103] The incarceration of the five men almost brought about a general strike throughout Northern Ireland. Thus two months before D-Day, the Royal Navy were to be found preparing to operate the Belfast Harbour power station, and the RUC were told that they might have to maintain essential services.[104] None of the strikes in Northern Ireland were directly intended to sabotage the war effort but both management and unions clearly took advantage of the vital importance of the province's war production as a bargaining counter in their disputes.* This period of industrial unrest was not one which the authorities viewed with much pride. The official history of the province in the Second World War devotes just one paragraph to the strikes.[106]

There was no evidence that workers from the twenty-six counties played any part in these events but the Northern Ireland Government became increasingly nervous about what it referred to as the 'infiltration' of Eire citizens into the province. Andrews told his Cabinet in 1942 that there was 'evidence of increasing public criticism of the ease with which workers from Eire could obtain employment of various kinds in Northern Ireland when numbers of Northern Ireland workers were being sent to Great Britain and others were unemployed at home.'[107] Brooke initially took the view that 'it would be comparatively easy for ill-disposed persons

---

* A much more opportunistic attitude towards the war – or rather, the effects of the war – was revealed when refugees who had lost their homes in the German air raids on Belfast in 1941 found themselves charged exorbitant rents for emergency accommodation. Intimidated by landlords who threatened to evict them from their new homes if they complained to the authorities, many families preferred to pay the new rents in silence. In September 1941, Dawson Bates proposed a tribunal to which tenants could appeal without fear of eviction.[105]

from Eire to obtain information of considerable value to the enemy regarding the manufacture in Northern Ireland of certain secret war materials.'[108] But there was no disguising the fact that the real reason for the Government's concern lay in the fear that their own citizens might return from Britain – or from the services – to find their jobs occupied by Eire workers. By 1944, Midgley, who was then Brooke's Minister of Labour, was worried that Irish citizens who had served in the British forces might seek employment in Northern Ireland 'and compete with our own ex-Servicemen and civilians in a falling labour market.' Many of these men, thought Midgley, would 'gravitate to the disloyal element in our population and increase our political difficulties.'[109] The Stormont Cabinet's anxiety, however, was partly of its own making. Between February and December 1941, for instance, almost 7000 Eire citizens legally entered Northern Ireland to take up employment in the province. But in November alone, over 900 of the 1180 new arrivals in the six counties had been brought in under the auspices of the Northern Ireland Ministry of Labour because they belonged to trades – shipbuilding and engineering – in which there was a shortage of local labour. These men were all included by the Government in the total number of Eire workers who had supposedly 'infiltrated' the province.[110]

If the Cabinet's concern appeared to be misconceived, the problem was at least not as trivial as other matters to which the Government turned its stern and occasionally obsessive attention. The wartime archives of the Stormont administration contain dozens of memoranda from civil servants and ministers, discussing – sometimes in words of outrage – the critical reports on Northern Ireland that were published from time to time in both Irish and British newspapers. An article in the Dublin *Irish Press* in July 1940, for example, was considered to be 'prejudicial to the interests of Northern Ireland' and worthy of debate within the Cabinet Secretariat.[111] When the *Manchester Guardian* neglected to publish an article on the province in a trade review but included a dispatch on Eire's ploughing policy, a senior civil servant came to the conclusion that the Irish Government had secured the editorial imbalance by placing an advertisement in the same issue of the paper.[112] In May 1940, Stormont wanted to know why *The Times* had included Eire in a supplement on trade and engineering in the British Empire but had left out any reference to Northern Ireland.* The paper irritated the province's civil service again in 1943 when it carried a report that held out hope of a united Ireland under a Dublin government. Wilfrid Spender suspected that Dulanty was responsible for the article. 'In my view,' he wrote, '*The Times* is doing its

---

* *The Times* Supplements editor replied, not unreasonably, by observing that Eire was part of the Empire while the province was part of the United Kingdom, and that if he had given the province separate treatment, 'there would be immediately a howl of protest that Northern Ireland is part of the United Kingdom.'[113]

best to cloak up its support of the disgraceful betrayal of the British Empire's interests in the past.'[114]

There were times when Unionist anger was justified. In 1944, Dr Bernard Griffin, the Archbishop of Westminster, saw fit to tell a meeting of Christians and Jews in London that 'today Roman Catholics are being persecuted in Germany and Poland – and I need hardly mention the persecution that is going on even at the present day in Northern Ireland.'[115] This extraordinary parallel between the behaviour of the Northern Ireland Government and the genocide of the Nazis naturally brought a bitter response from the Belfast Government. Edmund Warnock, Brooke's Minister of Home Affairs, wrote to Herbert Morrison, the Home Secretary, to condemn the Archbishop's 'odious' charge of persecution in the province. 'It is so highly provocative,' wrote Warnock, 'that it tends to stir up sectarian trouble from which during the war years we have happily been very free. In the shipyard and in the factories men and women, Protestants and Catholics, have been working together without any sign of sectarian feeling, but as you know this kind of mischief is much nearer the surface here than in England.' The assertion that Protestants and Catholics were co-operating in war work without any 'sectarian feeling' was difficult to sustain but Warnock was on strong ground when he pointed out to Morrison that since 1940, 'over 30,000 Eire citizens have applied to come and reside in our midst.' Speeches such as the Archbishop's could cause sectarian strife, he added, which 'inevitably leads to disputes in the workshops and the possible effect upon war production here might very well be serious . . .'[116]

Warnock's letter may have carried less weight than he would have wished because Unionist Governments and their supporters had for several years made a habit of interpreting any verbal attack on Northern Ireland – justified or not – as a danger to the province's war production and therefore to the Allied war effort as a whole. Even the most mundane and facile press criticism would provoke such complaints from Northern Ireland's Unionist defenders. Just after Craigavon's death in 1940, Lord Londonderry was offended by an article in the *Sunday Express* written by Viscount Castlerosse, an ex-Guards officer who was a director of Beaverbrook's newspaper chain. Castlerosse declared that Catholics in Northern Ireland had had 'an abominably bad deal' and told readers of his column that 'Christianity in Ulster, instead of being interpreted as a gospel of love, is well-known to be founded on loathing . . . I can assure you that the mentality of Ulster has to be seen to be believed. They are a strange, bitter and bigoted people.'[117] Londonderry wrote to Beaverbrook, an old acquaintance, to say that while he had not been in full agreement with Craigavon's policies, he did not want Andrews, the new Prime Minister, 'to have to go on fighting on an issue which is only raised by Britain's enemies. I want him to devote himself to production, unemployment . . .' Castlerosse's 'wholly unjustified and untrue statements' did not help

Andrews.[118] Assuring Londonderry that he was 'aware of the difficulties in Ulster after Craigavon's death', Beaverbrook replied that Castlerosse's opinions were 'strong and sincere', adding disingenuously that 'in any case, I must not interfere in any way with the conduct of the newspapers.'[119]

The problem, of course, was that the sectarian character of Northern Ireland politics was not something that was 'only raised by Britain's enemies'. Nor were claims of bigotry entirely misleading, as British and American troops realised when the Protestant Churches in the province objected to Sunday entertainment for the forces. Ecclesiastical protests had begun in May 1940, when the Congregational Union of Ireland sent a consequential letter to the Stormont Government, announcing that 'while the churches feel it their duty to do all they can to provide for the comfort and the happiness of the men who are serving their King and Country, it is felt to be unwise to encroach unduly upon the sanctity of the Day of Rest and worship, which is regarded among the citizens of Ulster generally as essential to the highest interests of the nation.'[120] Protests of a similar kind found their way to the British Parliament. Herbert Morrison thought it would be undesirable 'to attempt to override local opinion as regards Sunday opening'.[121] However, when the Reverend Dr James Little, the Westminster MP for Down, denounced the British Army for organising Sunday entertainments at theatres and music halls in the province, Sir James Grigg, the Secretary of State for War, said that he did not think 'wholesome amusement' was 'inconsistent with the worship of God or the defeat of our enemies'.[122] It was the wholesomeness of the amusement, or lack of it, that ostensibly concerned the clerics. The Protestant authorities in Londonderry – where dance-halls closed at 11.30 at night, even on weekdays – claimed that 'public feeling was outraged at the spectacle of young people – and more especially young girls, of whom, as you know, we have a plentitude [sic] – coming home at late hours, and often not in a normal condition . . .'[123] The Minister of Home Affairs himself believed that 'the conduct taking place at these dances and, more especially, on the way home, was in the nature of a public scandal.'[124] But the primary motive behind the campaign was religious. Objecting to Sunday entertainments, the Presbyterian Church in Belfast called upon its members 'to enter fully into the true meaning and significance of the Lord's Day.'[125] The Londonderry Temperance Council expressed 'strong disapproval' of Sunday cinema performances for Royal Navy personnel in the city and resolved to 'do all possible to preserve the principles of Christianity and the proper observance of the Lord's Day.'[126]

To the British troops preparing to defend Northern Ireland from invasion and to the naval crews resting in Londonderry after Atlantic escort duty, this seemed not only ungenerous but hypocritical. Andrews noted that there was 'a good deal of feeling' among servicemen stationed in the province[127] although the Northern Ireland Cabinet preferred to remain aloof from the issue, believing that it 'should not express any opinion or intervene . . .'[128] To the Government's embarrassment, the Protestant Churches in Belfast attacked General Franklyn when he requisitioned the Hippodrome Theatre for an army variety show one Sunday in March 1942. His action, stated the Churches' manifesto, had 'caused grievous hurt to the conscience and sentiments of a vast multitude of the citizens of this City and Province who are amongst the most loyal, law-abiding and devoted subjects of the British Crown and Government.'[129] To this pomposity, the Churches artfully added a warning of 'the known presence of certain reactionary, Anti-British elements which might easily seize the opportunity to inflict incalculable injury upon His Majesty's Forces.'[130] Why these supposedly revolutionary elements should be more dangerous to British troops on Sundays than on any other day of the week remained as much a mystery as the Churches' inability to see why such a warning might seem at odds with their equally forceful assertion that Northern Ireland's citizens were among the most law-abiding in the realm.

The Belfast Government were not the only Unionists to worry about the effect that the Churches' campaign might have on the servicemen stationed in the province. Major General Hugh de Fellenberg Montgomery, a prominent Ulster Unionist at the time of partition who had in 1938 founded an ecumenical movement to foster relations between Protestants and Catholics, told Andrews of his anxiety about 'the very obvious danger of we Ulster people getting an increasingly bad name, not only with the British Troops who are quartered here but also with our American visitors.'[131] A different if predictable concern over the newly-arrived American soldiers affected the local chairman of the Entertainments National Service Association – ENSA – who wrote to Brooke, warning of 'the very real need for countering subversive propaganda'. American troops, he claimed, 'are being invited, or inveigled, into places where no opportunity is lost to disseminate certain views, with the object of creating an unfavourable impression of Great Britain and our war aims . . .' In an effort to dissuade the American forces from accepting invitations to Catholic areas – for that is what his circumlocution referred to – the ENSA organiser believed that 'hospitality and entertainment by the loyal people of the Province' would effectively eliminate the dangers of hostile propaganda.[132]

The 'loyal people of the Province', 'a loyal and willing population', 'the most loyal, law-abiding and devoted subjects of the British Crown and Government'; the phrases, used before and to be heard again later, became a kind of antidote to the harsh evidence of Northern Ireland's social and political malaise. However justified or however unfair their opponents' condemnation, the Unionists of the province would emphasise – consistently and repeatedly – their allegiance to the monarch. Craigavon had told the British that his people were 'King's men' and Brooke faithfully perpetuated this idea. 'We are in this war just as you are,' he told a British audience in London in 1944. 'The pattern of our wartime life is identical with yours with the one exception of conscription.'[133] Even with this important qualification, the statement was untrue. Brooke could not possibly have believed it himself but he probably thought the British did. The assertion therefore had to be buttressed with figures and statistics, with painstaking endeavours to catalogue the province's contribution to the Allied war effort. The Belfast Government knew that this contribution would be challenged in later years; it was not by chance that when the Stormont Cabinet resolved in 1941 to commission an official wartime history of Northern Ireland,[134] Andrews himself decided that one of the authors' main tasks would be 'to prevent the possibility that the efforts and sacrifices of Ulster should hereafter be discredited or belittled.'[135]

But the British would not attempt to disparage the achievements of the six counties, partly because there were real efforts and sacrifices involved. Quite apart from the 140 warships and 1500 heavy bombers manufactured in Belfast, Brooke later computed the province's armaments production as 123 merchant ships, 500 tanks, 14,000 gun barrels, seventy-five million shells, 50,000 bayonets and two million parachutes.[136] Northern Ireland farmers produced a larger proportionate contribution to home-grown food supplies than any other area of the United Kingdom.[137] By November 1941, 23,000 men had joined the services[138] and regiments from the province served in almost every major British engagement of the war, from the defence of Arras and the retreat to Dunkirk in 1940 – in which seven Northern Ireland units were involved – to Egypt, Sicily, Italy, Normandy, the Rhine and Burma.[139] 'Most of Ballymena, Derry and Newtownards are in the Middle East to judge by the voices one hears,' a young RAF pilot from Northern Ireland wrote home from Egypt in 1942.[140] They took their share of casualties: 4735 servicemen from the province died in the war.[141] Among them were Craigavon's nephew, who was commanding a destroyer when it struck a mine,[142] and two of Brooke's own three sons. After the death of the second boy, shot by a sniper in Italy in 1945, Churchill sent the family a telegram, expressing sympathy for them in their 'proud sorrow'.[143] Brooke appreciated the message for he was an aristocratic man whose family had already provided Britain with one of her finest generals, Viscount Alanbrooke. Among the field marshals to whose ancestry the province also laid claim were Alexander, Dill, Auchinleck and Montgomery.[144]*

But it was not even this contribution that Britain chiefly valued. Only indirectly did the British esteem the presence of the 'King's men'. Craig-

* Montgomery's inclusion in this list was always questionable. His family had lived in County Donegal, part of the historic province of Ulster that was excluded from the new state of Northern Ireland in 1921. While he was therefore an 'Ulsterman', he was nonetheless raised in what was to become the Irish Free State. The Northern Ireland Government adopted him all the same, and Montgomery was never known to object.

avon touched upon the truth when he claimed just before his death that Northern Ireland had secured for Britain 'a *pied à terre* in Ireland', a base to defend Britain's north-western ports, and from which the Royal Navy would later fight the Battle of the Atlantic. This territorial advantage was Northern Ireland's principal contribution to the war, as Churchill himself acknowledged in 1943. The only remaining shipping lane to Britain stayed open in a dark and dangerous hour, he said, 'because loyal Ulster gave us the full use of the Northern Irish ports and waters and thus ensured the free working of the Clyde and the Mersey.' Churchill attributed this deliverance to 'the loyalty of Northern Ireland'.[145] Later, he would credit the province's existence at this time to providence. 'Here by the grace of God,' he was to write of Northern Ireland's strategic position on the north Atlantic sea lane, 'Ulster stood a faithful sentinel.'[146] Brooke was more prosaic. 'Before 1939,' he told his Guildhall audience:

> . . . Ulster was too often in the position of reminding Great Britain that she also was one of the great family of the British Commonwealth and Empire. During this war Great Britain and the Allies have had reason to be grateful for our insistence on remaining in the family group . . . We have never doubted that you are necessary to us. We hope that you now realise that we are necessary to you.[147]

It is still puzzling that during the early months of the war, the Northern Ireland Government did not realise that the cost of this mutual dependence might be higher than the inevitable death of servicemen overseas, that loyalty might demand a blood sacrifice more brutal if less costly than that which had been made by Carson's men on the Somme in 1916. Only occasionally did it occur to the authorities in Belfast that by enlarging the scope of their commitment to the war effort, they were also increasing the chances of becoming directly and dangerously involved in the conflict. 'I wonder,' mused Lindsay Keir, the Queen's University Vice Chancellor, in February 1941, 'if there isn't some force in the suggestion that the immunity of Northern Ireland from aerial attack may be connected with the absence of important munition plants here. It is at least possible, and the corollary might well be that immunity would cease were ordnance factories to be set up . . .'[148]

The idea never struck Herbert Shaw when he surveyed Northern Ireland's prospects in December of 1940. 'Taking a long view,' he wrote:

> . . . the future of Northern Irish politics is obscure. On the one hand the older generation of leaders grow old and there are virtually none of the younger desirous or capable of succeeding them. On the other, steadfast determination of the Protestant population to resist domination by the Catholic South seems scarcely to have diminished. There is, however, no reason to fear that the graver problems which may well lie ahead are likely to present themselves for some time. In so far as the purposes of the war are concerned all is well in Northern Ireland.[149]

Chapter 13

Many Fires Were Started . . .

> When we approached the target at half-past two we stared silently into a sea of flames such as none of us had seen before . . . in Belfast there was not a large number of conflagrations but just one enormous conflagration which spread over the entire harbour and industrial area . . .
>
> German radio reporter on the
> Luftwaffe bombing of Belfast *4/5 May 1941*

> There are in the country probably about 5,000 absolutely unbilletable persons. They are unbilletable owing to personal habits which are sub-human. Camps or institutions under suitable supervision must be instituted for these.
>
> Richard Dawson Bates, Northern Ireland Minister
> of Home Affairs, on refugees from the Belfast blitz
> *5 May 1941*

> I have been working nineteen years in Belfast and I never saw the like of them before. If something is not done now to remedy this rank inequality there will be a revolution after the war.
>
> The Moderator of the Presbyterian
> Church General Assembly in Belfast, speaking of
> the blitz refugees *3 June 1941*

Early on the afternoon of Saturday, 30 November 1940 – two days after Craigavon's funeral – a solitary Luftwaffe photo-reconnaissance aircraft flew at high altitude through the wintry sky above the great basin of Belfast Lough. Its crew could see the long finger of the Ards peninsula, with its patchwork of fields, stretching away to the south while to the west, beyond the industrial haze of Belfast, they could make out the runways of the RAF's fighter station at Aldergrove. As the plane soared gently towards the city, the photographer on board began to film the suburbs of the Northern Ireland capital passing slowly beneath him. He took a series of composite and well-defined pictures of possible targets which the Luftwaffe's Section 5 photo-reconnaissance unit found no difficulty in identifying: '. . . die Werft Harland & Wolff Ltd, die Tankstelle Conns Water, das Flugzeugwerk Short & Harland, das Kraftwerk Belfast, die Grossmühle Rank & Co, das Wasserwerk Belfast, die Kasernenanlagen Victoria Barracks . . .'[1]

It was a fine day, and the camera was able to pick out a few cars far below on the drab Belfast streets. One of the green-tinted photographic prints developed later by the Germans clearly showed the City Hall, its pale, grimy walls contrasting with the dark streets that lay at right angles off Donegall Square. A few small, feathery cirrus clouds drifted below the plane as it banked to the south-west – unmolested by RAF fighters – to afford the photographer a view of the Belfast gasworks; he expended several frames on the exposed and vulnerable gasometers beside the River Lagan. The Luftwaffe were pleased with the pictures. A bombing raid on the gas installations alone, they estimated, would produce a chaos of 'fire, explosions and collapsing buildings'.[2] They must have been even more delighted with what the photographs told them of Belfast's anti-aircraft defences. There was, they noted, a heavy anti-aircraft gun beside the Customs House two hundred metres north-west of the Queen's Bridge. There was another *flakbatterie* in the Clarendon Dock, one in Victoria Park and two on the coast at Holywood in County Down on the southern edge of the Lough.[3] But that was all. Belfast, with its shipyards and aircraft factories, its engineering works and its harbour-side power station, appeared to be defended by only seven anti-aircraft batteries.

It seems like something more than tragic irony that less than three years earlier, the Stormont Cabinet had been trying to coax rearmament work from the British Government with the assurance that 'it would hardly be possible to find in the United Kingdom any industrial area less vulnerable in time of war than Northern Ireland.'[4] At a time when no one in London – let alone in Belfast – imagined that the Germans would occupy the Continental coastline from Norway to Brittany, this was not an entirely foolish assumption. Spender had recorded how in March 1939 Major General Ismay derided the idea of a German attack on Northern Ireland. How could the Luftwaffe fly across the defended mainland of Britain, with little hope of reaching the province and none of returning safely to Germany? There were a few officials at Stormont – Spender among them – who did not take so complacent an attitude. But Craigavon's old Cabinet found it difficult to grasp the issues involved. Financial considerations tended to count for more than security, and parliamentary secretaries – though younger than their ministers – were themselves incapable of coping with decisions which would never normally fall to a provincial government.

In June 1939, for example, Edmond Warnock, then Dawson Bates's Parliamentary Secretary, advised the Stormont Cabinet against following

British civil defence proposals that placed an obligation on large factories and commercial firms to build air-raid shelters for their employees. Belfast, Warnock told the Cabinet:

> . . . is the most distant city of the United Kingdom from any possible enemy base. It is 535 miles from the nearest point in Germany. An attack on Northern Ireland would involve a flight of over 1,000 miles. For aeroplanes of the bombing type, loaded, this is a very big undertaking. To reach Northern Ireland and to get back again the enemy aeroplanes must twice pass through the active gun, searchlight and aeroplane defences of Great Britain . . . In coming to Northern Ireland the attacking plane would pass over targets which would appear to be more attractive than anything the North of Ireland has to offer. Bearing these facts in mind it is possible that we might escape attack altogether. But if Northern Ireland is attacked the above factors would suggest that at least we shall not be subject to frequent attack or to attack by large concentrations of enemy aircraft.[5]

Warnock acknowledged that during a recent visit to London, he had received 'no support for the view that Belfast was likely to escape attack' and mentioned that Sir Alexander Maxwell, the Home Office Permanent Secretary, 'would have scheduled Belfast as a vulnerable area' had the British civil defence proposals been applied to Northern Ireland. But Warnock was indecisive, telling the Stormont Cabinet at one point that any attack on Belfast 'would probably be all over in a matter of a very few minutes', at another point that he was planning to deal with up to eight hundred casualties in a raid. Even if the population was given Anderson shelters – dug into their back yards or gardens – raids would be so infrequent, he thought, that families would probably not bother to use them. As for ordering the city's factories to build shelters, it was Warnock's view that 'the risk of attack on Belfast is not sufficiently great to justify the Government in imposing this heavy burden upon industry . . .'[6] Three days later, an ARP memorandum was circulated to the Stormont Cabinet by the Ministry of Home Affairs, stating that fire was 'the most serious risk in Northern Ireland' but that the Belfast authorities were experiencing great difficulty in securing extra fire-fighting equipment from the British authorities.[7]

The most serious aspect of this last minute pre-war planning, however, was the Northern Ireland Government's failure to provide its people with air-raid protection of any kind. In Belfast, the authorities were hampered by geological factors. Beneath the older part of the city lay a wet, moving sub-soil known as 'sleech', a bog-like morass that made any kind of excavation for deep underground shelters impossible. Small Anderson shelters were being distributed to families in Britain but were still unavailable in Northern Ireland where the Ministry of Home Affairs had no desire to obtain them 'until the financial considerations as between the two Governments are settled.' The question of Britain's monetary contribution to Northern Ireland's ARP services was apparently sufficient reason to delay building shelters. Besides, there was no RAF squadron to protect Belfast, and there were few anti-aircraft guns. 'It will be noted,' the ARP memorandum stated with astonishing equanimity, 'that there are at present no plans for the direct protection of the people . . .'[8]

Craigavon was uneasy. The main consideration, he declared, must be 'the protection of our working people'. There were also political factors. John Gordon, the Minister of Labour, thought that the Northern Ireland Government would be open to 'serious criticism' if it did not give its people comparable protection to that available in Britain. The Cabinet would be accused of 'dereliction of duty' if it did not take advantage of the financial resources at its disposal. In the end, the Cabinet decided to designate buildings in which 'measures of protection' would have to be taken, and to institute compulsory ARP training in all businesses employing more than twenty people.[9] Craigavon, in a rare if futile display of personal initiative, had sought advice from friends who had witnessed air raids in the Spanish civil war. Only deep underground shelters were of use in a city, he was told – and they could not be built in Belfast. In the countryside, 'a slit trench or ditch was satisfactory'.[10] The fragile, useless earthen trenches which Spender had noticed beside the City Hall were products of this inquiry. When war began, therefore, Northern Ireland was almost totally unprepared for the possibility of air attack, and its population drew the obvious conclusions. 'All sorts of rot are going on here,' Lady Londonderry wrote to her husband from the province a few days after war was declared. 'Air raid warning and black outs!! As if anyone cared or wished to bomb Belfast . . .'[11]

The fall of France and the arrival of the German Army on the Channel coast in June of 1940 showed exactly how dilatory the Northern Ireland Government had been. In the ten months since the start of the war, they had built just two hundred public shelters in Belfast and supplied only 4000 householders with domestic shelters.[12] John MacDermott, appointed to the newly-created post of Minister of Public Security to take over Dawson Bates's civil defence responsibilities, was horrified to discover that his friend Warnock had actually been *returning* consignments of fire-fighting equipment to Britain on the grounds that they were not needed in Northern Ireland.[13] When Craigavon proposed to set up a non-party parliamentary committee to advise on air-raid precautions, Dawson Bates opposed the idea because Stormont MPs 'would be put in possession of information showing, for example, that we had not distributed gas masks on the scale we had promised, and that our shelter programme was far behind that in Great Britain.'[14]

MacDermott soon found out the effect that this official complacency had had upon the public. Told by the Army that Belfast would be 'the main target of attack' in Northern Ireland,[15] he ordered the evacuation of some 17,000 children from the city on July 7. But only about 7000 turned up. When he arranged a second evacuation in August, only 1800 of the 5000 registered evacuees reported to the boarding points.[16] Many people, it seemed, still believed that Belfast would not be bombed. MacDermott became convinced that it would. He told the all-party ARP committee that 'the collapse of France had altered the situation and they could no longer consider it probable that there would be long, if any, warning of an impending attack, nor could they still expect that raids would be of the "hit and run" type now that Germany controlled the whole French seaboard.' MacDermott believed that 'greatly increased demands for equipment and shelters were justified.'[17]

But the *Blitzkrieg* on England had begun and there were few supplies available for Northern Ireland. Having at last aroused themselves to the necessities of air-raid protection, the Stormont authorities were too late to do much about it. The strength of ARP personnel was raised from 15,000 to 22,000, and 135 new recruits were brought into the fire service.[18] But pumps, steel pipe fittings and extra fire engines were almost impossible to obtain, since the major cities of Britain – now under regular attack by the Luftwaffe – were desperately trying to augment their own fire-fighting equipment. MacDermott did his best to take advantage of the raids on Britain, sending his civil servants over from Belfast to watch the air attacks on London.[19] The Ministry of Public Security began building at high speed 'thousands of hideous brick shelters on the streets of Belfast, half blocking the footpath and half blocking the carriageway.'[20] But it was not enough. In December of 1940, MacDermott reported to his new Prime Minister, John Andrews, that 50,000 households were still without air-raid shelters.[21]

The full extent of the destruction that might follow an attack on Belfast, however, was only brought home to MacDermott two months later when Rear Admiral King, the Royal Navy's FOIC in Belfast, sent him a confidential report written by three naval officers who had visited Coventry on November 15, the day after the Luftwaffe incendiary raid on the city. MacDermott read carefully through the document, which contained none of the comforting, censored prose of newspaper accounts of the attack. The Luftwaffe had dropped 150,000 incendiaries, 1400 high explosive bombs and 130 parachute mines over Coventry. The first bombs had broken the water mains upon which the fire brigade depended, and successive waves of aircraft had stoked the fires. The anti-aircraft barrage was inadequate and night fighters were ineffectual. More than fifty thousand houses had been destroyed or damaged. Many of the city's factories were gutted. Two hundred gas mains were broken; sewage pipes were smashed. Power lines and telecommunications all collapsed. The railways and roads were blocked by heaps of rubble. More than five hundred people had died. 'The report was a pen picture of what a city looked like after a big raid,' MacDermott was to recall. 'It made my hair stand on end because I realised that this was what Belfast would be like.'[22]

He knew, as he told the Stormont Cabinet later, that 'the task of handling the situation after a "blitz" with the necessary speed and efficiency went beyond the powers of the local Civil Defence Authority.'[23]

MacDermott called Eric Scales and William Iliff, his two permanent assistants, into his office at Stormont Castle and told Iliff – a Dunkirk veteran – to construct a plan for an advanced government headquarters to operate in Belfast in the aftermath of a raid. The Hiram Plan – it was Iliff's idea to name the project after the Biblical king of Tyre[24]* – envisaged a government secretariat that would have authority to act on the Cabinet's behalf after a German air raid if all communications in Belfast had broken down; MacDermott would himself take the decision to put the Hiram Plan into effect. Spender was one of the few critics of the scheme, arguing that MacDermott's functions should terminate shortly after an air attack so that other ministers could take over their departmental duties. He believed that 'there may be certain districts in Belfast which are very badly damaged and which may perhaps have to be evacuated in whole or in part' but that these regions would be confined in area. Spender felt that Stormont ministers should at least be responsible for their department's work during 'the gravest crisis in our history'.[25]

Perhaps the Northern Ireland Government was spurred to such administrative effort by the realisation that there was now little hope of averting a tragedy if the Germans decided to bomb Belfast. MacDermott had taken to heart the experience of fire crews in Britain whose hoses had run dry when bomb explosions tore up the water mains. There were nearly two hundred fire engines in Belfast[26] but the large pumps and steel pipe fittings that would hopefully prevent such a calamity in Northern Ireland had only just arrived in the province and the Auxiliary Fire Service volunteers had had little time to train on them. By the spring of 1941, despite the feverish construction of pavement shelters, fewer than 15 per cent of the householders in Belfast had been provided with air-raid protection in their homes.[27] The air defence system was even more scandalous. In the entire province, there were only 24 heavy anti-aircraft guns, 14 light anti-aircraft guns, 1 RAF Hurricane squadron, 6 radar stations, just one bomb disposal unit and 2 small balloon barrages. Three Northern Ireland anti-aircraft regiments had actually been withdrawn from the province. There were no searchlights in Belfast, no night fighters and no provisions for a smoke screen.[28]

A few bombs had already fallen near the city. In the early spring nights, Luftwaffe aircraft engaged in the heavy raids on Liverpool and Glasgow occasionally strayed off course and unloaded their incendiaries over the Northern Ireland coast. Belfast Lough was regularly mined; each Sunday

---

* Hiram supplied the craftsmen and cedarwood to build Solomon's Temple in Jerusalem after peace had returned to the land of Israel (1 Kings 5). MacDermott's task was to be less glamorous.

morning, a minesweeper would cruise majestically down to Bangor, clearing the waterway for the merchant ships moored off the Copelands. James Kelly was sitting on Bangor promenade one morning when the crew of a cargo vessel anchored off the pier turned off their degaussing electrical system to adjust the ship's compass, attracting a magnetic mine to the hull. Before the citizens of Bangor, the ship was blown out of the water.[29] But there had been no determined attack, even on a small scale, to suggest that the Germans were about to divert their attention to Belfast. In March, MacDermott asked vainly for more guns, for searchlights and night fighters, adding with frightening prescience that 'the period of the next moon from, say, the 7 to the 16 April may well bring our turn.'[30]

They came on the night of April 7. It was a pin-prick, exploratory raid by six twin-engined Heinkel 111 bombers,[31] probably undertaken to test Belfast's air defences. The planes had detached themselves from a larger force on its way to attack Glasgow and flew in over the Lough at 7000 feet at four minutes after midnight. The barrage balloons were too low to hinder them and the city's anti-aircraft gunners, firing shells to an altitude of 12,000 feet, never made contact with the planes. So confident were the pilots that two of the Heinkels switched on their navigation lights as they made a preliminary run over the harbour and dropped flares around the Harland and Wolff shipyard. Several of the aircraft unloaded incendiaries onto the armed trawlers in the Pollock Dock; the vessels fired back with machine guns, earning for themselves a stern reproof from Rear Admiral King 'for wasting ammunition against invisible targets'.[32] Several high explosive bombs damaged sewers and a grain storage shed belonging to Rank's flour mill. But the only serious destruction was caused by a parachute mine, dropped by a Heinkel that swept in over the Lough at 3.30 in the morning, which floated innocently over the Musgrave Channel and exploded on the roof of Short and Harland's aircraft fuselage factory, burning the building to the ground.[33] In the overcast night, the RAF at Aldergrove scrambled a Hurricane which miraculously located two of the German aircraft off the County Down coast not far from Downpatrick, opened fire at one of them and blew it up in mid-air. The debris and Luftwaffe crew fell seven thousand feet into the sea. Thirteen people died in the raid – an insignificant figure beside the fatalities in the *Blitzkrieg* on British cities – but the Belfast authorities experienced one small technical problem that might just have warned them of a flaw in their meagre defences. Many of the merchant ships tied up at the Belfast docks that night were armed with anti-aircraft guns that could have contributed to the barrage; in the event, scarcely any of them opened fire because, as Rear Admiral King noted in a dispatch to the Admiralty, none of the vessels was connected by telephone to the shore batteries.[34] A similar failure of communication in the future – or a total collapse of communication between anti-aircraft units on the ground – might prove fatal.

From the morning of April 8 onwards, Belfast's air-raid sirens howled every twenty-four hours. But for six days, no German aircraft appeared over the city. Many people began to ignore the warnings and travelled to Bangor for the Easter weekend, taking the little steam train that ran along the southern shore of the Lough past the newly burnt-out fuselage factory. Rita Hegarty, a Protestant girl who worked as a stitcher making Army uniforms, paid no attention to the sirens, assuming that they were being sounded for a civil defence practice. She spent April 14 – Easter Monday– preparing for her cousin's marriage on the following day.[35] That night, the sirens were heard again in Belfast as a Luftwaffe reconnaissance aircraft glided over the city at 22,000 feet. A single gun belonging to the 102nd Heavy Anti-Aircraft Regiment fired impotently skywards before the plane vanished off the radar screens.[36]

Next morning, April 15, the sirens wailed again and several people in Belfast remember that they heard anti-aircraft fire around lunchtime. There is no record of such a barrage in the official archives but memories of this dull, overcast day have remained unusually vivid. The Reverend Eric Gallagher officiated at a wedding in his Methodist church that morning and still recalls how the bridegroom looked at the grey sky and commented that it was 'like a day a man would be hung.'[37] Rita Hegarty thought she heard gunfire as she walked down to St Stephen's Church in Millfield for her cousin's wedding. The service, she remembered, was punctuated by distant explosions which she identified as the anti-aircraft batteries at the harbour.[38] More than thirty years after the war – and at a time when Northern Ireland was enduring a different form of violent humiliation – her recollection of the period still had about it a remarkable clarity. Many of those who were to witness the events of the next three weeks – and especially the next few hours – were left with memories so terrible or so exhilarating that they would never shake them off. Even the Luftwaffe crews were to admit later that they could not believe their eyes when they set fire to Belfast.

The evening of April 15 was mild and clear with a light wind and some cumulus cloud. It was not until 22.40 hours that the sirens sounded again; the anti-aircraft gunners had already been ordered to 'stand to' at Castle-reagh on the gentle hills that overlooked the shipyards.[39] James Kelly had left his office in Belfast and taken the trolley bus home to the Glen Road off the Falls when he heard the alert. He thought it was another false alarm until he stepped off the bus and became aware of the anti-aircraft guns firing from across the city in east Belfast. Then, above the sound of the barrage, he made out a low humming sound that seemed to grow, sharply and clearly, from out of the south-east, from the hills away in County Down.[40] Rear Admiral King's post-raid report estimated that between a hundred and two hundred planes were flying towards Belfast and it confirmed Kelly's sense of direction. The majority of aircraft, it laconically observed, 'approached from S.E. and attacked on arrival.'[41]

In fact, the first wave of Heinkel 111s and Junkers 88s dropped flares,

417

creating an artificial daylight – momentarily blinding – over the entire city. Rodney Green of Queen's University watched them from the Lisburn Road in south Belfast. He could not see the aircraft, only the flares that 'came tumbling down out of the darkness and then sprayed out horizontally on several levels.'[42] Bathed in the intense white and orange light, figures in the streets stood out in surrealistic relief. 'The whole area seemed brighter than at noon in summertime,' one eye-witness was to write. 'I looked along the street and could recognise clearly two wardens who were a hundred yards away. I felt as if I were standing in the street stark naked.'[43] With other ARP men in west Belfast, Brian Moore heard the guns go briefly silent 'then, beautiful, exploding with a faint pop in the sky . . . a magnesium flare floated up in the stillness, lighting the rooftops in a ghostly silver.'[44] To Kelly, the flares were 'like a giant candelabra spreading out across the city'.[45] A mile away in the Grosvenor Road, Paddy Devlin, the young IRA volunteer, watched the flares 'go from white to bright orange to dull orange and then disappear.'[46]

Before the light had faded, scores of aircraft came in over the Lough, flying level at 7000 feet to clear the puny balloon barrage, and rained incendiaries, high explosive bombs and parachute mines onto Belfast.[47] From the north-west of the city – from the swathe of tiny streets and old Victorian slum houses that stretched from the docks at York Road near the LMS railway terminus up towards the Antrim Road and Cavehill – there came the noise of hundreds of explosions in such rapid succession that to those watching from the outskirts it seemed as if Belfast had been struck by one long rumbling burst of sound. Kelly recalls the ground vibrating under his feet and seeing 'droves of aircraft' caught for a few seconds in the gleam of the dying flares.[48] In the Lisburn Road, Rodney Green stared in fascination as the incendiaries fell from the darkness. They would come down in showers 'making a crackling sound when they hit the ground like the sparks of tram wires; then little points of flame would spring up.'[49]

Green also noticed that the fires were more thickly clustered west of the harbour, and indeed the Luftwaffe bomber force – German records show that 180 aircraft were over the Belfast target area[50] – were dropping all their high explosive bombs onto civilian districts. Instead of pouring onto the harbour and shipyards, well over a hundred tons of bombs were unloaded in sticks across thousands of back-to-back terraced homes where the poor of Belfast lay unprotected. Off York Road, in the Antrim Road and at the foot of the Shankill, huge fires were generated as the explosions rippled across the little houses. At least twenty parachute mines – intended to smash the pre-stressed concrete and steel defences of industrial targets – glided down among the fragile, decaying slums north of New Lodge; the force of their explosion tore down whole blocks of houses. Hogarth Street and Veryan Gardens, two unassuming red-brick terraces off the Antrim Road, were literally blasted to dust, their occupants with them.

Just as at Coventry – and just as MacDermott had feared – the massive bombing broke up the water mains. There were thirty-two fractures in all,[51] and the water pressure began to fall at the very moment when the Auxiliary Fire Service tried to bring the conflagrations around the Antrim Road under control. At 23.40 hours, exactly an hour after the raid began, Kelly walked outside his house in the Glen Road and looked northwards to see 'a river of flame across Belfast – it was as if the whole city was on fire.'[52] Rita Hegarty, who was only fifteen, fled with her relatives to the Percy Street Gospel Hall because they knew a public shelter had been erected beside it. But when she reached the hall, Hegarty found that the entire block of buildings was on fire and that pieces of human body lay across the street.[53] Joseph McCann, an 18-year-old Catholic ARP warden who had believed neither the 'yellow' nor the 'red' air-raid alerts until he heard the planes overhead, found many Catholics huddling in the vaults of the Clonard monastery half way up the Falls Road. From his perch beside the public baths, where he worked as an attendant, he watched the flames blossoming from streets at the bottom of the Shankill, holding his hands to his head to protect his ear-drums from the shriek of torpedo bombs. Only rarely, he noticed, did the constant rumble of explosions slacken off, and then only for a few seconds.[54] In some districts, whole communities were wiped out. The nineteenth-century brick-built factory of the York Street Flax Spinning Company had received several direct hits during the early hours of the raid; just after one o'clock in the morning, one of the back walls – six storeys high and sixty yards long – toppled over without warning and pulverised the forty-two houses that lay beneath it, killing thirty-five people.

Whether the Germans intended to strike at Belfast's civilian population is open to question. It was noticed at the time that the initial target flares drifted in the light wind north-eastwards across Belfast, away from the harbour;[55] ARP personnel came to the conclusion that many of the German bomb aimers mistook the waterworks at Cavehill for Queen's Island opposite Harland and Wolff, and bombed the residential district in error.[56] Against this is the evidence supplied by a Luftwaffe officer who took part in the raid and who, by a freak of history, found himself being interrogated by the Irish Army just after the war ended. Based in Denmark when the German forces surrendered in 1945, he and his crew had sought asylum by flying at low level across England to Eire. He told the Irish military authorities that during the April 15/16 raid on Belfast, he had been told to take bearings for his bombing run on the twin-spired Catholic cathedral just south of the Falls Road in the west of the city. If the harbour had been his objective, he would already have overshot his target by the time he saw the cathedral.[57] However, as Northern Ireland's official war historian has pointed out, German reports suggest that the Luftwaffe was unaware that it had concentrated its attacks on residential property.[58] The fact that the Germans were to return within three weeks to finish their work by fire-bombing the harbour area does indicate that the first raid was poorly executed rather than designed to kill civilians.

In nationalist areas of the city, there emerged a rumour that the Germans had been selective in their bombing and had concentrated their attacks upon Protestant districts because they regarded the Catholics as neutral.[59] This whimsical idea – which was widely believed at the time – did not stand up to examination. All those who died when the spinning factory wall collapsed behind York Street were Catholics and about a third of the night's fatalities were to be from nationalist districts of Belfast, a figure that accurately reflected the ratio of the two communities within the population. What *was* true, however, was that the Northern Ireland Government's plans to cope with an air attack had been quite overwhelmed by the heaviness and duration of the raid. The scale of the event totally outstripped the capacity of MacDermott's governmental machinery to make any impression on the chaos that was spreading across Belfast. In 1938, the authorities had considered the city almost immune from attack; in 1939, Warnock did not believe it would be raided by 'large concentrations of enemy aircraft'; Belfast would suffer a maximum of eight hundred wounded, he thought. Now even MacDermott's bloodiest predictions were being surpassed. The brief, sometimes garbled reports that were reaching him suggested that the injured already numbered about a thousand and that the dead were being counted not in dozens but in hundreds. A member of MacDermott's staff was to acknowledge later that 'all this destruction, killing, maiming, burning and upset far exceeded anything for which we had prepared. It made our schemes look woefully inadequate.'[60]

MacDermott scarcely needed to be told. From the windows of his home on Cairnburn Road not far from the Stormont parliament building, he could see a vivid orange glow suffusing the sky across Belfast, flickering occasionally but growing ever brighter as the fires took hold.[61] Parachute mines were now falling into the shipyards and the aircraft plant which lay less than two miles to the east of MacDermott's house. A high explosive bomb hit the Harland and Wolff boiler factory, bringing the overhead cranes crashing to the ground. The roof was blown off the electrical manufacturing shop and a bomb started a fire that set light to the planes parked on the Short and Harland runway.[62] Water pressure for the fire service was now down to 50 per cent of normal.[63] MacDermott knew that he needed assistance on an impressive scale. Explosions were shaking his own home, and one bomb landed so close that the windows blew in; he heard shrapnel clattering on the tiles of his roof. Retreating to his study at the rear of the house, he took the telephone and clambered beneath his desk for cover as the back windows shattered. The line was still connected. And so there, crouched on the floor as his home vibrated to the explosions outside, MacDermott did something that no Northern Ireland Government minister had done for his province before or would ever do again: he called Dublin and asked for help.[64]

MacDermott claimed later that he could not remember to whom he spoke in the Irish capital, only that he asked 'someone in authority' there to send fire appliances across the border as quickly as possible because Belfast was being bombed. The willingness of the Irish fire service to answer this mercy call and the arrival of Irish fire crews in Belfast a few hours later was to acquire enormous symbolic importance in the years after the war, apparent proof that despite their political and religious differences, Irishmen could still rely upon each other for help in time of mortal danger. The episode was to be turned into legend by the people of Belfast, many of whom still swear that the Irish firemen arrived in the city proudly flying Tricolours from their vehicles – which is untrue – and that the Irish crews spent their time bravely fighting fires for the Protestants in the Shankill Road, which is also untrue. But such stories were inevitable, for even today the facts of this extraordinary affair are still obscure.

Given the considerable political implications of his approach to Dublin, MacDermott's inability to remember details of his telephone call was somewhat intriguing although, as he said years after the war, 'the significance of what I was doing was nothing to what was going on outside my house at the time.'[65] More curious, however, is the apparent absence of any mention of Eire's fire brigade assistance in the relevant archives of the Stormont Government. In the records of the Ministry of Home Affairs, there is a file on cross-border fire service co-operation – an arrangement that came about as a direct result of the 1941 raids on Belfast – but the earliest documents there relate to 1943.[66] All papers before this date have disappeared. Still more puzzling is the lack of any reference to the Irish assistance on the night of April 15/16 in the files of the Taoiseach's Department in Dublin. Here too the earliest document on fire service co-operation between Eire and Northern Ireland – a memorandum by Frank Aiken – is dated 1943.[67]*

Nevertheless, a number of Irish firemen who volunteered to travel to Belfast early on 16 April 1941 are still alive, and from them it is possible to reconstruct some of the events that took place in the hours after the Northern Ireland Minister of Public Security made his historic request. According to MacDermott, he placed his call to Dublin at around 1.30 a.m. De Valera's biographers say that the first appeal for help from Belfast was made to the Dublin telephone exchange supervisor at about this time and that the Taoiseach was awoken at 2.0 a.m. with the news that Belfast was on fire. According to this account – which incorrectly places the date of the raid as May 1 – de Valera weighed the consequences of giving

---

* Even the Irish Fire Brigade do not seem to have taken much care of their records of this period. One of the fire engines to travel north on April 16 was from Dun Laoghaire; but when in 1979 the author asked the local fire service there to show him their files for April and May 1941, he was told that they 'cannot be traced'.

humanitarian assistance, then 'took what was possibly the fastest decision of his career', ordering the Irish fire service to Northern Ireland because 'the fact that it was Irish men and women who were in danger overruled his caution.'[68]

There can be little doubt, however, that de Valera was also influenced by Cardinal MacRory. When Dublin's Chief Fire Superintendent, Major Comerford, turned up at Tara Street fire station at about 2.30 a.m. to ask for volunteers to go to Belfast, he told his men that 'the Primate has spoken to de Valera about the bombing and "Dev" is asking us to help.'[69] Was there, one wonders, some contact between MacDermott and MacRory that night? Did MacDermott himself perhaps telephone to Armagh and ask the Cardinal to intercede with de Valera, judging that an appeal from the Catholic church would have more effect on the Taoiseach than a request from the Northern Ireland Government? There are, it seems, no surviving records to clarify the matter. At Tara Street, Comerford found thirty volunteers after giving an assurance that their families would be cared for by the Irish Government if the firemen were killed. Thirteen appliances – from Dublin, Dun Laoghaire, Drogheda and Dundalk – were sent north. Patrick Finlay, a 27-year-old fireman from the Rathmines sub-station, was allocated an Irish civil defence vehicle that towed a red painted trailer pump. Outside Drogheda, the trailer skidded into a telegraph pole but was hastily repaired.[70] John Kelly drove another of the pumps and found the night so cold that he had to sit on his hands every few minutes to stop them going numb.[71] At the Killeen border post, the thirteen crews were met by an RUC escort. It was then that Finlay first heard the drone of aircraft and saw several German planes caught in the beam of a searchlight over Newry.[72]

In Belfast, the anti-aircraft batteries around the city had continued to fire blindly into the sky, assisted by the guns of HMS *Furious* which was marooned in the Harland and Wolff dry dock for repairs. The barrage had grown steadily weaker, however, until just after 1.45 a heavy bomb exploded next to the city's central telephone exchange near the corner of Oxford Steet and East Bridge Street, severing all local and trunk lines out of Belfast. MacDermott had made his call to Dublin just in time. But the collapse of the telephones was catastrophic for the air defence system. The anti-aircraft operations control room lost its own communications and, in the words of the official historian, 'the gunfire practically ceased'.[73] The Oxford Street bomb also cut the RAF's fighter sector cross-channel operational circuits, breaking the radar direction plotting lines between Aldergrove and the filter station at Preston on the British mainland.[74] The RAF now had no idea of how many aircraft were raiding Belfast nor in what direction they were moving. Just before two o'clock in the morning, it seems, the RAF sector control unhelpfully decided to order its Hurricanes to keep outside a five mile radius of the city.[75] The Luftwaffe had the sky to themselves.

Belfast was now garlanded with fire, a sweep of flames that stretched down from Cavehill in the north to the docks below York Road, then south to the commercial centre of the city which was also ablaze. Many buildings were left to burn themselves out. In the Crumlin Road, civil defence men tried to carry wounded past the flames that were consuming St Mary's Church; a *Belfast Telegraph* photographer managed to take one hurried picture of the scene, a frightening image of running men against a backcloth of fire. Bruce Williamson, who only eight months earlier had lain on the cliffs above Fair Head watching the British convoys moving placidly through the North Channel, lived at the top of the Antrim Road and noticed that by three in the morning, no attempt was any longer being made to shoot at the German planes over the city. He was strangely excited by the raid, observing that 'because there was no opposition, it seemed as if the German aircraft were on a routine exercise – one felt they were there by right.'[76]

Twenty minutes later, the raid ended. Most of the bombers were tracked across to the west of the province where they flew over Donegal and then southwards down the coast of Eire.* But in the city, the fires went on burning. Fearful that the Germans would soon return, MacDermott now demanded help from Britain. At 4.25 a.m., the duty officer at the Public Security office at Stormont Castle sent an urgent telegram to the Home Security War Room in London, pleading for more fire appliances. Written in haste and at times almost illegible, the wire – now preserved in the Public Record Office of Northern Ireland – conveys something of the flavour of desperation in which the Northern Ireland authorities now found themselves:

MANY MAJOR FIRES HAVE BEEN CAUSED IN BELFAST. ALL PUMPS ARE HEAVILY ENGAGED. BELFAST FIRE CONTROL HAS ASKED FOR REINFORCEMENTS TO BE SENT TO STAND BY TONIGHT 16/17. PLEASE SEND 50 LARGE TRAILERS FROM GLASGOW OR LIVERPOOL UNDER ARRANGEMENTS RECENTLY MADE. ALL TELEPHONE COMMUNICATION IN BELFAST HAS BROKEN DOWN.[78]

Without phone lines, the Ministry of Public Security had little idea what was happening. 'Many fires were started in Belfast,' read its initial intelligence report, 'and some are still burning.' Across the city, there were four major conflagrations which were still spreading, nineteen serious fires requiring up to thirty pumps and 116 smaller fires.[79]

Daylight did not really return at dawn, for Belfast was cloaked in a

---

* Londonderry had been raided by a single aircraft about one and a half hours earlier; it dropped a parachute mine that killed fifteen people in the walled part of the city. A Royal Navy dispatch noted that the black-out was so poor at the time that the plane had not bothered to use flares.[77] Five people also died when a stick of bombs fell on Bangor in County Down.

dense cloud of smoke, ash and dust, a thick yellow fog that permeated every street and house and which settled in a soft, clammy skin over trees and fields up to ten miles from the city. After a night which had been turned into day, natural day had become darkness. Leading his column of fire engines into Belfast, Patrick Finlay saw 'hundreds of feet of smoke and fire' stretching far up into the sky and heard a long, constant rumble of collapsing buildings.[80] James Kelly made his way on foot through the dun coloured fog down to the city centre, noticing almost casually that the premises of the *Northern Whig* were on fire and that even the official censor's office was burning. But what caught his attention was the mood of panic. There were vans crammed with people trying to leave the city; the railway terminus in Great Victoria Street was crowded with old and sick people, with cripples and wounded men and women, all trying to get aboard the trains to Dublin.[81] When Finlay and his men tramped into the Chichester Street fire station for instructions, they found one of Belfast's senior fire officers sitting beneath a table, weeping with his head in his hands and refusing to come out.[82] Stunned by what had happened during the night, MacDermott went first to the City Hall where he was quietly greeted by Thomas Henderson, the Shankill MP. 'No one can blame you,' Henderson said, placing his hand on MacDermott's arm. 'How can you stop these things falling anyway?'[83]

The Belfast firemen had already lost many hoses – they had been broken by collapsing buildings – and even the Irish fire crews could not always help. The Drogheda appliance was fitted with $2\frac{3}{4}$-inch hose couplings that would not lock into the British standard $2\frac{1}{2}$-inch connections in use in Belfast. The Irish crews had no waterproofs to protect their legs from the freezing water and most of them had no idea of the geography of the city.[84] Laurence Carroll, a 29-year-old fireman from Dublin, was directed to a fire in a margarine factory, found the location but never discovered exactly where he was in the city.[85]* Finlay and his men were sent to the docks around York Road where they became aware of a light, warm wind that seemed to move in the direction of the fires. Several of the Irish firemen complained of the lack of oxygen which always exists in the vacuum that usually precedes a fire-storm.[86] Those fires which had been brought under control by the Belfast brigade were still smouldering and little attempt was being made to pull down dangerous walls and masonry. Near Flax Street at the top of the Crumlin Road, Finlay climbed a Belfast fire engine ladder to retrieve a hose that was fixed to the roof of a burning factory. When he reached the roof and turned to pull the slack on the hose, he was horrified to find the parapet of the wall moving gently with the weight of his foot: the ladder was all that was holding the wall up. Seconds after he had climbed frantically back down to the road, the entire factory collapsed

---

* He was in fact in Hudson Street off the Crumlin Road; most of the Irish crews were asked to tackle fires in this general area after the first raid.

inwards in a blaze of fire.[87]

But what shocked both the Belfast and the Irish crews was their growing awareness of the number of dead around them. There were corpses in the streets, spreadeagled on the pavements, sometimes even collapsed across the roofs of buildings where they had been blown by the explosions during the night. John Kelly, the Dublin fire engine driver, always remembered Belfast as a place of ruins in which there were 'human bodies and dead animals lying all over the place.'[88] Laurence Carroll was shocked to see how many corpses were loaded onto the back of military trucks in the Crumlin Road.[89] Bruce Williamson came across the dead, covered in blood, on the streets near Duncairn Gardens; later, looking at the shrapnel gashes in the stone façade of the public library in Royal Avenue, he found himself 'imagining what metal could do to flesh.'[90] Touring the city in a government car at daybreak with William Iliff, MacDermott noticed that 'a benevolent white dust had settled on the corpses.'[91]

Nowhere was the extent of the massacre more horrifyingly revealed, however, than in the overcrowded city mortuaries. Brian Moore, the ARP warden who had watched the flares floating so sublimely over Belfast the previous evening, volunteered to coffin many of the dead, and in his semi-autobiographical novel *The Emperor of Ice-Cream*, he described what he found in the mortuary:

> . . . in the stink of human excrement, in the acrid smell of disinfectant, these dead were heaped, body on body, flung arm, twisted feet, open mouth, staring eyes, old men on top of young women, a child lying on a policeman's back, a soldier's hand resting on a woman's thigh, a carter, still wearing his coal slacks, on top of a pile of arms and legs, his own arm outstretched, finger pointing, as though he warned of some unseen horror. Forbidding and clumsy, the dead cluttered the morgue room from floor to ceiling . . .[92]

At first, the authorities decided to lay out the coffined bodies around the public baths in the Falls Road and at Peter's Hill so that relatives could identify them. McCann, the pool attendant in the Falls, watched the first corpses arrive in a furniture lorry. The lids of the coffins had been removed for identification and the first victims to be brought into the building – a woman and child, stripped naked by the explosion that killed them – were laid beside the pool. As their number grew, however, the pool was emptied and the coffins were laid out side by side on the bottom of the baths. After an hour or two, there were no more coffins and the bodies – mostly women and children – began to arrive in nothing more than the torn clothes they had died in. McCann was puzzled by a heavy, bulky shroud that was brought in on a stretcher and found a label attached to it: 'Believed to be a mother and five children,' it said. In some cases, only parts of bodies had been found. McCann saw a human leg incongruously brought in on a plank.[93]

'There had been a particularly frightful carnage in Percy Street off the Shankill Road where a parachute mine had fallen on a public air-raid shelter. Rita Hegarty had witnessed the aftermath but Kenneth Taylor of the Auxiliary Fire Service – a Protestant lorry driver from Wilton Street – actually saw the mine drift past twenty feet above his head as he stood on the flat roof of a mill in North Howard Street. He thought the object on the parachute was a pilot who had bailed out of one of the German planes, until the mine hit the shelter. The explosion blasted the brick walls inwards and tore the people inside to pieces.[94] For days afterwards, local people who had been away for the Easter holidays returned to their homes to find bodies in their back yards.[95]

At the Falls Road baths, relatives arranged for the removal of victims whom they could identify but the building had become a charnel house of unrecognised or unrecognisable bodies, 150 of them within the first twenty-four hours. They stayed there for three days but as the weather grew warmer and more humid, they began to smell. The ARP put volunteers on the doors of the baths, carrying zip-guns to spray disinfectant over those entering or leaving the building.[96] On April 19, the Government ordered the cadavers to be taken to May's Fields, a wasteland between the river and the markets beside the GNR railway tracks, where families were given a last chance to identify their dead. What they saw there was sometimes almost obscene. Several people remember a young ARP man sitting amid hundreds of bodies, spraying them with cold water from a hose to keep them cool while eating a package of ham sandwiches.[97] Still more victims were found in the days that followed; even weeks afterwards, when the official casualty toll had risen above seven hundred, corpses were being discovered in derelict houses, disembodied arms and legs, green with corruption, trapped in trees and in the guttering of roofs.[98]

Five days after the raid, past crowds who stood four deep on the pavements,[99] a mass funeral of 150 of the dead made its way to the top of the Falls Road. The coffins had been piled on the back of five Army lorries because the forty-seven black Belgian funeral horses that belonged to Belfast's leading firm of undertakers had also perished in the Blitz.[100] The authorities had searched through the possessions of the unidentified dead and those on whom rosary beads had been found were placed with the Catholic victims in the leading truck.[101] When it reached the graveyards, the cortège therefore divided on clinically sectarian lines; the Catholics were taken to Milltown while the Protestants were placed in a mass grave in the City Cemetery a few hundred yards away, their anonymous bodies later commemorated by a depressing grey concrete memorial slab that announced their bleak and unnecessary fate.

Even today, there is no certain figure for those who died in the bombing. Two days after the raid, the Ministry of Public Security believed that 323 people had died; an hour after they recorded this estimate, the total was raised to 500.[102] The Ministry eventually decided that 745 lives had been lost in less than five hours on the night of April 15/16.[103]* This was far worse than Coventry where only 554 had been killed. MacDermott gave instructions to Belfast editors not to print the names and addresses of the dead because the newspapers would be 'in Lisbon via Dublin in two days and provide the Germans with the number of casualties.'[105] The Northern Ireland Government would subsequently claim, with some validity, that no other city in the United Kingdom apart from London suffered so heavily in a single night during the entire war.† It was a lamentable distinction. As Brian Moore commented long after the war, 'Belfast finally became important when the Germans paid attention to it.'[107]

The British gave to the city some momentary attention. On the day after the raid, forty-two more fire appliances arrived from Glasgow and Liverpool.[108] Herbert Morrison, the Home Secretary, wired Andrews to express his sympathy for the bereaved and to 'congratulate leaders and people on their grit and courage'.[109] There had indeed been a good deal of valour displayed on the night of April 15/16; three George Medals and six British Empire Medals were awarded for gallantry and brave conduct during the raid, official recognition of the Belfast firemen, civil defence and first-aid workers who risked their lives to rescue trapped and injured people while bombs were exploding in the streets around them. But there was another, less attractive side to the public's reaction to the raid. Among those who crowded the trains out of Belfast on the morning of April 16 were civil defence and ARP personnel; one senior air-raid warden, his helmet still in his hand, was seen walking out of Amiens Street station in Dublin with hundreds of refugees only hours after the bombing.[110] MacDermott was full of praise for the Auxiliary Fire Service but acknowledged that other civil defence workers 'sloped off'.[111] Spender thought that the Belfast Fire Brigade generally 'made a poor showing' and that the Dublin firemen must have gained 'a poor impression' of Belfast's civil defence organisation.[112]

Individual evidence – sometimes expressed in angry, intemperate language – began to arrive at Stormont suggesting that shipyard and aircraft factory hands had not always showed the 'grit' to which Morrison referred. An American employee of the Lockheed Aircraft Corporation, on loan to Short and Harland's, was to write home to his parents in California after the raid with a less than glowing account of the behaviour of his fellow

* The Ministry of Public Security's civilian casualty return for all of April 1941 – including the raid of April 7/8 – shows that in the whole province 775 people were killed: 315 men, 243 women, 54 children and 163 victims so mutilated that their sex could not be determined. The same return gives a total of 1661 wounded, 483 of them seriously. A man and woman in Belfast were listed as 'missing, believed killed' but their bodies were never found.[104]
† An estimated 720 died in a single night's raid on Liverpool just over two weeks later. London lost 1436 lives on the night May 10/11 1941.[106]

workers. The bombing, he said, 'really kicked hell out of the place and I'm not kidding square blocks were laid flat . . . You have heard about how tough the Irish are – well all I can say is that the tough Irish must come from S. Ireland because the boys up in N. Ireland are a bunch of chicken shit yellow bastards – 90% of them left everything and ran like hell. Short and Harlands the Aircraft factory that builds Stirlings here had 300 Volunteer fire fighters in the plant, after the raid they were lucky to get 90 of them . . .'[113]* In the emergency censor's office near Lombard Street, James Kelly found that his report on the raid was severely excised. All mention of parachute mines had been deleted but the most heavily scored passages were Kelly's observations on civilian morale.[115]

It was hardly surprising, for by midday on April 16 a mass exodus from Belfast had begun, not just a few hundred or even a few thousand people but tens of thousands – Protestants and Catholics – pushing their way onto trains or buses or walking through the streets of broken glass towards the countryside. Joseph McCann saw 'streams of people moving up the Falls Road, women and children with blankets and flasks, all heading to the country.'[116] The Northern Ireland Government was to suggest later that the shared suffering had brought about a new unity between Protestants and Catholics. Professor Lyons has spoken of 'the spontaneous coming together of Catholic and Protestant in their hour of crisis',[117] and it is true that the raid did briefly create a new political thought process that some-times took individuals by surprise. Watching hundreds of refugees pour-ing out of the city on the morning after the raid, Breandán Mac Giolla Choille, a young Catholic from County Down, took cover when he heard the sound of a low-flying aircraft and shouted urgently to a man near him: 'Is it one of ours?' When Mac Giolla Choille recognised the RAF roundels on the fuselage of the 245 Squadron Hurricane that raced over the roof tops, he relaxed but was nonetheless amazed at his instinctive use of the possessive 'our' in relation to a British plane. Would the Catholics of Northern Ireland, he wondered, now subconsciously take sides in the war?[118] A song was temporarily popular in Belfast that no doubt reflected some bond of friendship between the communities, even if it did have a sting in the tail:

> On the Shankill, on the Falls,
> You forget oul' Derry's walls.
> You'se run as the bombs begin to fall,
> Says good oul' Rule Britannia.[119]

---

* The writer sent his letter from Dublin because 'letters are not censored here', an unwise remark which immediately caught the eye of the British censorship authorities when the mail was being trans-shipped through Britain to the United States. A copy was sent to the Northern Ireland Government where a civil servant noted that it was 'certainly of interest . . . as an example of the American language!'[114]

But the citizens of Belfast were united not by common love but by grief and common fear. They moved, a frightening, uncontrollable army of terrified people, into the laneways and fields and ditches outside the city, swamping the post-raid evacuation centres that MacDermott's Ministry of Public Security had set up over the previous eight months. This was not 'a spontaneous coming together': it was panic. Official refugee reception areas became 'hopelessly jammed' by the hordes of people seeking shelter outside Belfast.[120] In the city itself, 40,000 people had to be accommodated in rest centres and 70,000 given meals in emergency feeding centres. In the countryside, small towns were inundated by refugees. The five hundred inhabitants of Dromara in County Down found 2000 people flocking into their village.[121] Many of the refugees were dirty; most of them were poor. They moved from their crushed streets, the 'submerged tenth' of the population,[122] bringing with them a danger of disease and a tide of people whose energy was galvanised by terror rather than homelessness. Up to a hundred thousand people joined this extraordinary trek to the countryside,[123] returning only at dawn to their vulnerable houses. MacDermott initiated the Hiram Plan on the morning of April 16[124] but was forced almost immediately to confine the work of his own ministry to the restoration of the city.[125] Such was the atmosphere at Stormont that when Spender dared to tell Andrews that the Cabinet had placed too much responsibility on MacDermott's shoulders, Andrews accused him of petty jealousy.[126]

In later years, MacDermott would hold Craigavon, his dead prime minister, partly responsible for the exodus of Belfast's population. 'Craigavon made one unfortunate pronouncement in 1940,' MacDermott remarked long after the war. 'When he was talking about air raid protection for the people, he said: "The country's near and they can take to the ditches." '[127] The 'ditchers' did just that. Each evening, Rita Hegarty watched them in their thousands moving up the Shankill to the hills above Belfast[128] to find shelter in the fields, in old barns, beside overgrown hedgerows. Thousands more – most but by no means all Catholics – travelled on special trains to Dublin. There, they were at one and the same time the subject of genuine compassion and an object lesson to those who thought Eire should have entered the war on the British side. If the British could not even defend Belfast and protect these people, how could they possibly have guaranteed Dublin's safety under air attack if Eire had allied herself to Britain in 1940? There were also those who saw some distant but hopeful outcome to the events in Belfast. 'Politically,' wrote *The Irish Times*, 'the border between the six and the twenty-six counties remains as firm as ever; actually it has been shaken by every train that has borne its burden of refugees from North to South, and by every train that has carried distraught relatives from South to North in search of their loved ones. A community of kindness means a closer and higher union than any political association.'[129]

Patrick Finlay had experienced some of this kindness at first hand in a city so alien to him that he did not understand why the people there spoke with 'Scotch accents'. Men and women came to him to shake his hand as he sat on a Belfast kerbstone to eat a Salvation Army meal of corned beef and cabbage. Only when he returned to Dublin was he asked why he had risked his life for the citizens of Northern Ireland. The British Government was less expressive in its gratitude: it formally paid each Irish fireman just five shillings to cover the cost of his lunch.[130] The Irish answer to Belfast's request for help had, of course, been a technical breach of neutrality. In Dublin, Hempel, the German Minister, understood the emotional and political reasons behind the act. 'Strictly speaking,' he told an Irish journalist long afterwards, 'I think we could have protested. But it would have been cruel . . . I know that the Irish Government felt a bit uneasy that the German Government might protest, but it was a deed of sympathy for your people, your Irish people, and we fully understood what you felt. Nobody from Germany protested and I had no intention of doing so. Your own people were in danger.'[131]

The Irish Government were fortunate that Hempel took this view, for they were unequivocal about what they had done. Aiken was in Boston on his abortive arms purchasing mission when Belfast was bombed and he was immediately asked by the American press if Irish fire crews should have been permitted to cross the border. 'Of course we should go to Belfast,' he told them. 'They are Irish people too.'[132] De Valera referred to the raid on Belfast as 'a disaster', rather as if it was a natural calamity than a man-made act of war. But he was publicly generous in his sympathy. Three days after the bombing, he spoke warmly about the people of Northern Ireland, both Protestant and Catholic:

In the past, and probably in the present too, a number of them did not see eye to eye with us politically, but they are all our people – we are one and the same people – and their sorrows in the present instance are also our sorrows; and I want to say that any help we can give them in the present time we will give to them wholeheartedly, believing that were the circumstances reversed they would also give us their help wholeheartedly.[133]

Against the conflagrations that had raged in Belfast, de Valera's aid could really only be symbolic. The Irish fire crews were withdrawn before dusk on April 16, no doubt for fear that Eire's relations with Germany might be complicated if their men were killed in a second night's raid. The Northern Ireland authorities believed that the Germans would indeed return and did nothing to prevent the nightly exodus to the countryside. MacDermott's Ministry of Public Security could do little to alleviate the threat. Indeed, one of its few recorded acts of public protection during this initial post-raid period was a decision to shoot the animals at Belfast

Zoo in case they escaped from their cages in another air attack.* The water supply was not fully restored for five days and even then eighteen roads in the city were still blocked by debris. War production fell by up to 25 per cent,[135] a remarkably high figure since the Germans had left the harbour area comparatively untouched. They were not to make the same mistake again. Just after midnight on Sunday, May 4, the Luftwaffe returned.

German records show that 204 aircraft arrived over Belfast that night and that they dropped well over 95,000 incendiaries across the eastern sector of the city, turning the harbour and shipyard district into an inferno. High explosive and oil bombs showered down onto the Short and Harland flight shed and airport; acres of Harland and Wolff's yards were consumed by a fire that swept through many of the workshops and cascaded into the densely populated Protestant Newtownards Road. Three corvettes under construction were bombed while the cargo ship *Fair Head*, moored to the side of the Dufferin Dock, was blown apart and sunk.[136] Unhampered by barrage balloons, several German aircraft left their formations and flew at low level across the waterfront area of York Road – already devastated in the April raid – raking the streets with cannon fire.[137] This time, the water mains – smashed in 67 places[138] – dried up and fire crews, lacking the steel pipe fittings which MacDermott had demanded of the British authorities the previous autumn, could make little use of the natural underground rivers which ran beneath the streets of Belfast. At 2.0 a.m. on May 5, the Belfast Chief Fire Officer made a distress call to his opposite number at Tara Street in Dublin.[139] The Belfast Brigade were trying, hopelessly, to control two conflagrations, 22 'major' and 58 'serious' fires – each of them attended by an average of 30 appliances – and 125 smaller fires.[140]

From the hills outside Belfast, watchers could see 'a great ring of fire, as if the whole city was ablaze, and every now and then the sudden glow in the sky as oil bomb or parachute mine suddenly erupted.'[141] From the air, the fires seemed even more apocalyptic. Having discovered the feebleness of the city's defences three weeks earlier, the Luftwaffe permitted a radio reporter attached to their squadrons, Ernst von Kuhren, to fly with them on the mission to Northern Ireland and record his own graphic account of the *Blitzkrieg*. 'When I saw Belfast,' he told his listeners on the German Home Service a few hours later:

. . . I revised all my ideas about the effects of German bombing. I can really say that I could not believe my eyes. When we approached the target at half-past two we stared silently into a sea of flames such as none of us had seen before. Then after some time our squadron leader, who has already made more

---

* Two RUC marksmen were called in to dispatch six wolves, two racoons, a puma, a hyena, five lions, two lionesses, a tiger, a black bear, two brown bears, two polar bears, a lynx, a vulture and a giant rat.[134]

than 100 flights, said 'One would not believe it' . . . in Belfast there was not a large number of conflagrations, but just one enormous conflagration which spread over the entire harbour and industrial area . . .[142]

In the bright moonlit night and clear visibility, the Germans experienced no difficulty in finding their target. The Luftwaffe crews in the second wave of bombers saw the fires of Belfast when they were still over the north-west coast of Britain, a blaze of light surmounted by a two-mile high column of black smoke.[143] Von Kuhren, whose report was to become steadily more propagandistic, though nonetheless precise, claimed that there were scarcely any fires in the outer suburbs of the city, but:

> . . . within the target area there was not one black spot. In the district of the docks, wharves, factories and storehouses, an area of about one and a half square kilometres, everything was on fire. Here are the large shipbuilding yards . . . Here was the last hide-out place for unloading war materials from the USA. Here the English had concentrated an important part of their war industries because they thought themselves safe far up in the north, safe from the blows of the German Air Force. This has come to an end.[144]

Von Kuhren was right, as Northern Ireland ministers must have realised when they read through the BBC's transcript of his report. The words were a cruel echo of those self-confident memoranda on Belfast's invulnerability which Stormont officials were composing only three years before. The German reporter's description of the 'enormous black pall of smoke' that hung over Belfast, of 'the black skeletons of burnt-out factories' and burning silos,[145] was painfully accurate.

Although this time only 150 people were killed, official statistics compiled after the raid showed that Harland and Wolff's shipyard did not return to full production for six months and that it was nearly a year before night-work resumed in the machine shop; immediately after the attack, war production was running at only 10 per cent. The destruction of workshops at Short and Harland's slowed production of the Stirling bomber.[146] The harbour power plant was badly damaged and the LMS railway station at York Road devastated. Even the City Hall – the towering landmark of central Belfast which stood out so prominently on the Luftwaffe photo-reconnaissance pictures – was partially burnt out by an incendiary which set fire to the balconies above Donegall Square.[147] In fact, every industry and factory listed on the Luftwaffe's target indicator chart the previous November had now been destroyed or seriously damaged. In all Belfast, German bombs had in less than three weeks blasted 56,600 houses, totally destroying 3200 of them,[148] a veritable Jerusalem for MacDermott to rebuild.

At 5.0 a.m. on the morning of May 5, Sub-officer William Kennedy of the Dun Laoghaire Fire Brigade – one of the thirteen crews who had again been sent up from Eire – was damping down a fire in a rope-works on the

Newtownards Road when he noticed far above him a Luftwaffe reconnaissance aircraft.[149] The Germans were assessing the results of their night's work and made little secret of their conclusions. 'German reconnaissance planes,' the German radio's Home Service told its audience, 'ascertained by means of photos that during the raid on Belfast harbour works . . . three ships under construction were most extensively damaged. They were a tanker of 10,000 tons, a merchantman of 8,000 tons and another of 7,000 tons. The almost completed ships were utterly destroyed . . .'[150] They were not, but the *Fair Head* was; she lay blocking the fairway throughout the summer.[151] There was one final, light raid on Belfast the next night when several German bombers, presumably mistaking the city for a town on the British mainland, dropped incendiaries and a parachute mine on some public shelters, killing fourteen people. An RAF Hurricane succeeded in destroying one of the planes, a Junkers 88, near Ardglass.[152]*

After almost a thousand deaths in just three weeks, it was only to be expected that ingenious and occasionally conspiratorial rumours would circulate among the people of Belfast; that de Valera had personally appealed to Hitler to stop the bombing of Northern Ireland, that Eire would now join the war against Germany, that the Luftwaffe bombers had used the lights of neutral Dublin to guide them north to Belfast. According to Hempel, de Valera had certainly been worried about the danger of a Luftwaffe attack on the six counties, telling the German Minister shortly before the outbreak of war that 'the North is also part of Ireland and you should be careful with it.'[154] But there is no record that the Taoiseach made any protest – formal or otherwise – to the German Government after the Belfast bombings. Hempel did receive a letter from Cardinal MacRory, however, in which the Primate asked him to do his best to prevent an air attack on Armagh. Hempel recalled that MacRory – who sent his note just after the Belfast raids – had 'explained that Armagh was the ecclesiastical capital of Ireland, and that it should be saved from destruction by bombing.' The German Minister passed this appeal to the Foreign Ministry in Berlin. There was no reply;[155] nor were there any more air raids on Northern Ireland.

That Dublin unwittingly acted as a navigation beacon for German aircraft on their way to bomb Belfast is a more difficult question to resolve. On the night of May 4/5, the Luftwaffe flew across the north west of Britain to attack their target, and neither then nor on the night of April 15/16 are there any records in the Irish Defence Department archives to show that belligerent aircraft infringed Irish air space. There is considerable evidence that planes *did* approach the Irish capital on other nights although they may not have been using Dublin as a marker; on the

---

* German records state that five of their aircraft were shot down on the night of April 15/16. A Belfast anti-aircraft gun battery was credited with a 'hit' during that raid[153] but no wreckage was ever found.

contrary, it seems possible that they were planning to attack it under the erroneous impression that it was a British city. There is, for instance, an intriguing entry in the Irish Air and Marine intelligence file for 28 May 1941, when the Air Corps noted that approximately fifty planes – presumably German although they were marked down as 'unidentified' – flew across the south-east coast of Eire just after midnight, heading northwards. 'It would seem,' the Air Corps mapping officer reported at the time, 'that large waves of aircraft flying in flights entered the country at three main points 1) Carnsore and Cahore 2) Kilmichael and Wicklow and 3) the Brownstown to Carnsore area. Apart from one flight, most of the activity was confined to the East Coast.'[156]

Then something very strange happened. The plotting map shows that the planes were heading in the general direction of Dublin; some aircraft did fly up the Wicklow coast, passing above the village of Dalkey at one end of Dublin Bay but then continued northwards towards Rush. Several planes flew on into Northern Ireland but one turned round when it reached the border at Cootehill while another was recorded by ground observers almost eighty miles to the south at Mountmellick. There were reports of 'Very lights, flashes and explosions', most of which the Irish military authorities thought were due to their own anti-aircraft batteries at Collinstown; they fired 28 Bofors shells and 210 rounds of heavy machine-gun fire at the intruders. 'Nevertheless,' the Air Corps stated, 'reports re explosions, which were definitely not A-A gunfire, were' also received from various posts mostly situated on the coast South of Dublin.'[157] The evidence – the formations of aircraft that suddenly divided up in confusion, the apparent disorientation of the pilots who flew in different directions after passing Dublin – strongly suggests that this was an air raid that was aborted at the last minute, perhaps when the aircrews realised they were over Ireland and not Britain. The explosions heard along the coast may well have been bombs which the Luftwaffe pilots unloaded into the sea after realising their mistake.

The incident is important because two nights later, the Luftwaffe did bomb Dublin, flying over the coast at 1.30 a.m. and dropping several parachute mines around the North Strand Road, east of the Post Office in O'Connell Street. They killed thirty-four people, wounded ninety and destroyed or damaged three hundred houses. Many of the deaths were caused by a 500 lb bomb that exploded on the tram-tracked roadway just north of Amiens Street railway station, deflecting the blast into the neighbouring houses.[158] Nothing as serious as this had happened in Eire since the war began and many people in Dublin found it hard to believe that their city had been attacked. Surviving newsreel film taken at dawn on May 31 portrays something of the impact that the bombings made on this neutral environment: there are shots of ARP personnel standing gravely to attention and saluting whenever bodies are extracted from the ruins, and of de Valera and Aiken staring dumbfounded at the crater made

434

by the bomb that hit the surface of the North Strand Road.

Hempel was no less shocked by the raid. 'I was staggered,' he would afterwards recall. 'I went immediately to Mr Walshe to find out about it and I also saw Mr de Valera . . . My first very immediate reaction was one of suspicion and I wondered if the bombing had been done by the British with captured German planes. It could have been easy for them to have done something like that to upset Irish neutrality and to get Ireland into the war. They could have said "Oh look what the Germans have done!" I may have wired that to Berlin.'[159] Hempel was not the first to consider this possibility. Some three weeks before the bombing of North Strand, there had been a curious transmission over the German radio's English language service that seemed to carry some foreknowledge of the incident. Commenting on Britain's need for the Treaty ports, the broadcaster had concluded that 'it is conceivable that, to gain their ends, the British intend to bomb Eire and then declare that this crime was committed by Germany.'[160] Did the Germans therefore really believe that the British might attack Dublin? Or were they preparing the ground for a raid of their own, a bombing that they would then blame upon the RAF?

The bomb fragments were of German origin and quickly proved that the Luftwaffe had been responsible. Aiken says that 'of course, we knew it was the Germans'[161] and indeed the Irish Government swiftly registered a diplomatic protest in Berlin. Hempel could not disagree with the evidence and sent a second message to his Foreign Ministry, advising caution.[162] Germany's embarrassment was evident in the news broadcasts transmitted in Axis countries some days later. The protest made by William Warnock, the Irish representative in Berlin, was given considerable publicity on Axis stations, followed always by assurances of Germany's moral innocence. Italians were told that a 'very careful enquiry will be held to establish responsibility. If this proved that German aircraft did in fact bomb the Irish capital, this was naturally in error, as it is absolutely absurd to consider the possibility of a deliberate attack.'[163] Warnock had been assured that it was 'impossible that the Germans bombed Dublin intentionally,' Budapest radio announced.[164]

The most likely explanation for the Dublin bombing was put forward by Churchill after the war: that it was an unforeseen result of British interference with the radio beams used by the Luftwaffe bombers to find their targets in Britain.[165] The Germans had for several months been transmitting radio navigation signals on intersecting lines to guide their planes to the British cities which had been selected for bombing; the British countered this by jamming the German radios and distorting the signals. They did not 'bend' the beams, as some writers have suggested,[166] but smothered them in such a way that the aircraft would start wandering around the sky in an attempt to trace the genuine signals.[167] This would produce just the pattern of events that occurred along the east coast of Eire on May 28 when the aircraft involved might have been targeted on

Cardiff, Swansea or Milford Haven. The same thing may well have happened two nights later, only this time the Germans realised too late that they were bombing the wrong country. Hempel eventually subscribed to this theory. With radar, he said, the British 'had the possibility of directing the bombing of Dublin and other Irish places. I think it was due to the interference with our planes that Irish towns were bombed. They thought they were attacking British towns.'[168] There is no evidence in German records to confirm that this is what happened, nor is there any suggestion in British files that the distortion of the Luftwaffe radio beams would lead directly to an attack on Dublin. Given Britain's mood at the time, however, it is unlikely that the British would have cared unduly if it had.

The bombing of the Irish capital was of political rather than military importance; the comparatively few casualties made it an almost absurd epilogue to the raids on Belfast. But in Northern Ireland itself, the authorities had no way of knowing that the *Blitzkrieg* was over. The Luftwaffe were able to bomb Belfast with 'almost complete immunity', a Stormont memorandum stated, partly because 'the neutrality of Eire gives facilities to the enemy aircraft . . . to elude our Fighting Force.'[169] At last, however, the Northern Ireland Government did bestir itself to give more adequate protection to its people. Acknowledging that the provision of air-raid shelters in Belfast and Londonderry had been 'below the scale of that which was available in comparable cities in Great Britain,' ministers determined to build more protection, emphasising 'the effect upon the morale of the population if they are called upon to face the coming winter without adequate shelter.'[170]

The Stormont Government therefore approved expenditure for air-raid shelters for a further 44,000 householders in the province. A new evacuation system was instituted while the British provided more anti-aircraft guns, more searchlights, a Defiant night fighter squadron and an extended balloon barrage and radar system. Hundreds of extra fire engines were brought into Belfast.[171] Since Stormont itself had been attacked, an alternative seat of Government was proposed at Hillsborough Castle.[172] Even now, however, a frightening parochialism dominated the Cabinet's deliberations. A disquieting illustration of this could be found in the attention which ministers devoted to Carson's statue. A larger-than-life bronze replica of the Unionist leader who had opposed Home Rule stood at the top of the ceremonial drive outside the Stormont Parliament building, his outstretched arm and hand beckoning to the indifferent city below. How could it be protected from possible bomb damage? The Cabinet debated this vexed question at some length, concluding that it should be surrounded with sandbags, although for good measure Andrews himself decided to consult Carson's widow.[173] Two months later, the statue was the first item on the agenda of a Cabinet meeting that proposed to remove it altogether for safekeeping.[174] Then, at a time when thousands of people in Belfast still had no air-raid shelters, the Stormont Government went so far as to set up a *committee* to pronounce on the best form of protection for this lofty replica of one of modern unionism's founding fathers.[175]* It was indeed just as well that after the night of May 5/6, the Germans were never to drop another bomb on Northern Ireland.

But the population was not to know this. The raids did not continue but the nightly exodus from Belfast did. Thousands of people, driven by the memory of what had happened on those two nights of bombing, still preferred the cold and damp countryside to their own homes at night. The 'ditchers' of Belfast became the subject of comment on Nazi radio stations. 'Fearing air raids,' Radio Paris told its listeners in mid-May, '20,000 women and children escape every evening from Belfast to the outskirts of the city.'[177] If anything, this was an underestimate. Two weeks after the last raid, 2000 people were crowding the suburb of Dunmurry alone. Apparently quite unnerved by the chaos outside the city, Dawson Bates presented an extraordinary memorandum to the Stormont Cabinet on May 15, insisting that the Northern Ireland Governor's residence at Hillsborough be turned over to refugees because all official country accommodation had been swamped. He wanted 'large houses, institutions or camps for respectable families who are at present billeted in the country in some cases at the rate [sic] of 30 to small houses.' And in a truly shocking passage, Dawson Bates announced that:

> There are in the country probably about 5,000 absolutely unbilletable persons. They are unbilletable owing to personal habits which are sub-human. Camps or institutions under suitable supervision must be instituted for these.[178]

Thus did the Northern Ireland Government regard the poorest of the poor in their divided community, who had abandoned their homes for want of the protection which their government failed to give them.

The Cabinet were becoming fearful rather than compassionate as they realised that their people were passing out of their control, reluctant to play their part in the crisis that had come upon the province. There was ample evidence to prove that this was true. MacDermott told his fellow ministers that during the rescue operations which followed the second air raid, he had 'heard several complaints of soldiers at work being watched by large crowds of idle but able-bodied men.'[179] There were 'signs of reluctance' on the part of fire-watchers to do their job at night, there was 'no equality of sacrifice throughout the country'.[180] The Admiralty had to be informed that Harland and Wolff's men refused to work night shifts. Labour difficulties grew in Belfast's war industries.[181] 'It is . . . impossible to resist the conclusion,' MacDermott told his Cabinet colleagues,

---

* MacDermott put an end to this nonsense. 'I saw Dawson Bates in the corridor at Stormont,' he recalled. 'I told him I didn't think old Ned would like to see himself in some backyard. Dawson Bates replied "Neither do I" and that was the end of the committee.'[176]

'that the morale of the city as a whole is not first class. Indeed it is in some ways definitely disappointing. There is much fear. Many are still leaving the town nightly to stay in the fields or walk the roads till the danger of a raid is thought to be passed, and there are far too many rumours of an alarming character going about.'[182] According to Spender, an 'appalling description of the situation in Belfast' was given to a Stormont Cabinet meeting at which both Dawson Bates and MacDermott 'made it clear that in their view there was far more panic amongst the people of Belfast than in the cities in Great Britain which had been subjected to worse bombardment.'[183]

But the panic went on. Every evening at dusk, MacDermott would sit at his home near Stormont and hear 'the pattering of feet up the lane outside'.[184] Nine months after the raids, James Kelly was to find an old man and his wife sitting beneath a country hedge at three in the morning, waiting for the daylight that would give them the courage to return home.[185] As the columns made their way out of Belfast each night, they were in some indefinable way recreating a medieval phenomenon, the flight of a people from the unknown contagion of the city. No Northern Ireland Government could comprehend it. Thomas Henderson, the Shankill MP who had comforted MacDermott after the April raid, was among the first to recognise the scale of the Stormont Cabinet's complacency and its implications. 'I broke down,' he told the Belfast Parliament:

> . . . when I saw lying dead men I had been reared beside. When I saw the whole district where I roamed in my bare feet razed to the ground . . . Will the Right Hon Member come with me to the hills and to Divis mountain? Will he go to the barns and sheughs throughout Northern Ireland to see the people of Belfast, some of them lying on damp ground? Will he come to Hannahstown and the Falls Road? The Catholics and Protestants are going up there mixed and they are talking to one another. They are sleeping in the same sheugh, below the same tree or in the same barn. They all say the same thing, that the government is no good.[186]

Even more disturbing was the awesome prophecy that came from the Moderator of the Presbyterian Church General Assembly, a normally reticent man who had been shaken by the poverty of those he now saw walking the bombed streets of his city. 'I have been working nineteen years in Belfast,' he said:

> . . . and I never saw the like of them before. If something is not done now to remedy this rank inequality there will be a revolution after the war.'[187]

Chapter 14

Consonant with the Law of God

> Unless Britain is prepared from a military point of view to seize the whole country it appears to be madness . . . Eighty thousand Irish volunteers in [the] British Army will be disaffected. A Government, a popular majority and an army inclined to be friendly to Britain rather than to the Axis will become definitely hostile, possibly giving active aid to Germany . . .
>
> David Gray, American Minister in Dublin, on
> British proposals to extend conscription
> to Northern Ireland *25 April 1941*

In the weeks that followed the air attacks on Belfast, the phrase 'equality of sacrifice' – initially MacDermott's words but later adopted by other ministers – was heard ever more frequently at Stormont. As the public's fear of renewed air raids failed to diminish, the nightly ritual of the 'ditchers' came to be regarded with increasing concern by the Northern Ireland Cabinet. It was not just that the exodus represented a vote of no confidence in the authorities. The Government had, after all, failed in one of their primary duties: the protection of their people. But the continued lack of trust displayed by the thousands who left the city and the growing signs of public apathy were also, in their way, a form of insurrection, a refusal to accept the burdens with which the war had rewarded Northern Ireland for its official protestations of loyalty. A unity of suffering was one thing but if this new-found social cohesion should be directed against the Government, it would raise infinitely more serious prospects for those at Stormont Castle who had until now paid scant attention to the social needs and inequalities of their citizens. Now that fire had embraced Belfast and bombs had blasted open the warrens of poverty in the city, it was necessary for the Government to control the forces that might be released. Ministers came to terms with this challenge in the same bland, generalised manner in which they had confronted so many other crises over the past twenty-one months. 'This country,' John MacDermott told the Cabinet, 'has suffered and is suffering from being only half in the war.'[1]

From the records of the Northern Ireland Government's discussions at this period, it seems sometimes as if ministers were unaware – unable to

439

grasp the fact – that one third of their population did not wish to be in the war at all. The butchery of the air raids prompted not reflection on their part but calls for discipline of a kind that was bound to meet resistance from the nationalists who felt no allegiance to the Stormont authorities. The official view was crystallised in the memorandum – understandably marked 'Secret' – which MacDermott placed before the Cabinet on May 12, six days after the last bombs had been dropped on Belfast. The province's semi-war status, he claimed, had brought about 'a general feeling that we are neither one thing nor the other, and I think this has contributed to the unsettling effects of the raids . . .' Civil defence personnel would have to be strengthened but it was doubtful if this could be done on a voluntary basis. 'There is no feeling,' said MacDermott, '. . . of equality of sacrifice throughout the country. The willing horse is bearing the brunt and we are in danger of working him to death.' The time had come to ask the British Government to 'reconsider most carefully' the application of conscription in Northern Ireland. MacDermott believed that 'its introduction would cause difficulties with the minority but I doubt if they would be as great as they were at the beginning of the war, and I feel that such difficulties would be more than offset by the benefits gained.'[2]

Previously, Unionists had always demanded the introduction of compulsory national service on the grounds that the province should play its part in the defence of the realm; 'equality of sacrifice' was intended then to represent the relationship between Northern Ireland and Great Britain, not between the people of the six counties. In 1939, Unionist newspapers used emotionally charged language in urging their readers to enlist. 'Whoever stands aloof at the present crisis,' trumpeted the *Belfast Telegraph* when Craigavon had called for conscription, 'is a friend to Fascist aggression and an enemy of democracy.'[3] In September 1939, the same publication had castigated the province's nationalist community for their lack of patriotic spirit. '. . . it is noticeable,' the paper commented then, 'that many Separatists in Ireland do not extend to other countries that zeal for the rights of small nations of which they talk so volubly when they themselves are concerned.'[4] This sort of political rhetoric had now largely disappeared and MacDermott's support for conscription was based on a far more pragmatic attitude, one that had apparently been inspired by Craigavon. MacDermott recalled that he was 'driving out of Belfast with the Prime Minister one day in 1940 and as we were going through a road-block at Glengormley, Craigavon turned to me and said: "You know, this war might go on for years and years and years." I thought about this for a long time and it made me think that the discipline of the community would stand stronger if we had conscription.'[5] It was a view that he was to develop over the coming months, the idea that national service – far from being divisive in the province – would create a renewed respect for authority among the people. Its effect, MacDermott told

Andrews, the Prime Minister, on May 17 – five days after his original memorandum – would be one of 'stiffening the social fabric so that it may withstand the tide of total war.'[6]

That the air attacks on Belfast were not the only factor behind the Northern Ireland Government's renewed interest in conscription is proved by the fact that Andrews had written to Herbert Morrison, the Home Secretary, on April 4 – eleven days before the first big raid – suggesting that national service should be extended to the six counties.[7] He had apparently heard that the British Army were thinking of conscription as a method of raising additional home defence battalions in the province.[8] For their part, the British Government were impressed by the apparent reservoir of manpower now available there; statistics suggested that about 48,000 men might be at the disposal of the armed forces if conscription was applied to Northern Ireland. Churchill was said to be particularly attracted by the arguments of the Unionist Government[9] and on May 20, this mutual interest was formalised by an official request to Andrews from Herbert Morrison, asking for the Stormont Cabinet's views on the introduction of conscription in the six counties. The British Government, wired Morrison, 'are disposed to think this might produce substantial accession of strength to [the] armed forces.'[10]

The only concern of Stormont ministers was to ensure that citizens from Eire did not take the jobs of conscripted men, and the Cabinet appointed a sub-committee to look into this question.[11] But there was nothing uncertain about their reply to Morrison, a two-paragraph telegram the text of which had clearly been heavily influenced by MacDermott. The Northern Ireland Government, it said:

> . . . is emphatically of opinion that conscription should be applied to Northern Ireland. It considers that in this matter a common basis for the whole of the United Kingdom is just. It further considers, particularly in the light of recent heavy enemy attacks, that the principle of equality of sacrifice and service underlying conscription is essential to promote the degree of corporate discipline which is necessary if our people are to withstand the tide of total war and play their full part in the national effort.[12]

Then, almost as an afterthought, the Stormont Cabinet added that it thought:

> . . . there may be Nationalist opposition to conscription. It is impossible to forecast the extent of such opposition accurately. It feels, however, that the difficulties of such opposition would be more than offset by the advantages gained.[13]

It was apparent from the outset that Northern Ireland ministers had scarcely considered nationalist opposition, let alone tried to forecast its extent. They had not bothered to consult either the Army or the RUC

Inspector General, who had to wait for a later approach from the British before being given the opportunity of expressing his views on potential Catholic reaction to conscription. Nor was any attempt made to seek the opinion of Cardinal MacRory whose advice, however unwelcome it might have been to the Unionist Government, would at least have left them in no doubt as to the strength of feeling within the Catholic Church. In fact, the Primate only heard of the Stormont Cabinet's plans when James Kelly, the *Irish Independent*'s persistent young correspondent in Belfast, picked up a rumour in the Stormont corridors on the evening of May 20 that some kind of national service measures were again being contemplated. Kelly telephoned the Cardinal's residence in Armagh and spoke to MacRory's secretary who had heard nothing of the report but immediately informed the Primate.[14]

On the same day that the Stormont Cabinet sent their reply to Morrison, Churchill told the House of Commons in London that the British Government was considering the extension of conscription to Northern Ireland. For some reason, the issue reawoke all Churchill's old animosity towards de Valera and his twenty-six county state; when John Dulanty called at Downing Street to pass on de Valera's condemnation on May 22, he apparently found the British Prime Minister in one of his most hostile moods. De Valera's biographers, who were permitted to read J.P. Walshe's report on the Downing Street encounter, record that Churchill lost his temper, claiming that the demand for conscription had come from Northern Ireland, that everybody there would be treated alike but that 'no obstruction would be put in the way of those who wanted to run away.' He was not interested in any trouble that might occur in Ireland, which would in any case be only a small addition to the bloodshed elsewhere in the world. The Anglo-Irish Treaty of 1921 once more loomed in Churchill's mind. De Valera had cast it aside. 'Since that date,' said Churchill, 'he had drawn the sword.'[15] The British Prime Minister calmed down towards the end of his conversation with Dulanty but on the evidence to reach de Valera, Churchill could not be reasoned with.

The public reaction to Churchill's announcement was as explosive as it was inevitable. Cardinal MacRory immediately recalled the statement made by the Catholic bishops of Northern Ireland almost two years earlier, that conscripting the province would be 'an outrage on the national feeling and an aggression upon our national rights'. Any attempt to impose such a measure would be a disaster. 'That the people of all creeds and classes in Belfast have recently suffered heavily at the hands of the Germans, however regrettable it may be,' he said:

> . . . does not touch the essence of the question which is that an ancient land, made one by God, was partitioned by a foreign power against the vehement protests of its people and that conscription would now seek to compel those who still writhe under this grievous wrong to fight on the side of its perpetrators.[16]

Melodramatic as this statement may have appeared, it nonetheless represented a view that was shared by tens of thousands of Catholics in Northern Ireland, as well as many trade unionists and several Protestant members of the Labour Party. Jack Beattie, the anti-partitionist Labour MP in the Stormont Parliament, thought that 'if Mr Churchill forces conscription on Northern Ireland his action will prove one of the biggest blunders in the history of Ireland or England.'[17]

Dulanty, whose arguments had made no impression on Churchill, called on Herbert Morrison on May 23 to explain de Valera's 'grave view' of the situation. According to Morrison's report of the visit, the Irish High Commissioner warned that there would be resistance from large numbers of nationalists in Northern Ireland, adding 'that the imprisonment of recalcitrants would no doubt be followed by hunger striking, and that much bitter feeling would necessarily be generated.' It was the prospect of conscription in 1916 'which contributed largely to the defeat of the Redmond policy and the rise of the extremists.'[18] It is unlikely that Dulanty would actually have used words like 'recalcitrants' or 'extremists', especially since his own prime minister would have to be numbered historically among the latter, but Morrison forwarded to the British War Cabinet an account of his conversation, together with verbatim transcripts of MacRory's and Beattie's statements. He also sought the opinion of Harry Midgley, the Commonwealth Labour Party leader in Northern Ireland, who was 'strongly in favour of conscription' but anticipated 'considerable opposition' within the province. Morrison's Private Secretary, who had spoken to Midgley on behalf of his minister, also dismissed 'the bogey that all loyal Ulstermen of military age are already enrolled as Special Constables or are in reserved occupations and that therefore all the conscripts would be "pro-Eire" if not "anti-British".'[19] Yet the idea that conscription *would* fall more heavily upon the nationalist community was widely believed in Catholic areas of Belfast. Of the estimated 212,000 males between the ages of eighteen and forty-one in Northern Ireland, some 104,000 were in 'reserved' jobs vital to the war effort. The authorities assumed that up to 30,000 of the remainder were already in the forces and that another 30,000 would either be medically unfit or might cross the border into Eire.[20] Nationalists reasoned that the outstanding 48,000 represented Catholics since the shipyard, engineering and aircraft works – industries with 'reserved' occupations – employed mostly Protestants, and since the 'B' Special defence force, which could not be conscripted, was Protestant to a man.[21]*

It is unlikely that the British realised the full extent of the crisis into which they plunged de Valera. If conscription was opposed with violence

---

* Many Catholics believed that the cancellation of the annual Protestant 'Twelfth' marches for the duration of the war was specifically approved by the Unionist Government lest people should realise how many able-bodied young Orangemen had failed to join the Colours.[22]

in Northern Ireland, with hunger strikes and street demonstrations, he would have to align himself with these protests; yet the opposition in the province would be partly led by the IRA, whose own reputation – on both sides of the border – would acquire a powerful new prestige and status. De Valera's biographers imply that the Irish Government even feared that Hermann Goertz, the Abwehr agent in Ireland, would have been able to take advantage of the chaos in the six counties to reactivate his connections with the IRA and Germany.[23] Anxious to obtain a united political front, de Valera met Fine Gael and Labour leaders on May 23. If Mulcahy's account of the meeting is to be believed, the Taoiseach was in a state of some considerable agitation, suggesting that the introduction of conscription in Northern Ireland would be 'only a prelude' to a British invasion of Eire. He thought that Dulanty 'has spoken to Churchill in a way that might have suited Chamberlain, but not Churchill.' The High Commissioner had contacted Sir Archibald Sinclair, the British Air Minister, who 'felt that there was nothing for Churchill to do but go ahead.' Morrison and Clement Attlee, the Lord Privy Seal, said de Valera, 'rather favoured our point of view.' He thought the situation was 'highly serious' and that conscription would be announced when the British Parliament met on May 27.[24]

It was proof of de Valera's perturbation that he considered travelling to London to speak personally to Churchill. But he saw dangers in this. According to Mulcahy, de Valera said that 'his personal arrangements with Churchill were very different from those with Chamberlain, that if he succeeded in stopping conscription it would be said that there were secret bargains, that the question of granting facilities might arise in the discussions . . .' He even suspected 'that if he stopped conscription the Germans might think there was some secret arrangement, and might attack us . . .' This remarkable assumption was buttressed by a *non sequitur* of equally stupendous reasoning when de Valera 'recalled that when Chamberlain went to Munich he was present at a meeting of the League of Nations, and everybody else but himself there thought it was a mistake for Chamberlain to go to Munich!' If de Valera was drawing a comparison between Chamberlain's mission to Hitler and his own notion of visiting Churchill, it was a particularly strange one. Mulcahy and his colleagues suggested 'that the move in the North was not necessarily a military move, that all the voluntary machinery had broken down in Belfast in the recent raids . . . They might want to control and distribute the industrial power of the men in Belfast.'[25] Fine Gael had touched upon the truth although this could have little effect on events north of the border.

As de Valera was talking to his political opponents in Dublin, a nationalist anti-conscription campaign with important historical antecedents was getting under way in Belfast. A conference attended by Nationalist MPs and Senators of the Northern Ireland Parliament drew up a pledge for

Catholics to sign in all the parishes of the province. 'Denying the right of the Churchill Government to enforce compulsory service in Ireland,' it said, 'we pledge ourselves solemnly to one another to resist conscription by the most effective means at our disposal, consonant with the law of God.'[26]* With appropriate emendations, this was essentially the same oath that the Catholic bishops had ordered to be read in every parish when the British tried to conscript Irishmen in 1918. De Valera had argued then that the morality of physical force was in direct proportion to the immorality of the effort to conscript the Irish nation,[28] and there can be no doubt that the 1941 pledge was intended to be invested with a parallel set of values. To oppose conscription with 'the most effective means . . . consonant with the law of God' was to go some way beyond passive resistance. But it was certain that the Northern Ireland Government would be swayed by such words.

With the support of the Ulster Unionist Council for 'whatever steps he thinks necessary to aid the war effort',[29] Andrews and four of his ministers – including MacDermott and Brooke – travelled to Britain on the evening of May 23 to persuade Churchill of the need for conscription in the province. The two prime ministers met at noon next day and the talks initially went in Andrews' favour. According to MacDermott, the Northern Ireland authorities proposed that conscription should be carried out in stages, that men would be 'called up in small batches so we could deal with resistance'. This would, it was hoped, avoid the pitched street battles that might develop if the RUC – or perhaps the Army – were required to round up thousands of men in one operation.[30] The discussions also appear to have been influenced by the personal contempt felt by some officials towards de Valera. At one point during the day, MacDermott – who was available for consultation but did not participate in the talks – received a note from a senior British Army officer who was present at the meeting. 'I think we have got the schoolmaster where we want him,' it said in reference to de Valera.[31] But one of the officials whom the Northern Ireland Prime Minister took with him to Britain, the Inspector General of the RUC, adopted a quite different view. Lieutenant Colonel Charles Wickham had not been asked to advise Andrews prior to the London meeting but Herbert Morrison – whose reservations over conscription had already been noted by Dulanty – now took the trouble to seek the Inspector General's views. They were devastating.

---

* The nationalist conference was not immune to a peculiar naivety that manifested itself in a comparison even more doubtful than that adumbrated by de Valera. At one point in their meeting, nationalists proclaimed that 'the British Government has no more right to conscript one Irishman in any part of Ireland than would Germany have to force into her armies the populations of Norway or any of those nations whose territory she has over-run.'[27] But Austrians had already been conscripted into the German armed forces as new citizens of the Reich while civilians in occupied European countries would shortly be employed *en masse* in forced labour for German war industries.

In a two-page memorandum, marked 'Secret' and forwarded to the War Cabinet, he totally refuted the arguments of the Northern Ireland Government and supported the nationalist claim that conscription would be primarily directed against the Catholic community. 'It is extremely doubtful,' he said:

> . . . if conscription has the whole-hearted support of either section of the population and there is considerable danger that it will drift into a local political issue and the main fact be overlooked that once the Bill is passed each individual must obey the law regardless of the attitude of his neighbour.
>
> It will fall more heavily upon the Roman Catholic section than the Protestant because a greater proportion of the latter are in reserved occupations, a fact which has already been exaggerated by Nationalist speakers.[32]

Wickham, whose brief hardly extended to Anglo-Irish relations, believed that if a 'popular clamour' arose in Eire, de Valera 'may well place himself at the head of it for no other reason than to gain popularity.' With the Church and the nationalists opposed to conscription, however, he thought that:

> . . . active organisation to resist it will commence at once in every parish and will not cease if a Bill is introduced and passed into law. Many will cross the Border but from those who remain wide resistance to the enforcement of the Act may be expected. This in the first instance will be demonstrated by failure to register. It will then be necessary for the Police to carry out arrests to which resistance may be expected even down to the use of firearms . . . conscription will give new life to the IRA and will attract into its ranks many who today are keeping well clear of it. It will provide it with a new strength and prestige which may last for a long while after the War is over. Further sectarian feeling will be embittered on both sides which will increase the risk of Protestants adopting the attitude that they go only if the Roman Catholics are taken.[33]

Unless the attitude of the nationalists and the Church changed, said Wickham, the RUC would have 'a difficult and dangerous task' ahead of them. 'It is as well to point out,' he added, 'that full use of press propaganda will be made and that every incident will be magnified. In places like Belfast incidents will be staged and the "Press Gang" up the Falls Road will get its full share of publicity on the Street and in the press.'[34]

It would be difficult to think of a more damaging assessment of the Northern Ireland Government's proposals, nor one which could more seriously undermine the credibility of the Stormont Cabinet in the eyes of the British authorities. Here was the head of the province's police force admitting that conscription would indeed strike unfairly at Catholics and acknowledging that Protestants did not fully support the idea of conscription. Even de Valera would have shared Wickham's view that the IRA would derive great benefit from such a measure. There is no record of

Churchill's reaction to this memorandum although evidence that opposition was already being mobilised in the province came from Brooke, who confided to MacDermott that 'the wires are hot with telegrams from Northern Ireland telling the Government not to think of conscription.'[35]

In Dublin, the Irish Cabinet agreed that de Valera should send a personal message to Churchill.[36] The note began in a calm, almost friendly way, a request rather than a demand that the British Prime Minister should reconsider his enthusiasm for extending conscription to Northern Ireland. De Valera recalled the feeling of 'better understanding and mutual sympathy' which had grown up between Britain and Eire in recent years. The imposition of conscription, he said, 'will inevitably undo all the good that has been done and throw the two peoples back into the old unhappy relations.' But this regretful tone changed after the first two paragraphs. The de Valera who had never accepted the Treaty or the partition of Ireland, the de Valera whom Churchill hated, now took over. 'The conscription of the people of one nation by another,' he wrote:

> . . . revolts the human conscience. No fair-minded man anywhere can fail to recognise in it an act of oppression upon a weaker people, and it cannot but do damage to Britain herself.
>
> The Six Counties have towards the rest of Ireland a status and a relationship which no Act of Parliament can change. They are part of Ireland. They have always been part of Ireland, and their people, Catholic and Protestant, are our people.
>
> I beg of you, before you enter on a course which can effect so profoundly the relations of our two peoples, to take all these matters into the most earnest consideration.[37]

De Valera had wondered if Dulanty approached Churchill in the right way but it was a sign of the Taoiseach's own lack of sensitivity that he chose to write to the British Prime Minister in this reproachful spirit. It was bound to infuriate Churchill, despite the apparently heartfelt final sentence. When Dulanty read the message to him on May 26, Churchill was stung by its contents. According to de Valera's biographers, who were given access to Walshe's account of this second confrontation, Churchill threw the note on one side 'asking whether de Valera wanted a public answer. "If he does," he said, "I will give it and it will resound about the world." Furiously he paced about the room, denouncing the Irish vehemently and in the strongest language. They had broken faith about the Treaty. Ireland had lost her soul. When he thought of John and Willie Redmond, and of Kettle – one of the best minds Ireland had produced in recent times:* when he thought of their courage and valour his blood

---

* Thomas Kettle, a founder and organiser of the Land League, was a member of the Irish Volunteers until the 1914–18 War when he decided that Britain was fighting for small nations and helped to recruit Irishmen for the British forces. He was killed on the Somme in September 1916.

447

boiled.'[38] If de Valera acted in character, so did Churchill, for he was still angrily condemning the betrayal of the Treaty and of the Irishmen whom be believed were truly loyal. The introverted nature of Churchill's rage was displayed by his failure to employ the arguments which the British normally used on such occasions; that they were fighting an evil regime and should therefore receive Eire's support. Dulanty described his visit as 'exceedingly unsatisfactory'.[39]

Churchill's anger may have been stirred by the realisation that conscription was after all likely to prove an unprofitable exercise in Northern Ireland. On the previous afternoon, a rally in Belfast – attended, so the *Irish Press* reported, by 10,000 men – had repeated the anti-conscription pledge. The meeting had even attracted the support of the largely middle class but nonetheless Protestant Ulster Union Club whose leader, Captain Denis Ireland, announced that 'after 150 years, Catholics and Protestants are once more united on the fundamental issue.'[40] This was not the sort of unity or discipline that Andrews and his ministers had in mind when they originally discussed conscription. The Northern Ireland Labour Party demanded a plebiscite to discover whether compulsory national service in the province would really increase British military strength. The Protestant Church began to protest.[41] The *Manchester Guardian* warned that the British Government was 'in danger of making a grave and irreparable political blunder'.[42] On the afternoon of May 26, de Valera addressed the Dail, demonstrating once more his claim to speak on an all-Ireland basis by condemning any attempt to compel the people of the six counties to serve in the British forces. It was a thoughtful speech, however, in which he urged the British not to change 'the policy which they have hitherto pursued' on conscription.[43] It was typical of him. As Frank Gallagher was afterwards to remark, de Valera 'did not demand that the British should drop a proposal, but that they should continue to do what they were already doing!'[44] He received the support of both Cosgrave and Norton, thereby securing his united political front.

As the Dail was meeting, the British War Cabinet received a 'Most Immediate' and 'Most Secret' telegram from John Maffey, reporting that public opinion in Eire had been 'suddenly and deeply stirred' by the conscription crisis. More important than this, the British Representative included in his dispatch the text of an urgent message which David Gray had just sent to Roosevelt. The American Minister had told his President that Irish opposition leaders believed that without a conscientious objectors' clause for Catholics, conscription in Northern Ireland would constitute 'a major irretrievable and fatal blunder' with grave consequences for American interests. 'They predict draft riots, the escape of draft dodgers to Southern Ireland who will be acclaimed as hero martyrs [sic] by three fourths of the population, and the fermenting of trouble by representatives and fifth columnists,' wrote Gray. 'The clearest headed leader predicts that de Valera will seize this opportunity to escape from economic and political realities by proclaiming himself the leader of the oppressed minority and with the blessing of the Cardinal will raise anti-British feeling and call a Holy War. I think it a very likely prediction.' This fanciful scenario was accompanied by more serious judgements. Gray considered the Irish conscription issue:

> . . . to be a repetition of the same fatal blunder made during the last war. Unless Britain is prepared from a military point of view to seize the whole country it appears to be madness . . . Eighty thousand Irish volunteers in [the] British Army will be disaffected. A Government, a popular majority and an army inclined to be friendly to Britain rather than to the Axis will become definitely hostile, possibly giving active aid to Germany . . .[45]

Gray passed on the gist of this message – leaving out the unflattering references – to de Valera, who reacted warmly at first but then telephoned the American Minister some hours later to say that 'an escape clause for Catholics would not do.' Maffey thought that such a clause would, in fact, solve the difficulty but he was still pessimistic. 'The case for conscription inside Ulster is no doubt unanswerable,' he wrote with diplomatic tact. 'But if we consider reactions in Ireland and possibly in America, expediency of measure appears most doubtful . . . Facilities on the West Coast are presumably vastly more important than Ulster's present needs.'[46]

The pressures were mounting on the British Government. Mackenzie King, the Canadian Prime Minister, also urged moderation.[47] Perhaps Churchill remembered 1918 when, as he himself had once written, 'Irish conscription was handled in such a fashion . . . that we had the worst of both worlds, all the resentment against conscription, and in the end no law and no men.'[48] On May 27, the British War Cabinet relented and in the House of Commons later that day, Churchill announced that it would be 'more trouble than it is worth to enforce such a policy' in Northern Ireland. His statement was drowned out in cheers.[49] Publicly, the Stormont Government pretended satisfaction; they had loyally supported the idea of conscription but the final decision had not been theirs to take. Churchill had praised their 'loyal aid and continued constant support'.[50] In reality, they had been humiliated. 'Andrews never got over it,' MacDermott was to recall. 'I saw him at his press conference. There were reporters all round him; they had to shout questions at him because he was deaf. The PM stood up to reply – but he got no further. He said nothing.'[51] When Andrews spoke to Spender two days later, he had recovered some of his self-confidence. 'He told me,' Spender wrote in his diary, 'that he thought that the best course had been taken and that he believed it had strengthened the position of Ulster across the water. I told him that I was sorry I could not agree with him and that I was afraid the very fact that this adverse decision had been cheered in the British Parliament showed that there was a large body of members in that House which would be prepared to play up to any demands made by de Valera . . . I pointed out that it would be very difficult for Mr Roosevelt to ask the American Nation to enter into the war when the British Government made excuses for its own citizens playing their proper part.'[52] Spender clearly did not appreciate the degree to which American pressure had been exercised against conscription, nor did he appear to realise that the 'timorous whisperings' in Northern Ireland,[53] to which he partly attributed the British Government's decision, had included some very forceful advice from the RUC Inspector General.

It seems certain, however, that Andrews' performance in London had not impressed Churchill's ministers. When Basil Brooke's Permanent Secretary later pointed out during an argument with Ernest Bevin, the British Minister of Labour, that the British Cabinet had been responsible for the absence of conscription in Northern Ireland, Bevin claimed – according to Spender – that the Stormont Government 'by a very weak and complaisant [sic] attitude had far greater responsibility for this than his own colleagues.'[54] Brooke, who had wanted to see conscription in the province but later thought this was a mistaken view,[55] alleged that Bevin used the issue as an argument during his bargaining for war contracts, suggesting that 'as Northern Ireland's manpower was not being tapped by the Services, workers should be moved into war industries in Great Britain.'[56] In Northern Ireland, too, Andrews' failure brought disparagement and contributed to his eventual resignation. Edmond Warnock accused the Stormont Cabinet of 'parochialism' over conscription and in 1942 urged Andrews to approach Churchill again. Spender noted that Andrews 'made out the best case he could for recruiting and instanced that 23,000 Ulstermen had joined the forces. This, however, seems to be rather an optimistic estimate.'[57]

It was principally because of the conscription débâcle that Stormont Governments were ever afterwards sensitive about the province's recruiting statistics. For when the war was drawing to a close, Irish sources produced figures which purported to show that far more citizens from Eire than from Northern Ireland had volunteered to serve in the British forces. This claim – so highly damaging to the province – was several times investigated in long and exhaustive detail by the British War Office, the Admiralty and the Air Ministry, usually at Brooke's request. Even before the war ended, ministry officials in London were instructed to comb through the records of every man and woman serving in the British armed forces to discover the true figures, a painstaking and often fruitless exercise because many men from both parts of Ireland had enlisted in England, giving British rather than Irish addresses and thus obscuring their place of birth. Moreover, many Eire citizens had travelled to Belfast to join up, unwittingly adding themselves to the total of recruits which Northern Ireland would later claim as its own. James Kelly, the *Irish Independent*'s correspondent in the city, used to see newly-enlisted men from Eire being marched down Lower Donegall Street to the docks by a recruiting sergeant, 'each one in an ill-fitting uniform and occasionally taunted by shipyard workers from the upper decks of trams.'[58] The situation was further complicated by desertions. About 7000 Irishmen absconded from the ranks of their own Army to serve in the British forces during the war,[59] partly, it seems, because they received better pay with the British.[60]

The Irish Consul General in New York was reported to have claimed that between 250,000 and 300,000 men from Eire had joined the British Army, the Royal Navy or the RAF.[61] British officials were told that the *New Yorker* had given a figure of a quarter of a million.[62] A letter in the *Daily Telegraph* suggested 150,000,[63] while the *Manchester Guardian* quoted an estimate of 300,000.[64] The Dominions Office, which had followed these ever more incredible claims in such detail that they even came across the 150,000 figure in a newspaper published by Catholic missionaries in Basutoland, wanted to supply 'a corrective to these fictions by publishing the facts' but wished at the same time to avoid controversy. This was indeed an ambitious undertaking.[65] In June 1945, a Dominions Office memorandum suggested that 'the total number of men born in both Eire and Northern Ireland and serving in the three armed forces would be approximately just over 40,000 in the case of each territory.' To claim that no government statistics were available, officials thought, 'seems unfair not merely to Northern Ireland but also to the belligerent Dominions. From the long term point of view also, it would seem to be desirable to prick the bubble of these inflated figures before the legend is too deeply rooted.'[66] According to a 1946 memorandum, the Dominions Office feared that the Irish claims, which had 'a direct bearing on the campaign which the Eire authorities are working up in America and elsewhere on the partition machine', were gaining ground. The document contained figures of 38,000 and 42,000 respectively for Eire and Northern Ireland, but civil servants admitted that their statistics were incomplete and 'not watertight'.[67]

Brooke wanted to clear the matter up. The Dominions Office believed that for Northern Ireland it was 'a question not of avoiding or provoking controversy, but of defending herself against a malignant, mendacious and dangerous attack, or of allowing her case, and incidentally that of truth, to go by default at the bar of world opinion.' Since the province had claimed a total of 27,000 recruits, 'the more fantastically Eire propagandists inflate their own imaginary figures, the more discreditable is Ulster's record made to appear.' De Valera, an official observed after the war, 'is one of the dupes of his own propagandists and really believes that his country sent 180,000 men to join the United Kingdom forces.'[68] Brooke described himself as being 'in a position of some embarrassment'[69] over the conflicting figures, and was given a set of statistics which showed that 37,282 men and women from Northern Ireland had served in the British forces.[70]* Figures for Eire that were compiled in 1945 had totalled 42,665[72]† but there is no explanation as to how this came to be reduced to 38,000 a year later. The whole affair became locked in controversy, just as the Dominions Office had thought it would. Eire's supporters pointed out that British figures did not take account of men from the twenty-six counties who had been killed in the Army before the end of 1944, of those discharged before this date, of those who were already serving when war broke out, and of other categories. If Eire's contribution was as low as the British claimed, it was asked, how could it be that as many as eight Victoria Crosses and a George Cross were awarded to Irishmen from the twenty-six counties when Canada, with a million of her citizens in the armed forces, received only ten?[74] If the real figure for Eire's contribution was indeed around 42,000 – a high figure for a neutral even though her population was about twice that of Northern Ireland – it did not stop the 'legend' gaining ground. As late as 1976, a British author was stating as fact that 'Ireland, in spite of her neutrality, had permitted 165,000 of her men to leave the country and serve in the British armed forces.'[75]

That Eire, after taking so rigid a stand on neutrality, should later wish to exaggerate her contribution to the army, navy and air force of the King, was an absurdity only balanced by the fact that partition was both a reason for her neutrality and for the propagation of recruitment figures which reflected so badly upon that part of Ireland which remained in the hands of the Crown. No less ridiculous was Stormont's concern over a proposal initiated by Churchill in 1941 to acknowledge 'the considerable help which we were receiving by the enlistment in our forces of volunteers from Southern Ireland.'[76] The British wanted to group the Royal Irish Fusiliers and the Royal Inniskilling Fusiliers – both Northern Ireland regiments – with the London Irish, a unit which drew many of its NCOs from Eire, under the title of the 'Irish Brigade'. The name was, of course, anathema to Stormont ministers. Andrews spoke to Brooke who agreed to take the matter up at once with General Sir Alan Brooke, the Commander-in-Chief of the British forces.[77] Stormont officials meanwhile learnt that an announcement of the Brigade's new status – in which General Gough was alleged to have had a hand – would not be made until it had 'covered itself with glory in the field of battle'.[78]

Before Irish soldiers had had time to participate in so auspicious an occasion, Andrews wrote to Attlee, the Lord Privy Seal, to say that while he had 'no objection to the service of these loyal men from Eire being fully recognised', the title of 'Irish Brigade' 'would inevitably be associated with the Irish who fought against England in the days of Marlborough, the Irish Brigade which fought against Britain in the Boer War, Sir Roger

* These were categorised as 29,549 (including 2087 women) in the Army, 4623 in the Royal Navy and Royal Marines, and 3110 in the RAF.[71]
† The classification showed that 30,900 (including 3060 women) were in the Army, 715 in the Royal Navy and 11,050 in the RAF.[73]

Casement's effort in the last war, and finally with a body of "Blue Shirts" [sic] organised in Eire a few years ago to fight in the Spanish Civil War.' Northern Ireland people would therefore 'strongly object to the absorption of Ulster regiments into an Irish Brigade . . .'[79] When Attlee failed to act on Andrews' advice, the Stormont Prime Minister wrote again, this time stating the real nature of his objection. 'In my view,' he stated, 'any policy calculated to obliterate or blur the distinction between the belligerency of Northern Ireland and the neutrality of Eire would confuse and mislead public opinion . . .'[80]*

It might have been easier for the British to have reconstituted the old Irish regiments disbanded after the Anglo-Irish Treaty of 1921 – units like the Connaught Rangers and the Dublin Fusiliers – if they wished to show their appreciation of Eire's contribution to their forces. Ironically, just such a suggestion had been made in 1938 by Sir Bindon Blood, a 96-year-old retired general from County Clare under whom Churchill had served in the Malakand Field Force at the turn of the century. Blood – whose ancestor Thomas Blood had once attempted to steal the Crown Jewels from the Tower of London – outlined his idea in a letter to Buckingham Palace. 'If you will kindly drop me a line and tell me what the King's wishes are,' he wrote, 'I will either shut up altogether, or commence work about recruiting, according to His Majesty's orders.'[84] The Dominions Office swiftly decided that 'the Eire authorities would not look with favour on the suggestion', observing with dark amusement that 'the last person . . . who took any interest in recruiting for the British forces in Eire was shot, and his assassins, though formally condemned to death, are now at large and regarded as highly respectable citizens!'[85] As it was, no 'Irish Brigade' ever existed to recognise the contribution that men from Eire made to Britain's eventual victory. The representations made by Andrews and Brooke evidently had their effect although their references to Casement's Irish Brigade in the 1914–18 War were inappropriate. When the Germans tried to form a similar brigade, composed of Irish-born POWs, in 1941, it turned into a charade, not least because the senior Irish officer – in civilian life the manager of the Theatre Royal in Dublin – was a British agent.[86] Northern Ireland ministers also assumed that men from Eire joined the British forces for exclusively pecuniary reasons; justifying proposed legislation that would prevent ex-servicemen from the twenty-six counties from settling in the province after the war, Harry Midgley told the Stormont Cabinet that 'a considerable number of Eire men

---

* The idea of an 'Irish Brigade' was then forgotten but strangely resurrected itself after the war when Brooke had to write off to the new Colonel of the Royal Ulster Rifles with identical objections to those made by Andrews six years earlier.[81] Brooke now suggested the titles of 'The Ulster Brigade' and 'The Northern Ireland Brigade', both of which were rejected by the British Government.[82] The name 'Irish Group' was then proposed and a brigade insignia of a shamrock containing the red hand of Ulster was sent to Brooke for his approval. 'I think there is too much Irish about it,' he replied.[83]

enlisted in H.M. Forces owing to economic pressure and without any sense of loyalty to the Empire.'[87]

The Northern Ireland Government did consider conscription on one more occasion, under Brooke's premiership in the spring of 1943, but their efforts were half-hearted and a Cabinet meeting heard that less than 30,000 men would be liable for call-up.[88] Wickham, the RUC Inspector General, once more gave it as his opinion that it was doubtful if conscription had the support of the people. 'The mass hysteria produced by the press publicity over the execution of Williams for the murder of a Catholic Constable,' he wrote, 'shows the extent to which feeling can be roused in Ireland especially when the press is not muzzled.' Feelings would be 'fanned and inflamed on both sides to an extent far deeper and more dangerous than the Williams case.' In its Easter manifesto, noted Wickham, the IRA had declared its intention to resist conscription 'by any means at its disposal.'[89] In fact, the IRA had staged a parade of volunteers near the Falls Road, each man carrying a machine gun on his shoulder, to show that it meant business.[90] Wickham reminded the Cabinet that 'there is behind the scenes a large amount of co-operation between the South and the Services and between London and Dublin generally. Conscription would kill this.'[91] In June 1943, Brooke briefly discussed conscription with Churchill but received no encouragement to pursue the matter further. His subsequent report to the Stormont Cabinet merited only a sentence in the formal written conclusions.[92] From then on, ministers heeded the advice of Lieutenant Colonel Wickham, that 'unless . . . there is a firm determination to see conscription through no matter what it may involve or what calls it imposes upon the Services then it should not even be mentioned.'[93]

Chapter 15

Phrases Make History

> . . . if it had not been for the loyalty and friendship of
> Northern Ireland we should have been forced to come to
> close quarters with Mr de Valera or perish for ever from
> the earth. However, with a restraint and poise to which,
> I say, history will find few parallels, His Majesty's
> Government never laid a violent hand upon them . . .
>
> Winston Churchill *13 May 1945*

> Mr Churchill makes it clear that, in certain circumstances,
> he would have violated our neutrality and that he would
> justify his action by Britain's necessity. It seems strange
> to me that Mr Churchill does not see that this, if accepted,
> would mean that Britain's necessity would become a moral
> code and that when this necessity became sufficiently great,
> other people's rights were not to count.
>
> Eamon de Valera *16 May 1945*

The entry of the United States into the war added a new dimension to Anglo-Irish relations but at the same time reduced their importance. As the danger of German invasion receded and the Anglo-American navies gradually broke the U-boats' stranglehold on the Atlantic sea lanes, Eire's strategic significance began to dwindle. The Treaty ports were no longer an issue of life or death to the British, and Irish neutrality – far from being a threat to Britain's security – now became a largely symbolic irritant. This new state of affairs was reflected in the changed substance of diplomacy, in which statements and requests were now made in order to place policies upon record rather than to achieve any kind of positive result. Gesture became more important than intention, a development which was more conducive to rhetoric than to political understanding.

Scarcely had the first American troops set foot on the Dufferin Docks in Belfast in January 1942 than de Valera was complaining that while 'the people of Ireland have no feeling of hostility towards, and no desire to be brought into conflict with, the United States . . . it is our duty to make it clearly understood that, no matter what troops occupy the Six Counties,

455

the Irish people's claim for the union of the whole national territory and for supreme jurisdiction over it, will remain unabated.' The maintenance of Ireland's partition, he said, was 'as indefensible as aggressions against small countries elsewhere.'[1] It was for de Valera a necessary re-statement of Ireland's claim to unity but it achieved no purpose and was not expected to. Its only result was to anger the Americans, for the statement contained that familiar arrow of insensitivity – on this occasion, the implication that British or American 'aggression' in the six counties was comparable to the German violation of European countries – which de Valera sometimes seemed incapable of avoiding. Similarly, when David Gray, the American Minister in Dublin, proposed in February 1944 to ask de Valera to 'clear out' the Axis missions in the Irish capital on the grounds that they represented a threat to Allied security in the months before D-Day, neither he nor the British Government expected the Taoiseach to comply. Gray assumed 'that this demand would meet with a negative reply, and the Eire Government would then be on record as having refused a request which had the object of safeguarding the lives of American soldiers, sailors and airmen at a vital moment in the war.'[2]

Gray, who developed something akin to hatred for de Valera – the feeling was mutual – certainly did his best to mobilise American public opinion against the Irish Government. In the United States, prominent Irish-Americans were induced to lend their support to a campaign to involve Eire in the war. In January 1942, for example, an entire edition of the magazine *The Nation*, a publication founded by abolitionists in 1865 which had in 1921 proposed the formation of a committee 'for the investigation of atrocities in Ireland', was devoted to the subject of Eire and the war, reminding de Valera of his 1921 valedictory that Ireland would not forget America's help in her struggle for freedom. 'I have no doubt,' wrote Senator George W. Norris, who had served on the 1920 committee, 'that, rather than see tyranny triumph, Ireland will render such assistance as is necessary to the United States and the other countries fighting aggression.'[3] The distinguished American journalist William L. Shirer claimed in the same edition that 'Mr de Valera's refusal to grant bases to the Allies will not save his country from attack by Hitler in the end . . . and once the Nazis are in Dublin, Irish freedom and independence, which were won so late and after so much sacrifice, will be snuffed out.'[4]

But the United States, after a long period of profitable neutrality, was really in no position to lecture Eire on the pitfalls of non-belligerency. Nor was the American Government in any great haste to acquire the Treaty ports, whatever Shirer may have thought. Indeed, the British Government were concerned rather than pleased at the prospect that Eire might after all become involved in the war. In 1944, Anthony Eden, the British Foreign Secretary, was distinctly unhappy at the remote possibility that de Valera might comply with Gray's request to remove the Axis missions, fearing that the Taoiseach would concede on the condition that Eire be given arms, oil and coal[5] which the Allies could not afford to supply. Anglo-Irish relations were now improving in almost exact proportion to the deterioration in Irish-American relations, an equation which could produce distinctly curious results. Thus when Gray was proposing to send his request to de Valera – a diplomatic note that was based on the assumption that Axis agents enjoyed 'almost unrestricted opportunity'[6] to send messages about Allied invasion preparations from Eire to Berlin – Eden was informing the War Cabinet in London that Britain was 'at present receiving considerable assistance from the Southern Irish Government, in matters of security, &c.'[7]

That Eire was not in fact a nest of German agents in this latter period of the war had already been secretly established by an agent of the American Office of Strategic Services, sent to Dublin in 1942 under the guise of being an economics adviser to David Gray's Legation. Ervin Marlin had been the Assistant Director of Personnel in the U.S. Government's Health, Education and Welfare Department when he was chosen for his task, chiefly, it seems, because he had been a student at Trinity College, Dublin. After being put through a Winchester rifle-firing course in Virginia, he was dispatched to Eire on the regular flying-boat to Foynes in July 1942 with the specific mission of discovering the truth of reports in the American press – and from Minister Gray – that Nazi spies were moving freely around the twenty-six counties. Marlin set up home in the University Club on St Stephen's Green, venturing out in a conspicuous car – by then, there was no petrol available for private motoring in Eire – to Cork, Kerry, Limerick and Galway. 'The whole thing was kind of a joke,' he afterwards recalled. 'I spoke to J.P. Walshe who told me that there were between fifty and a hundred thousand British sympathisers in Eire who were straining at the leash to report anything they heard about German spies. I never found any spies. I didn't discover any spy centres. I assumed that Irish intelligence had the place buttoned up; once they realised it was in their interest to keep us informed, they were very good to us.'[8]

Marlin suggested that Gray, whom he regarded as 'a privileged person, what is known as a testy old gentleman', was the origin of the American newspaper stories. He was later told that the American Minister had asked for his recall, which he thinks may be true, although he had already requested a transfer from Eire to London because 'Irish security arrangements were satisfactory.'[9] In his 1944 note to de Valera, Gray stated that 'it is our understanding that the German Legation in Dublin, until recently at least, has had in its possession a radio receiving set. This is evidence of the intention of the German Government to use this means of communication. Supporting evidence is furnished by two parachutists equipped with radio sending sets recently dropped on your territory by German planes.'[10] In rejecting the American demand, de Valera pointed out that the German Legation's transmitter had for some months been in the custody of the Irish Government, that the two parachutists – Lenihan and

O'Reilly – had been 'apprehended within a few hours' and that twelve men 'suspected of intention to engage in espionage' were now imprisoned in Eire.[11] After this diplomatic exchange, Hubert Will, the chief of the OSS counter-espionage branch in Europe, visited Dublin and put sixteen questions to Colonel Dan Bryan, to all of which the head of G2 replied. Details of their highly secret discussion have never been revealed although it is known that J.P. Walshe was present at the talks which particularly concentrated on the activities of the German Legation staff.[12] The Americans were then satisfied with Irish counter-espionage measures.

It was natural that the Allies should concern themselves with the security of Ireland in the months before D-Day. Many of the American troops who were to land on the Normandy beaches were based in the six counties and a few days before the invasion, an American battle fleet was moored off Bangor in County Down. Any information about their destination would have been of crucial importance to the Germans, and Ervin Marlin, though always sceptical of Gray's suspicions, wondered what the American Minister's position would have been if German agents 'had, by some means, been able to supply vital information to the Axis Governments at the critical moment.' It was not, Marlin thought, an easy question for Gray to solve 'and he chose the conservative position.'[13] So did Churchill. In March 1944, he gave instructions that Eire was to be physically isolated from the rest of the world, cutting off telephones and all air and sea links. 'The object of these measures is not spite against the Irish,' he informed Roosevelt, 'but preservation of British and American soldiers' lives and against our plans being betrayed by emissaries sent by sea or air from the German Minister in Dublin . . .'[14]

De Valera had at first thought that Gray's demand for the removal of the German and Japanese diplomats was an ultimatum from the American Government, and even a declaration from Roosevelt that the United States had no intention of invading Eire did not persuade the Taoiseach that his country was safe from the danger of attack by U.S. troops. Churchill saw no harm in allowing this idea to persist. 'It seems to me,' he told Roosevelt, 'that so far from allaying alarm in de Valera's circles we should let fear work its healthy process. Thereby we shall get behind the scenes a continued stiffening up of the Irish measures to prevent leakages, which even now are not so bad.'[15]* In the House of Commons, Churchill gave a second reason for the isolation of Eire. 'If a catastrophe were to occur to the Allied armies which could be traced to the retention of the German and Japanese representatives in Dublin,' he said, 'a gulf would be opened between Britain on the one hand and Southern Ireland on the

---

* Churchill did not appear to be aware that the Irish had confiscated Hempel's radio. In February, he had told Cranborne, the Dominions Secretary, that 'even if complete severance by sea was instituted it would not prevent the German Ambassador [sic] from sending a wireless warning of Zero, even though that was the last he was able to send.'[16]

other which even generations could not bridge.' But still there was that note of rancour which had always been present in Churchill's dealings with Eire. 'The whole question of Southern Ireland is anomalous from various points of view,' he told a Northern Ireland MP, 'and I can conceive that lawyers and high legal authorities might have very great difficulty in defining the factual relationship which prevails.'[17]

De Valera's refusal to expel the Axis diplomats afforded him a domestic political triumph. Fine Gael and Labour leaders united behind him in the Dail; his victory in the general election three months later – converting a minority government into an administration with an overall majority of fourteen seats – owed a good deal to the Irish public's newly-strengthened conviction that he would defend Irish neutrality, 'the logical consequence of Irish history and of the forced partition of the national territory,' as de Valera had described it in his reply to the State Department. The extensive file on the American 'note' in the Taoiseach's Department bears witness to the feeling of national unity which the incident encouraged. Even political enemies rallied to de Valera's side. 'Dear Chief,' began a letter from Sean MacBride, 'if in the course of the present crisis my services can be of any value to the Government I shall be at your disposal. If I may be permitted, I should like also to express my admiration at the manner in which you have handled the situation.'[18] Hempel, the German Minister, who had no way of communicating to Berlin at this stage of the war, made no official comment. Many years later, he praised de Valera because 'he refused to get on the bandwagon when Germany was winning the war and again refused when the Allies were going to win the war . . . He stuck courageously to his decision.'[19] According to Robert Smyllie, *The Irish Times* editor, the whole affair had provided de Valera with 'a God-given opportunity once more to demonstrate Eire's absolute independence of everybody, including on this occasion the United States and to figure in the eyes of his followers as one of the greatest statesmen since Abraham Lincoln.'[20]* When the Allies did land on the beaches of Normandy, de Valera had been safely returned to power, the diplomatic integrity of his neutrality policy as secure as the Allies' D-Day plans.

On the morning of June 6, Paddy Brosnan, the Dingle skipper of the trawler *Elsie Mabel*, was fishing off the Kerry coast when he thought he heard thunder. He looked north to see 'hundreds of fighters and bombers, so low I thought they'd take our masts off.' As the planes raced over him at sea level, sucking the Atlantic spray into the air around them, Brosnan could see the RAF and USAF markings on their wings. They were flying south towards Normandy;[21] the war was passing Ireland by. The Ger-

---

* The implications of the American 'note' and its aftermath fall outside the scope of this book. Readers who are interested in this and other aspects of Irish–American relations during the war should turn to Dr T. Ryle Dwyer's *Irish Neutrality and the USA 1939–47* (Gill and Macmillan, Dublin), especially pages 179–200.

mans were the first of the belligerents to lose interest in the island they had once considered invading as a bridgehead to England. Four days after the Allied landings in France, they lost the IRA leader in whom the Berlin Foreign Ministry had once placed such high hopes. Frank Ryan had been in declining health for at least a year, suffering a stroke and then pneumonia. He died in a Dresden sanatorium on June 10, delirious on his last night, shouting orders in Spanish as he fought again his lost war in Spain.[22] For the Germans, Ireland was by now an irrelevancy although the writer Francis Stuart apparently met a man in a Berlin bar in the winter of 1944 who pulled a wad of Irish bank notes from his pocket and claimed that he was being sent to Dublin by the Abwehr. Stuart mentioned the incident to Helmut Clissmann, describing the idea as 'lunacy'.[23] As the Allies closed in on Germany in the spring of 1945, the Department of External Affairs in Dublin sent instructions to Cornelius Cremin, the Irish representative in Germany, 'not to get caught in Berlin'. He travelled first to Salzburg and then to Babenhausen in Bavaria, thirty miles south of Augsburg. He had set up temporary office in a house there when the American Army arrived and a Limerick-born U.S. 7th Army Colonel, spotting Cremin's Tricolour hanging from a window, formally 'liberated' the Irish Legation to the German Reich.[24]

In Dublin, however, de Valera remained publicly neutral to the last. At 12.30 p.m. on April 30, David Gray called on the Taoiseach to ask for possession of the archives in the German Legation in Northumberland Road. The war had not yet ended – Hitler was still alive although he would commit suicide two hours later – but Gray wanted to ensure that Hempel had no time to destroy any material on submarine warfare, and presented de Valera with a memorandum to that effect. The American Minister's highly partial account of his meeting with the Taoiseach gives another indication of how low their relations had sunk. 'As I proceeded,' wrote Gray:

> . . . Mr de Valera grew red and looked very sour. He was evidently annoyed, but his manners were correct. When I finished, he slapped the copy of the memorandum which I had presented to him on his desk and said 'This is a matter for my legal advisers. It is not a matter that I can discuss with you now.'
> . . . He did not question my assertion that the German Government had ceased to exercise effective control over Germany and consequently *de facto* no longer existed. I told him that I had hoped that he would take advantage of this opportunity to show some mark of friendliness to us . . . He said that they [the Irish] were neutral and would continue to behave entirely correctly as neutrals.[25]

Gray explained to Walshe on the following day that data in the German archives might be 'important for the countering of U-boat warfare, which was likely to be continued for a considerable period.' Walshe agreed that the Irish would hand over the Legation upon the announcement of

German surrender. Gray accepted this but there was, as usual, another motive for his original request. The Allies, he told the State Department, had 'put upon record the refusal of the Irish Government again to seize the opportunity of co-operating with us in a friendly and non-legislative manner for allegedly internal political reasons.'[26] But the American Minister was shortly to have infinitely more combustible material to place on record.

When Roosevelt died, on 12 April 1945, de Valera sent a message to Truman, mourning 'a great man and a noble leader'.[27] On the afternoon of April 30, Hitler committed suicide in his Berlin bunker and the Taoiseach, accompanied by Joseph Walshe, paid a formal visit to the German Legation in Dublin to express his condolences on the death of the Führer. It was both a predictable and an extraordinary act; predictable because the visit would naturally have suggested itself to a man who applied so public – indeed, so balanced – a rigidity to the principles of neutrality; extraordinary and shocking because the German extermination camps had now been discovered by the advancing Allied armies and the truth of the Nazi policy of genocide had just been revealed to the world. De Valera's gesture, officially undertaken on behalf of the Irish people, immediately received international condemnation, and is still the subject of heated debate in Ireland. He explained his own reasons for paying his visit to Hempel in a personal letter to Robert Brennan in Washington some days later. He had expected that his call on the German Minister would be 'played up to the utmost', but had scorned the idea of having 'a diplomatic illness'. So long as Eire retained diplomatic relations with Germany, he said:

> . . . to have failed to call upon the German representative would have been an act of unpardonable discourtesy to the German nation and to Dr Hempel himself. During the whole of the war, Dr Hempel's conduct was irreproachable. He was always friendly and invariably correct – in marked contrast with Gray. I certainly was not going to add to his humiliation in the hour of defeat.[28]

To have failed to call on Hempel, thought de Valera, 'would establish a bad precedent.' He added, however, that 'the formal acts of courtesy paid on such occasions as the death of a head of State should not have attached to them any further significance, such as connoting approval or disapproval of the policies of the State in question, or of its head . . .' To have attempted to explain his action publicly, wrote de Valera, 'would have been interpreted as an excuse, and an excuse as a consciousness of having acted wrongly. I acted correctly, and, I feel certain, wisely.'[29]

Aiken always supported de Valera's decision. 'He went to see Hempel because it was protocol,' he said years later. 'The Germans had the representatives of their State here in Dublin and he had to show his sympathy for the situation.'[30] Maffey saw the incident according to his

461

own lights when he reported to the Dominions Office. De Valera, he wrote, had:

> . . . taken a very unwise step. Obstinately and mathematically consistent – stung perhaps by the most recent assault on his principles, ie. by the request for possession of the German archives before VE day – he decided to get a mention for a conspicuous act of neutrality in the field. He would at least show that he was no 'bandwaggoner'. He therefore called on the German Legation in Dublin to express his personal condolences on the death of Hitler. The public mind was too stunned to react quickly to this unnecessary but significant performance, but there came overnight the collapse of the Reich and with the sudden end of the censorship there came also atrocity stories, pictures of Buchenwald, etc. In the public mind Mr de Valera's condolences took on a smear of turpitude, and for the first time, and at a critical time, a sense of disgust slowly manifested itself and a growing feeling that Mr de Valera had blundered into a clash with the ideals of decency and right and was leading away from realities.[31]

John D. Kearney, the Canadian High Commissioner in Dublin, who regarded de Valera's action as 'a slap in the face', told Maffey that he had found the Irish Department of External Affairs 'profoundly depressed' after the visit of condolence and that 'Walshe even vaguely mooted some idea of apology.'[32] Neither diplomat seemed certain, however, as to why de Valera had placed himself in a position of such opprobrium. That he wished to insult Gray – to ruffle the feathers of the American eagle, as Professor Ryle Dwyer has put it[33] – was an idea that had occurred to Maffey. It is more likely that he wanted to show both the United States and Britain that Eire's neutrality had to be taken seriously, that it was not just a defensive posture adopted in time of war but a proof of Eire's freedom of action – however unpopular that action might be. Maffey's sarcastic reference to de Valera's refusal to be a 'bandwaggoner' came ill from a diplomat who would have drawn equally cynical conclusions at any new-found expression of enmity towards the Reich on de Valera's part. Indeed, the Allies' constant desire to have Eire established in history as an equivocal and erring nation seems in retrospect a very distasteful one. While the American and British press gave prominence to the Taoiseach's visit to Hempel, they paid little or no attention to the fact that the Portuguese Government – a more pliant neutral from the Allied point of view – had called for two days of national mourning for Hitler and ordered flags to be flown at half mast on public buildings.[34]

Yet de Valera's explanation is also unsatisfactory. In speaking of the 'unpardonable discourtesy to the German nation', had he considered what this nation was or what form of unforgivable insult he was now visiting upon the nations which Hitler had tried to destroy? And if such an act of courtesy had 'no special significance', what importance did de Valera attach to it? He would presumably have been the last to claim that a visit of condolence was a meaningless formality. In retrospect, one is led to the conclusion that his gesture was intended to shock, that while it may have been a deliberate affront to the Allies, it was for de Valera a necessary last act to an emergency policy that would now be as rigorously pursued in peace as it was in time of war. After the titanic conflict that had been waged outside Ireland, it was preposterous for de Valera to suggest – as he did in his letter to Brennan – that his visit to Hempel was an act of diplomatic courage. Morally, it was both senseless and deeply wounding to the millions who had suffered in the war; politically, it could have been disastrous. But symbolically, it could not be misunderstood: Eire had not accepted the values of the warring nations and did not intend to do so in the future.

The end of the war in Europe was marked in muted fashion in Dublin. *The Irish Times* celebrated the event by designing its front page display of photographs in the shape of a 'V', a contrivance that found its way past Frank Aiken's almost redundant censors. A more ugly commemoration occurred outside Trinity College, whose Anglo-Irish undergraduates decided to fly the Allied flags from the roof of their academy and tossed a smouldering Irish Tricolour into the street for good measure. Two students from University College – one of them an undergraduate named Charles Haughey – responded by burning a Union Jack in College Green.[35] Northern Ireland was able to honour the war's end in a more tangible way when dozens of Germany's surrendered U-boats were towed into Londonderry and tied up at the Lisahally quays. Basil Brooke watched this iron tribute to the province's help in the Battle of the Atlantic; and so did a man in civilian clothes who came up from Dublin uninvited but who nonetheless wanted to observe this little moment of history: Colonel Dan Bryan.[36]

There Ireland's small but critical role in the great world conflict might have come to a close had it not been for one last burst of Churchillian rancour. It came, surprisingly, in the British Prime Minister's victory broadcast, before a world audience and at a moment when the British were allowing themselves a measure of self-congratulation now that their tremendous struggle against Germany was at an end. Churchill recalled the Battle of Britain, the blitz and then the Battle of the Atlantic, when the U-boat fleets seemed about to throttle the Atlantic life-lines to the United States. 'The sense of envelopment,' he said:

> . . . which might at any moment turn to strangulation, lay heavy upon us . . . Owing to the action of Mr de Valera, so much at variance with the temper and instinct of thousands of Southern Irishmen who hastened to the battle-front to prove their ancient valour, the approaches which the Southern Irish ports and airfields could so easily have guarded were closed by the hostile aircraft and U-boats. This was indeed a deadly moment in our life, and if it had not been for the loyalty and friendship of Northern Ireland we should have been forced to come to close quarters with Mr de Valera or perish for ever from the earth.

463

However, with a restraint and poise to which, I say, history will find few parallels, His Majesty's Government never laid a violent hand upon them, though at times it would have been quite easy and quite natural, and we left the de Valera Government to frolic with the Germans and later with the Japanese representatives to their heart's content.[37]

When he thought of other episodes and personalities, of the Irishmen who had won VCs – including Fegen – he had to 'confess that bitterness by Britain against the Irish race dies in my heart. I can only pray that in years which I shall not see the shame will be forgotten and the glories will endure, and that the people of the British Isles as of the British Commonwealth of Nations will walk together in mutual comprehension and forgiveness.'[38]

It was a strange passage in an otherwise jubilant speech, a throwback to darker days and less generous thoughts. It was also the anger of an ageing man who was talking of a world that had already changed without his realising it. He was still regarding Eire as a colonial dependency whose Redmondite instincts – still alive in the deeds of Irishmen who had proved their valour in the service of the British – had been temporarily perverted by de Valera. The word 'frolic' was not idly chosen for it was meant to illustrate, cruelly, the abnormal nature of the political path which de Valera had chosen to follow. It was as if the Irish all-party demonstrations in favour of neutrality had never taken place. Non-belligerency, Churchill imagined, was 'at variance with the temper and instincts of thousands of Southern Irishmen'. He failed to see, even now, that the citizens of Eire were no longer British, that neutrality – far from being an unnatural course – was proof of their independence.

De Valera's reply was eagerly awaited but when it came, three days later, it was dispassionate and undramatic, scrupulously avoiding the excuse for personal abuse which Churchill had provided. 'I know the kind of answer I am expected to make,' he said. 'I know the answer that first springs to the lips of every man of Irish blood who heard or read that speech . . . I know the reply I would have given a quarter of a century ago.' But he would not add 'fuel to the flames of hatred and passion'. Allowances could be made, he said:

. . . for Mr Churchill's statement, however unworthy, in the first flush of his victory. No such excuse could be found for me in this quieter atmosphere. There are, however, some things which it is my duty to say, some things which it is essential to say . . . Mr Churchill makes it clear that, in certain circumstances, he would have violated our neutrality and that he would justify his action by Britain's necessity. It seems strange to me that Mr Churchill does not see that this, if accepted, would mean that Britain's necessity would become a moral code and that when this necessity became sufficiently great, other people's rights were not to count.[39]

De Valera gave 'all credit' to Churchill for successfully resisting the temptation of violating Irish neutrality. By doing so, the British Prime Minister, 'instead of adding another horrid chapter to the already blood-stained record of the relations between England and this country, has advanced the cause of international morality an important step . . .' But de Valera found it difficult to understand how Britons could fail to see the reason for Eire's neutrality. If Germany had occupied England and then, after many years, had conceded England's right to freedom but maintained control of her six south-eastern counties, would Churchill lead his partitioned country 'to join with Germany in a crusade'? De Valera did not think so. Churchill, he said:

> . . . is proud of Britain's stand alone, after France had fallen and before America entered the war.
>   Could he not find in his heart the generosity to acknowledge that there is a small nation that stood alone not for one year or two, but for several hundred years against aggression; that endured spoliations, famines, massacres in endless succession . . . a small nation that could never be got to accept defeat and has never surrendered her soul?[40]

It was an extremely clever reply, calm and at times even generous in its understanding of the British Prime Minister's wrath in his moment of triumph. Almost at once, Churchill seems to have regretted his attack on de Valera. Randolph Churchill once explained that his father told him it 'was a speech which "perhaps I should not have made in the heat of the moment. We had just come through the war and I had been looking around at our victories. The idea of Eire sitting at our feet without giving us a hand annoyed me." '[41] A few days after de Valera's reply, Randolph Churchill told Frank Gallagher that his father 'didn't like it and . . . was very quiet for a long time after hearing it.'[42] Years later, when Winston Churchill was completing the sixth volume of his history of the war, he made a significant alteration to the text of his speech attacking de Valera. The Taoiseach's name was deleted from the insulting personal references and in its place was substituted the more anodyne phrase 'the Dublin Government'.[43]

Maffey's assessment of the radio contest was a mixture of regret and thinly-disguised impatience with his Prime Minister. In Dublin, he reminded the Dominions Office, he pursued a policy of 'absent treatment' towards Eire; but Churchill, 'handling world problems on a vast stage, finds it expedient from time to time to come into collision with that policy . . . If milk happens to be spilt here it would be presumptuous on my part to suggest any criticism of the hand which spilt it.' But, wrote Maffey, 'in this day of judgement it was necessary for the Prime Minister to stress (a) the dangers to which we were exposed by Mr de Valera withholding from us the use of the ports, though the American Minister, the Canadian High

Commissioner and I felt something was lost in the moral plane by suggesting we might have seized them; (b) the services rendered to our cause by the Irishmen who fought for us – though all speakers on this subject would do well to remember that the majority of these gallant warriors are supporters of Mr de Valera and his policy of neutrality.' However, Maffey continued:

> . . . where we lost most tricks in the rubber here was in the fact that after five and a half years of world war the British Prime Minister, in a historic speech, gave prominence to Mr de Valera, attacking him personally and thereby introduced him to the spotlight and a world radio contest. There was balm for every Irishman in this, and with the Irish people today Mr de Valera is as great a hero as is the Irishman who scores the winning try at Twickenham. 'Absent treatment' would not have presented Mr de Valera with this opportunity of escape from the eclipse which had closed down on him and the Irish Question . . . Mr de Valera assumed the pose of the elder statesman and skilfully worked on all the old passions in order to dramatise the stand taken by Eire in this war. So long as he can work his *mystique* over Irishmen in all parts of the world Mr de Valera does not worry about the rest of humanity.[44]

Churchill's speech represented a 'setback' to Dominions Office policy in Eire, wrote Maffey. He quoted John Kearney's reaction to the way in which de Valera's visit to Hempel had been followed by his reply to Churchill's personal attack. 'We had him on a plate,' Kearney said of de Valera. 'We had him where we wanted him. But look at the papers this morning!' De Valera, observed Maffey, 'had the right of reply, saw his advantage, found the authentic anti-British note and did not put a foot wrong. Therefore today, for the Irishman in the Homeland and overseas, it is once again a case of "Up Dev!" '[45]

Maffey attached a slightly less discreet criticism of Churchill in a letter to Sir Eric Machtig, the Dominions Office Permanent Under-Secretary. 'I sympathise very deeply with the Dominions Office,' he wrote. 'This temperamental country needs quiet treatment and a patient, consistent policy. But how are you to control Ministerial incursions into your china shop? Phrases make history here.'[46] Machtig showed Maffey's letter to Cranborne who thought that while there had been benefit to de Valera in Ireland, this was not true in the rest of the world. De Valera, Machtig wrote back to Maffey, 'inflicted a profound and enduring shock on the American people by his visit of condolence on the death of Hitler which, unhappily for him, coincided with the Buchenwald revelations . . . The Prime Minister's severe remarks were therefore accepted and even applauded as a salutary rap over the knuckles.'[47]

When the Allies did enter Hempel's Legation, they found nothing of any worth; an empty combination-lock safe, a map projector, a teleprinter, two typewriters and some cheap furnishings. When they were sold at auction in Belfast four months later, they fetched £1760. A German eagle in plaster went for £3 15s, an edition of Hitler's *Mein Kampf* for a guinea and a copy of Goering's *Knight of the Air* for just ten shillings.[48] There, too, Ireland's wartime story might have ended were it not for the British Government's determination 'to get rid of the Germans in Eire.' By June of 1945, there were, according to Dominions Office files, 260 interned German sailors and airmen, 'a small handful of Nazi agents' and three or four former Legation staff still in the twenty-six counties.[49] The British were particularly interested in the German agents, especially 'the notorious Dr Hermann Goertz'. Maffey thought there would be no difficulty in transferring the service personnel to Germany since the only condition that the Irish attached to this was that they should not be sent to the Russian zone of occupation. Joseph Walshe saw more difficulties in handing over the imprisoned German spies since they were being held by the Irish authorities for offences committed against Eire. Maffey was given to understand that the Irish would eventually be prepared to transfer these men provided they were not executed by the Allies.[50] The former Abwehr agents were kept in Athlone jail and no more was heard of the matter until Gerald Boland gave them parole at Christmas 1945, contradicting an undertaking which had been made – unknown to him – between the Irish and British authorities that the prisoners would not be released from custody before being sent back to Germany. When Maffey called to complain to Boland, the Irish Minister for Justice informed him that as the Germans had been beaten, he 'would not agree to any policy of "woe to the vanquished" and told him that the Irish people always sympathised with the fallen.' When Gray arrived on the same mission next day, Boland told the American Minister, whom he thought 'an unprincipled old villain', that the United States would have to use force if they wished to take the prisoners out of Eire.[51]

But seventeen months later, the ex-Abwehr agents were suddenly re-arrested and informed that they were to be deported to occupied Germany. Little is known about the Anglo-Irish discussions which brought this about but most of the prisoners accepted the situation with equanimity, except for Goertz who became desperate to avoid a return to his homeland. 'I will never go back to Germany,' he told his fellow prisoner Gunther Schütz. 'I don't wish to fall into the hands of the British.' Schütz told Goertz that he was 'not that important' but Goertz replied – according to Schütz, who did not like him – that 'it was beneath his dignity to fall into the hands of the enemy.'[52] In his private papers, Boland recorded that Maffey had given an assurance that Goertz would be permitted to travel from Germany to the Argentine to live with his brother;[53] Hempel, who had been given asylum by de Valera, also tried to persuade the former German spy that he would not be harmed if he returned to Germany. But Goertz shouted at him: 'No, no, they will persecute me.' Hempel later heard that Goertz was contemplating suicide and even went to see Maffey who repeated his guarantee that he would

467

come to no harm.[54] Colonel Dan Bryan still believes that he could have persuaded Goertz to go to Germany of his own free will – he had earlier induced him to give up a hunger-and-thirst strike – but he was unable to see the German prisoner.[55] There is even now a suspicion in Eire that Boland had been given a choice – to send either the spies or the diplomats back to Germany – and that Hempel had convinced the Irish that the agents should be returned in order to save himself.[56]

Was Goertz, now a partially demented man, standing on what was left of his dignity or was he really frightened that he would be tortured by the British authorities? Helmut Clissmann was held at a camp at Bad Nenndorf in Germany after the war and was constantly interrogated by the British about his connections with Ireland. He says that he was beaten while being made to run naked down corridors and was forced to stand in cold water for more than a day in an effort to make him reveal his Irish contacts.[57] Did Goertz believe that he would be subjected to this sort of treatment?

Just before ten o'clock on 23 May 1947, he was brought to the Aliens Office at Dublin Castle and informed by a Garda Sergeant that he would be sent to Mountjoy before being deported. Goertz sat down and smoked his pipe but shortly afterwards another officer saw him put something in his mouth. Schütz, who was sitting in the next room, heard Goertz fall to the floor.[58] He had swallowed something from a glass phial which one of the policemen found in his hand. By coincidence, Patrick Finlay, the young fireman who had travelled to Belfast after the Luftwaffe bombing, was driving the ambulance that was summoned to the Aliens Office after Goertz's collapse. A police officer shouted to him: 'We've a guy in here who's had a heart attack' but Finlay realised this was not true when he saw 'a frothing at the man's mouth'. Finlay lifted Goertz in his arms, wrapped him gently in a blanket and put him on a stretcher. 'He muttered something to me but I couldn't hear what he said,' Finlay afterwards recalled. 'I got him in the ambulance to Mercer's Hospital where a Jewish doctor diagnosed that he had swallowed something. Goertz was staring with his eyes wide open all the time. They did everything they could for him. He was sick into a bowl and passed out. Then I smelt geraniums and knew that he had taken cyanide.'[59]

Hermann Goertz was buried in his Luftwaffe uniform at Dean's Grange cemetery in the south-eastern suburbs of Dublin on a bright afternoon three days later. The cemetery records described him as '56, Protestant, married' and gave his address as No. 7, Spencer Villas, Glenageary.[60] His coffin was covered in a Swastika flag and surviving photographs show female mourners crowding his graveside, hands upraised in the Nazi salute.

Chapter 16

Mr de Valera Got Away
with It . . .

> Historically, Ireland, which has never been able to protect herself against invasion, has been, as she is today, a potential base for attack on the United Kingdom . . . Failing some firm and satisfactory assurance as to the attitude in war of a United Ireland, of which the present Republic was a major part, there are strong strategic arguments for the retention of the friendly bastion of the Six Counties.
>
> Commonwealth Relations Office
> memorandum *1951*

When the Second World War started, George Bernard Shaw urged Eire to fight with the Commonwealth on Britain's side. With the careless good grace of a literary genius, he later admitted that his advice had been wrong. Neutrality, he announced, 'seemed a crack-brained line to take, yet Mr de Valera got away with it . . . that powerless little cabbage garden called Ireland wins in the teeth of all the mighty Powers. Erin go Bragh.'[1] Ireland did not win of course; she survived. The penalty for neutrality was to be exacted in the coming years, when the people of Eire emerged from Plato's cave, dazzled, into the light of day, into 'a new and vastly different world'.[2] It was a world in which they were excluded from the international forum that had been created as a successor to the League of Nations and in which the frontier between the two parts of Ireland had been branded even more deeply across the island. If neutrality was contingent upon the maintenance of partition – as de Valera had implied in his response to Churchill at the end of the war – it had served to consolidate that state of affairs by the time the conflict ended. Its logical outcome was manifest when the two parts of Ireland diverged in the late forties. Having proved her sovereignty in wartime, Eire declared herself a Republic in 1948. Having established her loyalty in war, Northern Ireland received formal affirmation from the British Parliament in 1949 that the province was part of the United Kingdom and would not cease to be so without the consent of the legislature at Stormont.

De Valera misunderstood the implications of the war for Northern Ireland, partly because he underestimated – or ignored – its largely Protestant population. While he constantly asserted the illegality of the province's secession, he failed to realise that most of its people could not be persuaded to move to the aegis of a Dublin government in the manner of repentant prodigals. The war created a strengthened bond between London and Belfast, a link that was accentuated and repeatedly emphasised throughout the war by Eire's refusal to stand by Britain in her hour of need. The Irish Treaty ports had been closed to the Royal Navy but Northern Ireland had stood a 'faithful sentinel' guarding the north Atlantic approaches to the Clyde and the Mersey. How could Britain abandon the province now? Stormont governments preferred to believe that Britain's faithfulness towards the six counties was a response to their manpower and industrial contribution to the war effort, that it was the *people* of the province who had secured Britain's undying gratitude. In fact, the individual Irishmen whom Churchill singled out for praise were the VCs from Eire, of whom he spoke so proudly in his victory broadcast. The only wartime event in Northern Ireland which seemed to move the British was the bombing of Belfast, a blood sacrifice infinitely more frightful than that enacted in Dublin in 1916 and one which was not voluntarily undertaken. Churchill was to refer to it briefly but significantly in his letter marking Andrews' resignation, claiming that 'the bonds of affection between Great Britain and the people of Northern Ireland have been tempered by fire and are now, I firmly believe, unbreakable.'[3] The idea that the province had finally earned its place in British hearts in this manner – that it had 'made good in blood its pledge to stand by Britain "come what may" '[4] – was to persist for many years although it was not a very safe structure upon which to base political confidence in the future. Basil Brooke came close to understanding the real relationship between Northern Ireland and Britain when he told his audience in London that while the province had never doubted that Britain was necessary to its survival, 'we hope that you now realise that we are necessary to you.' But would Northern Ireland be so indispensable when the war was over?

Ireland itself was a geographical location that only touched British consciousness at times of insurrection or external danger. Throughout the Second World War, it was the pressing need for the Treaty ports and the fear that Germany might use Eire as a platform for an assault upon Britain that dominated British strategic thinking on Ireland. John Maffey was to acknowledge the historical reasons for this policy years later when, as Lord Rugby, he told Sean MacBride, then Irish Minister for External Affairs, that the British Admiralty's claim to the Treaty ports 'formed part of a traditional psychological attitude that had been developed since the Napoleonic Wars . . .'[5] When the Irish anchorages were unavailable to the

Royal Navy in 1939, British frustration was mixed with an equally traditional suspicion of Irish motives and intentions, of secret co-operation with the Nazis or with fuel-starved U-boat crews. Opposition spokesmen in Eire were judged according to the sympathy they expressed towards the Allies rather than by the policies they pursued publicly inside the twenty-six counties; thus James Dillon was given undue attention by the British while his party, together with Labour, united behind the very neutrality which had deprived the Royal Navy of the ports.

The ambiguous nature of Churchill's own reaction to Irish neutrality added some confusion to Britain's policies. There were times when he seemed to loathe de Valera, unable to comprehend why the Taoiseach wanted to break away from Britain. 'There were some things Churchill did not see clearly and did not understand,' Malcolm MacDonald said shortly before his death in 1981. 'These old colonialists thought that those who wanted to be independent were wild men. He didn't attempt to understand Dev. Because Dev wanted to get away from the Empire, Churchill thought he should be regarded as an enemy of Britain. This dictated his attitude before the war, during the war and for some time afterwards. Dev would not let Britain use the ports in Britain's hour of greatest crisis. For Churchill, therefore, Dev was an enemy, an enemy, an enemy.'[6] De Valera was constantly identified as the man who had betrayed the great Anglo-Irish Treaty, who had lied his way out of the solemn covenant that Churchill had agreed with Collins, Griffith and O'Higgins. According to Churchill's own account, Collins had been convinced of Britain's strategic needs and had told Churchill during the Treaty negotiations: 'Of course you must have the ports. They are necessary for your life.'[7] It was Collins and O'Higgins who were extolled by Churchill when he opposed the handover of the harbours in 1938. He described Collins as 'a man of his word'.[8] The animosity against de Valera was personal as well as political, and Churchill's imperialist mind did really believe that Eire's neutrality was only a temporary aberration and that she would in good time return to the heart of the Empire. He never lost his conviction that Ireland could be united in a form of dominion home rule and the British never tried to expel Eire from the Commonwealth even though this was briefly considered. Eire, on the other hand, wanted to be regarded as a sovereign state and it was one of the ironies of the period that Northern Ireland – in its desire to promote the maintenance of partition – chose to emphasise Eire's 'foreign-ness' in a way which the British Government in London, anxious to preserve the Commonwealth and Empire, would never have encouraged.

Behind Churchill's vexation with Irish neutrality lay the problem of India. His pre-war journalism for Rothermere's *Daily Mail* had contained more warnings about the dangers of Indian independence than about de Valera's dismantling of the 1921 Treaty. The struggle for national freedom was a contagion that could spread through the Empire and any manifestation of the disease was to be resisted. Churchill had convinced himself that the real negotiators of Irish independence – Collins and Griffith and their associates – were reasonable men, but the new strain of revolutionary personified by de Valera, who had so ruthlessly rejected England's benign hand, were far more frightening. Such a mood for independence was almost incomprehensible and it was not surprising that Churchill's most influential advisers in wartime Eire – the brilliant Maffey and the incompetent Tegart – were both old India hands. The second could only feed suspicion although the first quickly realised that the credibility of Irish neutrality – and thus Eire's independence – lay in the degree of public support which it received. Churchill's telegram to de Valera in 1941, offering Eire the opportunity to 'regain her soul' by joining the Allies was in this context spectacularly inappropriate since the Irish were in the very process of regaining their soul – their political independence – by remaining neutral.

Malcolm MacDonald, who found himself in 1940 in the ambivalent position of trying to get back what he had given away two years earlier, came to the conclusion that Eire's benevolent neutrality was of more use to Britain than her participation in the war as an ally, a view later held by many other ministers. 'I was being a diplomat in June, 1940, and I would have been glad if Eire had come into the war,' MacDonald recalled. 'But by the time Dev had presented his arguments, I was inclined to think that he was right to say that on balance it was in Britain's interest for Eire to stay neutral. He knew that the vast majority of his supporters and countrymen agreed with his view. The retention of the ports by Eire was not only a symbol of independence but an *establishment* of independence – and Dev thought that any tiny qualification of the principle of sovereignty was a denial of that principle.'[9] The proof of that sovereignty, of course, was Britain's acceptance of Irish neutrality, a policy that was thus publicly unalterable inside Eire. Indeed, the most impressive aspect of Eire's foreign and domestic policy during the war was not the *act* of neutrality nor its later benevolence towards the Allies but the *consistency* with which that neutrality was expressed, from the late thirties until the last days of the Second World War.

Since it was also the only policy behind which the people of Eire could unite – and since they knew it was the only one – neutrality was successful in avoiding both internal and external disaster. Even Dillon was to admit in later years that it was 'a masterly political stroke'.[10] It fulfilled a psychological need[11] and if it was not legitimate in Churchill's eyes, if it was indeed 'anomalous', it was nonetheless viable – at a cost. The immediate political price – or punishment – that was exacted of post-war Eire was the rejection of her application for membership of the United Nations where she had been opposed by the Soviet Union. But there was a more long-term price of this neutrality, a result of wartime isolation but, more significantly, of the moral issues upon which Eire ostentatiously turned her back during the war. Elizabeth Bowen and the other visitors to Dublin in the winter of 1940 were all struck by the Irish predilection for ignoring the ideology of the war. True, Eire was unlikely to warm to the idea of a conflict fought on behalf of 'little nations'. Redmond had accepted that crusade and de Valera had later opposed it in an almost forgotten anti-conscription address in 1918. ' "Little Belgium" had a champion in many a generous Irish youth,' he wrote then. 'Their bones to-day lie buried beneath the soil of Flanders, or beneath the waves of Suvla Bay, or bleaching on the slopes of Gallipoli, or on the sands of Egypt or Arabia, in Mesopotamia, or wherever the battle line extends from Dunkirk to the Persian Gulf . . .'[12] Long after the 1939–45 War, de Valera was to tell Terence O'Neill, then the Northern Ireland Prime Minister, that Eire was neutral because 'I lost many good friends during the First World War and had no intention of doing so in the Second.'[13]

But if England's 1939 'crusade' was spurious, merely an excuse for another war between impersonal power blocs, what were Eire's moral values? The Irish resented the British habit of presenting themselves as a corporate Saint George, galloping off to save democracy from the forces of evil. But in previous years, de Valera had himself not been averse to raising the banner of Saint Patrick. In 1933, the Taoiseach had announced that since 'the Irish genius has always stressed spiritual and intellectual rather than material values', this characteristic eminently fitted the Irish people 'for the task . . . of helping to save Western civilisation.'[14] An echo of this speech was contained in de Valera's 1943 Saint Patrick's Day panegyric in which he conjured up images of a Ruritanian Ireland, whose countryside would be bright with cosy homesteads, athletic youths and comely maidens. Eire was to be a nation that struggled against materialism – the Germans played upon this in their wartime broadcasts, the British unwisely made fun of it – and so the war was seen as a conflict of materialism, a struggle between two opposing but equally unspiritual sides. Britain's ideals may have merited more initial sympathy but when she allied herself with atheistical Russia, with a state that represented materialism in its most powerful form, she muddied the ideological waters in Ireland. It became easier for the Irish to claim then that the belligerent nations were as bad as one another. Belsen could be compared to Katyn, Auschwitz to Nagasaki. 'Imagine,' wrote Gerald Boland after the war, 'the people who murdered the cream of the Polish Army and buried them in the Mass Grave in the Katyn Forest, those who bombed the City of Dresden which was undefended and full of refugees and those who atom-bombed Hiroshima and Nagasaki having the cheek to try anyone for war crimes!!'[15]

This argument had some validity but it also represented a sliding away from the issues that were involved in the war, a wilful refusal to acknowledge the evil nature of Hitler's Nazi regime and the terror it inflicted upon the world. As late as 1982, *The Irish Times* carried a letter alleging that

'World War II was a struggle between power blocs for global domination, and the destruction of European Jewry by one of those blocs was coincidental.'[16] Such views make neutrality more than honourable and de Valera's visit of condolence to the German Legation a mere bureaucratic nicety to which no odium could attach. Indeed, just after the war, Nazi atrocities were disbelieved in some parts of Eire.* If neutrality gave rise to such post-war emotions, how much easier must it have been during the war to regard the outside world as evil, a universe gone mad in which only Eire and a few other non-belligerent nations were able – or lucky enough – to retain their sanity. Censorship was so strict that it obfuscated the moral issues of the war and restrained free speech in a way not even contemplated by some other neutrals; the Swedish press, for instance, was comparatively free to criticise Germany even though the Reich lay much nearer to her shores than to Ireland's.[19] It was therefore almost possible to forget that neutrality – far from being above the conflict, in some way sacrosanct – was based on the very same values of self-interest of which the Irish always accused the belligerents. The nearest the Irish ever came to acknowledging this fact was in Frank Aiken's 1940 memorandum on censorship where neutrality was defined as 'a condition of limited warfare'.

Belated recognition of this may account for a growing realisation in the Irish Republic that de Valera's wartime policies, however necessary and successful they were at the time, should not necessarily be held up as a model for future foreign policy. In 1978, John Kelly, a former Attorney General and one of Fine Gael's front bench spokesmen, gave it as his personal view that during the war, Eire 'stood aside from a decisive contest against fearful cruelty and tyranny and did so for what, by comparison, were petty and parochial reasons. It would be shameful to make a similar mistake again . . .'[20] Kelly was not quite suggesting that neutrality was disreputable, merely that it was a good deal less holy than its supporters had previously suggested. 'We hypocritically pretended to sit on the fence during the Second World War,' wrote one Irish commentator, 'while with one foot we kicked the ball for Britain when nobody was looking.'[21] This

---

* In Kilkenny in 1945, a local newspaper reader declared that newsreel films of Belsen were 'all propaganda' and had been faked by the British using starving Indians; first prize at a fancy dress ball in the town went to 'the Beast of Belsen'.[17] This general air of incredulity may have been the reason why few people in Ireland raised objections when some of Hitler's former admirers decided to buy property there after the war. Pieter Menten, the SS officer later to be convicted of killing Jews in Poland, Otto Skorzeny, the SS leader who rescued Mussolini in 1943, and Oswald Mosley, the former British Blackshirt leader, all invested in expensive property in Ireland. These generally unrepentant old fascists never engaged in political activities in the Irish Republic and only when Menten was convicted in Holland for war crimes were there calls for him to be banned from the country. The *Limerick Leader* noted that 'the campaign against war criminals is strangely confined to those who happen to fight on the wrong side.' It conceded that 'Allied atrocities cannot excuse the monstrous barbarism of the Reich.'[18]

only recognises what all neutrals have discovered in time of war; that they have ultimately to pay less regard to the rules of neutrality than to the facts of power. A Swedish historian, writing of his own country's wartime experience, observed that when the tide of war was running against the great powers, 'they demanded respect for the obligations of neutrality. When they were winning, they demanded respect for their power.'[22]

But there was another, deeper consciousness in Ireland that the Soviet Union might ultimately have represented the greatest threat to humanity; this, too, has had its effect on post-war Irish reaction to de Valera's emergency policies. During the conflict, Eire temporarily impounded several merchant ships from the Baltic States which found themselves in Irish ports when the Soviet Union absorbed Latvia, Estonia and Lithuania, refusing to release the vessels until the states regained their freedom. It was a small gesture that has gone largely unremarked since, but a distrust – a fear – of the Soviets would certainly have provided another reason for de Valera's correct behaviour towards the Germans even in the later stages of the war. In an essay on Irish neutrality, Constance Howard has suggested that de Valera 'would have liked to see a lenient or even a compromise peace with Germany so that there might be some semblance of European balance at the end of the war to withstand Russia.'[23] This feeling that the Soviets are a potential enemy of Ireland has persisted to the present day. A former Irish Minister for Justice said in 1979 that Europe should unite to face 'the ideological threat' from Russia. 'What would our attitude to neutrality have been in the last war if we had been aware of the existence of Belsen?' he asked. 'But we do have evidence of the Russian system.'[24] The predilection for anti-communism that was prevalent in Ireland during the war can still be found, even in the pages of the Irish defence forces magazine. The Second World War, a retired Irish Army officer wrote in 1978, destroyed Nazism, but this was supplanted by 'the new style imperialism of Communism which few will dispute is one of the most fiendishly evil systems of human enslavement that history has yet spawned . . .'[25]

But would Eire's participation in the war have changed history? If de Valera had accepted Britain's offer of Irish unity in 1940, would the shape of the European conflict have been radically altered? If the Royal Navy had used Cobh, Berehaven and Lough Swilly, the Battle of the Atlantic might not have been so hard-fought, the U-boat menace might have been overcome at an earlier stage and fewer British seamen would have died. An Irish military historian has conjectured that with the Treaty ports in British hands and the Atlantic battles sooner won, the Normandy landings 'may have taken place before Russia could recross Poland and eventually emerge as a world power. Perhaps with the changed dispersal of forces even Singapore may not have fallen . . .'[26] If de Valera had entered the war in response to Britain's offer, however, would Irish unity have come about? De Valera did not believe it. A defence council may well have been set up but Craigavon and Andrews would have been able to ensure that the joint committee examining the constitution of the union became bogged down in procedural details.* Churchill would have supported the efforts towards union, but de Valera would not have accepted a dominion home rule that lasted for more than a few years, and Craigavon and his successors would have taken nothing less than that. Even supposing that the attempt had been made, would the British have left the Treaty ports again at the end of the war, disengaging themselves entirely from this new and united Ireland? Were a united Ireland really the supreme national aspiration of most Irish men and women, then perhaps de Valera would have given Britain's offer of a solemn undertaking more consideration. But Eire's new sovereignty was of more consequence than the ending of partition; at that stage of the war, the preservation of neutrality was more important than unity and has arguably remained so. It would be interesting to know to what degree it was also a *substitute* for unity.

Both the Dublin and the Belfast Governments used the war, the first to assert Eire's sovereignty, the second to secure further Northern Ireland's place within the United Kingdom. In Eire, domestic considerations – the need to demonstrate sovereignty and independence – overlapped with the neutrality upon which the country relied for its defence. For once, symbol and reality were one. In Northern Ireland, where the authorities had no control over external defence, the war effort was tuned to a domestic rather than a British national aspiration. The province was not so wholeheartedly in the war as the Stormont Government made out. And the raising of an all-Protestant defence force, the demand for a greater share of Britain's war production, the attempts to introduce conscription, to emphasise Northern Ireland's 'Britishness' at the expense of Eire; all these efforts were designed primarily to ensure the survival of the province as part of the United Kingdom rather than to preserve the United Kingdom from her enemies abroad. The war emphasised the blindness of both governments in the island; of the Irish towards Northern Ireland's Protestants and of Stormont towards Northern Ireland's Catholics. A united but neutral Ireland was an impossibility; equally conscription was never an option in the province, except in the mind of Unionist ministers and – briefly – of Churchill. Within the Stormont Government, the conflict between loyalty to Empire and loyalty to province – Spender exemplifying the former, Craigavon the latter – was resolved in the short term by the new but not indefinite lease of life which Unionists gained for their six counties. John Andrews' wartime achievement was to obtain the British Treasury's acknowledgement that it was Britain's duty to make up the

---

* The only gesture towards unity made by the British after 1940 was the Council of Ireland embodied in the 1973 Anglo-Irish agreement at Sunningdale. It was a pale shadow of the proposal that MacDonald presented to de Valera in 1940 and Protestant opposition in Northern Ireland ensured that it never came into being.

leeway in public services between Northern Ireland and the rest of the United Kingdom.[27] The British Parliament's declaration of the province's integral position within the realm was partly a response to the birth of the new Irish Republic but without the loyalty demonstrated by Northern Ireland in war, such an affirmation may not have been so fulsome or forthcoming.

And it remains a fact that Northern Ireland fought while Eire did not. 'I hope that somebody will explain . . . to the Pope,' wrote a Protestant reader of *The Irish Times* just before Pope John Paul's visit to Ireland in 1979, 'why it was that the Irish Free State . . . decided to remain neutral when the predominantly Roman Catholic country of Poland, the Pope's own country, was savagely attacked in 1939, while the predominantly Protestant part of Ireland went to the aid of Poland.'[28] The Irish reply to these arguments has always been the same: that it did Poland little good since the Allies later acquiesced at her subjugation by new masters. But in Britain, where Northern Ireland's status is decided, the province's wartime duty had been duly noted. Nor was the reciprocation of loyalty by Britain entirely unselfish. In 1951, the Commonwealth Relations Office noted that 'historically, Ireland, which has never been able to protect herself against invasion, has been, as she is today, a potential base for attack on the United Kingdom. It is the more important that a part of the island, and that one strategically well placed, should, and of its own free will, wish to remain part of the United Kingdom and of the United Kingdom defence scheme . . . Failing some firm and satisfactory assurance as to the attitude in war of a united Ireland, of which the present Republic was a major part, there are strong strategic arguments for the retention of the friendly bastion of the Six Counties . . .'[29] At almost the same time, the Americans were reassessing their defence policy towards the Irish Republic, which had already refused to join the NATO alliance. 'Despite strong anti-communist sentiments,' a National Security Council analysis stated, 'the Irish Government for domestic political considerations still adheres strongly to its traditional policy of neutrality which was militarily embarrassing to the Allies in World War II. In a war against communism, a policy of Irish neutrality would be more benevolent to the Western Allies than in World War II and less useful to the Soviet Union . . . The United States would welcome use of Ireland's port facilities and the air bases which could be developed there, although they are not considered essential at this time.'[30]

In September 1953, de Valera arrived for a luncheon at Downing Street to be warmly greeted by a Winston Churchill who had long ago come to terms with the Irish Republic's independence. Aiken was there and noted that the two leaders got on well together, discussing over their lunch nothing more volatile than higher mathematics.[31] The equation had been squared between them in the past; Churchill had been legalistic in his arguments against Eire's sovereignty but de Valera had been equally fascinated by the legal rights and complex details of statehood. Now Britain presented no threat to the Republic although she also felt there were no debts to be paid, least of all with the six Irish counties which remained to her. Her treatment of Ireland had been barbarous in the past but many Britons felt that their tolerance of Eire's wartime neutrality – which, they believed, few others would have shown – had now dispensed with any residual guilt.

In Ireland, there were those who thought that the new and more terrible weapons available to the super-powers had nullified the country's military significance, that missiles had 'deprived Ireland, possibly for all time, of her former strategic importance.'[32] But others did not agree, believing that Britain's defence posture still took Northern Ireland into account. If Britain were to withdraw her troops and sovereignty from the province, a leading British Conservative wrote in 1978, 'in favour of a neutral Republic or an "independent Ulster", the West could be denied the Northern Irish ports, over-flying rights and early warning. A new gap would open in NATO's defences.'[33] The neutrality debate opened anew in Dublin in 1981 with suggestions that the Irish Republic might trade in its traditional non-aligned military role in return for Irish unity. The British Secretary of State who now sat in Craigavon's old office at Stormont believed that both nations could discuss a defence pact since they had 'a common interest in resisting totalitarianism'.[34] De Valera's granddaughter, herself a member of the Irish Parliament, thought that 'a united and independent Ireland could well make possible a fresh approach to the consideration of our place within the scheme of Western defence'[35] while Charles Haughey, the Taoiseach, considered that if the European Community – to which the Irish Republic now belonged – should be organised into a full political union, then Ireland 'would accept the obligations even if these included defence.'[36] A week later, *Izvestia* announced that Britain was trying to bring the Irish Republic into a military alliance with NATO.[37] A year later, the retiring Irish Army Chief of Staff, Lieutenant General Carl O'Sullivan, defined the Republic's sovereignty as 'the ability to defend ourselves or to be defended' but he seemed to ignore the assumption that sovereignty also involved the right not to take sides in a conflict. 'The threat in the last war came from Europe and the UK,' he said. 'Now the Soviets have a strategic fleet sited in Murmansk. They have airborne divisions in the Kola peninsula which pose a threat to the north Atlantic and Ireland is in a crucial position there. So morally we owe it to Europe to consolidate our defences either on our own, or in consort with other people.'[38] Winston Churchill would have approved.

But the old suspicions remained, only to be reconfirmed in a fateful, ritualistic manner in the early summer of 1982 when the Royal Navy once more went to war in the Atlantic. It was a miniature conflict but it re-awoke all the ghosts of Anglo-Irish distrustfulness. The Irish were asked to support an economic boycott of Argentina but did so only temporarily.

Just as de Valera had urged the antagonists of 1939 to seek redress within the League of Nations, so Haughey now insisted that the Anglo-Argentine dispute over the Falkland Islands should be resolved at the United Nations. When a British submarine sank the Argentine destroyer *General Belgrano*, Ireland decided that she could no longer support Britain's claim to moral superiority. If this was a war against fascist aggression, Haughey would no more accept such a contention than de Valera had done four decades earlier.

Haughey, who liked to regard de Valera as his political inspiration, reinvoked Irish neutrality. Margaret Thatcher, who liked to model her personality upon Churchill, turned angrily upon Ireland for her apparent disloyalty. Thus history conspired again to torture Anglo-Irish relations. Perhaps the parallels were too many. For when the final British casualty lists were published, there was something familiar about them. One of the first British seamen to die in the South Atlantic came from Northern Ireland. And among the last to be killed fighting for the Crown was a young man from the Irish Republic.

Epilogue

The Irish Treaty ports are still there but history and more than forty years of Atlantic storms have done them more harm than any invader. At Berehaven and Lough Swilly, the only flotillas that moor now at the battleship anchorages are fishing smacks and sailing boats, indifferent to the crumbling forts above them. The guns are there too, pointing towards the Royal Navy's ghostly enemies, but the embrasures are overgrown, the great iron ammunition lockers welded shut with rust. On Bere Island, cows munch the grass by the wild roses and blasted rockery outside the derelict pavilion where British officers once took cocktails. The water tanks are broken, the windows of Rerrin Redoubt are smashed. The old British Army canteen has been assaulted by the wind, its tin roof peeled back towards the sky as if a giant had torn at it. The 6-inch guns stand forlorn amid the rye grass and honeysuckle, their breeches protected by corrugated-iron sheeting and their long, green-painted barrels resting impotently on little brick walls above the ruffled waters of Berehaven. The cramped square where Second Lieutenant John Griffin raised the Tricolour is carpeted with grass, the flag staff missing.

At Cobh, the hectic tide still races through the chasm between Forts Camden and Carlisle but the massive bastions are decaying, their black, mile-long tunnels filled with rubble, their ammunition railway tracks congealed into the concrete and weeds. Perhaps the Irish prefer it this way; who, after all, would covet a ruined fort? Only on Spike Island are the old British defences still intact. Fort Westmoreland has become Fort Mitchel – after the United Irishman who awaited deportation in its cells – and the cricket field has been turned into a hurling pitch. The young Irish Army gunners were not even born when the Union Jack was lowered on the barrack square to 'God Save the King' played by the Irish Army's No. 2 Band. But the 9.2-inch guns are in perfect working order to this day, their vintage shells still kept in the fort's underground corridors. The brass shell cases betray the date '1938', and along the walls still hang the Royal Artillery's gunnery instructions, surmounted by the Royal coat-of-arms. The British officers' quarters are near the parade ground, places of old oak panelling, banisters, empty billiard rooms, heavy doors, thick walls, dry rot and damp. The tiny harbour boats *John Adams* and *Raven*, handed over with such ill-mannered generosity by the British, still ply the short passage between Cobh town and the island. And in the Irish Army's mess, there is kept a large book with a faded gold British regimental insignia on its brown leather cover. It is inscribed 'Officers' Mess, Royal Artillery, Berc Island' and contains Second Lieutenant Griffin's entry – in slightly inaccurate Irish – on the day that the Army of Eire took possession of the sentinel towers.

The Heavy Regiment, Royal Artillery, which marched so blithely across Fort Westmoreland's wooden drawbridge in 1938, has since returned to Ireland, to duties more bloody and less predictable than those it carried out before the war. Belfast, too, has its wartime memorials. As late as 1981, the Royal Navy was defusing a Luftwaffe bomb in Bangor harbour, a relic of the German air attacks of 1941. The unknown victims of those raids still lie in the City Cemetery at the top of the Falls Road, their concrete memorial slab cracked, surrounded by bushes and the stone angels of Belfast's nineteenth-century linen barons. The cemetery is now in an area contested between the British Army and the IRA; relatives prefer to visit their dead on Sundays when they have safety in numbers. There, too, are the graves of Northern Ireland men who were killed in the British forces in the Second World War and who also became a tangible part of the province's sacrifice. Four years ago, at night, their headstones were smashed and the flowers around their graves uprooted. The bond of affection that they helped to cement did not save their parliament from extinction; nor did it prevent the British politician who lamented the wartime unemployment in the six counties from sneering more than thirty years later at the 'spongers' of Northern Ireland. Twelve miles to the south of Belfast, the airfield that General Kurt Student planned to capture at Long Kesh has become a prison for the political descendants of the men who once tried to co-operate with the Reich for the overthrow of British power in Ireland.

There are other mementoes of the war. It is still just possible to make out the huge, faded lettering of the word EIRE on the cliffs and headlands from Donegal to Kerry, alerting British and American pilots that they were approaching neutral territory. Those who did not – or could not – heed this warning have left their mark. On the wild slopes of Mount Brandon, the crushed aero-engine of a Wellington bomber and the broken fabric of a flying-boat can still be found amid the gorse and bracken. Wreckage from the Flying Fortress that crashed at Mullaghmore in County Sligo now hangs in a local public house together with the injured American pilot's flying hat, still stained with his blood. In Baltimore, County Cork, Captain Fell of His Majesty's Ship *Tamura* would today be amused to find more German tourists than Irish residents although the bomb which sank a small Royal Navy hydrographic survey vessel in the village harbour in 1971 might have reinforced his suspicions.

The German plans for the invasion of Ireland became a curiosity. In Brussels, a theatre company printed posters on the back of the maps that

481

the Wehrmacht were supposed to carry when they stormed the beaches of Waterford. The West Germans eventually paid compensation for the Luftwaffe's bombing of Dublin, and the East Germans returned Frank Ryan's body to Ireland in 1979. The *Irish Press* ennobled him as 'the laughing cavalier of Republicanism' which may have been true since every shade of mutually hostile republican accompanied his cortège to Glasnevin. There were other honoured graves at Spike Island, where Irish troops each year still scythe the long grass around the headstones of the anonymous Irishmen who died waiting for the convict ships. Of all the graves, however, none is more intriguing than that of Hermann Goertz, whose body was exhumed in 1974 and reburied in the official German War Cemetery in County Wicklow. He spent the three months before his death carving his own tombstone, sculpting a relief upon it which symbolised a belligerent's captivity in neutral Ireland; a sword sheathed in barbed wire.

Appendix 1

Extract from memorandum entitled *Neutrality, Censorship and Democracy* by the Irish Minister for the Coordination of Defensive Measures, dated 23 January 1940.

In these days one of the most important weapons of war is propaganda. Indeed it would not be surprising to find that the Germans were using more man and brain power in spreading their own propaganda and stopping that of the Allies, than in their submarine campaign. In these days, therefore, no matter what the old and very much out of date international conventions contain, it behoves neutrals who want to remain at peace to walk warily in the zone of the propaganda war.

So well was this realised that following upon the declaration of war by England and France on Germany the Government set up a Censorship Branch. This Branch immediately proceeded to ban the publication of statements which might endanger our neutrality. Since then the Dail has met on several occasions but no member tabled a motion declaring that the Government should allow a public discussion to take place on the question as to whether we should continue to be neutral or to participate in the war. Thus the legality of the Government's action in suppressing statements which might endanger our neutrality is reinforced not only by the great mass of public opinion but also, it can be fairly claimed, by the active consent of the Members of the Oireachtas.

Notwithstanding the fact that few would be found to question the legality of the Government's action in regard to censorship and neutrality, there may be some who will say that individual citizens and public representatives should be allowed to talk offensively about the belligerents and advocate the declaration of war on one or other of them. Freedom of this kind might have had certain usefulness in other countries in olden times in providing an outlet for a certain type of people who like blowing off steam, but in our country and in our circumstances it would be positively dangerous. As a nation we have a definite grievance against the nearest belligerent, but the Government have declared with general consent that we would be unwise, in the interests of the nation, to engage in war against this belligerent. Not all of our people approve this policy, and if a certain section were allowed to talk offensively about the morals of Germany in relation to its aggression in Poland and elsewhere, we can be quite sure that others would try to express in even more offensive terms their detestation of British morality. If we were a nation of Dillons words would only lead to words. But we are not. And if a competition of this sort were allowed to

483

start between gentlemen who would confine themselves to words, they would very quickly get supporters who would wish to use stronger arguments, and it might very well be that we would have a civil war to decide the question as to which of the European belligerents we should declare war upon. Consequently it would be the Government's duty, if it had not legal power to repress such activity, to seek that power immediately; and, as it has the power, it is its duty to use it.

Apart from the question of internal trouble arising through the expression of belligerent opinion, there is the question of international law and courtesy to friendly nations. There is nothing in the old Hague Convention which precludes neutrals from expressing sympathy with one belligerent and antipathy to the other so long as these feelings do not find expression in acts of war violating impartiality.

Nowadays, however, as has already been pointed out, propaganda is an important weapon of war, and the use of that weapon against a belligerent even by a neutral is coming more and more to be regarded as an act of war. But apart from the new status of propaganda, if a nation in its own interests prohibits the expression of antipathy to one belligerent and does not prohibit it in relation to the other, there is no doubt that the belligerent offended against will regard it as a departure from the impartial conduct which neutrality imposes. In our own interests and according to our declared policy we must suppress propaganda against the nearest belligerent and are thus led naturally to prevent propaganda against the other.

So much for the question as to whether censorship is legitimate and necessary to secure the continuance of neutrality. But what about democracy?

There are some self-styled democrats who would hold on to the peace time liberalistic trimmings of democracy while the fundamental basis of democracy was being swept from under their feet by the foreign or domestic enemies of their democratic State. Wise men, however, discard these trimmings when necessary in order successfully to maintain the fundamental right of the citizens freely to choose by whom they shall be governed. Wise Constitutions provide for such emergencies. Our own Constitution does so in Article 28. Under this Article the Dail wisely gave the Government the power to legislate, when necessary during the emergency, by Decree. Thus the much loved trimming of discussion before legislation went by the board. Thus was the Government given the power to do away with a lot of other trimmings if and when necessary 'for the purpose of securing the public safety and the preservation of the State'. But the Government must summon the people's representatives to meet from time to time, and the Dail has the power to ask all questions and to discuss all the affairs of Government and to change the Government if they think it wise. Between the meetings of the Dail no representative has any more right than has an ordinary citizen to do or say anything that might embroil our people in war or render it more difficult for them to stay out of war.

The right of declaring war is a corporative right of the Dail and no member of the Oireachtas or ordinary citizen has any reasonable grounds for complaint if he is prevented in time of war, in the interests of the preservation of the State, from expressing his opinion on the question of war and peace outside a meeting of the Dail, in a manner which might endanger peace, and, more particularly when the majority of the Members of the Dail have agreed to give the

Government the right to suppress the publication of such opinions outside the Dail.

Any argument that 'time of war' is different from 'time of neutrality' has no basis in our constitutional law and little or none in fact. The Constitution makes no legal difference but rather emphasises the identical gravity of the two emergencies. Neutrality is not like a simple mathematical formula which has only to be announced and demonstrated in order to be believed and respected. It has in fact always been one of the difficult problems in human relationship. Instead of earning the respect and goodwill of both belligerents it is regarded by both with hatred and contempt, 'He who is not with me is against me'. In the modern total warfare it is not a condition of peace with both belligerents, but rather a condition of limited warfare with both, a warfare whose limits, under the terrific and all prevailing force of modern total warfare, tend to expand to coincide with those of total warfare. In cold economic and military fact it is becoming more and more difficult to distinguish between the serious-ness of the two emergencies called war and neutrality, indeed in terms of expenditure of man power and resources, and the general upset of normal life, the difference is rather one of geographical location than of legal status as a belligerent or a neutral. In the last war the belligerent Japan spent less than neutral Switzerland. Neutral Belgium is already spending from £60 to £80 millions a year in this trouble. A neutral perilously located in regard to the main belligerents may have to make more extensive use of censorship and other emergency powers than a belligerent situated a long way from the main theatre of war.

If the Dail wishes, it can withdraw the right of censorship it gave the Government, but until it so decides the Government must use that power and all its other powers to maintain the neutrality of this democratic State.

When the Dail is not in session and a situation arises which, in the opinion of one or more members of the Dail necessitates a declaration of war, the proper constitutional democratic course for them to pursue is to ask the President, in pursuance of his powers under Article 13,2,3° of the Constitution to summon the Dail for that purpose, if the Government refuses to do so.

If newspapers or ordinary citizens feel aggrieved they can make representa-tion to their elected representatives.

Whoever says he is not satisfied with such a system of democracy in 'time of war' is either a very foolish democrat or an agent provocateur for those who want to overthrow democracy or to embroil us in civil or foreign war.

State Paper Office (Dublin) S 11586A

Appendix II

The revised terms of the final British offer of Irish unity, conveyed to Eamon de Valera on 28 June 1940 and signed by Neville Chamberlain.

(i)   A declaration to be made by the United Kingdom Government forthwith accepting the principle of a United Ireland. This declaration would take the form of a solemn undertaking that the Union is to become at an early date an accomplished fact from which there shall be no turning back.

(ii)   A joint Body, including representatives of the Government of Eire and the Government of Northern Ireland, to be set up at once to work out the Constitutional and other practical details of the Union of Ireland. The United Kingdom Government to give such assistance towards the work of this Body as might be desired, the purpose of the work being to establish at as early a date as possible the whole machinery of government of the Union.

(iii)   A joint Defence Council representative of Eire and Northern Ireland to be set up immediately.

(iv)   The Government of Eire to invite British naval vessels to have the use of ports in Eire, and British troops and aeroplanes to cooperate with the Eire Forces and to be stationed in such positions in Eire as may be agreed between the two Governments, for the purpose of increasing the security of Eire against the fate which has overcome neutral Norway, Denmark, Holland, Belgium and Luxemburg.

(v)   The Government of Eire to intern all German and Italian aliens in the country and to take any further steps necessary to suppress Fifth Column activities.

(vi)   The United Kingdom Government to provide military equipment at once to the Government of Eire in accordance with the particulars given in the annex.

Public Record Office (London) PREM 3/131/2

Notes

The primary documentary sources for this book can be found in the Public Record Office (PRO) at Kew, the State Paper Office (SPO) in Dublin and the Public Record Office of Northern Ireland (PRONI) in Belfast. Other sources which appear in abbreviated form are the University College Archives in Dublin (UCD Archives), the Imperial War Museum (IWM) in London, the House of Lords Record Office (HLRO) in London, the National Library of Ireland (NLI) in Dublin and the Radio Telefis Eireann (RTE) Film Library in Dublin. Sources which do not appear in abbreviated form are self-explanatory and are also referred to in the Acknowledgements.

The PRO papers are taken from the files of the British Prime Minister's Office (PREM), the War Cabinet (CAB), the Dominions Office (DO), the Foreign Office (FO), the Admiralty (ADM) and the Air Ministry (AIR). SPO documents relate either to Irish Cabinet minutes (CAB) or to memoranda in the archives of the Taoiseach's Department, all of which carry an 'S' classification. PRONI papers come from Northern Ireland Cabinet files (CAB), the Ministry of Commerce (COM) and the Ministry of Home Affairs (HA). Axis radio monitoring reports compiled by the BBC and sent to the Northern Ireland Government are in the Cabinet Secretariat files (CAB 9CD) and are abbreviated in the notes as BBCMR. Also in the PRONI archives are the Blake papers, the notes and documentation used by the official Northern Ireland war historian, and the diaries of Sir Wilfrid Spender (referred to in the notes as Spender diaries). IWM references are to the Enemy Documents Section (EDS) which contains captured German military material on Ireland. IWM private papers are classified under MISC. In HLRO, Beaverbrook's papers are classified under BBK. UCD Archives contain the papers of General Richard Mulcahy and NLI hold the Frank Gallagher Papers.

Shortly after the author consulted the archives of the Public Record Office of Northern Ireland, more than half the government documents which he used – and which are quoted in this book – were suddenly closed to the public. No explanation was given.

List of abbreviations
PRO ....Public Record Office, Kew (London)
  PREM ....Prime Minister's Office
  CAB...War Cabinet
  DO ....Dominions Office
  FO ....Foreign Office
  ADM..Admiralty

CHAPTER 1 THE SENTINEL TOWERS

1   PRO DO 35/895 Love to GOC 13.7.38.
2   *The Irish Times* Michael Bowles article 24.7.78.
3   PRO DO 35/895 Mins of Eire/UK meetings on ports 25–27–28.5.38.
4   Ibid.
5   PRO DO 35/895 Admin conf Spike Island 8–9.6.38.
6   PRO DO 35/895 Love to GOC 13.7.38.
7   *The Sapper* (Royal Engineers magazine) August 1938.
8   Interview with Lt Col John Griffin. Galway 7.5.78.
9   Interview with Michael Bowles. Dublin 19.1.79 and Bowles article op. cit.
10   Bowles interview 19.1.79.
11   PRO DO 35/895 Love to GOC 13.7.38.
12   Ibid.
13   Griffin interview 7.5.78.
14   PRO DO 35/895 See esp Stephenson to Nunan 1.12.38 and Loch to Stephenson 6.1.39.
15   PRO DO 35/895 Admin conf Spike Island 8–9.6.38.
16   Interview with Company Quartermaster Sgt William Robinson. Cobh Co Cork 6.7.78.
17   *An Cosantoir* (Irish Defence Journal) May 1978 'The Defences of Spike Island 1793–1815' by Paul M. Kerrigan.
18   Ibid.
19   *An Cosantoir* May 1978 Historical summary of Fort Dunree.
20   *An Cosantoir* May 1978 Dunree summary quoting Edward Wakefield *An Account of Ireland, Statistical and Political* (1812).
21   *An Cosantoir* July 1978 'Why Lough Swilly was Defended'.
22   Correlli Barnett *The Swordbearers* (Eyre and Spottiswoode) London 1963 pp 121–22.
23   Robinson interview 6.7.78.
24   Details from British War Office maps now in custody of Irish Department of Defence (Cobh) and author's visits to Treaty ports 5–6–23.7.78.

25 PRO FO 53/36 Draft Report Chiefs of Staff Sub-comm.
26 PRO DO 35/895 Mins of Eire/UK meetings on ports 25–27–28.5.38.
27 PRO DO 35/895 Admin conf Spike Island 8–9.6.38.
28 PRO CAB 27/525 Irish Situation Committee 6.4.32.
29 Ibid.
30 PRO ADM 1/9874 Director Local Defence memo 31.7.39.
31 Winston S. Churchill *The Second World War: The Gathering Storm* Vol I (Cassell) London 1948 p 215.
32 Nicholas Mansergh *Documents and Speeches on British Commonwealth Affairs 1931–1952* Vol 1 (OUP) 1953 p 385 (House of Commons Debates Vol 335 coll 1094–1105 5.5.38).
33 NLI MS 18,375 (6) Frank Gallagher Papers.
34 *Irish Independent* 12.7.38.
35 Ibid.
36 Griffin interview 7.5.78.
37 PRO DO 35/895 Mins of Eire/UK meetings on ports 25–27–28.5.38.
38 *Irish Press* 11.7.78 'British Withdrawal – 1938 Style' by Comdt Padraic O'Farrell.
39 PRO DO 35/895 Mins of Eire/UK meetings on ports 25–27–28.5.38.
40 *Irish Press* 11.7.78 O'Farrell op. cit.
41 *Defence Forces Handbook* (Dublin) 1968 p 10.
42 Griffin interview 7.5.78.
43 *Irish Independent* 12.7.38.
44 Ibid.
45 Ibid.
46 Interview with Capt William Glavin (Irish Army escort to de Valera) Cobh Co Cork 5.7.78.
47 The Earl of Longford and Thomas P. O'Neill *Eamon de Valera* (Arrow Books) London 1974 p 324.
48 F.S.L. Lyons *Ireland Since the Famine* (Fontana) London 1978 pp 26–7.
49 Mary C. Bromage *Churchill and Ireland* (University of Notre Dame) Indiana 1964 p 21, quoting H.M. Hyde *Carson* (Heinemann) London 1953 p 242.
50 Bromage op. cit. quoting W.S. Churchill *Irish Home Rule – A Speech . . . at Belfast 8 February 1912* (Liberal Publication Department) London 1912.
51 George Dangerfield *The Damnable Question: A Study in Anglo-Irish Relations* (Constable) London 1977 p 111.
52 Longford and O'Neill op. cit. p 19.
53 Lyons op. cit. p. 311.
54 A.T.Q. Stewart *The Ulster Crisis* (Faber) London 1967 p 241.
55 Dangerfield op. cit. p 156.
56 Dangerfield op. cit. p 158, quoting John Devoy *Recollections of an Irish Rebel* Shannon 1969 p 434.
57 Dangerfield op. cit. p 166, quoting Casement Diary Vol 2 in NLI.
58 Dangerfield op. cit. pp 285–90.
59 Lyons op. cit. p 431.
60 Articles of Agreement for a Treaty between Great Britain and Ireland 6.12.21.
61 Annex to Articles of Agreement 6.12.21 section 1 a–f.

62   Thomas Jones *Whitehall Diary* Vol III ed Keith Middlemass (OUP) London 1971 p 121.

63   Jones op. cit. p 122.

64   Ibid.

65   Jones op. cit. p 90.

66   Jones op. cit. p 120.

67   Mansergh op. cit. p 384 (Churchill in House of Commons 5.5.38).

68   Jones op. cit. p 124

69   Ibid.

70   Ibid.

71   Jones op. cit. pp 139–40.

72   Jones op. cit. p 143.

73   Jones op. cit. pp 143–4.

74   Longford and O'Neill op. cit. pp 74–5, quoting *Christian Science Monitor* 15.5.18.

75   Dangerfield op. cit. p 344.

76   Winston S. Churchill *The World Crisis: The Aftermath* (Thornton Butterworth) London 1929 p 298.

77   Lord Longford *Peace by Ordeal* (Sidgwick & Jackson) London 1972 p 249.

78   Longford and O'Neill op. cit. p 167.

79   Longford and O'Neill op. cit. p 169.

80   Bromage op. cit. p 91, quoting *New York Times* 29.6.22.

81   Lyons op. cit. pp 467–8 n.

82   *Emmet Dalton Remembers* Radio Telefis Eireann 7.2.78 (rpt 22.8.78).

83   For discussion on continuity of Irish political values, see Brian Farrell *The Founding of Dail Eireann* (Gill and Macmillan) Dublin 1971 esp pp 80–4.

84   Lyons op. cit. p 487.

85   Lyons op. cit. p 499, quoting Dail Debates XII 1101–2 (Longford and O'Neill op. cit. p 256 give the phrase as 'no other significance').

86   Longford and O'Neill op. cit. p 274.

87   Lyons op. cit. p 511.

88   Longford and O'Neill op. cit. p 279.

89   *The Times* 5.8.32.

90   *Irish Press* 24.4.33 (quoted in Longford and O'Neill op. cit. p 289).

91   Longford and O'Neill op. cit. p 277.

92   PRO CAB 27/525 Gen Staff memo to Irish Sit Comm 6.4.32.

93   Ibid.

94   PRONI CAB 3/4/21 Blake Papers Naval Information Papers/Comm Imp Def Nov 1931.

95   PRO DO 35/895 Report 19.10.37.

96   PRO CAB 27/525 Irish Sit Comm op. cit.

97   Ibid.

98   PRO CAB 27/525 Admiralty memo to Irish Sit Comm 7.5.32.

99   PRO CAB 27/523 Mins Irish Sit Comm 5.8.32.

100   Tim Pat Coogan *The IRA* (Fontana) London 1980 p 82.

101   Coogan op. cit. p 91.

102   Ibid.

103   Coogan op. cit. pp 93–7 (IRA General Army Convention directive 18.2.33).

104 Coogan op. cit. p 104.
105 Longford and O'Neill op. cit. p 304.
106 PRO CAB 24/262 Committee of Imperial Defence 4.2.36.
107 PRO CAB 24/262 MacDonald Cabinet memo May 1936.
108 *The Times* 29.10.35.
109 This and subsequent paragraphs based on author's interview with Malcolm MacDonald. Sevenoaks, Kent 18.4.78.
110 PRO CAB 24/262 Comm Imp Def 4.2.36.
111 William L. Shirer *The Rise and Fall of the Third Reich* (Pan) London 1960 p 357.
112 PRO CAB 24/262 Comm Imp Def 4.2.36.
113 Longford and O'Neill op. cit. p 304.
114 MacDonald interview 18.4.78.
115 PRO CAB 24/262 MacDonald memo May 1936.
116 MacDonald interview 18.4.78.
117 PRO CAB 27/523 Irish Sit Comm 25.5.36.
118 Ibid.
119 PRO CAB 53/6 Comm Imp Def 6.7.36.
120 Ibid.
121 PRO CAB 53/28 Joint Planning Sub Comm report 27.7.36.
122 PRO CAB 27/527 Appendix I Fisher to Dulanty 14.9.36.
123 PRO CAB 35/895 Report 19.10.37.
124 PRO CO 267/678 Comm Imp Def 4.12.36.
125 PRO CAB 24/271 MacDonald to Cabinet 12.10.37.
126 Ibid.
127 Patrick Keatinge *A Place Among the Nations: Issues of Irish Foreign Policy* (IPA) Dublin 1978 p 71, quoting Dail Debates 21,1455 (16.11.27).
128 Dail Debates Vol II col 2660.
129 Longford and O'Neill op. cit. p 307.
130 Longford and O'Neill op. cit. p 311, quoting Dail Debates Vol 67 coll 721–2 (19.5.37).
131 PRO CAB 27/524 Irish Sit Comm 14.12.37.
132 PRO CAB 53/35 Comm Imp Def 12.1.38.
133 SPO CAB 1/8 Cab mins 23.11.37.
134 Longford and O'Neill op. cit. p 314.
135 MacDonald interview 18.4.78.
136 Longford and O'Neill op. cit. p 314.
137 Longford and O'Neill op. cit. p 322.
138 PRO FO 800/310 Halifax to MacDonald 7.4.38.
139 MacDonald interview 18.4.78.
140 Ibid.
141 PRO CAB 27/523 Irish Sit Comm 25.5.36.
142 Mansergh op. cit. p 376, quoting Dail Debates Vol 71 coll 34–47 (27–28.4.38).
143 PRO CAB 24/523 Irish Sit Comm 4.2.36.
144 Mansergh op. cit. p 379, quoting House of Commons Debates Vol 335 coll 1072–8 (5.5.38).
145 Mansergh op. cit. p 384, quoting House of Commons Debates Vol 335 coll 1094–1105 (5.5.38).

146 Ibid.
147 Griffin interview 7.5.78.
148 Interview with Brendan Murphy. Bere Island Co Cork 6.7.78.
149 MacDonald interview 18.4.78.
150 Griffin interview 7.5.78.
151 *Irish Press* 11.7.78 O'Farrell op. cit.
152 Griffin interview 7.5.78.
153 Murphy interview 6.7.78.
154 PRO DO 35/895 Mins of Eire/UK meetings on ports 25–27–28.5.38.
155 *Irish Independent* 4.10.38.
156 *The Times* 1.10.38.
157 *Irish Press* 11.7.78 O'Farrell op. cit. quoting *Donegal Democrat.*
158 Irish Department of Defence *Fort Dunree Historical Summary* (see also *An Cosantoir* July 1978).

CHAPTER 2 A CERTAIN CONSIDERATION

1 PRO DO 35/895 see esp Mears–Stephenson discussions 10.4.39.
2 Ibid.
3 Lyons op. cit. p 710.
4 John W. Blake *Northern Ireland in the Second World War* (HMSO) Belfast 1956 p 537.
5 PRONI Spender diaries D 715/10 letter to Hannah 30.4.38.
6 PRONI Spender diaries D 715/10 October 1938.
7 *Northern Whig* 3.1.38.
8 Interview with Victor Fiorentini. Londonderry 13.12.78.
9 Lyons op. cit. p 717.
10 John A. Oliver *Working at Stormont* (IPA) Dublin 1978 p 22.
11 Ibid.
12 Patrick Buckland *Ulster Unionism and the Origins of Northern Ireland 1886–1922* (Gill and Macmillan) Dublin 1973 quoting Parl Deb (House of Commons) ser 5 cxxvii 29.3.20 col 989.
13 Lyons op. cit. p 716.
14 Ibid.
15 John F. Harbinson *The Ulster Unionist Party 1882–1973* (Blackstaff) Belfast 1973 p 136 quoting *Debates* (Northern Ireland House of Commons) 1, c36–7.
16 Harbinson op. cit. p 136.
17 *Debates* (Northern Ireland House of Commons) Vol XVI coll 1091–5.
18 Harbinson op. cit. p 137.
19 R.J. Lawrence *The Government of Northern Ireland: Public Finance and Public Services 1921–1964* (OUP) London 1965 p 61.
20 Lyons op. cit. p 714.
21 *Irish News* 1.7.38.
22 Oliver op. cit. p 17.
23 St John Ervine *Craigavon Ulsterman* (Allen & Unwin) London 1949 p 560 quoting *Northern Whig* interview 8.11.40.
24 MacDonald interview 18.4.78.
25 Longford and O'Neill op. cit. p 321.

26 PRONI Spender diaries D 715/15.
27 Ibid.
28 Ibid.
29 Ibid.
30 St John Ervine op. cit. p 70.
31 See, for instance, Carlton Younger *A State of Disunity* (Muller) London 1972 p 214.
32 *The Irish Times* 14.1.38.
33 PRONI Spender diaries D 715/9 letter to Powell.
34 *Northern Whig* 17.1.38.
35 *The Times* 15.1.38.
36 *Northern Whig* 8.1.38 and 6.1.38.
37 *Northern Whig* 4.1.38.
38 *Northern Whig* 3.1.38.
39 *Northern Whig* 7.1.38.
40 *Northern Whig* 14.2.38 quoting *The Sunday Times*.
41 PRO CAB 27/528 Effect of Proposed Treaty on Northern Ireland Industry.
42 PRONI Spender diaries D 715/10 Blackmore to Maxwell 31.3.38.
43 PRO CAB 27/528 Rearmament work in Northern Ireland. March 1938 (also in PRONI Spender diaries D 715/10).
44 Lawrence op. cit. Ch 3 passim.
45 *Northern Whig* 1.2.36.
46 *Northern Whig* 3.1.38.
47 PRONI CAB 9R/60/5 Andrews to Hoare 4.5.38.
48 PRO CAB 27/524 Irish Sit Comm 8.4.38.
49 PRO CAB 27/528 Rearmament work in Northern Ireland March 1938.
50 PRONI Spender diaries D 715/12 March 1939.
51 Blake op. cit. p 65.
52 PRONI Spender diaries D 715/10 October 1938.
53 PRO CAB 27/524 Irish Sit Comm 8.4.38.
54 Blake op. cit. p 51.
55 Blake op. cit. p 54.
56 PRO CAB 27/524 Irish Sit Comm 8.4.38.
57 Ervine op. cit. p 545.
58 Ibid and *The Times* 3.3.26.
59 Ervine op. cit. pp 544–5.
60 Bromage op. cit. p 104, quoting House of Commons Debates Vol 180 col 1666 23.2.25.
61 *Daily Mail* 29.3.32.
62 *Daily Mail* 15.2.33.
63 *Daily Mail* 29.3.32.
64 *Daily Mail* 1.5.35.
65 Ibid.
66 Winston S. Churchill *My Early Life: A Roving Commission* (Thornton Butterworth) London 1930 p 16.
67 *Daily Mail* 1.5.35.
68 *Daily Mail* 15.2.33.
69 NLI MS 18,375 (6) Frank Gallagher Papers.

70   PRO FO 800/310 Inskip/de Valera 8.9.38.
71   PRO DO 35/893/XII/247 Chamberlain note 4.10.38.
72   Shirer op. cit. pp 514–5.
73   PRO DO 35/893/XII/247 Devonshire note 4.10.38.
74   *Sunday Press* (Dublin) 'Ireland on the Brink' by Dr Eduard Hempel (as told to John Murdoch) 17.11.63.
75   Longford and O'Neill op. cit. p 339.
76   Shirer op. cit. p 438, 471n.
77   Speech to League 13th Assembly 26.9.32 (President de Valera *Recent Speeches and Broadcasts* (Talbot Press) Dublin 1933 p 39).
78   *Irish Press* 17.9.35.
79   Lyons op. cit. p 552.
80   SPO S8083 External Affairs memo 24.9.35.
81   Maurice Manning *The Blueshirts* (Gill and Macmillan) Dublin 1971 p 207, quoting Eoin O'Duffy *Crusade in Spain* (Dublin) 1938 p 248.
82   *The Irish Times* 3–4.9.35.
83   Patrick Keatinge *The Formulation of Irish Foreign Policy* (IPA) Dublin 1973 p 24 quoting Dail Debates 62,2660 18.6.36.
84   Keatinge *A Place Among the Nations* op. cit. p. 157, quoting Dail Debates 62,2655 18.6.36.
85   T. Ryle Dwyer *Irish Neutrality and the USA 1939–47* (Gill and Macmillan) Dublin 1977 p 23.
86   Longford and O'Neill op. cit. pp 338–9.
87   PRO FO 800/310 Inskip/de Valera 8.9.38.
88   PRO DO 35/894/X31/18 16.9.38.
89   PRO DO 35/894/X31/18 Harding memo 17.9.38.
90   PRO DO 35/894/X31/18 letter to Stephenson 17.9.38.
91   PRO DO 35/894/X31/18 Butler memo 26.9.38.
92   UCD Archives Deirdre McMahon *Malcolm MacDonald and Anglo–Irish Relations 1935–8* MA thesis 1975.
93   *Irish Studies in International Affairs* Vol 1 no 1 (Royal Irish Academy) Dublin 1979 'Ireland, the Dominions and the Munich Crisis' by Deirdre McMahon.
94   Keatinge *A Place Among the Nations* op. cit. p 157.
95   PRO DO 35/894/X31/18 Butler memo.
96   PRO PREM 1/249 De Valera to Chamberlain 27.9.38.
97   PRO DO 35/894/X31/18 Stephenson note 3.10.38.
98   SPO CAB 2/2 Cab mins 13.9.38.
99   SPO CAB 2/2 Cab mins 7.11.38.
100 PRO DO 35/893/XII/247 Devonshire note 4.10.38.
101 PRO DO 35/893/XII/247 Chamberlain note 4.10.38.
102 Keatinge *A Place Among the Nations* op. cit. pp 38–9, quoting *Irish Review* Vol III July 1913 224–5.
103 Churchill *The World Crisis: The Aftermath* op. cit. pp 424–9.
104 Interview with Dr Cornelius Cremin. Dublin 11.1.79.
105 De Valera *Recent Speeches and Broadcasts* op. cit. p 59 Broadcast to United States 12.2.33.
106 De Valera *Recent Speeches and Broadcasts* op. cit. p 11 Broadcast to United States 4.3.32.

107 Longford and O'Neill op. cit. p 338.
108 PRO FO 53/36 Comm Imp Def Appendix II.
109 Figures from Department of Defence, Dublin 4.4.79.
110 PRO FO 53/36 Comm Imp Def Appendix II.
111 Details from Department of Defence, Dublin 4.4.79.
112 *An Cosantoir* March 1975 'Armour in the War Years' by Denis J. McCarthy.
113 Ibid.
114 PRO 53/36 Comm Imp Def Appendix II.
115 Figures from Department of Defence, Dublin 4.4.79.
116 SPO S10826 and S8332A July 1938.
117 SPO S10826 Dept Defence 8.9.38 Ref no 2/55096.
118 PRO CAB 53/41 MacDonald note 12.10.38.
119 Ibid.
120 PRO FO 53/36 Comm Imp Def Draft Report and Appendix I.
121 PRO CAB 53/42 Inskip note 20.10.38.
122 Interview with Frank Aiken. Dublin 12.4.79.
123 Coogan op. cit. p 154.
124 PRO CAB 53/42 Inskip note 20.10.38.
125 PRO CAB 53/42 Comm Imp Def 26.10.38.
126 PRO CAB 53/42 Comm Imp Def 31.10.38.
127 *Evening Standard* (London) 17.10.38.
128 Liam de Paor *Divided Ulster* (Penguin) London 1977 pp 149–50.
129 PRONI Spender diaries D 715/7 7–22.12.35.
130 PRO DO 35/89311/XII/251.
131 PRO FO 800/310 MacDonald note 23.12.38.
132 Ibid.
133 PRO FO 800/310 American Dept note 30.12.38.
134 Longford and O'Neill op. cit. p 100.
135 Coogan op. cit. p 162.
136 Brendan Behan *Borstal Boy* (Corgi) London 1970 p 13.
137 Coogan op. cit. pp 162–3.
138 Coogan op. cit. p 156.
139 SPO CAB 2/2 Cab mins 10–20–25.2.39 see also 11.5.39.
140 PRO CAB 27/524 Irish Sit Comm 14.12.37.
141 *Sunday News* (Belfast) 28.1.68 'The Brookeborough Memoirs' as told to Ken Nixon.
142 PRONI CAB 4/408/5 Cab conclusions 10.1.39.
143 Coogan op. cit. p 153.
144 Kevin Boland *Up Dev!* (Kevin Boland) Dublin 1977 p 17.
145 See K.R.M. Short *The Dynamite War: Irish–American Bombers in Victorian Britain* (Gill and Macmillan) Dublin 1979.
146 Boland Papers 2(X).
147 Interview with Helmut Clissmann. Dublin 14.4.79.
148 Enno Stephan *Spies in Ireland* (Four Square) London 1965 p 20.
149 Carolle J. Carter *The Shamrock and the Swastika: German Espionage in Ireland in World War II* (Pacific Books) Palo Alto, California 1977 p 101.
150 Carter op. cit. p 103.
151 Stephan op. cit. p 30.

152   Clissmann interview 14.4.79.
153   Ibid.
154   Carter op. cit. p 28.
155   *Sunday Press* 17.11.63 Hempel op. cit. (and correction *Sunday Press* 29.12.63).
156   Shirer op. cit. p 577n.
157   PRO FO 800/310 Chamberlain note 27.3.39.
158   PRONI Spender diaries D 715/10.
159   Ibid.
160   PRONI CAB 4/410/4 Cab concl 10.2.39.
161   *Irish Press* 3.5.39.
162   *Irish Press* 1.5.39 and 3.5.39.
163   Blake op. cit. p 194.
164   SPO S12432 Cable to de Valera 1.5.39.
165   David Irving *The War Path: Hitler's Germany 1933–9* (Michael Joseph) London 1978 p 206.
166   Shirer op. cit. p 577.
167   *Manchester Guardian* 29.4.39.
168   *Daily Mirror* 1.5.39.
169   *The Times* 2.5.39.
170   *Evening Standard* 1.5.39.
171   *Manchester Guardian* 29.4.39.
172   *Belfast Telegraph* 26.4.39.
173   *Northern Whig* 14.1.38.
174   Stewart op. cit. p 62.
175   *Sunday News* 28.1.79 interview with Kirk.
176   Ervine op. cit. p 547, quoting Lady Craigavon's diary for 2.5.39.
177   *Irish Press* 5.5.39.
178   Ibid.
179   *Irish Press* 6.5.39.
180   *Irish Press* 5.5.39.
181   *Irish Press* 11.5.39.
182   *Irish Times* 5.5.39.
183   *Irish Press* 6.5.39.
184   *Irish Press* 5.5.39.
185   Blake op. cit. p 85.
186   Blake op. cit. pp 52–4.
187   Ervine op. cit. p 550.
188   Blake op. cit. p 537 Appendix I.
189   SPO S11394 Department of Industry and Commerce 18.4.39.
190   SPO S10823 Department of the Taoiseach 6.9.38.
191   SPO S10868A Department of Finance 24.9.38.
192   *An Cosantoir* August 1978 'Armoured Fighting Vehicles of the Army'.
193   SPO S10868A Dept Fin 24.9.38.
194   SPO S10823 Dept Taoiseach 6.9.38.
195   Dail Debates Vol 74 col 719.
196   *Documents on German Foreign Policy 1918–45* Series D Vol VII (HMSO) London 1952 p 471 Hempel to Foreign Ministry 31.8.39.
197   PRO FO 371/23966 Liesching 5.7.39.

198 Interview with William Warnock. Dublin 14.6.78.
199 Bernard Share *The Emergency: Neutral Ireland 1939–45* (Gill and Macmillan) Dublin 1978 p 2.
200 PRONI CAB 9CD/2/2 Scales to Gransden 2.9.39.
201 PRONI CAB 9CD/129 Situation report 2.9.39.
202 PRONI CAB 9CD/129 Wickham to Pim 2.9.39.
203 Interview with Professor Rodney Green. Belfast 10.9.79.
204 PRONI CAB 9CD/129 Harrison to Wickham 4.9.39.
205 Ibid.

CHAPTER 3 THE WEAPONS OF COERCION

1 Interview with Peggy Fanning (nee Bristow). Dalkey, Co Dublin 13.8.79.
2 SPO S11470 Department of Justice memorandum 7.10.39.
3 SPO S11133A External Affairs to Sarsfield 5.9.39.
4 SPO S11133A Revenue Commissioners to Hogan 5.10.39.
5 SPO S11470 Dept Justice memo 7.10.39.
6 *Sunday News* 28.1.68 Brookeborough Memoirs op. cit.
7 SPO S11470 Dept Justice memo 7.10.39.
8 Ibid.
9 Dail Debates Vol 77 cols 1–8 de Valera statement 2.9.39.
10 Nicholas Bethell *The War Hitler Won: September 1939* (Allen Lane) London 1972 p 233.
11 Lord Avon *The Eden Memoirs: The Reckoning* (Cassell) London 1965 p 69.
12 Longford and O'Neill op. cit. p 351.
13 SPO S11417A.
14 PRO CAB 66/1 Appendix I 12.9.39.
15 Coogan op. cit. p 172.
16 PRO CAB 66/1 Appendix II Maffey 14.9.39.
17 Avon op. cit. p 69.
18 PRO CAB 66/1 Eden memorandum 16.9.39.
19 PRO DO 35/1107 Maffey 20.9.39.
20 Ibid.
21 Avon op. cit. p 69.
22 PRO DO 35/1107 Maffey 20.9.39.
23 *The Irish Times* 26.9.39.
24 *The Irish Times* 11.9.39.
25 *The Irish Times* 15.9.39.
26 Ibid.
27 *The Irish Times* 8.9.39.
28 *The Irish Times* 9.9.39 Accounts by crew of *Olive Grove*.
29 PRO AIR 27/1955 RAF 502 Squadron Operations Record Book (abbreviated account of 502 ops can also be found in PRONI Blake papers CAB 3/A/1–46).
30 *The Irish Times* 25.9.39.
31 PRO CAB 66/1 Churchill memorandum 17.9.39.
32 Martin Gilbert *Winston S. Churchill Vol V 1922–1939* (Heinemann) London 1976 p 1026 (Churchill speech 6.12.38).
33 Gilbert op. cit. p 1036 (Churchill to wife 18.1.39).

34 Winston S. Churchill *The Second World War: The Gathering Storm* Vol I (Cassell) London 1948 p 335 Churchill to First Sea Lord and others 5.9.39.
35 Ibid.
36 Ibid.
37 Churchill *The Gathering Storm* op. cit. p 215.
38 PRO ADM 1/9874 31.7.39.
39 PRO ADM 1/9874 Wallworth note 8.9.39.
40 PRONI Blake papers CAB 3/A/22 (Transcript of original Admiralty file MO 13914/39).
41 PRO ADM 1/9874 16.9.39.
42 Churchill College Archives Inskip diaries 1/2 p 50 (Vol II) 18.9.39.
43 Churchill College Archives Inskip diaries 1/2 p 53 (Vol II) 19.9.39.
44 Churchill *The Gathering Storm* op. cit. pp 582–3 Churchill to First Sea Lord and others 24.9.39.
45 Ibid.
46 Bethell op. cit. p 243.
47 PRO AIR 27/1955 RAF 502 Squadron Operations Record Book.
48 *The Irish Times* 27.9.39.
49 Irving op. cit. pp 33–5.
50 PRO CAB 65/1 Cabinet mins 17.10.39.
51 PRO CAB 53/35 Committee of Imperial Defence 12.1.38.
52 PRO CAB 66/2 Phillips memorandum 18.10.39.
53 Lord Avon *The Eden Memoirs: Facing the Dictators* (Cassell) London 1962 p 116.
54 PRO FO 800/310 Malkin (plus Annex) 19.10.39.
55 PRO FO 800/310 Eden to Malkin 20.10.39.
56 PRO FO 800/310 Churchill note 20.10.39.
57 PRO FO 800/310 Halifax 23.10.39.
58 *Daily Mail* 29.3.32.
59 Mansergh op. cit. p 388, quoting House of Commons Debates Vol 335 coll 1094–1105 (Churchill speech 5.5.38).
60 PRO CAB 66/2 Maffey Appendix 20.10.39.
61 PRO FO 800/310 Eden to Malkin 20.10.39.
62 PRO CAB 66/2 Maffey report 21.10.39.
63 PRO FO 800/310 Extract from War Cabinet conclusions 24.10.39 Also PRO CAB 65/1.
64 PRO CAB 65/1 24.10.39.
65 PRO FO 800/310 Extract from War Cabinet conclusions 24.10.39 Also PRO CAB 65/1.
66 PRO CAB 67/2 Law Lords memorandum 7.11.39.
67 PRONI Blake papers CAB 3/A/21 Churchill to Eden 26.10.39.
68 Churchill *The Gathering Storm* op. cit. p 577 Churchill to Director of Naval Intelligence 6.9.39.

CHAPTER 4 ANY SORT OF STICK TO BEAT EIRE

1 PRO CAB 66/1 Eden memorandum 16.9.39.
2 PRO CAB 65/1 Cabinet minutes 15.9.39.
3 Churchill College Archives Inskip diaries 1/2 p 50 (Vol II) 18.9.39.

4   PRO CAB 66/1 Eden memorandum 16.9.39.

5   Dangerfield op. cit. p 286.

6   Maurice O'Sullivan *Twenty Years A-Growing* (OUP) 1975 p 1.

7   *The Irish Times* 21.7.79 'Aran in the Thirties' by Breandan O hEithir.

8   Niall Fallon *The Armada in Ireland* (Stanford Maritime) London 1978 p 214.

9   Frank O'Connor *Leinster, Munster and Connaught* (Robert Hale) London p 268.

10   Kevin B. Nolan and T. Desmond Williams (eds) *Ireland in the War Years and After 1939–51* (Gill and Macmillan) Dublin 1969 'Education and Language, 1938–51' by Donal McCartney p 88.

11   PRO AIR 27/1955 RAF 502 Squadron Operations Record Book.

12   PRO CAB 66/3 Index 131 (Folios 237 and 238).

13   PRO ADM 173/15709 Log of HM Submarine *H 33*.

14   Joseph T. Carroll *Ireland in the War Years 1939–1945* (David & Charles/Crane, Russak & Company, Inc) Newton Abbot and New York 1975 p 35.

15   PRO ADM 1/10138 Reports of Proceedings of *H 43* and *Tamura* 9–21.11.39.

16   PRO ADM 1/10138 Dunbar-Nasmith to Admiralty Secretary 3.12.39.

17   PRO ADM 1/10138 Intelligence Division to Captain Greig 14.12.39.

18   Confidential source. Dublin.

19   *Irish Press* 5.10.39.

20   *Irish Press* 6.10.39.

21   Ibid.

22   Ibid.

23   *The Irish Times* 6.10.39.

24   Interview with Michael O'Sullivan. Dingle, Co Kerry 14.4.78.

25   J.C. Taylor *German Warships of World War II* (Doubleday/Ian Allen) 1966 p 112.

26   PRO CAB 66/2 Maffey to Eden 26.10.39.

27   PRO AIR 24/366 Operations Record Book Headquarters Coastal Command 6.10.39.

28   PRO ADM 199/1829 Op orders for *Tamura* and *H 43* 11.1.40.

29   PRO ADM 199/1829 *H 43* narrative 12–26.1.40.

30   PRO ADM 199/1829 Staff minute sheet 9.2.40.

31   PRO CAB 66/1 Eden memorandum 16.9.39.

32   PRO CAB 66/1 Dulanty 12.9.39.

33   *The Irish Times* 3.9.79 (Supplement) 'The Days of Emergency' by Colonel Dan Bryan.

34   Carter op. cit. pp 142–6 and Stephan op. cit. pp 64–7.

35   Churchill *The Gathering Storm* op. cit. p 583 Note to First Sea Lord and Director of Naval Intelligence 24.9.39.

36   PRO ADM 199/1829 Report of proceedings *Tamura* 27.2.40 to 11.3.40.

37   Baltimore Harbour Commission register (F. Nolan) 30.3.40.

38   Interviews in Baltimore (interviewees requested anonymity) 7.7.78.

39   PRO ADM 199/1829 Report of proceedings *Tamura* 27.2.40 to 11.3.40.

40   PRO ADM 199/1829 Record of proceedings *H 43* 24–31.5.40.

41   IWM CVJ/8 C.V. Jack papers. Vice Admiral Campbell 11.4.40.

42   IWM CVJ/8 C.V. Jack papers. Jack to Rear Admiral Taylor 24.7.40.

43 IWM CVJ/8 C.V. Jack papers. Vice Admiral Campbell 11.4.40.
44 Gilbert op. cit. p 397.
45 Nicholas Bethell *The Palestine Triangle: The Struggle between the British, the Jews and the Arabs 1935–48* (André Deutsch) London 1979 p 37 see also *Journal of Palestine Studies* (Beirut) Vol VIII No 2 'Jewish Military Recruitment in Palestine, 1940–1943' by Ronald W. Davis p 56.
46 PRO PREM 3/131/2 Morton to Swinton 8.6.40.
47 Ibid.
48 PRO PREM 3/131/2 Chamberlain to Churchill 12.6.40.
49 PRO PREM 3/131/2 Morton to Swinton 8.6.40.
50 PRO PREM 3/131/2 Morton to Churchill 10.6.40.
51 PRO PREM 3/131/2 Churchill note to Chamberlain and Caldecote 11.6.40.
52 PRO PREM 3/129/2 Intelligence report 20.7.40.
53 PRO DO 3/151 Index.
54 PRO PREM 3/129/2. Intelligence report on west coast of Ireland 20.7.40.
55 Interview with Regina Boyd (née Hemersbach). Inver, Co Donegal 14.8.78.
56 Telephone interview with Stuart McIvor. Lisburn, Co Antrim 19.8.78.
57 Interview with Florence Dunleavy (formerly Coyle, née Hemersbach). Mountcharles, Co Donegal 17.8.78.
58 Interview with William Rose. Inver, Co Donegal 17.8.78.
59 Interview with Colonel Dan Bryan. Dublin 15.12.78.
60 PRO PREM 3/129/2 Intelligence report on west coast of Ireland 20.7.40.
61 Interview (anonymous at interviewee's request). Glenties, Co Donegal 17.8.78.
62 PRO PREM 3/129/2 Intelligence report on west coast of Ireland.
63 Bryan interview 15.12.78.
64 PRO PREM 3/129/2 Intelligence report. 20.7.40.
65 Ibid.
66 PRO PREM 3/129/2. RUC report 20.7.40.
67 Bryan interview 15.12.78.
68 SPO S12014A Marcus to Moynihan 6.6.41.
69 SPO S12014A Moynihan to Roche 19.6.41.
70 SPO S12014A Carroll to Roche 23.6.41.
71 SPO S12014A Roche to Moynihan 24.6.41.
72 SPO S12014A Moynihan to Marcus 26.6.41.
73 SPO S12014A Roche to Moynihan 29.8.41.
74 UCD Archives Mulcahy papers P7a/220 Mulcahy to Boland 8.6.40.
75 PRONI Spender diaries D 715/15 Note of conversation with Maffey 11.12.40.
76 Carter op. cit. pp 191–4 and Stephan op. cit. pp 124–8.
77 Winston S. Churchill *The Second World War: Their Finest Hour* Vol II (Cassell) London 1949 p 639.
78 Blake op. cit. p 302.
79 PRO PREM 3/129/2. Intelligence report on west coast of Ireland 20.7.40.
80 Ibid.
81 Interview with Frank Ward. Aranmore Island, Co Donegal 15.8.78.
82 Rose interview 17.8.78.

83   Murphy interview 6.7.78.
84   Interview with Paddy Brosnan. Dingle, Co Kerry 14.4.78.
85   Interview with Mort O'Leary. Dingle, Co Kerry 15.4.78.
86   O'Sullivan interview 14.4.78.
87   Ibid.
88   Glavin interview 5.7.78.
89   Interview with Michael Brick. Brandon, Co Kerry 15.4.78.
90   Interview with Hugh Wrenn. Brixton, London 18.5.78.
91   Winston S. Churchill *The Second World War: The Grand Alliance* Vol III (Cassell) London 1950 p 697.
92   PRONI CAB 61/861 Postal Censorship 'Dick' to Murphy 20.5.41.
93   PRONI CAB 61/861 Postal Censorship. Nottage letter 9.7.41.
94   Interview with Frank Aiken. Dublin 12.4.79.
95   *Eire–Ireland* (Irish American Cultural Institute) Vol XII 'Ireland: America's Neutral Ally, 1939–1941' by Carrolle J. Carter.
96   PRO ADM 1/17089 letter dated 24.3.44.
97   PRO ADM 1/17089 Admiralty to Little 1.4.44.
98   PRO ADM 1/17089 Private Office note 31.3.44.
99   SPO S9559A Transcript of de Valera reply in Dail Eireann 25.4.44.
100   Cecil Woodham-Smith *The Great Hunger: Ireland 1845–1849* (Hamish Hamilton) London pp 412–3.
101   Interview with Professor Rodney Green. Belfast 10.9.79.
102   Interview (anonymous) Glenties, Co Donegal 17.8.78.

CHAPTER 5 WITHIN THE WAR ZONE

1   *Sunday Press* 17.11.63 Hempel op. cit.
2   *Documents on German Foreign Policy 1918–45* Series D Vol VIII (HMSO) London 1954 p 242 Hempel to Foreign Ministry 8.10.39.
3   *Documents on German Foreign Policy 1918–45* Series D Vol IX (HMSO) London 1956 p 423 Hempel to Foreign Ministry 23.5.40.
4   *Documents on German Foreign Policy 1918–45* Series D Vol VIII op. cit. p 760 Woermann memorandum 10.2.40.
5   *Documents on German Foreign Policy 1918–45* Series D Vol VIII op. cit. p 405 Hempel to Woermann 14.11.39.
6   *Sunday Press* 17.11.63 Hempel op. cit.
7   *Documents on German Foreign Policy 1918–45* Series D Vol VIII op. cit. p 242 Hempel to Foreign Ministry 8.10.39.
8   SPO S5803A1 copy of Executive Council minutes 21.5.37.
9   PRONI Spender diaries D 715/15 Maffey conversation 11.12.40.
10   PRO Prem 3/129/2. RUC report 20.7.40.
11   *Sunday Press* 17.11.63 Hempel op. cit.
12   Ibid.
13   *Sunday Press* 29.12.63 Hempel op. cit.
14   Carroll op. cit. p 33.
15   Carroll op. cit. p 40.
16   Ibid.
17   PRO PREM 3/131/2 General Report on Position in Eire.
18   SPO CAB 2/3 Cabinet minutes 11.12.39.

19 SPO S8658A Department of External Affairs to President 6.11.36.
20 SPO S8658A Department of Defence October 1938.
21 SPO S8658A Department of Defence 25.8.38.
22 *The Irish Times* 21.10.38.
23 *Studies* March 1938 'The Vulnerability of Ireland in War' by Col J.J. O'Connell see SPO S8658A.
24 SPO CAB 2/2 Cabinet minutes 18.7.39.
25 SPO CAB 2/3 Cabinet minutes 29.11.39.
26 SPO S11342 Sean Moylan to Aiken 15.11.39.
27 SPO CAB 2/3 Cabinet minutes 17.5.40.
28 SPO S11101 Department of Defence to Government 3.6.40.
29 SPO CAB 2/3 Cabinet minutes 17.5.40.
30 SPO S11101 Department of Defence to Government 7.5.41.
31 Ibid.
32 Boland Papers 2 (d).
33 Ibid.
34 SPO CAB 2/3 Cabinet minutes 28.5.40.
35 Share op. cit. pp 58, 67.
36 Longford and O'Neill op. cit. p 363.
37 Interview with Enda Boland. Dublin 30.1.78.
38 UCD Archives Mulcahy papers P7/C/113 Note of 1.2.41.
39 Boland Papers 4(x).
40 UCD Archives Mulcahy papers P7/C/111 Note of 13.11.40.
41 UCD Archives Mulcahy papers P7/C/112 Note of 5.7.40.
42 Ibid.
43 SPO S11586A Emergency Powers Order 1939. Knightly.
44 SPO CAB 2/2 Cabinet minutes 1.9.39.
45 SPO S11450 Department of Justice memorandum 21.9.39.
46 Share op. cit. p 32.
47 SPO S11306 Connolly to de Valera 19.9.39.
48 SPO S9559A Knightly to Connolly 20.11.39.
49 SPO S11586A 'Neutrality, Censorship and Democracy' Aiken to Government 23.1.40.
50 Ibid.
51 Ibid.
52 SPO S11586A Connolly to Government 15.1.40.
53 SPO S11586A MacEntee to Government 6.2.40.
54 SPO S11586A Connolly to Government 3.7.40.
55 SPO S11586A Connolly to Government 25.1.41.
56 UCD Archives Mulcahy papers P7/C/113 proof from *The Irish Times* 20.5.41.
57 UCD Archives Mulcahy papers P7/C/113 Mulcahy–Smyllie correspondence 21.5.41.
58 PRO FO 371/89108 Balinski report 27.1.41.
59 SPO S11586A Connolly to Moynihan 30.7.41.
60 Ibid.
61 SPO S11586A Note to Moynihan 30.7.41.
62 Carroll op. cit. p 116.
63 SPO S11306 Department of External Affairs to de Valera and draft 15.2.43.

64 SPO S11306 Extract from Dail Eireann Debates 3.2.43.
65 *Irish Press* 12.7.40.
66 PRO CAB 67/6 Maffey memorandum 10.5.40.
67 Ibid.
68 *Eamon de Valera Speeches and Statements 1917–1973* ed Maurice Moynihan (Gill and Macmillan) Dublin 1980 p 435 de Valera at Galway 12.5.40.
69 *Sunday Press* 22.12.63 Hempel op. cit.
70 Ibid.
71 PRO CAB 67/6 Maffey telegram to Dominions Office 16.5.40.
72 PRO CAB 66/2 Maffey to Eden 26.10.39.
73 PRO PREM 3/129/2. RUC report 20.7.40.
74 Bryan interview 2.6.78.
75 Ibid.
76 Interview with confidential Irish Army source 2.6.78.
77 *Irish Press* 19.12.40.
78 SPO S12125 Collis to McNamara.
79 SPO S12125 Department of Justice memorandum 28.5.41.
80 SPO S12125 Walshe memorandum 20.11.40.
81 SPO S12094A Department of Defence to Cabinet Committee on Emergency Problems 11.10.40.
82 *An Cosantoir* August 1979 'The Mad Escape' by T. Ryle Dwyer (reprinted from *The Canadian* March 1978).
83 SPO S12094A Department of Defence to Government 14.1.42.
84 *An Cosantoir* August 1979 Dwyer op. cit.
85 Ibid.
86 SPO S12094A Walshe to Taoiseach's Department 3.1.42.
87 UCD Archives Mulcahy papers P7a/213 Notes of 29.12.40.
88 SPO S12026A Emergency Powers (51) Order September 1940.
89 SPO S12123 Department of Justice memorandum 17.10.40.
90 SPO S12123 Department of Justice memorandum 25.10.40.
91 PRONI CAB 9R/60/5 Dominions Office memorandum.
92 Carroll op. cit. pp 83–4.
93 PRONI CAB 9R/60/5 Dominions Office memorandum.
94 PRONI CAB 4/432/39 Cabinet conclusions 30.4.40.
95 PRONI CAB 9R/60/5 Andrews memorandum 30.4.40.
96 PRONI CAB 9R/60/5 Anderson to Andrews 3.5.40.
97 PRONI CAB 9R/60/5 Robertson to Gransden 6.5.40.
98 PRONI COM 61/113 Northern Ireland minutes of Ryan meeting 14.12.39.
99 PRONI COM 61/61 Scott memorandum 16.9.39.
100 PRONI COM 61/183 Cooke-Collis to Andrews and memorandum 30.11.39.
101 Blake op. cit. p 199.
102 Lawrence op. cit. p 64.
103 Blake op. cit. p 78.
104 *Sunday News* 28.1.68 Brookeborough Memoirs op. cit.
105 Ervine op. cit. p 554.
106 PRONI COM 61/61 Notes of Cooke-Collis/Gransden telephone conversation and minutes of Ministry of Information meeting 12.9.39.
107 Ibid.

108 Blake op. cit. p 82.
109 PRONI CAB 3/A/78 Inspector General's Office. Folder No 66. 1945.
110 Blake op. cit. p 82n3.
111 PRONI Blake papers CAB3/A/49.
112 Blake op. cit. p 82n3.
113 PRO PREM 3/131/2 Intelligence report 20.7.40.
114 Ibid.
115 Ervine op. cit. p iv.
116 Ervine op. cit. p 552.
117 PRONI CAB 4/438/3 Cabinet conclusions 20.5.40.
118 PRONI CAB 4/439/4 Cabinet conclusions 25.5.40.
119 PRONI Spender diaries D 715/14 6–11.5.40.
120 Churchill *Their Finest Hour* op. cit. p 23 Churchill to Roosevelt 15.5.40.
121 A. Hezlet *The 'B' Specials: A History of the Ulster Special Constabulary* (Pan) London 1973 pp 141, 151n3.
122 Ervine op. cit. p 553.
123 PRONI CAB 4/439/4 Cabinet conclusions 25.5.40.
124 Churchill College Archives Hickleton Papers A4/410/19/1A (microfilm) Halifax to Churchill 24.5.40.

CHAPTER 6 AN OFFER OF UNITY AND THE RULE OF 'EQUAL HOLDS'

1 PRO CAB 67/6 Anderson memorandum 17.5.40.
2 PRO PREM 3/130 Minutes of Machtig–Walshe meeting 23.5.40.
3 PRO PREM 3/130 Ismay to Churchill 29.5.40.
4 Ibid.
5 PRO CAB 66/8 Chiefs of Staff minutes 30.5.40.
6 Peter Fleming *Invasion 1940* (Hart-Davis) London 1957 pp 171–2 quoting Invasion Warning Sub-Committee.
7 PRO PREM 3/131/2 Chamberlain to Craigavon 12.6.40.
8 Longford and O'Neill op. cit. p 365.
9 PRO PREM 3/131/2 Chamberlain to Churchill 12.6.40.
10 PRO PREM 3/131/2 Chamberlain to Craigavon 12.6.40.
11 PRO PREM 3/131/2 Chamberlain to de Valera 12.6.40.
12 PRO PREM 3/131/2 Craigavon to Chamberlain 14.6.40.
13 Longford and O'Neill op. cit. p 365.
14 PRO PREM 3/131/2 Chamberlain to Craigavon 17.6.40.
15 Interview with Malcolm MacDonald. Sevenoaks, Kent. 18.4.78.
16 *The Diaries of Sir Alexander Cadogan* Edited by David Dilkes (Cassell) London p 341.
17 MacDonald interview 18.4.78.
18 PRO PREM 3/131/1 MacDonald memorandum 17.6.40.
19 PRO CAB 66/9 Cabinet minutes 20.6.40.
20 Cadogan Diaries op. cit. p 305.
21 Ibid.
22 PRO CAB 66/9 Cabinet minutes 20.6.40.
23 MacDonald interview 18.4.78.
24 PRO PREM 3/131/1 MacDonald memorandum 21–22.6.40.
25 Ibid.

26 PRO CAB 66/9 Chamberlain memorandum 25.6.40.
27 Ibid.
28 Ibid.
29 PRO PREM 3/131/2 British note to Eire Government 26.6.40.
30 Ibid.
31 PRO PREM 3/131/2 Craigavon to Chamberlain 26.6.40.
32 PRO PREM 3/131/1 MacDonald memorandum of meeting of 26.6.40.
33 SPO CAB 2/3 Cabinet minutes 27.6.40.
34 PRO PREM 3/131/1 MacDonald memorandum of meeting of 27.6.40.
35 Ibid.
36 Ibid.
37 Ibid.
38 Ibid.
39 PRO PREM 3/131/1 MacDonald to Churchill 27.6.40.
40 PRO PREM 3/131/2 Chamberlain to Craigavon 26.6.40.
41 Patrick Buckland *James Craig Lord Craigavon* (Gill and Macmillan) Dublin 1980 p 121, quoting Spender diaries for March–October 1938.
42 PRO PREM 3/131/2 Craigavon to Chamberlain 27.6.40.
43 PRO PREM 3/131/2 Chamberlain to Craigavon (undated).
44 PRO PREM 3/131/1 MacDonald to Churchill 27.6.40.
45 PRO PREM 3/131/1 Chamberlain to de Valera 28.6.40.
46 Ibid.
47 Ibid.
48 PRO PREM 3/131/2 Chamberlain to de Valera 29.6.40.
49 PRO PREM 3/131/2 Craigavon to Chamberlain 29.6.40.
50 PRO PREM 3/131/2 Craigavon memorandum 6.7.40.
51 Longford and O'Neill op. cit. pp 122–3.
52 Ervine op. cit. p 558, quoting *The Witness* 5.7.40.
53 PRO PREM 3/131/2 de Valera to Chamberlain 4.7.40.
54 Carlton Younger *A State of Disunion* (Muller) London 1972 p 212 (1925 election slogan).
55 MacDonald interview 18.4.78.
56 UCD Archives Mulcahy papers P7/C/112 Notes of de Valera interview 2.7.40.
57 Ibid.
58 Ibid.
59 MacDonald interview 18.4.78.
60 Aiken interview 12.4.79.
61 Boland Papers 5(x), 6(x), 7(x).
62 Boland Papers 7(x).
63 Aiken interview 12.4.79.
64 PRO CAB 66/10 Maffey to Dominions Office 17.7.40.
65 Longford and O'Neill op. cit. p 366.
66 Ervine op. cit. p 559.
67 Buckland op. cit. p 57, quoting PRONI CAB 4/30/9.
68 *Sunday News* 28.1.68 Brookeborough Memoirs op. cit.
69 Interview with Lord Brookeborough. Brookeborough, Co Fermanagh 12.8.78.
70 Interview with Lord MacDermott. Belfast 11.8.78.

71 Ibid.
72 PRONI Spender diaries D 715/15 Special Note.
73 Shirer op. cit. p 476, quoting British White Paper (Cmd 5847 no 2).
74 Churchill *Their Finest Hour* op. cit. p 180 Churchill to Reynaud 16.6.40.
75 MacDonald interview 18.4.78.
76 Churchill *Their Finest Hour* op. cit. pp 498–9 Churchill to Roosevelt 8.12.40.

CHAPTER 7 OPERATION 'GREEN' AND THE 'W' PLAN

1   IWM EDS M1/14/302 Box 356 *Militärgeographische Angaben über Irland* (Textheft) Berlin 30.9.40 p 15.
2   *An Cosantoir* March 1974 'Gruen, German Military Plans and Ireland, 1940' by Charles Burdick.
3   IWM EDS M1/14/302 Box 356 *Militärgeographische Angaben über Irland* (Textheft) op. cit. p 8.
4   *An Cosantoir* March 1974 Burdick op. cit.
5   Shirer op. cit. p 913.
6   Shirer op. cit. pp 375, 819, 1188, 375.
7   IWM EDS M1/14/302 Box 356 *Landing Irland (Grün)* (Plan 'Green') 12.8.40.
8   Fleming op. cit. p 250.
9   IWM EDS M1/14/302 Box 356 *Landing Irland (Grün)* op. cit.
10 Ibid.
11 *An Cosantoir* March 1974 Burdick op. cit.
12 IWM EDS M1/14/302 Box 356 *Landing Irland (Grün)* op. cit.
13 Ibid.
14 Fleming op. cit. p 243.
15 IWM EDS M1/14/302 Box 356 *Landing Irland (Grün)* op. cit.
16 Fleming op. cit. p 243.
17 Fleming op. cit. p 254.
18 Fleming op. cit. p 248.
19 IWM EDS M1/14/302 Box 356 *Landing Irland (Grün)* op. cit.
20 Walter Warlimont *Inside Hitler's Headquarters* (Weidenfeld and Nicolson) London 1964 p 106.
21 Fleming op. cit. p 262.
22 Fleming op. cit. p 262 n2.
23 *An Cosantoir* March 1974 Burdick op. cit.
24 David Irving *Hitler's War* (Hodder and Stoughton) London 1977 p 185.
25 A. Martienssen *Hitler and His Admirals* (Secker & Warburg) London 1948 Appendix II.
26 Ibid.
27 Ibid.
28 IWM EDS M1/14/302 Box 356 *Militärgeographische Angaben über Irland* (Textheft) op. cit. p 14.
29 IWM EDS M1/14/302 Box 356 *Militärgeographische Angaben über Irland* (Textheft) op. cit. p 15.
30 IWM EDS M1/14/302 Box 356 *Militärgeographische Angaben über Irland* (Textheft) op. cit. p 44.

31   *An Cosantoir* March 1975 'Militärgeographische Angaben über Irland' by Comdt Colm Cox.

32   IWM EDS M1/14/302 Box 356 *Militärgeographische Angaben über Irland* (Textheft) op. cit.

33   IWM EDS M1/14/302 Box 356 *Militärgeographische Angaben über Irland* (Bildheft).

34   IWM EDS M1/14/302 Box 356 *Stadtdurch/Fahrt/Planee* 1940.

35   *An Cosantoir* March 1975 Cox op. cit.

36   IWM EDS M1/14/302 Box 356 *Süd Und Ostküste* 31.5.41; *West Und Nordküste* 15.11.41.

37   *An Cosantoir* March 1975 Cox op. cit.

38   IWM EDS M1/14/302 Box 356 *Süd Und Ostküste* 31.5.41 see also *Letter from America* (US Office of War Information, Dublin) Vol III No 26 20.5.45.

39   IWM EDS M1/14/302 Box 356 *Küsten-Beschreibung des Irischen Freistaates (Eires)* (Oberfehldshaber der Luftwaffe) 1942.

40   UCD Archives Mulcahy papers P7/C/113 Note of 8.1.41.

41   Bryan interview 2.6.78.

42   Brosnan interview 14.4.78.

43   David Lampe *The Last Ditch* (Cassell) London 1968 p 40.

44   Lampe op. cit. p 176 (original in IWM EDS).

45   PRO PREM 3/130 Minutes of Machtig–Walshe meeting 23.5.40.

46   PRO PREM 3/130 Minutes of Machtig–Walshe meeting 24.5.40.

47   Carroll op. cit. pp 43–4.

48   Ibid.

49   Carroll op. cit. p 44.

50   Correspondence Public Record Office to the author 7.9.79 PRO WO 166/271 (War Diaries BTNI) is under 'restricted access'.

51   PRO PREM 3/130 Minutes of Clarke–Machtig meeting 28.5.40.

52   PRO PREM 3/130 Minutes of Machtig–Walshe meeting 24.5.40.

53   PRO PREM 3/130 Dominions Office. Annex 27.5.40.

54   Blake op. cit. p 157.

55   PRONI Blake papers CAB 3/A/49 BTNI War Diary 16.12.40.

56   Ibid.

57   Ibid.

58   PRONI CAB 3/A/52 'Q' (Movements) Northern Ireland September 1939 – June 1945 p 20.

59   *The Second World War: A Guide to Documents in the Public Record Office* (HMSO) London 1972 p 218.

60   PRONI Blake papers CAB 3/A/21 Note of 25.10.40 (British Cabinet Committee 235).

61   Carroll op. cit. p 98.

62   PRONI Blake papers CAB 3/A/49 BTNI War Diary 1942.

63   Carroll op. cit. p 98.

64   PRONI Blake papers CAB 3/A/49 BTNI War Diary February 1942.

65   PRONI CAB 3/A/52 'Q' (Movements) op. cit. p 21.

66   PRONI Blake papers CAB 3/A/49 BTNI War Diary November 1941.

67   Churchill *Their Finest Hour* op. cit. p 153 Churchill to Ismay 30.6.40.

68   PRONI Blake papers CAB 3/A/49 BTNI War Diary August 1941.

69 PRONI Blake papers CAB 3/A/49 BTNI War Diary October 1941.
70 PRONI Blake papers CAB 3/A/21 Admiralty memorandum 17.1.41.
71 PRONI Blake papers CAB 3/A/21 Admiral Forbes 4.5.41.
72 PRONI Blake papers CAB 3/A/21 (British Cabinet Committee 235) February 1941.
73 PRONI Blake papers CAB 3/A/21 Vice Admiral submarines memorandum 24.12.40.
74 PRONI Blake papers CAB 3/A/21 GOC BTNI 4.4.41.
75 Interview with James Kelly (*Irish Independent*) Dublin 10.6.78.
76 PRONI CAB 3/A/52 'Q' (Movements) op. cit. pp 21–2.
77 Ibid.
78 Carroll op. cit. p 98.
79 PRONI Blake papers CAB 3/A/49 BTNI War Diary August 1941.
80 H. Montgomery Hyde *The Londonderrys: A Family Portrait* (Hamish Hamilton) London 1979 p 255.
81 *The Memoirs of Field Marshal the Viscount Montgomery of Alamein KG* (Collins) London 1958 p 70.
82 Ibid.
83 Irving *Hitler's War* op. cit. p 185.
84 Churchill *Their Finest Hour* op. cit. p 172 6.11.40.
85 Carroll op. cit. p 71.
86 UCD Archives Mulcahy papers P7a/220 26.6.40.
87 Ibid.
88 Confidential Dublin source.
89 UCD Archives Mulcahy papers P7a/220 26.6.40.
90 UCD Archives Mulcahy papers P7/C/112 see also p 163 of this book.
91 UCD Archives Mulcahy papers P7/C/111 1.7.40.
92 Confidential Belfast source.
93 SPO S11101 Department of Defence memorandum 3.10.40.
94 Nolan and Williams op. cit. p 48 'Irish Defence Policy 1938–51' by G.A. Hayes-McCoy.
95 Share op. cit. pp 46–7.
96 *An Cosantoir* May 1980 'A Short History of the Air Corps' by Lt Col M. Cassidy.
97 Ibid.
98 Share op. cit. pp 95, 97.
99 UCD Archives Mulcahy papers P7/C/114 O'Higgins 3.3.41.
100 Carroll op. cit. p 98.
101 Interview with Kevin Boland. Rathcoole, Co Dublin 27.1.78.
102 Ibid.
103 *An Cosantoir* June 1980 'Autumn Exercises, 1940' by Lt Col M.T. Duggan Rtd.
104 Griffin interview 7.5.78.
105 UCD Archives Mulcahy papers P7/C/113 Note of 10.4.41 (Defence Conference of 3.4.41).
106 Griffin interview 7.5.78.
107 Ibid.
108 Boland interview 27.1.78.
109 UCD Archives Mulcahy papers P7/C/113 Note of 10.4.41 (Defence Conference of 3.4.41).

110 See Padraic O'Farrell *Who's Who in the Irish War of Independence 1916–1921* (Mercier) Cork 1980 *passim*.
111 *The Irish Times* 4.7.80.
112 *The Irish Times* 3.7.80.
113 PRO PREM 3/129/2 Intelligence report 20.7.40.
114 *An Cosantoir* April 1980 'The Development of the Irish Volunteers 1916–1922' Part III Risteard Mulcahy.
115 UCD Archives Mulcahy papers P7/C/111 Note 13.11.40.
116 Interview with James Dillon. Dublin 10.7.79.
117 UCD Archives Mulcahy papers P7/C/111 Note 14.6.40.
118 UCD Archives Mulcahy papers P7/C/111 Note 15.6.40.
119 UCD Archives Mulcahy papers P7/C/112 Note 5.7.40.
120 UCD Archives Mulcahy papers P7/C/114 Note 12.9.40.
121 UCD Archives Mulcahy papers P7/C/112 Note 18.10.40.
122 UCD Archives Mulcahy papers P7/C/111 Cosgrave memorandum 15.11.40.
123 UCD Archives Mulcahy papers P7/C/114 Dillon note 26.11.40.
124 UCD Archives Mulcahy papers P7/C/113 Mulcahy note 24.12.40.
125 UCD Archives Mulcahy papers P7/C/113 Mulcahy to de Valera 24.12.40.
126 UCD Archives Mulcahy papers P7/C/113 Note of meeting 27.12.40.
127 Carroll op. cit. pp 75–6.
128 Ibid.
129 *An Cosantoir* November 1979 'The Days of Emergency' (Copies of letters in *The Irish Times*).
130 Ibid.
131 Aiken interview 12.4.79.
132 Bryan interview 15.12.78.
133 SPO S11394 de Valera broadcast to United States.
134 *Sunday Press* 17.11.63 Hempel op. cit.
135 Carroll op. cit. p 37.
136 Carter op. cit. p 29.
137 Carter op. cit. pp 162–3, 166.
138 Carter op. cit. p 166.
139 Bryan interview 2.6.78.
140 Carter op. cit. p 163.
141 Bryan interview 2.6.78.
142 Griffin interview 7.5.78.
143 *An Cosantoir* May 1978 'Celtic Cloaks and Teutonic Daggers' Lt Col J.P. Duggan.
144 *The Irish Times* 27.8.80 letter from William P. Ryan.
145 Carroll op. cit. p 75.
146 *Documents on German Foreign Policy 1918–1945* Series D Vol XI (HMSO) London 1961 pp 882–3 Hempel to Ribbentrop/Weizsacker 17.12.40.
147 *Sunday Press* 17.11.63 Hempel op. cit.
148 UCD Archives Mulcahy papers P7/C/113 De Valera interview 30.1.41.
149 Ibid.
150 UCD Archives Mulcahy papers P7/C/113 Note of 1.2.41.
151 UCD Archives Mulcahy papers P7/C/113 Note of 24.5.41.
152 Ibid.

153   UCD Archives Mulcahy papers P7/C/114 O'Higgins 3.3.41.
154   UCD Archives Mulcahy papers P7a/213 Note of 7.4.41.
155   SPO S12014A Candy 1.8.40.
156   SPO S12014A Madigan 7.9.40.
157   SPO S12014A Extract from Cabinet minutes of 2.7.40.
158   SPO S11986A Department of Defence 11.7.40 see also *Irish Press* 7.2.41.
159   SPO S11986A Department of Finance memorandum 31.5.40.
160   SPO S11986A Office for the Coordination of Defensive Measures 25.7.40.
161   SPO CAB 2/3 Cabinet minutes 29.10.40.
162   SPO S11986A Taoiseach's Department memorandum 24.1.42.
163   SPO S11986A Memorandum from Mr T. Barry October 1942.
164   SPO S11986A Moynihan to Barry 14.1.43.
165   SPO S11986A Government memoranda 23.12.42.
166   Ibid.
167   SPO S12199 Draft of Taoiseach statement 28.10.40.
168   SPO S12199 Department of External Affairs memorandum 26.2.41.
169   Ibid.
170   SPO S12199 Government memorandum 21.9.41.
171   SPO S12199 Gallagher draft 30.10.41.
172   SPO S12199 Taoiseach's Department comparison Sweden/Ireland 5.6.44.
173   SPO S12067 Department of Defence memorandum 16.4.41.
174   SPO S12067 Secret Order 1940 signed Col Liam O hAodha.
175   SPO S12067 Draft of Information Bureau on Military Courts (No 2) Order January 1941.
176   Ibid.
177   SPO S12067 Memorandum for Cabinet Committee on Emergency Problems 4.3.41.
178   Ibid.
179   SPO S12273 Kinnane to Roche 23.1.41.
180   SPO S12273 Kinnane to Roche 14.2.41.
181   SPO S12273 Roche to Moynihan 25.2.41.
182   Ibid.
183   SPO S12273 Kinnane to Garda Siochana 28.2.41.
184   SPO S12273 Department of Defence memorandum 30.4.42.
185   SPO S12223 Department of Defence memorandum 19.12.41.
186   SPO S12223 POW (Internment) Regulations.
187   SPO S12223 Handwritten note Taoiseach's Department 6.12.40.
188   SPO S11992 Lemass to Moynihan 12.10.40.
189   SPO S11992 Walshe to Moynihan 25.10.40.
190   SPO CAB 2/3 Cabinet minutes 23.7.40.
191   SPO S11992 Walshe to Moynihan 25.10.40.
192   Ibid.
193   SPO S12199 Taoiseach's Department memoranda 19.11.40, 17.2.41.
194   SPO S12199 Taoiseach's Department memoranda 29.4.41, 15.5.41.
195   SPO S12156 Taoiseach's Department memorandum 23.7.40.
196   SPO S12156 Lemass to Moynihan 23.10.40.
197   SPO S12156 Walshe to Moynihan 1941 British military occupation of Samoa 1914.
198   SPO S12156 Department of Finance memorandum 26.11.41.

199 SPO S12156 Department of Finance to Moynihan 20.7.42.
200 Ibid.
201 *Irish Independent* 25.4.49 'A German Airborne Attack on the North' by General Kurt Student.
202 *Irish Independent* 26.4.49 'Airfields around Belfast as Paratroop Objectives' by General Kurt Student.
203 Ibid.
204 Ibid.
205 PRO PREM 3/129/2 Intelligence report 20.7.40.
206 Ibid.
207 Ibid.
208 PRONI CAB 3/A/41 RAF to Carr 29.6.40.
209 PRONI CAB 4/443/4 Draft Cabinet conclusion 15.6.40.
210 Ibid.
211 PRONI CAB 9CD/169/2 Hatty to Craigavon 31.5.40.
212 PRONI CAB 9CD/169/2 Gilbert to Craigavon 21.5.40.
213 PRONI CAB 9CD/169/2 Crawford to Craigavon 12.5.40.
214 PRONI CAB 9CD/169/2 Crawford to Craigavon 20.5.40.
215 PRONI CAB 9CD/169/2 Crawford to Craigavon 17.5.40.
216 PRONI CAB 9CD/169/2 Crawford to Craigavon 12.5.40.
217 PRONI COM 61/671 Guide to Co-ordination of Civil and Military Action in Northern Ireland 1940 (Guide).
218 PRONI CAB 9CD/169/1 Wilson Hungerford to Craigavon 24.5.40.
219 PRONI CAB 9CD/169/1 MacDermott memorandum to Cabinet 18.10.40.
220 PRONI CAB 9CD/169/1 MacDermott parliamentary reply 22.10.40.
221 PRONI CAB 4/453/4 Draft Cabinet conclusion 29.10.40.
222 PRONI CAB 4/455/13 Packenham-Walsh to Craigavon 22.11.40.
223 Ibid.
224 PRONI CAB 9CD/169/1 MacDermott memorandum to Cabinet 3.12.40.
225 MacDermott interview 11.8.78.
226 PRONI CAB 9CD/169/1 Maxwell to Gransden 11.3.41.
227 PRONI CAB 9CD/169/1 MacDermott note 25.9.41.
228 Hesketh op. cit. pp 144–5.
229 PRONI COM 61/568 Civil Administration in Extreme Emergency 1940 (Guide).
230 PRONI Blake papers CAB 3/A/21 Report of M15 visit to Belfast 28–30.8.40.
231 Blake op. cit. p 158.
232 PRONI Blake papers CAB 3/A/49.
233 Blake op. cit. p 163.
234 MacDermott interview 11.8.78.
235 Ibid.
236 PRONI COM 61/573 Franklyn to Andrews 29.6.41.
237 PRONI COM 61/568 Northern Ireland Defence Executive Committee 15.7.40.
238 PRONI COM 61/568 Northern Ireland Home Defence Executive 12.7.41.
239 PRONI COM 61/568 Northern Ireland Home Defence Executive 16.4.41.
240 PRONI COM 31/378 Spender to Scott 6.8.40 (also in PRONI COM 61/573).

241 Confidential Belfast source.
242 PRONI COM 61/568 Freer to Scales 27.1.42
243 PRO ADM 1/13032 Secretary of State for War to GOC BTNI August 1942.
244 Ibid.
245 PRO ADM 1/13032 Secretary of State for War to GOC Northern Ireland District 1943.
246 PRO ADM 1/13032 Noble to Secretary of the Admiralty 18.4.42 (also in PRONI Blake papers CAB 3/A/21).
247 PRO ADM 1/13032 Forbes to Secretary of the Admiralty 27.4.42 (also in PRONI Blake papers CAB 3/A/21).
248 PRO ADM 1/13032 Dominions Office to Maffey 15.10.42.
249 PRO ADM 1/13032 Maffey to Dominions Office 16.10.42.
250 PRO ADM 1/13032 Fremantle and Fletcher to Commander-in-Chief Western Approaches 13.12.42.
251 PRO ADM 1/13032 Irish Army Cork Harbour Defences (Major D.J. Collins) 27.11.42.
252 PRO ADM 1/13032 Fremantle and Fletcher Appendices 13.12.42.
253 PRO ADM 1/13032 Note of Admiralty Director of Plans 6.1.43.
254 NLI MS 18, 375 (6) Frank Gallagher Papers (p 52).
255 Clissmann interview 14.4.79.
256 PRONI COM 61/568 Home Defence Executive file. Pollock to Gransden 11.7.41 (also in PRONI COM 61/573).
257 Ibid.
258 Confidential Dublin source.
259 Ibid.
260 Ibid.
261 PRO PREM 3/131/1 Macdonald memorandum 17.6.40.
262 Confidential Dublin source. Irish Army exercise 28.6.41.

CHAPTER 8 THE NEUTRAL ISLAND IN THE HEART OF MAN

1   Interview with Bruce Williamson. Dublin 29.8.79.
2   PRO CAB 66/8 Chiefs of Staff to Cabinet 30.5.40.
3   PRONI Blake papers CAB 3/A/19 Director of Anti-Submarine Warfare minutes 23.8.40.
4   PRONI Blake papers CAB 3/A/19 Naval papers 2.9.40.
5   PRONI Blake papers CAB 3/A/19 Director of Local Defence minutes 25.8.40.
6   PRONI Blake papers CAB 3/A/19 Director Ordnance Depots minutes 13.9.40.
7   Bryan interview 15.12.78.
8   Blake op. cit. p 313.
9   Blake op. cit. pp 321–2.
10 Blake op. cit. p 332.
11 Blake op. cit. p 333.
12 Hugh Shearman *Northern Ireland 1921–1971* (HMSO) Belfast 1971 p 178.
13 Blake op. cit. p 319.
14 Churchill *Their Finest Hour* op. cit. p 529.

15   Erskine op. cit. p 560, quoting *Northern Whig.*

16   Erskine op. cit. p 560, quoting *Public Opinion.*

17   Erskine op. cit. p 560, quoting *Daily Express* 15.11.40.

18   Ibid.

19   Nolan and Williams op. cit. p 55 'Ulster During the War and After' by David Kennedy.

20   Nolan and Williams op. cit. p 55, quoting Hansard (Northern Ireland) xxiii, 1272 (28.5.40).

21   Nolan and Williams op. cit. p 55, quoting Hansard (Northern Ireland) xxiii, 2162 (25.9.40).

22   PRONI Spender diaries D 715/15 11–16.11.40.

23   Erskine op. cit. p 561.

24   Erskine op. cit. pp 563–4.

25   Erskine op. cit. p 561.

26   PRONI Spender diaries D 715/22 9–15.8.43.

27   Ibid.

28   Paul Bew, Peter Gibbon and Henry Patterson *The State in Northern Ireland 1921–72: Political Forces and Social Classes* (Manchester University Press) 1979 pp 82–4.

29   PRONI Spender diaries D 715/15 Special Note October 1940.

30   Ervine op. cit. p 562.

31   *Sunday News* 4.2.68 Brookeborough Memoirs op. cit.

32   Erskine op. cit. p 567.

33   PRONI CAB 4/455/15 Cabinet conclusions 5.12.40.

34   Harbinson op. cit. p 139.

35   PRO CAB 66/10 Maffey to Dominions Office 17.7.40.

36   PRO CAB 66/10 Caldecote to Maffey 16.7.40.

37   PRO CAB 66/10 Maffey to Dominions Office 17.7.40.

38   Ibid.

39   PRO CAB 66/10 Caldecote to Cabinet 20.7.40.

40   PRO CAB 66/10 Eden memorandum 'Equipment for Eire' 25.7.40.

41   PRO CAB 66/10 Eden to War Cabinet 17.7.40.

42   Churchill *Their Finest Hour* op. cit. p 639 Appendix B Table II.

43   Winston S. Churchill *War Speeches 1939–45* Vol I (Compiled by Charles Eade) (Cassell) London 1951 Speech to House of Commons 5.11.40.

44   Longford and O'Neill op. cit. p 374, quoting Dail Debates lxxxi 583–6 Speech to Dail 7.11.40.

45   PRO FO 800/310 Mrs Cameron (Elizabeth Bowen) Dominions Office file 9.11.40.

46   Churchill *Their Finest Hour* op. cit. pp 496–8 Churchill to Roosevelt 8.12.40.

47   PRO PREM 3/131/7 Churchill to Beaverbrook 13.11.40.

48   Lord Avon *The Reckoning* op. cit. p 70.

49   PRONI Spender diaries D 717/15 Special Note 16.11.40.

50   Ibid.

51   PRONI Spender diaries D 715/15 11–16.11.40.

52   B.H. Liddell Hart *History of the Second World War* (Cassell) London 1970 p 394.

53   Cyril Falls *The Second World War* (Methuen) London 1948 p 92.

54 *The Memoirs of General the Lord Ismay* (Heinemann) London 1960 p 152.

55 Ronald Lewin *Ultra Goes to War: The Secret Story* (Hutchinson) London 1978 pp 195–6.

56 David Kahn *Hitler's Spies: German Military Intelligence in World War II* (Hodder and Stoughton) London 1978 p 217.

57 Arnold and Veronica Toynbee (eds) *The War and the Neutrals* (OUP) London 1956 Part iii 'Eire' by Constance Howard p 240, quoting *Manchester Guardian* 21.11.40.

58 Henry Harrison *The Neutrality of Ireland: Why It Was Inevitable* (Robert Hale) London 1940 pp 72–7.

59 Nicholas Monsarrat *The Cruel Sea* (Cassell) London 1951 pp 151–2.

60 Ibid.

61 Ibid.

62 Louis MacNeice *Selected Poems* edited by W.H. Auden (Faber) London. 'Neutrality'.

63 PRONI Spender diaries D 715/15 Spender to Hankey 9.11.40.

64 PRONI Spender diaries D 715/15 Hankey to Spender 27.11.40.

65 PRONI Spender diaries D 715/15 Spender to Hankey 2.12.40.

66 PRONI Spender diaries D 715/15 26–31.5.41.

67 PRO CAB 66/14 Wood memorandum 6.12.40.

68 Ibid.

69 Carroll op. cit. p 85.

70 SPO S12235 Lemass memorandum 1.1.41.

71 SPO S12235 British reply to Lemass (undated).

72 SPO S12235 Lemass memorandum (and enclosure) 30.1.41.

73 PRO PREM 3/131/3 Maffey memorandum 20.1.41.

74 PRONI Spender diaries D 715/15 16–21.12.40.

75 UCD Archives Mulcahy papers P7/C/113 de Valera interview 30.1.41 (note dated 1.2.41).

76 PRO PREM 3/131/3 Maffey memorandum 20.1.41.

77 Ibid.

78 PRO PREM 3/131/3 Cranborne to Churchill 30.1.41.

79 Ibid.

80 PRO PREM 3/131/3 Churchill to Cranborne 31.1.41 (see also Winston S. Churchill *The Second World War: The Grand Alliance* Vol III (Cassell) London 1950 p 645).

81 PRO PREM 3/131/4 Cranborne to Churchill 17.2.41.

82 PRO PREM 3/131/4 Maffey note (with Cranborne to Churchill) 17.2.41.

83 PRO PREM 3/131/4 Churchill to Cranborne 19.2.41.

84 Churchill *Their Finest Hour* op. cit. p 690.

85 Longford and O'Neill op. cit. pp 378–9.

86 UCD Archives Mulcahy papers P7/C/113 Note of 24.12.40.

87 UCD Archives Mulcahy papers P7/C/113 de Valera interview 30.1.41 (note of 1.2.41).

88 Brendan Murphy interview 6.7.78.

89 Churchill *The Grand Alliance* op. cit. p 697 Appendix E.

90 UCD Archives Mulcahy papers P7/C/114 Fine Gael Front Bench meeting 4.3.41.

91 Ibid.

92   PRO PREM 3/131/7 Cranborne to Churchill 22.4.41.
93   PRO PREM 3/131/7 Maffey to Machtig 10.3.41.
94   PRO PREM 3/131/7 Extract from Dillon speech, attached to Maffey letter 10.3.41.
95   PRO PREM 3/131/7 Cranborne to Churchill 22.4.41.
96   PRO PREM 3/131/7 Maffey to Machtig 13.3.41.
97   PRO PREM 3/131/7 Maffey to Machtig 10.3.41.
98   Churchill *The Grand Alliance* op. cit. p 641 Churchill to Cranborne 17.1.41.
99   PRO PREM 3/131/5 Duff Cooper Exchange Telegraph report 7.5.41.
100 PRO PREM 3/131/5 Churchill to Duff Cooper 10.5.41.
101 PRO FO 800/310 Bradbury to Churchill June 1940.
102 PRO FO 800/310 Archer to Martin 7.6.40.
103 PRO PREM 3/131/7 Maffey memorandum 14.3.41.
104 Ibid.
105 PRO CAB 66/15 Cranborne memorandum 19.3.41.
106 PRO FO 371/29108 Maffey to Dominions Office 24.2.41.
107 Aiken interview 12.4.79.
108 PRO FO 371/29108 Maffey to Dominions Office 24.2.41.
109 Longford and O'Neill op. cit. p 225.
110 Williamson interview 29.8.79.
111 Dwyer op. cit. p 100.
112 Aiken interview 12.4.79.
113 Dwyer op. cit. p 112.
114 Aiken interview 12.4.79.
115 Dwyer op. cit. pp 112–3, quoting *Irish Press* 7.5.58 'My War-Time Mission in Washington' by Robert Brennan.
116 Aiken interview 12.4.79.
117 Dwyer op. cit. pp 112–3, quoting *Irish Press* 7.5.58 op. cit.
118 Aiken interview 12.4.79.
119 Carroll op. cit. pp 102–3.
120 Aiken interview 12.4.79.
121 UCD Archives Mulcahy papers P7/C/113 Copy of Aiken speech in Boston.
122 Ibid.
123 Dwyer op. cit. p 114.
124 Aiken interview 12.4.79.
125 Dwyer op. cit. p 114.
126 Carroll op. cit. p 107.
127 Carroll op. cit. p 106.
128 PRO FO 371/29108 Maffey to Machtig 15.5.41.
129 PRO PREM 3/131/7 Cranborne to Churchill 22.4.41.
130 PRO CAB 66/27 Chiefs of Staff to War Cabinet Annex I 6.8.42.
131 PRO PREM 3/129/6 Grigg to Churchill and extract from War Cabinet 27.7.42.
132 PRO PREM 3/131/6 Cranborne to Churchill 19.12.41.
133 PRO FO 371/32591 Brown to Lawford 5.2.42 containing Churchill minute of 5.2.42.
134 PRO CAB 66/27 Chiefs of Staff report to War Cabinet 6.8.42.
135 PRO PREM 3/130 Attlee to Churchill 12.3.42.

136   PRO PREM 3/130 Ismay to Churchill 16.3.42 and Churchill minute 25.3.42.
137   PRO PREM 3/130 Attlee to Churchill 23.3.42 and Churchill minute 25.3.42.
138   Winston S. Churchill *The Second World War: The Hinge of Fate* Vol IV (Cassell) London 1951 p 777 Churchill to Attlee 6.6.42.
139   SPO CAB 2/4 Cabinet minutes 8.10.41.
140   National Archives State Department RG 59 841 D. 24/11 Green memorandum 28.7.39.
141   National Archives State Department RG 59 841 D. 24/6 Green memorandum 17.5.39.
142   SPO S28208 Department of the President memorandum 'War. Essential Materials' 4.12.35.
143   SPO S11980 Report of the Interdepartmental Committee on Emergency Measures 4.7.40.
144   Nolan and Williams op. cit. p 34 'The Irish Economy During the War' by James F. Meenan.
145   SPO S10868A Department of Finance memorandum April 1939.
146   SPO S10868A Department of Finance 3.2.41.
147   SPO S11394 Taoiseach's Broadcast 29.1.41.
148   *Irish Press* 13.1.42.
149   SPO S11394 Dillon memorandum 7.2.41.
150   SPO S11394 Department of Supplies memorandum 15.2.41.
151   PRO CAB 72/25 Secretary for Mines memorandum 27.4.42.
152   Churchill *Their Finest Hour* op. cit. p 535 Churchill to Wood 1.12.40.
153   PRO CAB 72/25 Selbourne to Attlee 14.8.42 and Committee on Economic Policy Towards Eire 11.9.42.
154   PRO CAB 72/25 Attlee memorandum 16.3.43 and Dulanty to Attlee 23.2.43.
155   SPO S11394 Department of Supplies memorandum 16.8.43.
156   Ibid.
157   Ibid.
158   Churchill *Their Finest Hour* op. cit. p 536 Former Naval Person (Churchill) to Roosevelt, 13.12.40.
159   SPO S11394 Department of Supplies memorandum 16.8.43.
160   Frank Forde *The Long Watch: The History of the Irish Mercantile Marine in World War Two* (Gill and Macmillan) Dublin 1981 p 2.
161   SPO S12239 Interdepartmental Committee on Shipping 20.12.40.
162   Forde op. cit. p 36.
163   Forde op. cit. pp 68–80.
164   UCD Archives Mulcahy papers P7a/213 Note of 8.4.41.
165   Forde op. cit. p 71.
166   Brendan Murphy interview 6.7.78.
167   Forde op. cit. pp 26–7.
168   SPO S12203A, quoting Dail Debates 20.2.41.
169   SPO S12203A Copy of *Glencullen* Master's report.
170   Ibid.
171   SPO S12203A Department of Industry and Commerce to Taoiseach's Department 26.3.41.

172 SPO S12203A A. Moloney and Sons Ltd to Department of Industry and Commerce 31.3.41.
173 SPO S12203A A. Moloney and Sons Ltd to Department of Industry and Commerce 18.4.41.
174 Forde op. cit. p 110.
175 SPO S12203A Wexford Steamships Company to Department of Defence 26.4.41.
176 SPO S12203A MacEntee to Government 26.9.41.
177 Ibid.
178 Forde op. cit. pp 118–9.
179 Ibid.
180 Forde op. cit. pp 119–23.
181 PRO ADM 1/17075 Alexander to Cranborne 4.1.44.
182 PRO ADM 1/17075 Cranborne to Alexander 7.1.44.
183 Forde op. cit. p 105.
184 Forde op. cit. pp 46–7.
185 Forde op. cit. pp 15–7.
186 Forde op. cit. p 88 see also *An Cosantoir* March 1979 'SS "Kyleclare" of Limerick in World War II' by Frank Forde.
187 Ibid.
188 Bryan interview 2.6.78.
189 Glavin interview 5.7.78.
190 Copy of Supplement 3 to German Standing War Orders No 105 in possession of Douglas Gageby.
191 Copy of Supplement 3 to German Standing War Orders No 104 in possession of Douglas Gageby.
192 Forde op. cit. p 57.
193 Forde op. cit. p 90.
194 Guide to St Peter's Church, Malmo p 4.
195 *An Cosantoir* January 1978 'Irish Merchant Seamen's Memorial' by Captain Frank Forde.
196 PRO PREM 3/131/6 Churchill to de Valera 8.12.41.
197 NLI MS 18,375 (6) Frank Gallagher Papers (p 52).
198 Longford and O'Neill op. cit. pp 392–3.
199 Ibid.
200 PRO PREM 3/131/6 Maffey to Dominions Office 8.12.41.
201 PRO PREM 3/131/6 Note on Churchill to de Valera letter 8.12.41.
202 PRO PREM 3/131/6 Cranborne to Churchill 8.12.41.
203 Ibid.
204 PRO PREM 3/131/6 de Valera to Churchill 10.12.41.
205 PRO PREM 3/131/6 Churchill to de Valera 11.12.41.
206 PRO PREM 3/131/6 Dominions Office to Maffey 11.12.41.
207 Longford and O'Neill pp 394–5.
208 PRO PREM 3/131/6 Cranborne to Churchill 19.12.41.
209 Ibid.
210 Ibid.
211 PRO PREM 3/131/6 Churchill to Cranborne 20.12.41.
212 *Eamon de Valera Speeches and Statements 1917–1973* op. cit. pp 461–2 de Valera at Cork 14.12.41.

213 Confidential Dublin source.
214 PRONI Blake papers CAB 3/A/49 (Copy of Civil Defence file PR 535).
215 Carter op. cit. p 84.
216 PRONI Blake papers CAB 3/A/49.
217 Carter op. cit. p 77.
218 Carter op. cit. p 79.
219 Ibid.
220 PRONI Blake papers CAB 3/A/49.
221 Carter op. cit. p 84.
222 PRONI Blake papers CAB 3/A/49.
223 Brick interview 15.4.78.
224 Confidential Dublin source (report of 23.6.44).
225 Glavin interview 5.7.78.
226 Griffin interview 7.5.78.
227 Carroll op. cit. p 121.
228 PRONI Blake papers CAB 3/A/46 Air Ministry records 15.8.42.
229 Carroll op. cit. p 120.
230 Griffin interview 7.5.78.
231 Confidential Dublin source.
232 *An Cosantoir* December 1980 Official report dated 23.3.42 and article by Lt Col N.C. Harrington.
233 Brick interview 15.4.78.
234 Ibid.
235 PRONI Blake papers CAB 3/A/49.
236 *Hibernia Weekly Review* (Dublin) 28.6.79 Dermot McEvoy.
237 *An Cosantoir* May 1980 Air Corps History op. cit.
238 Dillon interview 10.7.79.
239 Carroll op. cit. p 116, quoting *Foreign Relations of the United States* papers 1942 Vol I.
240 Dillon interview 10.7.79.

CHAPTER 9 THE 'NATURAL' ALLY

1 *Documents on German Foreign Policy 1918–45* Series D Vol VIII (HMSO) London 1954 pp 241–2 Hempel to Foreign Ministry 8.10.39.
2 Ibid.
3 Ibid.
4 Ibid.
5 Stephan op. cit. p 50.
6 Stephan op. cit. pp 51–2.
7 Carter op. cit. pp 94–5, quoting Abwehr II War Diary and Paul Leverkuehn *German Military Intelligence* (translated by R.H. Stevens and C. FitzGibbon (Weidenfeld and Nicolson) London 1954.
8 Carter op. cit. p 96.
9 PRO PREM 3/131/2 Morton to Swinton 8.6.40.
10 Bryan interview 15.12.78.
11 Clissmann interview 14.4.79.
12 Information supplied by Bord na Mona, Dublin 9.8.79.
13 Clissmann interview 14.4.79.

14 Coogan op. cit. pp 176–7.
15 Boland Papers 2(x), 3(x).
16 Boland Papers 2(x).
17 *Documents on German Foreign Policy 1918–45* Series D Vol VIII op. cit. pp 405–6 Hempel to Woermann 14.11.39.
18 Ibid.
19 *Documents on German Foreign Policy 1918–45* Series D Vol VIII op. cit. pp 545–6 Hempel to Woermann 16.12.39.
20 PRONI COM 61/15 Ministry of Economic Warfare to York Street Flax Spinning Co 24.6.40.
21 Sean Cronin *Frank Ryan: The Search for the Republic* (Repsol) Dublin 1980 p 183.
22 Coogan op. cit. p 177.
23 Boland Papers 3(x).
24 SPO CAB 2/3 Cabinet minutes 23.2.40.
25 Coogan op. cit. pp 182–3.
26 Carter op. cit. p 112.
27 *Documents on German Foreign Policy 1918–45* Series D Vol VIII op. cit. p 693 Schmid to Foreign Ministry 24.1.40.
28 *Documents on German Foreign Policy 1918–45* Series D Vol VIII op. cit. pp 760–1 Woermann to Ribbentrop 10.2.40.
29 Ibid.
30 Cronin op. cit. p 177, quoting NLI McGarrity papers.
31 *Documents on German Foreign Policy 1918–45* Series D Vol VIII op. cit. pp 760–1 Woermann to Ribbentrop 10.2.40.
32 Ibid.
33 Carter op. cit. p 113.
34 Carter op. cit. p 114.
35 Clissmann interview 14.4.79.
36 Ibid.
37 Cronin op. cit. p 188.
38 Cronin op. cit. p. 189, quoting Abwehr II War Diary.
39 *Sunday Press* 17.11.63 Hempel op. cit.
40 Cronin op. cit. p 189.
41 *Eamon de Valera Speeches and Statements 1917–1973* op. cit. pp 420–2 de Valera 9.11.39.
42 Ibid.
43 Coogan op. cit. pp 187–9.
44 Stephan op. cit. p 95.
45 Boland Papers 13(x), 14(x).
46 SPO S11931A Record of third day of trial (MacCurtain) 13.6.40 sent to Taoiseach's Department.
47 Ibid.
48 *History of the 20th Century* No 46 (Purnell) p 1288 'De Valera Between the Wars' by David Thornley.
49 PRO PREM 3/131/1 MacDonald memorandum 17.6.40.
50 SPO S11931A Chief Superintendent J. Hannigan to Garda Commissioner 'C' Branch Section 3. 18.6.40 and Roche to Taoiseach's Department 24.6.40.

51 SPO CAB 2/3 Cabinet minutes 1.7.40.
52 Coogan op. cit. p 190.
53 PRO PREM 3/129/2. RUC report 20.7.40.
54 Ibid.
55 Carter op. cit. pp 144–5.
56 Carter op. cit. p 149.
57 Stephan op. cit. p 96.
58 Stephan op. cit. pp 78–82.
59 Carter op. cit. pp 154–5.
60 Irish Army Archives. Map of unidentified aircraft track 5–6.5.40.
61 Stephan op. cit. pp 102–4.
62 Carter op. cit. p 156.
63 *Documents on German Foreign Policy 1918–45* Series D Vol IX (HMSO) London 1956 pp 431–2 Hempel to Foreign Ministry 24.5.40.
64 *Documents on German Foreign Policy 1918–45* Series D Vol IX op. cit. p 432n5 Hempel to Foreign Ministry 25.5.40.
65 *Documents on German Foreign Policy 1918–45* Series D Vol IX op. cit. pp 490–1 Woermann to Hempel 1.6.40.
66 PRO PREM 3/129/2 RUC report 20.7.40.
67 *Documents on German Foreign Policy 1918–45* Series D Vol IX op. cit. pp 573–4 Woermann to Hempel 15.6.40.
68 Ibid.
69 *Documents on German Foreign Policy 1918–45* Series D Vol IX op. cit. pp 601–3 Hempel to Foreign Ministry 17.6.40.
70 Ibid.
71 *Documents on German Foreign Policy 1918–45* Series D Vol IX op. cit. pp 637–40 Hempel to Foreign Ministry 21.6.40.
72 Ibid.
73 Ibid.
74 Ibid.
75 *Documents on German Foreign Policy 1918–45* Series D Vol IX op. cit. pp 422–4 Hempel to Foreign Ministry 23.5.40.
76 Ibid.
77 *Documents on German Foreign Policy 1918–45* Series D Vol X (HMSO) London 1957 p 36 Hempel to Foreign Ministry 27.6.40.
78 *Documents on German Foreign Policy 1918–45* Series D Vol X op. cit. pp 89–90 Hempel to Foreign Ministry 1.7.40.
79 Ibid.
80 *Documents on German Foreign Policy 1918–45* Series D Vol X op. cit. pp 184–5 Ribbentrop to Hempel 11.7.40.
81 Ibid.
82 Carter op. cit. pp 159–61.
83 Stephan op cit. p 117.
84 Carter op. cit. p 167.
85 *Sunday Press* 24.11.63 Hempel op. cit.
86 Ibid.
87 Stephan op. cit. p 81.
88 Carter op. cit. p 173.
89 Stephan op. cit. pp 208–9.

90   Carter op. cit. p 175.
91   Coogan op. cit. pp 204–6.
92   Interview with Gunther Schütz. Avoca, Co Wicklow 11.4.79.
93   Stephan op. cit. p 186.
94   Schütz interview 11.4.79.
95   *Eire-Ireland* Spring 1975 'The Spy Who Brought His Lunch' by Carolle J. Carter, also Carter op. cit. pp 203–4.
96   Schütz interview 11.4.79.
97   Ibid.
98   Carter op. cit. pp 207–8.
99   Carter op. cit. p 210.
100   *Documents on German Foreign Policy 1918–45* Series D Vol X op. cit. pp 379–80 Hempel to Foreign Ministry 31.7.40.
101   *Documents on German Foreign Policy 1918–45* Series D Vol X op. cit. pp 420–1 Ribbentrop to Hempel 6.8.40.
102   *Documents on German Foreign Policy 1918–45* Series D Vol X op. cit. pp 262–3 Hempel to Foreign Ministry 22.7.40.
103   *Documents on German Foreign Policy 1918–45* Series D Vol X op. cit. pp 378–80 Hempel to Foreign Ministry 31.7.40.
104   *Documents on German Foreign Policy 1918–45* Series D Vol XI (HMSO) London 1961 pp 1198–9 Ribbentrop to Washington Embassy and New York Consulate 26.1.41.
105   *Documents on German Foreign Policy 1918–45* Series D Vol XI op. cit. pp 1213–4 Thomsen to Foreign Ministry 28.1.41.
106   Ibid.
107   *Documents on German Foreign Policy 1918–45* Series D Vol XI op. cit. pp 493–4 Hempel to Ribbentrop 7.11.40.
108   *Documents on German Foreign Policy 1918–45* Series D Vol XI op. cit. p 570 Weizsäcker to Hempel 13.11.40.
109   *Documents on German Foreign Policy 1918–45* Series D Vol XI op. cit. pp 572–3 Ritter memorandum 14.11.40.
110   *Documents on German Foreign Policy 1918–45* Series D Vol XI op. cit. pp 718–9 Ribbentrop to Hempel 26.11.40.
111   *Documents on German Foreign Policy 1918–45* Series D Vol XI op. cit. pp 727–8 Ritter memorandum 28.11.40.
112   *Documents on German Foreign Policy 1918–45* Series D Vol XI op. cit. pp 736–8 Hempel to Foreign Ministry 29.11.40.
113   *Documents on German Foreign Policy 1918–45* Series D Vol XI op. cit. pp 793–4 Ribbentrop to Hempel 6.12.40.
114   Ibid.
115   *Documents on German Foreign Policy 1918–45* Series D Vol XI op. cit. pp 804–5 Hempel to Foreign Ministry 7.12.40.
116   *Documents on German Foreign Policy 1918–45* Series D Vol XI op. cit. pp 572–3 Ritter memorandum 14.11.40.
117   *Documents on German Foreign Policy 1918–45* Series D Vol XI op. cit. pp 973–5 Hempel to Foreign Ministry 29.12.40.
118   Ibid.
119   *Documents on German Foreign Policy 1918–45* Series D Vol XI op. cit. p 975 n4 Foreign Ministry to Hempel 4.1.41.

120 Carroll op. cit. p 77.
121 UCD Archives Mulcahy papers P7/C/113 Note dated 30.1.41 on Defence Conference of 29.1.41.
122 UCD Archives Mulcahy papers P7/C/112 Defence Conference note 1940 (no date).
123 Bryan interview 15.12.78.
124 UCD Archives Mulcahy papers P7a/220 Mulcahy to Boland 8.6.40.
125 Bryan interview 15.12.78.
126 PRO ADM 1/17089 Little to Morrison 25.3.44.
127 Carter op. cit. pp 33–4.
128 Telephone interview with Brian Inglis. London 22.6.78.
129 Bryan interview 15.12.78.
130 Ibid.
131 *Irish Press* 5.10.39.
132 Warnock interview 14.6.78.
133 Carter op. cit. p 52.
134 Warnock interview 14.6.78.
135 *Documents on German Foreign Policy 1918–45* Series D Vol IX op. cit. pp 401–2 Woermann memorandum 21.5.40.
136 Warnock interview 14.6.78.
137 Ibid.
138 Cremin interview 11.1.79.
139 Cronin op. cit. p 240 Appendix I Ryan to Kerney 6.11.41.
140 Clissmann interview 14.4.79.
141 Ibid.
142 Ibid.
143 Carter op. cit. p 190.
144 Carter op. cit. p 196.
145 PRO PREM 3/129/2 Intelligence report 20.7.40.
146 Bryan interview 15.12.78.
147 Carter op. cit. p 139.
148 Stephan op. cit. pp 253–4.
149 Ibid.
150 Schütz interview 11.4.79.
151 *Sunday Press* 24.11.63 Hempel op. cit.
152 Interview with Francis Stuart. Dublin 13.6.78.
153 Schütz interview 11.4.79.
154 Stephan op. cit. p 254.
155 Clissmann interview 14.4.79.
156 Blake op. cit. p 83n2.
157 PRONI CAB 9CD/186/1 King to Iliff 27.7.40.
158 Interview with Paddy Devlin. Belfast 19.8.78.
159 Ibid.
160 *Sunday News* 4.2.68 Brookeborough Memoirs op. cit.
161 Devlin interview 19.8.78.
162 Coogan op. cit. p 231.
163 PRONI CAB 4/523/4 Petitions received over Thomas Joseph Williams.
164 PRONI CAB 4/523/6 Desmond Marrinan to Abercorn 31.8.42.
165 PRONI CAB 4/523/7 Andrews to Abercorn 1.9.42.

166 PRONI CAB 4/528/4 MacDermott to Dawson Bates 12.11.42.
167 MacDermott interview 11.8.78.
168 Devlin interview 19.8.78.
169 Ibid.
170 Fiorentini interview 13.12.78.
171 Clissmann interview 14.4.79.
172 Ibid.

CHAPTER 10 TODAY I SPOKE OF LIAM LYNCH . . .

1 Stuart interview 13.6.78.
2 See *Sunday Press* 23.7.78 'The Life and Times of Francis Stuart' by Emmanuel Kehoe.
3 Clissmann interview 14.4.79.
4 *The Irish Times* 21.2.81.
5 Stuart interview 13.6.78.
6 Ibid.
7 PRONI CAB 9CD/207 BBCMR 17.3.42 Stuart (in English for Ireland).
8 Ibid.
9 PRONI CAB 9CD/207 BBCMR 29.3.42 (in English for Ireland).
10 PRONI CAB 9CD/207 Wells to Gransden 5.11.42.
11 Cronin op. cit. p 229.
12 Stuart interview 13.6.78.
13 PRONI CAB 9CD/207 BBCMR 15.6.43 Hartmann (in Irish for Ireland).
14 PRONI CAB 9CD/207 BBCMR 25.11.43 Hartmann (in Irish for Ireland).
15 PRONI CAB 9CD/207 BBCMR 4.6.43 Hartmann (in Irish for Ireland).
16 PRONI CAB 9CD/207 BBCMR 5.4.42 Hartmann (in Irish for Ireland).
17 PRONI CAB 9CD/207 BBCMR 5.4.42 Stuart (in English for Ireland).
18 PRONI CAB 9CD/207 BBCMR 15.8.41 (in English for Eire).
19 PRONI CAB 9CD/207 BBCMR 8.6.41 (in Irish for Eire).
20 PRONI CAB 9CD/207 BBCMR 24.9.41 (in Irish for Eire).
21 PRONI CAB 9CD/207 BBCMR 2.2.43 Hartmann.
22 PRONI CAB 9CD/207 BBCMR 6.2.43 Stuart (in English for Eire).
23 Stuart interview 13.6.78.
24 PRONI CAB 9CD/207 BBCMR 7.1.42 Hartmann.
25 Cronin op. cit. pp 228–9.
26 PRONI CAB 9CD/207 BBCMR 7.1.42 Hartmann.
27 PRONI CAB 9CD/207 BBCMR 30.3.42 O'Brien.
28 PRONI CAB 9CD/207 BBCMR 6.4.42 (in English for Ireland).
29 PRONI CAB 9CD/207 BBCMR 1.4.42 Wolfe Tone statement (in Irish for Ireland).
30 PRONI CAB 9CD/207 BBCMR 13.11.41 (in English for Ireland).
31 Ibid.
32 PRONI CAB 9CD/207 BBCMR 18.11.42 (in English for Ireland).
33 PRONI CAB 9CD/207 BBCMR 31.12.41 (in English for Ireland).
34 Pathé Film Library Reel 40/50 'All for Defence'.
35 Ibid.
36 Ibid.
37 Pathé Film Library Reel 40/55 'Eire Menaced by Germany'.
38 Pathé Film Library Reel 40/58 'Mining the Coasts of Eire'.

39 Pathé Film Library Reel 41/4 'Eire Bombed'.
40 Pathé Film Library Reel 41/46 'Germans Bomb Dublin'.
41 RTE Film Library Accession No A/124 Can 1560 Paramount News 1942 'Ireland – The Plain Issue'.
42 Ibid.
43 Ibid.
44 Nolan and Williams op. cit. p 48 'Irish Defence Policy, 1938–51' by G.A. Hayes-McCoy.
45 RTE Film Library Accession No A/124 Can 1560 Paramount News 1942 'Ireland – The Plain Issue'.
46 Ibid.
47 Pathé Film Library Reel 44/25 'News From the Eire Border'.
48 Pathé Film Library Reel UN 262/F 'Basil Brooke'.
49 *Northern Whig* 1.2.44 review of 'Ulster at Arms'.
50 PRONI COM 61/661 Henderson to Scott 16.12.43, see also handwritten note marked 'Secret' 17.12.43.
51 PRONI CAB 9CD/207 BBCMR 9.9.42 'Lenin's Old Guard' Radio (in Russian).
52 PRONI CAB 9CD/207 BBCMR 2.9.42 Radio Paris.
53 PRONI CAB 9CD/207 BBCMR 6.9.42 Rome radio Hugo Andrea (in Spanish for Spain).
54 PRONI CAB 9CD/207 BBCMR 3.9.42 Italian Home Service.
55 PRONI CAB 9CD/207 BBCMR 3.9.42 Radio Paris group.
56 PRONI CAB 9CD/207 BBCMR 10.9.42 German Home Service via Friesland.
57 PRONI CAB 9CD/207 BBCMR 3.9.42 German Home Service via Frankfurt.
58 PRONI CAB 9CD/207 BBCMR 3.9.42 Finnish Home Service via Lahti.
59 PRONI CAB 9CD/207 BBCMR 11.9.42 Italian Home Service via Rome.
60 PRONI CAB 9CD/207 BBCMR 14.10.42 Calais transmitter (in English for UK).
61 PRONI CAB 9CD/207 BBCMR 15.10.42 Zeesen transmitter (in English for North America).
62 PRONI CAB 9CD/207 BBCMR 28.3.44 Japanese Telegraph Service (in English for Europe).
63 PRONI CAB 9CD/207 Handwritten Gransden note to Adams and Hackett 21.5.44 on BBCMR of 28.3.44 Japanese Telegraph Service.
64 PRONI CAB 9CD/207 BBCMR 1.5.44 'Free India Radio' (in English for India).
65 PRONI CAB 9CD/207 BBCMR 27.12.43 'Free India Radio' (in English for India).
66 PRONI CAB 9CD/207 BBCMR 29.4.44 'Free India Radio' (in English for India).
67 PRONI CAB 9CD/207 BBCMR 2.5.44 'Free India Radio' (in Farsee).
68 Donald N. Wilber *Afghanistan* (Hraf Press) New Haven 1962 pp 22–3.
69 PRONI CAB 9CD/207 BBCMR Pat O'Brien (in English for Eire).
70 PRONI CAB 9CD/207 BBCMR 2.8.42 Rome (in English for Eire).
71 PRONI CAB 9CD/207 BBCMR 14.1.43 (in English for Ireland).
72 PRONI CAB 9CD/207 BBCMR 14.1.43 (in English for Eire).

73 PRONI CAB 9CD/207 BBCMR 23.5.41 Deutschlandsender (in German for Germany).
74 PRONI CAB 9CD/207 BBCMR 23.5.41 (in German for South and East Asia and North America).
75 PRONI CAB 9CD/207 BBCMR 23.5.41 (in German for Africa).
76 PRONI CAB 9CD/207 BBCMR 28.5.41 Radio Paris, Hilversum, Zeesen (in Turkish for Turkey).
77 PRONI CAB 9CD/207 BBCMR 29.5.41 Hartmann (in Irish for Eire).
78 PRONI CAB 9CD/207 BBCMR 15.5.41 (in English for Ireland).
79 Ibid.
80 PRONI CAB 9CD/207 Adams to Gransden 13.4.40.
81 PRONI CAB 9CD/207 Handwritten reply on Adam's note to Gransden 13.4.40.
82 PRONI CAB 9CD/207 Adams to Gransden 13.4.40.
83 PRONI CAB 9CD/207 Gransden to Adams 15.8.42.
84 Interview with Elisabeth Clissmann 14.4.79.
85 Ibid.
86 PRONI CAB 9CD/207 BBCMR 15.1.42 Wagner (in French for Canada).
87 Brosnan interview 14.4.78.
88 PRONI CAB 9CD/207 BBCMR 10.7.41 Deutschlandsender (in German for Germany).
89 PRONI CAB 9CD/207 BBCMR 11.7.41 Radio Paris (in French for France).
90 PRONI CAB 9CD/207 BBCMR 15.7.41 Lille (Brussels group) (in French for Belgium).
91 PRONI CAB 9CD/207 BBCMR 28.6.41 Rome (Italian home stations).
92 PRONI CAB 9CD/207 BBCMR 23.3.44 German European Service (in English for UK).
93 PRONI CAB 9CD/207 BBCMR 26.3.44 'Workers Challenge' (in English for UK).
94 PRONI CAB 9CD/207 BBCMR 6.4.44 'Radio National' (in English for UK).
95 PRONI CAB 9CD/207 BBCMR 16.11.43 German European Service (in English for Eire).
96 Ibid.
97 PRONI CAB 9CD/207 BBCMR 5.8.42 Luxemburg (German home stations) (in German for Germany).
98 PRONI CAB 9CD/207 BBCMR 24.7.42 Jeloey (Norwegian home stations).
99 PRONI CAB 9CD/207 BBCMR 20.8.44 German European Service (in English).
100 Stuart interview 13.6.78.
101 Ibid.
102 PRONI CAB 9CD/207 BBCMR 14.10.42 Stuart 'In Irish Eyes' (in English for Ireland).
103 PRONI CAB 9CD/207 BBCMR 16.3.43 Stuart (in English for Ireland).
104 PRONI CAB 9CD/207 BBCMR 8.1.44 Stuart (in English for Eire).
105 Ibid.
106 Stuart interview 13.6.78.

107 *Hibernia Weekly Review* 3.7.80 'What Went Wrong?' by Francis Stuart.
108 *Hibernia Weekly Review* 5.7.78 letter from Tom Gallagher.
109 J.J. Lee *Ireland 1945–70* RTE Thomas Davis Lectures (Gill and Macmillan) Dublin p 124 'The Media 1945–70' by Douglas Gageby.
110 *The Irish Times* 29.8.81 'A Case of Emergency' by Hugh Leonard.
111 *The Irish Times* 21.7.79 'Aran in the Thirties' by Breandan O hEithir.
112 Stuart interview 13.6.78.

CHAPTER 11 PLATO'S CAVE

1   Lyons op. cit. p 556.
2   John Ryan *Remembering How We Stood* (Gill and Macmillan) Dublin 1975 p 5.
3   *The Irish Times* 21.8.81 'In Search of Patrick Kavanagh' by Caroline Walsh.
4   Interview with Rita McKittrick. Belfast 12.8.78.
5   SPO CAB 2/4 Cabinet minutes 17.2.42.
6   Kingsley Martin *Editor* (Hutchinson) London 1968 p 276.
7   PRO FO 800/310 Bowen to Dominions Office 9.11.40.
8   PRO FO 371/23966 Pakenham memorandum 23.10.39.
9   Ibid.
10 Ibid.
11 PRO FO 371/23966 Perth to Butler 31.10.39.
12 PRO FO 371/23966 Pakenham memorandum 23.10.39, handwritten note by Butler 6.11.39.
13 PRO FO 800/310 Cranborne to Halifax 25.11.40.
14 PRO FO 800/310 Bowen to Dominions Office 9.11.40.
15 Ibid.
16 Ibid.
17 Ibid.
18 PRO FO 371/89108 Shaw memorandum 1.1.41.
19 Ibid.
20 PRO FO 800/310 Loraine memorandum 21.12.40.
21 PRO FO 371/89108 Balinski report 27.1.41.
22 Pathé Film Library Dublin Reel 40/54 'Ireland, Outpost of Peace'.
23 PRO FO 371/89108 Shaw memorandum 1.1.41.
24 *Ireland Today* Vol 2 No 4 April 1937 'Ireland in the European Chaos' by Michael Tierney, quoted in Terence Brown *Ireland: a Social and Cultural History 1922–79* (Fontana) London 1981 p 170.
25 Lyons op. cit. pp 557–8.
26 SPO S9888 Government memorandum (Taoiseach's dept file) 13.3.41.
27 Ibid.
28 Ibid.
29 Keatinge *A Place Among the Nations* op. cit. pp 158–8.
30 SPO S9888 Walshe to de Valera 19.3.41.
31 SPO S12646 O Cochlain to Derrig 10.12.41.
32 Ibid.
33 Ibid.
34 PRO PREM 3/131/2 General Report on Position in Eire 20.7.40.
35 SPO S8658A Taoiseach's dept ARP conference 9.6.41.

36 *Eamon de Valera Speeches and Statements 1917–1973* op. cit. p 466 de Valera radio broadcast 17.3.43.
37 PRO FO 800/310 Bowen to Dominions Office 9.11.40.
38 PRONI Spender diaries D 715/15 note of Maffey conversation 11.12.40.
39 PRO FO 371/89108 Shaw memorandum 1.1.41.
40 PRO CAB 66/10 Maffey to Dominions Office 17.7.40.
41 PRO FO 371/89108 Shaw memorandum 1.1.41.
42 PRO FO 371/89108 Balinski report 27.1.41.
43 *Documents on German Foreign Policy 1918–45* Series D Vol IV op. cit. p 356 Hempel to Foreign Ministry 3.1.39.
44 Aiken interview 12.4.79.
45 *Documents on German Foreign Policy 1918–45* Series D Vol IV op. cit. p 356 Hempel to Foreign Ministry 3.1.39.
46 PRO FO 371/89108 Shaw memorandum 1.1.41.
47 UCD Archives Mulcahy papers P7/C/113 de Valera to Mulcahy 12.2.41.
48 *An Cosantoir* September 1979 'Cadets at Arlington' by Colonel Cyril M. Mattimoe (retd).
49 Brian Farrell *Chairman or Chief? The Role of Taoiseach in Irish Government* (Gill and Macmillan) Dublin 1971 p 80, quoting Lemass inverview in *Irish Press* (undated).
50 PRO FO 371/89108 Shaw memorandum 1.1.41.
51 PRO FO 371/89108 Balinski report 27.1.41.
52 Martin op. cit. p 276.
53 PRO FO 371/89108 Shaw memorandum 1.1.41.
54 *Eamon de Valera Speeches and Statements 1917–1973* op. cit. p 93 Dail Eireann Treaty debate 6.1.22.
55 SPO CAB 2/5 Cabinet minutes 11.12.42.
56 Dillon interview 10.7.79.
57 PRO FO 800/310 Bowen to Dominions Office 9.11.40.
58 Dillon interview 10.7.79.
59 PRO FO 800/310 Bowen to Dominions Office 9.11.40.
60 PRO FO 371/89108 Shaw memorandum 1.1.41.
61 Dillon interview 10.7.79.
62 PRO FO 800/310 Bowen to Dominions Office 9.11.40.
63 Dillon interview 10.7.79.
64 Aiken interview 12.4.79.
65 Dillon interview 10.7.79.
66 Boland Papers 5(x).
67 Aiken interview 12.4.79.
68 PRONI Spender diaries D 715/15 note of Maffey conversation 11.12.40.
69 PRO FO 371/89108 Shaw memorandum 1.1.41.
70 PRONI Spender diaries D 715/15 note of Maffey conversation 11.12.40.
71 PRO FO 800/310 Bowen to Dominions Office 9.11.40.
72 PRO FO 371/89108 Shaw memorandum 1.1.41.
73 Dillon interview 10.7.79.
74 Ibid.
75 Churchill *The Gathering Storm* op. cit. pp 582–3 First Lord to First Sea Lord 24.9.39.
76 PRO FO 800/310 Bowen to Dominions Office 9.11.40.

77 Manning op. cit. p 248.
78 Manning op. cit. p 171, quoting *Irish Press* 5.11.34.
79 For a discussion of the Blueshirts and European fascism, see Manning op. cit. pp 232–44.
80 Manning op. cit. p 237.
81 Dillon interview 10.7.79.
82 Ibid.
83 PRO FO 800/310 Bowen to Dominions Office 9.11.40.
84 Lyons op. cit. p 530.
85 Aiken interview 12.4.79.
86 Lyons op. cit. p 530.
87 Elisabeth Cullingford *Yeats, Ireland and Fascism* (Macmillan) London 1981 p 203, quoting *The Letters of W.B. Yeats* (ed Allan Wade) (Macmillan) 1954 p 812.
88 Cullingford op. cit. p 205.
89 Cullingford op. cit. p 226, quoting Mrs W.B. Yeats *Explorations* (Macmillan) London 1962 p 441.
90 Cullingford op. cit. p 199, quoting *The Letters of W.B. Yeats* op. cit. p 806.
91 *The Observer* 19.7.81.
92 Cullingford op. cit. p 235.
93 Boland Papers 1(x).
94 *The Irish Times* 11.2.81 letter from Borje Thilman.
95 Cronin op. cit p 251 von Grote to Woermann 5.4.43.
96 PRO FO 800/310 Bowen to Dominions Office 9.11.40.
97 Ibid.
98 Ibid.
99 Louis Hyman *The Jews of Ireland: From Earliest Times to the Year 1910* (Irish University Press) Shannon 1972 p 217, quoting *The Times* 10.4.04.
100 Hyman op. cit. p 217.
101 Carroll op. cit. pp 136–7, quoting *Irish Press* 28.4.73.
102 SPO S11470 Taoiseach's dept. draft of Dail reply 19.10.39.
103 *Hibernia Weekly Review* 20.3.80 letter from Manus O'Riordan.
104 Carroll op. cit. p 138.
105 Martin Gilbert *The Holocaust: A record of the destruction of Jewish life in Europe during the dark years of Nazi rule* (The Jerusalem Post) Jerusalem 1978 p 14.
106 Dail Debates Vol 91 colls 569, 572. 9.7.43.
107 see *Sunday Tribune* 10.1.82 'Sleepless Knight?'
108 *The Irish Times* 24.2.79.
109 Coogan op. cit. p 158.
110 Bryan interview 2.6.78.
111 Boland Papers 9(x).
112 Boland Papers 8(x).
113 UCD Archives Mulcahy papers P7a/220 Intelligence file. Agent's report 31.5.40.
114 Ibid.
115 Ibid.
116 UCD Archives Mulcahy papers P7a/220 Intelligence file. Agent's report 14.6.40 and 26.6.40.

117 UCD Archives Mulcahy papers P7a/220 Intelligence file. Agent's report 1.7.40.
118 Ibid.
119 Boland Papers 8(x).
120 Boland Papers 9(x).
121 PRO FO 371/89108 Balinski report 27.1.41.
122 PRO FO 371/89108 Shaw memorandum 1.1.41.
123 PRO PREM 3/131/2 General Report on Position in Eire 20.7.40.
124 PRO FO 371/89108 Robinson notes. Cavendish-Bentinck 17.2.41.
125 PRO FO 371/89108 Robinson notes. Randall 26.2.41.
126 PRO FO 371/89108 Robinson notes. Cavendish-Bentinck 27.2.41 and Makins 10.3.41.
127 PRO FO 371/23966 Dominions Information Department memo 25.10.39.
128 PRO FO 800/310 Bowen to Dominions Office 9.11.40.
129 PRO FO 371/89108 Balinski report 27.1.41.
130 PRO FO 800/310 Bowen to Dominions Office 9.11.40.
131 Leonard Mosley *Backs to the Wall: The Heroic Story of the People of London during World War II* (Random House) New York 1971 p 257n.
132 PRO FO 800/310 Bowen to Dominions Office 9.11.40.
133 Ibid.
134 PRO FO 371/89108 Balinski report 27.1.40.
135 Bryan interview 2.6.78.
136 Pathé Film Library Dublin Reel 42/89 'Defence Minister at LDF Parade'. Taoiseach's dept 26.3.43.
137 SPO S12077 Garda Siochana to Taoiseach's dept 26.3.43.
138 SPO S10785 A Traynor to O'Kelly 7.12.43.
139 PRO FO 371/89108 Shaw memorandum 1.1.41.
140 Ryan op. cit. p 15.
141 *Sunday Independent* 16.4.78.
142 Ryan interview 2.6.78.
143 Kim Philby *My Silent War* (Panther) London 1976 p 151.
144 *Sunday Tribune* (Magazine) 3.1.82 'The Men who Caught the German Ambassador Spying'.
145 Green interview 10.9.79.
146 PRO FO 371/89108 Shaw memorandum 1.1.41.
147 PRO FO 800/310 Loraine memorandum 21.12.40.
148 PRO FO 371/89108 Shaw memorandum 1.1.41.
149 UCD Archives Mulcahy papers P7/C/111 Note of 18.7.40.
150 UCD Archives Mulcahy papers P7/C/114 front bench meeting 4.3.41.
151 Ibid.
152 SPO S11306 Department of External Affairs to de Valera 15.2.43 and S11586A. 'Neutrality, Censorship and Democracy' Aiken to Government (Appendix) 23.1.40.
153 PRONI Spender diaries D 715/15 note of Maffey conversation 11.12.40.
154 SPO S12557 Green Cross Fund June 1942 and Cab mins 3.9.41.
155 SPO S12125 Walshe to Taoiseach's dept 20.11.40.
156 SPO S12244A Department of External Affairs to Government 31.12.40.
157 SPO S12244A Walshe to Taoiseach's dept 28.3.41 and External Affairs to Taoiseach's dept 17.2.41.

158 RTE Film Library Accession No A/378 Can 2027 Movietone. Ireland Review of the Year 1942.
159 Share op. cit. p 53.
160 PRO PREM 3/129/2. Intelligence report 20.7.40.
161 David Thomson *Woodbrook* (Penguin Books) London 1976 p 243.
162 Harbourmaster's Return of Arrivals and Sailings of Vessels, Fenit Pier, Co Kerry 24.4.40 – 27.6.45.
163 Telephone interview with Eamonn Sinnott of Wexford Harbour Board 8.4.78.
164 Donal Foley *Three Villages: An Autobiography* (Egotist Press) Dublin 1977 pp 53–4.

CHAPTER 12 A PIED À TERRE IN IRELAND

 1 PRONI CAB 3/A/52 'Q' (Movements) op. cit. pp 1–2.
 2 Interview with Kenneth Taylor. Belfast 11.8.78.
 3 Devlin interview 19.8.78.
 4 *Sunday News* 28.1.68 Brookeborough Memoirs op. cit.
 5 Devlin interview 19.8.78.
 6 PRO FO 371/89108 Pakenham memorandum 23.10.39.
 7 PRO FO 371/89108 Shaw memorandum 1.1.41.
 8 PRONI CAB 9CD/171 Belfast Protestant Churches manifesto to Stormont Government 30.3.42.
 9 PRONI Blake papers CAB 3/A/49 BTNI War Diary February 1942 App 7.
10 PRONI Blake papers CAB 3/A/23 Horton to Secretary of the Admiralty 4.5.43.
11 PRONI Blake papers CAB 3/A/23 Simpson to Horton 3.5.43.
12 PRONI CAB 4/438/3 draft Cabinet conclusions 20.5.40.
13 MacDermott interview 11.8.78.
14 McKittrick interview 12.8.78.
15 MacDermott interview 11.8.78.
16 Letter to the author from Lord MacDermott 9.9.78.
17 PRONI CAB 9CD/169/2 Gough, Harrison, Healy to Churchill 23.9.40.
18 PRONI CAB 9CD/169/2 Markbreiter to Gransden 12.10.40.
19 MacDermott interview 11.8.78.
20 PRONI CAB 9CD/169/2 Warner to Panter 9.6.40.
21 PRONI CAB 9CD/169/2 Warner to Panter 15.6.40.
22 PRONI CAB 9CD/169/2 Gransden to Panter 17.6.40.
23 PRONI Spender diaries D 715/15 Spender to Hankey 9.11.40.
24 PRONI COM 61/440 Northern Ireland's Manpower Resources J.H. Wilson 17.12.40.
25 Ibid.
26 Ibid.
27 PRONI COM 61/440 Lindsay Keir to Brooke (enclosure) 27.2.41.
28 PRONI COM 61/694 Andrews to Beaverbrook 10.2.42.
29 Blake op. cit. pp 420–1.
30 PRONI CAB 4/467/6 Cabinet conclusions 6.3.41.
31 *Northern Ireland in the Second World War: A Guide to Official Documents in*

PRONI (Public Record Office) Belfast 1976 p 24, quoting PRONI CAB 7CD/208 Morrison to Andrews 13.5.41.

32 HLRO BBK/D111 Beaverbrook to Brooke 20.11.41.
33 PRONI COM 61/694 Andrews to Beaverbrook 10.2.42.
34 *Sunday News* 28.1.68 Brookeborough Memoirs op. cit.
35 HLRO BBK/D/111 'W.B.B.' to Beaverbrook 20.11.41.
36 PRO FO 371/89108 Shaw memorandum 1.1.41.
37 MacDermott interview 11.8.78.
38 PRONI Spender diaries D 715/15 16–21.12.40.
39 PRONI Spender diaries D 715/15 17–22.2.41.
40 PRONI Spender diaries D 715/16 21–26.4.41.
41 Kelly interview 10.6.78.
42 PRO FO 371/89108 Shaw memorandum 1.1.41.
43 PRONI Spender diaries D 715/16 21–26.4.41.
44 PRONI CAB 4/462/3 Dawson Bates to Andrews 13.2.41.
45 PRO FO 371/89108 Shaw memorandum 1.1.41.
46 Harbinson op. cit. p 141.
47 *Sunday News* 4.2.68 Brookeborough Memoirs op. cit.
48 Harbinson op. cit. p 141.
49 *Sunday News* 4.2.68 Brookeborough Memoirs op. cit.
50 Ibid.
51 PRONI COM 61/861 *Daily Worker*/McColloch 20.5.43.
52 Devlin interview 19.8.78.
53 PRONI Spender diaries D 715/15 Spender to Hankey 2.12.40.
54 PRO FO 371/23966 Dominions Information Department memo 25.10.39.
55 PRO FO 371/89108 Shaw memorandum 1.1.41.
56 Devlin interview 19.8.78.
57 see, for example, SPO CAB 2/3 Cabinet minutes 2.7.40.
58 PRONI COM 61/568 Home Defence Executive 5.7.40.
59 Devlin interview 19.8.78.
60 Kelly interview 10.6.78.
61 Montgomery Hyde op. cit. p 261.
62 Montgomery Hyde op. cit. p 228.
63 Kelly interview 10.6.78.
64 Montgomery Hyde op. cit. p 259.
65 Kelly interview 10.6.78.
66 Irving *Hitler's War* op. cit. p 334.
67 Fiorentini interview 13.12.78.
68 Ibid.
69 PRO PREM 3/129/2 Intelligence report. Counties in Eire 20.7.40.
70 Fiorentini interview 13.12.78.
71 Ibid.
72 PRONI Spender diaries D 715/16 21–26.4.41.
73 PRONI Spender diaries D 715/15 note of Maffey conversation 11.12.40.
74 MacDermott interview 11.8.78.
75 Letter to the author from Lord MacDermott 9.9.78.
76 Letter to the author from Sam McAughtry 26.1.79.
77 Sam McAughtry *The Sinking of the Kenbane Head* (Blackstaff Press) Belfast 1977 p 117.

78 McAughtry op. cit. p 118.
79 Letter to the author from Sam McAughtry 26.1.79.
80 PRONI COM 61/861 Censorship intercept 27.2.42.
81 PRONI COM 61/861 Censorship intercept 25.2.42.
82 PRONI COM 61/861 Censorship intercept 8.1.42.
83 PRONI COM 61/861 Censorship intercept 10.1.42.
84 PRONI COM 61/861 Censorship intercent 24.3.42.
85 PRONI COM 61/861 Censorship intercept 31.8.42.
86 PRONI COM 61/861 Censorship intercept 22.8.42.
87 PRONI COM 61/861 Censorship intercept 16.2.42.
88 PRONI COM 61/861 Censorship intercept 26.1.42.
89 PRONI COM 61/861 Censorship intercept 21.11.41.
90 PRONI COM 61/861 Robinson to Scott 22.12.41.
91 PRONI COM 61/861 Parr to Gransden 17.11.44.
92 PRONI COM 61/861 Censorship intercept 27.3.42.
93 PRONI COM 61/861 Censorship intercept (undated).
94 PRONI COM 61/861 Censorship intercept (undated).
95 PRONI COM 61/861 Censorship intercept (undated).
96 PRONI COM 61/861 Censorship intercept 25.12.42.
97 PRONI CAB 12 notes of Andrews meeting with H M Forces 21.11.41.
98 *Northern Ireland in the Second World War: A Guide to the Official Documents in PRONI* op. cit., quoting CAB 7C/22 Churchill to Andrews 20.10.42.
99 PRONI CAB 3/A/78 Inspector General's Office. Folder No 66.1945.
100 PRONI COM 61/266 AEU to Ministry of Production (Belfast) (annex) 21.5.43.
101 PRONI CAB 3/A/78 Inspector General's Office. Folder No 66. 1945.
102 Kelly interview 10.6.78.
103 Devlin interview 19.8.78.
104 PRONI CAB 4/578/1 Cabinet conclusions 5.4.44.
105 PRONI CAB 4/482/14 Dawson Bates memorandum 11.9.41.
106 Blake op. cit. p 425.
107 PRONI CAB 4/507/7 draft Cabinet conclusions 28.4.42.
108 Ibid.
109 PRONI CAB 4/597/7 Midgley memorandum 9.9.44.
110 PRONI CAB 4/496/5A Gordon to Andrews (and annex) 15.1.42.
111 PRONI COM 61/61 Scott to Adams 2.2.40 and Adams to Scott 3.2.40.
112 PRONI COM 61/61 Adams to Scott 3.2.40.
113 PRONI COM 61/61 Adams to Scott 8.5.40.
114 PRONI Spender diaries D 715/22 9–15.8.43.
115 PRONI CAB 4/605/9 Cabinet conclusions 9.11.44, quoting Griffin 7.11.44.
116 PRONI CAB 4/605/16 Warnock to Morrison 9.11.44.
117 *Sunday Express* 1.12.40.
118 HLRO BBK/C/224 Londonderry to Beaverbrook 6.12.40.
119 HLRO BBK/C/224 Beaverbrook to Londonderry 12.12.40.
120 PRONI CAB 9CD/171 Congregational Union of Ireland to Government 8.5.40.
121 PRONI CAB 9CD/171 Extract from *Hansard* Vol 378 No 47 Col 1690 19.3.42.

122 PRONI CAB 9CD/171 Extract from *Hansard* Vol 379 No 58 Coll 820–1 28.4.42.
123 PRONI CAB 9CD/171 Simmons to Andrews 22.11.41.
124 PRONI CAB 9CD/171 Lowry to Glentoran 24.11.41.
125 PRONI CAB 9CD/171 Belfast Presbytery to Andrews 9.4.42.
126 PRONI CAB 9CD/171 Londonderry Temperance Council to Gransden 10.11.43.
127 PRONI CAB 9CD/171 Andrews to Simmons 20.11.41.
128 PRONI CAB C/501/7 draft Cabinet conclusion 31.3.42.
129 PRONI CAB 9CD/171 Belfast Protestant Churches manifesto to Government 30.3.42.
130 Ibid.
131 PRONI CAB 9CD/171 Montgomery to Andrews 23.3.42.
132 PRONI COM 61/865 ENSA Regional chairman to Brooke 14.9.42.
133 *News Letter* 28.4.44.
134 PRONI CAB 4/493/11 Cabinet conclusions 11.12.41.
135 PRONI CAB 4/493/9 Andrews memorandum 3.12.41.
136 *Sunday News* 4.2.68 Brookeborough Memoirs op. cit.
137 Shearman op. cit. p 178.
138 PRONI CAB 3/C/1 transcript of Andrews interview in *Glasgow Herald* 29.1.42.
139 Blake op. cit. pp 117–52, 439–99.
140 IWM MISC 227 C.W. Mann papers P/O O'Neill to Mann 11.2.42.
141 Blake op. cit. p 535.
142 Erskine op. cit. p 559.
143 *Sunday News* 4.2.68 Brookeborough Memoirs op. cit.
144 Nigel Nicolson *Alex: The Life of Field Marshal Earl Alexander of Tunis* (Weidenfeld and Nicolson) London 1973 p 7.
145 PRONI CAB 3/A/116 Churchill to Andrews 9.5.43.
146 Churchill *Their Finest Hour* op. cit. p 529.
147 *News Letter* 28.4.44.
148 PRONI COM 61/440 Lindsay Keir to Brooke (enclosure) 27.2.41.
149 PRO FO 371/89108 Shaw memorandum 1.1.41.

CHAPTER 13 MANY FIRES WERE STARTED . . .

1 IWM EDS M1/14/302 Box 356 Zielstammkarte (Grossbritannien Nord-Ireland) 30.11.40.
2 Ibid.
3 Ibid.
4 PRO CAB 27/528 Rearmament Work in Northern Ireland (Appendix C) March 1938, also in PRONI Spender diaries D 715/10.
5 PRONI CAB 4/408/12 Civil Defence memorandum 19.6.39.
6 Ibid.
7 PRONI CAB 4/415/17 ARP memorandum 22.6.39.
8 Ibid.
9 PRONI CAB 4/419/4 draft Cabinet conclusions 22.6.39.
10 Erskine op. cit. p 554.
11 Montgomery Hyde op. cit. p 254.

12   Blake op. cit. p 218.
13   MacDermott interview 11.8.78.
14   PRONI CAB 4/441/3 draft Cabinet conclusions 1.6.40.
15   PRONI CAB 4/446/3 draft Cabinet conclusions 1.7.40.
16   Blake op. cit. p 221.
17   PRONI CAB 3/A/76 Civil Defence Advisory Committee 11.7.40.
18   Blake op. cit. p 213.
19   MacDermott interview 11.8.78.
20   Oliver op. cit. p 65.
21   PRONI CAB 456/13 MacDermott memorandum 21.12.40.
22   MacDermott interview 11.8.78.
23   PRONI CAB 4/461/21 Cabinet conclusions 4.2.41.
24   MacDermott interview 11.8.78.
25   PRONI Spender diaries D 715/15 Spender *Blitz* memorandum 3.2.41.
26   Blake op. cit. p 215.
27   Blake op. cit. p 218.
28   Blake op. cit. p 208.
29   Kelly interview 10.6.78.
30   Blake op. cit. p 168.
31   Blake op. cit. p 236, quoting German Air Ministry records.
32   PRONI Blake papers CAB 3/A/60 King to Admiralty 16.4.41 on 8.4.41 raid.
33   Blake op. cit. p 227.
34   PRONI Blake papers CAB 3/A/60 King to Admiralty 16.4.41 on 8.4.41 raid.
35   McKittrick (née Hegarty) interview 12.8.78.
36   Blake op. cit. p 229.
37   *Belfast Telegraph* 15.4.71 'The Blitz' by Nevin McGhee.
38   McKittrick interview 12.8.78.
39   Blake op. cit. p 229.
40   Kelly interview 10.6.78.
41   PRONI Blake papers CAB 3/A/60 King to Admiralty 26.4.41 on 15/16.4.41 raid.
42   Green interview 10.9.79.
43   Blake op. cit. p 230–1.
44   Brian Moore *The Emperor of Ice-Cream* (André Deutsch) London 1966 p 199.
45   Kelly interview 10.6.78.
46   Devlin interview 19.8.78.
47   PRONI Blake papers CAB 3/A/60 King to Admiralty 26.4.41 on 15/16.4.41 raid.
48   Kelly interview 10.6.78.
49   Green interview 10.9.79.
50   Blake op. cit. p 235n1.
51   PRONI Blake papers CAB 3/A/60 Public Security intelligence summary 18.4.41.
52   Kelly interview 10.6.78.
53   McKittrick interview 12.8.78.
54   Interview with Joseph McCann. Belfast 13.12.78.
55   Blake op. cit. p 230.

56 *News Letter* 15.2.79 'Wardens keep *Blitz* memories burning'.
57 Confidential Dublin source.
58 Blake op. cit. p 235.
59 Devlin interview 19.8.78.
60 Oliver op. cit. p 65.
61 MacDermott interview 11.8.78.
62 PRONI Blake papers CAB 3/A/60 Public Security intelligence summary 18.4.41.
63 Ibid.
64 MacDermott interview 11.8.78.
65 Ibid.
66 PRONI HA 19/1/5/1 see Public Security-Northern Ireland fire service correspondence 10.3.43.
67 SPOS 12242 Aiken memorandum 30.8.43.
68 Longford and O'Neill op. cit. p 383.
69 Interview with Patrick Finlay of Dublin Fire Brigade. Dublin 25.8.79.
70 Ibid.
71 *Belfast Telegraph* 15.4.71 'The Blitz'.
72 Finlay interview 25.8.79.
73 Blake op. cit. p 231.
74 PRONI Blake papers CAB 3/A/46 RAF Ops Record Book July 1940 to July 1942. 15–16.4.41.
75 Blake op. cit. p 231.
76 Williamson interview 29.8.79.
77 PRONI Blake papers CAB 3/A/60 NOIC Derry to FOIC Belfast 26.4.41 on 15/16.4.41 raid.
78 *Northern Ireland in the Second World War: A Guide to the Official Documents in PRONI* op. cit., quoting PRONI HA 18/3/5 Public Security War Room to Home Security War Room 16.4.41.
79 PRONI Blake papers CAB 3/A/60 Public Security intelligence summary 16.4.41 & 18.4.41.
80 Finlay interview 25.8.79.
81 Kelly interview 10.6.78.
82 Finlay interview 25.8.79.
83 MacDermott interview 11.8.78.
84 Finlay interview 25.8.79.
85 *Belfast Telegraph* 15.4.71 'The Blitz'.
86 Finlay interview 25.8.79.
87 Ibid.
88 *Belfast Telegraph* 15.4.71 'The Blitz'.
89 Ibid.
90 Williamson interview 29.8.79.
91 MacDermott interview 11.8.78.
92 Moore op. cit. p 231.
93 McCann interview 13.12.78.
94 Interview with Kenneth Taylor. Belfast 11.8.78.
95 McKittrick interview 12.8.78.
96 McCann interview 13.12.78.
97 Confidential Belfast source.

98   Ibid.
99   McKittrick interview 12.8.78.
100   *Belfast Telegraph* 15.4.71 'The Blitz'.
101   *The Times* 7.10.74 'Learning to live with the segregated dead'.
102   PRONI Blake papers CAB 3/A/60 Public Security intelligence summary 18.4.41.
103   PRONI CAB 9CD/186/7 Civilian casualty return April 1941.
104   Ibid.
105   MacDermott interview 11.8.78.
106   Richard Collier *The City That Wouldn't Die* (Corgi) London 1959 p 260.
107   BBC World Service 22.11.81 'Six Irish Writers' Brian Moore in conversation with John Cronin.
108   PRONI Blake papers CAB 3/A/60 Public Security intelligence summary 18.4.41.
109   *Northern Ireland in the Second World War: A Guide to the Official Documents in PRONI* op. cit., quoting PRONI CAB 7CD/217 Morrison to Andrews 17.4.41.
110   Kelly interview 10.6.78.
111   MacDermott interview 11.8.78.
112   PRONI Spender diaries D 715/16 21–26.4.41.
113   PRONI COM 61/861 Censorship intercept 27.6.41.
114   PRONI COM 61/861 Note to Gransden 26.7.41.
115   Kelly interview 10.6.78.
116   McCann interview 13.12.78.
117   Lyons op. cit. p 730.
118   Information from Breandan Mac Giolla Choille. Dublin 16.10.78.
119   McCann interview 13.12.78.
120   PRONI CAB 4/473/10 MacDermott memorandum 12.5.41.
121   Blake op. cit. pp 240–1.
122   Ibid.
123   Blake op. cit. pp 238–9.
124   PRONI CAB 4/473/10 MacDermott mcmorandum 12.5.41.
125   Blake op. cit. p 239.
126   PRONI Spender diaries D 715/16 21–26.4.41.
127   MacDermott interview 11.8.78.
128   McKittrick interview 12.8.78.
129   *The Irish Times* 18.4.41.
130   Finlay interview 25.8.79.
131   *Sunday Press* 8.12.63 Hempel op. cit.
132   Aiken interview 12.4.79.
133   *Eamon de Valera Speeches and Statements 1917–1973* op. cit. p 458 de Valera at Castlebar 19.4.41.
134   *The Irish Times* Colour Supplement March 1981 p. 24.
135   Blake op. cit. p 235.
136   Blake op. cit. p 236.
137   *The Irish Times* Colour Supplement March 1981 p 21.
138   PRONI CAB 9CD/186/7 Public Security intelligence summary 13.6.41 on 4/5.5.41 raid.

139 Interview with Second Officer William Kennedy. Dun Laoghaire 28.2.79.
140 PRONI CAB 9CD/186/7 Public Security intelligence summary 13.6.41 on 4/5.5.41 raid.
141 Blake op. cit. p 237.
142 PRONI CAB 9CD/207 BBCMR 5.5.41 German Home Stations.
143 Ibid.
144 Ibid.
145 Ibid.
146 Blake op. cit. p 236.
147 *The Irish Times* Colour Supplement March 1981 p 23.
148 Blake op. cit. p 238.
149 Kennedy interview 28.2.79.
150 PRONI CAB 9CD/207 BBCMR 9.5.41 German Home Stations and 10.5.41 Koenigsberg (in Finnish for Finland).
151 Blake op. cit. p 236.
152 Blake op. cit. p 238.
153 PRONI Blake papers CAB 3/A/60 King to Admiralty 26.4.41 on 15/16.4.41 raid.
154 *Sunday Press* 8.12.63 Hempel op. cit.
155 Ibid.
156 Department of Defence Archives. Air and Marine Intelligence File Plot no 22. 28.5.41.
157 Ibid.
158 *An Cosantoir* September 1981 'The North Strand Bombing' by Lt Col Padraic O'Farrell.
159 *Sunday Press* 8.12.63 Hempel op. cit.
160 PRONI CAB 9CD/207 BBCMR 10.5.41 Bremen (in English for England).
161 Aiken interview 12.4.79.
162 *Sunday Press* 8.12.63 Hempel op. cit.
163 PRONI CAB 9CD/207 BBCMR 5.6.41 (in Italian for Italy).
164 PRONI CAB 9CD/207 BBCMR 5.6.41 Budapest (in Hungarian for Hungary).
165 Carroll op. cit. p 109.
166 Carter op. cit. p 85.
167 Lewin op. cit. p 98.
168 *Sunday Press* 8.12.63 Hempel op. cit.
169 PRONI CAB 4/474/11 Alternative accommodation memorandum 16.5.41.
170 PRONI CAB 4/475/13 Air Raid Shelter memorandum 16.5.41.
171 Blake op. cit. pp 243–9.
172 PRONI CAB 4/474/11 Alternative accommodation memorandum 16.5.41.
173 PRONI CAB 4/476/13 Cabinet conclusions 17.6.41.
174 PRONI CAB 4/482/5 draft Cabinet conclusions 23.9.41.
175 MacDermott interview 11.8.78.
176 Ibid.
177 PRONI CAB 9CD/207 BBCMR 18.5.41 Radio Paris (in French for France).
178 PRONI CAB 4/473/8 Dawson Bates memorandum 15.5.41.
179 PRONI CAB 4/473/10 MacDermott memorandum 12.5.41.

180 Ibid.
181 PRONI CAB 9CD/186/7 Public Security intelligence summary 13.6.41.
182 PRONI CAB 4/473/10 MacDermott memorandum 12.5.41.
183 PRONI Spender diaries D 715/16 30.5.41.
184 MacDermott interview 11.8.78.
185 Kelly interview 10.6.78.
186 Hansard (Northern Ireland) Vol XXIV col 828 13.5.41.
187 *News Letter* 3.6.41.

CHAPTER 14 CONSONANT WITH THE LAW OF GOD

 1 PRONI CAB 4/473/10 MacDermott memorandum 12.5.41.
 2 Ibid.
 3 *Belfast Telegraph* 27.4.39.
 4 *Belfast Telegraph* 4.9.39.
 5 MacDermott interview 11.8.78.
 6 Blake op. cit. p 196n1, quoting MacDermott to Andrews 17.5.41.
 7 Blake op. cit. p 195.
 8 Carroll op. cit. pp 107–8.
 9 Blake op. cit. pp 196–7.
10 PRONI CAB 4/475/16 Morrison to Andrews 20.5.41.
11 PRONI CAB 4/475/17 Cabinet conclusions 21.5.41.
12 PRONI CAB 4/475/15 Northern Ireland Government to Morrison 21.5.41.
13 Ibid.
14 Kelly interview 10.6.78.
15 Longford and O'Neill op. cit. p 384, quoting Walshe to de Valera 22.5.41.
16 PRO CAB 66/16 Morrison memorandum (Appendix II) 23.5.41; cf also *Irish Press* 23.5.41.
17 *The Times* 23.5.41.
18 PRO CAB 66/16 Morrison memorandum 23.5.41.
19 PRO CAB 66/16 Morrison memorandum (Appendix I) 23.5.41.
20 Blake op. cit. p 196n2.
21 Kelly interview 10.6.78.
22 Ibid.
23 Longford and O'Neill op. cit. p 384.
24 UCD Archives Mulcahy papers P7/C/113 de Valera conversation 23.5.41.
25 Ibid.
26 *Irish Press* 24.5.41.
27 Ibid.
28 Dangerfield op. cit. p 280.
29 *Irish Press* 24.5.41.
30 MacDermott interview 11.8.78.
31 Ibid.
32 PRO CAB 66/16 Wickham memorandum 24.5.41.
33 Ibid.
34 Ibid.
35 MacDermott interview 11.8.78.
36 SPO CAB 2/4 Cabinet minutes 24.5.41.

37 *Eamon de Valera Speeches and Statements 1917–1973* op. cit. p 459 de Valera to Churchill 25.5.41.
38 Longford and O'Neill op. cit. p 386, quoting Walshe to de Valera 26.5.41.
39 Ibid.
40 *Irish Press* 26.4.41.
41 Ibid.
42 *Manchester Guardian* 26.4.41.
43 Dail Debates Vol 83 no 4 coll 970–1 de Valera 26.5.41.
44 NLI MS 18,375 (6) Frank Gallagher Papers (p 51).
45 PRO CAB 66/16 Maffey telegram 25.5.41 (War Cabinet 26.5.41).
46 Ibid.
47 Carroll op. cit. p 108.
48 Winston Churchill *The Great War* Vol IV (Newnes) London p 1481.
49 *Irish Press* 28.5.41.
50 Ibid.
51 MacDermott interview 11.8.78.
52 PRONI Spender diaries D 715/16 26–31.5.41.
53 Ibid.
54 PRONI Spender diaries D 715/18 21.1.42.
55 *Sunday News* 4.2.68 Brookeborough Memoirs op. cit.
56 Ibid.
57 PRONI Spender diaries D 715/18 21.1.42.
58 Kelly interview 10.6.78.
59 Dail Debates Vol 99 no 19 coll 2320–1 Oscar Traynor 13.3.46.
60 John Furlong 'Irish Defence Policy 1940–1945' (unpublished MS), quoting UCD Archives Mulcahy papers M P/7/90 June 1941.
61 PRO DO 35/1230/WX132/1/140 Sedgwick to Costar 3.11.45.
62 Ibid.
63 *Daily Telegraph* 18.10.44.
64 *Manchester Guardian* 13.3.44.
65 PRO DO 35/1230/WX132/1/140 Sedgwick to Costar 3.11.45.
66 PRO DO 35/1230/WX132/1/124 Irish recruiting memorandum 31.1.45.
67 PRO DO 35/1230/WX132/1/124 Irish recruiting memorandum 25.2.46.
68 Ibid.
69 PRO DO 35/1230/WX132/1/124 Brooke to Chuter Ede 16.1.46.
70 PRO DO 35/1230/WX132/1/124 Machtig to Maxwell 26.3.46.
71 Ibid.
72 PRO DO 35/1230/WX132/1/124 Air Ministry to Costar 7.1.45; Admiralty to Costar 7.1.45; War Office statistics 13.12.44.
73 Ibid.
74 PRO DO 35/1230/WX132/1/124 'How Many?' by 'H.H.' 6.4.46 Dominions office file.
75 Cave Brown op. cit. p 542.
76 PRONI CAB 9CD/85/8 Extract from War Cabinet conclusions 9.10.41.
77 PRONI CAB 9CD/85/8 'Irish Brigade' handwritten note 22.11.41.
78 PRONI CAB 9CD/85/8 Freer to Gransden 13.11.41.
79 PRONI CAB 9CD/85/8 Andrews to Attlee 12.12.41.
80 PRONI CAB 9CD/85/8 Andrews to Attlee 23.1.42.
81 PRONI CAB 9CD/85/8 Brooke to Steele 5.2.47.

82   PRONI CAB 9CD/85/8 Chuter Ede to Bellenger 8.8.47.
83   PRONI CAB 9CD/85/8 Brooke to Gransden January 1948.
84   PRO DO 35/895 Blood to Hardinge 22.12.38.
85   PRO DO 35/895 Harding to Hardinge (two letters) 29.12.38.
86   Carter op. cit. pp 124–35.
87   PRONI CAB 4/597/7 Midgley memorandum 9.9.44.
88   PRONI CAB 4/540/6 Cabinet conclusions 28.4.43.
89   PRONI CAB 4/540/6A Wickham memorandum 28.4.43.
90   Kelly interview 10.6.78.
91   PRONI CAB 4/540/6A Wickham memorandum 28.4.43.
92   PRONI CAB 4/548/8 draft Cabinet conclusions 29.6.43.
93   PRONI CAB 4/540/6A Wickham memorandum 28.4.43.

CHAPTER 15 PHRASES MAKE HISTORY

1   *Eamon de Valera Speeches and Statements 1917–1973* op. cit. p 465 de Valera 27.1.42.
2   PRO CAB 66/46 Eden memorandum 1.2.44.
3   *The Nation* (New York) 31.1.42.
4   Ibid.
5   PRO CAB 66/46 Eden memorandum 1.2.44.
6   PRO CAB 66/48 Gray to de Valera 21.2.44.
7   PRO CAB 66/46 Eden memorandum 1.2.44.
8   Interview with Ervin 'Spike' Marlin. London 14.3.78.
9   Ibid.
10 PRO CAB 66/48 Gray to de Valera 21.2.44.
11 SPO S13450A de Valera to U.S. State Department 7.3.44.
12 *The Irish Times* 26–27.10.81 'The Germans' transmitter in Dublin' by Colonel Dan Bryan.
13 Marlin interview 14.3.78.
14 Winston S. Churchill *The Second World War: Closing the Ring* Vol V (Cassell) London 1952 Appendix C pp 614–5 Churchill to Roosevelt 19.3.44.
15 Ibid.
16 Churchill *Closing the Ring* op. cit. Appendix C p 607 Churchill to Cranborne 2.2.44.
17 Churchill *War Speeches 1939–45* (Eade) op. cit. p 94 Churchill 14.3.44.
18 SPO S13450A MacBride to de Valera 20.3.44.
19 *Sunday Press* 5.1.64 Hempel op. cit.
20 Ryle Dwyer op. cit. p 199, quoting *Foreign Affairs* Vol 24, p 324 January 1946 'Unneutral Neutral Eire' by Robert M. Smyllie.
21 Brosnan interview 14.4.78.
22 Cronin op. cit. p 232.
23 Clissmann interview 14.4.79.
24 Cremin interview 11.1.79.
25 PRO DO 35/1229/WX130/3/40 Maffey to Dominions Office 3.5.45, quoting Gray to State Department 3.5.45.
26 Ibid.
27 Longford and O'Neill op. cit. p 411.

28 Longford and O'Neill op. cit. p 411, quoting de Valera to Brennan. Whit Monday 1945.
29 Ibid.
30 Aiken interview 12.4.79.
31 PRO DO 35/1229/WX110/3 Maffey memorandum 21.5.45.
32 Ibid.
33 Ryle Dwyer op. cit. p 202.
34 *Irish Press* 3.5.45.
35 *The Sunday Times* 16.12.79.
36 Bryan interview 2.6.78.
37 Churchill *War Speeches 1939–45* (Eade) op. cit. p 441 Churchill 13.5.45.
38 Ibid.
39 *Why Ireland Was Neutral: Mr de Valera's Reply to Mr Churchill (Irish Press* publication) 16.5.45.
40 Ibid.
41 *The Irish Times* 5.2.79 'I've met them all' by Arthur Quinlan.
42 NLI MS 18, 375 (6) Frank Gallagher Papers (p 50a).
43 Winston S. Churchill *The Second World War: Triumph and Tragedy* Vol VI (Cassell) London 1954 (Appendix F) p 667 Churchill 13.5.45.
44 PRO DO 35/1229/WX110/3 Maffey memorandum 21.5.45.
45 Ibid.
46 PRO DO 35/1229/WX110/3 Maffey to Machtig 21.5.45.
47 PRO DO 35/1229/WX110/3 Machtig to Maffey 18.7.45.
48 *The Irish Times* 13.9.45.
49 PRO CAB 78/33 Emrys-Evans memorandum 2.6.45.
50 PRO CAB 78/33 Maffey memorandum 31.5.45.
51 Boland Papers 3(d), 4(a), 5(a), 6(d).
52 Schütz interview 11.4.79.
53 Boland Papers 6(d).
54 *Sunday Press* 1.12.63 Hempel op. cit.
55 Bryan interview 2.6.78.
56 Confidential Dublin source.
57 Clissmann interview 14.4.79.
58 Schütz interview 11.4.79.
59 Finlay interview 25.8.79.
60 Records of Dean's Grange Cemetery, Dublin.

CHAPTER 16 MR DE VALERA GOT AWAY WITH IT . . .

1 *Irish Press* 31.3.44.
2 Lyons op. cit. p 558.
3 PRONI CAB 3/A/116 Churchill to Andrews 9.5.43.
4 Lyons op. cit. p 730.
5 *The Irish Times* 5.1.82 letter from Sean MacBride.
6 MacDonald interview 18.4.78.
7 Churchill *The Gathering Storm* op. cit. p 215.
8 Mansergh op. cit. p 387, quoting House of Commons Debates Vol 335 coll 1094–1105 Churchill 5.5.38.
9 MacDonald interview 18.4.78.

10   Dillon interview 10.7.79.
11   Keatinge *A Place Among the Nations* op. cit. p 71.
12   Eamon de Valera *Ireland's Case against Conscription* (Maunsel) Dublin 1918 p 12.
13   Terence O'Neill *The Autobiography of Terence O'Neill* (Rupert Hart-Davis) London p 21.
14   De Valera *Recent Speeches and Broadcasts* op. cit. pp 52–3 Athlone speech 6.2.33.
15   Boland Papers 7(d).
16   *The Irish Times* 29.1.82 letter from Pól Ó Croidheáin.
17   *The Irish Times* 14.12.78 letter from Hubert Butler.
18   *The Irish Times* 18.12.78, quoting *Limerick Leader* in provincial press review.
19   See W.M. Carlgren *Swedish Foreign Policy During the Second World War* (Benn) London 1977 pp 20–1.
20   *The Irish Times* 20.10.78.
21   Dervla Murphy *A Place Apart* (Murray) London 1978 p 30.
22   Carlgren op. cit. p 229.
23   Arnold and Veronica Toynbee (eds) *The War and the Neutrals* (OUP) London 1956 'Eire' by Constance Howard p 254.
24   *The Irish Times* 5.4.79 Patrick Cooney, interviewed by Olivia O'Leary.
25   *An Cosantoir* November 1978 'European Defence – Is Neutrality an Option To-Day?' by Capt J. Doyle Rtd.
26   *An Cosantoir* July 1978 'The Treaty Ports' by John Buttimer.
27   Lawrence op. cit. p 69.
28   *The Irish Times* 25.9.79 letter from W.M. Abernethy.
29   *The Irish Times* 1–2.1.82 'Papers show British linked Irish unity to defence'.
30   *Irish Studies in International Affairs* Vol 1 No 1 (Royal Irish Academy) Dublin 1979 'The United States and Irish Participation in NATO: the Debate of 1950' by Ronan Fanning p 41, quoting NSC 83/1 President's Secretary's Files Box 209 Truman Papers Truman Library.
31   Aiken interview 12.4.79.
32   Nowlan and Williams op. cit. 'Irish Foreign Policy 1945–51' by Nicholas Mansergh p 146.
33   *The Daily Telegraph* 13.1.78 letter from John Biggs-Davison.
34   *The Irish Times* 26.2.81 Humphrey Atkins.
35   *The Irish Times* 28.2.81 Sile de Valera.
36   *The Irish Times* 12.3.81 Charles Haughey.
37   *The Irish Times* 20.3.81.
38   *The Irish Times* Lt Gen Carl O'Sullivan, interviewed by Olivia O'Leary.

Select Bibliography

Books

Avon, Lord *The Eden Memoirs: Facing the Dictators* (Cassell) London 1962; *The Eden Memoirs: The Reckoning* (Cassell) London 1965

Bethell, Nicholas *The War Hitler Won: September 1939* (Allen Lane) London 1972

Blake, John W. *Northern Ireland in the Second World War* (HMSO) Belfast 1956

Bromage, Mary C. *Churchill and Ireland* (University of Notre Dame) Indiana 1964

Brown, Terence *Ireland: A Social and Cultural History 1922–79* (Fontana) London 1981

Buckland, Patrick *Ulster Unionism and the Origins of Northern Ireland 1886–1922* (Gill and Macmillan) Dublin 1973; *James Craig Lord Craigavon* (Gill and Macmillan) Dublin 1980

Carroll, Joseph T. *Ireland in the War Years 1939–1945* (David and Charles) Newton Abbot 1975

Carter, Carolle J. *The Shamrock and the Swastika: German Espionage in Ireland in World War II* (Pacific Books) Palo Alto, California 1977

Churchill, Winston S. *The World Crisis: The Aftermath* (Thornton Butterworth) London 1929; *The Second World War Vol I: The Gathering Storm* (Cassell) London 1948; *The Second World War Vol II: Their Finest Hour* (Cassell) London 1949; *The Second World War Vol III: The Grand Alliance* (Cassell) London 1950; *The Second World War Vol V: Closing the Ring* (Cassell) London 1952; *The Second World War Vol VI: Triumph and Tragedy* (Cassell) London 1954

Coogan, Tim Pat *The IRA* (Fontana) London 1980

Cronin, Sean *Frank Ryan: The Search for the Republic* (Repsol) Dublin 1980

Cullingford, Elisabeth *Yeats, Ireland and Fascism* (Macmillan) London 1981

Dangerfield, George *The Damnable Question: A Study in Anglo-Irish Relations* (Constable) London 1977

De Paor, Liam *Divided Ulster* (Penguin) London 1977

De Valera, Eamon *Speeches and Statements 1917–1973* ed. Moynihan (Gill and Macmillan) Dublin 1980; *Recent Speeches and Broadcasts* (Talbot Press) Dublin 1933

Documents on German Foreign Policy 1918–1945 (HMSO) London Vol VIII (1954), IX (1956), X (1957), XI (1961)

Dwyer, T. Ryle *Irish Neutrality and the USA 1939–47* (Gill and Macmillan) Dublin 1977

Ervine, St John *Craigavon Ulsterman* (Allen & Unwin) London 1949

Fleming, Peter *Invasion 1940* (Hart-Davis) London 1957

Forde, Frank *The Long Watch: The History of the Irish Mercantile Marine in World War Two* (Gill and Macmillan) Dublin 1981

Gilbert, Martin *Winston S. Churchill Vol V 1922–1939* (Heinemann) London 1976

Harbinson, John F. *The Ulster Unionist Party 1882–1973* (Blackstaff) Belfast 1973

Harrison, Henry *The Neutrality of Ireland: Why It Was Inevitable* (Robert Hale) London 1940

Hezlet, A. *The 'B' Specials: A History of the Ulster Special Constabulary* (Pan) London 1973

Hyde, H. Montgomery *The Londonderrys: A Family Portrait* (Hamish Hamilton) London 1979

Irving, David *The War Path: Hitler's Germany 1933–9* (Michael Joseph) London 1978; *Hitler's War* (Hodder and Stoughton) London 1977

Jones, Thomas *Whitehall Diary Vol III* (OUP) London 1971

Keatinge, Patrick *The Formulation of Irish Foreign Policy* (Institute of Public Administration) Dublin 1973; *A Place Among the Nations: Issues of Irish Foreign Policy* (IPA) Dublin 1978

Lawrence, R.J. *The Government of Northern Ireland: Public Finance and Public Services 1921–1964* (OUP) London 1965

Longford, Lord *Peace by Ordeal* (Sidgwick & Jackson) London 1972; (with Thomas P. O'Neill) *Eamon de Valera* (Arrow Books) London 1974

Lyons, F.S.L. *Ireland Since the Famine* (Fontana) London 1978

McAughtry, Sam *The Sinking of the Kenbane Head* (Blackstaff) Belfast 1977

Manning, Maurice *The Blueshirts* (Gill and Macmillan) Dublin 1971

Mansergh, Nicholas *Documents and Speeches on British Commonwealth Affairs 1931–1952* Vol I (OUP) 1953

Martiensson, A. *Hitler and his Admirals* (Secker & Warburg) London 1948

Montgomery, Field Marshal *The Memoirs of Field Marshal the Viscount Montgomery of Alamein KG* (Collins) London 1958

Moore, Brian *The Emperor of Ice-Cream* (André Deutsch) London 1966

Nolan, Kevin B. and T. Desmond Williams *Ireland in the War Years and After 1939–51* (Gill and Macmillan) Dublin 1969

Oliver, John A. *Working at Stormont* (Institute of Public Administration) Dublin 1978

Ryan, John *Remembering How We Stood* (Gill and Macmillan) Dublin 1975

Share, Bernard *The Emergency: Neutral Ireland 1939–45* (Gill and Macmillan) Dublin 1978

Shirer, William L. *The Rise and Fall of the Third Reich* (Pan) London 1960

Stephan, Enno *Spies in Ireland* (Four Square) London 1965

Stewart, A.T.Q. *The Ulster Crisis* (Faber) London 1967

Toynbee, Arnold and Veronica (eds) *The War and the Neutrals* (OUP) London 1956

Warlimont, Walter *Inside Hitler's Headquarters* (Weidenfeld and Nicolson) London 1964

Younger, Carlton *A State of Disunion* (Muller) London 1972

Articles and Pamphlets

Bryan, Colonel Dan 'The Germans' transmitter in Dublin' *The Irish Times* 26–27.10.81

Burdick, Charles 'Gruen, German Military Plans and Ireland, 1940' *An Cosantoir* March 1974

Buttimer, John 'The Treaty Ports' *An Cosantoir* July 1978

Carter, Carolle J. 'Ireland: America's Neutral Ally, 1939–41' *Eire–Ireland* (Irish American Cultural Institute) Vol XII; 'The Spy Who Brought His Lunch' *Eire–Ireland* Spring 1975 pp 3–13

Cassidy, Lt Col M. 'A Short History of the Air Corps' *An Cosantoir* May 1980

Cox, Comdt Colm 'Militargeographische Angaben uber Irland' *An Cosantoir* March 1975

Doyle, Capt J. 'European Defence – Is Neutrality an Option To-Day?' *An Cosantoir* November 1978

Dwyer, T. Ryle 'The Mad Escape' *An Cosantoir* August 1979

Duggan, Lt Col M.T. 'Autumn Exercises, 1940' *An Cosantoir* June 1980

Fanning, Ronan 'The United States and Irish Participation in NATO: the Debate of 1950' *Irish Studies in International Affairs* Vol 1 No I (Royal Irish Academy) Dublin 1979

Forde, Frank 'Irish Merchant Seamen's Memorial' *An Cosantoir* January 1978; 'SS Kyleclare of Limerick in World War II' *An Cosantoir* March 1979

Kehoe, Emmanuel 'The Life and Times of Francis Stuart' *Sunday Press* 23.7.78

Kerrigan, Paul M. 'The Defences of Spike Island 1793–1815' *An Cosantoir* May 1978

McCarthy, Denis J. 'Armour in the War Years' *An Cosantoir* March 1975

McMahon, Deirdre 'Malcolm MacDonald and Anglo-Irish Relations 1935–8' (MA thesis 1975) UCD Archives; 'Ireland, the Dominions and the Munich Crisis' *Irish Studies in International Affairs* (Dublin) 1979

McMahon, Sean 'The Men who Caught the German Ambassador Spying' *Sunday Tribune* (Magazine) 3.1.82

Murdoch, John 'Ireland on the Brink' (Eduard Hempel interview) *Sunday Press* Nov–Dec 1963

Nixon, Ken 'The Brookeborough Memoirs' *Sunday News* January 1968

O'Connell, Col J.J. 'The Vulnerability of Ireland in War' *Studies* March 1938

O'Farrell, Comdt Padraic 'British Withdrawal – 1938 Style' *Irish Press* 11.7.78; 'The North Strand Bombing' *An Cosantoir* September 1981

O'hEithir, Breandan 'Aran in the Thirties' *The Irish Times* 21.7.79

Radcliffe, P.C.J. 'Northern Ireland in the Second World War: A Guide to Official Documents in PRONI' (PRONI) Belfast 1976

Student, General Kurt 'A German Airborne Attack on the North' *Irish Independent* 25.4.49; 'Airfields around Belfast as Paratroop Objectives' *Irish Independent* 26.4.49

Thornley, David 'De Valera Between the Wars' *History of the 20th Century*, No 46 (Purnell)

Williams, T. Desmond 'Neutrality' *Irish Press* 6–17.7.53

INDEX

A figure 2 in brackets immediately after a page reference means that there are two separate references to the subject on that page. NI stands for Northern Ireland.